CENTRAL ARKANSAS LIBRARY SYSTEM
1910 · 100 · 2010

A Gift of

Dickson Flake

in honor of

Linda Flake

Chamber Music

CHAMBER MUSIC
MUSIC
A Listener's Guide

JAMES M. KELLER

OXFORD
UNIVERSITY PRESS
2011

OXFORD
UNIVERSITY PRESS

Oxford University Press, Inc., publishes works that further
Oxford University's objective of excellence
in research, scholarship, and education.

Oxford   New York
Auckland   Cape Town   Dar es Salaam   Hong Kong   Karachi
Kuala Lumpur   Madrid   Melbourne   Mexico City   Nairobi
New Delhi   Shanghai   Taipei   Toronto

With offices in
Argentina   Austria   Brazil   Chile   Czech Republic   France   Greece
Guatemala   Hungary   Italy   Japan   Poland   Portugal   Singapore
South Korea   Switzerland   Thailand   Turkey   Ukraine   Vietnam

Published by Oxford University Press, Inc.
198 Madison Avenue, New York, NY 10016

www.oup.com

Library of Congress Cataloging-in-Publication Data
Keller, James M., 1953–
Chamber music : a listener's guide / James M. Keller.
p.   cm.
ISBN 978-0-19-538253-2
1. Chamber music—History and criticism.
2. Chamber music—Analysis, appreciation.   I. Title.
ML1100.K45 2010
785—dc22
2010009665

9 8 7 6 5 4 3 2 1

Printed in the United States of America
on acid-free paper

To Marc Dorfman,
for twenty-seven years of reasons

Introduction

"If I were in Berlin, I should rarely miss the Möser Quartet performances," wrote the poet and polymath Johann Wolfgang von Goethe, in 1829, to his musical adviser Carl Friedrich Zelter. This ensemble, headed by the violinist Karl Möser, stood at the core of Berlin's concert culture, and audiences crowded in to hear them play not only familiar quartets—by Haydn, for example—but also scores on which the ink was scarcely dry. Reviewing an 1828 concert in which they tackled Beethoven's String Quartet in A minor (Op. 132), published only a year earlier, the *Allgemeine musikalische Zeitung* of Leipzig worried that this "very difficult new quartet..., notwithstanding beautiful individual thoughts, did not please in its total effect, owing principally to the exhausting length of the movements and the overly rhapsodic development." And yet Goethe, who was no avant-gardist when it came to musical taste, found the foursome's repertoire uniquely satisfying. He continued in his letter: "Of all types of instrumental music, I have always been able to follow these best. You listen to four sensible persons conversing, you profit from their discourse, and you get to know the individual character of the instruments."

Goethe's pronouncement became the most famous summation of chamber music because it confirms what all listeners sense. A symphony orchestra may thrill us with the vastness of its resources, but a chamber group engages us on an entirely personal level. The musicians are wrapped in a web of intense communication with one another, and their parts, never so numerous as to confuse, project with a clarity that draws listeners in as rapt eavesdroppers on the conversation. Most often the subject is the music itself: the interweaving of melodies, the piquancy of harmonies, the architecture of construction, the timbre of sonic combinations. But chamber works can also give voice to less abstract matters; some composers have found such intimate forces ideal for conveying messages of love, for encoding tributes of musical respect, for proposing political commentary, for musing on their own lives.

The essays in this book are meant to help listeners deepen their appreciation of the chamber music literature. Many of them began as program notes, and as such they were crafted to assist listeners who were about to hear—or had just heard—the works performed. That is how I hope you will read them.

Whatever they aspire to convey is bound to be slight indeed if their reading is not accompanied by focused, committed listening.

There was a time when program notes tended toward extended musical analysis. To this approach we owe the revered program essays of Donald Francis Tovey from the first half of the twentieth century, as well as those of my beloved, departed colleague Michael Steinberg from the ensuing half-century; his insights will not be less enduring. My approach is usually more historical than analytical, and when it does drift toward analytical waters it takes care not to stray into deep currents. Music-lovers of 2010 are different from those of a century ago or even of a half-century ago. I cannot assume that they are able to read musical notation, and so I banish it from my program notes out of fear that it may alienate many readers rather than beckon them in. Some readers may find certain entries on the technical side, while others may wish they were more technical. My goal is to strike a happy mean that most people will find profitable most of the time. I have done my best to avoid jargon that nonprofessionals can find impenetrable; and, yet, one cannot write meaningfully about the content of musical compositions without using some vocabulary that is specific to the field. Readers who require help with the definition of musical terms, or who want to remind themselves precisely what "sonata form" or *stringendo* or basset horn are, might keep an ancillary reference book within reach; I would particularly recommend *The Harvard Dictionary of Music* (Fourth Edition).

Among the hallmarks of chamber music are the variety of its ensembles and the wealth of its repertoire. A guide of this size obviously cannot approach the repertoire in an exhaustive way, but the pieces discussed here all hold places of honor in the world of chamber music, and there is not a single one that a music-lover should go without hearing. In these pages readers will find most of the pieces they are likely to encounter most often in the course of their concert-going. Needless to say, the number of high-quality pieces that simply cannot be included within the available space is staggering; but I felt it would be better to say enough about the works that are included than to short-change them in order to touch lightly on more pieces. I have limited coverage to compositions that use between two and eight instrumentalists, normally playing without a conductor. (Two nonets and a decet were regretfully eliminated in the final cut.) I have not included any duos in which one of the participants is a piano, such as violin-and-piano sonatas. These may be legitimately considered chamber music, but much of that repertoire does invite a "soloist-plus-accompanist" aspect that is quite different from the general democracy of, say, a woodwind quintet; and so I drew the line.

Readers will find in these pages a strong representation of such seminal groupings as the string quartet and the piano trio, but I also have included pieces that suggest the variety of instrumental combinations that help make chamber music so endlessly interesting. Great names of the past dominate among the composers, but a number of living composers also find a place here, in every case thanks to chamber pieces that have begun to stake claims as classics. These reflect my perspective as an American listener; if I were British, I would probably have felt it essential to include works by Peter Maxwell Davies and Thomas Adès; if German, by Hans Werner Henze and Wolfgang Rihm; if French, by Henri Dutilleux. When a composer is represented by multiple works, I have presented the pieces in chronological order within the relevant chapter so as to suggest the historical flow of the composer's "chamber music career."

Some of these essays appear for the first time in this book, but many trace their ancestry to writings that appeared initially in the publications of musical establishments with which I have been affiliated over the years. I thank them for their support of this project, as organizations and as the individual professionals who have served as my special colleagues. At the New York Philharmonic and its chamber incentive, the New York Philharmonic Ensembles, Eric Latzky and Monica Parks (my cherished partner in program notes for the past fifteen years) have always offered unflagging encouragement, and I deeply appreciate president and executive director Zarin Mehta's constant support of communications that help engage audiences. The San Francisco Symphony maintains two separate chamber music series in addition to its orchestral programs, which affords me the pleasure of near-constant interaction with the editorial team of Larry Rothe, Katherine Cummins, and Jeanette Yu—friends, all; and I am grateful for the fervor the orchestra's executive director, Brent Assink, displays when it comes to upholding the storied standards of the orchestra's publications. I greatly value the camaraderie I enjoy with Janet Kessin and Heike Currie at the Juilliard School, and I always smile when my in-box holds an e-mail from Alison Latham, the genial and astute program editor of the Edinburgh International Festival. I have now written for six editors at *Chamber Music* magazine, a publication of Chamber Music America, most prominently (working backward) my esteemed collaborators Ellen Goldensohn, Karissa Krenz, Johanna Keller, and Clair Van Ausdall; I thank them all, as well as the organization's executive director, Margaret Lioi. There is nobody among these colleagues whose input is not in some way reflected in this volume. Thanks are also due to my *compadres* at *Pasatiempo/The Santa Fe New Mexican*, and especially to my editor there, Kristina Melcher, who gave me the gift of time.

The seed of this book was planted through conversations with Kim Robinson, then the music editor at Oxford University Press, and it was nurtured by her successor, Suzanne Ryan, who as executive editor of music books has kept everything on an even keel. Joellyn Ausanka and Madelyn Sutton are among those of her associates who have labored with consummate professionalism on behalf of this book. Joanne Wang proved to be both unflappable as my literary agent and unswerving as my friend.

Speaking of friends, these are a few who provided kindnesses specifically connected to the realization of this book: Alberto Bertoli and Eva Magdolen Bertoli, Linda Ciolek and the late Marty Streicher, Mary Lou Falcone, Annice Jacoby, Brian Kellow, Eloy and Anita Muñoz, Stuart and Linda Nelson, Roger and Kyla Thompson, Susan Wilber. I am grateful to my long-departed parents, Fred and Roberta Keller, who shuttled me to countless music lessons and in every way supported my incipient fascination with great music. Of my teachers, I am especially indebted to five who helped set me on the course of my life's work: the late Nancy Fisher, who cemented my love of languages; the late Virginia Zug, who challenged me to be a better writer; Frank J. Ferraro, who made space for chamber music in a high school's curriculum because it mattered to one of his students, and therefore to him; Maurice Bourgue, who guided me as an oboist and revealed musical secrets I will not forget; and Allen Forte, music theorist extraordinaire, who clarified that musical scores both provide answers and invite questions.

Last and most I thank Marc Dorfman, my indispensable other half for the past twenty-seven years. He has been and will remain my concert companion of choice.

Contents

Chamber Music

Anton Stepanovich Arensky

Born: June 30 (old style)/July 12 (new style), 1861 in Novgorad, Russia

Died: February 12 (old style)/25 (new style), 1906 in Terioki, Finland (now Zelenogorsk, Russia)

Piano Trio No. 1 in D minor, Op. 32

Allegro moderato—Adagio
Scherzo: Allegro molto
Elegia: Adagio
Finale: Allegro non troppo—Andante—Adagio—Allegro molto

Work composed: 1894

Work dedicated: "À la mémoire de Charles Davidoff" (To the memory of Karl Davïdov)

Work premiered: Probably December 1894 in either Moscow or St. Petersburg, by the violinist Jan Hrímalý, the cellist Anatoly Brandukov, and the composer as pianist

Instrumentation: Violin, cello, and piano

The generation of Russian composers who came of age during the 1860s and '70s were broadly split into two camps separated by a porous dividing line. Individual composers might occasionally creep over from one side to the other (and usually back again), but generally their allegiance lay either with the Nationalists (most prominently the composers of the "Russian Five" or "Mighty Handful"—Mili Balakirev, Alexander Borodin, Cesar Cui, Modest Musorgsky, and Nikolai Rimsky-Korsakov), who championed the use of music derived from Russian folk or liturgical sources, or with those who meshed more closely with the central Germanic tradition, most notably Tchaikovsky.

Arensky might have carried on the nationalistic tendencies of his teacher, Rimsky-Korsakov, with whom he studied in St. Petersburg, but instead he drifted toward the Tchaikovskian camp. Rimsky-Korsakov recalled him in generally unflattering terms, though one does not have to read between the lines very closely to sense that his account is hardly impartial: "According to all testimony, his life had run a dissipated course between wine and card-playing, yet his activity as a composer was most fertile. . . . He did work much at composition, but that is just where he began to burn the candle at both ends. Revels, card-playing, health undermined by this mode of living, gal-loping consumption as the final result, dying at Nice, and death at last in Finland. . . . In his youth Arensky had not escaped entirely my own influence; later he fell under that of Tchaikovsky. He will soon be forgotten."

An important professional opportunity came in Arensky's direction in 1894. Mili Balakirev, the opinionated chief of the Nationalist wing of Rus-sian composers, overcame his esthetic partisanship and recommended Aren-sky to be his successor as the director of the Imperial Chapel in St. Petersburg. Within a year Arensky would resign from the Moscow Conservatory and move to St. Petersburg to assume that position. In 1894 he also unveiled his second opera, *Rafael*, as a centerpiece of the First Congress of Russian Artists, and he composed two chamber works that continue to receive per-formances today: his Piano Trio No. 1 and his String Quartet No. 2. Both of these chamber works were memorial pieces—the quartet in honor of Tchai-kovsky, who had died the preceding year, and the trio to commemorate Karl Yul'yevich Davïdov, who had died in 1889. Born in 1838 in the Courland Governorate of Russia (now Latvia), Davïdov served a few years as principal cellist of the Leipzig Gewandhaus Orchestra before returning to Russia to become principal cellist of the Imperial Italian Opera, cellist of the Russian Musical Society's Quartet, cello professor at the St. Petersburg Conservatory, and from 1876 to 1887 the Conservatory's director. Writing commemorative chamber-music tributes was something of a tradition just then: Tchaikovsky had composed his A-minor Piano Trio (1882) as a memorial to his teacher Nikolai Rubinstein, and in 1893 Rachmaninoff wrote his Second *Trio élé-giaque* in honor of Tchaikovsky.

Arensky's D-minor Piano Trio is a full-scale work, its four movements running more than a half hour and covering a broad spectrum of styles in the process. The first movement is often compared to the corresponding section of Mendelssohn's much earlier D-minor Piano Trio (1839), though Arensky proceeds with more relaxed luxury than Mendelssohn had. Arensky's ingra-tiating themes seem born of the salon, and the composer manipulates them with consummate mastery and variety. The second movement is a *Scherzo* in the sparkling mode of Saint-Saëns, reminiscent of that composer's Piano Concerto No. 2 almost to the point of parody, and the pianist's fingers fly across the keys in most spectacular fashion before the movement reaches its whispered coda.

The Davïdov memorial is constructed specifically in the third movement, which is actually headed *Elegia*. The string instruments install mutes for the duration of this movement, which maintains quiet nobility: this is more a dignified, reflective memorial service than a grief-racked funeral. Davïdov had been a kind and encouraging presence during Arensky's student years in St. Petersburg, and the affection with which Arensky repays him is palpable in this tender movement, which appropriately begins with the cello singing the beautiful *adagio* melody in G minor. The middle of this slow movement— effectively a Trio section—speeds up a notch (*più mosso*) and moves into G major. Now it is the piano that is given the main melody as the strings waver gently in the background. The thought breaks off in a grand pause, and then Arensky offers the same "*più mosso*" music even more beautifully orchestrated, with the violin playing the melody against the pizzicato cello and flutter-ing figuration in the piano. One might argue that Arensky is treading water through these sequence-filled passages; but if that is the case, at least he is a swimmer of surpassing elegance, and he knows better than to stretch out his sequences longer than he does. This second go-round of the "*più mosso*" music also drifts off in silence, after which the violin picks up the train of thought with the beautiful G-minor melody from the opening. Again, Arensky does not settle for literal repetition. Instead he redistributes his music among the players, fleshes out the piano part into rich handfuls of chords, and enriches the texture through canonic gestures in which one instrument quietly con-curs with what another has just said. On the final page the cello exhales the principal melody one final time against the dotted rhythms of the piano's funeral-march accompaniment.

In the *Finale* we find not only original themes but also references to melodies heard earlier—the principal theme of the *Elegia* (turned into the major mode but still announced first by the cello) and, near the end, the gor-geous, somewhat nostalgic "*più mosso*" theme of the *Elegia*. Arensky travels well-worn paths in his D-minor Piano Trio, and listeners who put a premium on novelty may therefore find the piece easy to dismiss as reactionary and lightweight. And yet it is an easy piece to love thanks to Arensky's undeni-able skill in the time-honored methods of composing, his ever-delicate touch, and—perhaps most important—his undeniable sincerity.

Arensky's D-minor Trio was in the news in 2008, with the discovery of a cache of some two hundred cylinders recorded in the 1890s by the businessman and music aficionado Julius H. Block. Long thought lost or possibly destroyed in World War II, they were rediscovered in a library in St. Petersburg. Among the treasures were cylinders of portions of the D-minor Trio's first three movements, all played rhapsodically and at a vigorous pace. Whether this recorded performance suggests "ideal" tempos for the work is open to dispute; it is possible that the musicians were playing quicker than they might have liked simply because they wanted to squeeze as much music as they could onto the cylinders, which could only hold between two and just over four minutes of material. The recordings were made on December 10, 1894, and the performers are identified: Arensky, as pianist, is joined by the violinist Jan Hrímalý and the cellist Anatoly Brandukov. Details about the premiere of this work being vague, we may be tempted to surmise that these were also the musicians who first played the work in concert.

Johann Sebastian Bach

Born: March 21, 1685, in Eisenach, Thuringia (Germany)

Died: July 28, 1750, in Leipzig, Saxony (Germany)

BWV numbers: Johann Sebastian Bach's works are identified by "BWV" (sometimes "S") numbers assigned in Wolfgang Schmieder's *Thematisch-systematisches Verzeichnis der musikalischen Werke Johann Sebastian Bachs: Bach-Werke-Verzeichnis* (1950/1990).

Trio Sonata in G major for Flute, Violin, and Basso Continuo, BWV 1038

Largo
Vivace
Adagio
Presto

Johann Sebastian Bach left a modest legacy of true chamber music, if we understand the term to mean one-on-a-part compositions for small groups of instruments that don't invite doubling of multiple players on a single line. That's how it looks on the page, anyway; in practice, many of his apparently larger pieces may have been conceived, or at least performed, with hardly more than what we would consider chamber forces. Then, too, we find in Bach occasions where orchestral and chamber writing co-exist within a single piece. For familiar examples we could turn to the *Brandenburg* Concertos, all six of which are logically classified in his catalogue as orchestral works. Nonetheless, the variously constituted orchestras sit silent for the slow movements in three of these concertos while the solo instruments play exquisite pieces of chamber music: in the Second *Brandenburg* Concerto, an *Andante* that could have been plucked from a *sonata a quattro* for flute, oboe, violin, and basso continuo; in the Fifth, a corresponding *Affettuoso* (originally *Adagio)* for flute, violin, obbligato harpsichord, and basso continuo; and in the Sixth an *Adagio ma non troppo* for a trio sonata texture of two violas and basso continuo. In such pieces as these we find chamber music and symphonic music living cheek by jowl. We may even sense that we have stumbled into a historical moment when the orchestra is emerging, not yet fully or certainly formed, from the more intimate chamber formulations that gave rise to it.

Evidence relating to the surviving manuscript parts of Bach's Trio Sonata in G major (BWV 1038) suggests that it was written sometime between 1732 and 1735. This piece perfectly exemplifies the sort of musicological problems that swirl about his chamber works. There is no question that Bach wrote at least its bass part, which is identical to that of his G-major Violin Sonata (BWV 1021), also from that period. Considerable controversy reigns over the trio sonata's upper lines, which are for flute and violin. Few scholars today subscribe to the formerly widespread belief that Bach wrote the melody parts himself. Most posit that he had a student derive them from the pre-existent violin sonata, but a few plot the process in reverse, suggesting that the trio sonata came first and that the violin sonata represents a sometimes awkward student reduction.

In 1775 the composer's son (and pupil) Carl Philipp Emanuel Bach shared with the Bach biographer Johann Nikolaus Forkel a description of his father's mode of teaching composition, which jibes perfectly with the general idea of how this trio sonata came about:

> In composition he started his pupils right in with what was practical, and omitted all the *dry species* of counterpoint that are given in Fux and others. His pupils had to begin their studies by learning pure four-part thorough bass. From this they went to chorales; first he added the basses himself, and they had to invent the alto and tenor. . . . As for the invention of ideas, he required this from the very beginning, and anyone who had none he advised to stay away from composition altogether. With his children as well as with other pupils he did not begin the study of composition until he had seen work of theirs in which he detected talent.

If Bach did not write the upper lines himself, it remains a mystery who did. He taught numerous composition students once he moved to Leipzig in 1723, and many of them reached a level of accomplishment that would have enabled them to undertake such an exercise. The musicologist Stephen Daw has suggested that the melody lines may have been "written by a young, fashion-conscious Leipzig student, such as Friedrich Gottlieb Wild or Christoph Gottlob Wecker." Wecker (1706–74) studied with Bach from

1723 to 1729, as did Wild (1700–1762) from 1726 to 1735. Both of these now obscure souls went on to minor careers as church musicians, Wecker in Schweidnitz, Silesia, Wild in St. Petersburg. Wild might have an edge as a candidate since his study with Bach coincides more exactly to the period when this trio sonata was seemingly composed, and since a recommendation Bach wrote to support one of Wild's job applications mentions that he was a capable flutist as well as a keyboard player. Daw's description of the mystery student as "fashion-conscious" rings true. If the raison d'être for this piece was principally didactic, the composer nonetheless found an outlet for expressivity that sometimes strikes us as personal. Especially in the third movement we encounter a hyper-emotive style that is connected to both the dense mournfulness we find in some of J. S. Bach's sacred works and the highly charged, if stylized, sentiment that would grow popular with C. P. E. Bach's generation.

Notwithstanding the musicological complications, the G-major Trio Sonata is easy to love, with its melodic lines tracing contrapuntal coils above Bach's elegantly plotted bass. The sonata's four-movement form is typical of the Italian Baroque "church sonatas," with their characteristic succession of slow-fast-slow-fast. But within this structure, the work's procedure shows some distinctive aspects. In the broad opening *Largo*, derived from an initial upward scale motif, the composer writes out what would normally be notated as a literal repeat of both halves in order to create a variation on the material the second time around; in other words, instead of a simple A-A-B-B structure, the material is here massaged considerably into A-A'-B-B'. The fast movements—the second and fourth—are notable for their brevity. In the second-movement *Vivace*, less than a minute long, only one theme is brought into serious play, and in the concluding *Presto*, contrapuntal procedures are so telescoped that the movement sounds almost like a mere fugal exposition, rather than the complete (if miniature) fugue that it actually is.

Sonata sopr'il Soggetto Reale a Traversa, Violino e Continuo, from Musical Offering (Musikalisches Opfer), BWV 1079

Largo
Allegro
Andante
Allegro

Johann Sebastian Bach fathered twenty children, of whom eleven would survive to their adulthoods. Four among them became distinguished composers in their own right: Wilhelm Friedemann, Carl Philipp Emanuel, Johann

Christoph Friedrich, and Johann Christian. The third of the sons (but the second to live beyond childhood), Carl Philipp Emanuel ("C. P. E.") was appointed in 1740, at the age of twenty-six, as chamber musician to King Frederick II "the Great" of Prussia, who had just acceded to the throne. The music-loving Frederick surrounded himself with a stellar assemblage of about forty staff musicians, not counting singers, and C. P. E. was his star keyboard player.

Johann Sebastian visited C. P. E. twice during the latter's tenure at Potsdam, first in the summer of 1741, then again in May 1747, that time perhaps with his eldest son, Wilhelm Friedemann, in tow. The *Musikalisches Opfer* (*Musical Offering*) traces its genesis to the latter visit. Whether Bach had been expressly invited to Potsdam by the flute-playing monarch or whether Frederick was surprised to find Bach's name on his daily roster of visitors is unclear—sources differ—but there is little question that the king was pleased to find Germany's most learned musician in his presence, and he reportedly escorted Bach through the palace, stopping to have him improvise on the various keyboard instruments they encountered. These included a couple of newfangled fortepianos built by Gottfried Silbermann, which Bach seems to have generally liked and which he would go on to represent as a selling agent in Leipzig.

In 1754 the *Musikalische Bibliothek*, published by a music society to which C. P. E. belonged, ran an obituary of Johann Sebastian, who had died four years earlier. Prepared jointly by C. P. E. and Johann Friedrich Agricola (a devoted Bach pupil), the obituary made mention of Johann Sebastian's last visit:

> In the year 1747 he made a journey to Berlin and was graciously allowed on this occasion to perform in the presence of His Majesty the King of Prussia at Potsdam. His Majesty himself played a fugue subject for him, on which Bach improvised a fugue at once on the piano, to the especial pleasure of His Majesty. Hereupon His Majesty demanded to hear a six-part fugue, which command was also fulfilled at once, on a theme selected by Bach, to the astonishment of the King and the assembled musicians. After his return to Leipzig, he wrote a three-part and a six-part *Ricercar* besides various other smaller pieces based on the same theme presented to him by His Majesty, and dedicated the copper engraving of the work to the King.

The event generated great interest, and not just among musicians. On May 11, 1747, the newspaper *Berliner Nachrichten* devoted an enthusiastic article to the soirée—the only time in his life Bach appears to have achieved front-page coverage. It's not at all certain that Frederick the Great himself wrote the theme proposed; most musicologists agree that at the very least it was coached out of him by, for example, C. P. E. The theme's contours are distinctive and easily remembered and recognized: a rising minor triad leading to a minor sixth, from there a plummet of a diminished seventh, a return to the fifth and a sinuous, chromatic descent that zeroes in on the tonic, with a bit of melodic embellishment at the cadence.

The *Musical Offering* was published in September 1747, four months after the composer's visit to Potsdam. Bach had it printed in an edition of two hundred copies, each of which comprised five smaller booklets containing several movements apiece. Musicologists have debated whether this curious format was arbitrary or not, and whether Bach implied any particular order for the work's sixteen movements or, indeed, if he even envisioned most of it as music that would actually be performed.

The set comprises two ricercars (the word was anciently used as a rough synonym for "fugue"), ten canons of various sorts, and a four-movement trio sonata, which Bach titles *Sonata sopr'il Soggetto Reale* ("Sonata on the Royal Subject"). Problems with the ordering of selections at least do not affect the movements of the trio sonata, which unrolls according to the slow-fast-slow-fast plan typical of its genre. The question of intended instrumentation, which is unaddressed or vague nearly throughout the *Musical Offering*, is blessedly explicit when it comes to the trio sonata: it is scored for flute, violin, and basso continuo. That the flute should take a soloist's role is natural, given Frederick's predilection for that instrument. Bach's pupil Johann Philipp Kirnberger, who later published his solutions of several of the canons, actually wrote out a realization of the sonata's entire continuo part, the only such example created within hailing distance of the composer's supervision.

In the *Sonata sopr'il Soggetto Reale* Frederick's theme appears verbatim only in the second movement (*Allegro*)—and there abundantly. To ears by now accustomed to its contours it seems to hover at the edges from the outset. Suspense mounts until finally the subject is unleashed a minute into the movement, given out in the bass line first in the dominant key (starting on G), then a few measures later in the tonic (on C). That would be enough: Bach has met his requirements. But we move on to the movement's balancing second half, where the royal theme suddenly jumps out from the violin part and then (following a C. P. E.-like rhythmic caesura) from the flute prior to a return to music from near the movement's beginning, including a revisit of the bass-line royal-theme quotations.

Though these are the only verbatim iterations of the royal theme in the trio sonata, allusions to it surface throughout. Both of the slow movements are exquisite examples of Bach's highly expressive *affettuoso* style, though neither is expressly marked with that term. In the initial *Largo*—its opening bass line being a filled-out version of the royal theme—we find the intensity of emotional expression familiar from Bach's cantatas, while the third-movement *Andante* bathes itself in the sighing *Empfindsamer Stil* popular in the Potsdam Court. The concluding *Allegro* is cast as a high-spirited gigue in 6/8 meter. The movement's main motif is clearly a rhythmic variation on Frederick's theme, and it is worked out with exorbitant subtlety of counterpoint, expressive chromatic progressions, and layers of rhythmic contrasts.

Samuel Barber

Born: March 9, 1910, in West Chester, Pennsylvania

Died: January 23, 1981, in New York City

String Quartet, Op. 11

Molto allegro e appassionato
Molto adagio [attacca]
Molto allegro (come prima)

Work composed: Begun in the summer of 1935 and completed the next year in a provisional form; Barber continued to revise the work—particularly its finale—through 1943.

Work dedicated: To Louise and Sidney Homer

Work premiered: In its provisional form on December 14, 1936, by the Pro Arte Quartet at the Villa Aurelia in Rome; in its final form on May 28, 1943, by the Budapest Quartet at the Library of Congress in Washington, D.C.

Instrumentation: Two violins, viola, and cello

As its low opus number suggests, Samuel Barber's String Quartet was an early work. In May 1935 the twenty-five-year-old composer received two awards in quick succession: a Pulitzer traveling scholarship (announced on May 6) and the Prix de Rome (on May 9). That October he left for the two-year residency in Rome attached to the latter prize, and from there he undertook considerable travels elsewhere in Europe. This was a fine arrangement for him, as his long-term companion and fellow composer Gian Carlo Menotti came from Milan and was delighted that they could spend time so conveniently in Italy. From mid-May to the end of October 1936 the

couple lived in an idyllic mountain cottage in St. Wolfgang in the Salzkammergut, and that is where Barber's String Quartet began to germinate.

Before he left for Austria, Barber had alerted Orlando Cole, the cellist of
the Curtis String Quartet, that a string quartet was in the offing, and he suggested that the Curtis Quartet might introduce the envisioned piece during
a European tour they had already scheduled. But his work proceeded more
slowly than he had hoped, and by the end of August Barber alerted Cole that
the piece would not be ready in time for them to prepare it for their tour.
Work advanced, if slowly. On September 19 he wrote to Cole: "I have just
finished the slow movement of my quartet today—it is a knock-out! Now for
a Finale."

The finale he produced would become a bee in Barber's bonnet. It served
to conclude the work's premiere, on December 14, 1936, at the Villa Aurelia
in Rome, when it was played by the Pro Arte Quartet. Barber was distressed
that the honor of the premiere went to an ensemble other than the Curtis String Quartet, but the scheduling proved impossible for that foursome.
Immediately after the premiere Barber withdrew the finale for a rewrite; and
when the Curtis String Quartet finally played the piece—at a private pre-
birthday concert for Barber on March 7, 1937, at the Curtis Institute—they
presented only the opening Molto allegro and the ensuing Molto adagio. By
April Barber had finished rewriting his finale, which the Gordon Quartet
included when it played the work at the Library of Congress that month. The
finale was especially admired in this concert, but Barber remained uneasy
and ended up recasting it yet again. By the time the piece was published, in
1943, Barber had settled on the structure as we now know it: a solid opening
movement in sonata form, followed by the famous slow movement and then
a very telescoped finale—only two minutes long—that revisits themes from
the opening movement, thereby attaining a cyclic form for the quartet as a
whole. The finale is presented in the score not as an independent movement
but rather as an appendage to the second, from which it emerges attacca (i.e.,
without a break).

The opening movement begins with a strongly etched, ultra-dramatic
motif announced in unison by the four players; the effect recalls Beethoven's
Serioso Quartet (Op. 95). A second theme area involves chorale-like music
of a slinky personality, and a third focuses on Barber's characteristic ability to
spin out a lyrical melody of uncommon beauty, this one being of a yearning
sort that would have been admired in movie scores of the '30s and '40s.

The quartet as whole is in the key of B minor, but a part of the opening theme involves a starkly demarcated semitone. So it is that the opening
movement ends pondering the distance that separates notes a semitone apart;
and this serves to link the first movement, in B minor, to the second, in the

chromatically close but harmonically distant realm of B-flat minor. The tonic of B minor returns in the brief revisit of the fast material at the quartet's end, but this B-flat-minor second movement is the heart of the work. Its materials are slight: a very slow and extended melody built from stepwise intervals, slightly varied in its numerous repetitions, uncoiling over (or in the midst of) sustained chords that change with note-by-note reluctance, all of it building into a powerful climax at the high end of the instruments' range and then quickly receding to the contemplative quietude that ultimately defines this musical expanse. It is indeed "a knock-out," as Barber reported, and it rose to superstardom when Barber arranged it as a stand-alone Adagio for Strings for five-part string orchestra (two violins, two violas, and cello), which was first heard on November 5, 1938, in a broadcast by Arturo Toscanini and the NBC Symphony.

Toscanini soon included the piece in his European and South American tour programs, and this sparked a debate among esthetes over the merits of modernist versus retrograde musical style, with Barber being deemed to adhere to the latter. Though interesting, the argument was moot, and Barber's Adagio for Strings promptly became an icon of American music, particularly associated with grief-laden situations. It was played at the presidential funerals of both Franklin D. Roosevelt and John F. Kennedy, and in 1986 it contributed to the heart-wrenching impact of Oliver Stone's film *Platoon*. Even composers who would themselves be cited as more forward-looking presences in American music had no trouble applauding the special qualities of Barber's Adagio. In a 1982 BBC broadcast, Aaron Copland declared: "It's really well felt, it's believable, you see, it's not phoney....It comes straight from the heart, to use old-fashioned terms. The sense of continuity, the steadiness of the flow, the satisfaction of the arch that it creates from beginning to end. They're all very gratifying, satisfying, and it makes you believe in the sincerity which he obviously put into it." And William Schuman, in the same broadcast: "It's so precise emotionally. The emotional climate is never left in doubt. It begins, it reaches its climax, it makes its point, and it goes away. For me it's never a war-horse; when I hear it played I'm always moved by it."

After transcribing the Adagio for string orchestra Barber would go on to adapt it also for chorus, in 1967, as a setting of the Agnus Dei. He bestowed his *nihil obstat* on arrangements made for organ by William Strickland, for clarinet choir by Lucien Caillet, and for woodwind ensemble by John O'Reilly. Still, it is as a string quartet that this remarkable movement was conceived. The quartet was hard-won, and although Barber did accept a commission for a Second String Quartet in 1947, he never managed to move beyond a few pages of sketches for that work.

Summer Music for Wind Quintet, Op. 31

Slow and Indolent—With motion—Faster—Lively, still faster—Faster

Work composed: 1956 on commission from the Chamber Music Society of Detroit

Work premiered: March 20, 1956, at the Detroit Institute of Arts in Detroit, Michigan, in a concert of the Chamber Music Society of Detroit; played on that occasion by five principal players from the Detroit Symphony: flutist James Pellerite, oboist Arno Mariotti, clarinetist Albert Luconi, hornist Ray Alonge, and bassoonist Charles Sirard.

Instrumentation: Flute, oboe, clarinet, horn, and bassoon

Summer Music came about through an unusual commission, extended by the Chamber Music Society of Detroit in 1953, that received a good deal of publicity at the time. Instead of negotiating a lump-sum payment for his new work, Barber signed on to a plan whereby the Society would ask Detroit's music lovers to pledge whatever they wished toward underwriting the project. Most donations arrived in amounts ranging from one dollar to five dollars, but they arrived in abundance. I don't know how much Barber received, but the Society guaranteed that the sum would not be less than $2,000. Barber resisted at first, as he explained:

> The idea was if this caught on, music societies around the country would take up similar collections and use the funds to commission young local composers who needed experience and exposure. I made a speech against myself, essentially, telling them it was crazy that they didn't use local composers. It was certainly done in Bach's day. But they didn't like that idea. They wanted the same old tired names—Copland, Sessions, Harris, me—so it never got off the ground.

In any case, Barber signed on to compose a septet for three winds, three strings, and piano. As the piece emerged, its forces morphed into a sextet and finally into a wind quintet, the eventual scoring reflecting how impressed Barber had been by his exposure to the New York Woodwind Quintet during the summer of 1954 in Blue Hill, Maine. That ensemble would play a central role in the creation of Barber's piece. Back in New York during the winter of 1955 he observed them in rehearsals mastering exercises crafted by John Barrows, the group's hornist, to address advanced technical issues of wind-quintet playing. Armed with what he had learned, Barber turned some of those technical challenges to expressive use. On November 14 he arranged for the New York Woodwind Quintet to read through the piece, after which its flutist, Samuel Baron, reported: "We were completely gassed! What a wonderful new quintet conception. Barber has studied our charts and has written some of our favorite effects. The piece is very hard, but so far it sounds just beautiful to us."

They were understandably disappointed that the circumstances of the commission would not allow them to play the premiere, which was reserved for Detroit (on March 20, 1956). Perhaps they were fortunate in the long run. Although the Detroit premiere was warmly received and the critic for the *Detroit News* complimented the piece for its "mood of pastoral serenity," Barber felt, upon hearing the work in concert, that it was too long. He therefore set about effecting cuts, working with the New York Woodwind Quintet, who actually managed to dissuade him from deleting one section that made prominent use of some of the "problem chords" from Barrows' exercises. *Summer Music* reached its final form and the ensemble finally was able to program it for the first time on April 27, 1956, at a concert of the Harvard Musical Association. It would instantly become a standard item in their repertoire.

In addition to drawing inspiration from the group's technical exercises, Barber had also gotten himself going on the piece by borrowing thematic material from a work he had composed in 1945 for *The Standard Oil Hour*, a program on the NBC radio network. Titled *Horizon*, it was a short orchestral piece "on Arabian themes" (such was NBC's request), and it was played for the broadcast on June 17, 1945, by the San Francisco Symphony, conducted by Efrem Kurtz. What had been uttered by a pair of bassoons at the outset of *Horizon* was transposed up a step to become the beginning of *Summer Music*; and another motif a bit into the first movement—starting with three notes plunging by the interval of an eleventh—also derives from *Horizon*. By the way, I doubt that anyone not knowing in advance about the supposed "Arabian" content of *Horizon* would make that geographical connection. To me it sounds essentially French and particularly indebted to the Debussy of *La Mer* or *Images* for Orchestra.

Summer Music is a difficult piece from the performers' standpoint, but audiences are grateful for its placid, often witty, rather Gallic gentility. (Not *too* placid, though; Barber complained that interpreters tended to play the piece too slowly.) Cast as a single movement with five discrete sections, it conveys a sense of nostalgic lassitude such as we treasure so much in Barber's *Knoxville, Summer of 1915*, which would follow shortly, in 1947, though it bubbles with considerable energy in the middle. Near the end of his life Barber told an interviewer, "It's supposed to be *evocative* of summer—summer meaning languid, not killing mosquitos."

Heat and lethargy infuse the opening, which is marked "Slow and indolent." Horn and bassoon strike a bluesy pose à la Gershwin or (with their implications of bitonality) Milhaud, and above them flute and then clarinet release fluttering roulades that descend through the thickening texture, finally being buried deep in the bassoon. The oboe sings out a long-phrased melody, which is worked out in a mood of utmost relaxation. The tempo now picks up and the instruments putter in very quick staccatos (a naked test of ensemble precision). "Lively, still faster," urges Barber, and the music takes on something of a hoedown flavor—effectively a central trio to the scherzo of the staccato music, which returns to round out this section. (The unmistakably American sound of the quick "trio" section is not characteristic of Barber, who was often cited in his day for completely resisting the "yippee-yi-yay" tendencies of numerous mid-century scores by, for example, Aaron Copland and Roy Harris.) This gives way to a return of the oboe's languid melody. Now all the principal material is revisited through quick allusions: the staccato section (slowed down considerably), the indolent sounds of the opening. A new section emerges (marked "Faster"), dance-like, and modal, owing something to Dvořák and treated at considerable length. Memories of the listless opening return near the end, but the final page picks up energy and dies away in a quiet, rustling scurry.

Béla Victor János Bartók

Born: March 25, 1881, in Nagyszentmiklós, Hungary, now Sînnicolau Mare, Romania

Died: September 26, 1945, in New York City

BB and Sz numbers: The "BB numbers" attached to Bartók's compositions refer to entries in the chronological catalogue prepared by musicologist László Somfai and published in the volume *Béla Bartók: Composition, Concepts, and Autograph Sources* (Berkeley, 1996). Somfai's catalogue supersedes the one produced in 1957 by András Szöllösy, *Bibliographie des oeuvres musicales et écrits musicologiques de Béla Bartók*, but one still finds frequent references to the "Sz numbers" of that earlier reference book. These numbers really are helpful to the general music-lover since many of Bartók's compositions have very similar titles and since he stopped assigning opus number to his works in mid-career.

String Quartet No. 2, Op. 17 (BB 75; Sz.67)

Moderato
Allegro molto capriccioso
Lento

Work composed: 1914–17 in Rákoskeresztúr, Hungary (then a village just to the east of Budapest, but subsumed into the city in 1950)

Work dedicated: To the Waldbauer-Kerpely Quartet

Work premiered: March 3, 1918, in Budapest by the Waldbauer-Kerpely Quartet

Instrumentation: Two violins, viola, and cello

Hungarians revere Béla Bartók as their nation's greatest twentieth-century composer, and rightly so. But today any Hungarian who should decide to make a pilgrimage to pay respects at the site where Bartók was born would have to leave the country. He was indeed born in Hungary—or properly put, in the Greater Hungarian sector of the Austro-Hungarian Empire—in the small town of Nagyszentmiklós. The town hasn't moved, of course, but political boundaries in that part of the world have proved fluid over the years. So it was that the Treaty of Trianon, drafted in 1920 to divvy up the spoils of World War I, turned what had been Nagyszentmiklós, at the northern end of the southern Hungarian province of Torontál, into Sînnicolau Mare, in the state of Timiş in western Romania, just a few miles in from the border of modern Hungary.

Bartók grew up understanding that in his part of the world cultures were local and national borders capricious. He grew fascinated by the folk music of his region and beyond, collecting songs in Hungary, Romania, Ruthenia, Serbia, Croatia, Bulgaria, Turkey, and North Africa. Most of these excursions left their mark on Bartók's own compositions, sometimes in an obvious way (as in his many pieces that consist of harmonizations of intact melodies), sometimes more profoundly absorbed into his distinctive brand of modernism. But just as folk-inflected sounds waft through his music, so do echoes of important strands of the "high-art" musical avant-garde of his time (including very prominently the harmonic Impressionism of Debussy and the breaking-point post-Romanticism of Schoenberg) or of past generations (such as the contrapuntal proclivities of Bach or the formal balance and dramatic pacing of Beethoven and Brahms).

Frank Whitaker, a British journalist who in 1926 embarked on the first biography ever of Bartók but failed to get beyond the first chapter, did manage to contribute a pellucid description of the composer for a BBC publication in 1932: "Béla Bartók is a quiet little man with a springy walk and a complexion like faded parchment. His lean, alert face suggests the man of forty, his white hair and scholar's stoop the man of sixty.... The English words he uses oftenest to describe his music are 'provoking' and 'unaccustomed.' For instance, he will say, 'My Bagatelles were my first provoking work,' or 'My second string quartet was too unaccustomed for the public of the day.'"

This "too unaccustomed" Second String Quartet may reflect its composer's state of mind during World War I. Bartók was deeply affected by the outbreak of the war in the summer of 1914. Several months later, on October 30, he wrote to his friend Rev. Sámuel Bobál, a Slovak minister: "I also belong to the age-group which is to be called up for military service. There's a good chance that I shall be rejected on health grounds. But nowadays there's no knowing anything in advance." As it turned out, he received a medical deferment and instead was assigned by the state to collect folk songs from soldiers—a mission that agreed with him perfectly. Still, the cloud of war hung over everybody. To another friend, János Buşiţia-Belényes, he wrote on May 20, 1915: "My long silence has been due to the fact that every now and then I am thrown into a state of depression by the war—a condition which, in my case, alternates with a kind of devil-may-care attitude."

Perhaps we have that devil-may-care streak to thank for the fact that Bartók's productivity did not grind to a halt during the war. On the contrary, these proved to be relatively fertile years, and even in the straitened circumstances the composer continued to see some of his musical colleagues, including Imre Waldbauer and Jenö Kerpely. Bartók's elder son, Béla, Jr., spoke of his family's home life during the war in an interview published in 1976 in the *New Hungarian Quarterly*: "I knew quite certainly that the members of the Waldbauer String Quartet were here separately, and also together. I recall Waldbauer and Kerpely were here in uniform, being on war service. The Second String Quartet was completed on the occasion of a visit like this." The Waldbauer-Kerpely Quartet was honored with the dedication of this work, which they unveiled in Budapest on March 3, 1918.

In the Second String Quartet we find Bartók working in a freely chromatic and rhythmically complex idiom, meticulously molding his themes and motives into tight and rigorous musical proceedings. Bartók here continued to develop his originality as a structuralist. The relationships of tempos among movements are unorthodox compared to the progressive acceleration of the First Quartet: a *Moderato* leads to an *Allegro molto capriccioso* and then to a concluding, unearthly *Lento*. The spirit of the writing in every case mirrors what one might reasonably expect as typical of those tempos. Bartók's respected colleague Zoltán Kodály described the three movements as "1.) A quiet life; 2.) Joy; 3.) Sorrow." Otherwise put, it is a progression that may first evoke normality, then Bartók's "devil-may-care" exhilaration (and, in the brief middle episode of the second movement, outright nonchalance), and finally his lamenting depression over the sad state of things.

String Quartet No. 3 (BB 93; Sz.85)

> *Prima parte: Moderato (attacca)*
> *Seconda parte: Allegro (attacca)*
> *Ricapitulazione della prima parte: Moderato (attacca)*
> *Coda: Allegro molto*

Work composed: September 1927 in Budapest

Work dedicated: To the Musical Fund Society of Philadelphia

Work premiered: December 30, 1928, in Philadelphia by violinists Mischa Mischakoff and David Dubinsky, violist Samuel Lifschey, and cellist William Van der Berg

Instrumentation: Two violins, viola, and cello

Bartók composed his Third Quartet in Budapest in September 1927, completing it at the end of that month, and shortly thereafter embarked on a ten-week American tour. Usually reliable reference sources reflect considerable disagreement about the ensuing chronology—extending even to details of the premieres—but one credible explanation has Bartók learning in the course of his trip, from Hungarian-American friends, about a competition for new chamber works being sponsored by the august Musical Fund Society of Philadelphia. Following his return to Hungary he submitted his new quartet, which ended up sharing the first prize of $6,000 with a largely forgotten work by Alfredo Casella, his Serenata for clarinet, bassoon, trumpet, violin, cello, and piano. (Among the 643 entries they edged out was Szymanowski's String Quartet No. 2.) In appreciation he dedicated this quartet to the Society.

The work was played as part of the Musical Fund Society competition proceedings—though with the composer not identified—and it appears to have received its public premiere in Philadelphia on December 30, 1928, by the Mischakoff/Dubinsky/Lifschey/Van der Berg Quartet. This fell within the time during which the Society held exclusive performance rights for the winning works, a period of three months following the announcement of the awards. Other ensembles were waiting in the wings to champion this piece abroad. The Kolisch Quartet played a BBC broadcast performance of it in London on February 12, 1939, and the Waldbauer-Kerpely Quartet (identifying itself as the Hungarian Quartet when on tour) presented the first London concert performance of the piece precisely a week later, at Wigmore Hall on February 19, 1929 (some sources cite this as the world premiere, almost certainly in error). The Kolisch Quartet played it in Frankfurt two days later in a concert of the International Society of Contemporary Music (ISCM), and would go on to premiere Bartók's Fifth and Sixth Quartets in coming decades.

The Third and Fourth String Quartets stand as a pair, the latter being completed exactly a year after the former. Though not as "abstract" as the Third, the athletically dissonant Fourth shares its general musical vocabulary, to the extent that some commentators have referred to it as continuing the conversation begun in the Third. It is probably safe to say that of the six these are the most distant from traditional tonality in their harmonic behavior, although the Third is anchored on the note C-sharp and the Fourth is based on C. Having said this, we should also acknowledge that the centripetal force of C-sharp in the Third Quartet is not at all constant; but since that note reigns over the beginning and the end, it does seem to occupy a special place in the tonal hierarchy. The interval of the tritone fuels much of Bartók's structural development in this work, and the fact that it is the least stable of all note combinations adds greatly to the sense of tonal ambiguity and infuses the piece with an unremitting sense of tension that can prove unnerving. It has been remarked that this is the Bartók quartet that most approximates the general feel of the Viennese Expressionists; the music of Alban Berg comes particularly to mind in terms of this piece's general effect. As it happens, Bartók had traveled to Baden-Baden, Germany, in July 1927 to perform his Piano Sonata in a concert that also included Berg's Lyric Suite for String Quartet.

Unlike Berg, Bartók did not work within the twelve-tone method devised by Schoenberg (whose own Third String Quartet dates from the same year), but its sound-world is nonetheless dissonant, often to the point of harshness. In the Third Quartet rhythmic brashness overshadows melodic content, with captivating metric patterns providing the sense of continuity that in earlier music had been all but automatically assigned to well-developed melodies. A listener trying to follow this quartet as a succession of tunes will be constantly frustrated by a perpetual parade of melodic motifs that, when all is said and done, make slight effect in and of themselves. The motifs do develop locally, sometimes to the extent of being treated in canon or in inversion, but their variation is perpetual and it is Bartók's vibrant rhythms that sweep us along.

The architecture of the Third Quartet displays a rather simple layout in an A-B-A'-B' pattern. Such two-part (or four-part) balanced forms surface in other Bartók works from the 1920s, including his Second Sonata for Violin and Piano and his Rhapsodies for Violin and Piano and for Cello and Piano. The four movements—or perhaps we should call them sections—are all connected into a single fifteen-minute span, making this the shortest of Bartók's quartets. The character changes greatly along the way, offering typically Bartókian vistas: Magyar folk-scales and rhythms, mysterious "night music" of chirping insects, brilliant excursions of harmonically dense counterpoint, dreamlike reminiscence of vaguely remembered music (from the opening part) in the *Ricapitulazione*, mystical secretiveness in the *Coda*.

Among the early appreciators of this quartet was the philosopher-critic Theodor Adorno, who considered it the composer's best work to date. In a 1929 essay, he pointed out in detail how in the Third Quartet Bartók returned to this favored genre enriched in specific ways by the musical experiments he had conducted since completing his Second Quartet a decade earlier. Adorno concluded his article with an insightful observation about the essential sound of this piece:

He has wrested from neo-classicism, which he has left behind, the thing one would least have expected: new color. . . . The counterpoint has unloosed all its colors and injected the wealth of nuances into the tension between black and white that had otherwise dictated Bartók's sound. The remote possibilities of the instruments bend willingly to his hand, as do the broad spans of multivocal chords. In the Third Quartet, Bartók made his actual discovery of the productivity of color. It not only guarantees this masterwork but opens a perspective on what will follow.

String Quartet No. 4 (BB 95; Sz.91)

Allegro
Prestissimo, con sordino
Non troppo lento
Allegretto pizzicato
Allegro molto

Work composed: July through September 1928

Work dedicated: To the Pro Arte Quartet (violinists Alphonse Onnou and Laurent Halleux, violist Germain Prévost, and cellist Robert Maas)

Work premiered: February 22, 1929, in a London radio broadcast by the Waldbauer-Kerpely Quartet; the same group played the work's concert premiere, on March 20, 1929, in Budapest.

Instrumentation: Two violins, viola, and cello

In a number of pieces Bartók was drawn to "arch" forms, large symmetrical structures of which the five-movement layouts of the Fourth and Fifth Quartets are exemplars. The Fourth String Quartet, therefore, may be taken as a sort of palindrome (in a general sense), with the first and fifth movements (both being *Allegros*) bearing some kinship, the second and fourth similarly reflecting each other (both are scherzos), and the third standing as a fulcrum in the middle. That relaxed third movement, the central moment, is itself structured in a symmetrical form, its ternary A-B-A layout serving as an exquisite turnabout for the overarching A-B-C-B'-A' structure of the entire quartet.

These relationships are most immediately born out in the lengths of the movements and in their overall emotional casts. That the formal plan extends to the tonalities of the various movements may be less apparent to listeners in light of the work's very dissonant character, but in fact the balance—if not precise symmetry—is maintained in this regard as well. The first and fifth movements define C as the overall tonal center. The second movement is centered a major third above (in E) and the fourth movement a major third below (in A-flat). The slow movement, a fine specimen of Bartók's nervous "night music" style, is the most sinuous and equivocal in regard to its tonality, which centers on A. In this middle movement the cello sings out a long-spanning, highly ornamented melody that musicologists have identified (depending on their biases) as Bartók's original "take" on a folk lament of the Hungarian *verbunkos* variety or else on a Romanian *hora lungă*, a song form Bartók had encountered in 1912–13 during his ethnological work in northern Transylvania. Bartók himself described the *hora lungă* as "a single melody in numerous variants [whose] features are strong, instrumental character, very ornamented, and indeterminate content structure." The themes of the paired movements (I and V, II and IV) display considerable kinship, further unifying this tightly structured composition.

Bartók generally avoided providing commentary about his music but he did describe his Fourth Quartet briefly but cogently in an essay:

> The work is in five movements; their character corresponds to Classical sonata form. The slow movement is the kernel of the work; the other movements are, as it were, arranged in layers around it. Movement IV is a free variation of II, and I and V have the same thematic material; that is, around the kernel (Movement III), metaphorically speaking, I and V are the outer, II and IV the inner layers.

Such an observation does nothing to convey the bristling quality of Bartók's Fourth Quartet, the emotional landscape of which can turn on a dime. To be sure, this serves an especially useful function in monothematic movements, which cannot rely on the alternation of themes (and the development of a variety of material) to keep the ear intrigued. Perhaps monothematic is too strong a word here, since Bartók does introduce subsidiary themes. But they are very much subsidiary to the principal themes. The rugged first movement, for example, never strays far from the principal theme, a brief gesture consisting of a group of chromatic notes clustered tightly within the space of a minor third.

When all is said and done, however, the most memorable aspect of the Fourth Quartet is surely the sheer novelty of its sound. No previous quartet—certainly none that has claimed a place in the standard repertoire—had made such sustained use of unusual sonic effects available to a string quartet. This particularly characterizes the second half of the piece. In the *Non troppo lento* movement the cello's *espressivo* melody is supported by a chordal accompaniment by the other strings; but Bartók meticulously indicates at what point those chords are to be played with vibrato or without vibrato, yielding a timbre that is respectively more ascetic or more lush. Eventually the melody is handed off to the avian chirping of the first violin, and then to the viola. Against the viola's husky-toned rhapsodizing the other instruments play shivering tremolo chords *sul ponticello*—bowing their strings near the bridge of the instrument to yield a wispy, nasal sound. And yet, each of these *sul ponticello* chords is preceded by a quick, accented iteration of the same note, but played with normal bowing, not so near the bridge, yielding a momentarily fuller tone. The first violin and the cello, playing in counterpoint, lead the movement to its tranquil ending; but here, too, the sound is specific, with the violin playing in full voice (if softly) as the cello finally installs a mute to match the hushed tones of the other instruments. The fourth movement is an exercise in pizzicato. The players pluck their instruments' strings throughout, and sometimes they are instructed to attack so violently that the string rebounds against the fingerboard, creating a banjo-like twang. After this the huge chords that open the fifth movement sound all the more unbridled.

Through the originality of its very sound this often dense quartet transports us far from the Classical idea of the genteel quartettish conversation. Each of Bartók's quartets represents a significant step beyond those that preceded it, but even in this lineup the Fourth appears instantly to be an unusually "breakthrough" accomplishment, a decisive advance even beyond the brilliance of the quartet that had won its composer an award from the Musical Fund Society of Philadelphia the year before. In a letter to his fellow Hungarian Frigyes (Fritz) Reiner, Bartók reported: "I have written another string quartet, a much longer one this time; there are 5 movements (would there by any chance be another competition somewhere?!!)."

String Quartet No. 5 (BB 110; Sz.102)

> *Allegro*
> *Adagio molto*
> *Scherzo. Alla bulgarese (Vivace)*
> *Andante, Finale*
> *Allegro vivace*

Work composed: August 6 to September 6, 1934, in Budapest

Work dedicated: To Elizabeth Sprague Coolidge

Work premiered: April 8, 1935, by the Kolisch Quartet at the Library of Congress in Washington, D.C.

Instrumentation: Two violins, viola, and cello

In Bartók's Fifth String Quartet we again encounter an arch form. Much as in the Fourth Quartet, the first and fifth movements mirror each other in their general impression, as do the second and fourth, leaving the third to stand as the fulcrum in the middle. In this work Bartók finds a balance between the harsh outbursts and unremitting intensity that can prove downright terrifying in some of his works (in much of the Fourth Quartet, for example) and the melodic lyricism and glittering details that prove captivating in other scores. This balance between disparate Bartókian tendencies doubtless contributes to the fact that the Fifth is the most widely loved and most played of his quartets. Although it predates Bartók's American years—all of the quartets do—its impetus came from the United States as it was commissioned by the Elizabeth Sprague Coolidge Foundation, was dedicated to that great American patron of chamber music, and was premiered by the Kolisch Quartet on April 8, 1935, in Washington, D.C., at the Library of Congress, the venue most associated with Mrs. Coolidge's commissions.

Bartók composed this work in a mere month, from August 6 to September 6, 1934—an astonishing achievement, but one that was not atypical of the concentrated bursts of creativity that he occasionally experienced during his years of maturity as a composer. It was the only really original work he completed that entire year, which otherwise was given over to preparing orchestral transcriptions of folk-based arrangements he had previously made for piano or voice.

Where the Fifth Quartet has certifiable themes they are poured out generously, a contrast to the tersely telegraphed motivic statements of his most recently preceding quartets. Nonetheless, the opening music consists of vehemently hammered notes that set into motion a vibrantly energized movement that is itself a sort of palindrome: when its three principal themes return in the movement's recapitulation they appear in reverse order from how they were presented in the exposition, and two of them carry the "mirror image" idea further by becoming inverted in the recapitulation. In the second movement (*Adagio molto*) we encounter Bartók in his irresistible "night music" mode, providing a gentle tone poem full of bird calls and insect chirps (rather than developed melodies), not to mention wisps of folk-song phrases wafting in from a distance. In the Fourth Quartet the slow movement stood as the central keystone. In the Fifth the fulcrum is instead a scherzo-with-trio (itself a symmetrical structure), and its complex rhythmic patterns, as well as its modal melody, derive from Bulgarian folk style. (Pianists find similar metric patterns in the dances in Bulgarian rhythms in Bartók's *Mikrokosmos*, and we will encounter it shortly in his *Contrasts*.) In the trio of this middle movement—the quartet's exact midpoint—the viola plays an unassuming melody that would seem to be a folk song, or an excellent imitation of one. Having rounded the central point of the arch we return to another slow movement:

more "night music," but the evening has progressed and the atmosphere has grown altogether darker. The quartet concludes with a fascinating finale, its vivacity reflecting that of the first movement, that runs through an array of sections that include a bizarre fugue and (at the evocative marking *Allegretto, con indifferenza*) an amusing depiction of an organ-grinder whose instrument is none too well tuned, the utterly trivial tune being (to one's surprise) a variant, simplified to the point of banality, of the main theme of the whole movement.

As in the Fourth Quartet, the arch form lends a strong sense of structural coherence, which is reinforced by the subtle dovetailing of more surface details. For Bartók, knitting a piece together seems to be to a considerable extent an act of intuition. The composer Sándor Veress, who had studied piano with Bartók, recounted an incident that occurred in 1936. Following a performance of the Fifth String Quartet in Budapest, a commentary was published by the Hungarian musician Sándor Jemnitz. Recalled Veress: "Jemnitz sent his analysis to Bartók for approval and later, when he visited him to discuss his writing, Bartók revealed that he was surprised by reading about motivic, formal and harmonic connections Jemnitz discovered in the Quartet and of which he was quite unaware."

Sonata for Two Pianos and Percussion (BB 115; Sz.110)

Assai lento—Allegro molto
Lento, ma non troppo
Allegro non troppo

Work composed: Summer 1937

Work premiered: January 16, 1938, in Basel, Switzerland, by the composer and his wife, Ditta Pásztory-Bartók (pianists), with Fritz Schiesser and Philipp Rühlig (percussionists)

Instrumentation: Two pianos plus an array of percussion instruments played by two musicians: three timpani, xylophone, side drum with snares, side drum without snares, suspended cymbal, pair of cymbals, bass drum, triangle, and tam-tam

The billionaire philanthropist Paul Sacher married into a pharmaceutical fortune (his father-in-law had founded the Hoffmann-La Roche company), and he used his newfound resources constructively. In 1926 the twenty-year-old Sacher formed the Basel Chamber Orchestra and set about commissioning works from leading composers, which he would often conduct at their premieres. As a result, important scores by Richard Strauss, Hindemith, Stravinsky, Honegger, Tippett, and many other figures received their first performances in Basel. More than 200 works by major twentieth-century composers owe their existence to Paul Sacher and his foundation, which inhabits opulent facilities in Basel, houses the archives of such notables as Stravinsky, Webern, Frank Martin, and Bruno Maderna.

Bartók exercised the arts of victimhood and paranoia lavishly, but at least he seems to have had no reason to complain about this benefactor. Sacher not only commissioned both Bartók's Music for Strings, Percussion, and Celesta (1936, to celebrate the tenth anniversary of the Basel Chamber Orchestra) and his Divertimento for String Orchestra (1939) but also arranged for another party—the Swiss Section of the ISCM (International Society of Contemporary Music)—to commission his Sonata for Two Pianos and Percussion (1937) and then anted up the fee for that piece himself. The Basel Section of the ISCM was set to celebrate its tenth anniversary in January 1938, and Sacher felt that Bartók would be the perfect candidate to write a chamber piece to mark the occasion.

In the spring of 1937 Sacher approached the composer with the ISCM commission, and Bartók responded with a measure of anxiety about the short deadline and with a flurry of thoughts about the specific forces he might use. "What kind of chamber music should it be?" he asked in a letter to Sacher on May 24. "Could it be, for example, a quartet for two pianos and two groups of percussion? Or a piano trio? Would you perhaps consider a piece for voice and piano to be chamber music, or not?"

Sacher liked the first possibility, although for another month Bartók kept bringing up the idea of a piano trio or a voice-and-piano piece as more easily realizable within the time limit. The fact is that Bartók seems to have been contemplating for some time a piece for two pianists and two percussionists—one does not suggest a commission for such an unusual instrumentation by simply pulling it out of the blue—and as the weeks passed he, too, began to focus his thoughts on that grouping. Once he set about the composition he proceeded quickly, and by September 2 he was able to write to Sacher, "I am pleased to inform you that I have almost succeeded in completing the planned work—my choice fell on a quartet for two pianos and percussion; it may be counted on. It consists of three movements; the first and second movements are finished, and half of the third is ready, too."

Bartók, Ditta Pásztory (his wife and a pianist, like her husband), and two Swiss percussionists played the premiere on the anniversary concert, and the work scored so great a success that subsequent performances were quickly arranged for London, Brussels, Luxembourg, and Budapest. In 1940, Bartók's publisher convinced him to recast the piece as a Concerto for Two Pianos, Percussion, and Orchestra. This was not intended to supersede Bartók's original conception but rather to broaden the work's possibilities for performances, particularly in the American market, where he viewed as dim the likelihood of the chamber version's being programmed. As it happens, the concerto version is very rarely presented, and Bartók's original chamber conception is the one that has steadfastly hooked the public's fascination.

Prior to the premiere, Bartók penned an analytical introduction to the work, in German, which was published in the *Basel National Zeitung*. There he explained that he had initially planned to use a single piano but decided to use two, the better to balance the "frequently very sharp tones of the percussion instruments.... The role of the percussion sounds varies: sometimes they reinforce the more important accents; in places they carry motifs serving as a counterpoint to the piano parts; and the timpani and the xylophone frequently play themes that act as principal subjects. Only two players are required for the seven percussion instruments—timpani, bass drum, cymbals, tam-tam, side drum with snares, side drum without snares, and xylophone. Both of them play all the instruments."

The timbre Bartók achieves in this work is novel and striking. He largely eschews the lyric potential of the pianos, stressing instead their percussive qualities; at spots, one is tempted to view this as a quartet for four percussion players, some employing pitched instruments and others unpitched ones. (I can't imagine how Bartók failed to mention the triangle when he enumerated the instruments in his percussion section, but he does include one in the score; beyond that, he calls for suspended cymbal in addition to a pair of crash cymbals.) The work is cast in a three-movement plan, which is entirely traditional for a sonata, though in this case the center of gravity is heavily skewed to the opening movement, which is twice as long as either of the two that succeed it. The first movement traces a "standard" sonata-allegro form (though with a slow introduction that rises from untold depths to a pitch of high drama); the second adheres to a forthright A-B-A plan, here used to convey one of the composer's signature pieces in shivering "nocturnal" style; and the third is a rondo.

Bartók's analysis, however, suggests the subtlety and complexity that unifies the piece at a profound level, and the implications of his suggestions have been delved by many theorists in ensuing decades. This turns out to be a prime example of the strict mathematical ratios of the "golden section" and the related Fibonacci and Lucas sequences, which the composer embeds into the rhythmic evolution of his piece and which are underscored not only by rhythmic structures but also by emphases of melody, harmony, and timbre. Though such geometric relationships may not be perceived readily by the listener—and it is contested whether or not Bartók himself was consciously embedding them in this piece—many specialists in the psychology of music believe that they are perforce apprehended by a listener at a subconscious level, that they lend a sense of logic and inevitability to pieces that might otherwise seem overly rhapsodic in their plan.

Contrasts for Clarinet, Violin, and Piano (BB 116; Sz. 111)

> *Verbunkos (Recruiting Dance)*
> *Pihenö (Relaxation)*
> *Sebes (Fast Dance)*

Work composed: 1938, completed in Budapest on September 24

Work dedicated: Written for and dedicated to Benny Goodman and Joseph Szigeti

Work premiered: The first and third movements on January 9, 1939, at Carnegie Hall in New York, by Benny Goodman (clarinet), Joseph Szigeti (violin), and Endre Petri (piano); the complete three movements were first played together when Goodman, Szigeti, and the composer (as pianist) made a recording of the work in April 1940 in New York City; the same ensemble played the complete work's concert premiere on February 4, 1941, at Jordan Hall in Boston.

Instrumentation: Clarinet, violin, and piano

Whether Benny Goodman, the "King of Swing," qualifies to go down in the annals of music-making as one of the supreme classical clarinetists is open to debate; that he was sincere in his interest in classical music—and in *contemporary* concert music—is indisputable. In November 1938 he commissioned Bartók's *Contrasts*, the first of several important works he would usher into the clarinet repertoire (and the only chamber work of Bartók's to include a wind instrument). In the ensuing decade, he would similarly extract clarinet concertos from both Hindemith and Copland.

As he increased his participation in classical music Goodman developed close friendships with several notable instrumentalists. One was the Hungarian violinist Joseph Szigeti, Bartók's friend and musical partner of long standing, who by that time had emigrated to the United States. Szigeti "had a brainwave," as he put it, "about suggesting to Benny Goodman that he authorize me to ask Bartók to write a work for the three of us—Goodman, Bartók, and myself—to be underwritten financially by Benny." (The underwriting consisted of the hardly magnanimous sum of $300, which included reserving performing rights for Goodman for three years.) With Goodman's go-ahead, he sent a letter to Bartók in August 1938—the composer was on vacation in Switzerland at the time—asking for "a six-seven minute clarinet-violin duo with piano accompaniment." Though final decisions about the piece were left to Bartók, Szigeti (acting as Goodman's mouthpiece) suggested that the work should consist of two movements, each of which could stand alone as an independent piece, and that each movement should be short enough to fit on one side of a 12-inch 78-r.p.m. phonograph record; and he assured Bartók that some cadenzas would be welcome, too. Several Goodman recordings enclosed in the package sweetened the deal, and the composer set to work immediately.

The piece was completed in Budapest on September 24, and the two movements received their premiere on January 9, 1939, at Carnegie Hall, under the title *Rhapsody: Two Dances*. On that occasion, Goodman and Szigeti were joined by the pianist Endre Petri. Szigeti reported in a letter to Bartók: "The second part had to be repeated and we also played the second part of that movement because my E string had snapped!" The movements lasted about five minutes each, rather longer than Goodman had hoped, and Bartók was apologetic. In the letter sent to accompany the score, he wrote: "Generally the salesman delivers less than he is supposed to. There are exceptions, however, as for example if you order a suit for a two-year-old baby and an adult's suit is sent instead—when the generosity is not particularly welcome!" The following year Bartók traveled to New York and recorded the piece with Goodman and Szigeti in a now-classic reading made on April 29–30, 1940, for Columbia Records; even in the gloaming of the CD era it remains in print on rival CDs on the CBS Masterworks, Hungaroton, Pearl, Urania, and Membran labels. It was for that recording that Bartók added a further movement (placed in the middle), which he had composed back in September 1938 but for some reason kept secret, and assigned the name *Contrasts* to the set. The three musicians finally played the complete three-movement *Contrasts* in its concert premiere on February 4, 1941, in Boston.

The first movement, titled *Verbunkos* (at the tempo *Moderato, ben ritmato*), is based on a dance employed by recruiting officers in eighteenth- and nineteenth-century Hungary who hoped that their proud footwork would ensnare a few good men. All three instruments are shown off here with considerable flair before the clarinet takes off in a cadenza filled with roulades and folkloric scale fragments. *Pihenö (Relaxation,* marked *Lento)* was the late addition, and one can only marvel at how *Contrasts* benefits—indeed, earns its title—from the contrast this movement provides. Its sound is uniquely Bartókian—nocturnal, lyrical, mysterious, perhaps a bit ominous.

After this respite, the ear is ready for the high-spirited *Sebes* (*Fast Dance*, marked *Allegro vivace*). The movement begins and ends in strongly accented 2/4 time, but the central section is cast in what reads more like a mathematical formula than a meter mark: $\dfrac{(3+2+3)+(2+3)}{8}$. This is identified as a rhythm from Bulgarian folklore, though linked to a melody that is an original creation of Bartók's. In a lecture in 1938 Bartók explained, "Bulgarian rhythm is a type where these very short basic values are grouped into unequal values—that is, asymmetrically—within the bar." That is precisely what happens here: a grouping of three eighth notes plus two eighth notes plus three eighth notes is counterbalanced, asymmetrically, by a grouping of two eighth notes and three eighth notes. When the music returns to the relative squareness of 2/4 we may detect a faint whiff of jazz, especially in a few bars of sequential figuration. In 1940 in the magazine *Listen*, Goodman confirmed that there was indeed a jazz connection: "I think it's interesting to note that Bartók derived his inspiration to write *Contrasts* from listening to a number of records made by my old Jazz Trio, consisting of Teddy Wilson, Gene Krupa and myself."

In this finale the violinist uses an odd scordatura, playing an instrument with the bottom string tuned a half-step up and the top string a half-step down. The tuning is shown off unadorned in the opening measures. The effect is jarring, as one would expect, and unequivocally redolent of a peasant dance. In this movement the violinist gets a cadenza, balancing the clarinetist's in the first movement; by the time it arrives, the player has switched from the oddly tuned instrument to one with normally tuned strings. The violinist has only about four seconds to change instruments, but Bartók notes in the score that the pattern the clarinet and piano are playing in that tiny interlude "may be repeated several times if necessary," a thoughtful and pragmatic authorization that has probably saved a good many violins from physical damage in the heat of the moment. The clarinetist similarly alternates between two instruments in the finale, playing mostly on a clarinet in B-flat but briefly switching to clarinet in A (which is used uninterruptedly in the first two movements). When *Contrasts* was first published the clarinet part was provided in two versions: one requiring clarinets in A and B-flat, as described, the other transposed so the entire piece can be played using just a clarinet in B-flat. Peter A. Bartók, the composer's son, has rejected the legitimacy of amalgamating the part onto a single instrument, writing in the preface to the corrected edition of the score that "it was not part of the original concept prepared by the composer and, moreover, the A clarinet is called upon to play its lowest note," which sounds a half-tone deeper than the lowest note on a B-flat clarinet. So it seems that Bartók intended that the instruments themselves should reflect some of the contrasts in *Contrasts*.

String Quartet No. 6 (BB 119; Sz. 114)

Mesto—Più mosso, pesante—Vivace
Mesto—Marcia
Mesto—Burletta
Moderato, Mesto

Work composed: August–November 1939, begun in Saanen, Switzerland, completed in Budapest

Work dedicated: To the Kolisch Quartet

Work premiered: January 20, 1941, in New York by the Kolisch Quartet

Instrumentation: Two violins, viola, and cello

Bartók's life was growing uneasy by the time he reached his Sixth Quartet. The Second World War began while this piece was in progress, and although Hungary was not involved in the conflict at the outset, the war struck an everlasting blow to the composer's idealistic, humanitarian spirit. What's more, Bartók's mother, with whom he felt an intense bond, was in rapidly failing health; she would die on December 19, 1939, at the age of eighty-two, just a month after he finished this piece. He would grieve her loss profoundly, but her death also would prove a liberation of sorts. With her passing there would no longer be a compelling reason for Bartók to remain in his native Hungary. Before he had completed this quartet, with the death of his mother still imminent, Bartók decided to leave Hungary for the United States—"for an extended period," he wrote to another friend. Following a five-and-a-half-week concert-and-lecture tour in America, he returned briefly to Hungary before moving to the United States in October 1940 to spend the rest of his life, most of it unhappily. The Sixth Quartet is therefore sometimes interpreted as both bitter farewell to the European political tragedy and cathartic leave-taking of his mother.

By the time the piece received its world premiere, in New York on January 20, 1941, Bartók and his family had moved to America definitively, and he was able to attend the Kolisch Quartet's concert in person. He cannot have been strongly encouraged, as the audience's response to this profoundly personal work was tepid. But the Kolisch Quartet was firm in its commitment and the second New York performance, in 1944, was more warmly received. The critic Marion Bauer, writing in the *Musical Leader* about that second performance, offered a perspicacious summary: "If one is looking for a contemporary expression of a mental state produced on a sensitive person by conditions of recent years, it is to be found in this poignant, profoundly sad work"

The Sixth String Quartet deserts the arch forms of the Fourth and Fifth Quartets in favor of a four-movement plan. It is far from classic in the specifics of its layout, consisting as it does of an opening sonata form, two movements of parody (*Marcia* and *Burletta*), and a closing slow movement. We can count on Bartók to come up with novel takes on standard forms, and in this case he does so by launching each movement with a slow introduction. The introductions are not merely slow; they're sad—literally, since he heads them with the marking *Mesto* ("sad"). Each of the *Mesto* introductions grows from the same material into something progressively longer, more complex, and more richly textured. By the last movement, the *Mesto* turns out not to be an introduction at all, instead consuming the entire finale. The theme of the *Mesto* sections—and, accordingly, of the finale as a whole—is a doleful melody originally offered by the unaccompanied viola, spanning thirteen measures of swaying 6/8 meter, rhythmically asymmetrical, highly chromatic, covering two octaves, starting at a noncommittal *mezzo forte* but ranging as loud as *forte* and as soft as *pianissimo*. Whether it is correct to consider this theme to be thrice rejected before it is allowed to flower, as the musicologist Gerald Abraham suggested shortly after the piece was written, is up for debate. One might prefer to view it as unfolding gradually over the course of the entire quartet, not rejected at all but rather hibernating between its appearances—and, for that matter, wielding a measure of influence over certain contours of the work's other material.

The first movement (following the *Mesto* introduction) unrolls as a *Vivace* sonata-form structure with two basic themes, both of which reveal some kinship to the *Mesto* theme itself; the rhythm of the second is especially inspired by Hungarian folk music. A swaggering *verbunkos* passage reminds the listener of how ingrained Hungarian traditional music had become in Bartók's original vocabulary following many years of dedicated collecting, notating, codifying, and publishing folk songs and dances. In the introduction to the second movement, the theme (played now by cello) is accompanied by rapidly beating notes that evoke the sounds of a Hungarian cimbalom. The tune of the *Marcia* proper derives from a phrase of the *Mesto* theme, but the notes now convey an entirely different effect. Both this and the *Burletta* are sardonic parodies, hardly concealing the underlying bitterness. Both movements are clearly structured as scherzos with central trios. In the *Marcia's* trio, the cello offers a variant on the *Mesto* theme in its highest register, bizarrely accompanied by a combination of tremolo chords (on the violins) and crude strumming (on the viola). The *Burletta* is a weird, drunken movement. Following the *Mesto* section (which by now extends to a minute and a half), it proceeds into a succession of harsh, biting, dissonant attacks and a swooning melody that veers hideously out of tune: Bartók's score actually indicates that one of the violins is to play a quarter-tone flat. The fourth movement, profoundly mournful and completely overtaken by the *Mesto* material, is said to be a tombeau for the composer's mother, who was nearing death as he worked on this section. One senses that this is the most authentic expression of Bartók's sorrow, which is elsewhere disguised as satire or melancholy. Rarely in the history of chamber music does a movement combine restraint and powerful expression to achieve an impact as profound as Bartók does here, at the conclusion of his last quartet—and of his career as a chamber music composer.

Ludwig van Beethoven

Born: Probably on December 16, 1770 (he was baptized on December 17), in Bonn, then an independent electorate of Germany

Died: March 26, 1827, in Vienna, Austria

Piano Trio in C minor, Op. 1, No. 3

Allegro con brio
Andante cantabile con variazione
Menuetto quasi Allegro
Finale. Prestissimo

Work composed: Apparently sometime between 1794 (maybe even 1793) and 1795, in Vienna; in 1795 it was published in an elegantly engraved edition as the last of the three trios that together make up his first numbered opus.

Work dedicated: To Prince Karl Lichnowsky

Work premiered: Apparently 1794, maybe early 1795, at the Vienna home of Prince Karl Lichnowsky

Instrumentation: Violin, cello, and piano

Ludwig van Beethoven had made some formative attempts in the medium of the piano trio even before he moved from his native Bonn to Vienna in November 1792, intent on studying with Haydn, and he continued exploring the genre through 1811, when he arrived at the summit with his *Archduke* Trio. The Three Trios (Op. 1) date from his first years in Vienna, but we are not certain just when. His pupil Ferdinand Ries held that the C-minor Piano Trio, the final piece in the set, dated from 1793 and that the composer participated in its first performance, in early 1794, at the Viennese home of Prince Karl Lichnowsky (its dedicatee), with Haydn in attendance. Recent research suggests that Ries' memory failed him and that the C-minor Trio was instead written shortly before the Op. 1 set was printed (in 1795, by the firm of Artaria) and distributed to an extensive subscriber list laden with names of Viennese and Czech aristocrats. Obviously, word was out that something exciting was going to appear between the bindings of that collection; doubtless Prince Lichnowsky, Beethoven enthusiast that he was, had a hand in whipping up interest among the moneyed class for the composer he had "discovered."

Beethoven's formal studies with Haydn were neither long-lasting nor particularly productive—in later years Beethoven was quoted as saying that he had learned nothing from Haydn—but at least the two were not separated by any permanent rift, always a possibility with prickly Beethoven, and maintained reasonably cordial relations. When Haydn left for his second residency in England, Beethoven embarked on more influential lessons from the academically inclined Johann Georg Albrechtsberger and also availed himself of free composition coaching offered by the Viennese Imperial Kapellmeister, Antonio Salieri.

Haydn volunteered strongly worded praise for his erstwhile pupil's Trios— or, at least, for two of them. He had doubts about the Third, as Beethoven's pupil Ferdinand Ries would explain, recalling the circumstances of the set's first performance:

> Most of the artists and music-lovers were invited, especially Haydn, for whose opinion all were eager. The Trios were played and at once commanded extraordinary attention. Haydn also said many pretty things about them, but advised Beethoven not to publish the third, in C minor. This astonished Beethoven, inasmuch as he considered the third the best of the Trios, as it is still the one which gives the greatest pleasure and makes the greatest effect. Consequently, Haydn's remark left a bad impression on Beethoven and led him to think that Haydn was envious, jealous and ill-disposed toward him. I confess that when Beethoven told me of this I gave it little credence. I therefore took occasion to ask Haydn himself about it. His answer, however, confirmed Beethoven's statement; he said he had not believed that this Trio would be so quickly and easily understood and so favorably received by the public.

Mingled within the overall Viennese Classicism are striking marks of individuality that, in retrospect, we hear as Beethovenian hallmarks. The work opens with an *Allegro con brio* that is cast, predictably in a sonata form. A cautious, brooding beginning in C minor gives way to a second theme in the major mode, its sunny lyricism in complete contrast to the brow-furrowed opening. But even in this early work Beethoven expands the development section of the traditional sonata form into an audaciously dramatic scene with constantly changing character. One imagines that Schubert must have admired this development section; its abrupt alternation of conflicting sentiments, from the violent to the blissful, prefigures the sort of emotional flux Schubert would often favor.

Variations follow—five of them that explore the possibilities inherent in a placid *Andante cantabile*. In the first, the piano dresses up the theme with an overlay of ornamentation; in the second, violin and cello weave in counterpoint above the piano's simple chordal accompaniment. The piano governs the third variation, where strings take a decidedly subsidiary role—playing in self-effacing pizzicato, no less. The bittersweet potential of the theme becomes prominent in the fourth variation, where violin and cello turn the tune into poignant sighs; but the sadness is swept away by the piano's giddy figuration in the final variation. A deceptive cadence leads to a lightly chromatic coda and a gentle end.

A minuet in name only, the third movement documents Beethoven on the way to replacing that traditional dance movement with the more impish scherzo as the standard third movement of symphonies, sonatas, and large chamber works. The main section is made memorable by a surprising appoggiatura accent on the first beat of its phrases, while in the trio section piano scales interlock with a spacious melody from the cello.

With the outburst of its opening theme the *Finale* returns to the stormy spirit that had reigned over much of the first movement. As in that earlier section, Beethoven provides a second subject that contrasts strikingly, here with a temperament of proud nobility. Overall, the atmosphere is tense and moody, and the music makes countless abrupt, unnerving turns before dying in a whisper. If one were intent on finding precedent for such a work, there would be no choice but the always unpredictable music of Haydn. But even in the works of his so-called *Sturm und Drang* period Haydn was not wont to push tonal and formal boundaries quite so far as this. It's easy to see why the older composer was perplexed, and quite possibly frightened, by Beethoven's newfangled creation.

Trio in B-flat major for Clarinet, Cello, and Piano, Op. 11

> *Allegro con brio*
> *Adagio*
> *Tema: "Pria ch'io l'impegno": Allegretto*

Work composed: In late 1797 or 1798, in Vienna

Work dedicated: To Countess Maria Wilhelmine von Thun

Work premiered: Not known

Instrumentation: Clarinet, cello, and piano

Beethoven conceived his Op. 11 Trio for the combination of clarinet, cello, and piano, but when the work was published, in Vienna in 1798, the title page carried the observation that it could also be played, with very few emendations, by the more standard ensemble of violin, cello, and piano. This was a reasonable and very practical suggestion, given that the clarinet was still a relatively new instrument at the time and that Vienna boasted few competent players. Indeed, Beethoven makes substantial technical demands on both the clarinet and the cello, but at heart this music is centered on the composer's own instrument, the piano.

Here we find Beethoven near the beginning of his chamber music production, a freshly innocent composer still a year away from embarking on his first set of six string quartets (Op. 18), but one who was already plunged into the world of chamber music through his early piano trios, his first two cello sonatas, and his Quintet for Piano and Winds. He was not entirely naïve, though: he knew enough to dedicate this piece to Countess Maria Wilhelmine von Thun, who had been an important supporter of Mozart and who was the mother-in-law of two of Beethoven's own influential patrons, Prince Karl Lichnowsky and Count (later Prince) Andreas Kirillovich Razumovsky.

Beethoven was almost certainly inspired to write his Clarinet Trio by the otherwise obscure Austrian clarinetist Franz Joseph Bähr (1770–1819). He had scored great success in Vienna in 1796 while touring with his friend Friedrich Witt, a cellist who reported to a friend that "Bähr blows like a God." Beethoven was among those who were smitten with Bähr's artistry, and at least twice—in April 1797 and again a year later—Bähr and Beethoven (as pianist) took part in Viennese performances of the composer's Quintet for Piano and Winds. Bähr seems to have been the impetus behind every one of Beethoven's chamber works with especially prominent clarinet parts, all of which are clustered in the years 1796–1802. Although we don't know precisely when the Clarinet Trio was unveiled, there can be little doubt that Bähr was the clarinetist on that occasion; clear documentation testifies that he performed in the first public performances of Beethoven's Septet (Op. 20, in 1800) and Sextet (Op. 71, in 1805), with the *Allgemeine musikalische Zeitung* of Leipzig declaring his playing in the latter to be "absolutely perfect." We should note with sympathetic understanding that commentators have often confused Bähr with a different clarinetist with a similar name, the Bohemian Joseph Beer (1744–1812), who traveled in some of the same circles at the same period, and (spelling being an imprecise art at the time) sometimes found his surname spelled Beere, Paer, Pär, Pehr, Behr, Baer, Baher, Baehr, or—yes—Bähr. Critics tended to give Bähr more enthusiastic reviews than they did Beer.

The *Allgemeine musikalische Zeitung* smiled on the Clarinet Trio in a 1799 review. "This trio," it observed, "is by no means easy in parts, but it runs more flowingly than much of the composer's other work and produces an excellent ensemble effect without pianoforte and clavier accompaniment. If the composer, with his unusual grasp of harmony, his love of the graver movements, would aim at natural rather than strained and *recherché* composition, he would set good work before the public, such as would throw into the shade the stale hurdy-gurdy tunes of many a more talked-of musician." The critic's point about the piece making an excellent ensemble effect without the keyboard accompaniment seems odd at first, since the piano part represents an essential corner of the action; probably he was referring to Variation Two of the finale, in which the clarinet and cello play while the piano holds its silence. In 1799 Beethoven was still a relative unknown in musical circles and even a backhanded compliment such as the one provided by this review would have been better than no compliment at all.

The *Allegro con brio* opens emphatically, with the piano's double octaves reinforcing the unisons of the violin and cello, and it unrolls as a well-behaved sonata-allegro. The second-movement *Adagio* (in the subdominant key of E-flat) shows traces of being an old-style minuet in three-quarter time, here launched by a preparatory upbeat. The finale is a genial and amusing set of nine variations on the tune "Pria ch'io l'impegno," which had been composed by Joseph Weigl (1766–1846), the conductor of Vienna's Kärntnertor Theatre, for his opera *L'Amor marinaro* (later known among English speakers by its subtitle, *The Corsair*), which was premiered on October 15, 1797. This melody, which Weigl used in a comic trio, became enduringly popular; in 1828 Paganini would compose a Grand Sonata and Variations for Violin and Orchestra based on the same tune.

Precisely how Beethoven fixed on Weigl's theme is a matter of debate. *Thayer's Life of Beethoven*, the peerless compendium of Beethoveniana, relates that the Viennese music publisher Domenico Artaria claimed in 1797 "that he had given the theme to Beethoven and requested him to introduce variations on it into a trio, and added that Beethoven did not know that the melody was Weigl's until after the Trio was finished, whereupon he grew very angry finding it out." On the other hand, Beethoven's pupil Carl Czerny (of pianistic finger-exercise fame) reported, in the supplement to his *Pianoforte School*: "It was at the wish of the clarinet player for whom Beethoven wrote this Trio that he employed the ... theme by Weigl (which was then very popular) as the finale. At a later period he frequently contemplated writing another concluding movement for this Trio, and letting the variations stand as a separate work." Although these accounts do not concur, at least we can be sure that Beethoven's Clarinet Trio (its finale, anyway) was not composed earlier than late October 1797. The fact that the piece was not published by Artaria's company, but rather (in October 1798) by the competing firm that had just been established by the ex-Artaria employee Tranquillo Mollo, may give credence to the idea that Beethoven was indeed annoyed with Artaria.

String Quartet in B-flat major, Op. 18, No. 6

> *Allegro con brio*
> *Adagio, ma non troppo*
> *Scherzo: Allegro*
> *La Malinconia: Adagio—Allegretto quasi Allegro*

Work composed: Mostly during the spring and summer of 1800, in Vienna

Work dedicated: To Prince Karl Lobkowitz

Work premiered: Thought to be about 1800, in Vienna, played by the Shuppanzigh Quartet (first violinist Ignaz Schuppanzigh, second violinist Louis Sina or maybe on this occasion Heinrich Eppinger, violist Franz Weiss, and cellist Anton Kraft)

Instrumentation: **Two violins, viola, and cello**

When, in 1792, Beethoven left his native Bonn to seek his fortune as a pianist and a composer in the heady cultural capital of Vienna, he was entering a world dominated by the spirit of the late lamented Mozart and the still-living and universally revered Haydn. "By untiring work you will receive the spirit of Mozart from the hands of Haydn," Count Ferdinand von Waldstein (the future dedicatee of the Beethoven's C-major Piano Sonata, Op. 53) had written in the composer's autograph book shortly before he packed his bags for Vienna. Given the interest those two composers had shown in the medium of the string quartet, it was inevitable that Beethoven should have followed in their footsteps.

As in the case of his concertos and symphonies, Beethoven's early string quartets are clearly born of the tradition of his great predecessors, yet they already strain toward new directions. Succinct themes capable of extensive development; endlessly imaginative melodic manipulation; startling dynamic contrasts; complete, sometimes radical, formal mastery: these are all evident in Beethoven's first set of six quartets, Op. 18, which he composed between the summer or autumn of 1798 and the summer of 1800. After these, he set the genre on the back burner for several years, concentrating on other musical types, including symphonies, sonatas, and opera—and in the course of doing so, he became famous. But his Op. 18 quartets played an important part in launching his eventual renown. They were introduced at a series of private house-concerts given on Friday mornings at the Vienna home of Prince Karl Lobkowitz, the Austrian aristocrat to whom the set is dedicated. These performances were regularly attended by the city's cultural and philanthropic elite, and it comes as no surprise that, shortly after these quartets were unveiled, patrons showed an increasing interest in commissioning works from this intractable but inescapable genius.

The numbering of the Op. 18 Quartets bears a brief comment. The three bound sketchbooks Beethoven employed for recording and working out his ideas for these quartets reveal that the pieces were composed in a different order from how they were positioned when published, in 1801. The D-major Quartet (Op. 18, No. 3) was the first to be written; the Quartets in F major (No. 1) and G major (No. 2) followed, probably in that order; and those in C minor (No. 4), A major (No. 5), and B-flat major (No. 6)—again, possibly not in that order—came last. The chronology may be further confused by some overlap, assuming that Beethoven may have worked on more than one of the pieces simultaneously. In any case, at least some general revision took place late in the process, including a major rewriting of the first two quartets. In fact, the set served as a critical workshop for its composer. It's no surprise that by the time he finished penning the six he should have learned lessons that he wanted to incorporate into the earliest of them.

If the B-flat-major Quartet was not the last of the set to be written (maybe it was, maybe it wasn't), it surely fell late in the series, occupying its composer principally in the spring and summer of 1800. It does seem to stand apart from the other five as a more individualistic—one might even say, a more mature—work. The first movement, rich in dialogue between high and low registers, might best be viewed as a good-natured tribute to Haydn, who had not only defined the genre of the string quartet but was still composing his last ones at about the same time. Curious things start to happen in the second movement. Its opening is entirely traditional: a reserved but ingratiating song-like theme spotlighting the first violin. But Beethoven quickly switches into the minor mode, stating the tune with the instruments in unison, *pianissimo*, to rather unsettling effect. Contrasting textures, unexpected pauses, and starkly unadorned couplings continue to inform this movement to its end.

The real groundbreaking aspect of this quartet, however, comes with its last two movements. The *Scherzo* is positively frenetic, its syncopation making mincemeat out of its meter signature, which is a straightforward 3/4. The trio, with its flippant violin figures, passes so quickly as to leave little effect apart from suggesting that the violins have rather run amok vis à vis the unified quartet texture. In retrospect, we recognize this movement as a "typical" Beethovenian scherzo; to the work's first listeners it must have been baffling.

What follows is astonishing, too: a second slow movement, or at least so it seems until this three-and-a-half-minute passage is revealed to be the extended introduction to the quick finale. Beethoven attaches to this introduction the title "La Malinconia" ("Melancholy"), and adds the printed directive "This piece must be played with the utmost delicacy." Mostly *pianissimo*, though punctuated by sudden *forte* outbursts, the section's hushed harmonic questing yields a tense, mysterious atmosphere. Its flavor adumbrates the introspective, emotionally powerful style Beethoven would employ two decades later in his late quartets, and it also suggests traits that Schubert would find appealing. Following the "Malinconia" introduction, the finale begins as a country-dance, sometimes even making use of an oom-pah accompaniment. Still, there's nothing rampantly joyful in this conclusion. The tempo is itself tamed to a moderate *Allegretto quasi Allegro*, and its progress is broken by grieving reminiscences of the "Malinconia" introduction, much as, several years earlier, Beethoven had interrupted the *Allegro con brio* of his *Pathétique* Piano Sonata with ominous interpolations from that work's slow introduction. Even the main thematic material of the *Allegretto quasi Allegro* is slowed down to take on melancholy overtones before the final, action-packed coda.

Opinions are divided about whether one should impose much biography on the interpretation of musical compositions. Nonetheless, it would not be hard to imagine that if a composer begins to experience evidence of a hearing disorder, as Beethoven did while writing this piece, some expression of worry, doubt, and foreboding might easily enter his work. We cannot say for sure that the melancholy to which Beethoven refers in this piece, explicitly and implicitly, refers to the sometimes debilitating ringing in his ears, which he probably had not yet accepted as a sign of eventual deafness. What is indubitable is that, of his early string quartets, this is the most mysterious and personal in its tone.

Septet in E-flat major for Clarinet, Bassoon, Horn, Violin, Viola, Cello, and Double Bass, Op. 20

Adagio—Allegro con brio
Adagio cantabile
Tempo di Menuetto
Tema con variazioni: Andante
Scherzo: Allegro molto e vivace
Andante con moto alla Marcia—Presto

Work composed: Late 1799, in Vienna, though the Menuetto theme is drawn from a piano sonata he wrote in 1795–96

Work dedicated: To Empress Maria Theresia

Work premiered: Apparently in a private performance on December 20, 1799; the first public performance was on April 2, 1800, at Vienna's Burgtheater, on which occasion the performers were, according to advance publicity, "Herren Schuppanzigh, Schreiber, Schindlecker, Bär, Nickel, Matauschek, and Dietzel."

Instrumentation: Clarinet, bassoon, horn, violin, viola, cello, and double bass

At least on a professional level, things were going well for Beethoven as the old century yielded to the new. He had gained renown as a pianist, and aristocrats were beginning to seek him out to provide the piano lessons that were all but obligatory for their daughters (and some of their sons, too). He had composed quite a few pieces, some more inspired than others, and was already embarked on his earliest works in major, large-scale musical genres. On April 2, 1800, at Vienna's Burgtheater, Beethoven undertook his first benefit concert, a benefit concert being normally understood in those days to mean "for the benefit of the composer." The program included a Mozart symphony, excerpts from Haydn's newly unveiled oratorio *The Creation*, piano improvisations, one of Beethoven's piano concertos (whether the B-flat-major or the C-major we don't know), and two new Beethoven pieces: the Septet (Op. 20) and the Symphony No. 1 (Op. 21).

"This septet has truly delighted me," he wrote to his publisher following that successful concert; but as the years passed he began to resent the work's extreme popularity, feeling that other, more profound compositions he was producing more justly deserved the acclaim. By the time the Septet was unveiled in London, in 1815, Beethoven was heard to utter, "That damn work: I wish it could be burned." Once he even tried to silence an ecstatic listener by insisting that the piece had been written not by him but rather by Mozart. On the other hand, Beethoven himself fanned the flames of popularity by transcribing it for piano trio and publishing it in that very marketable form as his Op. 38.

Predictably, the Septet spawned numerous imitations. Louis Spohr's Nonet (Op. 31, of 1813) is surely a descendant, but perhaps none was so obviously inspired by it than Conradin Kreutzer's still-performed Septet (Op. 62, of ca. 1825)—also in E-flat major, with the same number (and design) of movements, calling for an identical ensemble and written with the same violinist in mind. That violinist was Ignaz Schuppanzigh, whose name is forever linked to Beethoven's: he headed the string quartet that premiered and championed the composer's essays in that genre, and his plumpness provided Beethoven abundant amusement. Schuppanzigh put up with the ribbing, and in return he got some good music to play, including this Septet with its very prominent, even soloistic, violin part.

The work's six movements adhere to the structure of an old-fashioned divertimento, here with an "extra" *Andante* (Theme and Variations) and *Scherzo* augmenting the four movements (fast—slow—minuet—fast) common to many Classical chamber works. Following a brief slow introduction, the opening movement makes clear that charm is the Septet's strong suit. This is a conservative work that provides delight without breaking new ground, which doubtless accounts for a good measure of its early success. In retrospect, though, we have the pleasure of glimpsing the future Beethoven in numerous turns of phrase, as when the lyrical second movement points the way to the *Pastoral* Symphony. Probably the third movement (*Tempo di Menuetto*) will ring most familiar: Beethoven here borrowed the opening theme from the G-major Piano Sonata he had written in 1795–96 (published later, and thus carrying the deceptive identification as his Op. 49, No. 2), and in that earlier version it has made its way into countless anthologies for beginning or intermediate piano students.

The theme of the fourth movement is presumably a German folk song, though the exact song has eluded researchers. In any case, its four-square phrases and elementary harmony make it sound like one, and each of its five variations spotlights a different combination: strings alone; solo violin (remember Schuppanzigh!) with a background accompaniment; rich-timbred winds with a modest string accompaniment (but with roles switched for one phrase); a mysterious episode in the minor, with long notes in the winds enhancing the almost Mendelssohnian atmosphere; and finally a placid variation making use of the entire ensemble, with a dash of Haydnesque surprise held in store for the coda.

This is the moment in Beethoven's career when he was replacing old-fashioned minuets with newfangled scherzos. In the Septet, we have an example of both; the lightweight Scherzo injects a charming cello tune as a trio to separate the two occurrences of the slightly unruly main section (with horn calls). Don't be misled by the minor-key solemnity that unaccountably opens the finale; within moments it yields to a skittish *Presto* that passes through a particularly luminous landscape with pizzicato strings—and even breaks for a violin cadenza—before sprinting to the finish.

Serenade in D major for Flute, Violin, and Viola, Op. 25

Entrata (Allegro)
Tempo ordinario d'un Menuetto

Allegro molto
Andante con variazioni
Allegro scherzando e vivace
Adagio (attacca subito)
Allegro vivace e disinvolto—Presto

Work composed: 1801, in Vienna

Work premiered: Not known

Instrumentation: Flute, violin, and viola

Through most of his career, Beethoven crossed the boundary separating bagatelles from masterpieces with seemingly carefree ease. The popular image of
the composer, ill-tempered and self-tormented, struggling with his own Olympian talents to create works of surpassing genius is certainly not inaccurate.
But the same Beethoven apparently had no trouble laying aside the pages
of a symphony or sonata destined for posterity in order to toss off a blithe
rondo or a menial set of variations that might pay a bill or two. Of course,
Beethoven didn't achieve works of masterpiece status from the very outset;
like most composers, he grew into them. But by 1801, when he composed the
genial D-major Serenade for Flute, Violin, and Viola, Beethoven had already
distinguished himself with a small handful of pieces that might claim that
designation. His first six string quartets (Op.18) were already behind him, as
was the *Pathétique* Sonata, and further indelible works were "on the burner."
The Op. 25 Serenade is roughly coeval with the abundantly witty Symphony
No. 1 (Op. 21), the supernal *Spring* Sonata for Violin and Piano (Op. 24),
and two of Beethoven's most beloved piano sonatas, the *Moonlight* (Op. 27,
No. 2) and the *Pastoral* (Op. 28).

The D-major Serenade is not a deep work, nor was it intended to be
one. The very genre of the serenade bespeaks casual lightheartedness. (The
word itself is derived from the Italian *sera*, or "evening," with a serenata, or
serenade, therefore being a piece of light music appropriate for the evening.)
Countless composers, from Haydn and Mozart to Elgar and Korngold, have
written works called serenades, and in nearly every case deep thoughts are all
but banished. Beethoven's Serenade adheres to the general structure of the
type: a loosely knit sequence of numerous short movements—seven, in this
case—of varying characters and tempos, all designed to tickle the ear rather
than to challenge the intellect. The instrumentation, which employs two
high-pitched instruments (flute and violin) and one of medium range (viola),
supports the work's pleasant character perfectly; it's hard to write deep music
without low-pitched instruments.

The movements follow one another in quick succession. The opening *Entrata* (an "entrance piece") is a jaunty march built on a fanfare motif. The ensuing minuet has a memorable character thanks to slight syncopation in its main tune, and to the distinctive personalities of the two interspersed trios. The first features running sixteenth notes in the violin, while the flute takes a breather, preparing for its own passage-work in the second. A blustery *Allegro molto* follows, and then the Serenade's high point: a stately, dignified theme introduced by the violin, three variations that spotlight each player in turn, and a beautifully crafted coda. An almost negligible *Allegro scherzando* flies past, leading to a brief *Adagio*, which turns out to be little more than an introduction to the final, energetic rondo. Though unusual in a musical context, the movement's designation *disinvolto* ("free and easy" seems a better translation than the also-possible "self-possessed") seems perfectly apt as the Serenade dashes *presto* toward the finish line.

Beethoven's D-major Serenade was brought before the public in 1802 as his Op. 25, under the imprint of the Viennese publisher Giovanni Cappi. It seems to have met with enough success to merit further dissemination in a new arrangement for smaller instrumental forces. Transcriptions were common in Beethoven's time, and the composer's chief concern about them seems to have been more monetary than esthetic; in an age before modern copyright laws, composers could not expect to receive royalties from arrangements others made of their works. It seems that Beethoven sometimes dealt with the situation by having assistants or lesser colleagues prepare transcriptions of his works (probably for a fee), which he would then review, amend slightly, and publish as his own. Such was apparently the case with the Op. 25 Serenade, one of two serenades recast by a certain Franz Xaver Kleinheinz; this one resurfaced in Leipzig as Beethoven's Serenade in D major for Piano and Flute or Violin, Op. 41. "The arrangements," a haughty Beethoven wrote to his publisher in 1803, "were not made by me, but I have gone through them and made drastic corrections in some passages. So do not dare to state in writing that I have arranged them.... I could never have found the time, or even had the patience, to do work of that kind."

String Quintet in C major, Op. 29

Allegro
Adagio molto espressivo
Scherzo: Allegro
Presto

Work composed: 1801, in Vienna

Dedicated: To Count Moritz von Fries

Work premiered: In Beethoven's apartment in Vienna on November 14, 1802

Instrumentation: Two violins, two violas, and cello

The medium of the string quintet was of great interest to Beethoven's eminent predecessor Mozart, who created five works for the combination of two violins, two violas, and cello. Beethoven's Op. 29 is his only completed work to continue that tradition, although he did arrange several of his other works for these same forces. It is perhaps most logical to approach the Op. 29 Quintet as a transitional piece representative of the moment when the "Classical" Beethoven began ceding to his distinctive maturity. Beethoven's "Early Quartets"—his Six Quartets, Op. 18—were composed in the two-year span of 1798–1800, and his "Middle Quartets" would begin with his Op. 59 set of 1806; this Quintet, dating from 1801, clearly falls in the interstice, both chronologically and stylistically. Its first two movements are planted in what came before while the last two stretch toward what lies ahead. Nonetheless, one finds plenty of surprises in the beautifully balanced phrases of the opening *Allegro*, particularly (at least for harmonic structuralists) in the fact that the second subject appears in the unexpected submediant key (A major, since the overriding key of the movement is C major), rather than in the Classically typical dominant (which in this case would be G major). The ensuing *Adagio molto espressivo* is one of Beethoven's most Mozartian expanses, a long-lined tribute of the most gorgeous sort.

The *Scherzo* is more radical. We spy what would become the Beethoven hallmark of generating much material from a very minimal motif; here a single measure comprising three notes is bounced around ceaselessly as the movement unrolls with unstoppable momentum, the motif being repeated by each of the five musicians and on every step of the scale. The finale also exhibits a supercharged character. It's an ambitious conception, embodying three principal themes, a patch of expert and imaginative counterpoint, and an unforgettable character. The strings' sizzling *tremolandos* buzz in an electrical way. Here, too, we encounter a fine example of Beethoven's unpredictability: the surprising insertion of a minuet-like passage just before the movement's recapitulation, a passage the composer marks *Andante con moto e scherzoso* (i.e., "Andante with motion and in the style of a joke"), after which he picks up where he had left off, but in a "wrong key" (F major) that requires some deft modulation to get back to a proper ending in C major.

Apart from its musical value, the String Quintet occasioned an emblematic moment in Beethoven's biography, one that underscores the pitfalls of becoming famous. The piece was written at the behest of Count Moritz von Fries, a music-loving Viennese banker who apparently commissioned it along with Beethoven's Violin Sonatas Op. 23 and Op. 24 (the *Spring*) of 1800–01. All three of these pieces were dedicated to him, as would be Beethoven's Seventh Symphony more than a decade later. Beethoven and his brother Carl, who at that time was acting as his business manager, then sold the piece for publication to the firm of Breitkopf & Härtel in Leipzig, which seems to have been within their rights. But while the ink was still wet on Breitkopf's pages, a rival edition appeared from the Viennese firm of Artaria, which also wanted to benefit from the increasingly popular composer. The Beethovens were furious over what they understandably considered Artaria's undercutting of their arrangement with Breitkopf, and they unleashed a flurry of letters to both publishers clarifying their thoughts on the matter in no uncertain terms. The conflict escalated into a lawsuit. Beethoven ran a newspaper notice decrying Artaria's presumed piracy, and then, on court order, published a half-hearted retraction. It seems, however, that the engravers at Artaria worked from a copy they had received directly from Count Fries, who also had legal standing concerning the disposition of the work. The matter dragged on for many months without reaching a firm resolution. Years later Ferdinand Ries penned an amusing account of Beethoven's cunningly arranging for Artaria to send him all the copies they had printed by offering to hand-correct various mistakes in the edition and then having Ries deface the sheets into an unusable state, a tale that may have been entirely fabricated in the interest of after-the-fact public relations.

String Quartet in F major, Op. 59, No. 1, *First Razumovsky*

> *Allegro*
> *Allegretto vivace e sempre scherzando*
> *Adagio molto e mesto (attacca)*
> *Thème russe: Allegro*

Work composed: 1806, begun on May 26 and completed in June, in Vienna

Work dedicated: To Count Andreas Kirillovich Razumovsky

Work premiered: Near the beginning of 1807, at the Vienna home of Count Razumovsky, by the Schuppanzigh Quartet (at that time comprising first violinist Ignaz Schuppanzigh, Razumovsky himself as second violinist, violist Franz Weiss, and cellist Joseph Linke, sometimes spelled "Lincke")

Instrumentation: Two violins, viola, and cello

Beethoven composed his three Op. 59 quartets on commission from Count Andreas (Andrei) Kirillovich Razumovsky (1752–1836), scion of a Ukrainian family that had begun to work its way up through aristocratic circles only at the beginning of the eighteenth century. Razumovsky achieved the rank of captain in the Russian Imperial Navy and then entered the diplomatic service, which led to postings in Venice, Naples, Copenhagen, and Stockholm before landing him in the plum position of Russian Ambassador to the Court of Vienna in 1792, the same year Beethoven arrived in town. Razumovsky was a deeply cultured man who amassed a splendid art collection and, for a period of about eight years, supported a string quartet, led by Ignaz Schuppanzigh, in which he himself occasionally played second violin. In addition to being immortalized through the dedication of the Op. 59 quartets, he was also the joint dedicatee, with Prince Lobkowitz, of Beethoven's Fifth and Sixth Symphonies. Additionally, he was connected to another important Beethoven patron, Prince Lichnowsky, having married Lichnowsky's sister-in-law in 1788. As it happens, Beethoven changed the dedication of the Op. 59 Quartets to Prince Lichnowsky for a short while, though he quickly reverted to Razumovsky, whose name remains popularly attached to them as an easy identifier.

The three quartets Razumovsky commissioned from Beethoven were considered tough fare when they were unveiled. A report survives about the Schuppanzigh Quartet playing through the F-major Quartet for the first time and exploding into laughter, thinking that Beethoven was playing a joke on them. The *Allgemeine musikalische Zeitung* found them to be "long and difficult...profound and excellently wrought but not easily intelligible—except perhaps for the Third, whose originality, melody, and harmonic power will surely win over every educated music lover." Long they were indeed: the First *Razumovsky* Quartet clocks in at about forty minutes, an extraordinary length for a string quartet in its day. It strains at its seams with such muscularity that some commentators have referred to it as the *Eroica* of the Beethoven quartets, connecting its expansiveness to that of the groundbreaking symphony the composer had completed a year earlier. It is of these three quartets that Beethoven replied to an uncomprehending violinist, "Not for you, but for a later age."

All the movements of Op. 59, No. 1 are cast in some kind of sonata form, the primus inter pares of Classical musical architectures, with the result that they enjoy a sort of structural parity. So it is that the opening movement (the traditional repository of sonata procedures) is not a priori more "weighty" than the others, the scherzo is proportionally far longer than one would expect, the slow movement is the longest section of all, and the finale is the shortest by such a degree that the end arrives almost as a surprise.

The first movement opens with a broad principal theme played by the cello against the pulsating accompaniment of the other strings. The theme is handed off to the first violin before reaching a high point in measure 19, after which the music breaks into a second theme and, shortly, a murmuring third. The movement runs to nearly twelve minutes, but even that considerable length does not include a repetition of the exposition section, which Beethoven audaciously chooses to omit. (Had he demanded a repeat, the piece would be almost three minutes longer.) For a while he was thinking of repeating the development and recapitulation but in the end he decided to repeat nothing at all, leaving us with an entirely through-composed movement. This opens the door to surprises, most especially when what we might imagine is the expected repetition of the exposition veers off into uncharted territory that involves even a fugal exploration of the main theme's potential.

Another fast movement comes second, an atypical placement since Beethoven was still favoring third-movement scherzos at this point in his career. The theme seems a joke: a rhythmic pattern rather than a real tune, played on one note by the cello alone with the other instruments adding their voices in a fragmented texture. The theme assembles itself gradually out of these bits and pieces, rather as if we are watching in reverse a film of a vase being broken into smithereens. The scherzo, as we have already suggested, is strikingly long for its function, but its curious and amusing turns have no trouble holding one's interest.

The *Adagio* attests to further kinship with the *Eroica* Symphony, which includes a funeral march that is not so different in tragic sentiment from this one. "A weeping willow or an acacia over my brother's grave" reads a cryptic inscription on a sketch page for this movement. Beethoven had already lost two brothers, but he did not really know either; one (the original Ludwig van Beethoven) had died a year before our composer was born, and the other died in infancy when our composer was thirteen. Some suggest the comment relates instead to the figurative "death" of his brother Caspar Carl, who had just married a woman Beethoven disliked. And then, of course, Beethoven was always eager to proclaim the sort of spiritualized brotherhood that connects all of humanity. Whatever we are to understand from this notation—and we are free to simply ignore it—the music is magnificent, a high point of Beethoven's expressiveness that draws on a wide instrumental range to enhance its poignancy. Near the end, the movement loosens into what may be considered an accompanied cadenza for the first violin; but in a deft act of telescoping, Beethoven has the cello launch the theme of the finale before the violin has finished playing its final trill.

That *Thème russe*, as Beethoven marks it, is an obvious nod to the piece's Russian patron; it's a folk tune (titled "Ah, my luck! Such luck!") drawn from a collection of a hundred Russian folk tunes assembled in 1790 by the Czech folklorist Ivan Prach (or, in German, Johann Gottfried Pratsch), assisted by Nikolai Lvov. The tune is intriguing; as it begins on the sixth note of the scale, it leaves the listener groping to locate the tonal center of the tonic. It was originally a sad song, but Beethoven pumps it up to a quick dance for his finale. In the course of the movement he puts it through all manner of development, much of it cleverly contrapuntal. Near the end, however, a dozen measures of *Adagio* suggest in passing the tune's original introversion.

String Quartet in E minor, Op. 59, No. 2, *Second Razumovsky*

> *Allegro*
> *Molto adagio*
> *Allegretto—Maggiore (Thème russe)*
> *Finale: Presto—più presto*

Work composed: 1806, in Vienna

Work dedicated: To Count Andreas Kirillovich Razumovsky

Work premiered: Near the beginning of 1807 (some sources suggest January), at the Vienna home of Count Razumovsky, by the Schuppanzigh Quartet (at that time comprising first violinist Ignaz Schuppanzigh, Razumovsky himself as second violinist, violist Franz Weiss, and cellist Joseph Linke)

Instrumentation: Two violins, viola, and cello

Beethoven produced all three of the Op. 59 quartets in 1806, apparently between May and the end of the year. Through a curious fluke of history we know that the first two movements of the E-minor Quartet were finished by late October, when Beethoven traveled back to Vienna from a country getaway in Silesia. He packed his manuscripts in a trunk that proved to be leaky when his coach passed through a storm on the way home. The manuscript of the first two movements is indeed water-stained, but the last two are not—pretty firm evidence that they were not written out until after that trip.

The first movement (*Allegro*) is taut and lean, tense with nervous energy that erupts and recedes throughout the duration of the movement. Of course drama is built from contrast, and Beethoven builds plenty of disparity into his music here: rhythmic clashes, interlaced themes of dissimilar mood, sudden starts and stops, surprising harmonic juxtapositions that, in this case, particularly emphasize half-steps. The second movement seems the polar opposite of the first, utterly unified in its mood of hymnic transcendence. "Si tratta questo pezzo con molto di sentimento," wrote Beethoven by way of performance advice: "This piece is to be played with great feeling." His notation was superfluous: no musician could approach this piece with anything less than the greatest feeling. Several accounts from Beethoven's contemporaries, including one from his pupil Carl Czerny, relate that he conceived of this E-major expanse while gazing at the night sky at Baden (near Vienna) and contemplating the music of the spheres, and it is easy to "hear" the vastness of eternal heavens in these pages.

Beethoven initially envisioned a minuet as his third movement, an unaccountably old-fashioned idea at that stage in his career. Instead he decided on an *Allegretto*, one that revisits the restive spirit of the opening movement. When he presented his commission, Count Razumovsky had requested that Beethoven work "some Russian melodies, real or imitated" into his quartets. Beethoven had already used a Russian tune in the finale of the first of the Razumovsky set, and now he rises to the occasion again in the contrasting trio section of this movement, marked *Maggiore* ("[In the] major [key]"). Lest the point be overlooked, he signals the tune with the words *Thème russe*. This section is based on a real (not an imitated) Russian traditional melody that Beethoven found in a collection by Ivan Prach (the publication also furnished the Russian tune of the preceding quartet), where it is indicated to be a stately melody in moderate tempo. The same tune would find its way into scores by several later Russian composers, most prominently Musorgsky's opera *Boris Godunov*. Beethoven was always fascinated with variations, and here he pokes and pulls the theme in all sorts of spirited directions, not feeling bound to present the tune even once with its original character. And, being Beethoven, he could not resist putting the material through strenuous contrapuntal paces, trying out its suitability as the subject of a rather boisterous fugue. Beethoven's score calls for the *Allegretto* section to be played through three times and the trio twice, yielding an A-B-A-B-A structure, but some ensembles today prefer to condense it into a simple A-B-A journey, perhaps a defensible decision in so substantial a work as this.

The energy of the variations continues in the *Finale*, which, like so much else in this quartet, delights in ambiguity. Here that is most on display in the curious theme heard at the very outset, which hovers oddly between the major and minor modes—again, arguably, an *à la russe* touch. This harmonic uncertainty flickers throughout the galloping movement before the quartet arrives at a very definitive E minor to close.

String Quartet in C major, Op. 59, No. 3, *Third Razumovsky*

> *Introduzione. Andante con moto—Allegro vivace*
> *Andante con moto quasi Allegretto*
> *Menuetto. Grazioso—Trio—Menuetto da Capo—Coda*
> *Allegro molto*

Work composed: Completed on July 5, 1806

Work dedicated: To Count Andreas Kirillovich Razumovsky

Work premiered: Near the beginning of 1807, perhaps in February, at the Vienna home of Count Razumovsky, by the Schuppanzigh Quartet (at that time comprising first violinist Ignaz Schuppanzigh, Razumovsky himself as second violinist, violist Franz Weiss, and cellist Joseph Linke)

Instrumentation: Two violins, viola, and cello

When the *Allgemeine musikalische Zeitung* of Leipzig proclaimed Beethoven's Op. 59 quartets to be "long and difficult...profound and excellently wrought but not easily intelligible," it made a hesitating exception for "perhaps...the Third, whose originality, melody, and harmonic power will surely win over every educated music lover." Whoever wrote that was not a normal listener by any stretch of the imagination; how could he single out the Third *Razumovsky* Quartet as more "intelligible" than the other two, given the harmonic meanderings of its exceedingly bizarre introduction and the very distinctive flavor of its second movement?

The first movement opens in mystery thanks to a slow introduction of twenty-nine measures that pokes into various harmonic nooks and crannies, sidestepping at all costs the C-major triad that would define the overriding key of this quartet. On paper, that C-major tonic is reached when the main part of the movement begins (*Allegro vivace*), but even here we fail to sense the tonal anchoring that had characterized earlier Classical expositions. The first violin announces its theme with only the most meager accompaniment from its colleagues, almost in the style of a cadenza, and it veers immediately from the tentative C major into D minor, such that the quartet is already forty-three measures old before it is grounded by what everyone can agree is a firm C-major cadence. At that point, with the cello thrumming octave Cs in the bass, the quartet finally seems to take off in earnest. Apart from signaling the harmonic imagination that will inform the entire quartet, this unusual opening alerts us to the freedom of texture Beethoven is allowing himself, a wide dispersion of lines and a vivid contrast among parts that, at times, will lend a frankly symphonic character to this chamber work.

The second movement boasts a characteristically complicated Beethoven tempo marking: *Andante con moto quasi Allegretto*, which at least connotes that the music is to flow with considerable liquidity. In an obvious nod to the patron, Beethoven's first two *Razumovsky* quartets make explicit use of Russian folk tunes; Razumovsky had actually requested that the composer work something of Russian import into the pieces. The C-major Quartet does not do this, so far as we know, but the principal melody of this slow movement nonetheless displays an exotic, vaguely Eastern character; and, as in the first movement, the tonality is somewhat destabilized at the outset by the cello's repeated pizzicato plucks of low E—the fifth, rather than the more firmly grounded first, step of the A-minor scale (A minor being the key of this movement). This lengthy movement is hypnotic in its unrelenting emphasis on flowing eighth notes in 6/8 meter, and its haunting quality foreshadows the intimate contemplations of the late quartets.

The composer Vincent d'Indy dismissed the third movement as hopelessly retroactive, "a return to the style of 1796" (by which he meant the style of the Op. 18 quartets). Certainly its Haydn-and-Mozart character is less visionary than the sorts of brave explorations Beethoven has pursued in the first two movements; and yet, by this time we are ready to relax a bit. And so we have a *Grazioso* respite for a few minutes, in the course of which we may empty out our ears to prepare for what is to come.

In truth, what follows is not necessarily heavy, though it is certainly learned and virtuosic. The *Allegro molto* that concludes this Third *Rasumovsky* Quartet is an imaginative hybrid of a sonata form with a fugue. Sonata forms and fugues operate according to different principles, such that we might be better off saying that this movement unrolls along the familiar lines of a sonata form, but that its principal material is fugal. What the form is or isn't may be principally of theoretical interest, but on a practical level it's worth observing that Beethoven here harnesses together the two most dramatic structural methods available to the Classical composer. The combined rhythmic-harmonic propulsion and psychological inevitability of sonata and fugue yield a movement of compelling momentum. It holds the potential to be one of the most exciting conclusions in all of chamber music.

Piano Trio in D major, Op. 70, No. 1, *Ghost*

Allegro vivace e con brio
Largo assai ed espressivo
Presto

Work composed: 1808, in Vienna

Work dedicated: To Countess Anna Maria (or Marie) von Erdödy

Work premiered: Date not known, but shortly after its completion at the Vienna home of Countess Anna Maria von Erdödy

Instrumentation: Violin, cello, and piano

The name of Countess Anna Maria von Erdödy surfaces quite a lot in the annals of Beethoven. In late 1808 her home on the Krugerstrasse in Vienna resounded with the first performance of Beethoven's two Op. 70 Piano Trios, which were dedicated to her when they were published in the summer of 1809. Several of the composer's new scores underwent their gestation within those same walls, since he lived there for several months from late 1808 until the spring of 1809. An accomplished pianist, she was a devoted friend and sup-portive patron of Beethoven at that time—he is said to have referred to her as his "Father Confessor"—and she was delighted to be able to include his music in her frequent at-home musical soirées, where Beethoven himself sometimes performed either pre-composed pieces or piano improvisations. In 1815 she would again achieve immortality as the dedicatee of Beethoven's Op. 102 Cello Sonatas, and she hosted their premiere at her country house outside Vienna.

The first of the Op. 70 Trios is far the more overtly dramatic of the two, beginning with its opening volley, a unison explosion that within five mea-sures both defines the tonic key (D major) and undercuts it when the last note of the theme veers to the note F-natural. This is a harmonic feint not unknown to Beethoven aficionados, who will recall related surprises at the opening of the *Eroica* Symphony or at the offstage trumpet calls in the *Leonore* Overtures No. 2 and No. 3. Such things are rarely red herrings in Beethoven. Although the music slips right back into D major in this opening moment, we will find that the sidestep has foreshadowed a structural idea when, in the movement's recapitulation, the key center is coaxed into remote B-flat major by way of that very note of F. The structuralists among us derive enduring satisfaction from Beethovenian niceties of this sort.

The slow movement is very slow and melancholy indeed. Its fragmented character skirts the boundaries of out-and-out weirdness. The piano some-times plays ominous tremolos, against which the violin and cello bat melodic motifs back and forth at such a snail's pace that the scene seems to be unroll-ing in slow motion. Much of this movement is, indeed, "spooky," and it is to this section that the work owes its nickname, *Ghost*, first attached to it (so it appears) in 1842 when Beethoven's pupil Carl Czerny wrote that the slow movement called to mind the initial appearance of the ghost in *Hamlet*. As it happens, a page of Beethoven's sketches for this trio also includes a short musical idea the composer was thinking of working out in an operatic setting of *Macbeth* he was contemplating at the time—another curious, though ultimately inconsequential, Shakespearean connection. (It would prove all the more fleeting since the *Macbeth* opera, which Beethoven was approaching via a libretto by Heinrich Joseph von Collin, was aborted early on.) You may discard as erroneous the oft-encountered claim that this movement of the *Ghost* Trio is a reworking of music Beethoven originally sketched as the Witches' Chorus for his *Macbeth*.

The work's finale brings us back to the world of normality, no doubt the best strategy after so extraordinary a slow movement. Nonetheless, Beethoven hardly retreats to Classical orthodoxy, and even in the unanticipated modulations of this finale we find aftershocks of the startling F-natural that had disturbed the Trio's opening phrase.

The proto-Romantic author and composer E. T. A. Hoffmann (of *Tales of Hoffmann* fame) wrote a good deal of music criticism in the course of his career, among which we find a glowing consideration of the *Ghost* Trio that was published in 1813 in the *Allgemeine musikalische Zeitung*. Writing of this finale, he says:

> The concluding movement, Presto, in D major, once again has a short, original theme, which continually reappears in many variations and meaningful allusions throughout the entire piece while a variety of figures are interchanged. . . . Just as the storm wind drives away the clouds, with light and shadow alternating in a moment, as forms then appear in the restless pursuit and commotion, disappear and appear again, just so does the music rush continuously onward. . . . Beethoven's style . . . shows itself in final movements primarily through continuous, ever mounting bustle and commotion. Regardless of the good nature that prevails in the entire trio, with the exception of the melancholy Largo, Beethoven's genius still remains serious and solemn. It is as though the master believed that deep, secret things can never be discussed in commonplace terms, but only in sublime, magnificent ones, even when the spirit, which is intimately familiar with them, feels joyously and happily uplifted.

Piano Trio in E-flat major, Op. 70, No. 2

Poco sostenuto—Allegro ma non troppo
Allegretto
Allegretto ma non troppo
Finale: Allegro

Work composed: 1808, in Vienna

Work dedicated: To Countess Anna Maria (or Marie) von Erdödy

Work premiered: December 1808 at the Vienna home of the Countess Anna Maria von Erdödy, on which occasion Ignaz Schuppanzigh played violin, Joseph Linke was the cellist, and the composer essayed the piano part

Instrumentation: Violin, cello, and piano

Compared to its Op. 70 companion, the intense *Ghost* Trio, the Trio in E-flat major is overwhelmingly genial and warmhearted: a yin-and-yang dyad. Listeners who gravitate toward the defiant Beethoven will have to make an adjustment for Op. 70, No. 2. At least on an emotional plane it seems more connected to the *Archduke* Trio, which lay a bit more than two years in the future, or, for that matter, to the style of the composer's younger years, although the harmonic subtlety of this trio surpasses anything Beethoven had achieved a decade earlier. In fact, this work entirely lacks a slow movement, which would have been a natural repository for deep thoughts, and the whole four-movement span remains within the bounds of relatively moderate tempos. An elegant, if not entirely unruffled, introduction launches the piece. Its carefully plotted, stepwise lines in slow but flowing counterpoint, canonic at the outset, invest this opening with a searching quality. This leads to the main section of the movement (*Allegro ma non troppo*), a lyrical effusion if ever one was, though its songfulness is infused with an aristocratic bearing. Just before the end the composer brings back a reminiscence of the "searching music" of the introduction, this time with the scoring altered.

Both of the middle movements are *Allegrettos*—one (most typically the first of them) might have been the spot for a real slow movement—but they have quite different characters. The second movement sounds resolutely old-fashioned, beginning with a neo-Baroque gavotte, though modernized with the wry sort of figuration beloved by Beethovenians, beginning with the raised eyebrows of the opening motif. Major-key variations on this alternate with minor-key sections based on a more vehement element; this too has a neo-Baroque cast, being uncannily reminiscent of the sort of blustery, pared-down variations one might encounter toward the end of a Baroque chaconne or passacaglia.

The marking *Allegretto* already represents a moderate tempo. Adding *ma non troppo* ("but not too much"), as Beethoven does in the third movement, seems not particularly helpful: does he mean that players should shade the *Allegretto* to the fast or the slow side? Perhaps the former, as this spot in a composition would most characteristically have been the place for a triple-meter minuet—or rather, at this point in Beethoven's career, a scherzo—and the movement is cast in the meter and structure of those forms, though with the main episode and the "trio" repeated, extending the movement from the usual A-B-A of a scherzo to a five-section A-B-A-B-A structure. But at heart we have no scherzo here. The spirit is Apollonian rather than Dionysian, and the phrases are studiously symmetrical, again displaying something of an antique character. In fact, the spacious main theme of the movement was, if not literally antique, at least not new, since Beethoven had already used it as the opening theme of his Piano Sonata in A-flat major (Op. 26) of 1800–1801, developing it in that sonata through a set of variations. Beethoven doesn't repeat himself verbatim in reviving this theme, but the similarity is unmistakable. One of his enhancements in the trio is memorable indeed: the odd passage in the principal-theme section (heard several times in the course of the movement) in which the unaccompanied piano slowly cascades down through a series of unlikely notes that leave us momentarily in tonal limbo before the main theme grounds the tonality once again.

With the *Finale* we finally have a full-fledged fast movement: not a rip-roaring *Presto* or *Vivace*, to be sure, but at least a solidly rapid *Allegro*. And yet, hardly does the movement get started with energetic, ascending piano flourishes than the strings pull on the reins. This proves to be a momentary interruption of the momentum, though it will not be the last, even apart from when this passage is heard again as the exposition is repeated. In general, though, the movement proceeds apace as it works through its episodes. "It is a continuous, ever mounting bustle and commotion—ideas, images chase by in a restless flight, and sparkle and disappear like flashes of lightning—it is a free play of the most highly aroused imagination": so says E. T. A. Hoffmann, writing in the *Allgemeine musikalische Zeitung* in 1813. Beethoven's pupil Carl Czerny maintained that in the G-major section in the middle of this finale Beethoven drew on Croatian melodies that were popular in Hungary, which would have been an appropriate nod from the composer to the Countess, who belonged to a family of Hungarian aristocrats.

This trio occupies a unique place in Beethoven's oeuvre. While many of its details are those of middle-period Beethoven, they seem to some extent overlain on an older template, almost as if Beethoven were rewriting a composition from his earlier years—which to some small extent he did by resurrecting a pre-existent theme in the third movement. The distinguished commentator Donald Francis Tovey rightly viewed this as a work "where Beethoven discovers new meanings for Mozart's phrases and Haydn's formulas." But when all is said and done it is in no way a retrograde composition. In its relaxed character (both in its moderate tempo markings and in the behavior of the instruments within the movements), the unfussy forthrightness of its technique, the distinctive contour of certain modulations, and its overall spirit of scarcely impeded *joie de vivre*, this piano trio brings us surprisingly close to the sound of another great composer who would not emerge until a decade later: Franz Schubert.

String Quartet in E-flat major, Op. 74, *Harp*

> *Poco adagio—Allegro*
> *Adagio ma non troppo*
> *Presto—Più presto quasi prestissimo*
> *Allegretto con variazioni*

Work composed: Summer and autumn 1809, entirely finished and delivered to its commissioner, Prince Lobkowitz, on July 2, 1810

Work dedicated: To Prince Franz Josef von Lobkowitz

Work premiered: When and where not known, but it was played by the Schuppanzigh Quartet (at that time comprising first violinist Ignaz Schuppanzigh, second violinist Joseph Mayseder, violist Franz Weiss, and cellist Joseph Linke)

Instrumentation: Two violins, viola, and cello

Vienna was in turmoil when Beethoven composed his Op. 74 Quartet in 1809. Austria was growing exhausted from a series of on-and-off wars with France that had marked the past eighteen years. That spring the French renewed their bombardment with particular ferocity. On May 4 the imperial family fled Vienna, and at the end of July Beethoven wrote to the Leipzig publisher Breitkopf & Härtel: "Let me tell you that since May 4th I have produced very little coherent work, at most a fragment here and there. The whole course of events has in my case affected both body and soul." Nonetheless, he soon embarked on this quartet and apparently completed it quickly. We should not automatically assume that Beethoven's compositions are a form of autobiography; and, indeed, one would not point to this quartet as an example of Beethovenian tumult, notwithstanding some punchiness here and there. Among the quartets of his maturity this one stands as an island of calm in the midst of what could often escalate into a hurricane, although even here the scherzo movement does not shy away in the least from being boisterous.

The first movement—and not just its quiet introduction (tantalizingly interrupted by a couple of one-chord outbursts)—projects an overwhelmingly gracious mien. On the surface this piece seems to look back toward Classical models rather than ahead to Beethoven's late style, much as does its near chronological neighbor the E-flat-major Piano Trio (Op. 70, No. 2). Analysis of its construction nonetheless reveals that the composer in no way lacks forward-thinking originality even while projecting a spirit of mellow intimacy. The nickname *Harp* (not Beethoven's idea) derives from an abundance of pizzicato in this opening movement. The ensuing *Adagio*, in contrast, does foreshadow the late quartets, its transcendent, even sentimental melody belying deeper intimations of anxiety. It is plotted as a slow rondo in which the refrain is considerably varied at each return. The final measures are a coda that, in the manner of Mozart, manage to summarize and even transcend the essential quality of what has come before.

The scherzo (*Presto*, with two go-rounds of the still quicker trio section) may remind us of ideas in the composer's Fifth Symphony, premiered just the preceding December—certainly the symphony's famous opening "fate motif" but also the contrapuntal trio, which evokes the corresponding section of the symphony. It is an odd expanse, its texture thinned down to very little as first the cello, then the first violin (with the other two instruments eventually joining in) engage in a boisterous game of tag. Like the symphony's scherzo, this movement is set overall in C minor (shifting to C major for the trio) and connects to the finale without a break. Here the concluding *Allegretto* consists of an unassuming theme with six variations. Extreme contrast is the order of the day here—between the widely spaced staccato arpeggios and contrary motion of the first variation and the gentle viola murmurings of the second, between the running sixteenth notes (with syncopated punctuations) of the third and the restrained elegance of the fourth (played "always soft and sweet," according to the score), between the violin's virtuosic yodeling of the fifth and the quiet but simmering energy of the sixth. After Beethoven has worked through the theme's possibilities the quartet escalates into a rambunctious, even hilarious conclusion.

String Quartet in F minor, Op. 95, *Quartett Serioso*

> *Allegro con brio*
> *Allegretto ma non troppo*
> *Allegro assai vivace ma serioso—Più allegro*
> *Larghetto espressivo—Allegretto agitato—Allegro*

Work composed: Summer through October 1810, in Vienna, but apparently revised in 1814, just prior to its premiere

Work dedicated: To Nikolaus Zmeskall von Domanovecz, a cello-playing friend of the composer

Work premiered: May 1814 in Vienna by the Schuppanzigh Quartet (first violinist Ignaz Schuppanzigh, second violinist Joseph Mayseder, violist Franz Weiss, and cellist Joseph Linke)

Instrumentation: Two violins, viola, and cello

The F-minor Quartet (Op. 95) closes out the sequence of quartets from Beethoven's middle period. After he wrote it, he gave up the genre for more than a decade. He would not accept a commission for another until late 1822 and wouldn't actually set to writing one until May 1824. But one might argue that if any composition of Beethoven's middle period adumbrates the spirit of his late works, it is this quartet. We may call it a middle-period quartet, but we can hardly fail to recognize that this Janus-like composition looks forward to the final five and backward to Op. 59 and Op. 74 in nearly equal measure.

The Op. 95 Quartet is the only one to which Beethoven himself gave a nickname, inscribing the words "Quartett serioso" on the manuscript. He reaffirmed the work's "serious" character by using the term again in the tempo heading of the third movement, the very unusually marked *Allegro assai vivace ma serioso*. The angry F-minor theme shouted in unison at the opening of the first movement sets the tone for the entire quartet. It is a strikingly compact work. Writing in *The Beethoven Compendium*, the musicologist Nicholas Marston observes, "The music exudes a sense of having been ruthlessly pared down until all that remains is the very essence of the musical material involved. The opening five bars are as good an example of this as any, but the sense of compression extends even to single notes or note pairs: in the first movement, D-flat–C and C–D-flat come to bear a huge musical weight." This would qualify as a forward-looking aspect of the quartet, prefiguring the sudden contrasts and telescoped transitions that will surface in the late works. The musical analyst Donald Francis Tovey also noted this quartet's density, remarking that in its opening movement Beethoven "contrives to pack a large symphonic tragedy into five minutes." Five minutes may have been a typical running time in Tovey's day, close to a century ago, but many modern interpretations clock in at closer to four. No sooner has the piece begun than it's over.

Despite some more placid gestures, the following *Allegretto ma non troppo* maintains the heated emotional pitch that has been established. Even the central section, a four-part fugue, provides little contrast in expression, based as it is on a worrisome subject carved out of a descending chromatic tune. A scherzo ensues, but a fitful one full of jagged rhythms, in no way amusing; remember that this is the movement marked *Allegro assai vivace ma serioso*.

Agitation reigns over the finale, too, a sonata-rondo hybrid that, following a slow and moody introduction, sustains the quartet's character through nervous repeated notes and truncated phrases. Felix Mendelssohn is known to have held this last movement particularly dear, an affection that must have attached in no small part to the curious conclusion. Not many measures before the end the music comes to rest on an F-major chord and then springs into a quicksilver coda (*Allegro*) that prolongs that major key to the end—rather as Beethoven also does in the *Egmont* Overture, written at about the same time. Generations of listeners have been perplexed by this passage, so seemingly out of character with the rest of the piece; some analysts have discovered—or imagined they discovered—thematic connections between this coda and material that has come before in the quartet. There is really no explaining it except to say that Beethoven wanted it that way. The composer Randall Thompson accepted it for the delightful conclusion it is and quipped, "No bottle of champagne was ever uncorked at a better time."

Piano Trio in B-flat major, Op. 97, *Archduke*

> *Allegro con brio*
> *Scherzo: Allegro*
> *Andante cantabile, ma però con moto—Poco più adagio*
> *Allegro moderato*

Work composed: 1810–11, mostly from March 3 to March 26, 1811; Beethoven appears to have revised it in 1814–15.

Work dedicated: To Archduke Rudolph

Work premiered: April 11, 1814, at noon, at Vienna's Hotel Zum Romischen Kaiser, on which occasion Ignaz Schuppanzigh played violin, Joseph Linke was the cellist, and the composer essayed the piano part

Instrumentation: Violin, cello, and piano

The archduke with whom the last of Beethoven's Piano Trio is identified was Archduke Rudolph (Rudolph Johann Joseph Rainer, to use all his given names), the youngest son of Emperor Leopold II and brother of the then-current Emperor Franz. Ill health prevented his following the military career his father had mapped out for him, and instead he took minor vows as a cleric and became an excellent pianist. Perhaps as early as the winter of 1803–04 he became a piano pupil of Beethoven (perhaps later; musicologists dispute this question), and in 1808 he was honored with the dedication of Beethoven's Fourth Piano Concerto, the first of a dozen works Beethoven would inscribe to him. This was more than Beethoven dedicated to any other individual, and the list is mighty impressive, continuing on through the Fifth Piano Concerto (the *Emperor*), three piano sonatas (*Les Adieux*, the *Hammerklavier*, and Op. 111), the G-major Violin Sonata (Op. 96), the *Missa solemnis*, and the *Grosse Fuge*—plus, of course, the *Archduke* Trio.

Archduke Rudolph continued to study piano, and later music theory and composition, with Beethoven at least through 1824. Beethoven complained that these lessons interfered with his own composing schedule, but he was careful not to voice such objections to the Archduke directly—at least not in the many of his letters to Rudolph that have survived. It was wise of Beethoven to behave tactfully in this regard, since Rudolph was one of his staunchest patrons, not that the composer normally worried overmuch about social niceties. Rudolph was one of the three aristocrats (along with Prince Kinsky and Prince Lobkowitz) who, in 1809, when Beethoven was considering a job offer from a brother of Napoleon, drew up a contract promising Beethoven a substantial annuity so long as he remained in Austrian lands—and of the three Rudolph was the most punctilious in making sure his share of the payments arrived promptly.

The B-flat-major Piano Trio surely marks the summit of Beethoven's production for the medium, and it is among the towering masterpieces of his entire chamber-music output. It is a spacious work—Beethoven in his Apollonian mode—and its four movements (the last two being connected) typically run past forty minutes in performance. The opening theme is nothing if not aristocratic; whether its inherent nobility fostered the popularity of the work's nickname I cannot say, but it is unquestionably music befitting an archduke. It sets the tone for the entire work, which ultimately comes off as beneficent and often tender. Nearly all of the principal themes are first presented at a soft volume, often with the admonition *dolce* appended. Of course, Beethoven develops his material exhaustively following those initial statements, frequently growing loud and sometimes gruff; but even so, first impressions count for a lot. A relatively lighthearted second theme provides essential contrast, and in the extended development Beethoven explores every imaginable permutation of the materials he has set forth. Throughout this trio the instrumental texture is meticulously balanced and full of variety—in the first movement's seductive episode in pizzicato, for example, or in the way in which Beethoven avoids doubling instrumental lines, the better to clarify contrapuntal intent and to avoid pitfalls of unison intonation.

In Classical four-movement structures a slow movement usually comes second and a lighter minuet or scherzo third. Here Beethoven reverses the order, a touch he would repeat from time to time in his mid-career and later works. We therefore move from the elevated tone of the opening movement directly into the *Scherzo*, which comes across as jocular and even boisterous in comparison. Both the scherzo proper and the central trio section are built on themes that rise from a low B-flat, but apart from that their characters could hardly be more different; the scherzo proper is derived from a forthright ascending major scale while the trio is a chromatic canon with creepy overtones. After playing out the standard scherzo-trio-scherzo structure, Beethoven extends the movement by summoning up the trio once again, followed by another repetition of the scherzo section, after which a coda refers yet again to the music of the trio section.

The slow movement follows—a theme with five variations that unroll leisurely in an atmosphere of pervasive calm, reminding us that the monumental slow movement of the *Hammerklavier* Sonata lies not far ahead in Beethoven's production. The hymn-like melody is transformed and decorated by ever-quickening rhythmic patterns as the variations unfurl: first in eighth-note triplets, then sixteenth notes, then sixteenth-note triplets, then thirty-second notes. An expressive coda follows the variations, and this leads without break to the finale. The mood transforms instantly from serenity to joviality in this rondo movement, the principal theme of which again begins with an ascending melodic pattern (as in the opening movements).

The *Archduke* Trio proved popular from the outset, notwithstanding the shortcomings of its premiere. *Thayer's Life of Beethoven*, the classic Beethoven biography, quotes the testimony of the composer Louis Spohr, who it says attended a rehearsal of the piece at Beethoven's home: "It was not a treat, for, in the first place, the piano was badly out of tune, which Beethoven minded little, since he did not hear it; and secondly, on account of his deafness there was scarcely anything left of the virtuosity of the artist which had formerly been so greatly admired. In *forte* passages the poor deaf man pounded on the keys till the strings jangled, and in *piano* he played so softly that whole groups of tones were omitted, so that the music was unintelligible unless one could look into the pianoforte part." This anecdote has been often repeated in connection with this piece, but this is a good moment to point out that consulting Spohr's *Autobiography*, the source of the quotation, reveals that the piece he heard was what he identified as "a new Trio (D-Major, 3/4 time)"—which is to say the *Ghost* Trio (Op. 70, No. 1, composed in 1808 and therefore still relatively new, certainly new to Spohr) rather than the *Archduke*. Still, Spohr's account of the state of Beethoven's pianism may be taken as generally accurate, and it's confirmed by an entry in the diary of the composer Ignaz Moscheles, who attended the premiere of the *Archduke* Trio: "In the case of how many compositions is the word 'new' misapplied! But never in Beethoven's, and least of all in this, which again is full of originality. His playing, aside from its intellectual element, satisfied me less, being wanting in clarity and precision; but I observed many traces of the *grand* style of playing which I had long recognized in his composition."

String Quartet in E-flat major, Op. 127

> Maestoso—Allegro
> Adagio, ma non troppo e molto cantabile
> Scherzando vivace
> Finale

Work composed: Sketches reach to 1822, and some work was done in April 1823, but mostly composed from summer 1824 through February 1825

Work dedicated: To Prince Nikolas Galitzin

Work premiered: March 6, 1825, in Vienna, by the Schuppanzigh Quartet (then comprising first violinist Ignaz Schuppanzigh, second violinist Carl Holz, violist Franz Weiss, and cellist Joseph Linke)

Instrumentation: Two violins, viola, and cello

By the time Beethoven embarked on his final five string quartets and the *Grosse Fuge*, he was pretty much surviving on a planet of his own, cut off by deafness from the hearing world, showing rather little interest in musical developments around him, wrapped up utterly in his uniquely advanced compositional technique and emotional expression.

The first three of his late quartets were written at the urging of the composer's Russian patron Prince Nikolas Borisovich Galitzin. An ardent amateur cellist, the prince made a peculiar specialty of creating chamber works that were assembled out of movements by Beethoven, such as a string quartet he published in St. Petersburg that was fashioned from movements of Beethoven's E-flat-major Piano Sonata (Op. 7), C-major Piano Sonata (Op. 53, the *Waldstein*), and A-major Cello Sonata (Op. 69).

Beethoven had eleven "real" string quartets under his belt when he was approached by Galitzin, but a decade had passed since he had last grappled with the genre. As early as June 1822 he was telling people that he'd like to produce more quartets, and in December of that year Prince Galitzin officially offered the commission that would ultimately yield the Quartets in E-flat major (Op. 127), A minor (Op. 132), and B-flat major (Op. 130). Galitzin gave Beethoven a fair amount of leeway, inviting him "to compose one, two, or three quartets, for which labor I will be glad to pay you what you think proper." Beethoven signaled that he would deliver one of these quartets by March 1823, giving himself nearly three months in which to complete the piece. At the end of November 1823—nine months after Beethoven's self-imposed deadline—the Prince wrote to the composer, urging him on while trying not to "pressure" him unduly: "I am really impatient to have a new quartet of yours; nevertheless, I beg you not to mind and to be guided in this only by your inspiration and the disposition of your mind, for no one knows better than I that you cannot command genius, rather that it should be left alone, and we know moreover that in your private life you are not the kind of person to sacrifice artistic for personal interest and that music done to order is not your business at all."

In the end, Beethoven missed his target by almost exactly two years, but we should be thankful, since much of the interstice was given over to working out the details of the Ninth Symphony and the *Missa solemnis*; the former, in fact, shares certain conceptual details with the Op. 127 Quartet. The E-flat-major Quartet was finally performed on March 6, 1825, in Vienna, by the Schuppanzigh Quartet. This long-suffering ensemble had done yeoman's service for Beethoven over the years, but in this case they had only two weeks in which to make sense of a work that was at all turns baffling, and their performance got the chilly reception it possibly deserved. "Few were moved; it was a weak *succès d'estime*," reported the violinist Joseph Böhm.

Unlike all but one of its companions among the late quartets, Op. 127 adheres to the four-movement format of most Classical string quartets: fast first and last movements (here with a slow introduction to the first), separated by a slow second movement and a scherzo. That's where the resemblance to tradition pretty much ends—and it almost didn't make it that far, since, for a while, Beethoven contemplated expanding even this work to six movements. (The extra movements would have been one titled "La Gaité," falling between the first two movements as they now exist, and a searching *Adagio* preceding the Finale.) The composer referred to his music of this period as involving "a new kind of part-writing," an intensely polyphonic style in which each line operates with considerable independence while still blending into the overall harmony (though not always in a way that listeners might anticipate). Similarly, he manipulates the larger structure of his pieces to stress the independence of sections: he extracts structural pieces as monumental blocks of music, highlighting their contours much as, at the end of the nineteenth century, Cézanne would extract and emphasize the elemental designs of his visual images without completely deracinating them from the overall image. The dense *Maestoso* introduction to the first movement, for example, is not forgotten once it's over; instead, Beethoven invokes it two more times before the movement is through, as if moving a monumental block of sound to places where the listener doesn't expect to encounter it.

The second movement sports a typically Beethovenian tempo direction of the sort that suggests that words weren't available to explicitly pin down what he had in mind: "Very slow, but not *too* slow, and in a singing style."

It unrolls as a theme with variations—actually, the variations involve two interlinked themes—in relaxed 12/8 meter, though two of the variations move into different meters. This is one of Beethoven's most deeply expressive, timeless statements. Robert Schumann, who (apart from being a composer) was one of the most perspicacious critics of the generation following Beethoven, remarked of this *Adagio*, "One seems to have lingered not fifteen short minutes, but an eternity."

In the third movement, a scherzo, rhythmic displacements confuse the triple-time meter—a trademark of Beethoven's teacher Haydn. Specifically, measures in 2/4 time are interpolated within the triple-time framework of this movement, which is rich in imitative counterpoint. The trio scurries giddily, marked *presto* in distinction to the movement's overall indication of *Scherzando vivace*.

Beethoven tried to be as specific as he could about the tempo of the second movement, but what can explain his complete lack of indication about the speed of the *Finale?* Certainly it must be something toward the rapid side of the spectrum, but it's up to the interpreters to decide. The general consensus is to underscore the bright spirit implied by the movement's tuneful effusion, which is introduced by a four-bar introduction, very likely the distillation of the separate *Adagio* movement Beethoven had initially imagined in that spot. The movement culminates, following a false ending, in a scurrying coda born of a nearly indeterminate trill.

String Quartet in A minor, Op. 132

> *Assai sostenuto—Allegro*
> *Allegro ma non tanto*
> *Molto adagio*
> *Alla marcia, assai vivace—Più allegro (attacca)*
> *Allegro appassionato*

Work composed: Sketched in 1824, mostly written in 1825 and principally finished in July, in Vienna and the spa town of Baden just south of the city, though perhaps some polishing continued through that autumn

Work dedicated: To Prince Nikolas Galitzin

Work premiered: November 6, 1825, in Vienna, played by the Schuppanzigh Quartet (first violinist Ignaz Schuppanzigh, second violinist Carl Holz, violist Franz Weiss, and cellist Joseph Linke)

Instrumentation: Two violins, viola, and cello

The A-minor String Quartet (Op. 132) is the second of the triptych Beethoven wrote for Count Nikolas Galitzin. It occupied the composer from about February through July 1825, and its content is very much wrapped up with the vicissitudes of his life during those months. By that time he had reached a sorry state, increasingly isolated through his deafness. In 1825 he was actually arrested as a vagrant—a mistake, but an understandable one in light of what was reported to be his increasingly slovenly appearance.

Beethoven was no stranger to ill health, but that April he was beset by an unusually serious illness: an inflammation of the intestine that sidelined him for about a month. His occasional physician since 1820, Dr. Anton Braunhofer, was unswerving in his demand that Beethoven give himself over to rest and follow a bland diet that he did not like. Presumably this ruled out the liver dumplings that he counted among his favorite foods, and he was specifically ordered to exclude spices, coffee, and wine. (The wine became a particular point of contention.) Whether the physician's treatment was responsible for the patient's recovery we cannot know—when reading of eighteenth- and nineteenth-century medical treatments we often marvel that patients ever improved at all—but after about a month Beethoven had returned to health and to his usual cantankerousness. At least Beethoven felt grateful enough toward Dr. Braunhofer to send him a letter that May that included a comical dialogue between doctor and patient, and also a canon to the text "Doctor, close not the door against Death, notes will help him who is in need." The pun involving the words notes (*Noten*) and need (*Not*) eludes translation.

The notes that most immediately summoned him back to productivity were those of the A-minor Quartet, which he completed that July. The cello launches the proceedings, perhaps an idea left over from Beethoven's original conception of this as a quartet with a concertante cello part (or at least so reported Joseph Linke, perhaps with unwarranted hopefulness). The angular motif of four notes begins on the leading tone (G-sharp), but it is nonetheless unambiguous about defining the key of A minor; and the four instruments enter sequentially, bottom to top, already exploring the motif's contrapuntal possibilities while it is being first announced. An effusion from the first violin (*Allegro*) is the jumping-off point to the principal theme. The movement progresses with a spirit of the fantastic, always inhabited by a sense of tragedy and generally unsettling.

Strange, too, is the mood of the *Allegro ma non tanto*, a minuet in all but name, a throw-back idea for a composer who years earlier had largely given up minuets to make way for scherzos in the space they had traditionally occupied. Beethoven is focused on counterpoint here, and the simple theme is viewed in a shifting variety of imitative contexts. The trio section of this ostensible minuet has a rustic air, with a long drone in the violins—then joined by viola and cello—evoking a peasant musette.

Nearly half of the length of Op. 132 is given over to the ensuing movement, the famous *Molto adagio* expanse that is most overtly connected to Beethoven's health issues and, we gather, the existential crisis they engendered. At its head the composer writes: *Heiliger Dankgesang eines Genesenen an die Gottheit, in der lydischen Tonart* ("Holy Song of Thanksgiving from a Convalescent to the Divinity, in the Lydian Mode"). The Lydian mode refers to a scale, particularly associated in the post-Renaissance era with sacred music, that is neither a major key nor a minor one but rather revolves around its own scale-pattern of notes. When based on the note F, as it is here, the Lydian scale resembles that of F major except that its fourth step is a B-natural rather than a B-flat. It yields an impression of austerity and purity, or at least it's part of what lends this movement its uniquely successful character of private meditation. The chorale is intoned as if through three verses, much varied at its repetitions, separated by more spirited episodes of textural and contrapuntal complexity. When Beethoven visits it for the last time, he marks the score *Mit inniger Empfindung* ("With earnest sentiment," though the German words suggest a deeper sincerity and passion than those English ones do). A hush descends in the final bars, and the listeners are left bathed in a silence that seems to prolong this most intimate of Beethoven's pages.

I have often wished that the piece ended at that point; but after the eyes have been dabbed, Beethoven helps us get on with life by way of a boisterous little march. It's a strange one, though, with its opening rhythm momentarily seeming to be in triple time, as if it were another minuet: oddly disorienting. Suddenly the flow is interrupted and, over tense tremolos in the lower strings (they can sound surprisingly like a harmonium), the first violin lets loose a passionate, quasi-vocal recitative (*Più allegro*) that seems ripped from an opera of considerable grandeur. This leads without break to a simmering triple-time *Allegro appassionato* that sounds at first as if it would serve admirably in a piano sonata. (In fact, Beethoven appears to have sketched the melody in connection with his Ninth Symphony, though he didn't use it there.) It builds in power and texture as it unrolls, and the instruments are eventually forced into extreme registers, particularly the soaring first violin. Finally the music sidesteps into A major for a coda that nonetheless remains edgy to the end.

String Quartet in B-flat major, Op. 130, and *Grosse Fuge*, Op. 133

Original version:
Adagio ma non troppo—Allegro
Presto
Andante con moto ma non troppo

Alla danza tedesca: Allegro assai
Cavatina: Adagio molto espressivo
Grosse Fuge
    (Overtura: Allegro—Meno mosso e moderato—Allegro
    Fuga: [Allegro]—Meno mosso e moderato—Allegro molto e con brio)

Revised version:
Adagio ma non troppo—Allegro
Presto
Andante con moto ma non troppo
Alla danza tedesca: Allegro assai,
Cavatina: Adagio molto espressivo
Finale: Allegro

Work composed: Mostly August through November 1825, in Baden, just south of Vienna; the replacement finale was written in the autumn of 1826 while Beethoven was staying at his brother's house in Gneixendorf, near Krems, Austria.

Work dedicated: The manuscript and the first version published version of Op. 130 carry a dedication to Prince Nikolas Galitzin, but when the *Grosse Fuge* was published as an independent item, it bore a dedication to Archduke Rudolph.

Work premiered: March 21, 1826, in Vienna, played by the Schuppanzigh Quartet (first violinist Ignaz Schuppanzigh, second violinist Carl Holz, violist Franz Weiss, and cellist Joseph Linke). The same musicians introduced the revised version of Op. 130, with its new finale, in Vienna on April 22, 1827. The *Grosse Fuge* was first offered as a stand-alone concert piece on January 20, 1853, played by the Quatuor Maurin (violinists Jean-Pierre Maurin and J.-B. Sabatier, violist Joseph Louis Marie Mas, and cellist Alexandre Chevillard).

Instrumentation: Two violins, viola, and cello

One sometimes reads that Beethoven tended simultaneously to the composition of his Quartets in A minor (Op. 132) and B-flat major (Op. 130), but that seems too liberal an interpretation of the facts. Indeed, sketch-work for the two did overlap to some extent, and ideas originally drafted to be part of Op. 132 were "saved" for Op. 130 instead. Nonetheless, when he moved into compositional high gear in 1825, he kept himself focused on each quartet in succession. The B-flat-major Quartet therefore falls chronologically between those in A minor and C-sharp minor, a fact that was obscured when it came time to assign opus numbers.

With rather few interruptions, Beethoven was able to plunge ahead into his new quartet without a break, and the first two movements flowed quickly onto the page in August 1825. The opening movement would be startling in its capriciousness. Its opening measures (*Adagio ma non troppo*) are lush in their dense voicing, prefiguring a sort of sound that would be cultivated imminently by Robert Schumann and some of his colleagues in the "Romantic generation." This introduction ends promptly as the first violin bursts into a bevy of scales, which are then picked up by the other instruments. But the momentum of this sonata-form movement is interrupted often by recollections of the music from the slow introduction. Overall, the impression is one of exorbitant fantasy that extends to both the dreamy and the vivacious ends of the spectrum.

The second movement is a mercurial scherzo (*Presto*), so fleet-footed that it runs only about two minutes in performance. That includes a trio section as well as some amusing solo braying from the first violin to enhance the transition from the trio into the revisitation of the scherzo proper.

After that, Beethoven became briefly stymied. His sketches show him experimenting in different directions, and not until the middle of August did he settle on the emotionally ambiguous expanse that would be the third movement, set again in the key of D-flat major. This sports a sort of tempo marking that we find often in later Beethoven; its wordiness suggests an attempt to convey something precise, yet it ends up settling nothing. *Andante con moto ma non troppo*, we read here: "In a walking tempo, with motion, but not too much so." If that weren't puzzling enough, Beethoven then adds, directly above the opening bar, the words *poco scherzoso*, surely meaning "a little bit jokingly," although, from a linguistic stance, one could argue that it could be read quite differently, as "not very jokingly." In any case, the "joke-like" idea does become clear beginning in the third measure, when the cello starts harrumphing away staccato down in the basement. Nonetheless, this sly, cryptic movement is hardly a "ha-ha" scherzo, and some interpreters choose to underscore its quizzical features more than its gruff ones. Robert Schumann described it as an "intermezzo"—an interlude, yes, but in practice the term is often attached to a movement of emotional restraint.

Next would be the finale, or at least that was Beethoven's initial assumption; but as he thought about it, the traditional four-movement layout seemed not so persuasive after all. He had broken that mold in Op. 132, and he was prepared to do it again. On August 24 he wrote a letter to his nephew, and another to Carl Holz, announcing that the new quartet would include not four but six movements. One of the added movements he had already drafted, thinking it would be a part of Op. 132. That was the *Danza alla tedesca*, originally planned in A major but well suited to the new context as long as it was moved to a more suitable key. In the event, that would be G; just as D-flat stands a minor third above the general tonic of B-flat, G stands a minor third below, yielding a nice symmetry of harmonic architecture. In this context, the original key of A would have seemed nonsensical to Beethoven. Here he provides a piece "in the style of a German dance," but it's a surprisingly complex rendering of what one might anticipate to be a simplistic peasant romp. Or is it that Beethoven is striving for overt parody here, rather as he did when, in his *Pastoral* Symphony, he ribbed country musicians who were uncertain about where their parts were to enter? We sense something of that spirit in the broken-up, halting phrasing of the first violin's tune and the offbeat accompaniments that emerge as the melody is explored through variation.

On then to the fifth movement, and down from G by another minor third to the key of E-flat major. Beethoven is now in a prayerful mood, and his gorgeous *Cavatina* unrolls in a placid spirit. At about this time Beethoven was having Bachian thoughts, vaguely pondering the idea of composing an overture on the motif B–A–C–H (which, using German nomenclature, translates to the notes B-flat–A–C–B-natural) and actually producing a short canon using that theme. We do hear something neo-Baroque in the solid harmonic progressions of this *Cavatina*, but the spaciousness perhaps evokes Handel more than Bach. "Beethoven valued most highly Mozart and Handel, then S. Bach," reported his disciple Ferdinand Ries. On his deathbed he consoled himself by paging through installments of a recently released forty-volume edition of Handel's music, which he had just received as a gift. "I have long waited for them," said Beethoven, "for Handel is the greatest, the ablest composer that ever lived. I can still learn from him." Holz stated of this movement, "Never did his music breathe so heartfelt an inspiration, and even the memory of this movement brought tears to his eyes." At one point its contemplation wells up and the first violin cries out with a rising, recitative-like figure, which the composer marks *beklemmt* ("afflicted"). Still, everything is brought back under control, and as the movement arrives at its hushed end, those of us who have been paying attention to the architecture of key relationships can be secure that this expanse of E-flat will cadence, for the final movement, into the grand tonic of B-flat, thus tracing a so-called plagal cadence, which is the sound of a churchly "Amen."

From an expressive viewpoint, the *Cavatina* would be a difficult act to follow, but to Beethoven the solution must have seemed obvious. Time and again we find a fugue, or part of a fugue, being folded into the "argument" in late Beethoven, and very often he adapts the rules in order to heighten even further the emotional impact of such a span. Even in his written indications Beethoven began to acknowledge the liberties he exercised in bending fugue to his expressive aspirations: the stunning finale of his *Hammerklavier* Sonata (Op. 106) is headed "Fuga a tre voci, con alcune licenze" ("Three-voiced fugue, with some licenses"), while the *Grosse Fuge* itself—the finale he proposes in this quartet—carries the words (possibly his publisher's rather than his own) "GRANDE FUGUE, tantôt libre, tantôt recherchée" ("Grand Fugue, as free as it is erudite").

The *Grosse Fuge* was strictly sui generis in its time, and it has never given up sounding avant-garde. Its subject is marked by immense leaps, the contours of its lines are jagged, its harmonic trajectory veers toward brash dissonance, and its progress is interrupted by extreme contrasts of tempo, mood, and dynamics. The germ of the material is presented in an opening few bars marked *Overtura*, after which the first violin gently proposes the basic contour of the subject as if hesitantly touching toe to water. Then the ensemble erupts into the fugue with a vengeance. It's an enormous piece by fugal standards, running in some performances close to twenty minutes. All things considered, it is shocking—musically blasphemous, one might even say—in its daring juxtaposition of elements, in its injection of gruffest humor into the most exalted of musical pursuits, in challenging its listeners to accept infringements of form, method, and style that had not been countenanced previously.

The Op. 130 String Quartet, with the *Grosse Fuge* as its finale, was introduced on March 21 (Bach's birthday!), 1826, in Vienna by the long-suffering Schuppanzigh Quartet, which had valiantly done its best to conquer Beethoven's increasingly challenging quartets as he produced them. For reasons that remain unclear Beethoven chose not to attend—he couldn't have heard much anyway—and instead passed his time in a nearby tavern. When the performance was over, his friend Carl Holz (who played second violin in the performance) arrived to report that the quartet had scored a success, with the audience demanding encores of the second and fourth movements. The fugue—that was different matter. The audience was understandably perplexed by it, and Beethoven responded to their confusion with typical forthrightness: "Cattle! Asses!"

Nonetheless, the publisher Matthias Artaria engraved the quartet for publication just as Beethoven wrote it, though it was not actually printed. Soon, however, Artaria approached Beethoven to ask that he compose a different finale, one that might be less unsettling to the public. That Beethoven consented to do this seems uncharacteristic—perhaps the promise of an extra fee helped lubricate the arrangement—but in the autumn of 1826, while visiting his brother in Gneixendorf (near Krems in Lower Austria), he did write a replacement finale, a far less stressful rondo *Allegro*. This he gave to Artaria on November 22, and the Schuppanzigh Quartet played it the following month. On April 22, 1827, the same foursome gave the first complete performance of the Op. 130 Quartet with the new finale, not quite a month after the composer's death.

In posterity, performers have had to make the difficult choice between playing the Op. 130 Quartet with the *Grosse Fuge* finale, as Beethoven originally intended, or with the substitute finale, which stands as his last word on the subject—and, indeed, as his last word on anything, since it was the final composition of his career. The rondo finale was long the conclusion of choice, but today one is just as likely to hear the *Grosse Fuge* as the last movement when the quartet is played. Recordings conveniently allow ensembles to offer both, leaving the decision to listeners.

The *Grosse Fuge* would go on to live a life of its own even apart from the medium of the string quartet. A month after the premiere, Artaria had in hand an arrangement of the piece for piano four-hands. This was the work of Anton Halm, a pianist and pedagogue for whom Beethoven nurtured a soft spot even after an error he committed during an 1814 concert of his Choral Fantasy brought the performance to a complete standstill. Beethoven had supported the selection of Halm for this project, and Artaria paid Halm for his work three weeks after it was delivered and surely intended to publish it. But when Beethoven reviewed Halm's transcription he didn't approve it and instead set about making his own arrangement, which he provided to Artaria that August. In May 1827 Artaria published the fugue as a stand-alone work in two versions: in its original quartet version as Beethoven's Op. 133, and in the composer's own transcription for piano four-hands as his Op. 134. Both carried a dedication to the composer's long-time patron Archduke Rudolph. Some musicologists believe that Beethoven created the four-hands arrangement as a first step in transcribing the entire Op. 130 Quartet. If this is the case, the project seems not to have progressed beyond this single astonishing movement.

String Quartet in C-sharp minor, Op. 131

> *Adagio ma non troppo e molto espressivo*
> *Allegro molto vivace*
> *Allegro moderato*
> *Andante ma non troppo e molto cantabile*
> *Presto*
> *Adagio quasi un poco andante*
> *Allegro*

Work composed: December 1825 through August 1826, in Vienna

Work dedicated: To Baron Joseph Stutterheim, who some years earlier had accepted Beethoven's troubled nephew Karl into an infantry regiment he commanded

Work premiered: December 1826 in Halberstadt, Saxony (Germany) by the Müller (Sr.) Quartet, which comprised four brothers (first violinist Carl, Sr., second violinist Georg, violist Gustav, and cellist Theodor)

Instrumentation: Two violins, viola, and cello

Beethoven finished the third installment of his "Galitzin" commission in November 1825 but found himself so captivated by the challenges of string-quartet writing that he immediately began to sketch another one, with no commission attached. This would become the C-sharp-minor String Quartet (Op. 131) which, along with his final quartet (in B-flat major, Op. 135), he completed the following summer. There's no need to play favorites when it comes to Beethoven quartets, but—without insisting too much on what may have been meant as a casual comment—the composer did suggest to his friend Carl Holz that he loved this one most of all. With typically bluff humor, Beethoven sent this work off to his publisher (who had imprudently spelled out that he expected an "original" work) with a note attached: "Scrambled together with pilferings from one thing and another." This sent the recipient into a panic, and a week later Beethoven restored order into the relationship by writing to assure the publisher that the quartet's music really was new, after all, and not just a bunch of strung-together leftovers.

There's no question that it is strikingly different from other Beethoven quartets, even in the basic matter of its number of movements. In his late works, Beethoven played fast and loose with traditional forms; here he expands the standard four-movement layout to a seven-movement struc-ture—or, perhaps more to the point, a single vast movement of seven discrete sections with no breaks between. Or is seven too many? Perhaps one should consider there to be only six, since the third is only eleven measures long and can easily be viewed as a mere prelude to the fourth, just as the sixth can be seen as simply an introduction to the seventh—at which point we would find ourselves not so far from a sort of Classical four-movement string quartet after all. Yet even those short movements pack a punch: the listener feels as if the entire weight of a full-scale movement has been compressed into these dense supernovas, which might explode at any time. The traditional sonata-allegro form is not discarded entirely, but here Beethoven holds its drama in reserve for the final section. Where one would have expected a sonata form in the opening movement we find instead a restrained but imposing, widely modu-lating slow fugue (which a more traditional composer might have actually put at the end) emerging bit by bit out of silence to proclaim its melancholy. Nothing in this work is predictable.

The fugue builds in its quiet intensity as Beethoven augments the note values of its subject. This gives way to an odd transitional movement in lighthearted 6/8 meter, though Beethoven interrupts its flow with occasional dynamic outbursts. This section leaves the listener uneasy, ungrounded; its contrasts confirm nothing about where the piece is leading. Brash chords announce the fleeting third section, a recitative in which all four instruments take part, with the first violin proving especially elaborate.

Finally, with the fourth section, we find ourselves in comfortable, familiar territory. The aware listener will recognize the tune as custom-made for variations, a compositional procedure in which Beethoven took great delight throughout his career. These are far removed from the simple diminutions and predictable road-plan of Classical variations. Instead, Beethoven offers us different points of view about the theme, really more akin to reinterpretations of the theme's very substance, rather than mere decoration—something along the lines of the *Diabelli* Variations, though still more condensed. Beethoven's last "complete" go at the tune suggests hymn-like transcendence, after which the variations collapse into fragmentary suggestions and half-remembered allusions.

All that remains is a final fast movement, rugged and gruff. Even this is interrupted (after a false ending) by a twenty-eight-bar *Adagio* recollection of sounds that have come before, particularly the spirit of the opening fugue, thereby serving to unify the entire forty-minute work.

The piece has never lacked for admirers. One of the earliest to single it out was Franz Schubert. He idolized Beethoven, and on his own deathbed he expressed a desire that he might hear Op. 131 performed. Five days before Schubert's death, four string players assembled to fulfill his wish. One of the violinists later characterized the event: "The King of Harmony had sent the King of Song a friendly bidding to the crossing."

String Quartet in F major, Op. 135

> *Allegretto*
> *Vivace*
> *Lento assai, cantante e tranquillo—Grave ma non troppo tratto*
> *Allegro*

Work composed: Sketched in July 1826, mostly written from August through October 30 of that year

Work dedicated: "À son ami Jean Wolfmeier," meaning Johann Nepomuk Wolfmayer, a cloth merchant who was one of Beethoven's long-standing admirers and supporters

Work premiered: March 23, 1828, in Vienna by the Schuppanzigh Quartet (first violinist Ignaz Schuppanzigh, second violinist Carl Holz, violist Franz Weiss, and cellist Joseph Linke)

Instrumentation: Two violins, viola, and cello

Beethoven worked on his String Quartet in F major (Op. 135), his final quartet, during the summer of 1826, while completing the quartet that immediately preceded it, Op. 131. Even within his final group of quartets, Op. 135 stands as something of an anomaly. First of all, it usually clocks in at twenty-five minutes or less, which makes it considerably shorter than any of the others. The listener does not sense that this is due to a compaction of material, that the piece is particularly more dense than its companions; in fact, this quartet has an altogether cheerier mien than we expect of late Beethoven. Nonetheless, the composer's style has grown tight by this point in his career, and not a note is sounded without a distinct purpose. In the opening movement, the viola proclaims a succinct motif to which the other instruments respond with the musical equivalent of a raised eyebrow. These figures spend the movement being developed (along with several other short motifs) in all imaginable permutations and contexts throughout the quartet texture, all within the general design of a classic sonata-allegro form.

The second movement is a wild thing, leading from a giddy game of musical tag to a practically untamed explosion of hysterical merriment in which the first violin lets loose with the subtlety of a five-year-old stoked up on birthday cake—and then back again to the game of tag. The first violin is unquestionably the center of this *Vivace* party, a point made especially clear in the movement's middle section, when the other three instruments settle back to support its antics with an almost endlessly sustained ostinato figure.

Beethoven referred to the key of D-flat major as "the key of sentiment," and that spirit certainly reigns over the third movement, a cavatina (*Lento assai, cantante e tranquillo*) that is likely to evoke memories of a slightly earlier cavatina, the renowned fifth movement of Beethoven's Quartet in B-flat major (Op. 130). Its tone of profound nostalgia maintains through a set of four quiet variations. This movement seems to have been an afterthought, as Beethoven initially imagined his quartet as a three-movement structure.

The finale of Op. 135 is as famous for its words as for its music. This being a string quartet, the words, of course, are not spoken—or, rather, they are "spoken" privately by Beethoven to his performers, since they are entered on the score itself. "Der schwer gefasste Entschluss," he inscribes by way of a preface—"The hard-won resolution." And then, above an unassuming three-note motif (played by viola and cello) that seems to end in an ascending question mark, Beethoven writes "Muss es sein?" ("Must it be?"). He follows with the two violins' answer: "Es muss sein! Es muss sein!" ("It must be! It must be!"). The players now know the "text" that goes with their music, and they repeat their parts all the more emphatically to make the point. Later in the movement, the busy proceedings are tentatively interrupted for another presentation of the question-and-answer, but this time Beethoven hardly pauses as his onslaught of music all but bludgeons the metaphysical cry out of existence.

Just kidding. Everyone wants to read it as a metaphysical cry, of course: this, after all, is the final string quartet by the composer who ensuing generations would romanticize to the highest degree. We want to view it as a summing-up of his overwhelming oeuvre, and we gleefully seize on his annotations as the stuff for profound interpretation. Such was the attitude of Walter Willson Cobbett, the doyen of chamber-music commentators, who, in his 1929 *Cobbett's Cyclopedic Survey of Chamber Music*, summarized this entire piece (and connects Beethoven's end to his beginning) by pointing out that "the F major, last of these miracles of musicianship, after symbolizing in a few sinister bars the inexorability of fate, fitly finishes by 'babbling of green fields' in the mood of the 'period of initiation.'"

But the facts seem to be less heady. Beethoven's biographer Alexander Wheelock Thayer reported that the words represent nothing more than the composer's poking fun at someone who he felt wanted to get something for nothing. Ignaz Dembscher, a government official, wanted to borrow the performance parts of Beethoven's B-flat-major String Quartet (Op. 130) so he could include the work in a private concert; but because Dembscher had not attended the premiere—that is, he had not paid an initial subscription for the piece—Beethoven was not inclined to provide copies. Beethoven's friend Carl Holz offered to play the middleman and told Dembscher that if he paid Beethoven the full subscription cost of fifty florins (which they would allow even though the subscription period was past), he could have a copy of the score. "Muss es sein?" ("Must it be?"), asked Dembscher. "Es muss sein" ("It must be"), replied Holz. Beethoven was so amused on hearing about this transaction that he wrote a little canon to memorialize the event: its words were "Es muss sein, es muss sein, Ja, ja, ja, ja! Heraus mit dem Beutel!" ("It must be, it must be, yes, yes, yes, yes! Out with your wallet!"). Beethoven was not one to undervalue his own jokes, and apparently he couldn't get this little jest out of his mind. So there it is again, as the theme of that canon pops up to head the last movement of his quartet—a prominent spot, to be sure.

When Beethoven composed this quartet, he was already thinking ahead to further projects, including an opera, a Requiem Mass, and a Tenth Symphony. The F-major Quartet, in fact, seems to have been a bit of a distraction for him, which perhaps accounts for its somewhat lighter tone when compared with the other late quartets. On the other hand, Beethoven himself stoked the fires of legend when, in October 1826, he wrote to his Parisian publisher, Moritz Schlesinger, that composing the piece "has given me much trouble, for I could not bring myself to compose the last movement. But as your letters were reminding me of it, in the end I decided to compose it. And that is the reason why I have written the motto: "The difficult decision—Must it be?—It must, it must be!" Elsewhere, he wrote that he decided to go ahead with the quartet "frankly because I had pledged my word and I needed the money. You can see from the motto 'Es muss sein' that I wrote it with reluctance."

In fact, this was not quite his last work for string quartet; although it was his last full piece in the genre, it preceded the replacement finale he composed for Op. 130. Nonetheless, Op. 135, combining as it does depth with levity, serves as a wonderful finale for what remains the most astonishing sequence of string quartets in the history of music.

Alban (Albano) Maria Johannes Berg

Born: February 9, 1885, in Vienna, Austria

Died: December 24, 1935, in Vienna

Lyric Suite for String Quartet

Allegretto giovale ("Jovial Allegro")
Andante amoroso ("Amorous Andante")
Allegro misterioso—Trio ecstatico ("Mysterious Allegro—Ecstatic Trio")
Adagio appassionato ("Passionate Adagio")
Presto delirando—Tenebroso ("Delirious Presto—Gloomy)
Largo desolato ("Desolate Largo")

Work composed: 1926

Work dedicated: To Alexander von Zemlinsky

Work premiered: January 8, 1927, in Vienna, by the Kolisch String Quartet

Instrumentation: Two violins, viola, and cello

Alban Berg did not get off to a promising start. He was a terrible student, and he had to repeat two separate years of high school before he could graduate. Then, too, a fling with the family's kitchen-maid led to his attaining fatherhood at the age of seventeen. Though passionate about music, he was clearly not cut out for academic success, and he sensibly accepted a position as an unpaid intern for a civil-service position.

He finally found his focus in 1904, when he signed up for composition lessons with Arnold Schoenberg. Berg made great progress during his formal studies with Schoenberg, which continued until 1911. Writing to his publisher that year, Schoenberg remarked: "Alban Berg is an extraordinarily gifted composer, but the state he was in when he came to me was such that his imagination apparently could not work on anything but lieder.... He was absolutely incapable of writing an instrumental movement or inventing an instrumental theme." Indeed, Schoenberg was successful in divesting Berg of his interest in writing lieder; of his approximately eighty songs, only one setting dates from after that time. He wouldn't give up on the voice entirely, as witness his irreplaceable operas *Wozzeck* (1917–22, and premiered in 1925) and *Lulu* (begun in 1929 and left incomplete at his death in 1935). But apart from those, the catalogue of his mature works consists almost exclusively of instrumental pieces.

Through its very name, the Lyric Suite for String Quartet seems to reach out across the vocal-instrumental divide. Berg's contemporaries would have instantly noticed the connection of the title to that of Zemlinsky's Lyric Symphony of 1922–23 (premiered the following year), a Mahleresque symphony with solo voices; the link was real, and Berg underscored it by dedicating his Lyric Suite to Zemlinsky and even quoting the Lyric Symphony in the fourth movement. The word "lyric" evokes song-like thoughts, and although no words—no "lyrics"—figure in Berg's piece, the movement or section headings are unusually suggestive of specific states of mind: jovial, amorous, mysterious, ecstatic, passionate, delirious, gloomy, desolate. It seemed to some that a narrative was at work here. The esthetic philosopher Theodor W. Adorno, who had begun studying composition with Berg in 1925, wrote an extended commentary on this piece in the study of the composer he published in 1968, a year before his own death. While allowing that it was deeply expressive of some condition of the heart or soul—"'Take my love, give me your happiness,' is its dream," wrote Adorno—he also seemed ambivalent about the extent to which it might trace a narrative per se: "Lacking as it does any illustrative intent it certainly cannot be mistaken for a tone poem in the *neudeutsch* [modern German] sense. And yet it is a latent opera."

A question mark continued to hover over this piece until 1977. That year the composer George Perle had an opportunity to view a copy of the score that Berg had presented to a certain Hanna Fuchs-Robettin, and which remained in the possession of her daughter. Perle knew more about Berg's music than anyone at that time; he was working on book-length analytical studies of Berg's two operas, and it was he whose analytical investigations of *Lulu* had first clarified how much closer the composer had gotten to finishing that work than had been previously imagined, thereby paving the way for its being completed in a stylistically sensitive fashion so it could be effectively presented on stage. Nearly every page of Fuchs-Robettin's score contained annotations by the composer, and within months Perle published an article that detailed the story they told, the secret narrative of the Lyric Suite.

In May 1925 Berg had traveled to Prague to hear his Three Orchestral Fragments from *Wozzeck* (with Zemlinsky conducting), and while he was there he stayed in the home of a wealthy industrialist, Herbert Fuchs-Robettin, and his wife, Hanna. She was the sister of Franz Werfel, the novelist who a few years later would become the third husband of Alma Schindler Mahler-Gropius-Werfel. Berg was utterly smitten by Hanna Fuchs-Robettin, and they embarked on an affair that would last for the rest of his life. His wife, Helene, whom he had married in 1911, became aware that something was going on but, at least to outsiders, downplayed the depth of the involvement, excusing her husband on the grounds that artists are naturally susceptible to inspiration of all sorts. That Berg was profoundly in love with Hanna is made clear, however, in the love letters he wrote her in the course of their ten-year involvement, which have also come to light.

Berg's annotations reveal that the Lyric Suite encodes his love affair through a four-note pitch-cell that generates the tone-row on which the piece is based and that wields influence on how that row is used structurally. A–B-flat–B-natural–F are its notes. In German nomenclature that's A–B–H–F, as in "Alban–Berg–Hanna–Fuchs." The date "20.5.25" is written at the top of the score; that's the date they met. The numbers 23 (which Berg considered connected to his identity) and 10 (which he associated with Hanna) figure critically in this score, reflected, for example, in the number of measures a phrase or musical paragraph may occupy or in the proportions of one section to another.

In a sense, the music had told the general story all along, but since 1977 we have been able to understand its details explicitly. The *Jovial Allegretto* describes the high spirits of the couple's earliest flirtations, before the writing grows by turns more coquettish in the *Amorous Andante*. This second movement, Berg's jottings reveal, was meant to portray Hanna and her two children. The quicksilver scampering of the *Mysterious Allegro* is rendered all the more skittish by a panoply of bowing techniques that produce enigmatic effects, and the instruments' tones seem all but whispered, thanks to the installation of mutes. These remain in place throughout the movement, even in the *fortissimo* outbursts of the *Ecstatic Trio* that breaks in midway through. "Always as loud as possible," Berg advises at that point, and playing both loudly and with mutes lends a hoarse quality to the timbre.

All of this stands as foreplay to the *Passionate Adagio*. This is where the Zemlinsky quotation appears, in the viola part, though it is unlikely that most of us would take note of it while the piece is in action, especially since Zemlinsky's Lyric Symphony is far less familiar today than it was among Berg's crowd in the 1920s. In the third movement of Zemlinsky's work the quoted notes set the text "Du bist mein eigen, mein eigen"—"You are my own, my own." The music works up to sustained frenzy and then wilts into luxurious quietude. Emotions reach another high pitch in the *Delirious Presto*, perhaps stretching even to panic, and the interruptions of *Gloomy* no doubt reflect the hopelessness of the relationship between these two otherwise-attached people. Berg's manuscript note on Hanna's score here cites "the horrors and pains which now follow, of the days with their racing pulses, of the painful *Tenebroso* of the night."

Thus are we deposited at the door of the *Desolate Largo*. On Hanna's score the composer reveals that this movement refers to Baudelaire's poem "De profundis clamavi," from *Les fleurs du mal*: "To you, you sole dear one, my cry rises out of the deepest abyss in which my heart has fallen." To underscore the idea, Berg instructs that the cello's C-string is to be tuned down to B, sending it even farther than normal into "the deepest abyss." Baudelaire is not the only reference in this movement; unmistakable is a passing quotation of the celebrated "Tristan chord" (indeed, of the entire Wagnerian motif that encompasses it), and that unhopeful allusion leads on to an ending that retreats into "love, yearning, and grief."

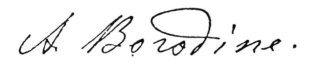

Alexander Porfiryevich Borodin

Born: October 31 (old style)/November 12 (new style), 1833, in St. Petersburg, Russia

Died: February 15 (old style)/27 (new style), 1887, in St. Petersburg

String Quartet No. 2 in D major

Allegro moderato
Scherzo: Allegro
Notturno: Andante
Finale: Andante—Vivace

Work composed: July and August 1881 while Borodin was on vacation in Zhitovo, outside Moscow

Dedicated: To Ekaterina Borodin, the composer's wife

Work premiered: February 25 (old style)/March 9 (new style), 1882—some sources give the date as January 26, 1882, not distinguishing which calendar—at a concert of the Russian Music Society in St. Petersburg by Nikolai Vladimirovich Galkin and Mr. Degtyerov (violins), Mr. Rezvetsov (viola), and Alexander Kuznetsov (cello)

Instrumentation: Two violins, viola, and cello

A curious bunch they were, the odd assemblage of scientists and military types who jelled into the "Russian Five," also known as the *Moguchaya kuchka* or "Mighty Handful," the group of composers who defined nineteenth-century Russian nationalism: the brilliant composer-and-pianist Mili Balakirev, Nikolai Rimsky-Korsakov, Cesar Cui, Modest Musorgsky, and Alexander Borodin. Only Balakirev had been principally trained as a musician, though even he had been a student of mathematics during his flirtations with college. Cui, who held the military rank of general, graduated from the Academy of Military Engineers and as a professor there was renowned for his expertise in military fortifications. Musorgsky was an army officer before he began composition lessons with Balakirev. Rimsky-Korsakov, scion of a military family, began his career in the navy; even after music took over his life, he remained for some years inspector of naval bands.

Borodin's biography is peculiar even by the standards of his cohorts. He was born the illegitimate son of a Georgian prince and his mistress, but, following the custom in such circumstance, was officially registered as the son of one of the prince's serfs. Nonetheless, the prince saw to it that young Alexander enjoyed privileges beyond what a serf might expect, with the result that Borodin received an excellent education. Music and science especially appealed to him. He completed the degree of Doctor of Medicine, served briefly as a medic in the army (where he met Musorgsky), and eventually became a research chemist and a distinguished professor specializing in the substances known as aldehydes.

His nonworking hours, however, were given over to music—to playing chamber music, to conducting ensembles, and to composing a small but choice catalogue of works. He fell into the circle of the "Mighty Handful" in 1862. Many of his masterworks from the 1860s on accordingly reflect that group's passionate embrace of folk sources, but he was also drawn to classic forms and genres, including those of chamber music, which was largely ignored by his fellow composers in the "Mighty Handful." Through a quirk of fate, he died an apparent peasant, just as he had been born one: he dropped dead while dressed as a Russian peasant at a Carnival-Week costume party at the St. Petersburg Medico-Surgical Academy.

His Second String Quartet, the last major work he completed, is probably his most frequently performed composition (or perhaps it's second to the Polovtsian Dances from his opera *Prince Igor*), and its popularity wasn't hurt any when Robert Wright and George Forrest pillaged from it, along with other Borodin works, when creating their Borodin-based score for the Broadway musical *Kismet* in 1953. The flip side, of course, is that for many of us it's all but impossible to listen to the second-movement *Scherzo* without mentally adding the lyrics of "Baubles, Bangles and Beads," or to hear the third-movement *Notturno* without imagining the words of "And This Is My Beloved." Forrest and White were not the first to harness the commercial possibilities in Borodin's score, by the way. In 1931 Nicolas Tcherepnin arranged and orchestrated a ballet for Ida Rubinstein titled *Ballet Borodin*, which drew on many of the same original Borodin pieces that would later star on Broadway.

Borodin usually composed slowly, but this piece he tossed off in a flash during two months of a summer vacation. He dedicated it to his wife, Ekaterina, intending it as a present to mark the twentieth anniversary of their engagement, which had taken place in August 1861. It is a richly Romantic piece, dripping in seductive melodies and appealing sentiment. While stopping short of calling this program music, Borodin acknowledged that the spirit of the movements coincided with certain romantic sensations: a nighttime rendezvous in the first movement, a waltz at a pleasure garden in the second, a love duet in the third, and a sunrise in the fourth. Notwithstanding these extra-musical allusions, the quartet is grounded in a balanced rhythmic naturalness and flow of material. It is not a complicated score. Glancing at its pages one is struck by how clear the texture looks, how unfussy the figuration, how unpretentious the musical means.

The rhapsodic flow and apparent naturalness of the opening sonata-form movement has inspired some commentators to characterize it as "Russian Schubert." The principal theme is granted first to the cello—not such a great surprise since that was the instrument Borodin usually played at chamber gatherings. (He was also adept on flute and oboe.) The *Scherzo*, which falls second in the lineup, is sometimes interpreted in the mercurial spirit of Mendelssohn, but the fact that Borodin marked it only *Allegro* leaves room for a more sedate reading, which brings it line with the waltz the composer said he intended. Listeners will expect the movement to unroll with a trio section in the middle and then a return to the *Scherzo* material. Borodin, however, surprises us by forgoing a trio and instead developing this movement in a sonata form. The development scampers along happily, unencumbered by the contrapuntal explorations many composers turn to in a development, and the recapitulation is not greatly expanded beyond the exposition's material. A coda takes on increasingly gossamer tones, finally playing out in a wisp of pizzicato.

The work's high point is the famously atmospheric *Notturno*, which became a salon favorite in countless arrangements long before Broadway got hold of it. (One early, well-known transcription, for violin and piano, was the work of Borodin's colleague Rimsky-Korsakov.) Again the cello is granted pride of place in introducing the rapturous melody, which is played against a repetitive rhythmic gesture in the second violin and viola. The melody is handed off to the first violin, at a far higher pitch level than anything we have encountered so far in this quartet (which mostly operates within relatively circumscribed pitch boundaries). The tempo ramps up (*più mosso*), and a second theme is introduced, this one ornamented with trilling figures in what Borodin surely imagined would be understood to represent the "Oriental" style. The themes interact with each other, and for a while the cello and first violin play the main theme in a loose canon. Borodin is obviously pleased with the effect, and he instantly repeats his technical tour-de-force by moving the canon to the two violins, which play it above a beautiful accompaniment of viola tremolandos and cello pizzicatos—delicious to all but the most jaded ear.

The *Finale* begins with questioning phrases alternating between the top two and the bottom two instruments. These *andante* ideas will return periodically to interrupt the flow of the main body of the movement, a *vivace* that works up to a brilliant climax while sustaining the appealing lyricism that underscores practically every measure of this delightful quartet. This concluding movement may not quite equal the earlier three in its overall effect, but it serves very nicely as dessert. The double bar arrives suddenly; the piece gives no hint of ending when suddenly the ensemble tosses off four concluding chords and the piece is over.

Johannes Brahms

Born: May 7, 1833, in Hamburg, Germany

Died: April 3, 1897, in Vienna, Austria

Piano Trio No. 1 in B major, Op. 8

Allegro con brio
Scherzo: Allegro molto
Adagio
Allegro

Work composed: Early 1854, in Hanover; it was published that year by the firm of Breitkopf & Härtel as Brahms' first "official" chamber work. Brahms severely revised the piece thirty-five years later, at Bad Ischl in the summer of 1889, and it is that revised version (published in 1891 by the firm of Simrock) that is nearly always heard today.

Work premiered: It is usually reported, including in the Brahms thematic catalogue (*Johannes Brahms: Thematisch-bibliographisches Werkverzeichnis*, by Margit McCorkle, drawing on the work of Donald McCorkle, 1984), that this piece received its premiere not in Germany but rather in Dodsworth's Hall in New York City, on November 27, 1855, on which occasion it was performed by three important figures in American music: Theodore Thomas (violin), Carl Bergmann (cello), and William Mason (piano). In 1991, however, the German musicological Michael Struck published his discovery that the work was played six weeks earlier, on October 13, 1855, at the Gewerbehaus in Danzig, Prussia (today Gdańsk, Poland), by performers identified only as Haupt (piano), Braun (violin), and Klahr (cello). The revised version of the trio was premiered on January 10, 1890, in Budapest, with Brahms (as pianist) joined by the violinist Jenö Hubay and the cellist David Popper.

Instrumentation: Violin, cello, and piano

In 1853 young Johannes Brahms made his way to Düsseldorf, where, on September 30, he appeared unannounced on the doorstep of Robert and Clara Schumann. Brahms had tried to contact Robert Schumann several years earlier and became furious when a packet of compositions he had sent was returned unopened. This time the reception was different; a letter of introduction from his violinist-friend Joseph Joachim made all the difference.

Brahms stayed on in Düsseldorf and grew close to the couple—to Robert, the acclaimed but volatile composer, conductor, and critic; to Clara, the exceptional pianist, insightful muse, and resilient survivor. They adored him, too, and their friendship deepened instantly, taking on both intellectual and vaguely erotic overtones. During that autumn Brahms traveled twice from Düsseldorf to Leipzig to meet with publishers whose doors had swung open on Schumann's recommendation. On October 28, Schumann published in the *Neue Zeitschrift für Musik* an effusive article titled "Neue Bahnen" ("New Paths"), which acclaimed Brahms as a sort of musical Messiah, "destined to give ideal presentation to the highest expression of the time, . . . springing forth like Minerva fully armed from the head of Jove."

At the beginning of the new year, now in Hanover, Brahms embarked on a new work, his B-major Piano Trio. Distractions soon loomed in his path. At the end of the month the Schumanns arrived in Hanover for a concert spotlighting Robert as composer and Clara as pianist. On February 6, back in Düsseldorf, Schumann wrote to thank Joachim for his hospitality during their visit, adding, "I'm enjoying the cigars very much. They seem to have a Brahmsian tang, as usual very strong but very good!" Exactly three weeks later Schumann pushed his way through carnival celebrators and leaped off a bridge into the Rhine in the dramatic suicide attempt that would signal the irretrievable progression of his insanity.

Word of the tragic event reached Brahms two days later, and he immediately left for Düsseldorf. He did what he could to console Clara, who was five months into her tenth pregnancy. (Robert was not there; at his own request, he had been removed to an asylum in Endenich, near Bonn, where he would die two and a half years later.) Brahms had plenty of help to distract Clara: his friends Joachim, Julius Grimm (a composer and cellist), and Albert Dietrich (a composer and fellow Schumann pupil) also clustered around. With such an assemblage looking for ways to fill the tense hours, it was inevitable that music should resound in the Schumann household, even in Robert's regretted absence. One of the pieces that appeared on the music stands was the piano trio that occupied Brahms when he could find time to work on it.

Clara found it a perplexing piece. "I cannot quite get used to the constant change of tempo in his works," she wrote in her journal, "and he plays them so entirely according to his own fancy that . . . I could not follow him, and it was very difficult for his fellow-players to keep their places." But by mid-April the piece had progressed considerably, and after playing it twice through one day she changed her tone: "Now everything in it is clear to me." Before long she wrote a letter to the firm of Breitkopf & Härtel, which published Robert's compositions as well as her own, urging them to add Brahms' new trio to their catalogue. This they promptly did.

But the B-major Piano Trio that Breitkopf & Härtel published is rarely heard today, since it was effectively superseded by Brahms' rewriting of the piece thirty-five years later. Brahms spent the summer of 1889 at Bad Ischl, which reigned for decades as a fashionable vacation hangout for Vienna's aristocracy and cultural crowd. He wrote to Clara: "With what childish amusement I while away the beautiful summer days you will never guess. I have rewritten my B-major Trio. . . . It will not be so wild as it was before— but whether it will be better—?" Apart from the assurance that, with so many years of experience under his belt, he could craft the work's material into a far more refined piece, there was a practical reason for this revision. Breitkopf & Härtel had sold the rights for Brahms' first ten published works to the rival firm of Simrock, which had since become the composer's regular publisher. Because Simrock would be printing a new edition anyway, Brahms felt the time was ripe to bring the piece up to his current level of ruthless self-appraisal. He assured Simrock that in its new guise, the trio would be "shorter, hopefully better, and in any case more expensive."

Certainly Brahms had grown more expert technically, and the considerable tightening to which he subjected the piece—the revision is two-thirds the length of the original—is widely viewed as an improvement. Today, the revised version is almost universally preferred by performers and audiences, but some of Brahms' friends resisted it. "You have no right to impress your masterly touch on this lovable, if sometimes vague, product of your youth," objected his trusted confidante Elisabet von Herzogenberg. Her husband wrote to Brahms that "though we both now understand the new form we quietly bemoan the traits of loveliness which have been taken away." Brahms maintained an ambivalent stance about the two versions and seems to have been perfectly content with the idea that both incarnations of the piece should be in circulation. One recalls his pronouncement, in another context, that "it is rare for a work which has once reached its conclusion to become better by revision."

The first movement (*Allegro con brio*; in the first version, Brahms had called it *Allegro con moto*) opens with a theme that is warmhearted and stately, a descendant of the finale tune of Schubert's *Great* Symphony, perhaps, and an ancestor of the finale theme from Brahms' own First Symphony, a work that would occupy him from 1855 to 1876. H. L. Mencken, writing in his capacity as music critic for the *Baltimore Sun*, declared this theme "the loveliest tune, perhaps, in the whole range of music"; although there may be other contenders, it would be hard to argue that Brahms' melody doesn't at least come close, growing from deep in the piano into a full-throated effusion for all three instruments. In his revision, Brahms did away with some neo-Bachian fuguing in the development section, ingenious but a bit self-indulgent. In its place he inserted some marvelous, intricate interlacing of rhythms and melodies in a section of sublime polyphonic mastery. Hemiolas and other rhythmic displacements—Brahms' characteristic fingerprints—appear here in abundance.

The *Scherzo* (*Allegro molto*) and its central trio section remained essentially unaltered when Brahms rewrote the piece, except for the appending of a concise coda in which the strings slip away toward silence. The tonic of B is relentless in this work. Here the *Scherzo* proper is cast in B minor, with the cello introducing its scampering, Schumannesque theme, but the relaxed contrast of the trio section, a slow waltz, is cast in the tonic major—in this case, the overriding B-major tonic of the whole composition.

The slow movement, an *Adagio* (*Adagio non troppo* in the first version) opens with a hushed, hymn-like melody, a sort of mystical chorale that bears some resemblance to correspondingly serene material in Beethoven's G-major Piano Concerto. In the 1854 version Brahms had worked in an allusion to Schubert's "Am Meer," a song about frustrated love; sometimes interpreted as an autobiographical detail referring to Brahms' feelings for Clara Schumann, this reference was eliminated in the revision. Like the first movement, the *Adagio* was profoundly rewritten, with a central fast section cut out and an entirely new second theme introduced to provide for greater variety in the development of material.

We return to B minor for the final *Allegro* (originally *Allegro molto agitato*), and indeed this ostensibly major-mode piano trio does close in the minor. Although it's not uncommon for minor-mode compositions to end in the major, the opposite is rare: Haydn's String Quartet in G major (Op. 76, No. 1; Hob. III/75) and Mendelssohn's *Italian* Symphony are two of the very few examples from the standard repertoire that jump to mind. In fact, the key of the principal theme is ambiguous; this tightly wound subject seems as much drawn in F-sharp minor as in B minor. Already in his original version Brahms had made compelling use of this contradiction by setting the second theme in F-sharp major, which, as the dominant of B minor, served to draw all of these keys into logical relationships. In the revision, he enhances the complex of keys by tossing in a spacious, broadly arpeggiated second theme in D major (the relative major of the tonic B minor and a firm thirds-relationship fulcrum for both B and F-sharp). Not everyone will immediately grasp the niceties of Brahms' structural improvements, but their underlying effect will certainly come through subliminally to all listeners. In any case, the movement's mounting passion will be evident to all.

String Sextet No. 1 in B-flat major, Op. 18

> *Allegro ma non troppo*
> *Andante, ma moderato*
> *Scherzo. Allegro molto—Trio Animato*
> *Rondo. Poco Allegretto e grazioso*

Work composed: 1859 through summer 1860

Work premiered: October 20, 1860, in the Saal des Museums in Hanover, by violinist Joseph Joachim and Messrs. Th. Eyertt, K. Eyertt, Prell, A. Lindner, and Herner. A second performance took place shortly thereafter at Joachim's home, on which occasion the guest of honor was the Hanoverian ambassador to Vienna. Then on the morning of November 27 Joachim and his friends played it at the Leipzig Conservatory, where (according to Clara Schumann) it "roused decided enthusiasm."

Instrumentation: Two violins, two violas, and two cellos

In November 1859, Brahms wrote a letter to Clara Schumann in which he referred to a string septet he was currently writing. We don't know much about what that piece was, but it quite likely played a part in the ancestry of the B-flat-major Sextet; it was not unusual for Brahms to go through several combinations of instruments before landing on one that seemed right for the material he had in mind. Brahms' conception seems to have quickly shrunk to a sextet—still a lush instrumental assemblage—and he sent the provisionally completed work to his violinist-colleague Joseph Joachim, along with a note that would prefigure many of the overly modest communications he would attach to his compositions over the years: "I'm afraid that as I've tarried so long over the piece, your expectations will not have been raised! But since God makes all things possible, I am sending you the parts, in case the *Rondo* should strike your fancy.... However, if you don't like the piece, then by all means send it back to me."

Joachim was delighted with what Brahms sent, promptly marked finger-ings and bowing indications into the string parts, and forwarded the piece to the publisher Fritz Simrock. Within a month Joachim presided over the sextet's premiere. In the course of rehearsals, however, he did come up with some suggestions for Brahms, and the composer incorporated a number of them into the score before it was published in January 1862. That one of the most prominent alterations involved moving the opening theme of the first movement from the first violin to the first cello—that is, taking it away from Joachim—reveals much about the objectivity that esteemed musician brought to the task.

The first movement unrolls at an unhurried pace, often reflecting the dance rhythms of the ländler, a sort of rustic Austrian slow-waltz. The prec-edent of Schubert inevitably comes to mind, especially that composer's C-major String Quintet, which came close to the instrumentation of Brahms' sextet, lacking only one of its violas. Brahms gives free rein to his penchant for rich sonorities, as well as to the bittersweet mood that infuses many of his works. The movement's character is basically serene, yet it is tinged with melancholy. As is his wont, Brahms flirts with both major and minor tonali-ties; perhaps better put, the flavors associated with both can surface irrespec-tive of the harmonic mode of the moment. This sense of twilight reverie pervades much of the sextet. The critic Eduard Hanslick, hearing this work in 1863, wrote "We believed ourselves suddenly transported into a pure world of beauty; it seemed like a dream."

The second movement is truly an extraordinary achievement. Brahms looks back into music history and creates a set of variations on a bass line and a harmonic sequence, a Baroque device that here seems particularly rooted in Bach's D-minor Chaconne for Unaccompanied Violin. Brahms adheres rig-idly to the metric divisions of his theme, but imaginative contrasts of sonori-ties mask the strictness of form. Again, the tonality inhabits a region that embraces both minor and major, a conflict inherent in the progression the composer has chosen as a theme. In the first three variations, the musical material is given with successively quicker subdivisions of the basic beat: four divisions to a beat in the first variation, six in the second (where the texture crackles in triplets), eight in the third (where cellos spin out turbulent scales). Tension is released in the fourth and fifth variations, both decisively in the major mode; the fourth is transcendent in its peacefulness, the fifth folk-like thanks to a musette-style drone in the violas. The sixth variation (consider it a coda if you wish) brings a return to the theme as it was heard at the opening, the variation aspect now limited to slight elaboration in the cello. Brahms was fond of this movement and prepared a piano transcription as a gift to Clara Schumann. (Film enthusiasts will recognize this movement as the soundtrack used to poignant effect in Louis Malle's *Les amants*, shocking in its day—1959—for a semi-nude scene of an adulterous affair. Screenings were banned in Ohio, one of the few times Brahms has been attached to such salacious proceedings.)

The concluding movements are lightweight in comparison. The third, a *Scherzo* with trio, is brief and rather Haydnesque in its bumptious vigor. It maintains its high energy throughout, not even slackening in the trio section. The finale returns to the luxurious Schubertian guise of the opening movement. Joachim worried a bit about this finale, fearing that it might come across as slack. The principal theme, announced by the first cello, is peaceful, but Brahms has good fun with it in the course of the movement, transforming the piece into a clever game of musical badminton in which fragments of the theme are batted back and forth by violins and first viola on one team and second viola and cellos on the other.

The B-flat-major Sextet stands as a milepost in Brahms' development as a composer. In his 1997 biography of the composer, Jan Swafford emphasizes the way it exemplifies its composer's position as straddling disparate musical esthetics. "In this work of his early maturity," writes Swafford, "Brahms appropriated traditional models of sonata, variations, scherzo, and rondo more or less at face value, then filled them in with his melodic and harmonic personality, his singular expressive world: Romantic emotion bridled by Classical form." Arnold Schoenberg, an ardent appreciator of Brahms, pointed to a less tradition-bound aspect of this piece. In his 1947 article "Brahms the Progressive," he cited the asymmetry that reigns over the opening of the sextet (a ten-measure phrase that can be broken down into cells of three measures, then two, then two, then two, then one) and of the second theme (two bars, then two, three, and two) as representing an "advanced phase of the development toward liberation from formal restrictions of musical thoughts, because they do not derive from a baroque feeling...."

Piano Quartet No. 1 in G minor, Op. 25

> *Allegro*
> *Intermezzo: Allegro ma non troppo*
> *Andante con moto*
> *Rondo alla Zingara: Presto*

Work composed: Principally in 1861, with preliminary work dating back as far as 1857

Work dedicated: To Baron Reinhard von Dalwigk (or, to use his full and glorious name—which the printed score did not—Baron Reinhard Ludwig Karl

Gustav Dalwigk zu Lichtenfels). He was in charge of the court Kapelle in the Lower Saxon city of Oldenburg.

Work premiered: November 16, 1861, in the Kleiner Wörmerscher Saal in Hamburg, with Clara Schumann appearing as pianist, joined by violinist John Böie, violist F. Breyther, and cellist Louis Lee

Instrumentation: Violin, viola, cello, and piano

The genre of the piano quartet—the somewhat rarely visited combination of violin, viola, cello, and piano—first occupied Brahms in 1855, when he began grappling with a piano quartet in C-sharp minor. Twenty years later he finally signed off on that work as his Piano Quartet No. 3 in C minor. In the intervening years he had produced two others: what we know as his First, in G minor (Op. 25), and his Second, in A major (Op. 26).

Brahms sometimes composed pieces in unmatched pairs—that is, working simultaneously on two pieces in the same genre but of strikingly different character. Such was the case with the G-minor and A-major Piano Quartets. They were very near contemporaries. The G-minor was composed between 1857 and the autumn of 1861 (but mostly intensely near the end of that span), and its Vienna premiere, on November 16, 1862, served as Brahms' debut as a pianist and composer in his adopted city, where he had moved only the preceding month. (That was the first anniversary, to the day, of the work's world premiere, which took place in Hamburg and included pianist Clara Schumann among the performers.) After a rehearsal for that Vienna performance the violinist Joseph Hellmesberger, a kingpin in the city's musical establishment and a member of the ensemble that played the quartet, declared, "This is Beethoven's heir!"

Nearly seventy years later the musical commentator Donald Francis Tovey would echo that sentiment, asserting that "the first movement is one of the most original and impressive tragic compositions since the first movement of Beethoven's Ninth Symphony." But in the years between Hellmesberger's pronouncement and Tovey's, the G-minor Piano Quartet was not consistently appreciated. Although it received numerous performances following its publication in the summer of 1863, many critics remained cool, perhaps baffled. The powerful Eduard Hanslick, who would soon become Brahms' chief acolyte, worried in print that he found the themes "dry and prosaic," and even Brahms' closest musician-friends—Clara Schumann and Joseph Joachim—voiced certain misgivings, particularly concerning the first movement. Clara, who provided an extensive critique in a letter to Brahms immediately after he shared the work-in-progress with her, in July 1861, found that this opening movement spent more time than she wished in the dominant key (D major), which she believed diluted the effect of the tonic

G minor. In time the musically sensitive came to appreciate that opening movement for its very special, indeed radical qualities. The musicologist Carl Dahlhaus insightfully observed that while the movement's opening theme does at first seem too condensed for the vast structure the composer develops from it, such "compositional economy, the building of music out of minimal capital, was taken to extremes by Brahms"—that, in fact, this is a quintessential demonstration of what makes Brahms Brahms.

The manuscript reveals that Brahms initially titled the second movement a *Scherzo*, but he crossed out that marking and replaced it with the heading *Intermezzo*. This was a very Brahmsian indication, one that would recur in his first three symphonies attached to mood pieces that display a character similar to this one, a touch introspective and perhaps nostalgic or unsettled—a character greatly underscored by the muted violin at the opening. Wrote Clara: "I cannot help thinking that if you had me in mind at all when you were writing it [i.e., the piano quartet] you must have known that I should be charmed with the scherzo in C minor. In fact, I should hardly call it a scherzo at all. I can only think of it as an allegretto." Brahms apparently agreed, once she pointed it out. "But it is a piece after my own heart!" she continued. "I find myself so tenderly transported to dreamland that it is as if my soul were rocked to sleep by the notes."

It is also a Brahmsian characteristic that the two middle movements of a four-movement piece often unroll at a similar tempo, which is the case here as the work continues through a placid, intimate *Andante con moto*. The central trio provides notable contrast. It's a march that sounds Schumannesque, at least at its outset. Yes, it is in three-quarter time, which generally has nothing to do with marches; but it seems a march nonetheless, quite in the spirit of such triple-meter "marches" as the "March of the Davidsbündler against the Philistines" from Schumann's *Carnaval* or the movement "An Important Event" from his *Scenes from Childhood*.

The earliest audiences for this quartet were lured in by the work's cumulative momentum: the tense tautness of the opening movement leading to the introspective *Intermezzo* and the warmhearted *Andante con moto*, finally to let loose with full abandon in the finale. Here Brahms offers a *Rondo alla Zingara*, a "Rondo in Gypsy Style," an exercise in the ostensible "Hungarian style" that had fascinated the composer ever since his early experiences accompanying the Hungarian violinist Ede Reményi on a concert tour in 1853. Brahms' dear friend Joseph Joachim had also grown up in Budapest (actually in Pest, since consolidated Budapest was not created until some decades later). "You have beat me on my own turf," wrote Joachim to Brahms; and apparently Brahms had, if one compares Joachim's relatively restrained Concerto in Hungarian Style of 1861 to Brahms' finale of the same year, by turns swashbuckling and achingly tender.

Piano Quartet No. 2 in A major, Op. 26

> *Allegro non troppo*
> *Poco adagio*
> *Scherzo. Poco allegro,*
> *Finale. Allegro*

Work composed: Between 1857 and the autumn of 1861, with most of the work taking place near the end

Work dedicated: To Frau Dr. Elisabeth Rösing, in whose home near Hamburg the composer lived in 1861–62

Work premiered: November 29, 1862, in the Musikvereinsaal in Vienna, with the composer (as pianist) joined by violinist Joseph Hellmesberger, violist Franz Dobyhal, and the cellist Heinrich Röver

Instrumentation: Violin, viola, cello, and piano

The A-major Piano Quartet, which occupied Brahms over precisely the same span as his G-minor Piano Quartet, was unveiled just thirteen days after its sister piece, on November 29, 1862, again with Hellmesberger and his string-playing colleagues and with the composer at the keyboard. (Also on that program were Brahms' Variations and Fugue on a Theme of Handel, Schumann's C-major Phantasy, and Brahms' piano transcription of a Bach organ toccata.) Listeners who had heard the powerful, extroverted G-minor Piano Quartet could scarcely have anticipated the very different flavor of its successor, which is overwhelmingly lyrical and far more introspective. Where the G-minor is taut, the A-major is luxurious; in fact, it is the longest of all Brahms' chamber works.

That's not to imply that it is in any way a flaccid piece. Brahms was never less than rigorous as a composer, and the A-major Piano Quartet is accordingly invigorated by the rhythmic complexity, melodic variety, and contrapuntal elegance that we expect of its composer. Together these two piano quartets gave fair notice to musical Vienna about the composer who would become its musical son. While Brahms was in town premiering these pieces he was being passed over back home as a candidate to be music director of the Hamburg Philharmonic Concert Association, a position he desired deeply. The following spring an offer arrived from the Vienna Singakademie; Brahms signed on as its director and moved to the city with which he would be forever associated thereafter.

When both piano quartets were written, Brahms was mostly dividing his time between Detmold and Hamburg, fulfilling various court obligations during the autumns in the former city, directing a women's choir in the latter. (The dedicatee of the A-major, Elisabeth Rösing, was his landlady in the Hamburg suburb of Hamm, where he lived when he was completing the piano quartets.) The A-major Piano Quartet bespeaks Brahms' admiration of, and debt to, one of his greatest predecessors in Vienna, Franz Schubert, both in large structural elements and in passing turns of phrases.

The first movement opens with a gently rocking theme that will pervade the leisurely unrolling of this sonata-form structure. The melodies are simple yet beautiful; they sound inevitable. The critic Eduard Hanslick, later to become a great Brahms enthusiast, sensed something unusual about the nature of Brahms' melodies when he penned a review following the premiere of the A-major Piano Quartet. "Brahms," he wrote, "has a tendency to favor themes whose contrapuntal viability is far greater than their essential inner content. The themes of this Quartet sound dry and prosaic. In the course of events they are given a wealth of imaginative derivatives, but the effectiveness of the whole is impossible without significant themes." I suspect his reticence in loving the melodies on their own terms disappeared with further exposure. You don't get far into the piece before encountering the hemiolas that are Brahmsian hallmarks, the contraposition of two notes against three. By the end of this extensive movement—in performance it can last sixteen or seventeen minutes—the innate lyricism escalates into something with quite a lot of passionate sweep, and yet, the listener is left feeling that it has been a calming experience.

So it is with the second movement, which Brahms' friend the violinist Joseph Joachim described as the "wonderful *Poco adagio* with its ambiguous passion." It opens as a soothing nocturne, perhaps a love song, but as soon as the opening tune is out, the piano unleashes a series of mysterious, even ominous diminished-seventh arpeggios against the unwavering stubbornness of the muted strings. It's a familiar moment. Where have we heard this eerie interpolation before? Schubert's late song "Die Stadt," from the set gathered at the end of his life under the title *Schwanengesang*; surely Brahms knew it. More nocturne music ensues, and then some Hungarian Gypsy flavor intrudes via the broad, deeply pitched phrases of the central section, certainly on the passionate side of Joachim's "ambiguous passion" equation. The tonal plan of this movement itself evokes Schubert: the relatively stormy F-minor section in the midst of this E-major movement mirrors exactly the tonal architecture of the transcendent *Adagio* of Schubert's C-major String Quintet, which Hellmesberger and his associates had premiered as recently as 1850, long after the composer's death. Passionate, too, are the achingly beautiful phrases of the most "romantic" passage when the strings sing in sixths against the raindrops of the piano's slowly broken chords.

Perhaps Brahms was showing off a bit in the third movement. Nobody would expect more in that spot than a scherzo and trio, but here the composer creates a complicated fusion of scherzo-and-trio with sonata form—no mean feat, and one that was sure to impress listeners of a more academic persuasion. So it is that the *Scherzo* (a rather relaxed one, to be sure) has a pair of contrasting themes that are worked out at some length, followed by a development and a recapitulation that follow classic key patterns. And then the trio section arrives: another tour de force, with the piano (in three octaves) and the strings playing in canon at the distance of one measure, *fortissimo* lest anyone miss the point. Some commentators have remarked that this trio recalls the third movement (a minuet in canon) of Haydn's D-minor String Quartet (Op. 76, No. 2, the *Fifths*), a real possibility since Brahms was a devoted aficionado of Haydn's music.

The *Finale* is the shortest of the movements, but at a brisk pace even its 519 measures clock in at ten minutes. Some of the modulations, unanticipated journeys from a point of departure to a harmonic destination a third away, will again remind us of Schubert, the more so when Brahms repeats the process over and over, much as his predecessor would have. In the minor-key passages one may find a Hungarian Gypsy spirit resurfacing, and perhaps also in the very vigorous *animato* conclusion.

Piano Quintet in F minor, Op. 34

> *Allegro non troppo*
> *Andante, un poco adagio*
> *Scherzo: Allegro*
> *Finale: Poco sostenuto—Allegro non troppo*

Work composed: 1862–64

Work dedicated: To Princess Anna of Hesse

Work premiered: June 22, 1866, at the Leipzig Conservatory; the earlier piano duet version of this piece had already been premiered on April 17, 1864, at the Vienna Singakademie, played by Carl Tausig and the composer.

Instrumentation: Two violins, viola, cello, and piano

Brahms was twenty-nine years old in 1862 when he embarked on this seminal masterpiece of the chamber-music repertoire, though the work would not reach its final form as his Piano Quintet until two years later. He was no beginner in chamber music when he began this project. He had already written dozens of chamber works before he dared to publish his B-major Piano Trio of 1853–54 (Op. 8, which he would revise extensively many years later); and in the final years of the 1850s he wrote his First String Sextet and his Piano Quartets in G minor and A major.

Having wrestled with the implications of writing for ensembles of three, four, and six instruments, Brahms now confronted five: a string quintet for two violins, viola, and two cellos. This instrumentation suggests that Brahms may have been thinking of Schubert's C-major String Quintet as his textural model, rather than the more common, Mozartian quintet arrangement of two violins, two violas, and cello. The violinist Joseph Joachim, a close friend of Brahms, voiced reservations about the quintet's effectiveness as string music; and when a revision failed to convince, Brahms started over with a completely new texture in mind.

In the course of 1863, the music of Brahms' String Quintet slowly reemerged as a vast piano duet, which the composer premiered in Vienna in 1864, with Carl Tausig seated at the other piano. Ironically, critics complained that the work lacked the sort of warmth that string instruments would have provided. Unlike the original string-quintet version, which Brahms burned, the piano duet was published—and is still performed and appreciated—as his Op. 34b. By this time, however, Brahms must have grown convinced of the musical merits of his material and, with some coaxing from his friend Clara Schumann, he gave the piece one more try, incorporating the most idiomatic aspects of both versions. The resulting Piano Quintet, the composer's only essay in that genre (and no wonder, after all that trouble), is one of the towering creations in Brahms' catalogue. Few works rival its masterful mingling of moods: majesty, serenity, tension, foreboding, anger, out-and-out joy.

In the summer of 1871 a young British pianist named Florence May arrived in Baden-Baden to take piano lessons from Clara Schumann. After a number of weeks Frau Schumann needed to leave on a trip, so Brahms gallantly agreed to take over Ms. May's instruction. In 1905 she would publish a two-volume biography of the composer, *The Life of Johannes Brahms*, which furnished a trove of anecdotes about the composer. She recounted how his Op. 34 would earn its composer generous recompense:

> Brahms' sonata for two pianofortes was heard privately in Baden-Baden several times in the course of the summer [of 1864]. Receiving the manuscript from the composer in July, Frau Schumann at once found opportunities of trying the work.…Later in the season she performed it with Brahms himself before the Princess Anna of Hesse, and the work…made its mark on this occasion. It appealed strongly to the royal listener, who, at the close of the last movement warmly expressed to the composer her sense of its beauty. Brahms, gratified and pleased at the Princess's unreserved appreciation, called on her the following

day, and begged permission, which was readily granted, to dedicate the work to her; and on its publication the following year in its final form—a quintet for pianoforte and strings—Her Royal Highness's name appeared on the title page. The Princess acknowledged the compliment of the dedication by presenting Brahms with one of her treasures—the autograph score of Mozart's G minor Symphony. It passed after his death, as part of his library, into the possession of the Gesellschaft der Musikfreunde, Vienna.

The opening movement (*Allegro non troppo*) is a vast sonata-form structure whose exposition contains at least five themes that undergo extensive development. Nothwithstanding the considerable contrast born of such melodic generosity, resoluteness informs the movement throughout. The musical ideas are themselves precise and concentrated, as tense as a tigress preparing to spring from a camouflaged crouch to a no-holds-barred chase. Brahms doesn't overindulge himself in working out this material, and the actual development section is strikingly brief here. As if to compensate, he gives himself what might be considered almost another development section at the end in the form of a lengthy coda.

The slow movement (*Andante, un poco adagio*) is as serene and tender as the opening movement is anxious. Here Brahms enters a shadowland, a hushed environment poised on dreams and often rendered quietly quirky through Brahms' accustomed rhythmic displacements. After this the *Scherzo* bursts forth with pent-up energy, its three musical "cells" following on each other's heels: a nervous, syncopated melody (its off-beatedness contrasting with the insistent on-the-beat pizzicatos of the cello); a crisp, staccato motif in the strings; and a grand, rather pompous, summation by the entire ensemble. A *cantabile* trio section provides a moment of relaxation before the main section of the *Scherzo* returns for another hearing.

The *Finale* balances the first movement in its colossal scope. A brooding introduction (*Poco sostenuto*) begins the proceedings, but it soon gives way to an ebullient tune with Hungarian Gypsy overtones, introduced by the cello. The movement builds gradually until, nearly exhausted, it reaches a coda marked *Presto, non troppo* (nearly an oxymoron, calling for the fastest tempo but, even then, tempered). Surely Beethoven was the inspiration for this unexpected sprint, and particularly the Beethoven of the volatile late quartets. The end seems more a dance of death than a victory: the whirlwind of its final chords hammer the last remaining breath out of this passionate creation.

String Sextet No. 2 in G major, Op. 36

Allegro non troppo
Scherzo: Allegro non troppo

Poco Adagio
Poco Allegro

Work composed: Begun in September 1864 in Baden-Baden, drawing on material from the 1850s; completed the following May.

Work premiered: October 11, 1866, at a concert of the Mendelssohn Quintet Club in Boston, Massachusetts, played by William Schultze, Karl Hamm, Thomas Ryan, Eduard Heindl, Rudolph Hennig, and Alexander Heindl; the European premiere took place on November 20, 1866, in the Great Hall of the Zurich Casino.

Instrumentation: Two violins, two violas, and two cellos

Brahms' Second String Sextet ushers us into the not very happy domain of his love life. With the benefit of history we know that he would live and die a bachelor, although many have also speculated that his abiding friendship with Clara Schumann, during her husband's decline into insanity and following his death, may have reached a level that involved the physical. But it was not Clara who was on Brahms' mind when he composed this sextet. While on vacation in Baden-Baden during the summer of 1864, he was overcome with nostalgia connected to a love affair he had enjoyed six years earlier in Göttingen. The girl he had courted then was named Agathe von Siebold, a twenty-three-year-old soprano, daughter of a professor at the University of Göttingen, long of hair and full of figure, a student of musical composition, no less, working under the aegis of Brahms' old Düsseldorf friend Julius Otto Grimm, who had settled in Göttingen as director of two women's choirs there.

At the end of the summer Brahms left Göttingen for Detmold, where he was then living; but the infatuation continued to be expressed through the mail, and Brahms arranged to spend the first week of January in Göttingen with Agathe. That's when the two exchanged engagement rings, and before he left, Johannes had his photograph taken with the ring proudly displayed on his finger. The bliss would be short-lived. Within weeks his D-minor Piano Concerto received its Leipzig premiere—a total failure—and Brahms reassessed the state of his life. Although he didn't doubt his talent, he had no reason to believe that it would ensure him professional stability let alone the dependable base from which he might support a family. Many years later he reported to his friend George Henschel: "At the time I should have liked to marry, my music was either hissed in the concert hall, or at least received with icy coldness.... If, in such moments, I had had to meet the anxious, questioning eyes of a wife with the words 'another failure'—I could not have borne that!... If she had wanted to comfort me—a wife to pity her husband for his lack of success—*ach!* I can't stand to think what a hell that would have been."

And so Brahms and Agathe parted ways, apparently with Brahms not acting gallantly in the situation (even to the extent that his friend Grimm stopped having anything to do with him). The breakup is not well documented, but late in her life Agathe wrote a novel based on their love affair, and from this we can surmise something of the desperate unhappiness that surrounded the situation. During his summer vacation in 1864 Brahms was suddenly beset with memories of what might have been. He wrote to his former friend Grimm, who responded with the information that in the ensuing five years Agathe's father had died and, consumed by woe, she had moved to Ireland to work as a governess to "get away from the shadowed pages of her life." Thus learning that there was no chance of his running into Agathe, Brahms hurried off to Göttingen to revisit the site of his earlier dreams and to work through his lingering apprehensions. Shortly after returning to Baden-Baden he set to work on his G-major Sextet.

Agathe is literally present in this composition. Brahms was bound to notice that her name translated nicely into musical notation, so long as he replaced the "T" with a "D," which is phonetically close. ("H," in German, refers to the note English-speakers call "B.") Right at the climax of the first movement's exposition we find a theme consisting of the notes A-G-A-D-H(=B)-E (with the D and H overlapping in harmony). Some also read another line working in counterpoint: A-D-E, with "Ade" being German for "adieu." It may be a stretch to accept that Brahms managed to translate an entire sentence into musical notation—"Agathe, adieu!"— but, then again, we shouldn't underestimate our composer. Brahms was known to be fond of this sort of musical gamesmanship early in his career, with one famous result being the Scherzo he contributed to the corporately composed "F.A.E. Sonata," built on notes signifying the personal motto of his violinist-friend Joseph Joachim, "Frei aber einsam" ("Free but lonely"). There is no question that the G-major Sextet represented a process of psychological liberation for Brahms. To his friend Joseph Gänsbacher he wrote, "By this work I have freed myself of my last love." In a musical sense, the wide-eyed passion and youthful vigor of Brahms' First String Sextet matures here into a subtler and wiser work born of a more finished experience of adulthood.

We may make much of Brahms' inclusion of the Agathe theme, but as important as it obviously was for him in personal terms it is not allowed to stick out as an obvious statement. That, in the end, is one of Brahms' great achievements in this piece—that his private message is made to operate entirely within the musical logic of the composition. It is certainly not necessary to know about the encoding to grasp the wonder of this work as a strictly musical achievement, although it is also unlikely that Brahms would have written the piece just as it is but for the whole Agathe affair.

In general this sextet tends toward moderation: the tempos of the first two movements are both tempered by the qualifier *non troppo* ("not too much"), and the last two by *poco* ("a little bit"). A current of nervous instability runs beneath the usually sunny surface of the opening movement. Sometimes this is obviously born of the murmuring figuration of the inner lines (as heard at the opening and very often throughout the movement), but the sensation also springs from the general harmonic and rhythmic patterns of the piece, rich in poignantly charged suspensions and harmonic sleights-of-hand. The second movement is also a nervous one, a curious *Scherzo* in 2/4 time (as opposed to the triple meter more commonly associated with such a movement); the meter does, however, shift to 3/4 for the galumphing country-dance that serves as the relatively boisterous trio (marked *Allegro giocoso*). The principal theme of the *Scherzo* was drawn from an earlier work, a Gavotte in A minor for piano (WoO3, No. 1) that Brahms had penned in the 1850s but never used as a stand-alone piece.

The *Poco Adagio* is a set of variations, again derived from earlier material, as Brahms had sent a sketch for this theme to Clara Schumann back in 1855. The variations are approached in free style, yielding a sense of rhapsodic outpouring and musical evolution that foreshadows a characteristic that would become a hallmark of the composer's late works. The theme is not so much a strongly etched melody as a vague meandering of notes; but its contour bears a good deal of similarity to the theme of the first movement's opening.

The finale is overwhelmingly upbeat and vivacious, though with gentle dance-like passages mixed in along the way—the idea being, some have said, that our composer is enjoying his last dance with Agathe before getting on with his life. But even in this last movement (if not quite to the degree elsewhere in this sextet), Brahms does not allow optimism to unroll unfettered; the piece can seem to subvert to its own sunshine. The musicologist Jan Swafford, in his biography of the composer, rightly refers to "a twilight quality, wistful and high-Brahmsian but still particular to this piece."

Trio in E-flat major for Horn, Violin, and Piano, Op. 40

Andante
Scherzo: Allegro
Adagio mesto
Finale: Allegro con brio

Work composed: Spring 1865, completed in May

Work premiered: November 28, 1865, in Zurich, Switzerland, played by Friedrich Hegar (violin), a Mr. Gläss (horn), and the composer (piano)

Instrumentation: Horn, violin, and piano

One early critic encountering Brahms' new Horn Trio was so taken aback by its unusual instrumentation that he declined to accept this as a legitimate piece of chamber music. Instead, he would deign only to consign it to the Brahmsian bin of "occasional works." That critic—his name was Selmar Bagge, should you wish to pray for the redemption of his soul—found the combination of horn, violin, and piano to be indefensibly unwieldy. Indeed it can be; an imprudent horn player can easily overwhelm the texture. But we count on musicians to tend to such problems, and there is no reason that Brahms' Horn Trio *has* to be unbalanced, even when played on a modern horn, as it usually is today. Brahms himself must have been considering this issue when he denoted that the piece was for the natural horn (or "hand horn," as he termed it) rather than for the more newfangled valve horn. It was a rather quaint decision in 1865; some years had passed since the valve system had been perfected, enabling hornists to alter the length of the instrument's tubes—and thereby broaden its chromatic possibilities—with the flick of a finger. Brahms' own mentor, Robert Schumann, had produced a small passel of pieces for valve horn in 1849.

But the natural horn exerted a pull on Brahms, perhaps partly because the composer's father, himself a professional hornist, had given his young son lessons in playing the "hand horn." (Brahms got pretty good at it, and in the late 1850s he played first horn in the orchestra at Detmold.) Then, too, the valve horn's facility came at a price—in this case, a straitening of the instrument's evocative timbre and in particular a smoothing out of the haunting, muted quality that ensued when a player inserted his hand into the instrument's bell to alter the pitch. "Notwithstanding its imperfections," wrote Louis-Ferdinand Dauprat of the natural horn, "it is of all the wind instruments the most beautiful in respect of timbre and intrinsic quality of tone, while the feelings aroused by its charm are generally admitted to be irresistible." It's only fair to note that Dauprat was himself a horn player; his observation appears in the monumental *Method for Alto Horn and Bass Horn* he published in 1824. But the fact is that the instrument's character completely corresponded to the mellow sonic sentiments of the early nineteenth century. Historically associated with the hunt (as well as postal delivery), the horn had long been pressed into service by composers who wanted to depict hunting or, by extension in either direction, pastoral or bellicose scenes. In his Horn Trio, Brahms requires the instrument to summon up both its lyrical and its dramatic sides, the former principally in the first and third movements, the latter in the other two.

Notwithstanding his Romantic sensibilities, Brahms was a great defender of the enduring value of Classical forms. He liked to pour new wine into old bottles like sonata forms, which is the structure that nearly always reigns over his first movements. But it does not here. Instead we have a rhapsodic piece, with episodes set off by different metric pulses, that avoids the exigencies of modulation inherent in an extended development section, modulation that would have been difficult to reconcile with the chromatic limitations of the "hand horn." The spirit of the mysterious Romantic forest is captured here; one could say that it reflects the character of the wooded landscape around Lichtenthal near Baden-Baden, in the Black Forest, where Brahms worked on this piece. In the second movement the Romantic haze lifts to reveal a boisterous rustic scene, although the contrasting trio section in the middle (in the arcane key of A-flat minor—seven flats!) reveals a brooding character.

The *Adagio mesto* ushers us into one of Brahms' most deeply felt slow movements, its melancholy possibly induced by the death of the composer's beloved mother only three months earlier. A passionate outburst erupts from this dolefulness but recedes into quiet contemplation. Near the movement's end the horn (with the violin providing harmony beneath it; then the roles switch) proposes a hushed premonition of what will soon recur as the upbeat principal theme of the finale. Both are said to refer to a German folk song, "In der Weiden steht ein Haus" ("In the Meadow Stands a House"). That *Finale* restores the good spirits that had been suggested in the *Scherzo* and it bustles its way to the end with scarcely a stop for breath.

String Quartet No. 1 in C minor, Op. 51, No. 1

> *Allegro*
> *Romanze: Poco Adagio*
> *Allegro molto moderato e comodo*
> *Un poco più animato, Allegro*

Work composed: Apparently over many years, though most emphatically beginning in 1866, and finished only in the summer of 1873, concurrently with his String Quartet No. 2

Work dedicated: To Brahms' physician-friend Theodor Billroth

Work premiered: December 11, 1873, in the Musikvereinsaal in Vienna, by the Hellmesberger String Quartet: the Joseph Hellmesbergers, Sr. and Jr. (violins), Sigmund Bachrich (viola), and Heinrich Röver (cello)

Instrumentation: Two violins, viola, and cello

"I shall never write a symphony!" Brahms famously declared in 1872. "You can't have any idea what it's like to hear such a giant marching behind you." The giant was Beethoven, of course, and although his music provided essential inspiration for Brahms, it also set such a high standard that the younger composer found it easy to discount his own creations as negligible in comparison. Nonetheless, Brahms proved relentless in confronting his compositional demons; rather than lead to a creative block, his self-criticism pushed him to forge ahead even when his eventual path seemed elusive. The result was that he made enormous strides as he created and then rejected material that he hoped might lead to the breakthroughs he sought in the realms in such genres as the string quartet or the symphony, the classic Beethovenian genres that caused him the most anxiety. We find Brahms producing two piano quartets, two string sextets, a piano-and-strings quintet, and a horn trio (all of these being non-Beethoven genres, or at least touched only in a minor way by the earlier master) before finally signing off on his first two string quartets (Op. 51) in 1873—and this, by his own account, after disposing of twenty exploratory string quartets. In truth, he did get some interim use out of those twenty early string quartets; he used them to paper the walls and ceilings of his apartment. "I had only to lie on my back to admire my sonatas and quartets," he once reminisced of his room in Hamburg. Of Brahms' early chamber works, only his B-major Piano Trio could be said to beg direct comparison to important chamber works in Beethoven's catalogue, and Brahms ended up completely rewriting that piece later.

He finally managed to bring not one, but two, quartets to fruition in the same year of 1873. When the C-minor and A-minor Quartets were published as a set, the C-minor was placed first. Its progress can be traced through many years of Brahms' correspondence. As early as 1865 the violinist Joseph Joachim wrote to ask if the C-minor Quartet (very possibly this one) would be ready for an impending concert date. It wasn't. Four years later Brahms had the piece read through privately by the Becker (also called the Florentine) Quartet, but this only led to further severe revisions. Not until the summer of 1873, which Brahms spent in the Bavarian summer resort of Tutzing on the Starnberger See, did he announce the piece's birth to his anxious publisher, Fritz Simrock, and this he did in typically self-deprecating terms: "I always take great pains, hoping that I will come up

with a great and terrible [work]—and they always turn out small and pitiful!
I can't wait for them to get better!"

In fact, he had created a masterwork, one that throughout bears his immediately identifiable language, rich in poignant harmonic suspensions, rhythmic displacements, nervous passion, and melting lyricism. All four movements
are bound by a propensity toward themes that prominently employ dotted
rhythms and the interval of the second. The quartet displays an austere character overall, growing out of the very serious tone of the opening measures.
Some interpreters find heroism in this tightly constructed opening movement, others a more romantic passion, but on the whole I would suggest that
tension is its hallmark. We can indeed sense the ghost of Beethoven hovering
over the second movement which, especially at its beginning, exhibits the
Classical restraint of some of the earlier composer's quartet slow movements.
The third movement unrolls as an intermezzo; yet the chain of descending
seconds in the principal theme yields a sobbing effect that to a great extent
undercuts the unbroken charm typical of many Brahms intermezzos. The
prominent use of the viola intensifies the darkness of this interlude. An abundance of themes fills the finale, a hybrid sonata-rondo that mirrors the tight
intensity of the opening movement.

String Quartet No. 2 in A minor, Op. 51, No. 2

> *Allegro non troppo*
> *Andante moderato*
> *Quasi minuetto, moderato—Allegretto vivace*
> *Finale: Allegro non assai*

Work composed: Probably over many years, though most emphatically beginning in 1866; Brahms finished it only in the summer of 1873, concurrently
with his String Quartet No. 1.

Work dedicated: To Brahms' physician-friend Theodor Billroth

Work premiered: October 18, 1873, in at the Berlin Singakademie, by the
Joachim String Quartet (violinists Joseph Joachim and Heinrich de Ahna, violist Eduard Rappoldi, and cellist Wilhelm Müller)

Instrumentation: Two violins, viola, and cello

Although the A-minor Quartet appears to have hatched over a long period,
Brahms' final, intensive efforts with it are documented especially in his

correspondence with his musical physician-friend Theodor Billroth. In July 1873, when Brahms was spending the summer at the Bavarian summer resort of Tutzing on the Starnberger See, he wrote, in the overly modest fashion that was characteristic when he discussed his new compositions:

> I am in the act of publishing for the first time—but not writing for the first time—a string quartet. It is not only the affectionate thoughts of you and of your friendship which prevail upon me to dedicate this to you. I just happen to think of you with such pleasure as a violinist and sextet player. A volume of tremendously difficult piano variations you would probably take even more to your heart, and they would certainly do you more justice. But there's no help for it. You have to accept this dedication as it stands.

As with his first two piano quartets, Brahms' two Op. 51 Quartets were born as a pair, but their contrast is not as marked as with those earlier works. Both of these quartets are in minor keys, and the C-minor is more intense and compact-sounding than the A-minor, which makes more room for more expansive lyricism. Both are deeply serious and uncompromising pieces that are frankly appreciated more by devoted Brahmsians than by the general public, who have been known to find both pieces somewhat forbidding.

The principal theme of the first movement works itself around the sequence of notes F-A-E, which are the second, third, and fourth notes of this rhapsodic melody. This was a musical encoding of the first letters making up the words of the personal motto of Brahms' violinist-friend Joseph Joachim, "Frei aber einsam" ("Free but lonely"). Some scholars have taken this as evidence that Brahms may have initially intended to dedicate this work to Joachim, whose string quartet played through provisional versions of the piece as Brahms worked on it and would midwife the piece at its premiere. As it happened, a bit of a misunderstanding clouded their friendship briefly at this time—a far more serious breach lay a decade in the future—and this may account for Brahms' decision to inscribe the two works to Billroth instead. Brahms' own complementary motto was "Frei aber froh" ("Free but happy"), and analysts have found *its* musical translation (F-A-F, or the inversion thereof) woven into the musical texture. I fear that the ear is not so likely to land on that, and I wonder if Brahms intended that as musical encoding at all, so common are figures based on thirds in music generally.

Listeners who worry that the Brahms string quartets are severe may take heart in the A-major second movement, which is a supremely beautiful expanse. Its phrases unroll at unhurried length, not wanting to end but rather unfurling into extensions of themselves and then, seamlessly, into the phrases of new themes. The effect is magical. A brief change of character inhabits a central *marcato* passage in which the first violin and the cello play in canon a strongly accented melody—with emphatic dotted-note rhythms and violently disjunct intervals—after which the spacious calm returns for the conclusion. Among this movement's particular admirers was Arnold Schoenberg, who found this piece altogether laudable in the subtle complexity of its interlocking phrases.

It was an odd, perhaps even perverse idea for Brahms in 1873 to refer to the ensuing movement in terms of the minuet, even if only *Quasi minuetto* ("To some degree a minuet"). The minuet was the quintessential Classical third-movement form, but here Brahms, the ultimate "Romantic Classicist," offers us something quite different from what had been inherently a dance movement. Instead we hear ominous, even spectral music that shares only its triple meter with a real minuet—and here the music moves considerably slower, in any case. The overall structure does echo that of the Classical minuet, which had a contrasting trio section in the middle. Here Brahms' "trio" section is an animated, possibly skittish *Allegretto vivace* (though interlaced with lyrical passages related to the main *quasi minuetto*); and when the opening material returns, Brahms invests it with an added degree of contrapuntal brilliance rather than merely repeat his music wholesale.

The *Finale* is not less intense than what has come before, but Brahms does season it, sparingly, with a slight Magyar flavor that might be considered overtly audience-friendly. On the other hand, this movement is every bit as uncompromising in its intellectualism as anything previous to it in this quartet, filled as it is with complicated rhythmic dissonances and with tight junctures worked out according to strict canonical procedures. I'm not sure I would go as far as Daniel Gregory Mason, who in his classic 1933 study of Brahms' chamber music declared this *Finale* to be "a hilarious rondo on two themes." Doubtless it depends on the musical interpretation the piece receives, but to my ears an overriding earnestness and seriousness inhabit Brahms' brilliant Second String Quartet from start to finish.

Piano Quartet No. 3 in C minor, Op. 60

> *Allegro ma non troppo*
> *Scherzo: Allegro*
> *Andante*
> *Finale. Allegro comodo*

Work composed: 1855–74

Work premiered: November 18, 1875, at the Musikvereinsaal in Vienna, with the composer (as pianist) joined by members of the Hellmesberger Quartet

(violinist Joseph Hellmesberg, Sr., violist Sigmund Bachrich, and cellist Friedrich Hilpert)

Instrumentation: Violin, viola, cello, and piano

Since Brahms was quite private in his work and scrupulous about destroying traces of compositions he abandoned, we are left with only tantalizing suggestions of chamber works that might have been. Such is the case with a piano quartet in C-sharp minor that occupied the twenty-two-year-old Brahms in 1855, at the same time as he was trying to mold some promising material into what would have been (but did not survive to be) his first symphony, in D minor. The symphony project gradually evolved to become his First Piano Concerto, which retained the material's key of D minor. The piano quartet would not even hold on to its original key; by the time Brahms brought it to completion and finally published it twenty years later, the whole conception had dropped a half-step to become his Piano Quartet No. 3 in C minor.

In a sense, the C-minor is both the first and the last of Brahms' three piano quartets. Between its origin and its completion, the composer wrote and published both of his other essays in the genre, in G minor and A major. It seems that only the first movement and the *Scherzo* (which may have been initially intended to serve as the finale) are actually derived from the early C-sharp-minor piece, and that Brahms wrote the other two "from scratch," polishing the whole work while he was on vacation in Rüschlikon, Switzerland, overlooking the Lake of Zurich, during the summer of 1874. Before he sent it off to his publisher, he played it through for Clara Schumann, who wrote afterward to share her impression: "I have been thinking about the quartet a great deal, and the last three movements have quite taken hold of me, but—if I may say so—the first does not seem to me to be on the same level; it has not the same freshness, though there is freshness in the first theme."

These words must have moistened Brahms' eyes a bit, for the piece—especially its first movement—had been born of the sentiments surrounding a poignant period of his complicated relationship with Clara Schumann. In 1854, Robert Schumann (Clara's husband and Brahms' mentor) had been committed to a psychiatric institution, manifesting evidence of severe mental illness that had led to an apparent suicide attempt. Schumann would spend his remaining two and a half years there, having good days and bad. On Schumann's doctor's advice, Clara did not see her husband during that entire time until only two days before he died. Brahms, on the other hand, visited Schumann regularly and mourned the dissolution of a close friend and a superlative mind. All the while, his passionate adoration of Clara only intensified. That they loved one another is unquestionable. Whether they hid a physical involvement behind veils of discretion—during or after Robert Schumann's lifetime—or whether they engaged in music history's longest Platonic love affair remains undisclosed.

What is certain is that Brahms was walking an emotional high-wire during those couple of years. He was well aware of how his sentiments were making their way into his music, and specifically into his piano quartet. It is a dark and stormy work, concise in its expression, unusually insistent upon emotional *Sturm und Drang*. In 1868, when the piece was midway through its evolution, Brahms described the first movement thus in a letter to his friend (and first biographer) Hermann Dieters: "Now imagine a man who is just going to shoot himself, because there is no alternative." Later, he would habitually describe the C-minor Piano Quartet with language invoking the outfit associated with the character of Werther, Goethe's young, sorrowful hero (or antihero) who ultimately commits suicide as a result of his unrequited love for his friend's wife. (Sound familiar?) So it is that Brahms tells his friend Theodor Billroth in an 1874 letter that the piece as it stands is "a curiosity—an illustration for the last chapter in the life of the man in the blue coat and yellow vest" (this was Werther's outfit), and that he cynically advises his publisher, Fritz Simrock, just before the work's publication, in the autumn of 1875: "On the cover you must have a picture, a head with a pistol pointed toward it. Now you can form an idea of the music! For this purpose I will send you my photograph! Blue coat, yellow breeches, and top-boots would do well, as you seem to like color-printing." At least Brahms had the good sense to have the piece published; only a couple of months earlier he had written to Simrock, "the Quartet is half old, half new—the whole thing isn't worth much."

The piano's raw octaves at the outset alternate with a descending two-note motif in the strings that at least one commentator has declared to be a sighing of the name "Clara"—this in the movement that Clara complained had not "taken hold of" her. And yet, Brahms retains a sense of composure even when verging on the maudlin, and the second theme possesses the nobility we expect of its creator; the piano introduces it, and it undergoes considerable variation throughout the exposition, and then returns in the recapitulation to be worked out through two further variations. This must be the melody that Clara identified as the "first theme," which she allowed had some freshness to it. The second-movement *Scherzo* (biting and angry) and the *Finale* (a sonata-rondo, replete with Brahms' beloved falling-thirds motifs) reinforce the spirit of the opening movement, with which they share the key of C minor and a sense of tight-wound dramatic tension.

But it is the third movement, the supernal *Adagio*, that is likely to linger longest in the listener's mind. It was long assumed from its harmonically distant key—E major—that it was a holdover from the early version of the work, since C-sharp minor and E major share a signature of four sharps. Research has confirmed, however, that this was *not* the slow movement that Clara Schumann had once admired. The cello has the honor of intoning the principal melody, against a simple piano accompaniment, and then continuing in counterpoint when the violin takes over the lead. (This movement may have begun life as a portion of an aborted cello sonata.) Both the theme's spacious lyricism and the way it is worked out strongly recall the flavor of corresponding movements of Robert Schumann's Piano Quartet and Piano Quintet. A quiet calm pervades the movement, reaching a magical moment at the start of the recapitulation, when the cello melody, now assigned to the piano, is accompanied by the pizzicato strumming of the viola and cello.

String Quartet No. 3 in B-flat major, Op. 67

> *Vivace*
> *Andante*
> *Agitato (Allegretto non troppo)—Trio*
> *Poco Allegretto con variazioni—Doppio movimento*

Work composed: 1875

Work dedicated: To Theodor Wilhelm Engelmann, a physiologist who taught at the University of Utrecht; his wife, Emma, was especially loved within the circle of Brahms' friends.

Work premiered: October 30, 1876, at the Berlin Singakademie, by the Joachim String Quartet (violinists Joseph Joachim and Heinrich de Ahna, violist Eduard Rappoldi, and cellist Wilhelm Müller)

Instrumentation: Two violins, viola, and cello

Brahms' three published string quartets were born in rather quick succession: the first two (a pair created almost simultaneously and published together as his Op. 51) were written in 1873, and the Third (Op. 67) followed in 1875, after which he abandoned the medium forever. In the summer of 1875 Brahms found himself in Ziegelhausen, a pleasant outpost on the Neckar River a few miles upstream from picturesque Heidelberg. It was a relaxed time for Brahms, who refused to allow anything to interrupt it. When his friend Franz Wüllner invited him to travel to Munich (perhaps 150 miles distant) to hear a performance of the composer's own German Requiem, Brahms demurred: "Your letter was a temptation to leave my pretty house...but all the same I stay sitting here, and from time to time write highly useless pieces in order not to have to look into the stern face of a symphony."

Among the "highly useless pieces" that occupied him were his C-minor Piano Quartet (Op. 60) and his B-flat-major String Quartet (Op. 67). Clara Schumann, to whom he supplied a copy of the string quartet, wrote expressing her pleasure with the piece, finding it "too delightful for words, with its delightful, mocking conclusion." What she found so appealing may have been the rhythmically off-kilter rollout of the *Finale's* tune, or perhaps the composer's recalling of themes from the first movement at the work's very end. It is indeed the most delightful of Brahms' three quartets. Where the first two impress with their technical brilliance and monumentality, they both come off as demanding and unremitting (the C-minor especially so), perhaps revealing their composer's discomfort in confronting the shade of Beethoven. In the Third Quartet, by contrast, we find Brahms not less proficient in his mastery—Brahms always astonishes—but he seems to a large degree freed from his compositional demons. Many music-lovers assume that the quintessential Brahms is the ultra-serious Brahms, echoing the composer Hugo Wolf's shrugging observation, "He cannot exult." But even if Brahms' feet seem always firmly planted on the ground, he most certainly had a playful side, and that aspect of his art is no less authentic. In the Third Quartet we find an example of Brahmsian cheerfulness, and the composer seems to have liked the piece as much as we do; some years later he told Joseph Joachim that of his three string quartets this was his favorite.

Folkish melodies abound in the Quartet No. 3, particularly in the first and last movements. In the opening *Vivace* we hear this in the opening theme, a "hunting tune" that would not have been out of place in his Horn Trio. A similar character informs the second theme, the Bohemian cast of which is likely to suggest Dvořák (a switch from the usual, since Dvořák so often drew inspiration from his mentor Brahms). For this tune Brahms changes meter from the overriding 6/8 to 2/4; and he effects this with particularly elegant dovetailing, teeter-tottering between the two meters before finally giving in (for a while) to 2/4. Such metrical shifts are unmistakable Brahmsian fingerprints, and this movement is full of them, with the 2/4 versus 6/8 tension resurfacing as the movement progresses.

The *Andante* is born of a different mold. It begins as a tender "song without words," an outpouring of Victorian sentiment in a Mendelssohnian mode. Brusque chords interrupt the mood, giving rise to a contrasting section with some neo-Baroque harmonic turns. The manuscript reveals that this portion was an afterthought, pasted over the composer's original, less adventurous conception. This D-minor interlude proves to be a momentary alarm, and the heartfelt opening melody returns, this time with its melody varied with

ornamentation and its accompaniment embroidered through more complicated rhythmic interlocking among the parts.

In the *Agitato* Brahms employs a novel sonic effect: the two violins and
cellos install mutes for the duration, but the viola is heard unmuted, in full
voice. The viola does indeed enjoy particular prominence here as a purveyor
of themes (as it does to an unusual extent throughout this quartet), but the
other instruments are active in this regard, too; and, though they are muted,
they are often asked to play out loudly. It is instead a question of Brahms
finding a way to achieve a particular sonority to serve the nervous, rustling
musical ideas that occupy him in this movement (a second theme, full of
nobility, is cut off before it can impose its mood). In the central trio section
the full-voiced viola remains silent for the opening measures—this begins
as both structurally and texturally a trio—while its muted colleagues trace
eight measures of arpeggio figures in contrary motion. We assume this to be
a new theme, but when the violins and cello repeat these measures unaltered
the viola joins in to play a more obvious melody in their midst, one bearing
much the same character as the movement's main theme and rhythmically
at odds with the other instruments (in characteristic Brahmsian fashion).
After this trio the main section of the *Agitato* returns verbatim, altered only
through a little coda in which the music drifts away at the end. The composer
held this movement in particular esteem, at one point remarking that it was
"the most amorous, affectionate thing I have ever written." We should know
better than to take Brahms too seriously when he comments on his own
music, and, for all the movement's strengths, "amorous" and "affectionate"
are not words anyone would propose to describe its attributes. Joachim wrote
to Brahms in May 1876, a month before the violinist's quartet premiered the
work, "You yourself have hardly written chamber music any more beautiful
than the D-minor movement and the finale; the former full of enchanted
Romanticism, the latter full of sincerity and grace while [maintaining] the
very artful form." That rings perfectly true, but about "amorous" and "affectionate" I'm not so sure.

Mutes come off for the finale, which is a set of variations on a folkish theme (though entirely Brahms' creation, without a doubt). Such an
odd rhythmic structure its opening displays: an unremarkable four-measure
phrase, then repeated, followed by a six-measure phrase (also repeated) that
sounds curtailed, or at least telescoped, as it veers in a sudden modulation into the minor mode; then an eight-measure bit (two times four, standard enough) and another six bars, again repeated. And so this variations
movement continues, curiously lopsided in its bearing, although by the end
repeated exposure makes it all seem normal enough. Brahms proceeds in
this fashion through six variations, exploring various melodic alterations
and increasing the harmonic complexity such that in the fourth, fifth, and

sixth variations we find ourselves respectively in the keys of B-flat minor, D-flat major, and G-flat major—logical territories to be explored at a time when harmonies based on thirds-relationships were at the forefront of composers' concerns. (B-flat minor reinforces the "B-flatness" of the overriding key of B-flat major, while D-flat major takes us a minor third above, and G-flat major a major third below, the tonic.) At that point something far less predictable occurs. Brahms moves into what we take to be Variation Seven, and with it returns to the home key of B-flat major. But now the theme is not the one that has reigned over the movement so far, but rather the "horn call" that had launched the opening *Vivace* movement. In the ensuing variation (the Eighth) he revisits another theme from the first movement, and then in the movement's conclusion he interweaves these themes with the finale's melody in a prolongation of the tune, an inspired and technically remarkable achievement that knits the whole piece into an unassailable whole.

Piano Trio No. 2 in C major, Op. 87

Allegro
Andante con moto
Scherzo: Presto
Finale: Allegro giocoso

Work composed: 1880–82; more specifically, in March 1880 in Vienna and in June 1882 in Bad Ischl

Work premiered: December 29, 1882, in Frankfurt, with the composer (as pianist) joined by violinist Hugo Heermann and cellist Wilhelm Müller; the program also included the premiere of Brahms' String Quintet in F major (Op. 88).

Instrumentation: Violin, cello, and piano

The C-major Piano Trio, the second of Brahms' three efforts in that genre, crept into being over a period of two years at the outset of the 1880s, when he was at the height of his creative powers and still blessed with bursting creative energy. When he began it, he was midway between the completion of his Second Symphony (in 1877) and his Third (in 1883). Within months of completing the Trio's first movement in March 1880, he composed his two great orchestral overtures, the *Academic Festival* and the *Tragic*, and by the time he returned to his Trio to shepherd it to completion two years later he had also signed off on his massive Piano Concerto No. 2. Brahms was actually occupied with the opening movements of two separate piano trios in the winter of 1880. He often worked on pieces in pairs—in contrasting pairs, typically—and in this case he produced the *Allegro* movement of the C-major Trio in tandem with another in E-flat major. Both works sat as torsos for some time, but at some point Brahms decided to destroy what he had completed of the projected E-flat-major Piano Trio, and not until the summer of 1882, when he was on vacation at Bad Ischl, did he get around to finishing the one in C major.

The C-major Piano Trio shares some territory with the Second Piano Concerto and the Third Symphony, which the contemporaneous conductor Hans Richter dubbed Brahms' *Eroica*. Certainly the Trio's first movement conveys something of an Olympian and heroic character. But the Trio does not invite much relaxation. The piece sounds not an eighth-note longer than it needs to be, and its four fully packed movements fill less than a half-hour. Power is the watchword at the beginning, and the movement's solid opening unisons (for violin and cello) are soon joined by rich-textured piano writing. Indeed, the piano part is so sumptuous that the strings occasionally team up in precisely the sort of octave-writing heard at the outset, the better to offset their partner's potentially overwhelming force. At the movement's precise midpoint the development section arrives with a stroke that could not have been accomplished except by a great master: the music follows an astonishing modulation to D-flat—only a half-step above the overall tonic, but very distant in terms of traditional harmonic behavior—and the cello presents a leisurely variant on the upward-surging principal theme, then taken up by the violin, all against rippling figurations in the piano. It's an insuperably Brahmsian moment. Here the composer has renewed the excitement of his piece through simultaneous alterations of the tonal center, the instrumental texture, and the melody itself. Toward the end of the movement Brahms restates his principal melody again, this time enriching it with what seems a vocal character. The cello's noble phrases seem practically extracted from a Schubert lied.

For the slow movement (*Andante con moto*) Brahms moves to the relative minor key of A minor, and he presents a theme-and-five-variations set based on a melody redolent of Magyar flavor. The mournful but proud tune makes much use of the rhythmic device known as the "Scotch snap," the dividing of a beat into a fast-slow figure (here a sixteenth-note followed by a dotted eighth-note), and Brahms further enhances the rhythmic plan by making extensive use of off-beat syncopations throughout this movement. (At one point, a particularly modal extension of the melody comes surprisingly close to Musorgsky's depiction of the Bydlo, the infinitely weighty Polish oxcart section in *Pictures at an Exhibition*.) The variations cover considerable emotional territory, even to the point of visiting the ethereal domain of the Brahmsian intermezzo.

The *Scherzo* flutters nervously, requiring the players to effect great agility while upholding a hushed and mysterious atmosphere. One might find certain affinities between these interior movements and certain works by Bartók, with the *Andante con moto* evoking any number of Bartók's modal, folk-inflected melodies and the *Scherzo* prefiguring his rustling "night music" movements. A listener is scarcely prepared for the trio section, which ushers forth via an elegant elision. This trio is again a hyper-Brahms expanse: not the most learned music he ever wrote, but a brilliant demonstration of how he makes his music ascend through soaring phrases into the empyrean. Nobody else ever wrote this kind of music as compellingly: it perfectly captures a sort of noble, triumphant, heart-swelling joy that may fill us with ecstatic contentment before we return to the will-o'-the-wisp of the *Scherzo* proper.

Some commentators have objected that the *Finale* of Brahms' C-major Trio is too lightweight compared to what came before. I don't agree with that assessment, although it is certainly true that Brahms presents his themes here in rapid succession and works out their implications with a minimum of fussiness: it is Brahms veering in the direction of Saint-Saëns. We have already experienced quite a lot of monumentality in this trio, and for this movement Brahms imagines a function different from what came before, much as the recessional at a wedding plays a distinct role from the processional that preceded it by not so very long.

String Quintet No. 1 in F major, Op. 88

> *Allegro non troppo ma con brio*
> *Grave ed appassionato—Allegretto vivace—Tempo I—Presto—Tempo I*
> *Allegro energico—Presto*

Work composed: Spring 1882 at Bad Ischl, Austria, drawing on some previously composed material

Work premiered: December 29, 1882, in Frankfurt, by violinists Hugo Heermann and Johann Naret-Koning, violists Fritz Bassermann and Mr. Welcker, and cellist Valentin Müller

Instrumentation: Two violins, two violas, and cello

During the mid-1850s Brahms plunged into the study of Baroque dance music—specifically that of Bach and Handel—and at that time he even composed a series of keyboard movements cast as sarabandes, gavottes, and gigues. He seems to have viewed them as personal composition exercise and didn't bother to publish them. But nearly three decades later, in the spring of 1882, he turned to his A-major Gavotte and Sarabande as a source for the second movement of his F-major String Quintet (Op. 88). Though the Quintet's roots in this way reach back at least a century and a half, the piece has nothing of an antique feel to it. It's pure Brahms—mature, subtle, and endlessly inventive, but with a lighter, less insistently serious quality than listeners often expect of him.

Written for two violins, two violas, and cello, the F-major Quintet adheres to the tradition of "viola quintets" that had been established by Mozart, Beethoven, Mendelssohn, and Spohr, as opposed to the "cello quintets" (two violins, one viola, two cellos) that had occupied Boccherini, Schubert, and even Brahms himself. This represents Brahms' second foray into the texture of the string quintet, following by twenty years an F-minor String Quintet with one viola and two cellos that he destroyed after finding its musical material ill-suited to the forces for which he had cast it. He recycled some of the early quintet's material, though, transforming it first into a large-scale work for two pianos and finally into an Everest among musical masterpieces, the F-minor Piano Quintet (Op. 34).

When Brahms returned to the forces of the string quintet for Op. 88, its mysteries no longer eluded him. The work's texture is lusciously rich, its "extra" viola allowed the composer more than the usual opportunities to spotlight an instrument he especially loved, and the ensemble's timbral possibilities seem to have released him from some of the procedural tightness that inhabits his string quartets. It was composed in the spring of 1882 at Bad Ischl, a resort near Salzburg, and because Brahms dated each of his manuscript's movements "in the Spring of 1882," the work is very occasionally called the *Spring* Quintet, though that has not proved to be one of classical music's more enduring or necessary nicknames.

The F-major Quintet has only three movements instead of the usual four, though, in a sense, the second movement combines slow and fast movements into one. Brahms noted this structure with typically dry humor when he sent the piece to his publisher, Fritz Simrock, not renowned as a big spender: "Of course the quintet has only three movements—you could cut the price down on that account—but in the trio there are variations, and in that line folks have an idea that I amount to something." Brahms also told Simrock "You have never before had such a beautiful work from me." It seems that he received his full fee.

The first movement opens with a theme that is unmistakable Brahms—full-timbred, warmly content, and infused with F-major dignity. The lyrical second subject, whose triplet figures inject interesting contrast, appears in the key of A major. This sets up the juxtaposition of key relationships a third apart, a structural process that was by then challenging the traditional

supremacy of fourths and fifths as the intervals of greatest structural importance. But don't imagine that Brahms turned his back on the ultimate logic of
tonic-dominant progressions. In the first movement's development, the cello
intones an enormously long low C that serves as a dominant pedal point to
the eventual F-major resolution of the recapitulation. In 1884 the composer
Hugo Wolf, reviewing a performance by the expanded Rosé Quartet, was surprised to find himself enjoying this work. After complaining about Brahms'
recent symphonies ("absolutely repulsive"), he allows of the Quintet that
"the chilly November fog that usually hangs over his compositions, stifling
every warm utterance before it has a chance to be heard—of this not a trace
here....An enchanting emerald green envelops this fairyland spring vision.
Everything is verdant and budding. One actually hears the grass growing—all
of nature so mysteriously still, so blissfully radiant."

The second movement, as already noted, employs Brahms' earlier Sarabande and Gavotte, but the material is here transformed into something
that could not comfortably be described as "neo-Baroque." The movement
unrolls in five sections (A-B-A-B'-A), rather after the fashion of a rondo
or—perhaps more precisely—a minuet with two related trios. The A sections
are very slow, derived from the Sarabande; the B sections are very fast, and
the second of them grew out of the earlier Gavotte. Third-relationships are
also at work in this movement, with the composer sounding the harmonic
distance between A major and C-sharp (in both its major and minor modes).
Again the purple prose of Hugo Wolf: "Deep meditation and silence. It is as if
glowworms were dancing their rounds, so glowing and sparkling is the rushing
instrumental figuration."

The third movement, marked *Allegro energico*, is no less brilliant in its
architecture, combining the disparate procedures of fugue and sonata form
into an exciting and ebullient finale. Such a union of forms was far from
unprecedented, to wit the finale of Mozart's *Jupiter* Symphony or Beethoven's
Third *Razumovsky* Quartet (Op. 59, No. 3)—not to mention Brahms' own
First Cello Sonata. All of these pieces are tours de force; but in the F-major
Quintet, Brahms obscures the challenge behind such buoyant nonchalance
that he makes it sound like the musical equivalent of tic-tac-toe rather than
the Rubik's Cube it really is.

Piano Trio No. 3 in C minor, Op. 101

Allegro energico
Presto non assai
Andante grazioso
Allegro molto

Work composed: Summer 1886

Work premiered: December 20, 1886, in Budapest, played by Joseph Joachim (violin), David Popper (cello), and the composer (piano)

Brahms passed the three summer months of 1886 at Hofstetten, near Lake Thun in Switzerland, and in that short span he produced a remarkable freshet of masterworks: his F-major Cello Sonata (Op. 99), his Second Violin Sonata (in A major, Op. 100), his C-minor Piano Trio (Op. 101), most of his Third Violin Sonata (in D minor, Op. 108), and several songs, including the evergreen "Wie Melodien zieht es mir" and "Immer leiser wird mein Schlummer." This is an extraordinary lineup by any measure, not just for its consistently superb quality (which, after all, we expect of Brahms) but also for the density of achievement in so little time and the variety of emotional terrain these pieces cover. Compared to the noble F-major Cello Sonata and the lyrical A-major Violin Sonata, the C-minor Piano Trio is a tightly coiled composition, tense and nervous, so compact that its span of four movements lasts about as long as the mere three movements of the Violin Sonata and considerably less than the three movements of the Cello Sonata.

The Trio springs into action with a furious outburst, rather in the mode of a Beethovenian eruption, and Brahms then provides contrast through a second theme, played in octaves by the violin and cello, that encapsulates aristocratic poise. These materials are investigated with extreme economy and in a way that seems unusually abstracted, to the extent that the rhythmic pulse sometimes is obscured into apparent irrelevance in the face of contrapuntal push-and-pull. "Smaller men," wrote Brahms' friend Heinrich von Herzogenberg, "will hardly trust themselves to proceed so laconically without forfeiting some of what they have to say." Indeed, Brahms says what he needs to with exceptional concentration here, even to the extent of deleting the traditional repetition of the exposition section.

The second movement is so reticent as to seem almost to apologize for its existence, the more so in light of the granitic toughness of the first movement. Here we have a mere wisp of a scherzo, and if we sometimes glimpse it only indistinctly—its evanescence underscored by the muting of the strings—at least we are back on terra firma so far as the rhythm is concerned, since Brahms casts this in a more reliably discernible duple meter.

With the third movement we turn to an oft-encountered Brahmsian landscape: an intermezzo, characteristically marked *Andante grazioso*. But where most Brahms intermezzos are calm and consoling, perhaps dreamy, this one may leave listeners feeling uneasy in a way that is hard to pin down. Again, it's the rhythm that's unstable, much as it had been in the development of the first movement. This time Brahms sets his music in groupings of three measures—specifically, a measure in 3/4 meter followed by two measures in 2/4 meter, with that pattern then repeated over and over. Otherwise put, he is here writing in virtual 7/4 meter, which in "standard practice" composition would be considered highly unorthodox, asymmetrical, even wobbly. (A central section is cast in the pattern of one measure of 9/8 time plus one of 6/8 time, effectively equivalent to 15/8—or 5/4 with the principal beats subdivided into triplets.) There is no musical reason Brahms could not have written this music in 7/4 and (in the middle) 5/4 meter, and a composer living a generation later would not have hesitated to do so. As it is, however, the more fragmentary division of the phrase allows Brahms to plot incontrovertibly where he wants the phrases' subtle accents to fall. This becomes especially significant when the opening material returns after the central interlude, now redistributed so that we hear one measure of piano followed by two measures of strings, and then one of strings followed by two of piano. It's all quite teasingly ambivalent. In any case, in 1886 a meter signature of 7/8 would have appeared quite outré; an exotic Russian composer might have essayed it for fun, but surely not a self-respecting German. Two years later, in fact, Brahms would go out on a limb by composing his vocal quartet *Nächtens* entirely in 5/4 meter; but we should not be surprised that Brahms preferred to notate his music for this intermezzo in a way that would translate into normally encountered time signatures. The Brahms biographer Jan Swafford wondered if this rhythmic daring might reflect Brahms' appreciation of Hungarian traditional music, with its sometimes complex rhythmic juxtapositions, and the musicologist Michael Musgrave avers that this movement testifies to Brahms' "love of the irregular meters of Serbian folk song." The rhythmic business provides sufficient complication for this brief movement. Apart from that it's quite straightforward in its tendency toward clear-cut alternations of phrases between the strings (still muted) and the piano.

By now we understand that this piano trio is to a large extent "about" rhythmic variety and bravery, and the finale carries through the idea to the end. (Surely it is "about" many other things as well, not least of which is the integration of the all-important four-note ascending melodic motif that permeates this composition.) One of Brahms' favorite rhythmic hallmarks is the hemiola, which is, as *The New Grove Dictionary of Music and Musicians* correctly defines it, "the articulation of two units of triple meter as if they were notated as three units of duple meter." (Leonard Bernstein provided a fail-safe demonstration in *West Side Story*; just sing "I want to be in A-me-ri-ca.") Hemiolas abound in this final movement of Brahms' trio, as are other falsely placed accents, and the cross-rhythms can throw a listener into rhythmic puzzlement. Finally, at the end the rhythmic restiveness is tamed into regularity, and the darkness of the minor mode yields to C major for a coda that seems almost out of place in these torrential surroundings. This brief coda brings the work to a relatively upbeat end, but it does not convey hard-won triumph so much as a stern forging of order out of chaos.

Connoisseurs have been split in their reactions to this work, though even doubters acknowledge that it is an important achievement and a signal accomplishment in the often-ignored area of rhythm. Through a curious coincidence, this work played a part in the first meeting, on December 20, 1887, between Brahms and Pyotr Ilyich Tchaikovsky, who crossed paths in Leipzig. Tchaikovsky reported in his diary: "Going to Brodsky's for the one-o'-clock dinner, I heard sounds of the piano, violin, and cello. They were rehearsing for the next day's performance of Brahms' new Pianoforte Trio, Op. 101, and the composer himself was at the piano. Thus it chanced that I saw the famous German musician for the first time.... During the rehearsal I took the liberty of making some remarks as to the skill and execution of the relative tempo 2–3 and these remarks were very good-naturedly received by the composer." It is perhaps not a coincidence that six years later, in 1893, Tchaikovsky would cast the captivating *Allegro con grazia* of his Sixth Symphony in 5/4 meter, perhaps an echo of Brahms' *Andante grazioso*.

String Quintet No. 2 in G major, Op. 111

> *Allegro non troppo, ma con brio*
> *Adagio*
> *Un poco allegretto*
> *Vivace ma non troppo presto*

Work composed: Spring and summer 1890, in Bad Ischl and Vienna

Work premiered: November 11, 1890, in Bösendorfer Hall in Vienna, by the Rosé Quartet (violinists Arnold Rosé and August Siebert, violist Sigmund Bachrich, and cellist Reinhold Hummer), with the violist Franz Jelinek

Instrumentation: Two violins, two violas, and cello

As he brought his pieces into existence Brahms sometimes tried out a variety of instrumentations before settling on one that satisfied him. Such was the case with his G-major String Quintet. The genealogy of its first movement reaches back to the spring of 1890, when Brahms, vacationing in Italy, sketched its principal material as a draft for what he envisioned would be his Fifth Symphony. It's not difficult to imagine an orchestra playing at the outset. The performers are faced with a challenge of balance from the first bar.

The opening theme is introduced by the cello, which must project through an overlay in which the four upper instrumental parts play vigorous, fluttering chords (*forte*, no less) that threaten to obscure the deep tones of the melody. Brahms' trusted friend Joseph Joachim, whom the composer often consulted on matters of string playing, begged him to thin out the texture, and Brahms did experiment with ways to do this before finally deciding to stick to his guns and retain the thick, energetic writing he had envisioned all along. Robert Haven Schauffler, a cellist who published a biography of the composer in 1933 (the centennial of Brahms' birth), drew on personal experience when he described this passage: "One of two things happens. Either the Master's directions are swept aside, or the agonized cellist saws so desperately that one hears considerably more resin, sheepgut, copper wire, horse-tail, and bow-wood than Brahms. And there are some who feel that this serves the composer right for wanting to have his dynamic cake and eat it too."

Though it may stretch the interpreters' ingenuity, the opening does impart a sense of unbounded joy, a rapturous mood that will define this overwhelmingly positive work. "The person who can have invented all this must be in a happy frame of mind!" wrote Brahms' friend Elisabet von Herzogenberg after studying the piece in the fall of 1890. "One feels you must have been celebrating—say, your thirtieth birthday." During a rehearsal, another friend, Max Kalbeck, confessed to the composer that the first movement suggested to him images of the Prater, the principal public park of Vienna. "You've guessed it," exclaimed Brahms, "and with all the pretty girls there, right?" Surely the "Prater" passage must be the second theme and its answer—lyrical, carefree, and managing to incorporate the rhythmic alternation of two and three beats that serves as a Brahmsian signature. "Never has Viennese Gemüthligkeit, even in its supreme poets, Schubert and Brahms, reached a more perfect and touching expression than in this...expectant question and confident answer, in which happiness and sadness mingle as they always mingle in simple hearts"—so wrote Daniel Gregory Mason in his analytical study of Brahms' chamber music, also published in the composer's centennial year.

The second movement, an *Adagio* in D minor, injects a more somber note, culminating in a dark close on the lowest strings of all the instruments. The ensuing *Un poco allegretto* inhabits the graceful, nostalgic, quizzical, emotionally ambiguous world of Brahms' piano intermezzos. The specter of Schubert hovers over this movement, too, especially in the trio section's folksy tunes and sleight-of-hand modulations. A broader sense of humor launches the finale in the decidedly "wrong" key of B major, but through an ingenious harmonic progression everyone lands emphatically on G major, reaffirming the expected—indeed, necessary—tonic. Brahms expends considerable contrapuntal skill in examining his material, and he makes several references to the oscillating motif that had accompanied the cello's announcement of the first-movement theme. Finally, a brief coda lets loose with a hearty, animated Hungarian dance, or perhaps a Slavonic polka, with off-balance phrases of five measures each.

After so buoyant a finale to so upbeat a work, it comes as a surprise to realize that Brahms thought of this as his farewell to composition. Though only fifty-seven, and not yet experiencing symptoms of the cancer that would eventually kill him, he was tired. Signing off on his final changes before the score was processed into print, he attached a letter to his publisher: "With this note you can take leave of my music, because it is high time to stop."

Trio in A minor for Clarinet, Cello, and Piano, Op. 114

> *Allegro*
> *Adagio*
> *Andante grazioso*
> *Allegro*

Work composed: July and August 1891, at Bad Ischl, Austria

Work premiered: November 24, 1891, in a private concert in Meiningen, by clarinetist Richard Mühlfeld, cellist Robert Hausmann, and the composer (as pianist). The public premiere, with the same performers, followed on December 12, in Berlin.

Instrumentation: Clarinet, cello, and piano

History is full of examples of composers who are motivated by specific performers, as Brahms was on various occasions by (among others) the pianist Clara Schumann, the violinist Joseph Joachim, and the clarinetist Richard Mühlfeld (1856–1907). Brahms first met Mühlfeld during a visit to Meiningen to hear Hans von Bülow conduct some of his works in the spring of 1891. Mühlfeld had entered the ducal orchestra in 1873 as a violinist and then taught himself to play the clarinet, becoming the orchestra's principal clarinetist in 1876. Brahms was so struck by his artistry that he spent hour after hour in his company exploring the technical possibilities of the instrument with an eye toward applying them in works of chamber music.

Brahms had recently begun announcing to his friends that his composing career had reached its end, but these sessions inspired him to compose not one but four masterpieces for the clarinet: the Trio in A minor (Op. 114, for clarinet, cello, and piano, in 1891) and the Quintet in B minor (Op. 115, for clarinet and string quartet, of the same year), plus the two Sonatas for

Clarinet and Piano, in F minor (Op. 120, No. 1) and E-flat major (Op. 120, No. 2), both from 1894. When Brahms sent a copy of the Clarinet Trio to his friend Eusebius Mandysczewski, he attached a characteristically self-effacing note saying that it was "the twin sister of an even bigger folly," by which he meant the Clarinet Quintet. Probably nobody since then has considered either a folly.

When the Trio was published (by the firm of Simrock, in March 1892), the title page allowed the possibility that a viola could substitute for the clarinet. During the rehearsal period preceding the work's premiere, Brahms is known to have tried out the piece in its viola version with Joseph Joachim handling that part. Nonetheless, there is no question that the clarinet was the composer's first choice, and that suggesting the viola as an alternative was principally a marketing decision. The clarinet Brahms calls for, by the way, is pitched in A. The clarinet in B-flat is more common today, though clarinets in A are still routinely sighted among professionals. The slightly larger instrument (in A) is required in order to reach low C-sharp (untransposed), which is prominent as the penultimate note of the first movement's main theme. Mühlfeld's clarinet still exists in healthy, playable condition. It displays two characteristics of salient interest: an unusually dark tone and a surprisingly high pitch for its time, just a slight notch below modern concert pitch. This latter detail bears out contemporary reports that pianos had to be "tuned up" for the early performances of Brahms' Trio.

The piece's timbre is more dark than sunny, but Brahms lightens the atmosphere somewhat by making full use of the clarinet's wide range and its facility with arpeggios and other rapid passagework. This in turn creates occasional challenges for the cellist, who is asked to mirror an agility that lies less comfortably on his instrument than on the clarinetist's. As a consolation prize, the cello gets to introduce most of the main themes, including both pairs of principal subjects in the first and last movements. The clarinet's subtleties are perhaps most deeply explored in the *Adagio*, which leads the player through ample opportunities to explore the instrument's wide range of pitch and dynamics, all the while rendering a free-flowing musical excursion in which intimate fantasy mixes with heart-on-sleeve passion.

The *Andantino grazioso*, which one might expect to be the brief, relaxed moment of contrast in this minor-key opus, turns out to be quite extensive, and it provides opportunities for Brahms to indulge in the sort of metric complications that are his hallmark. Its mood does serve as a balm, recalling the nostalgic tenderness of the *Liebeslieder* Waltzes or some of the late piano intermezzos. Early commentators tended to consider this movement unworthy of its composer, though their expressions of dismissal beg to be read in view of their writers' biases. Near the turn of the twentieth century the English scholar John Alexander Fuller-Maitland found in this movement "a beauty of such ripeness that the slightest touch must make it over-ripe" suggesting that it "comes very near to the border of the commonplace" and (in the ultimate England versus Ireland insult) that "Balfe himself might have written something very like it." Daniel Gregory Mason gleefully quoted these comments in his 1933 analytical guide to Brahms' chamber music, adding for his own part, "compared with the exquisite simplicity of so many of the intermezzi, this over-dressed tune is like the pretty peasant maiden who has spoiled herself, for a holiday at the fair, with finery and cosmetics." Most listeners today find more to appreciate in this movement, and, indeed, in the work as a whole. At the same time, they would have to agree that Brahms' Clarinet Trio is a notably serious work, even to the point of grim bleakness. Mason captured the essence of its mood in his poetic description of the "murmurous" last page of the first movement: "Here sky as well as earth is gray; charm is not offered, it is not even expected or desired. In recompense for its absence we find a high, unyielding sincerity, a grave dignity, a kind of stoic Roman virtue."

Quintet in B minor for Clarinet and Strings, Op. 115

Allegro
Adagio
Andantino—Presto non assai, ma con sentimento
Finale. Con moto

Work composed: Summer 1891, in Bad Ischl, Austria

Work premiered: December 12, 1891, in the Singakademie Hall in Berlin, with clarinetist Richard Mühlfeld and the Joachim Quartet (violinists Joseph Joachim and Heinrich de Ahna, violist Emanuel Wirth, and cellist Robert Hausmann)

Instrumentation: Clarinet, two violins, viola, and cello

"The clarinet cannot be better played," Brahms wrote to Clara Schumann after hearing Richard Mühlfeld perform a Weber concerto in Meiningen. The artistry of Mühlfeld (whom we met in connection with Brahms' Trio for Clarinet, Cello, and Piano, Op. 114) provided the impetus for Brahms to get back on track as a composer, to jump-start his energy, which had disappeared to such an extent that he had suggested to his publisher and his friends that his work as a composer was done. When he finished writing the Trio and Quintet, during his summer vacation at the spa of Bad Ischl in the spectacularly beautiful Salzkammergut, he alluded to Mühlfeld in another letter to Clara: "I look forward to returning to Meiningen if only for the pleasure of hearing them. You have never heard a clarinet player like the one they have there. He is absolutely the best I know of." When she finally heard Mühlfeld play the Quintet, in 1893, Clara wrote Brahms: "What a magnificent thing it is, and how moving! Words are inadequate to express my feelings. He plays so wonderfully, he must have been born for your music." Actually, the reverse was true.

We have no way of knowing how Mühlfeld really played, since he made no known recordings. An interesting reminiscence, however, is related by the late British clarinetist Jack Brymer in his 1976 book, *Clarinet*. In the 1930s, he reports, someone interviewed an ancient violist who had sometimes played in Joachim's quartet and had performed Brahms' Clarinet Quintet with Mühlfeld on several occasions. "He used two clarinets, A and B-flat, for the slow movement," recalled the violist, "to simplify the gypsy section; he had a fiery technique with a warm tone—and a big vibrato." Continued Brymer: "Asked again by a startled questioner if he didn't mean to say '*rubato*' the old man looked puzzled. 'No,' he said, 'vibrato—much more than Joachim, and as much as the cellist."

Brahms was fifty-eight years old when he wrote the Clarinet Trio and the Clarinet Quintet, and both evince the rich maturity of a composer who had a way of sounding autumnal practically from his youth. Nonetheless, the Quintet is the greater of the two, less constrained than the Trio in its inspiration, vaster in both its resources (employing five instruments instead of three) and its dimensions (spanning about thirty-five minutes, compared with the Trio's twenty-five), complete in its employ of the clarinet's range and timbral variety, secure in the strength of its classic construction yet rhapsodic in its poetry. Not all listeners were won over by its scope. In 1892, George Bernard Shaw, who was a busy music critic before he got distracted by other things, observed of a London performance: "It surpassed my utmost expectations: I never heard such a work in my life. Brahms' enormous gift of music is paralleled by nothing on earth but Gladstone's gift of words: it is a verbosity which outfaces its own commonplaceness by dint of sheer magnitude." A far more appreciative stance was struck by Brahms' biographer Florence May, who in her 1905 book on the composer wrote: "A fullness of rich melody, a luscious charm of tone, original effects arising from the treatment of the clarinet, 'olympian' ease and mastery, distinguish every movement of this noble and attractive work, which, taking its hearers by storm on its first production, has grown more firmly rooted to the hearts of musicians and laymen with each fresh hearing."

The Quintet's overall effect is one of nostalgic melancholy, although even the ultra-Romantic *Adagio* (where the strings install mutes for a particularly veiled tone) includes a central section rich in the Hungarian Gypsy-music proclivities of which Brahms was unapologetically fond. Where others would

have placed a third-movement scherzo (a light-hearted musical conception that does not much coincide with Brahms' natural tendencies) we find
instead a lyrical song-like movement; here, too, the music alternates with
more buoyant, vigorous passages, but in both this movement and the concluding theme-and-variations Brahms allows an atmosphere of introspective
resignation to dominate.

The theme-and-variations was a favorite device for Brahms, and imaginative examples of it run throughout his production. His *Finale* begins with
the announcement of a theme whose simplicity and ambivalent minor-ma-
jor modality suggest a folk song. Each of the ensuing five variations adheres
strictly to thirty-two measures, with the second sixteen repeating the first
sixteen exactly. Variation One spotlights the cello, and Variation Two, full
of the rhythmic displacement so dear to Brahms, recalls the agitation of the
"Hungarian Gypsy" interlude of the second movement. Variation Three
involves the fragmentation of the melody, elaborated by idiomatic clarinet
figuration. In the Fourth, written in the contrasting major mode, Brahms
shows off his skill as a contrapuntist; and in Variation Five, an impassioned
waltz, he directs the spotlight toward the viola, one of the composer's favorite, deep-hued instruments. After that, a coda, referring to thematic material
from the quintet's opening movement, brings the proceedings to a well-
rounded, serious end.

Benjamin Edward Britten

Born: November 22, 1913 (the feast of Saint Cecilia, the patron saint of music, as he was pleased to point out), in Lowestoft, Suffolk, England

Died: December 4, 1976, in Aldeburgh, Suffolk, England

Phantasy for Oboe and String Trio, Op. 2

Andante alla Marcia
Allegro giusto
Con fuoco
Tempo I—Andante alla marcia
(The sections are played without break.)

Work composed: In four to six weeks beginning September 9, 1932. At the end of his composition draft he placed the date "Oct. 19th (Oct. 10th) 1932," and in his diary he reported that the piece occupied him until October 10—and then later until October 25; these discrepancies must reflect revisions he effected to his initial drafts.

Work premiered: August 6, 1933, on a BBC National broadcast, by oboist Leon Goossens (to whom it is dedicated) and members of the International String Quartet: violinist André Mangeot, violist Eric Bray, and cellist Jack Shinebourne. The same players presented its concert premiere, on November 21, 1933, at the Music Club, St. John's Institute, London.

Instrumentation: Oboe, violin, viola, and cello

Early in his career Benjamin Britten was principally an instrumental composer. Only later did he develop the gifts for vocal writing that would cement his position in music history as a preeminent composer of songs, of choral music, and of operas. This comes as no particular surprise, since he was raised as an instrumentalist: he studied piano seriously as a child and soon took up the viola as well. The noted composer and teacher Frank Bridge encountered the thirteen-year-old musician at the Norwich Festival and was sufficiently intrigued by his talent to accept him as a private composition student. In 1930 Britten entered London's Royal College of Music, where the composer John Ireland and the pianists Arthur Benjamin and Harold Samuel continued to refine his musicianship. He still worked with Bridge on the side, and this proved an important aspect of his education; while his conservatory studies concentrated on "the classics," Bridge kept steering his young charge toward more up-to-date developments in scores by Mahler, Schoenberg, and Stravinsky. This equipped him to rebel definitively against the musical esthetic his generation inherited, that of Elgar and, most directly, the crepuscular, last-gasp-Romantic sublimity of Ralph Vaughan Williams and the so-called English Pastoral Tradition in music. Though he was rooted in the musical tradition of his nation, Britten pushed boldly forward. While many of his finest scores sound instantly British, they also sound resolutely of the twentieth century.

In the summer of 1932, in the course of a mere three weeks, Britten composed one of the first works he would deem a mature composition, his fifteen-minute-long Sinfonietta for a mixed ensemble of ten instruments. Displaying a degree of obeisance to Schoenberg, it exemplified what he would later describe as "a struggle away from everything Vaughan Williams seemed to stand for." He viewed it as a breakthrough achievement, and when it was published by the respected firm of Boosey & Hawkes in 1935, he designated the Sinfonietta as his Opus 1. Several months later he wrote what would appear in print (also in 1935) as his Opus 2: his *Phantasy*, a quartet for oboe and strings, which remains very much in the active repertoire of oboists today. The *Phantasy* was the first work to gain international attention for Britten, who was not quite nineteen years old when he wrote it. Together, the Sinfonietta and the *Phantasy* marked Britten's turning the corner to being a professional composer.

Britten's is one of many "phantasy" pieces produced by British composers in the first half of the century, for a reason of particular interest to lovers of chamber music. Walter Willson Cobbett (1847–1937), the wealthy chamber music aficionado who would author the fascinating and quirky *Cobbett's Cyclopedic Survey of Chamber Music* (first published in 1929), used the word—in its curious spelling—to describe the pieces he invited aspiring composers to submit for consideration in a competition he founded in 1905. According to Cobbett's guidelines, the competition "phantasies" were to be rather short pieces in a single movement, though potentially sectional or episodic, that were not worked out according to the strictures of the "classical" forms. They were rather analogous in this regard to the fantasias that English Renaissance composers turned out for lutes, viols, or keyboards. The *Phantasy* Piano Trio by Frank Bridge, Britten's composition teacher, won the second installment of the competition, in 1907, and ensuing victors would include such figures as John Ireland and Herbert Howell—and Britten, too, with his *Phantasy* Quintet for Strings in May 1932. That plush, almost Edwardian piece brought him a prize of thirteen guineas, which he used to buy a new suit and a copy of the score of *El Amor Brujo* by Manuel de Falla.

It does not appear that Britten wrote his ensuing *Phantasy* for Oboe and String Trio with the intent of submitting it to the Cobbett competition; it seems instead that he was simply on a "Phantasy" roll. In any case, this piece is structured according to Cobbett's ideal, unrolling as a single, continuous movement of about thirteen minutes' duration, which is divided into four distinct but organically connected sections. Though not planned out as a sonata form, the work does employ a late recapitulation of material heard early in the movement. But where a sonata form would require that the principal material be explored through a development section, Britten writes instead an extended slow expanse. A generally questing spirit reigns over much of this, underscored by the imaginative structure, a deliberate vagueness in dealing with tonal centers, a constant exploration of how themes can be varied, and a complexity in the instrumental textures. The final segment is remarkable for its resemblance to the sort of English folk modality we associate more with Vaughan Williams and the "pastoral tradition" than with the younger Britten—a reminder that Britten was just beginning to spread his wings and fly in directions that English music had not yet visited.

The *Phantasy* Quartet proved to be a momentous work for Britten. In August 1933 the BBC broadcast it in a performance with the eminent oboist Leon Goossens. (Goossens' brother Eugene, by the way, had won a Cobbett prize in 1915 for his own *Phantasy* Quartet for string quartet.) When the same ensemble reprised it at a live concert in Westminster, the *Phantasy* earned firm praise from the *Times*, which recognized it as "original...arresting...natural and unforced." Soon the *Phantasy* received another high-profile performance, at a concert of the International Society for Contemporary Music, in Florence, on April 5, 1934, this time with members of the Griller Quartet joining Goossens. The composer, by then twenty-one-years-old, traveled to Italy for the performance and wrote in his diary, "Goossens and the Grillers really play my Phant. very beautifully & it's quite well received."

String Quartet No. 2 in C major, Op. 36

> *Allegro calmo, senza rigore*
> *Vivace*
> *Chacony: Sostenuto*

Work composed: 1945 in Snape and London, completed on October 14

Work dedicated: For Mrs. J. L. Behrend—Mary Behrend, who underwrote the commission

Work premiered: November 21, 1945, at Wigmore Hall in London, by the entirely distaff Zorian String Quartet: Olive Zorian and Marjorie Lavers, violins; Winifred Copperwheat, viola; and Norina Semino, cello.

Instrumentation: Two violins, viola, and cello

On November 21, 1945, Great Britain marked the 250th anniversary of Henry Purcell's death with the first of two consecutive evenings of tribute concerts at London's Wigmore Hall, with the programs including works by both Purcell and Britten. Britten, in a somewhat accusatory mood, wrote of his ancient predecessor in a pamphlet produced for the occasion: "Henry Purcell was the last important international figure of English music. Ironically the continent of Europe has been more aware of his greatness than this island which produced him. But that he should be to the English public little more than a name in history books is not altogether strange, for he is the antithesis of the music which has been popular for so long in this country."

Britten had already been championing Purcell's music on the recital stage with his musical and spousal partner, the tenor Peter Pears, and he was on the verge of publishing some of the editions of Purcell's songs he had prepared for those performances. His reverence for Purcell was further reflected through original compositions he produced in the months immediately following the premiere of his groundbreaking opera *Peter Grimes*: his beloved *Young Person's Guide to the Orchestra*, Op. 34 (which is formally, and accurately, subtitled *Variations and Fugue on a Theme by Henry Purcell*), and his String Quartet No. 2 (Op. 36), which would be unveiled the first night of the Purcell celebration.

The first of the three movements of the Second Quartet includes as part of its opening texture eleven measures of the viola playing the note C plus the E a tenth above it, a musical molecule that is then taken up as an ostinato by the other instruments (though grounded on different notes). Britten's biographer Humphrey Carpenter suggests that this opening viola drone is "probably modeled on Purcell's Fantasia upon One Note, throughout which a viola sustains a middle C." In Purcell's day the part would have been played almost inevitably on tenor viol, but apart from that Carpenter's assumption seems likely, the more so since that particular Purcell work was played in the concert in which Britten's quartet was premiered, and since Britten chose it to round out the 1946 HMV set of the Second String Quartet made by the Zorian foursome, on modern instruments, of course—with the composer playing the unswerving viola part. (The Britten quartet took up seven 78-r.p.m. sides, leaving one further side available in the set.)

The movement is cast as a free take on a sonata form, with three principal theme groups presented in quick succession at the outset. Each of these thematic areas, all enunciated in octaves by the two violins and cello, begins with a melodic leap of the interval of a tenth, the same distance as that defined by the sustained viola part. The first, beginning on the tonic note C, jumping to the E an octave-plus higher and lasting eleven measures, recalls the calm of Britten's seascape-painting in *Peter Grimes*; the next—again eleven measures, G leaping to B—includes a wavering figure and picks up more vigor, building melodic momentum; and the third—tracing the rising interval D to F-sharp—includes aspects that are related to both, incorporating sustained calm plus wavering figures, yet tracing contours all its own. It's hard to know just where this third phrase ends, as it gradually cedes into a passage of wide-spanning arpeggios in the first violin, a pattern that will play a supporting role in this movement.

In the first movement's recapitulation these three melodic sections are sounded all together *fortissimo* in superimposition, a classical-music equivalent to those Broadway songs in which different characters sing apparently unrelated music that is then piled up simultaneously into an ensemble. (Think of "Playing Croquet/Swinging/How Do You Do?" which is set as an ensemble of two groups of girls and one of Canadian Mounties in Rick Besoyan's *Little Mary Sunshine*, or "Now/Later/Soon," the ingenious trio of the three Egermans—Fredrik, Henrik, and Anne—in Stephen Sondheim's *A Little Night Music*.) Britten has already offered a foretaste of the possibility of such superimposition in the exposition, where the first two of these melodic ideas coincide briefly; now when all three are played together, they sound above the rolling arpeggiated figure, entrusted here to the cello. The three-in-one overlap is certainly a tour de force, but Peter Evans, in his analytical study of Britten's music (*The Music of Benjamin Britten*, second edition) worries that "repeated hearings may make one wonder whether too much weight has not been thrown on this contrivance." It's a fair point; we should keep things in perspective and remember that this bit of legerdemain is only a passing, if clever, device in a movement remarkable from start to finish. It closes in a mood of surpassing beauty, with twenty-three quiet measures of interrupted C major spread out over five octaves of sustained notes and harp-like pizzicatos, embellished by only the tiniest harmonic shivers.

The C-minor scherzo makes use of the wide-spaced arpeggios already familiar from the first movement, now taking the role of the principal theme. The mood is anxious to the point of panic—shades of Britten's future friend Shostakovich—and the composer's instruction that all the instruments should install mutes for the duration of the movement further intensifies the breathless quality. A light-textured trio dispels the uneasy atmosphere only slightly.

The quartet's most overt homage to Purcell arrives with the last movement, the Chacony, a form Purcell often employed for expressions of emotional intensity. A stalwart form of Baroque music, the triple-meter chaconne, or ciacona, is a structure in which a bass progression repeats over and over as upper lines evolve in constantly shifting melodic and rhythmic patterns above it. Britten goes so far as to use the "olde Englishe" spelling of Chacony. This may strike us as twee, but it is indeed the spelling Purcell used, as in his famous Chacony in G minor (Z.730) for strings, of which Britten prepared an orchestral arrangement in 1955. Here the chaconne theme, nine measures long, is strongly dotted, although its character changes considerably as it is heard through twenty-two iterations (in two of which the pattern is truncated to only eight measures). A larger structure than just the repeating pattern is at work here. The variations are apportioned into four spans, which are demarcated by solo cadenzas, the first for cello, the second for viola, the third for first violin. Together these four sections practically add up to a whole string quartet within a string quartet: an introductory slow section (the theme plus five repetitions of the bass pattern), then a scherzo (six variations), then an adagio (six variations), and, to conclude, a fast coda (three variations). Each of the four sections explores a different mode of variation technique; in the brief program note he wrote for the work's premiere Britten explained, "The sections may be said to review the theme from (a) harmonic, (b) rhythmic, (c) melodic, and (d) formal aspects." The last go-through, extended to thirteen measures, is punctuated by twenty-one explosions of a C-major chord, surely corresponding to the twenty-one variations of the chaconne theme. These outbursts are thickly voiced, with each instrument quadruple stopped to yield sixteen notes in the final three blasts—an emphatic counterpart to the drawn-out C-major serenity that had ended the first movement.

Elliott Carter (signature)

Elliott Cook Carter

Born: December 11, 1908, in New York City

Eight Etudes and a Fantasy for Woodwind Quartet

I *Maestoso*
II *Quietly*
III *Adagio possibile*
IV *Vivace*
V *Andante*
VI *Allegretto leggero*
VII *Intensely*
VIII *Presto*
IX *Fantasy: Tempo giusto*

Work composed: 1950

Work dedicated: To the conductor and composer Richard Franko Goldman

Work premiered: October 28, 1952, in New York City, by members of the New York Woodwind Quintet (flutist Murray Panitz, oboist Jerome Roth, clarinetist David Glazer, and bassoonist Bernard Garfield)

Instrumentation: Flute, oboe, clarinet, and bassoon

Elliott Carter has been recognized as one of the United States' leading composers for more than half of his hundred-plus years, and even in his post-centennial phase he continues with relentless vigor to add important works to a catalogue that is already brimful with notable contributions to all the major musical genres: orchestral music, opera, ballet, choral repertoire, and chamber music. In his early works Carter tended toward a mainstream

Modernism that was in line with coeval scores by Prokofiev, Stravinsky, Milhaud, or Copland. But in the mid- to late-1940s he began to exhibit an absolutely distinctive style built on the drama of musical contrasts—contrasts of instrumental timbres, of rhythmic plans, of tempos. "I'm always concerned with context—with preceding and succeeding ideas," Carter told the music journalist David Ewen. "Making things that go along, changing in very slight degrees, bit by bit. Or dealing with things that change abruptly. And making all this *significant*."

His Eight Etudes and a Fantasy for Wind Quartet grew out of an orchestration class he was teaching at Columbia University. Long an essential feature of instrumental training, etudes are traditionally short pieces that focus on a single aspect of mechanical technique. Most offer negligible musical value apart from the refinement of technique (which is to some extent a musical value, or at least lends to the realization of musical values), but others have managed to be enduringly interesting as music. Nobody would banish Chopin's etudes from the concert stage, and wind players have similarly embraced the Carter set as essential repertoire, fodder for technical development yet deeply satisfying as concert compositions. These pieces call for an unusual grouping of instruments: four-fifths of a standard wind quintet—the woodwind complement only—with no horn (which, after all, is a member of the brass family and therefore operates according to entirely distinct mechanical principles from its four colleagues). A few other composers have written for such a quartet—Arthur Berger, Larry Sitsky, Eugène Bozza, and the fecund Heitor Villa-Lobos among them—but Carter's Eight Etudes and a Fantasy remain unchallenged in combining esthetic consequence with technical challenge for individual and ensemble skills. Etudes can also be "study pieces" that refine the techniques of *composers*, and Carter's set unveiled numerous ideas that he would develop in later pieces.

The first etude focuses on leaps of intervals. Among the challenges are precision in matching timbres from register to register, for each musician and for the ensemble as a whole, along with the need for spot-on accuracy of pitch, the handing-off of lines, and the balance of parts among subgroups within the ensemble. In the fleeting second movement, mercurial lines arch delicately in every instrument (*un poco espressivo*), with all the musicians eventually playing their tingling thirty-second notes at once—an unforgiving moment for rhythmic precision. Carter has compared the effect to four birds all repeating the same bird song but starting at different times.

The third etude investigates the timbral possibilities offered by a simple D-major chord. Each instrument plays only the three notes of that triad (D–F-sharp–A), the four instruments tucked together in formation. Carter asks that the instruments strive for "sneak entrances" as this short movement unrolls. Harmonic analysis would tell us that everything is static here; but much is going on in terms of voicing in this exercise in Schoenberg-style *Klangfarbenmelodie*, the "melody of sound colors." Minimal material also generates the athletic fourth etude: a two-note ascending semitone figure that bounces among the parts. Carter has spoken of this kind of musical construction as the aural equivalent of fitting together tiny mosaics into a large image, or (as the composer once analogized it in a speech) to a parquet floor in which "it is all made of small blocks of wood—all of the same dimension." The Carter of the future is glimpsed in the fifth etude, where the parts proceed with a degree of contrapuntal independence while balancing their lines according to the composer's precise instructions concerning dynamics. The sixth is lighter than air, making advanced technical demands in the domain of tonguing (including flutter-tonguing) and the quick alternation between possible fingerings of a single note (with a concomitant wavering of tone color).

The most famous movement is the seventh, a study related to the third but here reduced to a single pitch, G, which is bantered among the instruments. The voices shift in and out of prominence according to their dynamics and the effect of their attacks—and of course all four instruments must play perfectly in tune. This technique traces at least to the slow movement of Ruth Crawford Seeger's *String Quartet 1931*, and it points forward to the imminent moment when tonal manipulation of this sort would be achieved through electronic means. In an article he published in *Current Thought in Musicology* (1976), Carter explained that this piece "draws out the four possible tone colors and their eleven combinations and many variants due to dynamic and attack differences, a musical discourse entirely dependent on contrasting various types of 'entrances': sharp, incisive attacks as opposed to soft entrances." The hugely virtuosic eighth etude focuses on cells of scale passages—not the simple major and minor scales all instrumentalists can play in their sleep, but rather finger-twisting combinations of figures drawn from more complicated step-by-step arrangements.

Carter concludes with a Fantasy, a freely conceived fugue, or at least something that resembles a fugue, even if departs from "textbook" behavior. This crowning summation makes reference to all of the techniques explored in the preceding numbers, and even the tempos of its sections allude to the speeds of the individual etudes.

The entire set runs about twenty minutes and is normally performed in its entirety. Carter does, however, allow that various partial groupings may be performed, though in a preface to the score he imposes specific limitations on which may be played with which, including: "The Fantasy must not be played alone; it must be preceded at least by Etudes 1, 4, 7, and 6 (or 8), in that order, and it must be the final piece of any group containing it."

String Quartet No. 3

Duo I	Duo II
Violin and Cello	Violin and Viola
(playing quasi rubato throughout)	(playing in quite strict rhythm throughout)

Furioso	*Maestoso*
Leggerissimo	*Grazioso*
Andante espressivo	*Scorrevole*
Pizzicato giocoso	*Pizzicato giusto, meccanico*
	Largo tranquillo
	Appassionato

Work composed: 1971

Work dedicated: For the Juilliard Quartet

Work premiered: January 23, 1973, in New York City, by the Juilliard String Quartet (violinists Robert Mann and Earl Carlyss, violist Samuel Rhodes, and cellist Claus Adam)

Instrumentation: Two violins, viola, and cello

In his long career, Elliott Carter has created a body of work marked by rigorous explorations of the precise and complicated interactions of musical materials, and this interest has accordingly led to the creation of an oeuvre of escalating intricacy. The music theorist Jonathan Bernard astutely observed: "In a musical age dominated by simplification, what has made Carter's music increasingly attractive is, paradoxically, its very complexity: the sense it often conveys of many things going on at once, producing the most violent sorts of contrast alongside the smoothest of continuities, offering not an escape from the demands of modern existence but a meaningful engagement with them."

A Carter score demands a listener's uninterrupted concentration and perhaps a leap of faith. Most of us have trained our listening brains to synthesize what we hear in a musical performance, to find the relationships among dissimilar sounds and contrasting musical lines, to make sense out of the plentiful variety of material a composer presents. Whereas composers have usually worked out their music in a way that underscores how the parts of a composition are organically connected, Carter often emphasizes the extent to which the parts of his pieces are *unconnected*. This invites a different mode of listening; and if it goes against the grain compared to how we have trained our "listening brain" to process music, at least we can be sure that we are neurologically capable of a different approach. Most of us are entirely within our comfort zone when hearing and sorting out the disparate, independent streams of sound that come our way all at once in the course of daily life. As we drive our cars, for example, we may be simultaneously processing all sorts of unrelated sonic input without becoming discombobulated: the whoosh of traffic, the honking of a horn, the automated voice of a GPS system, all against the background of the Vivaldi being aired on drive-time radio. Approaching Carter in the same unedited way can prove rewarding. He brings our concert music into the era of multitasking.

A particular fingerprint that has become associated with Carter is an idiosyncratic way of plumbing the possibilities of instrumental textures in the ensembles he uses. Very often he derives subgroups from his orchestras and chamber ensembles, and then uses these smaller combinations of instruments in succession, or sometimes superimposed, until he has used up those of the available possibilities that seem relevant to the piece he's composing. In a sense, he creates dialogues among several players within a larger group.

The most famous application of independence in Carter's music comes in his String Quartet No. 3, which, like the quartet that preceded it, was awarded a Pulitzer Prize (in 1971). Here the foursome operates as two pairs of duos (Duo I comprising first violin and cello, Duo II containing second violin and viola) that happen to be occupying the same time and space but otherwise seem, for the most part, to be progressing with no regard to each other. (Perversely, Duo II is placed above Duo I in the score.) The composer instructs that they should be located "as separated from each other as is conveniently possible, so that the listener can not only perceive them as two separate sound sources but also be aware of the combination they form with each other."

The two dyads operate on very different rhythmic planes; Duo II adheres to a generally strict rhythmic pulse while Duo I is instructed to infuse its part with more rhapsodic *rubato*. The music for Duo I consists of four movements; Duo II gets six movements. Carter advises that "segments of the four movement of Duo I (first played in the order given...and then later resumed in other orders) are combined with segments of each of the six movements of Duo II." The separate material of the two groups is therefore shuffled so as to collide and contrast in different permutations, although sometimes one group sits silent while the other plays alone. The head spins.

The heading "Scorrevole" in the third of Duo II's movements is an unusual one, but it is a familiar marking on the Carterian landscape since the composer famously attached it to movements in his First and Fifth String Quartets, as well to a stand-alone orchestral piece, *Allegro scorrevole*. *Scorrevole* might be translated as "flowing," "gliding," or "scurrying." Many a more standard marking is far less helpful.

Aaron Copland

Born: November 14, 1900, in Brooklyn, New York

Died: December 2, 1990, in Peekskill, New York

Two Pieces for String Quartet

Lento Molto
Rondino

Work composed: The *Rondino* in spring of 1923 in Paris; the *Lento Molto* in 1928 (completed in April) in New York, when the two movements were harnessed together to become the Two Pieces for String Quartet

Work premiered: The Rondino in September 1924 at the American Conservatory in Fontainebleau, France; the Two Pieces were first presented as a set on May 6, 1928, when the Lenox String Quartet played them at the second of the Copland-Sessions Concerts of Contemporary Modern Music in New York

Instrumentation: Two violins, viola, and cello

Aaron Copland struck many of his earliest listeners as a brash, in-your-face Modernist, but history would prove that he was merely up-to-date. He did not simply keep up with his times; one might say that he *defined* the sound of his times—or at least a certain strain of modern sound—to the extent that the musical vocabulary and syntax he formalized in the 1930s and 1940s continues to connote deep-rooted "American-ness" to this day. Especially in his later years, the appellation "Dean of American Composers" became so over-used as to seem almost a part of Copland's surname. Nonetheless, he surely deserved the title for many reasons, among which an important qualification was that, as he himself put it, he could help out as "a good citizen of the Republic of Music."

Following early training in New York, Copland sailed for France to spend the summer of 1921 at the American Conservatory in Fontainebleau. At first he studied there with the prominent conductor and pedagogue Paul Antonin Vidal, but soon he moved on to instruction from the American Conservatory's founder, Nadia Boulanger. He worked with her from 1921 through 1924, both at Fontainebleau and in Paris, becoming one of the earliest in a succession of "Boulangerie"-trained American composers that would include Virgil Thomson, Roy Harris, Elliott Carter, and Philip Glass. Boulanger showed the gift (at least with many of her pupils) of developing their unique talents without bending them to adhere to any particular method. This proved to be a congenial approach for Copland, such that even his earliest "mature" works do afford glimpses of his distinctive voice.

The Two Pieces for String Quartet began (at least the second of them did) while he was under Boulanger's tutelage. Copland related the origins of this work in an interview conducted by Vivian Perlis and published in *Copland: 1900 through 1942*, the first installment of her essential, two-volume oral history of the composer. Said the composer:

> The *Rondino* was written in the spring of 1923 in Paris as the second part of an "Hommage à Fauré."...Preceding the *Rondino* had been an arrangement for string quartet of the Prelude IX from Fauré's *Préludes pour Piano* (Op. 103). The *Rondino* was based on the letters of Fauré's name. Mixed with his influence can be heard a hint of American jazz and a bit of mild polytonality. Mademoiselle [Boulanger] got together a professional quartet to read through it one Wednesday afternoon. Nadia often did this for students, and the hearing of one's imagined instrumentation did more toward the learning of instrumentation and orchestration than many hours of spoken instruction.
>
> The first performance of "Hommage à Fauré" took place in September 1924 at Fontainebleau. The old master, Fauré, was then seventy-eight and within a few months of his death....It is strange that the musical public outside France has never been convinced of his special charms, the delicacy, reserve, imperturbable calm—qualities that are not easily exportable....My arrangement of Fauré's *Prélude* was appropriate to the occasion in 1924. In 1928 it was replaced by *Lento Molto*, which, when paired with *Rondino*, became Two Pieces for String Quartet.

Writing short homage compositions based on the name of the honoree was a popular tradition in French musical circles. Such pieces grace the catalogues of quite a few notable figures of twentieth-century French music, pieces like Ravel's *Berceuse sur le nom de Fauré* (1922), Poulenc's *Piece Brève sur le nom d'Albert Roussel* (1929), and Duruflé's *Prelude et fugue sur le nom d'Alain* (1942). Composers crafted various codes to translate these names into musical notes. Copland approached the task by connecting the letters in the name "Gabriel Fauré" to the notes of a simple scale and then devising his theme from the correlating notes. Most of the letters in the name G-A-B-R-I-E-L F-A-U-R-É translate directly into note names: G, A, B, E, F, and again A and E. But what about the other letters, R, I, L, and again R? Copland must have devised a chart that looked rather like this, and he just kept filling in rows of letters beneath the solfège headings until he had used up the whole alphabet:

C	D	E	F	G	A	B
					A	B
C	D	E	F	G	H	I
J	K	L	M	N	O	P
Q	R	S	T	U	V	W
X	Y	Z				

Thus does R fall in the column of the note D, I under B, and L under E. In this musical translation, therefore, the letters G-A-B-R-I-E-L F-A-U-R-É are transformed into the note sequence G-A-B-D-B-E-E F-A-G-D-E. Copland allows himself the leeway to alter those basic notes chromatically, and the seventh note he moved entirely. The theme of the Rondino accordingly begins with the notes G–A–B-flat–D-flat–B-flat–E–G–F-sharp–A–G–D (natural)–E, and the piece rolls with pleasant briskness at *Allegro moderato*.

The *Lento Molto* (far slower than its companion piece, at *Tranquillo legato*) is energized by the tension between major and minor modes. The piece combines strength and calm in a way that would become increasingly associated with Copland's style. When Boulanger received a copy of this movement, she wrote to the composer, "This piece for string quartet is a masterpiece—so moving, so deep, so simple." Another of its admirers was the composer Marc Blitzstein, who made a transcription of it for two pianos.

It was long believed that these two movements were the only works Copland ever produced for the seminal medium of the string quartet, but in 1983 Vivian Perlis discovered among Copland's papers in the Library of Congress a further single movement for that ensemble, which dated from about the same time as the *Rondino*. It was soon published, with Copland's blessing, under the title *Movement* for string quartet, but, so far as I know, there has been no push to graft *Movement* onto the existing Two Pieces for String Quartet, although such an experiment might be justified. All three of these early works are of roughly similar length—three to five minutes each, more or less—and the *Movement* (itself a tripartite structure comprising a haunting introduction, a lively middle, and a lilting conclusion) might stand as a pleasant finale appended to the *Lento Molto* and the *Rondino*. As it is, the Two Pieces were separated by five formative years and, although both are appealing miniatures, they cannot be said to cohere as an organic unity.

Vitebsk (Study on a Jewish Theme)

Work composed: 1927–28, completed at the MacDowell Colony in Peterborough, New Hampshire

Work dedicated: To the composer Roy Harris

Work premiered: February 16, 1929, in New York City, at a concert of the League of Composers, performed by the pianist Walter Gieseking and two members of the Pro Arte Quartet, violinist Alphonse Onnou and cellist Robert Maas

Instrumentation: Violin, cello, and piano

During the 1926–27 season, the Neighborhood Playhouse in New York City presented a production, in English translation, of *The Dybbuk*, a play that had been written some years earlier by Semyon Ansky, that being the nom de plume of Shloyme Zanvl Rappoport (1863–1920). The play had to do with Jewish folklore and mythology as it intersected with daily life of the Hasidim in an impoverished Jewish *shtetl* in White Russia (roughly, the modern Belarus). According to the theatre director and drama critic Harold Clurman, this production interpreted the play "as a kind of phantasmagoria of a past civilization, a world beautiful in its depth of feeling but condemned for its practical organization." The production was shot through with incidental music that made a particular impression on Copland.

The beginning and ending of the play were accompanied by a mournful Jewish folk song titled "Mipnei Mah." Its lyrics ran: "Wherefore, O wherefore has the soul fallen from exalted heights to profoundest depths? Within itself, the fall contains the ascension." Ansky had known the tune from his youth, when he was growing up in his hometown of Vitebsk in White Russia, a town that also happened to be the birthplace of the artist Marc Chagall. Copland was struck by the song, which he borrowed to serve as the basis for this piano trio. He named his piece in honor of the town in which Ansky had first heard it. Any romantic illusions Copland may have had about the place were eventually punctured. He told Vivian Perlis, "Years later when I traveled in the

Soviet Union, the Russians were amazed that any composer would name a piece of music after the city of Vitebsk, a large industrial complex resembling Pittsburgh or Cleveland!"

Copland casts his trio as a single movement that is sectionalized into a slow opening, a fast middle (*subito allegro vivace*), and a slow conclusion, a favorite tempo trajectory of the composer. The outer sections are grim; his early biographer Julia Smith spoke of the work's "austerity and acid dissonance." The composer makes use of quarter-tones in the first and third sections. An example is heard at the very outset in the violin and cello: a series of identical rhythmic figures consisting of a very quick note falling to a lower one, effectively an appoggiatura. In each case the first note of the dyad is "on pitch," and the second is microtonally altered a quarter-tone above or below the standard note. (Please do not assume when you hear this performed that the musicians are playing out-of-tune—although, of course, they may be.)

The Hasidic song is given voice following this stern opening, sung out by the cello in B minor. "The cello's deep tone seemed appropriate for the *molto espressivo* I hoped to achieve," said Copland. Not long after this outpouring begins the boisterous middle. "The fast section," said Copland, "is a Chagall-like grotesquerie that reaches a wild climax and interrupts itself in mid-course."

Some commentators have viewed *Vitebsk*—particularly its use of "bluesy" quarter-tones—as the culmination of several years during which Copland had been exploring ways to integrate aspects of jazz vocabulary into his works, as he did in his *Music for the Theatre* (1925) and his Piano Concerto (1926). Others see its use of folk material as foreshadowing the composer's future fascination with the folk songs of the United States and Latin America. All told, its character stands rather apart from what we think of as "typical" Copland, but it enjoyed considerable success from the outset all the same. "Performers and audiences have told me that they find *Vitebsk* a strangely moving work," the composer said.

Perhaps it was not very moving at its first performance, at a concert of the League of Composers in New York City. The composer and conductor Lehman Engel shared his memories of *Vitebsk's* premiere with Vivian Perlis:

> It resembled nothing less that a Mack Sennett comedy. The cellist was heavyset (to put it politely), and as he came on stage carrying his large instrument, he knocked over the violinist's stand. While bending over to retrieve the music, he dropped his cello, and it knocked over the violist's stand. There was music all over the floor. Finally, when they were seated and ready to begin, a cello string broke with a loud noise! It was hilarious. For some reason, the nature of the piece and its strange name continued to strike the audience as funny! Laughter was mixed with applause at the end.

Ruth Crawford (Seeger)

Born: July 3, 1901, in East Liverpool, Ohio

Died: November 18, 1953, in Chevy Chase, Maryland

Name: She was Ruth Crawford when she wrote this piece, but upon marrying in 1932, would assume her husband's surname, Seeger.

String Quartet 1931

I *Rubato assai [attacca]*
II *Leggiero [attacca]*
III *Andante [attacca]*
IV *Allegro possibile*

Work composed: February to June 12, 1931; the *Andante* was revised into its final form in 1938.

Work premiered: November 13, 1933, at the New School in New York City, by the New World String Quartet

Instrumentation: Two violins, viola, and cello

One of the United States' most remarkable Modernists, Ruth Crawford (later Seeger) enrolled in 1921 in the American Conservatory of Music in Chicago with the goal of acquiring a teacher's certificate in piano. During the second half of the 1920s she figured as an important force in Chicago's new-music scene. She earned the respect of Henry Cowell, a mover and shaker of contemporary music, who appointed her to the board of his New Music Society. In 1929 she left for New York, where a place was waiting for her in Cowell's avant-garde circle, next to (among others) the music theorist and ethnomusicologist Charles Seeger. She became Seeger's student and, in 1932, his wife.

She was devoted to her husband and seemed so awed by his impressive intellect and imagination that she buckled under when it came to her own creativity. It appears that Charles supported her emotionally and intellectually at important moments in her career; and yet one gets the feeling that as the one hand was giving, the other was taking away. We need not enmesh ourselves in this complex relationship apart from its possible reflection in Ruth Crawford Seeger's producing a very small catalogue of music, with nearly all of her most significant works dating from the minuscule span of 1930–33, effectively ending just after her marriage. Following her "miracle years," she devoted a good deal of time to her family—her husband, his son Pete (the product of an earlier marriage), and their children Mike and Peggy—and she funneled most of her musical activities into the folk song revival movement, with which all the Seegers would become deeply associated. So it is that the musical maverick who turned the heads of avant-gardists in the early 1930s ended up being most widely known for the anthologies of folk songs she arranged for children.

Her masterpiece is the *String Quartet 1931*, which was composed in (can you guess?) 1931. Crawford was not yet Mrs. Seeger but she had by then become Charles' protégée and had embarked on a free-spirited love affair with him. She had mastered and internalized Charles' major contribution to music theory, the principle of "dissonant counterpoint," a through-the-looking-glass method whereby centuries-old rules were reversed such that dissonances were now considered stable and consonances unstable.

In 1930 she became the first woman to be awarded a Guggenheim Fellowship in composition, a boon that enabled her to spend about a year in Europe, beginning in autumn 1930—which, far from incidentally, enforced her physical separation from Seeger. The first half of her stay she spent in Berlin, where she made a point of *not* meeting Schoenberg, and then she moved on to Paris. She also scheduled excursions to Vienna, where she got along well with Berg, and to Budapest, where she managed to spend a few minutes with Bartók.

Throughout this time her *String Quartet 1931* was thrusting its way into existence, and that achievement in and of itself justified her Guggenheim grant, even though she was supposed to have written an orchestral composition instead. For years it went practically unperformed, but quite a few quartets have been championing it in recent years. It answers the need for something edgily challenging in the quartet program without pushing the limits of audience frustration. Strenuously Modernist and constantly dissonant, its four movements are varied and brief, with the whole piece lasting just short of twelve minutes.

The third of its four movements (*Andante*), in which each of the instruments stays planted on a single pitch for many measures, is widely regarded as the most remarkable expanse. This section is based on a novel idea that the composer described thus:

> The underlying plan is heterophony of dynamics—a sort of counterpoint of crescendi and diminuendi. The crescendo and diminuendo in each instrument occurs in definite rhythmic patterns, which change from time to time as the movement proceeds.... The melodic line grows out of this continuous increase and decrease; it is given, one tone at a time, to different instruments, and each new melodic tone is brought in at the high point in a crescendo.

Also distinctive is the fourth movement, again based on an ingenious and rigorous structure. The composer explained:

> The movement is written in two voices. Voice I is played by Violin I, Voice II by the three other instruments. Voice I begins with a single tone; at each succeeding entry one more tone is added until, at measure 52, 3 and 4, and again at measures 55–57, there are 20 tones in the group or entry. Voice II begins with 20 tones, decreasing to one tone at measure 57. At the Turning Point in measure 57 and 58, both voices settle on a single tone, and the two processes are then reversed.

Crawford's analysis goes on to discuss the melodic behavior of the piece (the lower strings play a ten-tone row ten times through, "each repetition beginning on a successive note of the row") as well as the organization of rhythm and dynamics (Violin I starts with its single tone *ffz*, decreases gradually to *pianissimo* as it adds notes to its motif, and then works its way back to *ffz*). A lot of this sounds similar to what would become known as serialism, although Crawford pursued her ideas almost always outside a twelve-tone idiom, which was the launching pad for classic serialism. Crawford serves up high drama, yet the structural elements will be apprehensible to most listeners, at least after the underlying method is pointed out (which is why we have program notes). This technically challenging mode of expression somewhat resembles the muscular aspect of Bartók (whose Fourth String Quartet she "liked tremendously" when she heard it in Europe in 1930), and the way in which her counterpoint sends the instruments tracing what can sound like entirely autonomous lines points the way toward Carter.

Looking back on the most important of her compositions, Ruth Crawford Seeger enumerated what she termed the salient principles informing the aspirations of modern American music of the sort that interested her—and, by extension, her own music: "Clarity of melodic line; Avoidance of rhythmic stickiness; Rhythmic independence between parts; Feeling of tonal and rhythmic center; Experiment with various means of obtaining at the same time, organic unity and various sorts of dissonance." There's something endearing in the way she expressed all that: none of it cites specific technical principles or compositional methods, yet it bespeaks a spirit of uncompromising pursuit of esthetic goals. When we listen to Ruth Crawford Seeger's *String Quartet 1931* we marvel at its technical cleverness but we love it for its principled upholding of specific musical aims. It cannot be said that she enriched the world with a string of masterpieces, but at least in this unique work she made a claim to immortality.

George Crumb

George Henry Crumb

Born: October 24, 1929, in Charleston, West Virginia

Vox Balaenae (Voice of the Whale) for Three Masked Players

Vocalise (. . . for the beginning of time)
Variations on Sea-Time
  Sea Theme
  Archeozoic
  Proterozoic
  Paleozoic
  Mesozoic
  Cenozoic
Sea-Nocturne (. . . for the end of time)

Work composed: Completed in June 1971, at the composer's home in Media, Pennsylvania

Work dedicated: For the New York Camerata

Work premiered: March 17, 1972, at the Library of Congress in Washington, D.C., by the New York Camerata

Instrumentation: Electric flute, electric cello, and electric piano

For much of the period between 1965 and 1985, George Crumb enjoyed a nearly unique position among living American composers: although he did not adhere to the dodecaphonic style that prevailed in academic circles, he commanded widespread respect among those who made pronouncements about the intellectual integrity of new compositions—and at the same time, audiences actually seemed to like his music, unabashedly modern though it was. He generously acknowledges other composers whose music has influenced him deeply: Webern, Schoenberg, Debussy, Bartók, Messiaen, Mahler, Ives...and also the folk music of the Appalachian hills that he heard during his boyhood in West Virginia. He was born there on October 24, 1929, and it's characteristic of his dark sense of humor that he delights in pointing out that this was "Black Thursday," the day the stock market crashed and set off the Great Depression.

For most of his career Crumb released his compositions grudgingly on the world, averaging only about a piece per year; happily, he seems to have grown ever-more productive since 1997, when he retired from his thirty-two-year tenure as professor of composition at the University of Pennsylvania. In these works modernity is linked to timeless emotions. For more than half a century this composer has asked his interpreters to make sounds that had not previously been imagined, but the results invariably transcend those sounds themselves, however captivating and momentarily surprising they may be. At the end of a Crumb composition, a listener understands profoundly what is meant when we say that, in the best music, the notes are merely a means toward an end. Although Crumb's music has no overlap with the pabulum of the so-called New Age composers, the "cosmic" aspects of his oeuvre have curiously endeared him to many listeners of that persuasion, an allegiance inevitably strengthened by his own predilection for attaching astrological or numerological symbolism to his works. Crumb's music conveys qualities that we encounter rarely in music: a sense of the visionary, the celebratory, the ecstatic.

Vox Balaenae was completed in 1971, a few years after a commercial recording of the whistling sounds of humpback whales had been released and gained widespread attention. Crumb first encountered these eerie noises in 1969, and he was so struck by their sound that he was inspired to emulate them in this work. It is hard to imagine that only flute, piano, and cello (all electronically enhanced) are capable of producing the sounds of this piece. Crumb asks for many "non-traditional" sonic effects. The pianist sometimes plucks the instrument's strings and also produces eerie harmonics by damping strings at critical points of vibration. In his instructions to the performers, Crumb notes (as if sending the keyboard player off on a scavenger hunt): "The pianist will need a paper clip, a chisel, and a solid glass rod (about nine inches in length) for certain special effects. A strip of plate glass may be substituted for the glass rod, if more practical." (When it is called for in the "Sea Theme," the pianist is advised, with still greater precision, that the chisel needs to have "a smooth cutting edge" to generate the desired sound as it is slid along the length of a piano string.) The flutist, who is directed to stand throughout, employs a full range of "extended technique" effects and is called upon to sing and speak (though not real words) while playing; this performer even doubles as a percussionist by adding delicate touches on four crotales (antique cymbals) in the concluding "Sea-Nocturne." The cellist plays in *scordatura*, with strings tuned to B, F-sharp, D-sharp, and A (an unusual combination of pitches for tuning), and joins the flutist in a call-and-response of whistling at the beginning of the "Sea-Nocturne."

Many of Crumb's works capitalize on the overt theatricality of performance, ranging from what he has called the "inherent choreography of performers playing instruments" to relatively complex indications of costuming, set decoration, and staging. In the case of *Vox Balaenae*, Crumb advises:

> Each of the three players should wear a black half-mask (vizor-mask) throughout the performance of the work. The masks, by effacing a sense of human projection, will symbolize the powerful impersonal forces of nature (nature dehumanized). *Vox Balaenae* can be performed under a deep-blue stage lighting, if desired, in which case the theatrical effect would be further enhanced.

Vox Balaenae is cast in three sections, of which the second is a theme (a "Sea Theme," actually) with five variations (played without pauses between them). The first and third movements carry the subtitles " ...for the beginning of time" and " ...for the end of time," phrases that perforce conjure up the highly spiritual chamber work *Quartet for the End of Time* by Olivier Messiaen, for whose music Crumb professes great admiration. While the outer movements capture a spirit of timeless mystery, the middle movement serves as the dramatic heart of the piece, its theme being marked "solemn, with calm majesty." Each of the variations inhabits a unique, subtly shaded sound-world, often drawing inspiration from Asian musics, and together they cover eons of Earth's history. "Archeozoic" ("Timeless, inchoate") includes what the composer has likened to the cries of seagulls, while the buzzing drone and sinuous cello line in "Proterozoic" ("Darkly mysterious") has an Indian flavor. In "Paleozoic" ("Flowing") the cello's whale songs sound distant compared with the brilliant punctuations of the piano and the flute. The glass rod is placed over the piano's strings to create what the composer calls the "jangling" timbre of "Mesozoic" ("Exultantly!"), a passage in which Messiaen's angels are dancing very near. This leads to "Cenozoic" ("Dramatic; with a sense of imminent destiny"), where the flute suggests a Japanese shakuhachi, and brief reference is made to a phrase from Richard Strauss' tone poem *Also sprach Zarathustra*, to which the piano had already alluded in the first movement. (The later reference corresponds to the emergence of humankind in Earth's time line.) The work concludes in a hovering "Sea-Nocturne," ("serene, pure, transfigured"), its shimmering sounds augmented by the delicate touches of the crotales, and the work floats away into silent mystery.

Black Angels: Thirteen Images from the Dark Land (Images I)

I. Departure
1. THRENODY I: Night of the Electric Insects
2. Sounds of Bones and Flutes
3. Lost Bells
4. Devil-music
5. Danse macabre

II. Absence
6. Pavana Lachrymae
7. THRENODY II: BLACK ANGELS!
8. Sarabanda de la Muerte Oscura
9. Lost Bells (Echo)

III. Return
10. God-music
11. Ancient Voices
12. Ancient Voices (echo)
13. THRENODY III: Night of the Electric Insects

Work composed: "Finished on Friday the Thirteenth, March, 1970 (in tempore belli)"

Work dedicated: Commissioned by the University of Michigan and dedicated to the Stanley Quartet (G. Ross, G. Rosseels, R. Courte, J. Jelinek)

Work premiered: October 23, 1970, in Ann Arbor, Michigan, by the Stanley Quartet

Instrumentation: Electric string quartet, with the players doubling on maracas, tam-tams, and crystal goblets

At the head of *Black Angels*, George Crumb inscribed the date on which he completed the piece: "in tempore belli, 1970." The notation "in tempore belli"—"in time of war"—gave rise to the widespread misunderstanding that this work bore a direct connection to, or was even descriptive of, the United States' undeclared war in Vietnam. Semantics notwithstanding, certainly it was a time of war. By March 1970, the United States was nine years deep into what was proving a quagmire. The nation was bitterly divided, the vice president had recently dismissed antiwar protestors as "impudent snobs," and the termination of American involvement still lay five years in the future. Yet Crumb always denied that he intended the piece to be interpreted in so specific a way, although he acknowledged that the war contributed to the dire essence the work reflects and confronts. "I didn't set out to write an anti-war piece," he later explained. "But at the end of the writing process it struck me—music can do this—that *Black Angels* just pulled in the surrounding psychological and emotional atmosphere." It was, he said, "conceived as a kind of parable on our troubled contemporary world."

The phrase "in tempore belli" also serves as a music-historical reference, summoning as it does the title of Franz Joseph Haydn's *Missa in tempore belli* ("Mass in Time of War") of 1796. Crumb's compositions often reach out to figures of the musical past, particularly through verbatim quotation of masterworks. It is left to the listener to decide what meaning these references have, but at the very least they express the composer's awareness that his work is anchored in a deep-rooted and ongoing tradition. These flashes of recognition can help orient listeners who may otherwise lack landmarks in Crumb's uncharted sonic universe. In *Black Angels* the most obvious quotations are of Schubert's *Death and the Maiden* Quartet (in the "Pavana Lachrymae" section that opens Part Two, then revisited on the final page of the quartet), Saint-Saëns' *Danse macabre* (in the identically named movement), and the plainchant "Dies irae," from the Roman Catholic Mass for the Dead, which is cited several times. (Another "antique" passage in this work, the "Sarabanda de la Muerte Oscura," is actually original, composed by Crumb.) There is nothing overtly Haydnesque about *Black Angels*, although this was at the time, and still is, Crumb's only published essay in the genre of the string quartet, which honors Haydn as its first great exponent. Then, too, Haydn provided some of music's most memorable portraits of angels: the same year he wrote his *Missa in tempore belli* he embarked on his oratorio *The Creation*, the story of which is related by the angels Gabriel, Uriel, and Raphael. They are all "good angels," but Haydn's libretto included among its sources John Milton's epic poem *Paradise Lost*, which thrust Lucifer and his band of rebellious angels to center stage. They were "black angels." "The image of the 'black angel,'" Crumb has stated, "was a conventional device used by early painters to symbolize the fallen angel."

At the end of the score Crumb writes: "finished on Friday the Thirteenth, March, 1970 (Media, Pa.)." It is in no way surprising that he should mention Friday the Thirteenth, a day superstitiously associated with bad luck; that is quite in keeping with the composer's ghoulish streak—which, by the way, contrasts extraordinarily with the sweet-tempered, gentle persona he projects to the public. But it turns out that the number 13 pervades this piece, which is shot through with a web of numerological associations. "These 'magical' relationships," says Crumb, "are variously expressed; *e.g.*, in terms of phrase-length, groupings of single tones, durations, patterns of repetitions, etc. An important pitch element in the work—descending E, A, and D-sharp—also symbolizes the fateful numbers 7 [and] 13. At certain points in the score there appears a kind of ritualistic counting in various languages, including German, French, Russian, Hungarian, Japanese, and Swahili." At one of these points the first violinist and the cellist count, in whispered Hungarian, to the number 7; at another, the number enunciated in several languages is 13. Crumb spells out the most basic numerological proportions of his piece in an introductory page in the score designated "Program." All of the sonic relationships to which he alludes in that table reduce to proportions of the numbers 7 and 13. These mathematical relationships will not be audible, but they are symbolic.

This quartet, which runs twenty minutes in performance, is divided into three principal sections: "Departure," "Absence," "Return." Crumb has elaborated on their meaning: "Departure (fall from grace), Absence (spiritual annihilation) and Return (redemption)." They are separated by thirteen-second pauses. Three "threnody" movements serve as structural pillars: one to open, one to close, and one at the precise midpoint. From these the other movements are draped as ominous, sometimes funereal, garlands. All told, there are thirteen of these submovements, and through their succession Crumb deploys his forces to create an overarching symmetry. The first movement ("THRENODY I: Night of the Electric Insects") uses all four players; the second movement, three; the third movement, two; the fourth movement, one (playing what Crumb describes as "the intensely obscene sounds of the Devil-music"); the fifth movement, two; the sixth movement, three; and back up to all four for Movement Seven, the central threnody ("THRENODY II: BLACK ANGELS!"); and then he repeats this pattern precisely in the work's second half, finally arriving at the full texture again in the closing number ("THRENODY III: Night of the Electric Insects"). "Night of the Electric Insects" is the portion of this work that was fragmentarily employed in William Friedkin's 1973 horror film *The Exorcist*. The *Wall Street Journal* reported the next year that for this contribution to the soundtrack the composer received forty times what he had earned to date from sales of scores for *Black Angels*.

The string players are required to double as percussionists, enlarging the sonic variety of this quartet with maracas, tam-tams, and (in "God-music") crystal goblets filled with water to different levels and then stroked with a bow to evoke the sounds of a glass harmonica. The instrumental effects are astonishing: at one point the musicians bow their strings *above* where their hands are positioned on the fingerboard; at another, they execute trills while wearing thimbles. And yet, one uses the word "effects" with caution; it cheapens the importance of the gestures. All the sounds are meticulously calibrated and balanced to achieve overarching import. "It's difficult to conceive particular sounds independent from the work as a whole," Crumb insists. "A sound is never an effect. It must be an integral part of the whole piece. I often use the term 'ethos': it's the total work that is the sound."

An Idyll for the Misbegotten (to be heard from afar, over a lake, on a moonlit evening in August), for Amplified Flute and Drums

Work composed: Completed in August 1985

Work dedicated: To the flutist Robert Aitken

Work premiered: November 16, 1986, at the Premiere Theatre, Harbourfront Centre, Toronto, Ontario, by flutist Robert Aitken and percussionists Beverley Johnston, John Brownell, and Ricahard Sacks

Instrumentation: Flute (amplified), percussion I (bongo drums, African log drum, five tomtoms, small bass drum), percussion II (bongo drums, African log drum, five tomtoms, medium bass drum), percussion III (large bass drum)

A number of Crumb's works, particularly from the mid-1960s through the mid-1980s, were implicitly tied to sentiments involving the natural world and man's stewardship of it, and this is where *An Idyll for the Misbegotten* fits into the scheme of Crumbiana. The composer wrote:

> I feel that "misbegotten" well describes the fateful and melancholy predica-
> ment of the species *homo sapiens* at the present moment in time. Mankind has
> become ever more "illegitimate" in the natural world of plants and animals.
> The ancient sense of brotherhood with all life-forms (so poignantly expressed
> in the poetry of St. Francis of Assisi) has gradually and relentlessly eroded, and
> consequently we find ourselves monarchs of a dying world. We share the fer-
> vent hope that humankind will embrace anew nature's "moral imperative."
>
> My little *Idyll* was inspired by these thoughts. Flute and drum are, to me
> (perhaps by association with ancient ethnic musics), those instruments which
> most powerfully evoke the voice of nature. I have suggested that ideally (even
> if impractically) my *Idyll* should be "heard from afar, over a lake, on a moonlit
> evening in August."

Should the performers find themselves unable to accommodate Crumb's "impractical suggestion" about scheduling and location, the listener's imagi-nation will need to summon up the requisite spirit of environmental stillness.

As is usual in Crumb's music, all the players read off identical scores, as opposed to parts reduced to include only their individual lines. This is essential given the rhythmic license of the music (which typically unrolls without bar lines) and the complexity of musical interaction among the participants. Notwithstanding the sense of freedom that inhabits all of Crumb's music, his scores are ultra-precise in their notation, with indications clarifying dynamics, attack, or character (sometimes several at once) being attached to nearly every pitch. In *An Idyll for the Misbegotten*, the flute is required to draw on an advanced technical arsenal that includes an expressive range of vibrato, flutter-tonguing, harmonics, multiphonics (also called double harmonics), whistle tones (third-partial harmonics), key-clicking, bent pitches to achieve microtones, and trilling at a wide interval to create what Crumb calls a "turtle-dove effect." Phrases of contrasting characters follow one another, sometimes in momentary succession—a passage marked *leggierissimo* ("very lightly"), for example, turns on a dime into *languidamente* ("languidly").

The large bass drum sounds the opening note (marked "molto portentously") and quickly fades to *pianississississimo*. It occasionally swells in volume and then recedes again as it underscores nearly the first four pages of music, and it will return at the piece's end, though then in an uninterrupted *pianississississimo*. Against this underpinning the flute begins—"semplice (like a primitive instrument)"—playing low in its register and with phrases that include signature Crumb-style phrases with disjunct grace-notes. At the end of this opening solo the flute plays the first of the "turtle-dove effects," after which two percussionists enter very quietly playing tomtoms in canon; bongo drums also will be heard playing in canon in this piece.

The low bass drum dies out as the ensuing section begins. The flute now briefly becomes a "Speak-flute" (Crumb's term), the player whispering a text over the mouthpiece of the instrument so that both the words and the flute's pitches project distinctly (as the composer insists in his score). The text is from the eighth-century Chinese author Ssŭ-K'ung Shu: "The moon goes down. There are shivering birds and withering grasses." In the midst of this quotation the flute (sounded normally, not as a "Speak-flute"), plays a short, literal quotation from Debussy's *Syrinx*, a classic work for unaccompanied flute.

Musical and literary quotations are inherent to Crumb's method, expanding the historical suggestions built into his compositions. In this case, the Debussy quotation evokes a chaste nymph of mythology who flees the amorous advances of Pan and hides in a river. Pan, not finding her where she is concealed, cuts down reeds growing there and forms them into his panpipes. Possibly this reference may intensify the image of the rape of the natural world. It may also be said that this quotation connects all flutists who play this work to Louis Fleury—his surname connotes the ides of "flowering"—their great predecessor who played the premiere of *Syrinx*, written as incidental music for a stage play in which it served as the last piece of music before Pan's own death.

The energy dies down toward the end, the melodic and rhythmic phrases grow shorter, and the low bass drum resumes its inexorable, subterranean roll—a cosmic hum. The last sound is a final evocation of nature: the flute's "turtle-dove effect," now played without accompaniment and sounding very lonely.

Achille-Claude Debussy

Born: August 22, 1862, in St. Germain-en-Laye, just
outside Paris, France

Died: March 25, 1918, in Paris

String Quartet in G minor, Op. 10

Animé et très décidé
Assez vif et bien rhythmé
Andantino, doucement expressif
Très modéré

Work composed: 1893 (possibly begun in 1892), completed in August 1893

Work dedicated: To the Ysaÿe Quartet

Work premiered: December 29, 1893, at a concert of the Société Nationale
de Musique at the Salle Pleyel, Paris, performed by the members of the Ysaÿe
Quartet: violinists Eugène Ysaÿe and Mathieu Crickboom, violist Léon Van
Hout, and cellist Joseph Jacob

Instrumentation: Two violins, viola, and cello

Claude Debussy has sometimes been said to occupy a similar place in music
as Paul Cézanne does in painting and Stéphane Mallarmé in literature;
all represent not only summits of French culture in their own right but
also points of departure to Modernism, pivots to the artistic aspirations of a new
century. In 1889, the young composer wrote: "Music begins where words are powerless to express. Music is made for the inexpressible, and I should like it to seem
to rise from the shadows and indeed sometimes to return to them." Debussy's

eventual style was not to display the sort of firm, unmistakable architecture that most composers up until that time had cherished. His method would evolve into something more intuitive, with brief themes that invite little development, with harmonies that inspire momentary excitement rather than underscore long-range trajectory.

Impulses in this direction are to be found in Debussy's String Quartet, his only contribution to that genre, but here the composer is still making use of some traditional structures, as in the sonata-style movements that open and close the piece. The quartet's opening melody (meaning the succession of tones but also, very importantly, the rhythm), which is densely scored and narrow in its range, informs much of what follows, though often in greatly disguised form. Material in the second and fourth movements traces its ancestry to this theme, following the influential model of thematic transformation championed by César Franck, whose own string quartet had appeared less than four years earlier. The spirit of Tchaikovsky seems also to inhabit the simmering passion of this piece, perhaps not surprising since Debussy would have heard a good deal of the Russian composer's music during his summers working in the household of the Russian music aficionado Nadezhda von Meck, who was also Tchaikovsky's musical patron.

Although Debussy identified his piece as being in G minor, his writing really departs from the assumptions of major-minor harmonic practice and often settles into a sort of Phrygian mode instead. The third movement, a retreat into muted introspection, is set in D-flat major, which inhabits almost the farthest distance possible from G minor on the harmonic spectrum, indicating that Debussy was stretching harmonic boundaries as far as he could. We also find radical touches in Debussy's approach to scoring, nowhere more than in the vivacious second movement, rich in persistent repetitions and in subtle cross-rhythms; here the composer experiments with the rapid alternation of bowed notes and pizzicato attacks.

The last movement of the quartet gave Debussy an inordinate amount of trouble. "I can't get it into the shape I want," he complained in a letter to the composer Ernest Chausson, his friend and sometime benefactor, "and therefore am starting it again for a third try. It's a hard slog!" The two composers were accustomed to sharing their satisfactions and frustrations with one another, and, as thanks for Chausson's input, Debussy resolved to dedicate the quartet to his slightly older colleague. On October 23, 1893, he reported to Chausson: "I've sold 'your quartet' to the Barbarians of the Place de la Madeleine [i.e., the Durand publishing house] for 250 francs! They were cynical enough to admit that what they were paying me didn't cover all the labor this 'work' entailed. At any rate, it will always be a pleasure for me to see your name attached to it. It represents for me the beginning of a friendship which, in time, is due to become the best and most profound of my life."

In the event, Chausson seems not to have cared much for the piece, and told Debussy why in some detail. They were accustomed to being blunt in their critiques of each other's works, and Debussy responded with a letter assuring Chausson of how much he valued their friendship, while nonetheless adding, somewhat cryptically: "Need I also say that for a few days I was very much grieved by what you said about my quartet, for I had only made you like *certain things* more, whereas I had hoped that it would make you forget them. Well, I shall write another one, just for you, and I shall try to clothe it in more dignified forms." The second quartet never materialized, but that Debussy was serious in his intent is clear from the fact that the title page of this work identifies it as his Premier Quatuor. (Why it was labeled his Op. 10 is a mystery; it is the only one of his compositions to have been published with an opus number.) And the published score did not carry a dedication to Chausson. Instead, Debussy dedicated it to the Ysaÿe Quartet, which premiered it at a concert of the Société Nationale de Musique in Paris to no particular acclaim.

The piece scored greater success two months after its world premiere, when it was played in forward-looking Brussels at an all-Debussy concert organized by the esthetic mover-and-shaker Octave Maus, in an exhibition room hung with paintings by Renoir, Gauguin, Redon, Sisley, Pissarro, and Signac, among others. "The Brussels concert was a marvelous occasion for me," Debussy wrote to Chausson a week later. "Ysaÿe played like an angel. The Quartet moved people in a way it didn't in Paris." The compliment was sincere; Debussy did not hand them out idly. The soprano Maggie Teyte, a notable interpreter of Debussy's opera *Pelléas et Mélisande*, recalled sitting with Debussy offstage waiting for a performance of his quartet to finish before they continued the program with a group of songs. "I noticed Debussy beginning to work himself up into one of his rages," she later reported. "Eventually the music came to its end, and the leader of the quartet came into the room. 'How did you like it, *Maître?*' he asked—only to be told by the furious composer: 'You played like a pig!'"

Sonata (No. 2) for Flute, Viola, and Harp

> *Pastorale (Lento, dolce rubato)*
> *Interlude (Tempo di Minuetto)*
> *Final (Allegro moderato ma risoluto)*

Work composed: Late September and October 1915

Work dedicated: To the composer's wife, Emma Debussy

Work premiered: November 7, 1916, at the Longy Club in Boston, Massachusetts, played by A. Brooke, F. Wittman, and T. Cella; the work received its public premiere February 2, 1917, at London's Aeolian Hall, played by flutist Albert Fransella, violist H. Waldo Warner, and harpist Miriam Timothy.

Instrumentation: Flute, viola, and harp

Despite widespread interest in his work and acceptance of many of his compositions, Debussy sank into deep depression when World War I broke out in 1914. As France's prospects grew increasingly dim amid the German military onslaught, Debussy also confronted a critical health issue: he seemed to be losing his personal battle against rectal cancer. His work came to a standstill until the summer of 1915, when he took lodgings in the village of Pourville, along the English Channel. The change of scenery proved salutary. Among other projects he resolved to embark on a series of six sonatas, each for a different combination of instruments. "The reason I haven't written before," he apologized in a letter to a friend, "is that I'm relearning about music....The emotional satisfaction one gets from putting the right chord in the right place can't be equaled in any of the other arts. Forgive me. I sound as if I've just discovered music. But, in all humility, that's rather what I feel like." While making new musical discoveries Debussy was also revisiting an earlier moment in his musical development, perhaps with a measure of nostalgia. Speaking of the Sonata for Flute, Viola, and Harp, he told his friend Robert Godet, self-effacingly: "It belongs to that era when I still knew something about music. It even recalls a very early Debussy, that of the Nocturnes, it seems to me."

During the summer of 1915 Debussy completed the first two of his sonatas—the First Sonata for Cello and Piano and the Second Sonata for Flute, Viola, and Harp. The terminology invites confusion: he wrote only a single sonata for each combination of instruments, but he also thought of his projected six sonatas as a group—First Sonata, Second Sonata, Third Sonata, and so on. The ordinals are rarely used in practice, and little is lost thereby.

The second of these sonatas was originally conceived for flute, oboe, and harp. The decision to substitute a viola for the oboe adds to the work's refined subtlety, enlarging the timbral variety and providing a sonic middle ground. When bowed, the viola allies itself to the sustained tones of the flute; when played *pizzicato*, it enriches the plucked-string timbre of the harp. Though Debussy tends to use all three instruments at once, he occasionally pairs them briefly into duos, aligning more rapid shifts of timbres with quicker tempos. Even at its densest moments the sonata is slender, and its translucent melodies are sometimes little more than evanescent thematic suggestions that truly seem "to rise from the shadows and indeed sometimes to return to them." Though the composer makes ample use of polytonality, the harmony seems soothing rather than dissonant. Nostalgic melancholy pervades all three movements, most especially the languorous opening "Pastorale," in which phrases are visited only fleetingly, and sometimes (it would seem) merely alluded to: wisps of memory, perhaps. The mood somewhat brightens in the central "Interlude," in which Debussy reinterprets the eighteenth-century minuet. Though he is far from doctrinaire about sticking to the triple meter of that courtly dance, the music does skip with carefree abandon in several passages. The final movement is quite vigorous, even a bit threatening at one point; but the mere sound of this trio of instruments, so instantly evocative of a highly perfumed French style, ensures that the pastoral spirit maintains to the work's emphatic end.

Debussy's productivity would prove short-lived. By the end of 1915, his cancer had progressed to the point where he required a colostomy. This left him depleted—"I'm suffering the tortures of the damned," he wrote—and again curtailed his work. The composer Darius Milhaud left a portrait of Debussy at precisely this moment. The publisher Durand asked Milhaud if he would like to participate as violist in what was thought to be the private premiere of this work—the answer, of course, was a resounding "Yes!"—and arranged for Milhaud to call on the composer at his home to work through the score. Milhaud recalled: "This was the first and only opportunity I ever had of meeting the master. . . . He was already afflicted with the disease which was to carry him off, his face was deathly pale and his hands affected by a slight tremor. He sat down at the piano and played me his sonata twice. Through excessive modesty and discretion, . . . I made no mention of my own compositions." (In fact, the piece had already been given a private performance at the francophile Longy Club in Boston. The performance in which Milhaud participated was, however, the French premiere.)

On December 10, 1916, the composer ventured out to hear that perfor-mance of the Second Sonata at Durand's home. The next day he related in a letter to a friend, "The harp part was taken by a young lady who looked like one of those priestess musicians you see on Egyptian tombs—nothing but profile! She's just back from Munich, which she had some difficulty getting away from; she spent a little time in prison and eventually left without her harp . . . worse than losing a leg. Even though it was chromatic (not her leg, the harp she played on yesterday), which distorts the sonority rather, it didn't sound bad, all things considered. It's not for me to say anything about the music. . . . Although I could do so without blushing, because it's by a Debussy I no longer know! . . . It's terribly sad and I don't know whether one ought to laugh at it or cry? Perhaps both?"

In the event, crying comes easier. The cancer continued to wear Debussy down, and another fallow year went by before he could achieve the third sonata of his series, which he scored for violin and piano. It would be his last substantial composition; the remaining three sonatas—the Fourth for oboe, horn, and harpsichord; the Fifth for trumpet, clarinet, bassoon, and piano; the Sixth for "various instruments" including double bass—went unwritten. Debussy died a year later, leaving his chamber-sonata cycle only half completed but having nonetheless enriched the repertoire with a trilogy of near-masterpieces.

Ernst von Dohnányi

Born: July 27, 1877, in Pozsony (also known as Pressburg or Bratislava, depending on how national borders were drawn at any given moment), in the Austro-Hungarian Empire; it is today the capital of Slovakia.

Died: February 9, 1960, in New York City

Name: The composer's name is sometimes given in its Hungarian form as Ernö Dohnányi (or, as Hungarians would present it, Dohnányi Ernö)

Serenade for String Trio, Op. 10

March
Romanza
Scherzo
Theme and Variations
Rondo

Work composed: 1902 through June 7, 1903

Work premiered: January 5, 1904, in Vienna, by members of the Fitzner String Quartet

Instrumentation: Violin, viola, and cello

Ernst von Dohnányi honed his skills as a pianist and composer at the Budapest Music Academy so convincingly that in 1896, the year he graduated, his F-major Symphony won the Hungarian Millennium Prize, a prestigious national award. For the next two decades he led the busy life of a touring pianist. Dohnányi was a powerhouse at the keyboard, according to reports and from the evidence of numerous recordings, but he was not one to allow his formidable technique to serve as a stand-in for thoughtful interpretation. In 1915 he returned to Budapest, where he distinguished himself as a piano pedagogue (at the Budapest Academy of Music), teacher of composition (also at the Budapest Academy), and conductor (of the Budapest Philharmonic), composing all the while.

World War II brought a full share of tragedy: one of his two sons was killed in combat; the other was executed for participating in a failed plot to assassinate Adolf Hitler in July 1944. (This latter son also left behind a son, Christoph, the well-known conductor.) Following the war, he emigrated to America, first to Argentina, then (in 1949) to Tallahassee, Florida, where he spent many years fostering an extraordinary musical climate at Florida State University.

His impact on the international music scene was enormous. Bartók avowed that it was Dohnányi who had revealed to him the genius of the famous sonata of their compatriot-predecessor, Franz Liszt; and the pianist Mischa Levitzki, who spent four years under Dohnányi's tutelage, expressed his admiration bluntly: "I know of no greater teacher." Brilliant musicians flowed from his studio, Géza Anda, György Cziffra, Annie Fischer, and Georg Solti among them.

As a composer, Dohnányi tended to look backward to what had been rather than ahead to unknown musical terrain. Such composers as Schoenberg and Stravinsky started with their feet planted in the musical language of the late nineteenth century but quickly broke through to radically new territory. Not so Dohnányi, who from the outset revealed his sympathy with the central Germanic tradition—especially with the sound-world of Schumann, Brahms, and Dvořák—and never belied his innate conservatism, not even flirting much with the folk-inflected styles of his slightly younger fellow-Hungarians Bartók and Kodály. As a composer, he left progressive musical experimentation to others; as a conductor, however, he championed their works along with the classics. The eminent music commentator Donald Francis Tovey wrote, in 1929: "In his compositions we have art in which the form arises organically from the matter. We also have mastery, describable in academic terms and traceable beyond anything that academies have codified. Fortunately there is no need for Dohnányi to justify himself to the critics of the future by writing feeble passages to show his modernity, for he is a musical administrator as well as a composer, and the contemporary composer, whatever his tendencies, has no grievance against either the programmes or the performances of the Philharmonic Orchestra of Budapest as directed by Dohnányi."

Dohnányi's Serenade in C major (Op. 10) was among his earliest works. Composed in 1902–03 and published in 1904, it marked a step in the

direction of his mature style, in which lush Romantic textures became somewhat more reined in than in his very first pieces. The five short movements of
Dohnányi's Serenade pack in a good deal of wit, suggesting that the smiling
spirit of Haydn hovers not far away. Haydn, in fact had been born only about
twenty miles from Dohnányi's hometown.

An opening *March*—energetic, tightly wound, and including a touch
of learned melodic inversion—leads to an introspective *Romanza*, its sense
of wistfulness breathed out in long lines by the viola. The violin and cello
interrupt with a passionate outburst but then tone down to support the viola's recapitulation with gentle counterpoint. In his published analysis of this
Serenade, Tovey observes that this second movement "ends on the dominant
with an effect akin to that of the Mixolydian mode and also to the tendencies
of much recent Spanish music," specifically Granados's *Goyescas*—rather a
surprise from a Hungarian composer. The *Scherzo* is a wry musical prank, a
mock-menacing fughetto that Mendelssohn would have appreciated. (It is
Brahms, however, who seems to drop by in the *Scherzo's* lyrical middle section.) A proud but mournful theme opens the fourth movement, its modal
turns lending a neo-Renaissance flavor. Five brief variations develop out
of it, growing progressively more intense (especially in the fourth) before
concluding in a luminous glow. The *Rondo* finale bubbles along *à la* Haydn
or Mendelssohn. At the very end, a transformation of the opening march
reappears—and quite nearly disappears, in *pianississimo*—before an eruptive
final chord.

Antonín Dvořák

Born: September 8, 1841, in Nelahozeves, Bohemia, about eight miles north-northwest of Prague, Bohemia

Died: May 1, 1904, in Prague

String Quartet in C major, Op. 61

Allegro
Poco adagio e molto cantabile
Scherzo
Finale: Vivace

Work composed: October 25 through November 10, 1881, in Prague

Work dedicated: To the violinist and Viennese Court Kapellmeister Joseph Hellmesberger, Sr., who commissioned the piece

Work premiered: Perhaps November 2, 1882, in Berlin, by the Joachim Quartet; perhaps December 6, 1882, in Bonn (suggested in Jarmil Burghauser's thematic catalogue of Dvořák's works; at the latest, at its Czech premiere, which was given January 5, 1884, in Prague, by violinists Ferdinand Lachner and Julius Raušer, violist Josef Krehan, and cellist Alois Neruda

Instrumentation: Two violins, viola, and cello

As a child, Antonín Dvořák did not reveal anything resembling precocious musical talent. In 1857 he entered the Prague Organ School, where he received a thorough academic grounding in theory and performance and graduated second out of a class of twelve students. Before long he secured a spot as violist in a dance orchestra. The group prospered,

and in 1862 its members formed the founding core of the Provisional Theatre orchestra. Dvořák would play principal viola in the Provisional Theatre
orchestra for nine years, in which capacity he sat directly beneath the batons
of such conductors as Bedřich Smetana and Richard Wagner.

In 1874 he received his first real break as a composer: he was awarded
the Austrian State Stipendium, a grant newly created by the Ministry of
Education to assist young, poor, gifted musicians—which defined Dvořák's
status at the time. That he received the award on four ensuing occasions
underscores how his financial situation was improving slowly, if at all, in the
mid-1870s. Fortunately, the powerful music critic Eduard Hanslick took a
shine to some of his music and in 1877 encouraged him to send some scores
to Johannes Brahms. Brahms was so delighted with what he received that he
recommended Dvořák to his own publisher, Fritz Simrock, who took Dvořák
into his fold and promptly launched him on the path of becoming the most
internationally famous composer from the Czech Lands. Dvořák was already
entering his fifth decade by the time his career began to take off, but once it
did it flourished vigorously. In 1891 he was installed as professor of composition and instrumentation at Prague Conservatory, but he would not remain
in that post for long. That June he was approached by the American philanthropist Jeannette Thurber, who recruited him as director of the National
Conservatory of Music in New York, an establishment she had been nurtur-
ing into existence over the preceding several years and was just then managing to get chartered through an act of the United States Congress. After three
years in New York (1892–95), Dvořák returned to his native land to live out
his remaining decade.

He composed this eleventh of his eventual fourteen quartets with the
haste that typified his compositional process: running thirty-five to forty
minutes in performance, it came into being in the course of perhaps three
weeks. In this case, practical matters added to the time pressure. Dvořák composed the C-major Quartet in response to a request from the Hellmesberger
Quartet, led by the renowned Viennese concertmaster Joseph Hellmesberger,
Sr. (to whom this piece is dedicated). On October 1, 1881, Dvořák wrote to
Hellmesberger promising to carry out the commission "with all enthusiasm
and mustering all my ability and insight to the endeavor in order to provide
you with something good and solid." He also conveyed the information that
"beloved God has already whispered a few melodies to me" and that he hoped
to complete the piece within five to six weeks.

Hellmesberger therefore went ahead and scheduled the work's premiere,
though he apparently failed to communicate that fact to Dvořák, who was
quite busy at the moment working on his opera *Dimitrij*. Dvořák wrote to a
friend on November 5: "I have read in the newspapers that on December 15
Hellmesberger is playing my new quartet, which I have not yet in any way

completed. There is no choice but to set aside the opera in order to write the quartet." Markings on the manuscript suggest that Dvořák may have been exaggerating a bit, and that the quartet's first three movements were at least tentatively finished by the time he wrote that letter. As it happened, the theatre in which this concert was to take place—the Vienna Ringtheater—suffered a fire and the concert was postponed. Hellmesberger was slow to reprogram it, and Dvořák grew increasingly annoyed that the piece was going unplayed. He ended up sending a copy of the work to the Joachim Quartet in Berlin, which, after delays occasioned by the illness of its first violinist, perhaps played it in that city on November 2, 1882.

Maybe the sudden deadline explains why Dvořák derived several of the themes in this quartet from sketches and completed works that he had written earlier: the beginning of the second movement grew out of a sketch for his F-major Violin Sonata (Op. 57) of the preceding year, and the principal themes of the third and fourth movements employ motifs from his A-major Polonaise for Cello and Piano (1879). (Maybe these were the melodies God had "already whispered" to him, as he had reported in his letter to Hellmesberger.) The first movement, however, is entirely new, its triadic themes embodying a swaggering, heroic quality, though they are sometimes rendered tenderly. Right at the outset of the *Allegro* we find a typical "Dvořák sound" in the wavering between major and minor modes within a single theme; from an initially ominous introduction the violins and viola climb upward in triplets (above a pedal in the cello) to achieve a radiant glow that, at least for a moment, evokes the characteristic sound of Wagner's *Lohengrin*. But the music also points to the future; in the movement's exposition, a bridge passage between the second and third themes includes hammering figures in the high strings and a degree of chromatic vagary that deposits us practically on the doorstep of Janáček (who was, after all, only thirteen years his junior).

The second movement (*Poco adagio e molto cantabile*) recalls Schubert in its pastoral unhurriedness. The lyrical *cantilena* of its melody (again, with a dollop of major-minor ambivalence) unrolls against murmuring figures in the accompaniment, sometimes enlivened by intriguing cross-rhythms. Notwithstanding the overall sense of relaxation, certain passages develop into passionate outpourings, and the coda grows mysterious through a rich infusion of chromaticism.

This work is sometimes described as Beethovenian in the dramatic tautness of its formal concerns. That connection is most obvious in the *Scherzo*, though even here Beethovenian vigor and intensity happily cede to contrasting expanses of broad lyricism. Arthur Cohn, in *The Literature of Chamber Music*, observes of this *Scherzo*, "This is the classical language receiving a bit of national accent, for, though the form is classic, the thematic material is foreign to it." That remark that could apply to Dvořák's Quartet as a whole, or at least to everything but the *Finale*, which seems more in line with "mainstream Dvořák"—overflowing with thematic variety and even informed by a folkloric dance rhythm, in this case, the *skočná*, or "skipping-dance," from the Slovácko region of Moravia.

Piano Trio in F minor, Op. 65

Allegro ma non troppo—Poco più mosso, quasi vivace
Allegro grazioso—Meno mosso
Poco adagio
Finale. Allegro con brio—Meno mosso—Vivace

Work composed: February 4 to March 31, 1883, in Prague

Work premiered: October 27, 1883, in an all-Dvořák concert in Mladá Boleslav, Bohemia, at a concert of the Boleslav Choral Society (where he had recently been elected a member), by violinist Ferdinand Lachner, cellist Alois Neruda, and the composer (as pianist)

Instrumentation: Violin, cello, and piano

Of the four piano trios of Dvořák's maturity (he appears to have destroyed two earlier works in the genre), the most famous is surely his last, the *Dumky* Trio (Op. 90) of 1890–91. The F-minor Piano Trio was written about eight years earlier, at a moment of personal turmoil. The death of Dvořák's mother, in December 1882, had left the composer severely depressed, and, although by that time certain of his works were receiving a considerable measure of applause, he entertained private doubts about whether he deserved the accolades that were coming his way, particularly the compliments of those who viewed him as the greatest hope of musical nationalism in Bohemia. His inner questioning may even extend to the fact that the manuscript of the F-minor Trio is one of very few to lack the composer's sign-off, *"Bohu díky!"* ("Thanks be to God!"). Perhaps that's stretching rather far; among his chamber works, the notation also fails to appear on the autograph of his Piano Quintet, an altogether less troubled composition.

In any case, the F-minor Trio went through a difficult birth. Dvořák commenced work on February 4, 1883, and completed the piece seven weeks later, on March 31. It was at Simrock's behest that Dvořák had embarked on this piece, and he kept his publisher current on its progress through a series of letters, reporting that he is deciding to forgo traveling to Vienna to attend a concert of his Sixth Symphony rather than risk breaking his concentration (February 24), that he has finished the *Adagio* movement (March 7), and that he will be traveling to Berlin a few days hence and will bring the completed Trio with him (March 28). By many other composers' standards, such a gestation period might seem rapid; for Dvořák, who usually composed with amazing speed, it was tortuously slow as he found himself continually rethinking the piece. He completely recast the first movement after he composed it, reversed the order of the middle two movements, and subjected the entire piece to quite a lot of tightening before he was ready to unveil it the following November.

The F-minor Trio is a serious, sometimes stern, work. Its somewhat Brahmsian cast reflects the esteem in which Dvořák held his older colleague. The deepness of its emotions, combined with the care exercised over the details of musical logic and ensemble writing, have led many aficionados to cite this as among the works signaling the peak of Dvořák's accomplishment. Here he manages to find a balance between nationalistic elements and the abstract Germanic mainstream as defined by Brahms. The opening movement generally stresses the passionate over the lyrical, although the latter is richly represented in the tenderness of the second theme. The second movement is a folk-like polka (here serving as a scherzo) with an especially prominent piano part, and the elegiac third movement (*Poco adagio*), with its spacious cello melody, is perhaps the most thoroughly Brahmsian music Dvořák ever wrote. In the *Finale* we again find Dvořák drawing on folk inspiration, with swirling dance rhythms alternating with music of inbred nobility.

Terzetto in C major for Two Violins and Viola, Op. 74

> *Introduzione: Allegro, ma non troppo*
> *Larghetto*
> *Scherzo: Vivace*
> *Tema con variazioni: Poco adagio—Molto allegro*

Work composed: January 7–14, 1887, in Prague

Work premiered: Apparently immediately upon its completion, in private and not very well, by violinists Josef Kruis and Jan Pelikán, with the composer himself playing the viola part. The public premiere took place in Prague, at a concert of the Umělecká Beseda cultural group on March 30, 1887, by violinists Karel Ondříček and Jan Buchal, with violist Jaroslav Šťastný.

Instrumentation: Two violins and viola

Chamber music was practically a constant through the course of Dvořák's career, but he did take a break from it for three years in the mid-1880s. His return to the field was marked by his Terzetto for Two Violins and Viola, which he wrote in a week and a day from January 7 to 14, 1887.

The circumstances of its composition are charming. Lodged in a spare room of the Dvořáks' home on Žitná Street in Prague was a chemistry student, Josef Kruis, who also was an enthusiastic amateur violinist. Kruis and his violinist-friend Jan Pelikán (who played in Prague's National Theatre orchestra) would often play violin duets, and Dvořák had the happy inspiration to write a piece for them to use in their at-home sessions, the idea being that he would assist as violist. The piece turned out to be too difficult for Kruis, so Dvořák immediately penned for them another, easier set for the same three instruments, titled *Miniatures* (Op. 75a), which he completed on January 18. (Within days he would rework the *Miniatures* into his Four Romantic Pieces for Violin and Piano, Op. 75b, which were premiered at the end of March by Karel Ondříček, concertmaster of the National Theatre orchestra, with Dvořák accompanying at the piano.) When the original Terzetto was introduced to the public, on March 30, the physician Jaroslav Šťastný took Dvořák's place as violist and was joined by Ondříček and Jan Buchal, a judge and therefore an amateur as a violinist, though apparently more proficient than Kruis was.

This is a lyrical, sweet-toned piece, although Dvořák injects passages of emotional and technical variety that keep it from becoming saccharine—a potential hazard in a composition employing only high strings. The violins occasionally play in canon, while the viola typically adheres to what functions as the bass line (though in the alto register). The *Larghetto* is a graceful study in Victorian harmony (surprisingly dense when you consider that only three instruments are involved), with some neo-Classical passages built into its central section; and the *Scherzo*, rich in rhythmic surprises, recalls Schubert in both its quirky harmonic turns and its countrified vigor. The finale unrolls as a folk-like (but not literally folk-derived) tune with ten short variations, which in turn spotlight the capacities of the various players. The movement opens with recitative-like passages of indistinct harmonic direction, and the end is also strikingly ambivalent about whether it's in the major or the minor mode. The final chords are C major, to be sure, but there are so many E-flats and A-flats leading up to them that Dvořák's Terzetto very nearly earns a place on the diminutive list of pieces that begin in the major mode and end in the minor.

Piano Quintet in A major, Op. 81

Allegro ma non troppo
Dumka: Andante con moto

Scherzo (Furiant): Molto vivace—Trio: Poco tranquillo
Finale: Allegro

Work composed: August 18 to October 3, 1887

Work dedicated: To Professor Bohdan Neureuther

Work premiered: January 6, 1888, in Prague at a concert of the Umělecká Beseda cultural group, played by violinists Karel Ondříček and Jan Pelikán, violist Petr Mareš, cellist Alois Neruda, and pianist Karel Kovařovic

Instrumentation: Two violins, viola, cello, and piano

One of the first works Dvořák wrote after deciding to commit full time to composition was a piano quintet, a three-movement work in A major that came into being in 1872. The piece was premiered late that year, and Dvořák was displeased enough with what he heard to destroy his manuscript. Still, the work interested him, and fifteen years later, in 1887, having borrowed a score from a friend who had kept a copy, he set about revising the early piano quintet. In the end, he seems to have found the piece unsalvageable. (It was published long posthumously, in 1959, as his Op. 5, which is the opus number he placed on its manuscript.) In the course of the revision Dvořák became hooked on the medium, and he soon embarked on a new piano quintet, the one that, as his Op. 81, would become recognized as one of the finest piano quintets ever written, a freshet of melodic inspiration and a model of how to balance the five participating instruments.

It is a relatively long piece by chamber-music standards, clocking in at about forty minutes, but it passes quickly thanks to its elegantly constructed dramatic logic. The best of Dvořák's most endearing characteristics are encapsulated here: arresting melodies (each balancing the others with a distinct personality), rhythmic vitality, elegant scoring, and a broad emotional palette. In this work Dvořák also gives free rein to his nationalistic tendencies. Folk-flavored touches abound throughout: quick alternation of major and minor modes, smile-provoking rhythmic displacements (as in the principal theme of the polka-like *Finale*), phrases that depart from the four-square.

The cello proposes the opening, ultra-lyrical subject of the first movement (*Allegro ma non troppo*), and a nostalgic second subject is announced by the viola. This second theme is soon repeated at the mediant—that is, at the distance of a third above its original pitch, a relationship particularly associated with Wagner and his disciples (among whose ranks one would not normally place Dvořák, though he did go through a blatantly Wagnerian phase).

Throughout the movement, major and minor modes alternate with such natural ease that one begins to sense a tonic key that encapsulates both—a characteristic of many modal folk musics, and certainly of the Bohemian songs and dances Dvořák loved so intensely (and a tendency we have already noted in his Terzetto). Nonetheless, it is in the two ensuing movements that the composer's nationalistic leanings emerge most obviously. The second movement is a dumka, an ancient and melancholy form of Slavonic (originally Ukrainian) folk ballad. In this case, the rather gloomy melody alternates with sunnier sections to form an expansive musical palindrome: A-B-A-C-A-B-A. Dvořák underscores the character of his melodies through his instrumentation, with the rich-toned viola and cello reigning over the principal melody (along with the piano), and the brighter violins growing more prominent in the contrasting sections.

Dvořák identifies the ensuing *Scherzo* as a *Furiant*, though with some poetic license, since it is more a quick waltz than a proper furiant (which is an energetic Bohemian folk dance marked by the alternation of duple and triple meters). In folk usage, furiants often followed dumkas; at the very least, Dvořák recaptures the spirit of the furiant's function in such a coupling, which is to eradicate the melancholy of the slow movement. Though the *Finale* is not cast in any specific "folk form," it evinces a vigorous spirit of earthy good humor. Rather than toss it off as a mere exercise in peasant jollity, however, Dvořák works a learned fugue into the movement's development section and builds up into a joyful secular chorale near the end.

Piano Quartet in E-flat major, Op. 87

> *Allegro con fuoco*
> *Lento*
> *Allegro moderato, grazioso*
> *Finale*

Work composed: July 10 through August 19, 1889, completed in Vysoká, Bohemia. Dvořák notes on the manuscript that he completed the piece "at the house of Councilor Rus," about whom he adds, "he died after an operation in the hospital…and was buried in the Olšany cemetery…on Sunday, at two p.m."

Work premiered: November 23, 1890, in Prague, in a concert of the Umělecká Beseda cultural group, played by violinist Ferdinand Lachner, violist Petr Mareš, cellist Hanuš Wihan, and pianist Hanuš Trneček

Instrumentation: Violin, viola, cello, and piano

Dvořák composed the first of his piano quartets, in D major (Op. 23), in the space of three weeks of 1875. The medium of the piano quartet, though not widely explored by that time, proved congenial to the composer. Beginning in 1885, the publisher Fritz Simrock began urging Dvořák to consider return-ing to the genre, which he had not touched for ten years apart from revising the D-major Piano Quartet just prior to its publication in 1880. Inspiration suddenly hit the composer while he was spending the summer at his little country house in the village of Vysoká. On August 10 he wrote to his close friend Alois Göbl: "I've now already finished three movements of a new piano quartet, and the Finale will be ready in a few days. As I expected, it came easily, and the melodies just surged upon me. Thank God!" In fact he did complete it within a few days—nine, to be precise, although more than a year would pass before the work received its premiere.

This was the first chamber work Dvořák had composed since 1887, when he created his famous A-major Piano Quintet (Op. 81), and the extreme popularity of that work has served to somewhat overshadow this piano quar-tet. Nonetheless, this is a fine contribution to its medium, logically compel-ling and brimful with enchanting melodies. The work's opening, with the strings and piano working in opposing camps, raises fears that Dvořák may fall prey to the lack of timbral integration that troubles many efforts in the medium. Such concerns are soon dispelled, however, as all the players soon join to create a beautifully unified texture. Although the first movement is structured according to the general plan of a sonata form, it comes across as consisting of strongly demarcated sections, some blustery and melodramatic, some meltingly delicious.

Dvořák's biographer Hans-Hubert Schönzeler has remarked of this work that "if anything, it is perhaps melodically *too* rich in its inventive-ness." Perhaps when he penned those words he had in mind the *Lento*, since its inventive richness extends to at least four distinct themes of strikingly diverse character: a lyrical effusion for the cello, a more formal melody from the violin, an excitable bit from the piano, and a blustery out-burst from the whole ensemble. As in the opening movement, the listener had better accept the spirit of rhapsody—though never flabbiness—that compels this work.

Third movements are often dance-derived, and in this case the composer offers something akin to a ländler, the forthright Austrian dance in triple-time whose popularity dimmed when the waltz came into vogue. This is a particularly winsome example. If the opening tune summons up images of Central European peasants, the second theme sounds oddly Middle Eastern. It has been suggested that its minuscule range and its evocative augmented seconds might just as easily allude to certain strains of Bohemian folk music, though for most listeners something considerably to the southeast may well come to mind. A rapid middle section—sometimes flickering, sometimes heroic—leads to a verbatim repetition of the movement's opening.

The *Finale* exhibits a full measure of energy and rich texture. Its second theme conveys a particularly Slavic flavor, and Dvořák takes care to provide contrast through lyrical episodes in which the tempo and the harmonic rhythm slacken mightily. The composer cannot be said to under-employ his resources here: the Dvořák biographer Alec Robertson may or may not be right when he objects that "to the final page only a full orchestra could do justice," but it's indisputable that the ending invites the foursome to let out all its stops.

Piano Trio in E minor, Op. 90, *Dumky*

> *Lento maestoso; Allegro vivace, quasi doppio movimento*
> *Poco adagio; Vivace non troppo*
> *Andante: Vivace non troppo*
> *Andante moderato (quasi tempo di marcia); Allegretto scherzando*
> *Allegro*
> *Lento maestoso; Vivace, quasi doppio movimento*

Work composed: November 1890 to February 12, 1891

Work premiered: April 11, 1891, in Prague, by violinist Ferdinand Lachner, cellist Hanuš Wihan, and the composer (as pianist)

Instrumentation: Violin, cello, and piano

Precisely what does *Dumky* mean? The term pops up a fair amount as one traverses Dvořák's works and here it is again, attached to one of his most famous compositions. It's best to work backward: *dumky* is actually the Czech plural form of *dumka*, which is itself a diminutive form of the word *duma*, the name of a folk genre that, as well as anyone can tell, originated in Ukraine at least three (and probably more) centuries ago. Initially, the Ukrainian *duma* seems to have been a sort of epic song, specifically a psalm or lament of captive people; by the time the genre was widely popularized by blind bards in the early nineteenth century, the *duma* had evolved into a nonstrophic song that typically recounted a grand historical event (usually one with dire consequences for the Ukrainians). When nineteenth-century composers in other Slavonic countries began adopting the *duma* (and its name) for "classical" settings, they endowed it with a specific form: a work of ruminative character but with cheerful sections interspersed along the way. In fact, the word *dumka* is often used in Czech today to refer to a slow, pondering consideration of something.

This is the *dumka* that Dvořák put to use in many of his works, including his Dumka for piano solo (Op. 35), Slavonic Dance No. 2, String Sextet, E-flat-major String Quartet, and—as we have already seen—his Op. 81 Piano Quintet. In the *Dumky* Trio, the entire piece is a succession of nothing but *dumky*—six of them; and, in a stroke of compositional bravery, Dvořák manages to wed this inherently folk-inspired form to the four-movement structure of a Classical chamber work. The risk, of course, is that such obsessive use of a single dance type could lead to monotony; that the *Dumky* Trio has persisted as one of Dvořák's most popular compositions suggests that the composer was fully up to the challenge.

In November 1890 he wrote to a friend: "At the moment I am working on something very small, indeed very small.... These are little pieces for violin, cello, and piano. The work will be happy and sad! In some places like a meditative song, in others like a joyful dance." Within several months, Dvořák would complete the piece, his fifth and last essay for piano trio, and would play the piano part at its premiere, in Prague, at a concert marking his acceptance of an honorary doctorate from the Charles University. Shortly after that, he and his partners, the violinist Ferdinand Lachner and the cellist Hanuš Wihan (to whom Dvořák would later dedicate his Cello Concerto), included the *Dumky* Trio in a forty-concert tour throughout Bohemia and Moravia.

The piece was therefore firmly established by the time Dvořák left for his extended residence in the United States as director of the National Conservatory of Music in New York. The Simrock publishing house was eager to publish the trio before the composer left Bohemia, but Dvořák insisted that he was in no hurry to see it in print. He didn't send it to Simrock until 1894, and since the composer was in America at the time and therefore not available to oversee the details of publication, his good friend Johannes Brahms was called into service to proofread the *Dumky* Trio before it went to press.

The first three of the trio's six *dumky* are played without pause, which effectively turns them into a single movement that serves as a full-scale opening. The first is heady and impassioned, with fast and slow sections alternating; the second (*Poco Adagio*) is downright funereal, with a cello lament intensified by the violin's muted whispers (again with vigorous tempo alternations); and the third, its theme announced by single notes in the piano, is simple and plaintive. In each of these, the mood of lamentation is leavened by contrasting sections that can be downright jovial, a characteristic that was not lost on the Irish poet John Todhunter (1839–1916), whose final volume of verse, *Sounds and Sweet Airs* (1905), included a five-page poem ("Inscribed to Sir C. Hubert Parry, Mus. Doc.") titled "Dvořák's 'Dumky' Trio. Here's how he described these alternations:

O tell me what forgotten tale,
What village tale of tragic sorrow,
Breathes in the strings' reiterated wail,
Dying slow in long-drawn sighs,
As the wind's gusty lamentation dies—
Outwearied with lone sorrow dies!

Tell me why, skipping suddenly in,
With change abrupt, that freaksome strain,
With its mirth remote and thin
Has now possest the violin?

The fourth *dumka* represents the trio's second stand-alone movement—again, a doleful melody, initially given to the cello, alternating with brighter sections. In the fifth *dumka* (movement three) Dvořák reverses his basic scheme: here (not counting a few slow introductory measures) he begins with a skittish fast tempo that should strictly be attached to an interlude, and reserves the slow section for contrast in the middle, where he displays some very serious canonical counterpoint. The finale opens with a stentorian *Lento maestoso* introduction, and after considerable development and alternation with quicker material, the trio ends buoyantly, in the major mode. Or, as Mr. Todhunter put it, "Then, like a wild thing roused from brief repose, / It leaps to a sudden close."

String Quartet in F major, Op. 96, *American*

Allegro ma non troppo
Lento
Molto vivace
Finale: Vivace ma non troppo

Work composed: June 8–23, 1894, in Spillville, Iowa

Work premiered: January 1, 1894, in Boston, Massachusetts, by the Kneisel Quartet (violinists Franz Kneisel and Otto Roth, violist Louis Svècenski, and cellist Alwin Schroeder)

Instrumentation: Two violins, viola, and cello

Two of Dvořák's chamber pieces share the same nickname: the *American* String Quartet (Op. 96) and the *American* String Quintet (Op. 97, although the name is less de rigueur for the latter one). The nickname comes from the fact that Dvořák composed these works while he was living in the United States, a period that also saw the creation of his Symphony *From the New World* (Op. 95). All three of these pieces were premiered in the United States; the Quartet and Quintet were unveiled in Boston (the Quartet on January 1, 1894, by the Kneisel Quartet), and the symphony by the New York Philharmonic in New York, where Dvořák served as director of the National Conservatory of Music from 1892 to 1895.

At the end of his first year in that capacity he traveled with his family to Spillville, Iowa, an agricultural community whose small population included a large Czech component. It is there, surrounded by the dual cultural influences of Czech traditions and the American Midwest, that he composed his *American* Quartet and Quintet. Work on the quartet proceeded quickly, as was his wont. He apparently set down sketches for this quartet for three days beginning June 8 (three days after his arrival in Spillville) and then completed the first movement on June 15, the second on the 17th, the third on the 20th, and the fourth on the 25th. One can only marvel at the pace Dvořák was able to maintain when in the flush of inspiration.

Dvořák certainly had some exposure to Native American music during his time in the United States. We know that in the spring of 1893 he attended one of Buffalo Bill Cody's "Wild West" shows in New York, which would have included more-or-less authentic singing and dancing from a group of Oglala Sioux who belonged to Cody's troupe. (These particular Indians, as it happened, hailed from the Pine Ridge reservation in the Dakota Territory, which just two years earlier had been the location of the notorious massacre at Wounded Knee.) A few months later, during his summer vacation in Spillville, Dvořák encountered performers of a different tradition at a performance given by the Kickapoo Medicine Company. (The Kickapoos, originally centered in what is now southern Michigan and northwest Ohio, were by that time mostly in what is today Oklahoma.) Still, for all his interest in cultural diversity, Dvořák was not in any way, shape, or form an ethnomusicologist. He was happy to derive folkish inspiration at arm's length and subsume it to his own artistic vocabulary. This was common practice in the 1890s, when a considerable roster of classical composers (such as the so-called American-Indianists) provided American audiences with a repertoire of purportedly "ethnic" music gussied up in concert-dress clothes. This was to some extent analogous to what James Fenimore Cooper and Henry Wadsworth Longfellow had achieved in their literary works infused with purported Indian lore, or to the carefully styled photographs Edward S. Curtis began taking in the 1890s, which would pave the way toward his monumental photographic collection *The North American Indian*.

In any case, it is widely held that some of the sounds Dvořák heard at those performances by Native Americans worked their way into both of his

American chamber pieces, although debate swirls around how deep his indebtedness was. Nearly all the themes of the Op. 96 String Quintet are pentatonic melodies, including the two principal themes of the first movement—the first announced staunchly by viola against a shimmering accompaniment, the second offered more hesitatingly by second violin. These may sound somehow "Indian" but, in truth, five-note scales are redolent of any number of folk musics. Some commentators have argued that they may be considered every bit as much Czech as they may be specifically American, and one is tempted to wonder whether any Native American connection would occur to most listeners were it not for the work's nickname.

Having spent many years as an orchestral violist, Dvořák left a thoughtful legacy to the viola players of posterity: it is remarkable how often he gives that instrument the honor of announcing themes. A fine example comes at the outset of this quartet, where the violins and cello ease the piece into being by defining nothing more than a chord, with the viola entering last, enunciating the principal melody with husky richness. Following the classically worked-out first movement, the second (*Lento*) is a hyper-Romantic reverie with touches of harmonic suspension adding to its yearning quality; the French musicologist Pierre Barbier has cunningly referred to this movement as a sort of "Bohemian blues." The third movement is a dance-like scherzo (again with a pentatonic theme), with the principal section alternating with a variant on itself to create an alternating A-B-A-B-A form. Dvořák reported that some violin figuration in the middle of the A sections represents a transcription of the song of the scarlet tanager, which he heard at Spillville. Good humor reigns over the *Finale*, although halfway through, the music slows down and assumes a pious attitude, presumably echoing the singing of a hymn—perhaps at the Church of St. Václav in Spillville, where Dvořák sometimes played the organ during his summer vacation.

String Quintet in E-flat major, Op. 97, *American*

> *Allegro non tanto*
> *Allegro vivo*
> *Larghetto*
> *Finale: Allegro giusto*

Work composed: June 25 to August 1, 1893

Work premiered: January 1, 1894, in Boston, Massachusetts, played by the Kneisel Quartet (violinists Franz Kneisel and Otto Roth, violist Louis Svècenski, and cellist Alwin Schroeder) and violist Max Zach; the piece was first played in Europe on October 10 of that same year in Prague, by the Bohemian Quartet (violinists Karel Hoffmann and Josef Suk, violist Oskar Nedbal, and cellist Hanuš Wihan) with violist Ferdinand Lachner assisting.

Instrumentation: Two violins, two violas, and cello

The *American* String Quintet (Op. 97) is a sister piece to the F-major String Quartet (Op. 96), and Dvořák allowed himself a break of only one day after finishing the quartet before he embarked on the quintet. In an article titled "For National Music," which the *Chicago Tribune* published on August 13, 1893, Dvořák wrote: "I have just now completed a quintet for string instruments, written lately at Spillville, Ia....In this work I think there will be found the American colour with which I have endeavored to infuse it. My new symphony is also on the same lines—namely: an endeavor to portray characteristics, such as are distinctly American." Elsewhere in the same article he explained that his method was to internalize these folk sounds, making them part of his personal expression: "I study certain melodies until I become thoroughly imbued with their characteristics and am enabled to make a musical picture in keeping with and partaking of those characteristics....My plan of work in this line is simple, but the attainment is subtle and difficult because of the minute and conscientious study demanded and the necessity to grasp the essence and vitality of the subject."

The first movement's opening theme is a pentatonic melody. It is true that five-note scales are used in the indigenous musics of many regions, but since the composer was so forthright in declaring this piece's Americanism he must have intended this as a typically American sound. The second main theme was identified by Dvořák's secretary, Josef Kovařík, as resembling a melody that was performed by the Kickapoos. The "drumming" effects heard from time to time in this quintet, including the dotted-note rhythms of prominent themes and the viola pattern at the outset of the second movement (*Allegro vivo*), have been cited as reflecting further Indian influence. Dvořák's Indian influences have proved hard to pin down, and doubters point out that he had already begun this quintet before the Indian troupe arrived in Spillville—though unquestionably after he attended the Buffalo Bill Cody show. On the whole, the first and second movements have as much of the Old World in them as the New, including great doses of subtle counterpoint, and the minor-key trio of the second movement (which is essentially a scherzo) is a splendid example of Dvořák in one of his pensive, viola-prone moods.

There is a chance that this work would seem even more "American" than it already is if Dvořák had stuck to his original plan of using the second part of the slow movement's theme as a new melody for the words of the patriotic anthem "My Country, 'tis of Thee," replacing the traditional melody borrowed from "God Save the King/Queen." (The relevant, major-key portion begins just after the sixteen-measure "sentence" in the minor mode with which the movement begins.) Josef Kovařík recalled: "I brought a few of these [patriotic songs] home with me; next day, the Master carefully studied those texts and made some comment that it was a pity for America to use an English tune for her anthem. He sat down at the piano, improvised a tune, noted it in his sketchbook and declared: 'There! This is going to be the new American anthem for the future.'" Dvořák went so far as to tell his publisher: "In this Quintet there is, in the second movement, an Andante with variations—its melody being part of an unpublished song composed to fit an English text, which I intend to publish later as an independent composition." Noble as this aspiration was, it did not come to pass. In any case, the *Larghetto* is a set of five variations on a hushed, hymnic theme (presented by the viola) that includes minor-mode as well as major-mode phrases. The composer works out his variations with a certain "by the book" formality, in every case preserving the distinctive harmonic contours of his melody.

With the *Finale* (*Allegro giusto*) we find ourselves in a Bohemian dance hall, and the sometimes raucous material rushes headlong through a vivacious rondo. In a long analytical article he published in the *New York Daily Tribune* on January 7, 1894, just following the quintet's premiere, the critic Henry Krehbiel observed, from his typically lofty perch: "In the last movement Dvořák permits his innocently playful mood to run riot. Here he is, even to the ears of the least discerning, the naïve musician to whom the simplest themes are factors to be multiplied into a product of beauty and the seemingly vulgar is aristocratic. The spirit of Haydn breathes through the movement.... What American suggestions lie in this merry tune we scarcely dare suggest, as not wishing to mar innocent and pure enjoyment with hints of the ignoble; but that it reflects some of the pleasures of the lowly is obvious enough. And it is delightful music."

Edward Elgar

Born: June 2, 1857, at Broadheath, Worcestershire, England

Died: February 23, 1934, in Worcester, England

Piano Quintet in A minor, Op. 84

Moderato—Allegro
Adagio
Andante—Allegro

Work composed: September 15, 1918, through February 9, 1919

Work dedicated: To Ernest Newman, the music critic of the Manchester *Guardian*

Work premiered: Played privately on April 26, 1919, at the home of Elgar's friend Frank Schuster in Westminster, London; the public premiere followed on May 21, 1919, at Wigmore Hall in London, by pianist William Murdoch and the British String Quartet (violinists Albert Sammons and William Henry Reed, violist Raymond Jeremy, and cellist Felix Salmond).

Instrumentation: Two violins, viola, cello, and piano

Edward Elgar stands as the pinnacle musical representative of the Edwardian Era, the late-Imperialist moment of British history named after the monarch who reigned over it—Edward VII, who on July 4, 1904, turned the composer into Sir Edward. The son of an organist in Worcester, Elgar enjoyed a none-too-spectacular career early on, deputizing for his father in church lofts, picking up a bit of instruction on violin, serving as bandmaster at the Worcester County Lunatic Asylum, and, in 1882, acceding to the position of music director of the Worcester Amateur Instrumental Music Society. By the mid-1890s he was deemed a name to reckon with, and in 1899 interested ears turned in his direction to take in what would become the most performed—and most discussed—of his major instrumental compositions, his Variations on an Original Theme (Op. 37), popularly known as the *Enigma Variations*. The following year his oratorio *The Dream of Gerontius*, presented at the Birmingham Festival, established Elgar as Britain's leading composer, a perfect embodiment of the well-upholstered, hearty spirit of the Edwardian moment.

He continued to compose vigorously until about 1920, when his beloved wife died. After that his production fell off precipitously and he completed no further works of more than modest consequence. Many of his compositions are deeply admired by connoisseurs, including such major orchestral works as his two completed symphonies and his concertos for violin and for cello. But Elgar did not lack the popular touch, and two of his pieces managed to leap across the divide separating the concert hall from everyday culture: his *Salut d'amour* (also called *Liebesgrüss*, 1888), for violin and piano, a delectable salon piece that graced the music stands of many a palm-court orchestra in its time, and the work widely identified as the *Pomp and Circumstance* March No. 1, without which generations of graduating students would be milling about expectantly in auditorium lobbies wondering what to do next.

He completed very little in the line of chamber music, and his only contributions of note were clustered together near the end of his composing career: his E-minor Sonata for Violin and Piano (1918), his E-minor String Quartet (1918) and his A-minor Piano Quintet (1918–19). World War I was dragging on, and the composer of "Land of Hope and Glory" (the patriotic adaptation of the *Pomp and Circumstance* March No. 1) was in no way exempt from the national disquiet. What's more, he was suffering from generally poor health that stubbornly defied diagnosis but eventually seemed to be related to a swollen tonsil, which he had removed in March 1918. A month later, the convalescent and his wife settled in at Brinkwells, a country property near Fittleworth in West Sussex that they had first rented the previous year, and it is there that Elgar turned his attention to chamber music.

Elgar's walks in the sylvan surroundings often took him past a grove of ancient, gnarled trees that had at best a spooky appearance and, according to the violinist W. H. Reed, were "a ghastly sight in the evening." A local legend had grown up about this grove. As Basil Maine put it, in his 1931 biography of the composer, "Upon the plateau, it is said, was once a settlement of Spanish monks, who, while carrying out some impious rites, were struck dead; and the trees are their dead forms." Precisely why Spanish monks would have been carrying out their impious rites in West Sussex is rather a puzzlement, but legends not infrequently take improbable turns as they are passed down through the generations. It appears that these trees affected Elgar powerfully, and the legend seems to have provided inspiration for the last of his chamber works, the Piano Quintet.

The first movement begins with eerie shivering from the strings, against which the piano plays a drawn-out line, in three octaves, that resembles nothing so much as plainchant. This haunted music breaks into a galloping 6/8 *Allegro* of a Brahmsian cast, and then that yields to a *Moderato* in 3/4. Here we encounter not the sort of second subject we might anticipate. It's a quiet, undulating theme, and it sounds positively Spanish. ("Spanish, Moorish, or possibly Oriental in character," H. R. Reed called it, but I don't think we have to cast our net so wide.) One assumes that it's meant to evoke the Spanish monks, but there's nothing monastic about this theme, which seems more redolent of guitars on the Mediterranean breeze or—let's be honest—the sort of music a salon orchestra might have been playing just then in any number of watering holes (or would have been if the continent had not been torn by war). There's a lightly jazzy lift to it, which is hardly what we expect of Elgar; but then we remember how adept he was when it came to morsels like *Salut d'amour*, and perhaps it seems not so entirely out of character after all. This material, which is worked out in the course of the movement, has come into some criticism as an exhibition of bad taste, and indeed one may greet its returns with bemusement, perhaps even recalling the inarguable truth uttered in Noël Coward's 1930 comedy of manners, *Private Lives*: "Extraordinary the power of cheap music." There's no reason we can't enjoy it, though the "Spanish theme," the plainchant, and the ghostly shivers do make for strange bedfellows.

Our real motivation for being here, though, is the second movement, a statement infused with broad nobility, its melody pulling on the heartstrings right from its first presentation by the rich-hued viola (playing *pianissimo* and *espressivo*). The music reaches back through nearly two decades to capture something of the profound peacefulness conveyed in the Angel's Farewell at the end of *The Dream of Gerontius*, a fusion of consolation and aristocratic bearing that Elgar would again capture, in 1908, in the *Adagio* of his First Symphony. Wrote W. H. Reed, "It appears supererogatory to attempt technical analysis of such a piece of music, which expresses all the higher emotions of which humanity is capable. It expresses them so truly and sincerely, and goes so much farther into the hidden meaning of things than can any mere words, that it seems to be a message from another world." George Bernard Shaw, who heard the movement played through privately when it had just come into being, found it the finest *Adagio* of its sort since Beethoven.

The questing motif that opens the last movement is drawn from the first, and many further references to the earlier movements surface in this finale, including the plainchant, the ghostly scurrying, and the swaying palms. There is no evidence that Elgar's Piano Quintet is an example of program music, that it encapsulates some more-or-less specific narrative; but it does seem at least born of tangible images that, in the composer's mind, were deeply interconnected.

George Enescu

Born: August 19, 1881, in Liveni Vîrnav, near Doro-
hai, in the Moldavian region of eastern Romania

Died: During the night of March 3–4, 1955, in Paris,
France

Name: The composer is also known by the French
form of his name, Georges Enesco

Octet for Strings, Op. 7

Très modéré
Très fougueux
Lentement
Moins vite, animé, mouvement de valse bien rhythmé
(The four movements are played without pause)

Work composed: 1900

Work dedicated: To the composer's counterpoint teacher André Gédalge

**Work premiered: Apparently December 18, 1909, in an all-Enescu "Soirées
d'Art" concert in Paris**

Instrumentation: Four violins, two violas, and two cellos

If you were to look for the village of Liveni Vîrnav on a modern map of
Romania, you would not find it. The place itself hasn't fallen off the
globe, nor was its existence denied through the sort of quirk that rewrote
Romanian history at regular intervals in the course of Nicolae Ceauşescu's

Communist regime. Instead, it changed its name at some point in the last century to honor its most celebrated native son, which is why today that spot on the map is identified by the name Enescu.

Enescu proved to be a double threat, gaining renown as both a performer and a composer. His instrument was the violin, which he began studying at the age of four, and he was acknowledged as one of the leading players of his generation. He was only seven when he entered the Vienna Conservatory, where he studied violin with Joseph Hellmesberger, Jr., and chamber music with Joseph Hellmesberger, Sr. (both had served as concertmaster of the Vienna Philharmonic). He earned his diploma in 1893, but stayed on for an additional year of work with his harmony and composition professor, Robert Fuchs.

After Vienna, he was off to Paris, where the Conservatoire put this impressive up-and-comer through its paces in the composition studios of both Jules Massenet and Gabriel Fauré and the legendary counterpoint and fugue courses of André Gédalge. By the time he graduated from the Conservatoire in 1899 (with a Premier Prix in violin), his resume included an all-Enescu chamber concert in Paris, the premiere of his *Poème roumain* (Op. 1) in the same city (conducted by the esteemed Édouard Colonne), and his presiding at the podium when the same piece was unveiled in Bucharest two months later, earning him enthusiastic coverage by the Romanian press. France and Romania would exert roughly equal pull on him through most of his career. In Romania he was honored by the patronage of the royal family and quickly achieved such eminence that in 1912 he established the Enescu Prize to encourage emerging Romanian composers. When the Communist Party took over the reins of government following World War II, Enescu left Romania for good and lived out his remaining decade in exile.

In France his circle of musical friends included Maurice Ravel, Florent Schmitt, and Charles Koechlin. It was in Paris that his opera, *Oedipe*, consumed him for a decade and a half, from its initial composition in 1921 to its premiere at the Paris Opéra in 1936. It was also in France, and elsewhere in the West, that he flourished as a performer—as a violinist, a pianist, a chamber musician, and a conductor. In 1923 he began to make regular concert tours in the United States as well, appearing both as a violinist and as a conductor. It was while on tour in San Francisco in 1925 that he met the youngster who would become his most acclaimed pupil, Yehudi Menuhin.

In the early phase of his career, Enescu displayed a chameleon-like ability to compose in the various musical approaches prominent at the turn of the twentieth century: incorporating folkloric elements into classical works, building on the Teutonic traditions of Schumann and Brahms, exploring transparent textures à la Saint-Saëns and Fauré, developing a sort of neo-Classicism some years before Stravinsky and Prokofiev looked in that direction. Post-Wagnerian chromaticism came to the fore in his Octet for Strings

(1900) and his Symphony No. 1 (1905), as did the chromatic modernity of Richard Strauss in his Symphony No. 2 (1914).

During the year 1900, when he composed his Octet, the teenaged Enescu was busy with concert engagements in Paris and Bucharest (playing, among other works, violin concertos by Bach, Beethoven, and Saint-Saëns) and introducing many of his own compositions, sometimes conducting them or assisting in chamber works as a pianist. The Octet does display certain attributes that we might associate with early works, most particularly a tendency to make sudden allusions to definable styles of other composers; its occasional Wagnerisms and Dvořákisms, but especially its Brahmsisms and Wolfisms, have a way of jumping off the page. On the other hand, this early work also suggests a distinctive voice, one that would become increasingly pervasive in Enescu's ensuing works. "What is important in art is to vibrate oneself and make others vibrate," he would later observe; and, on another occasion, "Something trembles in my heart incessantly, both night and day." And so it is that a listener may be moved by a sense of nervous energy, of fluttering, that underscores page after page of the Octet. Great drama is invested in this piece, borne proudly by a string ensemble—a "double quartet"—that approaches symphonic textures. At the end of the first movement, a full-bodied piece in sonata form that shows off the composer's adeptness with tightly knit linear (sometimes even canonical) writing, the second cello sustains a low B (achieved by tuning the bottom string down in *scordatura*) for almost a full minute, as the music winds down and fades away above it.

The second section—the Octet's four parts are not separated so decisively as to merit being called separate movements—is marked *Très fougueux* ("Very Impetuous"), an unusual but absolutely apt descriptive for this music of propulsive rhythms and angular melodies. The slow third section (*Lentement*) strikes a more muted pose, again with suggestions of canon in its interweaving lines; and yet its relative quiet is far from restful, and the frequently pulsating lower lines convey even here an underlying tension notwithstanding the remarkable beauty of its melodies. Only in the final minute of the movement does the mood change, with the upper voices finally expressing only optimism as the lower voices accompany with light-hearted pizzicatos.

The levity is short-lived, and the transition to the fourth section injects the sense of anxiety that will be familiar by now. The principal theme of this finale is craggy, and it gives way to a sort of drunken waltz, rather like proto-Prokofiev (even to the extent of involving unusually wide intervals and octave displacements). Already as a teenager, however, Enescu projected a unique accent. A distinct voice is clear even among the adept reflections of worthy influences that surround it in this masterly and complex chamber work.

Gabriel Urbain Fauré

Born: May 12, 1845, in Pamiers (Ariège), France

Died: November 4, 1924, in Paris, France

Piano Quartet No. 2 in G minor, Op. 45

Allegro molto moderato
Allegro molto
Adagio non troppo
Allegro molto

Work composed: 1885–86

Work dedicated: To the conductor Hans von Bülow

Work premiered: January 22, 1887, at the Société Nationale de Musique in Paris, by violinist Guillaume Rémy, violist Louis Van Waefelghem, and cellist Jules Delsart, joining the composer (as pianist)

Instrumentation: Violin, viola, cello, and piano

While the outer world has not failed to respect the subtle artistry of Gabriel Fauré, the French have generally showered him with adulation. Though he frequently faced financial difficulties, he was widely honored at home even during his lifetime, when he enjoyed acclaim as organist at some of the most respected churches in Paris (including St. Sulpice and the Madeleine), as director of the revered Conservatoire, as music critic for *Le Figaro*, and as the beloved teacher of such composers as Ravel, Enescu, Florent Schmitt, Charles Koechlin, and Nadia Boulanger.

To this day, the French rank Fauré roughly on a par with Schumann, a credible position in light of his songs, piano works, and chamber music. Fauré's strength lay with the smaller forms, and among his compositions for large forces, only his Requiem has achieved international status. Since the prestige of nineteenth- or early twentieth-century composers tended to rest on their large-scale works, such as operas and symphonies, Fauré's reputation in the esthetically intense climate of France was—and to a certain extent still is—reflected only dimly in the export market.

The G-minor Piano Quartet falls relatively early in Fauré's catalogue of chamber music, though he had already reached his fortieth birthday when he wrote it, following up on the success of his C-minor Piano Quartet of several years earlier. He would not return to that combination again, though in his later chamber production he would work his way through two piano quintets and, at the very end of his life, a piano trio and a string quartet. (The String Quartet was born of considerable trepidation. The composer wrote to his wife, "It's a medium in which Beethoven was particularly active, which is enough to give all those people who are not Beethoven the *jitters!*") The composer's seductive, gossamer sound, redolent of the salon, does little to conceal the turbulent passion that lurks just beneath the surface of the Second Piano Quartet. This aspect was appreciated by Pyotr Ilyich Tchaikovsky, who happened to be passing through Paris just after this work was published. He wrote about Fauré to his composer-friend Sergei Taneyev: "I very much approve of him, both as a man and a musician....I've heard an excellent Quartet by him." When he returned to Russia he was proud to be the possessor of a score of the Second Piano Quartet bearing a warm inscription from the composer, "with all my affection and respect."

While remaining resolutely French in its sound, the Second Piano Quartet also suggests something Brahmsian in its overall grandeur, its disciplined treatment of inherently luxurious material (particularly in the opening movement), and some of its thematic contours (especially the propulsive second theme of the finale, introduced by the piano a minute into that movement). In this work, Fauré constantly reviews his material from new perspectives; almost nothing is literally repeated, with the transformations subtly altering as if being viewed through a constantly revolving prism. The first movement begins dramatically, with the strings in unison proclaiming a passionate theme in the Phrygian mode. Phrase endings take on fluidity that we recognize as a Fauré signature: through the composer's harmonic legerdemain at cadences, listeners are often launched into a new paragraph of the piece before they are aware that the old one has ended.

The scherzo-without-trio (*Allegro molto*), in C minor, is brief, giddy, and nervous—even frantic—overrun by scale passages and syncopations. The ensuing *Adagio non troppo* is a summit achievement of chamber music. It

makes a programmatic reference in the piano's deep, tolling figure at its opening, an absolutely unique event for Fauré, who was otherwise an undeviating
believer in music for music's sake. He wrote to his wife: "I realize that, without really meaning to, I recalled a peal of bells we used to hear of an evening,
drifting over to Montgauzy from a village called Cadirac whenever the wind
blew from the West. Their sound gives rise to a vague reverie, which, like
all vague reveries, is not translatable into words. It often happens, doesn't
it, that some external thing plunges us into thoughts that are so imprecise,
they're not really thoughts at all, though the mind certainly finds them plea-
surable. Perhaps it's a desire for something beyond what actually exists; and
there music is very much at home." Quipped Fauré's pupil Charles Koechlin,
"The viola would have to be invented for this *Adagio* if it did not already
exist." This is one of Fauré's most moving creations, nowhere more than in
the almost intolerable pathos of its muted ending, which the listener strains
to grasp even as, powerless, he accepts that it must slip away.

One would be hard-pressed to find an appropriate tone for a finale following such a movement, but Fauré confronts the challenge with great energy.
This *Allegro molto* rarely pauses for reflection; on the other hand, the overall effect in performance can be more solid than frenetic. Skittish triplets
race through the texture, punctuating the contours of phrases as if they were
stones skipping across the surface of a lake. The work culminates in a coda
where, boosted by a crescendo and the request for "still more" (*più mosso*), the
Brahmsian second theme is heard in one final transformation.

Piano Quintet No. 2 in C minor, Op. 115

Allegro moderato
Allegro vivo
Andante moderato
Allegro molto

Work composed: September 1919 through mid-February 1921, completed in
Nice

Work dedicated: To the composer Paul Dukas

Work premiered: May 21, 1921, in the Salle du Conservatoire in Paris, at a
concert of the Société Nationale de Musique, played by André Tourret and
Victor Gentil (violins), Maurice Vieux (viola), Gérard Hekking (cello), and
Robert Lortat (piano)

Instrumentation: Two violins, viola, cello, and piano

"One could no more analyze a work of Fauré's than one could dissect the wing of a butterfly," wrote the French critic Bernard Gavoty, invoking an apt metaphor. An examination of Fauré's scores—or of a butterfly's wing—reveals structures that are strong but never bulky. Their magic resides apart from their sturdiness, in the luminous, elusive beauty with which their melodies, harmonies, and counterpoint interact. Without discarding the dramatic tension inherent in the ebb and flow of tonic and dominant, Fauré often imbued the standard progressions of tonality with the tinges of modality he had absorbed through his early study of plainchant and church accompaniment. His ethic was to express much with no more noise than was necessary. The pianist Alfred Cortot, one of Fauré's leading interpreters, summed it up: "Using a language which has never tried to astonish or compel attention, he has set on his masterpieces the hallmark of a surprising and permanent freshness."

Cortot's words are à propos to Fauré's Piano Quintet in C minor, written in the twilight of his long career. His final decades had been full of trials and tribulations. Fauré had ascended to the directorship of the Paris Conservatoire in 1905. Through an ironic twist of fate, he was beset at about the same time by hearing problems that would grow worse as the years passed. In his later years, his eyesight also began to fail, and he suffered from sclerosis and emphysema. A letter to his wife, dated August 21, 1921, strikes a typical tone: "I'm suffering from bronchial, stomach, liver, and kidney ailments. I've had to stay in bed and diet, living on drugs and milk."

After fifteen years at the head of the Conservatoire, Fauré was invited to resign in 1920. His admiring biographer Émile Vuillermoz related the composer's dismay at "that painful period when the state, noticing that its prisoner, weakened by age and infirmities, could no longer perform as many duties for it, brutally notified him of his dismissal and cast him, almost without funds, into the Parisian jungle." At least this encroaching decrepitude did not impede his creativity. Fauré realized his creative height during his final decade, with a string of chamber masterpieces that included his Second Piano Quintet (1919–21), Piano Trio (1922–23), and String Quartet (1923–24)—all of these being minor-key works. Fauré's pupil Charles Koechlin wrote of the C-minor Piano Quintet, "It was with pleased surprise that people found such vigorous and youthful music in a veteran composer," adding that the work sports what, in his opinion, may be "the finest first movement of Gabriel Fauré."

Fauré composed this piano quintet from the center out, working on the two middle movements during a visit to Monte Carlo and the Côte d'Azur in September 1919. Writing on September 2, from Annecy-le-Vieux, to his wife, Marie, he remarked: "I have begun a quintet. But as yet there are only sketches. So for the moment I'm not speaking of it to anyone." Nearly a year later, on August 23, 1920, he reported that the second and third movements were complete, and that he was in the middle of the first movement. Though all of his other late chamber works adhere to a three-movement plan, it is clear that in this case four movements were inherent to Fauré's conception from the beginning. The finale followed, with the final touches being achieved in Nice in February 1921. The genesis of this work, therefore, encircles Fauré's forced retirement from the Conservatoire, but even that upheaval in his pro-fessional life fails to mar the serene ecstasy of this score. The pianist Robert Lortat, who performed in the work's premiere, kept a watchful eye through-out the work's composition. In the same September 2, 1919, letter to his wife, Fauré noted that Lortat was in the region preparing for a performance of the composer's Fantaisie for Piano and Orchestra, "which suits him remarkably." Shortly thereafter, Fauré would support Lortat's candidacy for a position at the Conservatoire, declaring him to be "not only a very brilliant virtuoso among those at present in the public eye, [but also] an excellent musician, who loves music and makes others love it." The composer therefore worked with the assurance that his quintet would be entrusted to a performer attuned to his idiosyncratic style.

From the opening page, there can be no mistaking who wrote this piece. The first notes hover in midair harmonically, ambiguous in key, revealed in retrospect to be built on the unstable second inversion of the tonic chord. But even that remains almost arguable since the tonality stays in constant flux. Not until the arrival of a fugato passage for strings, three-and-a-half minutes into the piece, does anything sound compellingly to be in the minor key, and that relatively defiant passage passes quickly into harmonic territory that is, again, more suggestive than definite. Finally the movement officially modulates into unquestionable C major for its last twenty-eight measures.

The second movement, a scherzo, similarly refuses to be pinned down in the matter of its harmonic roots, its underlying key of E-flat major being expanded through the bitonal implications of its fleet scales. Here Fauré serves the musical equivalent of many wines of Champagne or Vouvray, light yet flavorful, achieving interest—if not actual depth—through the lyric arch of its long phrases yet always dazzlingly *pétillant* as it sparkles across the palate. In the ensuing *Andante moderato* we encounter the Fauré familiar from the renowned Requiem, the artist at prayer perhaps, the virtuoso reining in his expansive abilities to achieve humbled intensity. The resources are reduced to the lightest, whispered textures, with the simplest figurations serving as accompaniment ("a murmur of pianistic droplets," the biographer Émile Vuillermoz called them).

Something of the scherzo's spirit resurfaces in the finale, whose wide-ranging string melodies are underpinned by strikingly light-textured piano writing, and in which the material is enlivened by rich use of cross-rhythms. Fauré's son Philippe recalled the premiere of the C-minor Piano Quintet:

As the work continued, passionate feelings were roused, mixed perhaps with remorse at having underestimated the old man who had such a gift to offer. As the last chord sounded, the audience were on their feet. There were shouts, and hands pointing to the box in which Fauré was sitting (he had heard nothing of the whole occasion). He came to the front row all alone, nodding his head...and looking so frail, thin and unsteady in his heavy winter coat. He was very pale.

Piano Trio in D minor, Op. 120

Allegro ma non troppo
Andantino
Finale: Allegro vivo

Work composed: The *Andantino* in August and September 1922, in Annecy-le-Vieux (Haute-Savoie), the other two movements completed in mid-February 1923, in Paris

Work dedicated: To Madame Maurice Rouvier

Work premiered: May 12, 1923, at a concert of the Société Nationale de Musique in Paris, played by violinist Robert Krettly, cellist Jacques Patté, and pianist Tatiana de Sanzévitch, all past prize-winners from the Paris Conservatoire; the next month, on June 29, it was given all-star treatment by the trio of violinist Jacques Thibaud, cellist Pablo Casals, and pianist Alfred Cortot, also in Paris.

Instrumentation: Violin, cello, and piano

Although Fauré lived well into the era that shattered tonality, his works always purveyed a refined classicism. Viewing his musical style as essentially traditional, he wrote: "In whatever realm of thought one takes—literature, science, art—an education which is not based in the study of the classics can be neither complete nor fundamental....In the wide reaches of the human spirit, all those who have seemed to create ideas and styles hitherto unknown have only been expressing, through the medium of their own individualism, what others have already thought and said before them."

He composed his D-minor Piano Trio near the end of his long career, over the course of about a half-year in 1922–23, at the suggestion of his publisher, Jacques Durand. It would be his last completed work but one, followed only by his E-minor String Quartet. Initially Fauré planned to allow for clarinet to serve as an alternate instrument to the violin, but by the time it was published the clarinet was no longer in any part of the piece's sound-world. The composer modestly referred to this as "a little trio." It is indeed short compared to many specimens of the genre, but it is dense with grace and elegance, with melodic and harmonic felicities, with an energizing momentum that belies the advanced age and poor health of its creator. All of Fauré's late works share a sense of abstraction and contrapuntal conception, and allow for a rhapsodic sort of harmonic architecture quite unlike what one customarily finds in the Germanic mainstream. They reveal his meticulous concerns for timbral coloration, and they demand the performer's precise attention to voicing, balance, and (for the string players) vibrato and bow-work.

Shortly after its premiere, Fauré received a letter from the work's dedicatee, no less a personage than Queen Elisabeth of the Belgians. "Dear Master," she wrote, "I have heard your fine trio, which has moved me deeply. This work is so great and full of the charm of poetry, and I was enveloped by that inexpressible exaltation which emanates from your compositions....Its dedication by the great, beloved Master is a precious thing to me." It was a thoughtful expression, although the business about the dedication is perplexing, since the printed score unquestionably bears a dedication to Madame Maurice Rouvier, the wife of a former, by then deceased, high official in the French government.

We sometimes forget to think of Fauré as a twentieth-century composer, which he assuredly was by virtue of not only chronology but also musical style. Certainly Fauré did not personally tread the revolutionary routes charted by such composers as Debussy, Schoenberg, Webern, Stravinsky, and Bartók; but neither did he stop extending his own path. The Piano Trio is an unmistakably tonal work, yet one needs look no further than the long-spun principal theme of the first movement—marked *cantando* ("singing")—to marvel at how Fauré maintains a sense of tonal rootedness (in B-flat major) while allowing his melody to range through distant realms, here including allusions to the keys of D-flat and A-flat. There is also something old-fashioned about the composer's diaphanous sound, which conveys a sense of restrained passion that lurks just beneath the polite surface; surely this is on display in the poignant *Andantino*. The music of the *Finale* was initially sketched to be a scherzo, and although plans for that movement were scrapped, the attendant vivacity remains. And yet, this scherzo-finale never oversteps the bounds of good behavior; it was in Fauré's nature to be ultra-civilized. The composer Albert Roussel summed it up the year of Fauré's death: "Without noise or fuss or meaningless gestures, he pointed the way towards marvelous musical horizons overflowing with freshness and light."

César-Auguste-Jean-Guillaume-Hubert Franck

Born: December 10, 1822, in Liège (sometimes spelled Liége), in the French-speaking area of the Walloon district of the Low Countries (which would later become Belgium)

Died: November 8, 1890, in Paris, France

Piano Quintet in F minor

Molto moderato quasi lento—Allegro
Lento con molto sentimento
Allegro non troppo, ma con fuoco

Work composed: Autumn 1878–July 1879

Work dedicated: To Camille Saint-Saëns

Work premiered: January 17, 1880, at a concert of the Société Nationale de Musique at the Salle Pleyel in Paris, with pianist Camille Saint-Saëns and the Marsick Quartet (violinists Martin Marsick and Guillaume Rémy, violist Louis Van Waefelghem, and cellist Richard Loys)

Instrumentation: Two violins, viola, cello, and piano

For composers, nineteenth-century French musical life was a very clubby affair; Joël-Marie Fauquet's exhaustive and indispensable *Dictionnaire de la musique française au XIXe siècle* helps guide the confounded through more than sixty musical *sociétés* and *associations* of that era. One of the groups to which Franck belonged, the Société des Compositeurs de Musique, had since 1873 sponsored annual competitions for new works, typically calling for entries in three or four different genres, which changed from year to year. Their 1878 installment invited submissions in six distinct areas, including piano quintet. Franck was in his sixth year as organ professor at the Conservatoire, but a post on the composition faculty eluded him. When a position opened up in July 1878, Franck lost no time applying to fill the vacancy. It must have seemed to him that winning a prize from the Société des Compositeurs de Musique would propitiously boost his profile at this crucial moment, and so he began pondering a piece in one of the year's designated genres. His hopes were vanquished on October 1, when Jules Massenet, flush with an operatic success with *Le Roi de Lahore*, was named to the Conservatoire position instead.

Nonetheless, Franck's mind was now on his new piano quintet, and without the possibility of a new job at the Conservatoire, the benefit of winning a prize was moot. He did not meet the submission deadline of December 31, and, in the event, prizes were awarded (to now-obscure applicants) in every category except piano quintet, for which no winner was declared.

The lore of this piece has long attached to another musical figure, Franck's gifted pupil Augusta Holmès, who had been studying with him since 1875. In a biography published in 1951, the notable musicologist and music critic Léon Vallas maintained that Franck fell in love with her and that it was their passionate affair that released a flood of inspiration in his final years. Joël-Marie Fauquet, who (apart from his monumental dictionary) published the reigning biography of Franck in 1999, looked at this legend in the cold light of day, without the gender assumptions that had been rife a half-century earlier, and found nothing in the historical record to support it. Yes, Franck held Holmès in special esteem among his pupils, but (says Fauquet) it was because she was exceptionally talented. Yes, Madame Franck shunned the Piano Quintet, but she had long since grown distant from her husband and was manifestly uninterested in the "modernity" his musical language assumed after 1870. Still, it is hard to resist good gossip, even if it's not true, and music-lovers may enjoy a telling of this questionable tale through the novel *César and Augusta* (1978) by the playwright Ronald Harwood, where it is properly consigned to the domain of fiction.

A different brouhaha involved the work's premiere, by the Marsick Quartet, with Camille Saint-Saëns handling the piano part. When the piece was finished, Saint-Saëns walked offstage and left the score—copied out by Franck expressly for the premiere—on the piano, a gesture that was considered rude and was interpreted as representing his disdain for the work he had just performed.

Vallas reports that "this precious document was later offered, bearing a second dedication, to Pierre de Bréville," one of Franck's students—a factoid that has been repeated in some ensuing Franck biographies. Again beware. In a 1935 reminiscence published in the *Mercure de France*, Bréville recounted that Franck did indeed present him with that manuscript, telling him: "In truth, this is not the first manuscript; it's the copy of it I made for the performance. I had given it to Saint-Saëns, who played the piano part and, as you see, I had written at the end (the work being dedicated to him): 'To my good friend Camille Saint-Saëns.' On departing from the stage he left it on the piano. I retrieved it and, with my whole heart, I give it to you. You . . . you shall be its keeper." At some point the manuscript made its way to the Bibliothèque Nationale de France, where it resides to this day. When the piece appeared in published form, issued by the firm of Hamelle in 1880, the "my good friend" business had been suppressed—the title page proclaimed merely "À Camille Saint-Saëns"—but the piece certainly was never rededicated to anyone else.

The Piano Quintet is precise in its contrapuntal writing and its expressive notation, and it calls repeatedly for the broadest possible range of dynamics, from *pianississimo* to *fortississimo*. No previous work in the French chamber-music repertoire had come close to the torrid emotional power of Franck's writing in this piece; his fellow-composer Édouard Lalo spoke of it as an "explosion." Fauquet points out similarities between this piano quintet and that of Brahms. Apart from both being hugely powerful pieces and their composers' unique efforts in the genre, they share the key of F minor, an unusual choice for Franck, who was preternaturally drawn to the sharp keys. Brahms' Piano Quintet began life as a sonata for two pianos; Franck, conversely, engaged himself in creating a two-piano transcription of his own quintet, though he left it far from complete when he died. And the same publisher, Hamelle, undertook the Parisian editions of both works.

The work is cast in three movements. In typical Franckian fashion, themes wend their way throughout the cyclic unrolling of this piece, evolving through ingenious transformations to take on ever new characters. For example, following a slow introduction (*Molto moderato quasi lento*), the body of the first movement (*Allegro*) gets under way with a pair of themes, the second of which—a sequence of varying intervals above a stable bass note—reappears, in a series of disguises, in both of the ensuing movements. The generally serene *Lento, con molto sentimento* comes across as an uncomplicated sort of song, with generous, lyric writing for all the instruments. There is no scherzo to lighten the demeanor of this piece—if there had been one, it probably would have come at this juncture—but the finale opens with a rather lengthy prologue, separate from the body of the movement proper, which might be taken as analogous to an independent movement, though an abbreviated one. In the agitated *Allegro non troppo, ma con fuoco*, a motif first heard near the end of the second movement resurfaces as an important theme, and in the coda the Quintet's overriding theme returns, now transformed into triple meter, to round off the proceedings into a unified whole.

M. Glinka [signature]

Mikhail Ivanovich Glinka

Born: May 20 (old style)/June 1 (new style), 1804, in Novospasskoye, Smolensk District of Russia

Died: February 15, 1857, in Berlin, Prussia (Germany)

Trio pathétique in D minor for Clarinet, Bassoon, and Piano

> *Allegro moderato*
> *Scherzo—Vivacissimo*
> *Largo*
> *Allegro con spirito. Alla breve ma moderato*

Work composed: Fall 1832

Work premiered: Shortly after it was finished, in Milan, by the composer (as pianist) with the clarinetist Pietro Tassistro and the bassoonist Antonio Cantù

Instrumentation: Clarinet, bassoon, and piano

Mikhail Glinka was so revered as a fountainhead by later Russian composers that we easily fall into the trap of imagining that he sprang into being through some miraculous act of spontaneous generation. Figures such as Tchaikovsky, Rimsky-Korsakov, and Stravinsky implied as a matter of faith that all Russian music stemmed from him—"an unprecedented, astonishing phenomenon in the sphere of art" is how Tchaikovsky described him in 1888—but in fact Russian music evolved from a more complicated intersection of traditions, as did Glinka's music itself. In the late eighteenth century, the cities of Eastern Europe—St. Petersburg, Moscow,

Riga, Tallinn—were viewed as belonging to the European cultural circuit, even if they were considerably more remote than more easily accessed cities in, say, France, Italy, or Germany. St. Petersburg was the jewel among them, and it exerted increasing magnetism on vagabond musicians—mostly Italian—during the late eighteenth century and on through the nineteenth. Italian opera continued to impassion Russians in the following century, and much of the homegrown music that began to be produced in the nineteenth century reflected deep acquaintance with the music of Cherubini, Bellini, Donizetti, and Rossini.

Glinka, the scion of a well-to-do family (its roots ultimately traced to Poland), drank deeply from this well of Italianate inspiration, but in his *Memoirs* he also recalled his early fascination with the folk songs the family's serfs would not only sing but also play when they assembled into a private orchestra on his uncle's estate. He received a firm musical education while growing up, and as a student in St. Petersburg he even took a few piano lessons from the acclaimed Irish pianist and composer John Field, who was just concluding a stint there. For a young aristocrat, however, a career as a composer was out of the question; so, at his father's insistence, Glinka passed several years in "respectable" jobs in the governmental bureaucracy. It was at that time that he became friendly with the poet Alexander Pushkin.

In the fall of 1830 Glinka found himself at a crossroads, torn between filial duty and artistic yearnings. He did what any number of post-adolescents still do today to sort things out: he took a trip abroad, in his case (quite naturally) to Italy. It was a watershed moment to be in Milan, where that winter Glinka heard Donizetti and Bellini conduct the premieres of their respective operas *Anna Bolena* and *La sonnambula*. Finally, away from his father's pressures, Glinka's musical juices started to flow freely. By the time he returned to Russia, upon his father's death in 1834, there was no turning back on his career as a composer. He would make his enduring mark on Russian musical history principally through his operas, works steeped in the Italian tradition yet incorporating aspects of decidedly Russian inspiration. His first opera, *A Life for the Czar*, met with great enthusiasm at its premiere, in 1836, and Glinka quickly set his sights on a second opera, which he would base on the satirical fairy tale *Ruslan and Ludmila* by his friend Pushkin. In 1844 he headed to Paris, where Berlioz promoted his music in the concert hall and in the press, declaring Glinka to be "among the outstanding composers of his time." The ensuing years would find him in Spain, in Smolensk, in Warsaw, and finally in Berlin. In that last city he was honored to hear the trio from *A Life for the Czar* conducted by Giacomo Meyerbeer at a concert at the Prussian Court in January 1857. He came down with a cold immediately afterward and grew alarmingly debilitated. Three weeks later he was dead, apparently of stomach cancer.

Always given to hypochondria, Glinka felt he was not in good health when he composed his *Trio pathétique*, complaining that his fingers had grown numb from touching a stomach plaster that had been applied to assist with his digestion. "But somehow," he wrote in his *Memoirs*, "I still managed to struggle with my sufferings and I wrote a trio for piano, clarinet, and bassoon. My friends, who were musicians at La Scala, the clarinetist Tassistro and the bassoonist Cantu, accompanied me on the piano, and after the finale was over, Cantu exclaimed, 'Ma questo è disperazione!' ['But that is really despair!'] And as a matter of fact I was in despair....My limbs became numb, I felt suffocated, I lost my appetite and my ability to sleep and fell into the most bitter despair—despair which I expressed in this Trio." Another plaintive accretion is to be found in the work's original edition (though not in ensuing ones): a motto, in French, at the head of the score, reading "Je n'ai connu l'amour que par les peines qu'il cause" ("I have known love only through the sorrows it causes").

Notwithstanding some soulful melodies and the rich timbre occasioned by this particular combination of instruments, we are not likely to find the trio nearly as despairing as its composer did. (One occasionally hears an alternative instrumentation of this work—for violin, cello, and piano—which was created by an editor without Glinka's involvement or blessing.) What we have instead is a short (four movements in sixteen minutes), firmly constructed, well-developed, not very nationalistic, four-movement chamber piece in which Beethovenian solidity is wed to bel canto lyricism. The opening *Allegro moderato* is overwhelmingly graceful, and it leads without a break to the miniature, good-humored *Scherzo;* here contrast is provided by a slower trio section, where the piano seems to mimic the guitars of evening serenaders, portrayed by the two woodwinds. The most unusual formal aspect of the *Trio pathétique* is the bridge that links the *Scherzo* to the slow movement; we hear it initially as a coda to the *Scherzo*, but realize in retrospect that it belongs equally to the two sections it connects. From the piano tremolos of this passage flows the slow movement (*Largo*), the work's high point. First clarinet and piano, then bassoon and piano measure out the movement's grave pace, with the full trio texture flowering only at the change of spirit to a more optimistic *maestoso e risoluto*. In this slow movement we find unmistakable echoes of the bel canto masterpieces Glinka was hearing at the opera house during his Italian sojourn—or perhaps the piano writing of Chopin, who was similarly influenced by the Italian bel canto composers. After such profound expression, which leads to the only full stop in the whole trio, the composer was probably wise to limit his finale to a modest summation that spends some of its two minutes recalling music from the opening movement.

Osvaldo Golijov

Born: December 5, 1960, in La Plata, Argentina, about thirty miles southeast of Buenos Aires

The Dreams and Prayers of Isaac the Blind

Prelude: Calmo, Sospeso
  I. Agitato—Con Fuoco—Maestoso—Senza misura, oscilante
  II. Teneramente—Ruvido—Presto
  III. Calmo, Sospeso—Allegro Pesante
Postlude: Lento, liberamente

Work composed: 1994, on commission from the Schleswig-Holstein Musik Festival, the University Musical Society at Ann Arbor, and the Lied Center of Kansas

Work dedicated: To Silvia Golijov

Work premiered: August 10, 1994, in the St. Johannis Church on the island of Föhr, Germany, by clarinetist Giora Feidman and the Cleveland Quartet

Instrumentation: Clarinet ("regular" clarinet plus basset horn and bass clarinet), two violins, viola, and cello

It was about as remote a premiere as one could imagine, but on August 10, 1994, all of musical Germany seemed to have made its way to the tiny island of Föhr in the North Sea, ten miles off the coast of Germany's northwest corner and about the same distance from the Danish border.

Getting there took some effort. From Hamburg, where most visitors to the Schleswig-Holstein Musik Festival were staying, one drove northwest for two hours until reaching Dagebüll, an unremarkable seaside town with a beachful of changing cabanas and sun-shielding umbrellas. From there travelers boarded a ferry that, forty-five minutes later, deposited them in Wyk, the only full-fledged town on the island. Rose bushes rambled up the walls of ancient cottages and spilled onto thatched rooftops. Unhurried locals chatted in the curious tones of the North Frisian language.

Somehow people made their way to the minuscule village of Nieblum and its St. Johannis Church, a Romanesque cathedral on the south side of the island, a much larger church than seemed likely or necessary for such an unassuming locale. It was in that medieval structure that international forces convened to offer the first performance of *The Dreams and Prayers of Isaac the Blind*. The clarinetist Giora Feidman from Israel, the Cleveland Quartet from the United States, and the composer Osvaldo Golijov, an Argentine journeying in from his home in Massachusetts, gathered in this isolated corner of Europe, in this hulking church that had begun as an outpost of Roman Catholicism but had long since turned Lutheran, to breathe life into a work drenched in the ancient traditions of Jewish mysticism that lived on through the *klezmorim* in distant *shtetls* and ghettos.

A couple of hours before the concert was to begin, I strolled past the church in the company of the festival's director. A long line snaked from the makeshift box office, across the lawn and down a hillock. I expressed surprise that attendees were lining up so early, since the tickets were clearly designated for assigned seats. "But those people aren't ticket-holders," the director explained. That's the line for people hoping to get tickets that are turned back in." I struck up conversations at several points along the line, which already numbered more than a hundred of the hopeful. In every case the people with whom I spoke had traveled there from Hamburg—for hours—just in case they were lucky to get a seat for what had long been a sold-out event.

Golijov embodies the national diversity of Argentina, and by extension the multiculturalism that has informed an important strand of contemporary composition throughout the concert world. Of Eastern European Jewish heritage, he grew up listening not only to European-style classical music but also to Jewish liturgical and klezmer music and the "new tangos" of Astor Piazzolla. Giora Feidman, also from an Eastern European Jewish family in Buenos Aires, had played for twenty years in the Israel Philharmonic, but his ancestors had been musicians of the klezmer tradition, and he was therefore born to carry on that enterprise. As *The Dreams and Prayers of Isaac the Blind* laughed and cried and argued and danced its way through its three movements (plus prelude and postlude), Feidman was called on to play not only the regular "treble" clarinet but also bass clarinet and basset horn, sometimes shifting from one to another in quick succession. His diversity of clarinets gave the impression of being a single instrument with a hugely extended range.

This is a seductive work, a bit more than a half-hour long (perhaps ten minutes were judiciously shaved from the piece following its premiere). It reveals a deeply rooted ethnic flavor, exquisite musical beauty, and an intense, poignant sense of humanity. Golijov has spoken at some length about the piece:

> About eight hundred years ago, Isaac the Blind—who was the greatest Kabbalist rabbi of Provence—dictated a manuscript saying that everything in the universe, all things and events, are products of combinations of the Hebrew alphabet's letters.
>
> *The Dreams and Prayers of Isaac the Blind* is a kind of epic, a history of Judaism. It has Abraham, exile, and redemption. The movements sound like they are in three of the languages spoken in almost 6,000 years of Jewish history: the first in Aramaic; the second in Yiddish; and the third in Hebrew. I never wrote it with this idea in mind, and only understood it when the work was finished. But while I was composing the second movement, for example, my father would sit out on the deck with the newspaper, the sports pages, and every once in a while he would shout, "There you go! Another Yiddish chord!"

The work begins with a Prelude, which the composer has described as "like a celestial accordion, rising and falling like breathing, like praying...like air...then the air is transformed into a pulse and heart." The piece takes form out of some inchoate, mournful matter. Near the movement's end the clarinet emerges from the texture to offer a keening phrase, in the "speech-like" style especially cultivated by klezmer clarinetists.

The first movement "proper" begins without a break, suddenly energized, with the clarinet sounding long lines above the quartet's obsessive, minimalist chord repetitions. "It's built on a single chord, rotating like a monolith," says Golijov. The movement builds up terrific momentum and the clarinet "is caught up in the gravitational spin" before returning to quiet contemplation at the end.

Quiet wailing from clarinet and first violin opens the next movement. The impression, says the composer, resembles "those Bashevis Singer stories told in a poorhouse on a winter night: the same four notes, the same theme, playing in endless combinations." But the spirit of the dance is never far away—moods are never allowed to linger too long in this piece—and the movement's central expanse is given over to an ever-escalating klezmer romp. Here the music is marked *ruvido* ("coarse" or "scratchy"), an unusual indication, but one that is also to be found in György Ligeti's Six Bagatelles for Wind Quintet.

In the third movement the composer likens the opening tones to "a shepherd's magic flute." Golijov is an enthusiastic recycler of his own music, and this movement provides an example. Composed before the rest of this quintet, it's an instrumental version of his *K'VAKARAT*, premiered earlier the same year, which originally was set for a cantor plus string quartet. The movement's origins are unmistakable as the clarinet lets loose volleys of highly decorated Hebraic cantillation. "In this final movement," says Golijov, "hope is present but out of reach. There is a question woven into the hardening, inescapable pulse: why this task? Repairing a world forever breaking down, with pockets full of screws. The question remains unanswered in the postlude."

Edvard Hagerup Grieg

Born: June 15, 1843, in Bergen, Norway

Died: September 4, 1907, in Bergen

String Quartet in G minor, Op. 27

Un poco Andante—Allegro molto ed agitato
Romanze. Andantino—Allegro agitato
Intermezzo. Allegro molto marcato—Più vivo e scherzando
Finale. Lento—Presto al Saltarello

Work composed: 1877–78

Work dedicated: To Robert Heckmann

Work premiered: October 29, 1878, in Cologne, by the Robert Heckmann Quartet

Instrumentation: Two violins, viola, and cello

In the summer of 1877, Edvard Grieg and his wife settled into lodgings at a farm in the dramatic Hardanger country of Norway, inland from Bergen. They liked it so much that they decided to stay for the following winter, too, and moved to a slightly less rustic guesthouse in the village of Lofthus. At first Grieg used the village schoolhouse as a work studio, but shortly he arranged to have a log hut constructed on a remote hillside. It was just large enough to hold a table, a chair, and a piano but that was all Grieg needed to compose, apart from solitude. "However," Grieg later recalled, "it was just my bad luck that a time-honored old footpath—about whose existence I was ignorant—led right up to the place. And the farmers—let me tell you, they found that path in no time at all! They wanted to 'listen in.' All winter, when the weather was not too bad, I had the dubious pleasure of hearing stealthy footsteps outside the house while I sat working." Just before Easter, Grieg decided to make some changes. He enlisted some fifty neighborhood farmers, stoked them with beer one fine morning, and had them carry the cabin to a more sheltered and private spot some distance away, above a fjord and affording a spectacular view of the Folgefonna Glacier. In this new location the structure served Grieg as a holiday retreat for some years. After Grieg vacated "The Compost," as the hut was curiously dubbed, it was used as a dollhouse in a nearby rectory in Ullensvang, was moved to another town to serve as a washhouse for steamship employees, and eventually made its way back to where it started from, where it can now be visited as a Grieg museum on the grounds of the Ullensvang Hotel.

On February 10, 1878, Grieg wrote to his friend Gottfred Matthison-Hansen: "I recently finished a String Quartet which I still have not heard. It is in G minor and is not intended to deal in trivialities for petty minds. It aims at breadth, flight of imagination, and above all sonority for all the instruments for which it is written." Two years earlier Grieg had composed a set of six songs to poems by Henrik Ibsen, and the first seems to have stuck particularly in his mind. In 1900 he recalled, "Ibsen's poem 'Spillemaend' ['Fiddlers']—Album III, no. 34 [Op. 25, No. 1]—captured my imagination so vividly and lastingly that I used the beginning of the song as the core motive in the string quartet that was composed a short time later [Op. 27, G minor]." Ibsen's text has to do with a wicked sprite that lures minstrel fiddlers to its waterfall by promising them the gift of music, but invariably reneges and gives them grief instead. Some have suggested that Grieg found some autobiographical import in this tale, perhaps the frustration of a composer who finds his artistic goals out of grasp; and, indeed, Grieg copied the opening of Ibsen's poem in a letter to a conductor friend in 1898 and commented, "Herein lies, as you will understand, a bit of a life story, and I know I had to endure a great spiritual struggle and I expended a great deal of spiritual energy in giving shape to the first part of the Quartet."

It is an interesting motif in that it incorporates Grieg's melodic fingerprint, the falling interval connecting the tonic to the fifth below by way of the seventh. (For a prominent example, think of the opening flourish of Grieg's Piano Concerto.) This the four musicians play in unison, *forte* and accented, punctuating their prelude with athletic, widely spaced chords. In fact, the sonority immediately following the motto motif consists of a thirteen-note texture achieved through multiple-stopping: three notes each from

the second violin, viola, and cello, four notes from the first violin. The opening quickly cedes to a more standard four-voice texture, which launches the
main section of the movement with nervous scurrying; but as the movement
progresses, such writing alternates with contrasting sections of denser texture.
The "Fiddlers" motto seems never far from the action, and Grieg transforms
it throughout the movement—and beyond—through variations of timbre,
rhythm, and harmony.

The second movement begins as vintage Grieg—gentle, gracious, sweetly
melodic, richly harmonized—but here, too, more violent interludes interrupt
the flow, and listeners will have little trouble spotting a transformation of
the motto theme, especially in the more passionate passages. It stands at the
beginning of the third movement as well, again announced in big, muscular
chords. Nonetheless, this *Intermezzo*, thanks especially to its ingratiating trio
section, suggests on the whole a folk tune, the sort of piece the Hardanger
farmers who eavesdropped on its creation might have danced to on their
nights off. The motto motif is prominent in the *Finale* as well, both in the
introduction—where it is tossed down successively through the entire range
of the quartet, from the first violin at the top to the cello at the bottom—and
in the concluding coda. In between comes what Grieg describes as a saltarello, a vivacious Italian folk dance, although this may be the most Nordic
sounding saltarello ever penned.

A quartet headed by Robert Heckmann, concertmaster of the orchestra
in Cologne, introduced the piece on October 29, 1878. A year later Grieg
was delighted to receive a letter from Heckmann saying (as Grieg related to
someone else) "that after a performance of my String Quartet at a gathering
of musicians in Wiesbaden, Liszt came up to him and spoke at length and in
detail about the deep impression the quartet had made and the significance
it had. He said, 'Not for a long time has a new work—especially a string
quartet—interested me so deeply as precisely this singular, excellent work by
Grieg.'" Liszt was one of many composers who admired this work. In 1888
Grieg met Tchaikovsky at a private concert that included a performance of
this quartet, and the Russian expressed such enthusiasm that Grieg wrote
to a colleague, "In Tchaikovsky I have gained a warm friend for my music."
The same year marked the beginning of what would become a voluminous
correspondence between Grieg and Frederick Delius. The first letter in their
eighteen-year exchange was occasioned by this piece; Delius began, "I should
like to let you know what pleasure your Quartet gave me & in what a strange
mood it left me."

Nonetheless, it is a sad fact that even though Grieg's String Quartet was
a popular success from the outset it was treated roughly by the critics, largely
due to what they considered "orchestral" textures unbecoming of a string
quartet. Grieg's usual publisher, the Peters firm in Leipzig, was so swayed by

the negative reviews that it chose not to issue the piece. (A smaller firm did instead, and Peters ruefully purchased it from that company several years later, at very considerable expense.) Some suggested that the piece might succeed better with a different chamber medium. But when Grieg asked Heckmann for his thoughts on the matter, the violinist, writing on behalf of the entire membership of his quartet, insisted: "In our unanimous opinion there is not the slightest reason for rewriting your work either as a piano quartet or a string quintet. The sound effects in all four movements are characteristic of, and designed for, string instruments rather than the piano...; it would be a pity if the quartet were to lose its present sonority and characteristic form." Critical hostility would stalk the composer for years, and in 1901 he wrote to his friend Robert Henriques about further bad reviews that attended a group of songs he had recently written. "When I saw all these scornful dismissals of my songs," wrote Grieg, "I felt the same as I once did in Leipzig when, after the premiere of my String Quartet in G minor, all the critics trashed it. I had given my best, my very soul, and I received nothing but scorn. I was so sad that I wanted to burn my piece. But time has proven that the critics were wrong."

Franz Joseph Haydn

Born: March 31, 1732, in Rohrau, Lower Austria

Died: May 31, 1809, in Vienna, Austria

Hob. listings: As most of Haydn's major chamber works were published during his lifetime, their opus numbers provide a generally accurate indication of chronology. His oeuvre was put into more all-inclusive order by the Dutch musicologist Anthony van Hoboken, whose thematic catalogue of Haydn's works (*Joseph Haydn: Thematisch-bibliographisches Werkverzeichnis*) was published in two volumes in 1957 and 1971. Though much Haydn research has been carried out since then, these volumes remain invaluable, and they represent an essential step in unraveling the confusion that for so long rendered Haydn's output of nearly fifteen hundred pieces largely inaccessible to performers and audiences. Hoboken arranged Haydn's works in categories by genre (denoted by a Roman numeral), and then the entries within each genre chronologically. String quartets, for example, make up category III; the *Emperor* Quartet is listed as Hob. III:77, meaning it is the seventy-seventh string quartet Haydn composed.

String Quartet in F minor, Op. 20, No. 5 (Hob. III:35)

Allegro moderato
Menuetto—Trio
Adagio
Finale: Fuga a due soggetti

Work composed: 1772

Work dedicated: Haydn's Op. 20 Quartets carried no dedication when they were first published, in 1772, but when a new edition was brought out, in 1800, Haydn added a dedication to Prince Nikolaus Zmeskall von Domanovecz, Secretary of the Hungarian Chancellery in Vienna and an amateur cellist, to whom Beethoven's *Quartett serioso* would also be inscribed.

Work premiered: Not known

Instrumentation: Two violins, viola, and cello

F ranz Joseph Haydn took the most momentous step in his career when, on May 1, 1761, he entered the service of Prince Paul Anton Esterházy as Vice-Kapellmeister. In that capacity he traveled with Paul Anton and his successors to spend time at the court's palace in Vienna and at its summer residences in Eisenstadt (some thirty miles to the southeast) and the castle of Kitsee, overlooking the Danube.

Paul Anton died not quite a year into Haydn's tenure. It was tragic that the man who set the stage for Haydn's remarkable flowering should not live to enjoy the fruits of his efforts. But the Esterházy dynasty persisted, with Paul Anton's brother, Nikolaus, succeeding him as ruler of the family's estates. Nikolaus spent freely when it came to entertainment, acquiring the nickname Nikolaus "the Magnificent," thanks to the lavish festivities he underwrote for occasions of special political or social significance. In 1766, Haydn was elevated to the post of Kapellmeister, overseeing music in all genres, sacred as well as secular. Through many ensuing years Haydn labored assiduously for the Esterházy court, and his music began to leak out into the musical mainstream of Europe. No one was more surprised than Haydn himself to discover that he gradually became the most famous and universally respected composer in all of Europe. Commissions arrived from Paris and from distant Spain, and invitations were extended to Haydn for visits even to the heady musical capital of London. Although he avidly took on freelance commissions—some of his mature string quartets seem to have been written for non-Esterházy music-lovers—he stayed at home for nearly three decades, until the death of Prince Nikolaus in 1790 changed the cultural climate of the court and released Haydn to explore the wider world.

String quartets occupied Haydn for his entire mature career, from early works penned around the time he signed on with the Esterházys until his last, unfinished quartet, in D minor, a two-movement torso he wrote in 1803, when he was seventy-one. Between 1770 and 1772 he had pretty much focused his activities on composing opera, this in response to his Prince's opening a theatre at his new castle palace at Esterháza, Hungary. But around those years he also produced three sets of string quartets that demonstrate an increasing finesse in working in what would become the most exacting of genres. Each of these sets—Op. 9 (ca. 1770–71), Op. 17 (1771), and Op. 20 (1772)—contained six separate quartets (or divertimentos, as Haydn was calling them at that point). Whether he composed these for use at the Esterházy court or for musical colleagues or patrons in Vienna remains unclear. What is certain is that these three sets were the first to solidify the genre into its Classical four-movement form, with a pair of quick outer movements framing a minuet and a slow movement.

The Op. 20 String Quartets became known as the *Sun* Quartets thanks to the image that graced the cover of the first edition, which appeared in 1774. They generally surpass any that came before in overall dimensions, expressive range, and musical sophistication. One of two from the Op. 20 set that is composed in a minor key (the other is the Third, in G minor), the Fifth displays many characteristics of the hyper-emotive aesthetic movement known as *Sturm und Drang* (Storm and Stress), which would shortly be seized by European literary types, particularly those in German-speaking lands. The name originally belonged to a play by Maximilian Klinger; the work had initially sported a different title, but Klinger renamed it *Sturm und Drang* in 1776 and it became a keystone of the style. *Sturm und Drang* literature flourished for only a brief span, perhaps two decades from about 1767 to 1786, during which time it achieved pinnacles in such works as Goethe's *Götz von Berlichingen* (1773) and *Die Leiden des jungen Werthers* (1774), as well as Schillers' *Die Räuber* (1781).

It used to be accepted as indisputable that Haydn's minor-key works of the years surrounding 1770 were a musical expression of the *Sturm und Drang* literary esthetic. In recent decades, however, some scholars have argued that any connection is coincidental, maintaining that Haydn's veering into this style was no more than an outgrowth of his abstracted musical inclinations. Indeed, many of Haydn's scores from this period display no particular *Sturm und Drang* esthetic; those that do may simply reflect his experiments with what might prove interesting and successful when writing in a minor key, which, in Haydn, is not very common. In any case, a number of Haydn's works from around 1770 do share histrionic characteristics apart from their use of minor mode, including rhythmic syncopation, unanticipated modulations, fragmented themes, "sighing" melodic figures, and violent dynamic contrasts.

At the outset of the F-minor String Quartet, the first violin sets the tone of intensity by pouring out an emotionally charged melody, in its deep register, over a rich accompaniment of the lower strings. The tension relaxes a good deal with the more cheerful second theme, in the major mode, which is presented by all four instruments together, but even here chromatic inflections lend a deeper hue. The passion returns in force for the movement's conclusion, especially its searing coda.

The inner movements of string quartets—the minuet and the slow movement—would eventually settle into the opposite arrangement as a matter of standard practice. But in the early years of the string quartet, it was considerably more likely for them to unroll in fast-slow order, as they do here. Here, the minuet sticks to *Sturm und Drang* orthodoxy and displays none of the lightheartedness we expect of dance movements. The contrasting trio provides respite, to be sure, but on the whole the first movement's restlessness perseveres through this second movement.

The spirit of the dance is actually more evident in the *Adagio*, which is an old-fashioned siciliano in disguise, its simple and leisurely melody largely entrusted to the first violin (which effects considerable melodic elaboration). Haydn, however, has a virtuosic tour de force up his sleeve, and he reveals it in the *Finale*, a technically impeccable fugue built on two independent subjects. The first, which the first violin introduces at the outset, is a dramatic theme made up of wide leaps of intervals: its Baroque ancestors include the chorus "And with His stripes we are healed," from Handel's *Messiah* and the A-minor Fugue from Book Two of Bach's *Well-Tempered Clavier*. The second subject is enunciated before the first is finished; it's a quicker, mostly stepwise melody sounded initially by the viola. Haydn weaves these two subjects into a large tapestry of counterpoint, leading them through a wide palette of modulations. The composer keeps all four instruments active in an atmosphere of intense concentration, building up tension and ever thicker complexity before two powerful chords ring out to signal that this highly "intellectual" movement—and one of Haydn's most fascinating quartets—has reached its end.

String Quartet in E-flat major, Op. 33, No. 2, *Joke* (Hob. III:38)

> *Allegro moderato cantabile*
> *Scherzo: Allegro—Trio*
> *Largo e sostenuto*
> *Presto*

Work composed: 1781

Work dedicated: Haydn's Op. 33 Quartets carried no dedication when they were first published, in 1772, but when a new edition was brought out, in 1796, Haydn added a dedication to the Russian Grand Duke Paul Petrovich.

Work premiered: Possibly on December 25, 1781, at the Viennese home of Grand Duke Paul's wife, the Grand Duchess Maria Feodorovna, by the violinists Luigi Tomasini and Franz Asplmayr, violist Thaddäus Huber, and cellist Joseph Weigl

Instrumentation: Two violins, viola, and cello

The year 1782 marked a watershed for the genre of the string quartet. That April the Viennese publishing firm of Artaria issued a set of six new quartets by Franz Joseph Haydn to which it attached the opus number 33. Haydn had composed these quartets the preceding year, and shortly after completing them he sent manuscripts to a number of well-heeled music lovers whom he hoped would respond with honoraria prior to the formal publication of the quartets in Vienna. As part of that exploratory process, he provided copies to at least three potential patrons on December 3, 1781, with accompanying letters that repeated substantially the same "pitch": "As a great patron and connoisseur of music, I take the liberty of humbly offering Your Reverence and Grace my brand new à quadro [Quartets] for 2 violins, viola et violoncello concertante correctly copied, at a subscription price of 6 ducats. They are written in a new and special way, for I have not composed any for 10 years. The noble subscribers who live abroad will receive their copies before I issue them here. I beg for your favor, and a gracious acceptance of your offer." In the event, Artaria advertised the works' formal publication earlier than Haydn had expected it would. This led to a minor contretemps, since it put the composer in the embarrassing position of not yet having supplied his foreign subscribers with their manuscript copies before the published version appeared. A publication delay was negotiated, and Haydn proved himself ever the gentleman by writing promptly to Artaria to smooth over the misunderstanding: "Well, it happened that way; another time both of us will be more cautious." Haydn's behavior was rather less unimpeachable when he promptly sold the set to a second publisher, Hummel, and then, when Artaria protested, tried to lay the blame (illogically) on Artaria's presumably forgiven rush to publication several months before.

The set carried no dedication in its original edition, but an Artaria edition from the beginning of the nineteenth century is printed with a dedication "To the Grand Duke of Russia." Whether this was Haydn-approved or not we don't know. This would have referred to Grand Duke Paul (later Czar Paul I), and it is because of this dedication that the set became known as the *Russian* Quartets. Paul and his wife, the Grand Duchess Maria Feodorovna, were visiting Vienna in late 1781, and at least some of the Op. 33 quartets were first played at the Grand Duchess's apartments there on Christmas Day of 1781. The *Pressburger Zeitung* reported that their performance "was received with gracious applause by the illustrious audience, who were pleased to present Herr Haydn, as composer, with a magnificent enameled golden box set with brilliants, and each of the other four musicians with a golden snuff-box."

The Quartet in E-flat major opens with a sense of cheerful good humor that is entirely characteristic of the set. The "cantabile" of its marking *Allegro moderato cantabile* appears in some editions and not in others, but it would be hard to imagine conveying the principal melody in anything but a singing, "cantabile" style. This is the only sonata form we will encounter in this quartet; in Op. 33, Haydn effectively declares that sonata form is for first movements only. The movement's form unrolls without complication, and its development section is especially well wrought, with all four instruments exploring the principal theme in close imitation.

The second movement is quick. The standard practice of the time would have cast this section as a minuet, and what Haydn supplies looks on the page like a minuet, at least at a quick glance; if you did not see that it is labeled *Scherzo*, it would not enter your mind that something significant is going on here, at least conceptually. And yet surely Haydn meant something by using this nomenclature, which he employs consistently through the Op. 33 set. (An alternative nickname for this group, in fact, is *Gli scherzi*—"The Scherzos." Still another, used in German-speaking lands, is *Jungfern*—"Young Ladies"—which derives from the fact that the early Hummel edition of Op. 33 put an illustration of a comely maiden on the cover.) Sometimes musicians play this movement as if it were a minuet pure and simple; but those who try to invest it with an extra measure of vigor or jollity would seem to be going down the right path, a path that will eventually lead to Beethoven. The trio section takes the first violin up to the limits of what would have been considered normal string-quartet range. One often hears the trio's melody played with comical portamentos. They're not in the score, but they might support the scherzo idea Haydn was after.

The slow movement is particularly elegant. It opens with the viola playing a spacious melody, supported by the cello; and as soon as they reach the melody's end the two violins echo this opening, but with the cello adding a nervous flutter below. Powerful chords from the full ensemble interrupt occasionally, but on the whole this movement flows through to its coda unscathed.

It is the finale that gave rise to the nickname *Joke* that is widely attached to this quartet in English-speaking countries. The German-turned-British musicologist Hans Keller, who wrote a book on Haydn's quartets, recalled the shocked outrage he felt when he first countenanced this nickname: "To reduce what I thought was a doubly revolutionary compositorial device to the level of a joke which, by its very nature, makes it strongest effect when it is first heard, seemed to be equivalent to a childish misunderstanding, and the intervening decades have done nothing to improve my impression." And yet it *is* comical, and so "partial spoiler alert": from here on I give away Haydn's musical joke. The setup is that this *Presto* finale is cast in a very regular rondo form with a memorable if air-headed refrain built of four two-bar phrases, which is then repeated in its entirety. The movement behaves as rondos are supposed to behave: refrain, episode, refrain, episode, but toward the end of that second episode things start to break up a bit—a fragmented motif here, an inserted silence there. Still, the rondo tune returns and it's halfway through another go-round when suddenly the music lurches into an *Adagio* that is dramatic at the least, and we might say overwrought. But it's a feint, and the rondo tune rears its head again. This time each of its four phrases is heard independently, separated by a silence precisely as long as the phrase (or at least that long, I should say, since the marking of "GP"—"grand pause"— above those silences could be interpreted to beg an extension). The tune thus struggles to its end, and then it begins to repeat itself yet again, but not before a rest that is now twice as long as those that preceded. The ensemble manages to exhale the first two-bar phrase of this re-repetition and . . . is there more?

String Quartet in C major, Op. 33, No. 3, *Bird* (Hob. III:39)

> *Allegro moderato*
> *Scherzando: Allegretto*
> *Adagio ma non troppo*
> *Rondo: Presto*

Work composed: 1781

Work dedicated: Haydn's Op. 33 Quartets carried no dedication when they were first published, in 1772, but when a new edition was brought out, in 1796, Haydn added a dedication to the Russian Grand Duke Paul Petrovich.

Work premiered: Possibly on December 25, 1781, at the Viennese home of Grand Duke Paul's wife, the Grand Duchess Maria Feodorovna, by the violinists Luigi Tomasini and Franz Asplmayr, violist Thaddäus Huber, and cellist Joseph Weigl

Instrumentation: Two violins, viola, and cello

Everybody went wild for Haydn's Op. 33 Quartets, including a minor composer from Mainz who submitted them to Artaria as his own work that he wished to have published. He was unsuccessful, since Artaria (under whose imprint the pieces had appeared) was already quite familiar with them, obviously; but at least that composer scored high for chutzpah. This set proved so popular with musicians that it effectively reinvigorated widespread interest in the composition of string quartets. It gave rise directly to the great quartets of Mozart's maturity (most immediately to the younger composer's six quartets dedicated to Haydn), and, at a gap of about fifteen years, to the early quartets of Beethoven, who was briefly Haydn's composition pupil. Beethoven, poring over this score, surely learned lessons on every page, beginning with the quartet's first ten seconds. Its opening notes are frankly radical: a mere accompaniment chugging away, its melody withheld for a measure, and then that melody revealing itself reluctantly, unfolding only after a few long notes that on their own seem to be going nowhere. But even those long notes are enlivened by sprightly grace notes, a device that will permeate the movement and that perhaps gave rise to the nickname first attached to this quartet in the nineteenth century, the *Bird*. (Then, again, the theme of the concluding *Rondo* is birdlike, too, with the first violin chirping a staccato pattern that fits into a strikingly narrow range.)

It seems that as pupil and teacher, Beethoven and Haydn didn't manage to build up much of a rapport. Beethoven's lessons continued from the time he moved to Vienna, near the end of 1792, until the beginning of 1794. Years later Beethoven would tell his disciple Ferdinand Ries that he had learned nothing from Haydn during that year, which was perhaps true to the extent that Haydn kept trying to drill in certain principles of harmonic preparation and Fuxian counterpoint, which by then seemed too old-hat to keep the young Beethoven interested. They maintained at least a cordial relationship—normal for Haydn, not so normal for Beethoven—but apparently they were temperamentally mismatched. Aloys Fuchs, an early nineteenth-century collector of music memorabilia (including important Beethoveniana), passed along an anecdote that he said came from "the worthy hand of a contemporary." It chronicles an awkward encounter that took place three years after Haydn's oratorio *The Creation* (known in German as *Die Schöpfung*) had been unveiled to extraordinary success, and it involves a pun (involving the words *Geschöpfe* and *Schöpfung*, "creatures" and "creation") that seems to have fallen flat:

> When Beethoven had composed the music to the ballet *Die Geschöpfe des Prometheus* ["The Creatures of Prometheus"] in 1801, he was one day met by his former teacher, the great Joseph Haydn, who stopped him at once and said: "Well, I heard your ballet yesterday and it pleased me very much!" Beethoven replied: "O, dear Papa, you are very kind; but it is far from being a *Creation*!" Haydn, surprised at the answer and almost offended, said after a short pause: "That is true; it is not yet a *Creation* and I can scarcely believe

that it will ever become one." Whereupon the men said their adieus, both somewhat embarrassed.

Nonetheless, what Beethoven learned from Haydn's music was legion. The Quartet in C major (Op. 33, No. 3) suggests a few specific avenues that Beethoven would end up developing: how a theme can be crafted so as to lodge in the memory and yet embody endless possibilities for development; how the time-honored minuet might be replaced by an inner movement of a different character, like this *Scherzando*; how a composition can pivot on the contrasting characters of its sections, as in the captivating slow movement; how a work of high art may be leavened with allusions to popular or folk music, as in the finale; how a sense of humor can keep a composition fresh for two and a quarter centuries and even then make the piece sound still young. As with many of Haydn's earlier quartets, however, the texture in this one is much dominated by the first violin, and not until the finale do the lower voices play a part that is more democratic.

String Quartet in D major, Op. 50, No. 6, Frog (Hob. III:49)

Allegro
Poco Adagio
Menuetto: Allegretto—Trio
Finale: Allegro con spirito

Work composed: 1787

Work dedicated: To Friedrich Wilhelm II, King of Prussia

Work premiered: Apparently before it appeared in print in October 1787

Instrumentation: Two violins, viola, and cello

In an interview with his biographer Georg August Griesinger, Haydn would recall of his years working for the Esterházy princes, "As I was shut off from the world, no one in my surroundings would vex and confuse me, and so I was destined for originality." But he was less "shut off from the world" than he may have thought. By the 1770s several Parisian publishers were issuing editions of his music and he was receiving commissions from there and even from Spain. It was not a total surprise, therefore, when, in the winter of 1787, the Prussian minister to the Viennese court broached the idea of Haydn's dedicating a piece to King Friedrich Wilhelm II, the music-loving,

cello-playing monarch up in Berlin. The King himself followed up by sending Haydn a ring as a token of appreciation after receiving copies of Haydn's
Paris Symphonies, whereupon the composer suggested to his principal Viennese publisher, Artaria (headed by two brothers of that name), that the set
of six string quartets he was currently writing be dedicated to the Prussian
monarch.

What Haydn failed to mention to Artaria was that he was simultaneously
promising the very same quartets to the London publisher William Forster.
He had two manuscripts copied out; one went to Artaria on September 16,
the other to Forster four days later. Forster's edition appeared at lightning
speed, being issued on October 5 as Haydn's Op. 44, and Artaria's followed
on December 19 as Haydn's Op. 50—the opus numbers representing the only
major variance in the competing versions. What's more, in October Artaria
was dismayed to learn that manuscript copies of the quartets were already
being purchased by music-lovers. When confronted, Haydn insisted that the
leak must have emanated from Artaria's copyists, as his own were impeccably
trustworthy. The next month Artaria inevitably discovered that "its" new
quartets had just appeared in print in England, and the company's communications with Haydn grew chilly. Haydn assumed a reprehensible posture
and blamed Artaria for the state of affairs: he argued that if they had taken
the trouble to arrange for the quartets to be promptly issued by the London
firm of Longman & Broderip, with which they had a business arrangement,
then Forster would have had no incentive to print the pieces and this whole
situation wouldn't have arisen. We are accustomed to thinking of Haydn as a
kindly soul, and for the most part he was; but he was also capable of deceitful
business dealings, as he had shown prior to this affair and would demonstrate
again in the future. In Haydn's day the rules of the publishing business were
not spelled out as clearly as they are today, by a long shot, and on numerous
occasions the composer found himself on the receiving end of unscrupulous
shenanigans in this regard. That doesn't justify his behavior, which on this
occasion was literally duplicitous.

Six quartets issued from this adventure, with the Sixth (as Haydn situ-
ated it in both the Forster and the Artaria editions) becoming the most
popular over time. Its fortune was secured thanks to a distinguishing feature
that permeates its Finale. The opening theme of that movement begins with
ten iterations of the same pitch played while alternating the bow between
two adjacent strings, and the effect goes on to resurface often in the course
of the movement. String players call this a type of bariolage, from a French
word meaning "daubing with various colors" or, more anciently, from the
Latin *variolagium* ("alternation"). This technique usually involves playing an
identical note alternately on an open (unstopped) string and on the next-
lowest string (fingered), and the rapid contrast creates an unusual sonic

effect. At some point the effect was likened, not unreasonably, to the sound a frog makes. Germans took to calling this piece the *Froschquartett*, and from there English-speakers dubbed it the *Frog* Quartet. This is potentially misleading in that "frog" also happens to be the word for the mechanism on a violin (or viola, or cello, or whatever) bow that anchors and adjusts the horsehair at the end where the bow is held. It might be amusing to attack this passage of Haydn's *Frog* Quartet at the frog of the bow, though if that is what was intended the music would be marked *au talon* (signifying "at the frog"), which it is not. In any case, compositions that boast a nickname are more likely to gain a prominent spot in the repertoire than works that are not so endowed, particularly in a crowded field like the eighty-three string quartets of Haydn.

This quartet is extraordinary right from its beginning, which does not seem like a beginning in the least. The first violin starts off alone on the note E and continues through a falling-scale trajectory (accompanied by the other three players after a measure) that finally cadences on a D—harmonized by the tonic D-major chord—at the fourth measure, at which point the cello starts propelling the piece forward with hopping eighth-notes. In other words, this quartet begins by ending.

We might have assumed that Haydn's "preface" was nothing more than one of his accustomed jokes, but it becomes apparent that the violin's descending phrase is in fact the principal theme, and it keeps showing up, often in fragmented form, as the engine behind the whole movement. A wonderful moment arrives when the development ends and the recapitulation begins; the principal theme of course sounds like the end of a phrase in the development, and, at the instant we grasp that we are witnessing the return of the opening material, Haydn has the first violin repeat the phrase an octave lower. A listener might well wager that, since the four measures of the principal theme sound like an ending, Haydn will use them as his closing cadence—which he does not, thereby doling out one last laugh.

The slow movement is cast in a sort of three-part "song form" but with a heavy dose of variations, since the thematic material is constantly showing up in differently elaborated form. The theme is simplistic rather than searching, and the ear is titillated by the stratospheric reaches of the first violin or the quick arpeggios of the violin and the cello. A minuet is de rigueur for the third movement, and Haydn provides one that might be judged crazy. Anyone trying to dance to the opening strains of this minuet would surely trip and fall, so odd are its rhythms. The immense trio seems at first to be more surefooted, but then it turns out to have a lot invested in syncopation, and its phraseology becomes anything but balanced. Just when we think the dance may be getting back on track, Haydn inserts a grand pause, and then another, at which points it's anyone's guess where things are headed. Except, of course, that we will eventually find our way back to the minuet proper, because that's what always happens in Classical minuet-and-trio movements.

And so to the *Finale* and the frogs, and one really must admire not only Haydn's wit with the bariolage but also his insightfulness when it comes to tone color. I can't think of another piece of eighteenth-century music in which an observation about tone color generates an entire movement to the extent it does here. We find related uses of bariolage elsewhere in Haydn (in his *Farewell* Symphony, for example) but in the *Frog* Quartet this device is the heart of the matter rather than an incidental comment. I might not accompany Hans Keller (in his book *The Great Haydn Quartets*) all the way to his final argument, which is that we must view Haydn as the progenitor of *Klangfarbenmelodie*, the "melody of tone colors" that Schoenberg took credit for inventing in the early twentieth century. Still, in his eighteenth-century way, Haydn was certainly stretching the boundaries through a means that would prove unique in his quartets.

String Quartet in B-flat major, Op. 64, No. 3 (Hob. III:67)

> *Vivace assai*
> *Adagio*
> *Menuetto. Allegretto—Trio*
> *Finale. Allegro con spirito*

Work composed: The second half of 1790

Work dedicated: To Johann Tost

Work premiered: Not known

Instrumentation: Two violins, viola, and cello

For five years near the end of Haydn's tenure at the Esterházy court, the principal second violinist of the court orchestra was a certain Johann Tost, who had been engaged on March 1, 1783, for the annual sum of 400 gulden, 24 pounds of candles, and three fathom cords of firewood, as well as a new uniform each year. He left the orchestra in 1788, traveled to France, and later returned to Austria, where he married one of Prince Esterházy's housekeepers and became a prosperous cloth merchant.

Haydn is thought to have dedicated to Tost three sets of string quartets, totaling twelve pieces: the three quartets (Op. 54), three quartets (Op. 55), and six quartets (Op. 64). (Op. 54 and Op. 55 are often viewed as two halves of a single production, which is why Op. 64 is known as the second set of *Tost* Quartets.) Some scholars have suggested that Haydn inscribed only the Op. 64 set to Tost, with the earlier pieces mistakenly carrying a similar dedication due to the error of an early catalogue compiler. In any case, Tost's name has become popularly attached to all twelve works. As Tost's commercial aspirations increased, he became more and more mercenary in his dealings with musicians. In 1787, he proposed a business venture at the Esterházy court that would enable him to purvey "black market" copies of unpublished works by Haydn, a scheme he tried to engineer behind the composer's back.

Haydn's Op. 64 string quartets appear to have been written just at the juncture when Haydn's active employment at the Esterházy court drew to an end, which is to say with the death of Nikolaus "the Magnificent" in September 1790. It seems likely that the set was begun during the final months of Prince Nikolaus' life and completed by the end of 1790, by which time Haydn had moved from the rather isolated court in Esterháza to Vienna. That's where the set was published, early in 1791. The composer's earlier works would have been performed as soon as they were written, but since the Esterházys' musical establishment was on hiatus, the new set of quartets may not have been played until the composer took them with him to England later that year.

In Op. 64, Haydn returned to the intimate style of chamber writing that he had favored some years earlier, rather than the somewhat extroverted style of his more recent quartets, which often displayed flamboyant first violin parts and generally virtuosic writing. In these six pieces, the musical conversation is shared almost equally among the four participants. Nonetheless, Haydn's mastery of composition never stood still, and in the Op. 64 set he gives free rein to his experimental bent, perpetually trying out new ways to develop thematic material and expand the structures of his movements in novel directions.

Of the Op. 64 quartets, the most famous is surely the Fifth, nicknamed the *Lark*, but the Third, in B-flat major, is as fine. The arbitrary championing of one Haydn work over another is an issue that pervades his symphonies, string quartets, piano trios, and piano sonatas, but in the end, familiarity breeds more familiarity. The B-flat-major Quartet is rich in thematic and dynamic contrasts. The first movement brims with an unusual extravagance of melodies, and Haydn imaginatively adjusts the contours of his sonata-plan movement so that the classic development and recapitulation sections are rather telescoped into one another. A galloping rhythmic figure pops up in all the parts, helping create unity throughout the melodies of this movement.

The contemplative slow movement, in E-flat, is laid out on a familiar A-B-A plan, with the central section being cast in the tonic minor, the dark and rarely encountered key of E-flat minor. The *Menuetto* also hews to a strictly

Classical format, though Haydn has some fun by displacing accents here and there in a way that seems to throw the proceedings momentarily into duple time, as opposed to the overlying triple meter. Haydn also plays with rhythmic displacement in the trio section, although here the punch comes from having some instruments anticipate bar lines by a full beat, creating a syncopated push-and-pull that greatly prefigures Beethoven. (Metric displacements were nothing new to Haydn, to be sure; they are to be found in many of the minuet movements of his quartets and would shortly become nearly a hallmark of his *London* Symphonies.) More syncopation is built into the main theme of the quartet's *Finale*, a rollicking movement in which the action stops a couple of times to draw chordal, hymn-like breaths, *pianissimo*.

String Quartet in D major, Op. 64, No. 5, *Lark* (Hob. III:63)

> *Allegro moderato*
> *Adagio cantabile*
> *Menuetto: Allegretto—Trio*
> *Finale: Vivace*

Work composed: 1790

Work dedicated: To Johann Tost

Work premiered: Not known

Instrumentation: Two violins, viola, and cello

The *Lark* Quartet is justly hailed as one of Haydn's finest. Certainly the soaring quality of its opening theme (to which it owes its nickname) announces the work's exorbitant beauty from the very outset; as the movement unrolls the listener is also struck by the sheer boldness of imagination. In the second subject, powerful cross-beats throw the ear off kilter, assisted in this by dense and chromatic harmonic progressions. The development—the section in which anything can happen—is already "somewhere else" harmonically with its opening sonority, and in the recapitulation the syncopated figure is extended as Haydn capitalizes on what had already been a capital idea.

The *Adagio cantabile* is a pensive movement, potentially nostalgic and even mournful in places. It upholds its grace even while groping toward some indistinct destination. At this point in his quartet career, Haydn was still happy to consider the first violin as *primus inter pares*, and in this slow movement it is asked to render some quite lithe and acrobatic figuration while maintaining the overriding eloquent and gentle mood. The end seems practically a violin cadenza.

The minuet never relinquishes its dancelike swing, even in the face of some wry, off-beat business involving accented grace notes. The viola seems to pick up on this witticism a bit late and echoes the effect—rather as if it had the hiccups—in the rests left open by the other instruments. The trio, in D minor, has an ominous feel to it. Here the viola is terribly serious, playing a descending chromatic line while the other three instruments scurry about with much imitation among their parts. The effect is a bit academic and old-fashioned, inviting the description "post-Baroque."

Haydn concludes with an inimitable *Finale*. Here the first violin is instructed to play *piano* and always staccato, which further invigorates a line that already approaches a bout of folk-fiddling and at one point evokes the "Sailor's Hornpipe." Although it is the most overtly virtuosic in its demands, this is also the most democratic of the movements in terms of giving each instrument its moment in the spotlight, especially during the tempest-in-a-teapot fugal interlude in the middle. The cascade of sixteenth-notes never comes to rest, yielding the very definition of a *moto perpetuo*. Oh, dear: I have previously had reason to mention Hans Keller's 1986 volume *The Great Haydn Quartets*, and I see that he insists that it is a "so-miscalled *moto perpetuo*," adding, "How can one thus describe a complex, monothematic ternary form with a fugal middle section wherein the brilliant, stressedly homophonic theme suddenly discloses its contrapuntal potentialities?" If truth be told, Keller (*that* Keller, not me) seems to have resented that which proves popular, and this is probably the most popular, and hence the most frequently programmed, of all the Haydn quartets. He finds that the *Finale* "satisfies listeners and leaders alike on a fairly superficial level which, needless to add, hides its considerable musical substance." I would like to imagine that even people who resist smiling will be won over to doing so before this romp reaches its hilarious end.

String Quartet in B-flat major, Op. 71, No. 1 (Hob. III:69)

> *Allegro*
> *Adagio*
> *Menuetto: Allegretto—Trio*
> *Vivace*

Work composed: Summer 1793

Work dedicated: To Count Anton Apponyi

Work premiered: **Not known**

Instrumentation: **Two violins, viola, and cello**

For nearly three decades Haydn was steadily and (for the most part) happily employed in the service of the Esterházy princes. For all but his first year the court was headed by Prince Nikolaus Esterházy, who moved the court's base to the lavish palace he constructed at Esterháza, in a remote area of Hungary. Nikolaus died on September 28, 1790. He was succeeded by his son, Anton, a military man who did not much care for music and wasted no time acting on that fact: a mere two days after his father's death, he fired the entire court orchestra and opera company, retaining only a small wind-band for ceremonial occasions. Similar things were going on at other European courts at the time, the events that rattled France in 1789 being viewed as unpropitious for aristocratic establishments in general. Although Anton kept the composer on staff as his nominal musical director, he made it clear that no particular duties—or even attendance—would be required. At least this did not leave the fifty-eight-year-old Haydn in perilous financial straits. The old prince had stipulated in his will that Haydn should receive an annuity of 1,000 florins, and the new one added to that a pension of another 300 florins per year. For the first time in decades, Haydn was free to explore.

The turn of events proved to be a blessing in disguise. Musical innovator though he was, Haydn was essentially conservative in professional matters, preferring the stability of a long-term appointment to the risk entailed in scurrying from one noble patron to another in quest of incremental improvements of fortune. Anton's accession forced Haydn to effect a change. Establishing himself in a rented apartment in Vienna, he turned down an immediate job offer from another prince and briefly considered the idea of accepting a position with the King of Naples. In the end it was the German-born violinist Johann Peter Salomon, now working as a concert impresario in England, who prevailed among competitors, securing the promise of a tour from the eminent composer. Salomon had been angling to present Haydn for some time, and on learning of the changes at the Esterházy court he quickly showed up without an appointment at Haydn's doorstep in Vienna, reputedly introducing himself with the words: "I am Salomon of London and I have come to fetch you. Tomorrow we will arrange an accord."

An accord was reached whereby Haydn would travel to London and be richly rewarded for new works he was to unveil there, not to mention income from publication deals and a benefit concert. Haydn, who had never traveled significantly apart from making the rounds of the various Esterházy residences, appears to have looked forward to his trip with no trepidation. Following his first voyage aboard a ship, Haydn arrived in London on January 1, 1791, and embarked on a leisurely schedule of music-making and social appearances that included accepting a doctorate from Oxford University.

He returned to Vienna in the summer of 1792, having enjoyed the experience enormously, and he happily accepted a second invitation to visit London in 1794–95, during which his social calendar included even dinners and musicales with the royal family. The composer may have been thinking about settling in London permanently, but an unanticipated reversal of circumstances made him reconsider. The music-hating Prince Anton died abruptly, the result of a wound sustained while battling French forces. His successor, Prince Nikolaus II, quickly moved to restore some of the court's cultural programs to their former glory. Ever the loyal employee, Haydn consented to return to Austria at the conclusion of his London commitments in the 1795 season, and he remained formally attached to the Court of Nikolaus II for the rest of his life. He no longer had to worry about his financial needs at all. His biographer Georg August Griesinger said that Haydn's two London visits had netted him 13,000 gulden, which would have taken him twenty years to earn through his Esterházy paychecks.

In Haydn's final two decades he would devote himself to the composition of symphonies and to two musical fields that lay close to his heart: sacred works and chamber music. The sets in which his late quartets were published became known by the names of the persons who commissioned them, or at least to whom they are dedicated: the six *Tost* Quartets (Op. 64) in 1791, the six *Apponyi* Quartets (Op. 71 and Op. 74) in 1793, the six *Erdödy* Quartets (Op. 76) in 1797, and the two *Lobkowitz* Quartets (Op. 77) in 1799, leaving only a final, unfinished D-minor Quartet (Op. 103).

Anton Georg, Count von Apponyi (1751–1817), oversaw a court in Pressburg. An active Freemason, he was also one of the two members of the Viennese Lodge "Zur wahren Eintracht" (to which Mozart also belonged) who nominated Haydn as a member in 1785, although Haydn never ended up becoming very active himself. Apponyi was also a regular at Baron Gottfried van Swieten's Gesellschaft der Asociirten in Vienna, the circle whose explorations of Bach and Handel left a deep mark on Mozart and led to his updated arrangement of, among other works, Handel's *Messsiah*.

The two sets of three quartets each that are dedicated to Apponyi date from the time Haydn spent at home in Vienna between his two residencies in England. His six Op. 64 string quartets having proved a big hit during his first visit, in 1790, Haydn assumed that these new works would make a similar impact on his return in 1794, which they did. In general, the Op. 71 and Op. 74 Quartets mark a leap ahead in the composer's development of the genre. Several open with attention-getting "summons" motives, which the musicologist Reginald Barrett-Ayres imagined as a response to the concert-rooms of London, busy with conversation until the music began (although one wonders how different that was from the court atmosphere Haydn had previously experienced in Austria). Certain textural devices in these works seem borrowed from the world of the symphony, and the harmonic practice of these pieces is very forward-looking indeed. The first-violin parts tend toward brilliance, not surprising since Haydn knew that, at least in England, the first-violin part would be played by Salomon, who was internationally acclaimed as a violinist.

All of these characteristics make an appearance early in the B-flat-major Quartet (Op. 71, No. 1): the frankly symphonic "call to attention" of the opening two measures, with the texture expanded to as many as nine parts thanks to double- and triple-stopping; the dominance of the first violin through the first theme and beyond; and the appearance of occasional nondiatonic melodic intervals (particularly the minor sixth), which adumbrates later harmonic explorations. The chords of the opening seem at first to be no more than a prelude, but even they play a small thematic role, being echoed at the end of the exposition section and prefiguring the decisive final chords at the movement's end. For the very last chord, each of the players sounds a triple-stop, yielding a truly orchestral voicing of twelve notes—not often encountered in string quartets. Still, these references are incidental; ultimately, the movement is almost entirely spun out from the first violin's principal theme.

At this point in his career Haydn often made a slow movement serve as a work's center of gravity. This intensely tender *Adagio* is a case in point. Here he has the ensemble create a rich diversity of textures—sometimes playing in near-homophony, sometimes pairing off in combinations—all the while providing the first violin with an emotionally loaded line that in places seems so free in its rhythm as to suggest improvised embellishment. In the ensuing movement, the *Menuetto*, the cello has a way of disappearing briefly to allow the upper three parts to play alone, sometimes creating echo effects. This behavior forces us to focus on the comings and goings of the cello line. Doing so we spot a detail that the musicologist Cecil Gray pointed out years ago—that the contours the cello plays at the beginning of the *Menuetto* are essentially the same as the contours played by the first violin a half minute into the first movement and which that same instrument will revisit in the *Finale*. For the rest, Haydn lets loose with his signature wit in his *Finale*—not so much a barrage of laugh-out-loud jokes (though there are a few) as the sort of genial, well-bred good humor that has been charming listeners for two centuries and more.

String Quartet in G, Op. 74, No. 3, *Reiter* ("Rider") (Hob. III:74)

> *Allegro*
> *Largo assai*
> *Menuetto (Allegretto)—Trio*
> *Finale (Allegro con brio)*

Work composed: Summer 1793

Work dedicated: To Count Anton Apponyi

Work premiered: Not known

Instrumentation: Two violins, viola, and cello

The Quartet in G (Op. 74, No. 3) was the last of the second Apponyi set to be written. Its nickname, *Reiter* ("Rider" or, as it is sometimes translated, "Horseman"), popped up after Haydn's death; whether it refers to the galloping material of the first movement (in which case we have a three-legged horse) or that of the *Finale.* is both unknown and moot. In a catalogue as vast as Haydn's, the existence of a nickname can often spell the difference between fame and obscurity; in the case of the *Rider* Quartet, one imagines that it would be viewed as a seminal work either way.

Its most extraordinary idiosyncrasy is its key. Nine times out of ten you will find Op. 74, No. 3, referred to as being in G minor. And yet, as the first movement progresses, you are bound to have the feeling that you are listening to a piece in the major, rather than the minor, mode. In fact, the notation shifts blatantly into G major for the movement's last twenty-nine measures. The third movement, too, is written in G major, though with a contrasting trio in G minor; and the *Finale* mirrors the first movement by moving from G minor at its opening to G major two-thirds of the way through, after which it maintains the major mode to the end. That the work is "in G" is indubitable, but it is a sort of "bimodal" G, one that embraces both G minor and G major, and in which the former can never avoid veering into the latter.

What's more, the second movement is not in G at all; it is in E major. This tonal contrast has sometimes been cited as hideously jarring; and, indeed, traditional harmonic geography places E major very distant indeed from G minor. But if we acknowledge that the movements that surround the *Largo assai* are in a G that is at least as much major as minor, then we find that the contrast of the slow movement is a far less remote thirds-relationship of the sort that would become increasingly popular in the nineteenth century. Another harbinger of things to come resides in Haydn's prominent use of the ländler-like "yodeling" theme that the first violin plays on a single string, above a pizzicato bass and a broken-chord figure in the second violin; it motivates much of the movement. This, again, is an idea we associate with the nineteenth century far more than the eighteenth—that a movement's opening theme need not prove to be its most important one. Since this second theme is in the major mode, it contributes greatly to the general major-minor blend of the tonality.

This E-major slow movement serves as the center of gravity in this quartet. The movement became intimately familiar to generations of music students through its inclusion, in a piano transcription not by Haydn, in a hugely popular album of easy piano solos published by the G. Schirmer company. What a keyboard version could not really suggest, however, was the brilliance of Haydn's orchestration—the stunning contrasts of dynamics, of string color, of movement and rest. All of this peaks in two audacious measures where the melody continues uninterrupted while the texture shifts from sustained tones to a buzz of repeated thirty-second notes, an effect rendered positively shimmering by a concomitant shift from *forte* to *pianissimo*.

The minuet-and-trio is unusual principally in that the trio section represents an increasing of tension compared with the minuet proper; the opposite would be more typical. The *Finale* is a subtle movement, complex in its harmonic plot, and as already noted, ultimately moving from the minor mode of its anxious opening to a major-mode conclusion that is a more virtuosic bit of composition than its apparent modesty suggests. The final page is, in fact, an exercise in invertible triple counterpoint that superimposes thematic fragments from throughout the movement, a process that may bring to mind the finale of Mozart's *Jupiter* Symphony, which had preceded this quartet by only five years.

Piano Trio in A major (Hob. XV:18)

Allegro moderato
Andante
Allegro

Work composed: Probably 1794; perhaps begun in 1793

Work dedicated: To Princess Maria Anna Esterházy, along with the other two trios making up what was published as Haydn's Op. 70

Work premiered: Not known

Instrumentation: Violin, cello, and piano

We laud Haydn today as the "father of the symphony," but he was also a fountainhead of two of the central groupings of chamber music: the string quartet
and the piano trio. (One hesitates to make claims of his being absolutely "the
first" with any of these genres, but there is no gainsaying that he towered over
all contemporary efforts in all of these areas, rivaled by nobody until Mozart
came of age.) Whereas the string quartet enjoyed a somewhat intellectual
reputation, a vehicle for exploring the implications of four-part harmony and
counterpoint, the piano trio was a more "popular" genre. The piano was a
fixture of the well-appointed home, and Haydn's era was full of skilled prac-
titioners who were eager to put their instruments to use for at-home entertainment. Although Haydn's trios do show a progression toward an increased
democratization among the three participants, they invariably reflect his
era's propensity to view such ensembles as pianocentric. It is entirely typical
that in 1775 Carl Philipp Emanuel Bach should have published a group of
pieces that were identified on their title page as "Sonatas for the Piano, which
may equally well be played solo, or accompanied by violin and violoncello."
Haydn's attitude toward the genre did not differ fundamentally. In 1803, for
example, Prince Anton Esterházy asked his wandering Kapellmeister for a
violin sonata he might supply to a friend. Haydn responded by tendering
an arrangement for violin and piano of his E-flat-minor Piano Trio, easily
achieved by simply suppressing the cello line, which mostly duplicated the
left-hand of the piano part anyway. Even in his most advanced piano trios,
Haydn customarily placed the piano at the forefront of the texture.

Haydn composed his first keyboard trios in the early 1760s, which is to
say at about the time of his appointment with the Esterházy princes, and his
last in 1797, and in the course of that time he produced about forty-five piano
trios (the numbers being somewhat disputed due to a handful of lost and
questionably authentic works). Fifteen of his piano trios date from between
1794 and 1797, placing them within the high tide of his mature mastery.
During those three-and-a-half decades musical practice developed considerably, with one salient change being the supplanting of the harpsichord by the
piano. During his visits to London, in 1791–92 and 1794–95, Haydn became
acquainted with English pianos, which were more robust and extroverted in
their sound than were the Viennese instruments he had known previously.
The set of three trios he published in November 1794—the A-major plus the
two that immediately followed it in his catalogue—are cited as being tailor-
made to exploit the strengths of the new English pianos that had so impressed
the composer, and their piano parts accordingly sparkle a shade more effu-
sively than do the corresponding parts of his earlier trios.

Probably composed during Haydn's second London visit—possibly shortly
before—the three trios of this set stand in marked contrast to each other. The
second trio of the group (in G minor) is dark and troubled, and the last (in B-flat

major) is pastoral, but this opening trio is an upbeat and good-humored piece. That doesn't mean it's simplistic. The first movement ranges widely in its modulations, and its development section meanders into the realm of introspection before the cheerfulness returns with the recapitulation. At one point Haydn even works in an ultra-learned exercise in canon—so naturally, in fact, that this touch is very likely to escape the ear; it is one of Haydn's nods to the cognoscenti. By this point in his career Haydn had moved well beyond simple restatements of his material, and this opening movement provides an object lesson of how creatively the composer manipulates his material through varied touches of melodic, harmonic, and contrapuntal variation when themes are revisited.

The second movement, a pensive *Andante* in lilting 6/8 meter, maintains the tonic key of A, but it is based in the minor mode, though with a major-key episode separating the minor-mode outer sections. The movement is cast in a straightforward A-B-A form, but again we find that the returning "A" section is anything but a literal repetition of the opening one; instead it is richly ornamented to yield a texture of gracious elegance. The slow movement ends on a semicolon rather than a period. The listener may well expect it to continue into another contrasting episode, but after the slightest pause we move on instead to the last movement. The finale is a rollicking *Allegro*, the sort of Haydn movement that one would have difficulty listening to without breaking into a broad smile. This triple-time movement might be described as a sort of polonaise, and it seems a close cousin to the famous *Rondo all'Ongarese* (the "Gypsy Rondo") of the composer's G-major Trio (Hob. XV:25), which would follow in 1795.

Piano Trio in G major, *Gypsy Rondo* (Hob. XV:25)

> *Andante*
> *Poco adagio—Cantabile*
> *Rondo all'Ongarese*
> *Presto*

Work composed: Summer 1795, in London

Work dedicated: To the pianist Rebecca Schroeter

Work premiered: Not known

Instrumentation: Violin, cello, and piano

The G-major Piano Trio (Hob. XV:25) has been a popular favorite since it seduced its first London listeners through its vivacious finale. The first movement seems Mozartian in the songlike tunefulness of its opening theme, although even here the bass line dovetails with a degree of contrapuntal interest that Mozart might not have chosen if he had been presenting this melody in one of his unassuming lieder. In any case, Haydn subjects this unencumbered melody (with its arresting bass line) to a good deal of elaboration in the course of the variation movement. The melody is imaginatively presented first in G major, then in G minor—the two faces of G—and the variations proceed in a "double form," always reflecting that balance of major and minor (though the second minor variation provides variety by being cast in the related key of E minor). Haydn has traveled a great distance from his stance in his early trios; where those had been essentially piano sonatas spiced up through the timbral enhancements of two almost dispensable string instruments, the violin emerges in this trio as a full partner, even if the cello remains somewhat subservient.

The beginning of the *Poco adagio* is more what early Haydn trios had sounded like from a textural point of view, with the piano front and center and the violin and cello hovering in the background—although a less mature and experienced composer might not have captured quite the same combination of simplicity and expression, which here combine to poignant effect. The violin emerges in the central *Cantabile* section, which seems hardly less dreamlike than corresponding poetic expanses that will lie ahead in the more Romantic effusions of Schubert and Schumann. This is an exceptionally beautiful slow movement, even for Haydn. That it is set in E major clarifies why one of the variations in the opening movement had surprised us by being in E; we understand retroactively that it was not a passing fancy but rather the first step toward making this entire trio a well-woven whole.

But it is the vivacious finale that cemented this trio's status as a popular favorite from the outset. It's a tour de force in the so-called Hungarian Gypsy style that was wildly popular in Vienna and environs in the late eighteenth and nineteenth centuries, through (and even a bit beyond) the era of Haydn's great admirer Johannes Brahms. Haydn must have lived in proximity to music of this sort during his years at Esterháza in Hungary; one period engraving of the palace in Esterháza shows a Gypsy band playing at the edge of the scene. Haydn incorporated folk themes into his original works on a number of occasions, surely to the surprised delight of the Esterházy entourage. A famous example is to be found in the finale (marked *Rondo all'Ungherese*) of the most famous of Haydn's piano concertos (actually, his *only* famous piano concerto), the one in D major that he published in 1784 and that is often the first "grown-up" concerto that developing pianists master, one that can afford them pleasure for the rest of their careers. In that case the rondo melody is presumably based on a Croatian folk dance. In the *Gypsy Rondo* Trio, the source of the finale theme has proved more elusive, but its contours suggest music that it might have emanated from Komitat Veszprém (a county of western Hungary perhaps fifty miles southeast of Esterháza) and particularly from the tradition of the *verbunkos*, dances that figured in the process of military recruitment. The Austrian soldiers, wearing elegant uniforms, would entertain unsuspecting Hungarian peasants with vigorous music, athletic dances, and abundant beverages, at which point (though perhaps never thereafter) life in the regiments must have seemed irresistible. One of the themes in Haydn's *Gypsy Rondo* finale—the swaggering minor-key bit (over a cello drone) that falls just at the movement's mid-point and returns near the end—relates to a melody found in a four-volume collection, *Original Hungarian National Dances for the Piano*, that was issued in Vienna beginning in 1805. It certainly seems to give credence to the authentic folk origins of Haydn's piece, though a nagging "chicken-and-egg" question does surround such matters; sometimes "composed" melodies become adopted into the popular repertoire and are assumed to be folk pieces when they aren't really.

Haydn dedicated this trio to Rebecca Schroeter, an amateur pianist and the widow of a composer. They had met during Haydn's first residency in London, often dined together, and apparently became romantically involved (not a unique arrangement for Haydn, who had little in common with his wife and lived largely estranged from her). Haydn described Schroeter to his biographer Albert Christoph Dies as "a beautiful and amiable woman whom I might very easily have married if I had been free then."

Piano Trio in C major (Hob XV:27)

Allegro
Andante
Finale—Presto

Work composed: Apparently in 1796 or 1797, in Vienna

Work dedicated: To Therese Jansen Bartolozzi

Work premiered: Not known

Instrumentation: Violin, cello, and piano

The C-major Piano Trio (Hob XV:27) was one of Haydn's final group of three, and he composed it, just following his second English trip, for the piano virtuoso Therese Jansen Bartolozzi. Born in Aachen, she had moved to London and studied piano with Muzio Clementi, one of the most eminent virtuosos of the day. Haydn got to know her during his visits to England and admired her playing so much that he composed at least two (perhaps all three) of his last piano sonatas for her, as well as three piano trios (Hob. XV:27–29). Also unveiled at her home was his *Jacob's Dream*, a stand-alone program-matic movement for piano trio that would later be augmented by an intro-ductory movement to become the Trio in E-flat minor/major (Hob. XV:30). In May 1795 Haydn served as a witness at her wedding to Gaetano Bartolozzi, a violin- and viola-playing picture dealer and import-export wheeler-dealer whose father, Francesco, had engraved Haydn's portrait in 1791. (Therese and Gaetano would later separate; their elder daughter became famous as the dancer Madame Vestris.) Haydn had first met Gaetano when the latter trav-eled to Esterháza in the winter of 1785–86. On January 29, 1786, the London *Public Advertiser* carried an interesting, if exaggerated, report of their meeting, which was newsworthy in light of efforts then in the works to bring the com-poser to England—a project that would not be realized until five years later:

> A musician, it would seem, has as little honour in his own country as a prophet, and of this the celebrated Haydn furnishes a remarkable proof. The Prince of Esterhagy [*sic*], to whom this great composer is Maître de Chapelle, though he affects the highest admiration of the works of Haydn, who is constantly employed in his service, yet his only reward is a pittance which the most obscure fiddler in London would disdain to accept, together with a miserable apart-ment in the barracks, in which are his bed and an old spinet, or clavichord. In this situation, so unworthy of his genius, was Haydn found by Mr. Bartolozzi, who lately went to visit him. He seemed to be highly pleased with Bartolozzi's account of the encouragement given to his music in England, and of the high estimation in which his compositions were held. It was upon this occasion that Haydn first expressed a desire to visit London, which was the origin of the negociations [*sic*] now on the tapis between him and the managers of the Hanover-square Concerts.

The sonatas and trios Haydn composed for Therese Jansen Bartolozzi stand at the summit of his keyboard production in terms of requisite virtuosity (including notable specimens of octave playing and hand crossing), creative use of available technical effects, and harmonic and structural imagination.

The first movement opens with a theme of abrupt vigor, crafted beau-tifully for the keyboard, and the exposition unrolls busily from there. The development section begins lugubriously but makes its way to a span of strict, finely wrought counterpoint—the corresponding section of Haydn's Sym-phony No. 98 comes to mind—and then is rounded off with the expected recapitulation. But this is no apish recasting of the opening exposition; where the exposition had been rich in deceptive cadences, the recapitulation plunges forward with no such sidesteps.

The central *Andante* is cast in a simple A-B-A form, with the B section being a violent, minor-key interlude. A little cadenza for the piano pops up near the end. For his *Finale* Haydn serves up one of his irresistible sonata-rondos. In the main theme the music hops from register to register all over the piano's keyboard. This whirlwind of a movement leaves the performers practically breathless and the listeners grinning, if not laughing outright. The piece brims with humor, some of it of a gruff sort that points ahead to Beethoven. Among this trio's admirers was no less estimable a personage than Felix Mendelssohn, who played the piano part at a concert on February 22, 1838, and was proud to purvey this "find." He wrote to his sister, "The people couldn't get over their astonishment that such a lovely thing could exist, and yet it was published long ago by Breitkopf & Härtel." Once discovered—or rediscovered—it's not a piece a music-lover would want to let go of again.

String Quartet in G major, Op. 76, No. 1 (Hob. III:75)

Allegro con spirito
Adagio sostenuto
Menuetto: Presto—Trio
Finale: Allegro ma non troppo

Work composed: 1797

Work dedicated: To Count Joseph Erdödy

Work premiered: Not known

Instrumentation: Two violins, viola, and cello

The Erdödy family was an aristocratic Hungarian clan, several of whose members took their music very seriously. Count Joseph Erdödy (1754–1824) kept a string quartet handy at both his main palace in Pressburg and his summer palace in Freystadtl an der Waag (also called Galgócz, or Hlohovec) in Slovakia, and he commissioned a full set of six quartets from Haydn in 1796. The first editions, published in 1799 more-or-less simultaneously by the German firm of André, the Viennese firm of Artaria, and the London firm of Longman, Clementi & Co., accordingly bore a dedication to him, with Artaria identifying him grandly as Count Joseph Erdödy de Monyorokérek, the Current Chamberlain and Privy Councilor of State to his Majesty the Emperor and King, Supreme Count of the County of Neuttra.

Three of Haydn's Op. 76 Quartets have become well known by their nicknames: No. 2 (the *Fifths*), No. 3 (the *Emperor*), and No. 4 (the *Sunrise*). The Count was in no way shortchanged by the others. In the spring of 1799 the eminent British musical historian Charles Burney wrote to Haydn: "I had the great pleasure of hearing your new quartetti (opera 76) well performed before I went out of town, and never received more pleasure from instrumental music: they are full of invention, fire, good taste, and new effects, and seem the production, not of a sublime genius who had written so much and so well already, but one of highly-cultured talents, who had expended none of his fire before."

Haydn was greatly drawn to monothematic movements, and this G-major Quartet opens with a near example. Although the first movement certainly sports secondary motifs, no melody comes close to wielding the importance of the opening one, which (following three chords that serve as a call to order) is announced playfully by the cello, with a response coming from the viola. The viola will also attend to this theme at the launch of the development section, but here the second violin superimposes a sort of neo-Baroque descant, paving the way for more old-fashioned Baroque writing: a modulatory circle-of-fifths passage, practically unadorned, of the sort that Haydn must have heard endlessly in his youth. For the remainder of the movement the principal theme and the countermelody work often in tandem as a sort of double theme.

The *Adagio sostenuto* begins as a rapt hymn, a quietly sublime chorale that expands into more lyrical figuration in which the top and bottom lines play a little motif that is really nothing more than an arpeggiated chord enhanced with appoggiaturas. This complex will return (its music always transformed to some extent, but maintaining its unmistakable mood) to punctuate the entire movement, which is laid out as a slow rondo. Alternating with this principal theme is more lively, yet emotionally ambivalent, music in which the first violin, usually alone but on one occasion paired with second violin for added intensity, plays syncopated off-beats against the relentless pulse of the rest of the quartet.

Commentators have remarked that the profundity expressed in the slow movements of Haydn's Op. 76 quartets is counterbalanced by a commensurate change in the spirit of the third movements that follow. This is traditionally the domain of the minuet-and-trio, but by this time in the history of music the once courtly character of that genre was transforming into what we recognize in retrospect as the Beethovenian scherzo. That is certainly the case with this quartet, in which the minuet is actually marked *Presto* (so will be the corresponding movement of Op. 76, No. 6, the last of the Erdödy group) and the music positively scurries, with nearly every note marked staccato, no less. The trio section provides fleeting contrast by way of a genial ländler in which the first violin's countrified melody is accompanied by the pizzicato strumming of the other three players. Although it is not so marked in the score, nearly all interpreters intuitively relax the tempo for this central section before returning for another go-round of the high-intensity minuet-scherzo.

With the arrival of the *Finale* we hear something very quirky: a committed expanse of minor-key music, which until now has been visited only in passing in the course of harmonic migration in the first and second movements. Here Haydn offers a strongly etched minor-mode theme that might have found a place during his so-called *Sturm und Drang* period of circa 1770. This *Finale* is cast in a sonata form, and by this point in Haydn's production we know that all sorts of surprises can emerge in a development section. Even so, nobody could anticipate the novelty of this development section, in which Haydn takes us on a tour of the most arcane harmonic modulations—F minor, A-flat major, A-flat minor, D-flat minor, A major (which in this context is a simplified, "enharmonic" way of notating what in harmonic terms is B-double-flat major), and on and on: all quite prescient of Schubert.

It's a rare and risky business, this idea of ending a major-mode piece in the tonic minor key, and Haydn was not quite ready to take such a turn and then leave his listeners sitting at the end in tonal tumult. After these esoteric exertions, Haydn therefore delivers us to—of all places—the comfort zone of G major, which by now we surely have forgotten is supposed to be the overriding tonality of this whole quartet. (He'll do effectively the same thing two quartets later, in his *Emperor* Quartet, a work in C major with a C-minor finale until almost the end.) He underscores this maneuver by completely changing the texture at this moment, arranging for the first violin to sing out an entirely cheerful, even nonchalant, major-mode version of the principal melody, accompanied by sustained notes from the rest of the musicians. We have now reached the movement's recapitulation. Even here some of the more threatening music we have heard earlier will sneak in, but the final pages are overwhelmingly of good cheer. This adds up to a highly experimental work that often gives the impression of being an example of well-behaved Classicism, though to the attentive listener, it ends up being anything but that.

String Quartet in C major, Op. 76, No. 3, *Emperor* (Hob. III:77)

Allegro
Poco adagio. Cantabile
Menuetto: Allegro—Trio
Finale: Presto

Work composed: 1797

Work dedicated: To Count Joseph Erdödy

Work premiered: Not known

Instrumentation: Two violins, viola, and cello

Haydn's *Erdödy* Quartets were born into troubled times. European political life had been shattered by the French Revolution, and in its wake much of the continent erupted in war. Austria was heavily engaged in fighting against the French on two fronts: in the west for control of territories in southern Germany and in the south in defense of its holdings in Italy, the latter against troops directed by the brilliant young Napoleon Bonaparte. It was the Habsburg Holy Roman Emperor Franz II who had gotten Austria deeply involved in these wars, eschewing diplomacy that might have led to a less painful result. Probably Napoleon relished the fact that he was trouncing an emperor who was the nephew of the now-decapitated Marie Antoinette. The political ins and outs of Austria's involvement in the Napoleonic Wars are too complicated to recount here, but in the end Austria was a decisive loser and ended up ceding its preeminence among German-speaking lands to its rival Prussia. During the early years of the nineteenth century, Vienna spent a good deal of time under French occupation. In fact, when Haydn lay on his deathbed, Napoleon saw to it that an armed sentry stood guard outside his home to enforce as peaceful an atmosphere as was possible.

Several compositions with vaguely propagandistic overtones emanated from Haydn's pen at this time, including, in early 1794, his Symphony No. 100 (the *Military*) and, in 1796, his *Missa in tempore belli* ("Mass in Time of War"). The Austrian government was ever on the alert for ways to whip up patriotic fervor, and at the beginning of 1797, Count Franz Joseph Saurau, president of the Government of Lower Austria, made a suggestion to Count Moritz Dietrichstein, director of Court Music: "I have often regretted that unlike the English we had no national anthem fitted to display in front of the whole world the devoted attachment of the people to its wise and good National Father, and to awaken in the hearts of all good Austrians that noble pride of nation which is indispensible if they are to execute energetically each disciplinary measure considered necessary by the princes of the land." After rambling on about how awful the French were, he announced his solution: "I had text fashioned by the worthy poet Haschka, and to have it set to music, I turned to our immortal compatriot Haydn, who, I felt, was the only man capable of creating something which could be placed beside the English 'God Save the King.'" (Another account has Haydn coming up with the idea in the first place, and his friend Baron van Swieten conveying it thence to Saurau.)

So was born the anthem "Gott! erhalte Franz den Kaiser" ("God Preserve Emperor Franz"), which was unveiled at the emperor's birthday celebrations on February 12, 1797, at the Burgtheater in Vienna. Broadsides with Lorenz Haschka's text (in four verses) and Haydn's music (in piano score) were hastily printed so that attendees could join in singing the new hymn, which, needless to say, was greeted rapturously when unveiled during the festive evening, with an orchestral accompaniment prepared by the composer. The piece became instantly famous, and over time various other words were fitted to it. (It would enter Protestant hymnody as "Glorious Things of Thee Are Spoken.") It was officially adopted as the Austrian national anthem and served as such through the end of the World War I. At that point a new anthem was put in place, but it failed to take hold and Haydn's tune was officially reinstated in 1929, with non-Franz words. The melody also grew fanatically popular in Germany, and in 1841 it was fitted with a text that began, "Deutschland, Deutschland über Alles" ("Germany, Germany above all others"). In that form it would become the national anthem of a second nation, adopted by Germany in 1922 under the official title "Das Lied der Deutschen" ("The Song of the Germans"), and the fact that it thus served as a theme song for the Third Reich would be a most unfortunate byway of Haydn in posterity. After World War II the Allied Commission, hoping to sweep away all possibly lingering attachments to former times, nixed it as the Austrian National Anthem, and an entirely different song with identical scansion, "Land der Berge, Land der Strome" (its music sometimes attributed dubiously to Mozart) was adopted in 1947. Haydn's tune, however, lives on as the national anthem of Germany, adopted by the Federal Republic of Germany ("West Germany") as its official song in 1952, and by the entire reunified Germany in 1990.

Already when the piece was young many composers wrote variations on Haydn's tune, among them Carl Czerny, Wenzel Matiegka, Simon Sechter, and (ominously) an obscure figure named Führer—Robert Führer (1807–61), an unsavory church musician from Prague whose nefarious deeds included foisting off Schubert's G-major Mass on a publisher as his own. But the best variations were written by Haydn himself, as the second movement of the *Emperor* Quartet. The melody is inherently serious and elegant, and Haydn respects its character when he varies it. In the first variation, reduced to only two instruments, the first violin sings a sprightly filigree as the second violin plays the theme. The cello takes up the tune in the second variation, with the second violin sticking to a close harmonization and the other instruments filling out the texture (again, with the first violin being particularly decorative). Texture is again explored in the third variation: the three upper voices, then the three lower, then all four together, with the viola carrying the theme throughout. A slight reharmonization informs the hushed fourth variation, where the melody lies high in the first violin, and the foursome weaves its way to a magically contrapuntal coda.

The other movements seem to lead to, and then from, this obvious highpoint. The generously scaled opening *Allegro* is nonetheless entirely captivating in its own right, nowhere more than when in the development section it veers into a rowdy country dance, with the violins letting loose over an extended musette-style drone in the viola and cello. The *Menuetto* is forthright, its minor-key trio section assuming an expectant poise. A lyrical, major-key phrase within the trio sounds as if it were—odd concept—a trio within the trio. As in the G-major String Quartet (Op. 76, No. 1), Haydn begins his *Finale* in the tonic minor (C minor), although most of the exposition is actually spent in E-flat major. The development section, which bristles with triplets, builds up massive power, and finally the music finds its way to C major for a stentorian conclusion.

String Quartet in D major, Op. 76, No. 5 (Hob. III:79)

> *Allegretto—Allegro*
> *Largo cantabile e mesto*
> *Menuetto*
> *Finale. Presto*

Work composed: 1797

Work dedicated: To Count Joseph Erdödy

Work premiered: Not known

Instrumentation: Two violins, viola, and cello

Haydn's Quartet in D major (Op. 76, No. 5) is experimental in both its form and its musical working-out. Its first movement is structured not according to any sort of sonata form, contrary to expectation, but instead as a sort of siciliano (*Allegretto*) and an ornamented variation upon it, separated by a relatively tumultuous middle section. All of this is brought to a conclusion via an extended, vigorous, highly contrapuntal coda (*Allegro*); you might consider it a further variation that takes off on material from both the siciliano and the middle section.

The marking *Largo cantabile e mesto* ("Slowly, in a singing, mournful manner") is an indication we would expect to find more in a nineteenth-century quartet than an eighteenth-century one (which this one still is, just barely). In his late quartets Haydn very much straddles the divide; his pupil Beethoven, after all, was composing his first set of six quartets at about the same time Haydn was producing Op. 76. What's really notable is not so much the marking itself as the fact that it so quintessentially reflects what is embedded in the music. Haydn's late-in-career slow movements take on a sense of introspection and melancholy that had scarcely been expressed before. They are true harbingers of the slow-movement expressivity that Beethoven and his successors would soon be pushing toward an extreme. The late, regretted H. C. Robbins Landon, in his monumental *Haydn: Chronicle and Works*, described this as one of Haydn's "late-period slow movements with a profound but objective sense of melancholy—as if its composer were mourning for some lost antique thing of beauty." It is probably no coincidence that Beethoven's B-flat-major Quartet (Op. 18, No. 6), with its searching section titled "La Malinconia" ("Melancholy") followed this Haydn movement by only two or three years, if that (and on the very heels of the publication of Op. 76, which appeared in print in 1799). Haydn casts this unhurried slow movement in the rather arcane key of F-sharp major, a key attached to several of his most expressive compositions and one that here gives rise to a specific string tone. This movement is so greatly admired by connoisseurs that it did at one time give rise to a nickname for this entire quartet—the *Largo* Quartet—although that usage seems never to have been widespread and has by now fallen into complete desuetude.

Classical minuet movements are often the "least among equals," relatively lightweight palate-cleansers preparing the way for a sparkling dessert of a finale. In this case Haydn's minuet displays considerable gravitas in and of itself, its opening set deep in the instruments' registers and its central trio section full of minor-key seriousness in which the cello, and for a while the upper strings, scurry nervously, as if they had recently been visiting the furtive garden scene of Mozart's *Le nozze di Figaro*.

The *Finale* is one of Haydn's comic masterpieces. To begin with, the opening chords sound like closing chords of a particularly clichéd sort. (In his book *The Great Haydn Quartets*, the musicologist Hans Keller, whom I can't resist needling, complained that he couldn't figure out why everybody considered this a joke. He preferred to view the opening measures instead as a particularly compressed introduction. It seems that Hans Keller was not much one for jokes, though he appreciated Haydn deeply for other reasons.) After that feint the inner lines start chugging away like a motor that will hardly let up until the piece ends; their chords are strikingly similar to the ones that launched this fleeting movement less than four minutes earlier. In this concluding movement listeners finally get the sonata-form satisfaction they would have anticipated in the opening *Allegro*, but it's presented in a folksy guise and with economy and concentration of material that are unusual even for Haydn.

String Quartet in G major, Op. 77, No. 1 (Hob. III:81)

> *Allegro moderato*
> *Adagio*
> *Menuetto: Presto—Trio*
> *Finale: Presto*

Work composed: 1799

Work dedicated: To Prince Franz Joseph Maximilian von Lobkowitz

Work premiered: Not known

Instrumentation: Two violins, viola, and cello

There has been considerable speculation about why the *Lobkowitz* Quartets, Haydn's last complete works in the genre, are merely a pair, while all the others were produced in sets of six. It is certainly possible that Haydn intended to add at least one more to the set, and there are indications that Prince Lobkowitz may have expressly requested a group of six. But in 1799 the composer authorized his publisher, the Viennese firm of Artaria, to issue just the two together. This Artaria did, only a few months after they issued the set of Six Quartets (Op. 18) of Haydn's former pupil Ludwig van Beethoven—a set that bore a dedication to the same noble patron. It was the only Haydn dedication that Lobkowitz would receive, but many more from Beethoven would be forthcoming: the Triple Concerto; the Third, Fifth, and Sixth Symphonies; the E-flat-major Quartet (Op. 74); and the song cycle *An die ferne Geliebte.*

Listening to Haydn's Op. 77 Quartets one senses that they were composed to some extent in the shadow of Beethoven's Op. 18. Haydn, of course, was the grand old man of the genre, and Beethoven was still just a beginner; and yet Haydn was doubtless more aware than anybody that with the appearance of the Op. 18 Quartets, the ground rules had changed. His Op. 77 Quartets display all the imagination and polish one would expect from Haydn at that advanced point in his career, but certain traits seem to reflect the new experiments of Beethoven more than the ongoing logic of Haydn's own stream of quartets: sudden dynamic explosions, vigor in the minuets that seem to be turbulent Beethoven-style scherzos in all but name. In the G-major Quartet we are also struck by a pervading melancholy in the fantasia-like slow movement; at times the musical dialogue seems operatic, even foreshadowing the sort of vocal characterization that would emerge little more than a decade later in the works of Rossini.

The outer movements of the G-major Quartet are more firmly rooted in Haydn's accustomed practices. The opening *Allegro moderato* exhibits the flavor of a march, though, of course, it is developed with greater sophistication than one would expect of that genre. Some scholars maintain that the main theme is based on an ancient Hungarian recruiting song, from the same *verbunkos* tradition we found reflected in the *Gypsy Rondo* Piano Trio. Folk music has also been cited in connection with the *Finale*, the droll, oddly accented principal theme in this case being a Croatian round dance. (Croatian folk music had also provided some direct inspiration for a boisterous expanse of the *Gypsy Rondo* Trio.) Whatever inspired the tune, it does trace an odd contour. It seems to begin with the melody already in mid-phrase, not at all anchored, with some harmonic puzzlement, and only as the tune unrolls does it seem somehow logical in retrospect. The second time around it makes a quite different impression, as by that time our ear has figured out how to contextualize it. (A relative is found in the *Allegretto* movement of his Symphony No. 82, the *Bear*.) Haydn presents it forcefully, assigning it to all four instruments in unison. He puts it through all kinds of clever and inspired exercises, and at one points works up such an energetic frenzy that one can imagine Felix Mendelssohn using it as a starting point for the surpassing vigor of his Octet for Strings.

(signature) Fanny Hensel

Fanny Cäcilie Mendelssohn Hensel

Born: November 14, 1805, in Hamburg, Germany

Died: May 14, 1847, in Berlin, Prussia (Germany)

Surname: Hensel, following her marriage in 1829

Piano Trio in D minor, Op. 11

Allegro molto vivace
Andante espressivo
Lied (Allegretto)
Allegro moderato

Work composed: The winter of 1846–47

Work premiered: April 11, 1847, in Berlin

Instrumentation: Violin, cello, and piano

When music-lovers hear the name Mendelssohn they naturally think first of Felix, who was one of the most remarkable prodigies in the history of music. But he was not the only musical prodigy in the Mendelssohn family. In fact, the path for Felix was paved by his sister Fanny, three and a quarter years his senior and the eldest of the four Mendelssohn siblings. In the early years it was not uncommon for visitors to find Fanny even more remarkable than Felix. The two remained intertwined artistically and intellectually for their whole lives, which ended within months of each other's. She died suddenly of a stroke (as her father and grandfather had), on May 14, 1847, while conducting a rehearsal for one of the Sunday salon concerts she regularly hosted. In the aftermath of this devastating loss Felix sought solace in Switzerland, where he composed his despondent F-minor

String Quartet. His spirit was broken, and in October and November, back in Germany, he suffered three strokes in quick succession, surviving his beloved sister by less than six months.

One hesitates to speak of Fanny's as a tragic life, even though it lasted only forty-two years. She was born into privilege, was afforded an education of rare distinction, benefited from tremendous talent, was widely liked, and seems to have been generally happy. In 1829 she married the Prussian court painter Wilhelm Hensel. She was content in her marriage, and although she lost a child as a stillbirth, the Hensels' surviving son, Sebastian, grew up to become the chronicler of his astonishing family, producing a lengthy history of the Mendelssohns to which later historians are indebted. Beginning in the early 1830s she reinvigorated the family's earlier tradition (which had since lapsed) and began presiding over the vibrant and influential salon in Berlin, where she regularly performed as a pianist and premiered her new compositions. She cultivated friendships with people she found artistically stimulating. One such was the composer Charles Gounod, who wrote of her in his *Memoirs*: "Madame Hensel was a musician beyond comparison, a remarkable pianist, and a woman of superior mind; small and thin in person but with an energy that showed itself in her deep eyes and in her fiery glance. She was gifted with rare ability as a composer."

And yet, looking back from our vantage point, we can hardly help feeling that her life *was* tragic—or at least became so in one particular shortly after she started to compose: she was not encouraged to excel in a professional sphere. This was because she was a woman, of course, but more specifically it was because she was an upper-class woman, and Berlin society simply did not admit the idea of upper-class women pursuing any profession at all. It is something of a miracle that even Felix was encouraged in this direction, since music hardly counted as a "real profession" in those circles. For Fanny it was unthinkable. Her career would essentially be a private one, played out before appreciative listeners in her salon but not in any more public forum. She performed precisely once in a public venue, in February 1838, and then only because of special circumstances, which she detailed in a letter to her (and Felix's) friend Karl Klingemann:

> Last week there was a concert which caused a sensation in elegant society here. It was of a kind often given elsewhere: amateurs playing to benefit the poor, with tickets twice the normal price. The chorus was almost exclusively composed of countesses, ambassadors' wives, and officers. As a lady of acceptable rank I too was earnestly invited to play, and so for the first time in my life I played in public, choosing Felix's Concerto in G minor. I was not at all afraid—my acquaintances were kind enough to be nervous for me, and despite a rather wretched program the concert as a whole aroused so much curiosity and interest it raised 2500 thalers.

She began to release a few of her compositions publicly during her last years. Her published oeuvre ran to eleven opus numbers (although the Op. 11 Piano Trio was not actually published until after her death) and another sixteen short pieces that appeared with no opus numbers attached. These represent a tiny fraction of her output, which runs to about five hundred works, and modern editions of her music did not begin to appear until the late 1980s. As a result, our conception of Fanny Mendelssohn Hensel as a composer remains today very much in formation.

She composed her Piano Trio during the winter of 1846–47, and it was first played at a musicale marking the birthday of her sister Rebecka, on April 11. There is no getting around how similar this music is to her brother's—not surprising, given that the two were all but joined at the hip, enjoying essentially the same upbringing, musical and otherwise, and remaining always interested and involved in each other's work. Individual themes or phrases in the trio may well suggest corresponding passages in some of Felix's compositions, although Fanny certainly generated high-quality melodies of real originality. In the opening movement, the piano's initial rumblings are not distant from those in Felix's C-minor Piano Trio, and some of the fleet-fingered passage-work might be drawn from his piano concertos. As in several of Felix's chamber compositions with piano, the piano does sometimes tend to dominate the proceedings; in this piece, the violin and the cello often work in tandem "versus" the piano, though the cello has the honor of introducing the gorgeous second theme. In July 1847, an anonymous critic in the *Neue Berliner Musik Zeitung* commented of this movement: "We [find] in this trio broad, sweeping foundations that build themselves up through stormy waves into a marvelous edifice. In this respect the first movement is a masterpiece, and the trio most highly original."

The second and third movements reveal Fanny in her "lieder mode." Either could easily be imagined as songs, and the third movement is actually titled thus. This *Lied (Allegretto)* is short, forthright, and seductively beautiful, and it is an overt tribute to Felix as its theme is spun out of the opening phrase of the aria "If With All your Hearts" from his recently premiered oratorio *Elijah*, which Fanny had just then gotten to know. The opening of the finale, a piano flourish that evokes Bach's Chromatic Fantasy, reminds us of the conservative German musical tradition from which the Mendelssohns emerged. But this beginning is something of a red herring; the principal theme, which ensues directly, is nostalgic and stately, rather *à la* Chopin, perhaps with a touch of the "style hongrois" that was popular among the composers of the Romantic generation. A memorable theme from the first movement makes a repeat appearance in this finale, serving to bind this large-scale piece together.

Fanny Mendelssohn Hensel's Piano Trio is an impressive piece of music, and one feels churlish saying that it makes one wonder what she might have achieved if her circumstances had been different—if she had been in her brother's place. To have achieved a composition such as this is, in a sense, enough; and yet, one can only regret that this would be a unique entry in what, in another day and age, might have been a more formidably developed oeuvre. She appears to have been broadening her path of self-determination when she composed this piece; but a month and three days after its premiere, she reached her double bar.

Paul Hindemith (signature)

Paul Hindemith

Born: November 16, 1895, in Hanau, near Frankfurt, Germany

Died: December 28, 1963, in Frankfurt

Kleine Kammermusik for Wind Quintet, Op. 24, No. 2

Lustig. Mässig schnelle Viertel
Walzer. Durchweg sehr leise
Ruhig und einfach.—Im gleichen ruhigen Zeitmass (nicht scherzando!)
Schnelle Viertel [attacca],
Sehr lebhaft

Work composed: 1922

Work dedicated: "Written for the Frankfurt Wind Chamber Music Society"

Work premiered: July 12, 1922, in Cologne, Germany, by the musicians of the Frankfurt Wind Chamber Music Society (Frankfurter Bläser-Kammermusikvereinigung)

Instrumentation: Flute (doubling piccolo), oboe, clarinet, horn, and bassoon

When the twentieth century was at its midpoint, Paul Hindemith was regularly cited as one of the most influential composers of his era, along with Stravinsky, Schoenberg, and (at least by connoisseurs) Bartók. Not long after that, his public stock fell sharply. The style with which his name is most strongly connected is that of a punctilious, emotionally cool musical craftsman writing according to strict harmonic rules of his own devising (developed out of an idiosyncratic interpretation of musical acoustics) that, while sounding firmly tonal, wends its way through musical hierarchies that are not exactly those of the time-honored tonic-dominant system. (In short, his music is shot through with the interval of the fourth.)

In the early 1920s, Hindemith was reveling in the variety of styles that swirled through the musical atmosphere. He had already proved adept in a multitude of languages that seemed more innate to other composers: Puccini's melodic lyricism, Strauss' rich-blooded late-Romanticism, Schreker's Symbolist synthesis, Schoenberg's Expressionism (found in Hindemith's Second String Quartet, of 1921), Ravel's orientalism (as in Hindemith's 1920 one-act opera *Das Nusch-Nuschi*), Bartók's modality and rhythmic intricacy (which Hindemith explored in his Third String Quartet, of 1922), and the inevitable allure of American jazz (evident in Hindemith's *Suite '1922'* for piano). Through all this imitation and experimentation, Hindemith was developing his own angular and contrapuntal voice. Chamber music proved central to his evolving style, which marked some of its most important breakthroughs in his string quartets (neglected today), his witty *Kammermusik* No. 1 (1921), and his vocal chamber works (inspired, perhaps, by Stravinsky's *The Soldier's Tale*, Schoenberg's *Pierrot Lunaire*, and exotically timbred works by Ravel and Maurice Delage). Hindemith had no trouble keeping busy. In 1922 he wrote, "I've got a chronic mania for work."

Hindemith attached the term *Kammermusik*—literally "chamber music"—to a series of seven pieces in the 1920s, the first a modern-day concerto grosso for small orchestra, all the others concertos for solo instrument with a large chamber ensemble or small chamber orchestra. The *Kleine Kammermusik* ("Little Chamber Music") of 1922 does not for the most part share the contrapuntal abstraction of those works, which stand as testaments to his temporary involvement with the esthetics of the so-called *Neue Sachlichkeit* ("New Objectivity"). This is a more inviting piece, a genial five-movement "little suite" that doesn't ask to be taken too seriously. The opening movement (*Lustig. Mässig schnelle Viertel*; "Merry. Moderately fast quarter-notes") bustles with the sort of energy we might associate with Stravinsky and the composers of Les Six (who were active just then in Paris), but the harmonic writing sounds like nobody but Hindemith. The Waltz (*Durchweg sehr leise*— "Very soft throughout") might be the last dance of an evening in which a good deal of champagne has been consumed and everyone already should have gone to bed; in this movement alone the flutist switches to piccolo, to add a further air of wispiness. Again, Hindemith's trademark harmonies inform the peaceful third movement, which unrolls over ostinato figures (*Ruhig und einfach.—Im gleichen ruhigen Zeitmass (nicht scherzando!)*—"Peaceful and simple," leading to a section marked "In the same peaceful tempo" but "not in a playful fashion!"). In the minuscule fourth (*Schnelle Viertel*—"Fast quarter-notes"), lasting only twenty-three measures, solo proclamations from each of the instruments alternate with pounding, machine-age rhythms from the ensemble as a whole. The finale (*Sehr lebhaft*—"Very lively") is an earnest march—but not too earnest.

The piece was premiered by the Frankfurt Wind Chamber Music Society in July 1922, in Cologne, and was quickly welcomed by wind players as a consummate addition to their chamber repertoire. When the piece was given in a Town Hall recital in New York, in 1935, Hindemith wrote in his journal of his delight in finding the hall filled, with many young people figuring among the listeners. "Someone told me later," he continued, "that in a radio critique, which is considered most important here and which compares the value of programs by stars like a bottle of Cognac, [they] had given me four stars. This never happens to modern music—only to Greta Garbo."

Septet for Flute, Oboe, Clarinet, Bass Clarinet, Bassoon, Horn, and Trumpet

> *Lebhaft*
> *Intermezzo: Sehr langsam, frei*
> *Variationen*
> *Intermezzo: Sehr langsam*
> *Fuge: Alter Berner Marsch: Schnell*

Work composed: November through December 7, 1948, in Taormina and Rome, Italy

Work premiered: December 30, 1948, in Milan, by members of the Teatro Nuovo Orchestra

Instrumentation: Flute, oboe, clarinet, bass clarinet, bassoon, horn, and trumpet

The years following 1932 proved difficult for Hindemith. He did not immediately recognize the threat posed by the rise of the National Socialist Party in Germany, apparently assuming it would be a passing, short-lived development. He went on expressing his personal anti-Nazi views, performing with Jewish colleagues, and failing to recognize that his own wife's part-Jewish background might be used to squash his career. In November 1934, the Kulturgemeinde—an independent organization that served early on as unofficial cultural guardians for the Nazis—effected a boycott on all performances of his music, and in January 1935 he was placed on a leave of absence from his teaching position at the Hochschule für Musik in Berlin. By 1937 his situation grew so dire that he left for Switzerland, and in February 1940 he and his wife, Gertrud, proceeded to the United States, which he had visited on concert tours in each of the three previous years. He applied for American citizenship almost immediately on his arrival and was finally naturalized in 1946.

Several colleges and universities vied for him to grace their faculties, and in the end Yale was the successful suitor. In the autumn of 1940 he joined its faculty (first in a visiting position, soon in a permanent one), and he would remain there until 1953 as professor of music theory, at which point he and his wife returned to live in Europe. At Yale, he gained the reputation of being a tough taskmaster but earned a following among especially devoted students of theory and enthusiasts of early music, since he also directed the university's collegium musicum.

Hindemith composed his fifteen-minute-long Septet in 1948, during a visit to Europe that was largely given over to conducting engagements in England, Germany, and Italy. He wrote most of it in Taormina, Sicily, in November, and completed the finale in Rome, on December 7, 1948. Hindemith later recalled: "I wrote the piece in Taormina in one of the most beautiful gardens anyone could possibly imagine, with the sea at my feet and the snow-capped Aetna in the background. If one believes that one's surroundings influence the quality of a composition in some indescribable way, then one would expect that only the finest ideas would be found in such a place."

The Septet was premiered in Milan, by members of the Teatro Nuovo Orchestra, on December 30. It seems to have made rather little splash until four years later, when it was programmed on a concert by the New Friends of Music chamber orchestra (with the composer conducting, as was deemed required), at New York's Town Hall, on December 7, 1952. This was an important concert, an all-Hindemith event that included his *Kammermusik* No. 1 (from 1921), *Kammermusik* No. 3 (from 1925), and Concert Music for Piano, Brass, and Two Harps (from 1930), in addition to the Septet, which was the only recently composed piece on the program. The New York critics had been complaining for some time that Hindemith refused to have any of his early, European-period works played in America, and they were delighted (as was the audience) to finally hear three of them at one setting. Nonetheless, it was the Septet that made the deepest impression, since in early 1953 the New York Music Critics Circle named it 1952's "Best New Chamber Work of the Year." It was a curious selection given that the piece had already been premiered four years earlier—but no matter. Gertrud Hindemith wrote to their friend Willi Strecker, head of the Schott publishing firm: "The nice little Wind Septet has suddenly become famous because the New York critics voted it the best chamber music piece of the year. We have no idea what the award really means, but congratulations are raining down on all sides. The Septet is suddenly on the lips of all grocers and fishmongers, who have now admitted us into the ranks of their most important customers."

The Septet is cast in five movements, though it is crafted in such a way as to suggest a single, unified span divided into discrete sections. "Crafted" is a word that often comes to mind when listening to Hindemith's music, and even the first hearing suggests that this piece is as carefully turned as one expects of its composer. The opening movement (*Lebhaft*—"Lively") is indeed spirited, and it displays tremendous good humor. Its principal theme, which involves all the woodwinds trilling at once (but not the brasses), comes across as so sarcastic that one might imagine it accompanying a cartoon film. The ensuing *Intermezzo* (*Sehr langsam, frei*—"Very slow, free") sounds improvisatory at heart, and the composer's direction that it should be played freely stretches it further in the direction of the rhapsodic. Nine variations on a lyrical melody, each with a distinct rhythmic character, follow as the third movement; the "accompanying" texture displays striking imagination in terms of the sonic possibilities of the ensemble. A second brief *Intermezzo*, as fluid as the first (and again *Sehr langsam*), leads to a finale in which Hindemith melds the scholarly and popular sides of his musical personality. He casts it as a fugue, that doughtiest of academic compositional genres—indeed, parts of it are a double fugue, with two subjects going on at once—but there's a twinkle in the composer's eye. Suddenly the trumpet lets loose with a chunky, four-square phrase of a piece identified as the "Old Bern March," a tune then taken up and elaborated by other instruments, and even turned into a little fugato itself. After the whirlwind has gone on just long enough, Hindemith extinguishes everything with a couple of concluding chords, laughing all the way.

Jacques Ibert

Born: August 15, 1890, in Paris, France

Died: February 5, 1962, in Paris

Trois pièces brèves ("Three Short Pieces"), for Wind Quintet

Allegro
Andante
Assez lent—Allegro scherzando

Work composed: 1930

Work premiered: March 21, 1930, as part of a theatrical production at the Théâtre de l'Atelier in Paris

Instrumentation: Flute, oboe, clarinet, horn, and bassoon

Jacques Ibert represents the quintessence of the Parisian composer of the early to mid-twentieth century: cultivated but not pompous, technically adept but self-effacing, blending the "serious" with the "popular," typically good-spirited and often witty. He was born in Paris during the Belle Epoque and died in the same city seventy-two years later, having weathered two world wars. His mother, who was distantly related to the Spanish composer Manuel de Falla, had studied piano at the Paris Conservatoire and encouraged his musical education as a child. He was drawn to both music and the theatre, but his first professional steps after high school were hardly distinguished: he started working as a movie-hall pianist and writing popular songs under the pseudonym William Berty.

Realizing that he needed systematic artistic training, he enrolled at the Paris Conservatoire in 1910, initially as a drama student. Soon he began studying harmony and in 1912 moved on to the renowned counterpoint classes of André Gédalge; his fellow students included Arthur Honegger and Darius Milhaud, with whom he would enjoy lifelong friendships. In 1913 he also began studying composition with Paul Vidal, a teacher who was interested in up-to-date developments in music, of which there were plenty at that moment. Unfortunately, World War I intruded just when Ibert would have begun the Conservatoire's orchestration curriculum, and instead he spent several years as a nurse and stretcher-bearer. When the war ended, in 1918, he instantly returned to his composing and—little short of miraculously, given the interruption and his lack of orchestration training—he was awarded the prestigious Prix de Rome on his first try, in 1919.

Ibert would extend his activities to include music administration, and in 1937 he was named director of the Académie de France at the Villa Medici in Rome, which is where he had spent time as a Prix de Rome winner. He held that position until 1960, commuting between Paris and Rome frequently throughout that period, though with a break during the years of World War II. The Vichy Régime found him particularly abhorrent (to his great credit) and banned his music. He responded by retreating from Paris to Antibes on the Riviera—hardly a penance in and of itself—then on to other locales until the war was over. In 1955, Ibert was named administrator of the Théâtres Lyriques Nationaux, in which capacity he oversaw both of Paris's principal opera houses, the Opéra de Paris and the Opéra-Comique. Ill health forced him to resign less than a year later, but his spirit was boosted when, shortly thereafter, he was elected to the Académie des Beaux-Arts.

Ibert never departed much from an essentially traditional method of composing, and he used explicitly modern harmonies principally as surface details in his scores. He steadily produced an oeuvre that included contributions to most of the major musical genres (except sacred music), including orchestral works (most famously *Escales* and his Flute Concerto), operas (one of which, *L'Aiglon*, he composed jointly with Honegger), ballets (his neo-Renaissance *Diane de Poitiers* score is occasionally played), film scores (including the "Circus" section of the 1956 *Invitation to the Dance*, devised, directed, and danced by Gene Kelly but a flop nevertheless), and even, by way of curiosity, two cadenzas each for Mozart's Bassoon Concerto and Clarinet Concerto.

From 1924 on, he also composed a good deal of incidental music for dramatic productions, a natural intersection of his double-threat background in music and theatre, and it was one such project that gave rise to the *Trois pièces brèves*. The play was the five-act comedy *The Beaux' Stratagem*, by the

Irish author George Farquhar (1677 or 1678–1707), one of the cleverest play-wrights of the Restoration stage; the plot involves two rakish brothers and their hilarious quest to better their lot by marrying well-positioned young ladies in the peaceful countryside. It was adapted by Maurice Constantin-Weyer into a French version that was purveyed under the title *Le Stratagème des roués*, and when it was unveiled in Paris in 1930, it was graced with a charming score by Ibert. With a view toward practicality, he crafted his music for a standard wind quintet, which the theatre could accommodate with little space and a modest budget.

Within months, Ibert selected three of the morsels from his incidental music to stand on their own as a concert triptych. After a *fortissimo* call to attention, the first movement proper (*Allegro*) is insouciance itself, built on an oboe tune that, ironically, is both absent-minded and unforgettable. In the minuscule, more pensive second movement (*Andante*) the texture is pared down to a duo of flute and clarinet, though at its end the other instruments join in to rock the movement to sleep. A not-too-hearty reveille (*Assez lent*) announces the finale, in which upper lines sing out with what briefly seems a touch of alarm (from the flute) above a puttering accompaniment (*Allegro scherzando*). Gradually good order is restored, and the music waddles off cheer-fully. There's nothing complicated about this score, which in its entirety lasts only six minutes or so. On the surface it offers some moderately spicy bito-nality that is reminiscent of Stravinsky's *Pulcinella*, but it certainly wouldn't have pushed any of its initial listeners out of their comfort zone. Nonetheless, this amiable, lightweight suite proved perfectly suited to its medium, and it wasted little time establishing itself as the most frequently programmed piece in the entire literature of the wind quintet.

Chas. E. Ives.

Charles Edward Ives

Born October 20, 1874, in Danbury, Connecticut

Died: May 19, 1954, in New York City

String Quartet No. 2

  I. *Discussions: Andante moderato—Andante con spirito—Adagio molto*
 II. *Arguments: Allegro con spirito—Andante emasculata—Allegro con fisto—Largo—Allegro—Largo soblato—Allegro con fuoco—Andante con scratchy (as tuning up)—Allegro con fistiwatto (as a K.O.)*
III. *"The Call of the Mountains": Adagio—Andante—Andante con spirito—Adagio primo—Adagio maestoso*

Work composed: **1907–13**

Work premiered: **September 15, 1946, at the Yaddo Music Festival in Saratoga, New York, by the Walden Quartet**

Instrumentation: **Two violins, viola, and cello**

C harles Ives had the advantage of growing up surrounded by musical open-mindedness (or, better put, open-earedness). His father, George Ives, was a Connecticut bandmaster who took enormous pleasure from musical coincidences that most people found revolting—playing the melody of a tune in one key and its harmony in another, for example, or savoring the overlapping sounds of separate bands playing at once on a parade ground. Charles Ives grew up with the resultant polytonality sounding logical to his ears, a situation that did not endear him to the music faculty at Yale, where he spent four years (1894–98) and earned a D-plus grade average.

Following graduation, Ives sensibly took a position with an insurance firm. He proved exceptionally adept in that field, and in 1906 he started planning the creation of his own company—the eventual Ives & Myrick—in New York City. He would enter the annals of insurance for his advances in the recruitment and training of insurance agents and his pioneering concept of estate planning. His success as a businessman, combined with chronic but not entirely debilitating health concerns, led him to spend much of his adulthood pursuing his passion for composition in private. He was not particularly pleased that most of his works went unperformed, but at least his finances were such that he could go on composing whether people were interested in his work or not. Recognition was a long time coming, but when it finally arrived it did so decisively. In 1945 he was elected to the National Institute of Arts and Letters, and in 1947 he was honored with the Pulitzer Prize for his Third Symphony. "Awards and prizes are for school children, and I'm no longer a school boy," he harrumphed, keeping up appearances as the cranky Yankee he often was; but his friends recounted that, deep down, he seemed pleased and even honored by this turning of the tide.

Ives' Second String Quartet is now recognized as a hallmark of Modernism, but it wasn't premiered until thirty-three years after it was completed, and then it waited another eight years to appear in print. Throughout his career, Ives jotted memos to himself to capture thoughts on his music, his intended projects, his experiences, and a plethora of other topics. From time to time he would go through these to pluck out items appropriate to some current enterprise—an article in progress, a train of thought—with the result that many became misplaced. After the composer's death, his acolyte John Kirkpatrick managed to reassemble a great many of the memos, and he published them in 1972. Though that volume can prove frustrating—its very nature is to be fragmentary and desultory—it's packed with flashes of reminiscence and insight for anyone interested in the composer and his works. Here's a memo Ives jotted at some point that has relevance to the work at hand. Be forewarned: Ives was an alpha male among composers, given to withering, exasperating pronouncements about persons or music he considered insufficiently masculine:

> It used to come over me—especially after coming from some of those nice Kneisel Quartet concerts—that music had been, and still was too much of an emasculated art. Too much of what was easy and usual to play and to hear was called beautiful, etc.—the same old even-vibration, Sybaritic apron-strings, keeping music too much tied to the old ladies. The string quartet music got more and more weak, trite, and effeminate. After one of those Kneisel Quartet concerts in the old Mendelssohn Hall [in New York City], I started a string quartet score, half mad, half in fun, and half to try out, practise, and have some

fun with making those men fiddlers get up and do something like men. The set of three pieces for string quartet called: I. Four Men have Discussions, Conversations, II. Arguments and Fight, III. Contemplation—was done then. Only a part of a movement was copied out in parts and tried over...—it made all the men rather mad. I didn't blame them—it was very hard to play—but now it wouldn't cause so much trouble.

A characteristic element of Ives' style is the rampant use of musical quotations. At the very least they can surprise and amuse listeners, but often they serve to enlarge his compositions by reaching out beyond the score at hand to grasp the audible culture that stands without. Ives was all-embracing in his quotations and borrowings, which within a single piece can range from revival hymns and Civil War songs to patriotic anthems, popular tunes, college cheers, famous melodies from the classics, and even other works of his own composition. The musicologist Clayton W. Henderson has catalogued all (or darn near all) the borrowings in Ives' compositions and published them as *The Charles Ives Tunebook*, which Ives aficionados will find endlessly useful. Henderson spots allusions to fourteen outside pieces in the Second String Quartet (with several providing multiple borrowings), ranging from the Prelude to Wagner's *Tristan und Isolde* to "Columbia, the Gem of the Ocean" (a favorite Ivesian theme song) and "Turkey in the Straw." The most extraordinary superimposition comes in the second movement with the vast pileup of "Hail, Columbia!," Tchaikovsky's Sixth Symphony, Brahms' Second, Beethoven's Ninth, "Marching through Georgia," and "Massa's in de Cold, Cold Ground." If, as you listen, you fleetingly sense a familiar contour, your ears are probably not deceiving you.

Slow outer movements frame a fast middle one. The opening movement strikes a serious tone; it is a discussion in earnest, if discussion is quite the right word for a convocation in which all the parties constantly talk and never listen, rests being almost entirely absent from these densely inscribed pages.

Differences of opinion escalate in the fast second movement, although the exuberant outbursts do subside for a few moments—and I do mean moments—of calm in which we may imagine our participants gathering their thoughts. The second violin seizes a few opportunities to emit banal pleasantries. Ives assigned a name to that instrument on a sketch, though not in the published score: Rollo, the name of an overly well-behaved lad who was the hero in a series of children's books Ives had known in his youth. Rollo was the kind of obsequious person Ives abhorred. In the middle of the movement Ives doles out a fugato; it's horribly dissonant, and clearly he's proud of it. The texture is less abrasive in the final movement, although even here all the voices are active nearly all the time. Ives manages to build up and sustain a sense of mystical awe that culminates in an almost static *Adagio maestoso*. Here the first violin does its best to render double- and even triple-stopped sonorities somewhere high in the ether before everything wafts off in a cloud of relatively certain, but still slightly ambiguous, F major.

Leoš Janáček

Born: July 3, 1854, in Hukvaldy, Moravia

Died: August 12, 1928, in Moravská Ostrava, Moravia (Czechoslovakia)

Mládí ("Youth") for Wind Sextet

Allegro
Andante sostenuto
Vivace
Allegro animato

Work composed: July 1924, completed on July 24 in Hukvaldy, Czechoslovakia (drawing in the third movement on music written that May)

Work premiered: October 21, 1924, in Brno by an ensemble of professors from the Brno Conservatory

Instrumentation: Flute (doubling piccolo), oboe, clarinet, bass clarinet, horn, and bassoon

Since nearly all of Leoš Janáček's best known works date from the twentieth century—in most cases, from well into the twentieth century—we are likely to forget that this greatest of Moravian composers was anchored in the late-Romantic and nationalist traditions of the Czech lands. He was actually a near-contemporary of his Bohemian colleague Antonín Dvořák, who was only thirteen years older; but because Janáček enjoyed reasonable longevity and because his most notable output came later in life, he appears to us as belonging to an entirely later generation, and as such has been increasingly revered as an important modernist.

Nearly all of his most famous works date from his final decade. Among the great composers only César Franck rivals him for winning the race to the pantheon largely during the last lap. Janáček was approaching his seventieth birthday when he composed his wind sextet *Mládí* ("Youth"). It is such a buoyant piece that one imagines the composer in a kind of second childhood, devoid of premonitions that his end lay in the rather near future. It seems he had been inspired to write a chamber work for winds upon hearing a concert by the Société Moderne des Instruments à Vent, a Parisian ensemble he happened to encounter when they performed Albert Roussel's Divertissement for Wind Quintet and Piano at an International Society of Contemporary Music (ISCM) Festival in Salzburg in 1923. In April 1924 the ensemble followed up with a performance in Brno that reinforced the initial impression the group had made on Janáček. In the event, he did not mimic Roussel's instrumentation exactly in *Mládí*. Instead, he dispensed with the piano and employed an expanded version of the standard wind quintet, the unorthodox combination of flute (doubling piccolo), oboe, clarinet, bass clarinet, horn, and bassoon. Certainly the subject of youth was much on Janáček's mind as at that moment he was working with his biographer Max Brod on recounting the early period of his own life. On May 19, 1924, he had composed his *Pochod modráčků* (usually translated as *March of the Blue-Boys*), a merry little thing for piccolo, glockenspiel, and tambourine (or piccolo and piano) that depicted a memory from his school days, the blue-boys referring to the choristers—of which he had been one—at the ancient monastery in Brno. When it was published in the magazine *Hudební besídka* ("Bower of Music"), this inscription was appended: "Whistling go the little songsters from the Queen's Monastery—blue like bluebirds." This piece itself traced its ancestry to Janáček's sketch of a piece for piccolo, drums, and glockenspiel called *Siegesallee (Victory Boulevard)* meant to depict a musical contingent of the Prussian Army he had witnessed in Brno during the Austro-Prussian War (the "Seven Weeks' War") of 1866. The color blue would have been common to both scenes: the Prussian-blue uniforms of the soldiers, the blue cassocks of the choristers. The same music would shortly evolve into the third movement of *Mládí*.

The sextet occupied Janáček for about three weeks while he was ensconced at the cottage he had purchased a few years previously in his native village of Hukvaldy in Moravia, which by that time had become a part of the democratic republic of Czechoslovakia, formed six years before. From Hukvaldy, Janáček wrote to Kamila Stösslová (who will play a starring role in the Janáček story later), "While here I have composed a kind of reminiscence of my youth."

The first of the work's four movements is built around a main theme based on the falling third of A to F, intoned by the oboe at the outset, then in response by the flute; it is said that Janáček intended this motif as a sort of wordless text-setting of the phrase Mládí, zlaté mládí! ("Youth, golden youth!"). For decades Janáček had been fascinated by the idea of "speech melody," through which a strictly musical phrase might be crafted to follow the natural modulation of verbal speech. As early as 1897 he published a series of essays on Dvořák's tone poems. In Dvořák's Zlatý kolovrat ("The Golden Spinning Wheel") Janáček was struck by a melody that perfectly reflected the contour of an unusual spoken phrase found in the poem that inspired Dvořák's score. He approved entirely: Czech composers, he summarized, "ought to be, in the style of Czech music, phoneticians as well as symphonists." This principle would become central to his operatic text-settings, and here we find an example of his applying it also to a strictly instrumental piece. A sparkling central section is heralded by an unbuttoned outburst from the solo horn, playing con splendore. The movement, which is worked out in rondo form, includes a good measure of the nervous fluttering that is a Janáček fingerprint. It ends in a whirlwind, but for some comical pauses in the final bars. In contrast, the ensuing Andante sostenuto, with its unmistakably Slavic theme, seems introspective and nostalgic. The third movement is a scherzo (Vivace) that alternates twice with a more tender trio (and is that melodic figure of a gruppetto and a leap up a fourth or sixth intended to be a reference to Wagner's love music from Tristan und Isolde?). Here the flutist plays piccolo, recalling this music's original instrumentation as the March of the Blue-Boys. The finale is a joyful romp (though not without its pensive moments) that brings this brief work to its good-humored close.

Mládí was unveiled in Brno on October 21, 1924, when it was played by a group of teachers from the Brno Conservatory. The performers were in principle unimpeachable, and they had rehearsed the piece long and hard, but they were no match for the severe difference in temperature between their unheated warm-up room and the concert hall itself, which was uncomfortably hot. Disaster resulted. Matters of intonation aside, a key on the clarinetist's instrument chose that moment to stop working, putting that player out of the action. When the fiasco of a performance reached its end, Janáček leapt to the stage crying: "Ladies and Gentlemen, this was not my composition. Mr. Krtička [the clarinetist] was only pretending to play but in fact was not playing at all." By all reports, the work fared far better at its Prague premiere, at the Vinohrady Theatre on November 23 of the same year, when it was played by seven members of the Czech Philharmonic Orchestra—seven, rather than six, because separate players handled the flute and piccolo parts, notwithstanding the fact that Janáček had taken care to write in such a way that a single player could double on both. The piece was better received this time, and the Czech Academy honored Mládí, along with Janáček's First String Quartet, with its 1924 composition prize.

Capriccio for Piano Left-Hand and Chamber Ensemble

Allegro
Adagio
Allegretto
Andante

Work composed: June to October or early November 1926

Work premiered: March 2, 1928, in Smetana Hall, Prague, by pianist Otakar Hollmann and members of the Czech Philharmonic Orchestra: Václav Máček (flute); Evžen Šerý and František Trnka (trumpets); Antonín Bok, Jaroslav Šimsa, and Gustav Tyl (trombones), and Antonín Koula (tenor tuba), with Jaroslav Řidký conducting

Instrumentation: Flute (doubling piccolo), two trumpets, tenor tuba, three trombones, and piano left-hand.

A host of works featuring piano left-hand appeared in the years immediately following World War I. For many of them we must thank the Viennese pianist Paul Wittgenstein, the brother of the famous philosopher Ludwig Wittgenstein; after losing his right arm in the war, he developed an ambitious left-hand technique and commissioned left-hand works (mostly concertos or concerto-like pieces) from a lineup of composers that included Ravel, Prokofiev, Korngold, Hindemith, Britten, and Richard Strauss.

But he was not the only pianist forced into one-handedness by World War I. A similar fate befell Otakar Hollmann (1894–1967), a Czech pianist who emerged from the war with his right hand shattered and his arm bereft of feeling. He was the impetus for a number of works by Czech composers, including at least three notable additions to left-hand literature dating from 1926: Janáček's Capriccio for Piano Left-Hand and Chamber Ensemble, Bohuslav Martinů's Concertino for Piano Left-Hand and Chamber Orchestra, and Ervín Schulhoff's Piano Sonata No. 3. When Hollmann first approached Janáček about writing such a piece, the composer turned him down with a tactless comment: "But—my dear boy—why do you want to play with one hand? It's hard to dance to that which has only one leg." But then on November 11, 1926, Janáček wrote to Hollmann to impart the surprising news that he had in fact completed the proposed piece. "You know," he said in his letter, "just to write for left hand would have been willful to the point of childishness. More reasons were necessary: subjective and objective. When all three got together and came into conflict, the work came into existence." Janáček's initial reaction stuck painfully with Hollmann, who recalled arriving to read through the Capriccio at the composer's home in Brno in February 1928: "Hardly had I arrived in front of his garden house when I was overcome by desperate fear of how the Master would judge my dancing with one leg."

Nobody seems entirely sure about how to crack the code of the Capriccio, if, indeed, a subtext exists at all. At first Janáček titled the piece *Vzdor* ("Defiance"). The musicologist Jarmil Burghauser, in an essay included in the original printing of the score, opined that it was "Janáček's protest against the senselessness and horrors of war while the soloist—the work's hero—may be said to wage an unflinching struggle with one of war's crimes." Could be; but then again, the title Capriccio does seem flippant for such heavy matter. Another scholar, Bohumír Štědroň, thought the work had a biographical basis that involved Janáček's relationship with Kamila Stösslová, which was more incontrovertibly celebrated in the composer's String Quartet No. 2, *Listy důvěrné* ("Intimate Letters"), and he accordingly argued that the work was "an expression of peace and joyful contentment at the time of Janáček's affection for Kamila in defiance of the opinion of the rest of the world." The Janáček biographer Jaroslav Vogel doesn't agree with the "Kamila theory." He worries that "there is rather too little peace and joyful contentment in the work" apart from the last movement, and even there it's a stretch. The rest of the piece he finds "sometimes pugnacious, sometimes embittered, mocking, ironical, nostalgic and again even skeptical."

Asked to discuss the Capriccio in an interview, Janáček reputedly said, "It is capricious, nothing but pranks and puns." What then of the working title *Defiance*? Well, the composer actually did put that title to sarcastic use in a letter he wrote on March 1, 1928, the eve of the premiere, to Jarom John, a newspaper editor: "In the Capriccio which Mr. Hollmann will play," he wrote, "already defiantly the famous trombonists of the famous Philharmonic learn their parts at home! At home! It is necessary to record this to their eternal memory." I suppose this was intended to express mock surprise that trombone players actually practice from time to time; but his using the adverb "defiantly" (*ve vzdoru*), so odd in this context, surely represents some sort of wordplay relating to the discarded title *Vzdor*. The composer's wife, Zdenka Janáčková, had little to say of the piece, and certainly nothing regarding any bearing *l'affaire Kamila* might have on it. For her part, she noted in her memoirs only that "the pianist Hollmann played my husband's Capriccio excellently." The Capriccio was premiered by Hollmann and members of the Czech Philharmonic in a concert played to raise money for Czech veterans handicapped through injuries in World War I, and, since Janáček's health deteriorated shortly thereafter, it would turn out to be the last premiere of one of his own compositions he would ever attend.

The instrumentation is peculiar: in addition to the piano left-hand, a barrage of brass (two trumpets, tenor tuba—an unusual instrument for which bass flugelhorn is sometimes substituted—and three trombones) and the unlikely companion of flute (doubling piccolo), which participates in only the last three movements. Still more curious is Janáček's decision to use the more stolid trombones practically as coloratura instruments; apparently he intended that the players should use valve trombones, as opposed to slide trombones, and it is sometimes played on such instruments today, the better to address the exceptional agility required in the first and second trombone parts. Responding to Hollmann's inquiry about the choice of instruments, Janáček volunteered: "A long time ago I was asked to write something for a military ensemble, and when I was pondering the composition for you, I suddenly remembered this request and so it occurred to me: I'll combine wind instruments with the piano and the wind music with you."

The opening *Allegro* (*Allegro lugubre* in an early edition) bustles at its opening, but within a few measures the cross rhythms between piano and brass grow so out-of-sync that it sounds as if the piece may be falling apart. The movement's character changes almost erratically: the opening march yields to a nostalgic waltz, then to a vigorous pulsating bit that leads to a cadenza-like riff from the first trumpet, and so on until the music reaches its end with the piano trilling mysteriously above muted trombones.

The *Adagio* is also marked by mercurial changes—Impressionistic languor ceding to almost violent outbursts. The *Allegretto* comes across as a scherzo, galumphing at the outset but alternating "mystery music" in which the piano plays a filigree of scales against the sustained notes of the ensemble (a device revisited at the movement's conclusion). After this, the Capriccio ends with, of all things, a slow movement—or at least, at *Andante*, a relatively slow one. The flute's theme is indeed tender, and the writing is sometimes reminiscent of Debussy, with the piano imitating the Debussian timbre of the harp and with the melodic contours often tracing that composer's beloved whole-tone scales. Yet on the whole the effect is unmistakably of its composer, transcendent and celebratory, and the Capriccio ends in a spirit of sustained ecstasy that is a Janáček fingerprint.

String Quartet No. 2, *Listy důvěrné* ("Intimate Letters")

Andante
Adagio
Moderato
Allegro

Work composed: January 29 to February 19, 1928

Work premiered: September 11, 1928, in Brno by the Moravian String Quartet

Instrumentation: Two violins, viola, and cello

Janáček composed two string quartets, both late in his life and both rich in extra-musical associations. The first, written in 1923, bears the subtitle *Inspired by Tolstoy's "Kreutzer Sonata,"* and is understood to be a musical protest against the violence to women that Tolstoy pictures in his novella of that name, in which the heroine is murdered by her husband for infidelity. The tragedy of an unhappily married woman surely was connected in Janáček's mind with his own love for Kamila Stösslová. He was sixty-three years old and she was twenty-five when they met at the spa resort of Luhačovice in the summer of 1917. Though both parties were married, neither marriage was very satisfying. Janáček's wife, Zdenka, was dedicated to supporting her husband's career, but the magic had drained from their relationship. Kamila's husband, an antiques dealer, was frequently on the road, leaving her to cultivate her social life largely on her own. At first the two couples got along quite well, but over time Zdenka came to resent Kamila for having so obviously captured Janáček's heart.

Through the course of eleven years Janáček wrote to Kamila several times each week, at some periods even daily, yielding an archive of some six hundred letters. He occasionally traveled to visit at her home in the southern Bohemian town of Písek, a hundred miles distant from where the Janáčeks lived in Brno. The Stössls visited on Janáček's home turf only once. In July 1928 they paid a visit to their cottage in Hukvaldy, bringing along their eleven-year-old son. One afternoon the son went missing and Janáček headed out to search for him in the woods. It turned out the son wasn't as lost as people assumed, but Janáček overexerted himself in this adventure and came down with a chill. Pneumonia developed, and within a week he was dead. Zdenka held Kamila responsible. Through the entire eleven years Kamila seemed to have done little to encourage him. She responded to only a fraction of his letters and always insisted that he destroy what she wrote to him—which in most cases he did. At least that's how things stood until the final year, when Kamila's letters took on a more personal tone and her language suggested that she might be moving in the direction of mirroring his affections. There is no evidence that a physical relationship ever developed; Kamila vehemently maintained that it was always strictly platonic.

Nonetheless, from the composer's standpoint it *was* a love affair, if one sustained by hope and fantasy, and many works of his final decade were overtly connected to this relationship. She was the direct inspiration for his String

Quartet No. 2, written in a whirlwind of inspiration at the outset of 1928. It would be his last substantial work.

In a letter from Brno to his distant beloved in Písek, Janáček reported: "Now I've begun to write something nice. Our life will be in it. It will be called *Love Letters*. I think that it will sound delightful. . . . There will be little fires in my soul and they'll be set ablaze with the most beautiful melodies." In the end he decided to change the title to the more circumspect *Intimate Letters*. (The title is sometimes translated as *Intimate Pages*; in any case, the Czech name is *Listy důvěrné*.) Janáček's initial idea was to substitute a viola d'amore for the standard viola in the quartet, the viola d'amore being a Baroque-era viola in which a set of extra strings, never touched by the player, vibrates in sympathetic resonance to the main set of strings, yielding a veiled, mystical effect. Once he got to work he realized that the viola d'amore would not balance well with the other three instruments, and he sensibly resorted to a standard string quartet instead. It was an idea born more of linguistic than musical intent, viola d'amore being, of course, a "viola of love."

The musicologist Otakar Šourek, who incorporated into his 1948 edition of the piece various revisions presumably authorized by the composer, provided the following explanation of the quartet's "program":

> The first movement describes Janáček's first impressions of Madame Stössl, . . . and the second movement, the events occurring at the Luhačovice Spa, in Moravia in the summer of 1917. . . . It was during this time that love blossomed between Janáček and Madame Stössl. Janáček describes [the] third movement by saying, "It is bright and carefree, but dissolves into an apparition which resembles you." According to Janáček, the fourth movement is "the sound of my fear for you, not exactly fear, but yearning, yearning which is fulfilled by you."

There can be little doubt that this exercise in musical autobiography is filled with specific allusions that only Janáček and Kamila Stösslová could have discovered. The traditional musical roles of the movements have been overridden here—no opening sonata structure, no soulful *adagio* second movement, and so on—and one assumes that the plan of action is indeed extra-musical. Melodies undergo some thematic transformation or recur to provide underpinning at critical junctures, as when a poignant barcarolle opens and closes the third movement. But on the whole, the piece proceeds according to the loose yet satisfying lyrical judgment that characterizes much of Janáček's music.

Though Janáček did not live to hear the quartet's first public performance, which was given by the Moravian String Quartet, he did attend a private run-through by that ensemble. On May 18/19, 1928, he wrote to his muse: "Now, at 3 o'clock the Moravian Quartet should be coming to my place to play my—*your* composition! I'm already panting to hear it." The rehearsal over, he picks up the thread: "So they played me the first and the third movement! And Kamila, it will be beautiful, strange, unrestrained, inspired, a composition beyond all the usual conventions! Together I think that we'll triumph! It's my first composition that sprang from directly experienced feeling. Before then I composed only from things remembered. This piece, *Intimate Letters*, was written in fire, earlier pieces only in hot ash. The composition will be dedicated to you; you're the reason for it and to compose it was the greatest pleasure for me."

The public premiere took place three weeks after he died. In a lengthy memoir she dictated from 1933 through 1935, titled *My Life with Janáček*, Zdenka revealed: "When the Moravian Quartet were due to play his Second String Quartet, dedicated to Mrs. Stösslová and called *Intimate Letters*, I tried as hard as I could to prevent the work from carrying this title. I didn't succeed. For a long time I didn't go to concerts where I'd hear that passionate rearing up of Leoš's longing for another woman—a longing which destroyed him." The work remained unpublished until 1938, the same year Zdenka passed away. By then Kamila had been dead for three years. In the event, the printed score carries no dedication.

Zoltán Kodály [signature]

Zoltán Kodály

Born: December 16, 1882, in Kecskemét, Hungary,
some fifty miles southeast of Budapest

Died: March 6, 1967, in Budapest

Duo for Violin and Cello, Op. 7

Allegro serioso, non troppo
Adagio
Maestoso e largamente, ma non troppo lento—Presto

Work composed: Completed March 1914

Work premiered: May 7, 1918, in Budapest, by the Waldbauer-Kerpely Duo

Instrumentation: Violin and cello

If I were to name the composer whose works are the most perfect embodiment of the Hungarian spirit, I would answer, Kodály. His work proves his faith in the Hungarian spirit. The obvious explanation is that all Kodály's composing activity is rooted only in Hungarian soil, but the deep inner reason is his unshakable faith and trust in the constructive power and future of his people." So wrote Béla Bartók, whose opinion, emanating from the apex of twentieth-century Hungarian music, holds considerable authority.

Zoltán Kodály was the son of a frequently transferred stationmaster for the Hungarian railroads. Kodály spent his early years in a succession of small Hungarian towns (some of which would later be reassigned to Czechoslovakia). He expressed delight in the Magyar folk music that surrounded him and simultaneously developed an interest in mainstream European chamber music. His parents were enthusiastic musical amateurs, and Kodály learned piano, violin, viola, and cello well enough to perform creditably on each.

While still in his mid-teens he started to compose, producing a Mass at the age of sixteen, and he naturally proceeded to conservatory and university studies in music. From the Budapest Academy of Music he received diplomas in composition and in teaching, as well as a doctorate in musicology, culminating in a dissertation on the structure of Hungarian folk song (of which he collected some 3,500 examples). He joined with Bartók in organizing trips around the countryside to collect folk songs. As with Bartók, the musical material of these traditional pieces in turn inspired the language of his original compositions.

After polishing his compositional skills in Paris with the famous organist Charles-Marie Widor, Kodály returned to Budapest, where he taught at his alma mater, wrote music criticism for newspapers and magazines (including important analyses of Bartók's works), edited and published folk-song collections, and continued to compose. In 1919 he was appointed assistant director of the Budapest Academy of Music (reporting to Dohnányi), but quickly found himself on the losing end of a national political imbroglio, and left. He returned to the school in 1922, as a teacher. The three disciplines of composer, musicologist, and educator, too often uneasy counterparts among the musical professions, coexisted and reinforced one another in Kodály.

Composed in 1914, the Duo for Violin and Cello (Op. 7) is without precedent in the principal chamber-music literature, prefiguring and possibly inspiring Ravel's Sonata for Violin and Cello of 1920–22. The piece was not premiered until 1918, when it was heard on an all-Kodály program in Budapest, sharing the bill with the composer's Unaccompanied Cello Sonata (Op. 10, from 1915) and newly completed String Quartet No. 2. (Most of his chamber works include the cello, his favorite of the instruments he had mastered.) Kodály composed the Duo immediately upon returning from an expedition to collect folk songs in Transylvania; the rhythm, melody, and harmony of this traditional repertoire all exercise an influence on the Duo, which even includes direct quotations from folk dances and children's songs. All the same, the Duo is no folk song recital. Here, as in the rest of his "art music," Kodály has profoundly absorbed the material of his native Hungary and made it unequivocally his own.

Kodály's Duo exploits the similar technical possibilities of the two instruments, with their differing timbres and ranges enhancing the flavor of contrast. The work is rich in imitation and in explorations of minute subtleties of timbre. The opening *Allegro serioso* announces the Duo as a relatively extroverted, rhapsodic work, not unrelated in spirit to aspects of Ravel and other French contemporaries. The *Adagio* is nervous and simmering in its emotions, veering rapidly from the extremes of the two instruments' ranges to passages of overlapping pitch and even unisons. The finale opens with cadenza-like roulades from the violin, punctuated by pizzicatos and sweeping chords from the cello, before proceeding to an ebullient *Presto* section, announced by the cello's repeated-note motif, that proclaims its heritage in Magyar traditional music. Kodály's idiosyncratic brand of modernism is everywhere apparent, embracing classic sonata forms and contrapuntal procedures, the fervor of Romantic expressiveness, the experimental sense of the twentieth century, and nationalistic references to folk music—all synthesized into a convincing, authentic voice.

Serenade for Two Violins and Viola, Op. 12

> *Allegramente—Sostenuto, ma non troppo*
> *Lento, ma non troppo*
> *Vivo*

Work composed: 1919–March 1920

Work premiered: Unknown, but presumably in Budapest shortly after its composition

Instrumentation: Two violins and viola

If Bartók preferred the more percussive aspects of Hungarian and Balkan folk music, Kodály was drawn more strongly to its melodic and harmonic suggestions; both composers, however, were fascinated by the repertoire's metrical complexity. Kodály developed a recognizable style that, even in strictly instrumental pieces, emphasized the vocal contours of melodies and the influence of speech inflection on the shaping of phrases, much as Janáček had done among the Czechs. Many of his works exude a sense of introspection. A precise stylist, he stands as a classicist among twentieth-century ethno-nationalists.

His very first chamber work, written in 1899, was a Trio for Two Violins and Viola, an unusual combination practically without recent precedent apart from Dvořák's Terzetto for the same combination, which had appeared in 1887. That early trio was strictly a student work, but the combination of instruments must have appealed to Kodály, since he returned to it for his Serenade, composed in 1919–20, just when he was going through a period of uncertainty following his temporary departure from the Budapest Academy of Music.

Bartók wrote a review of this piece in 1921, commenting:

> Like Kodály's other works, this composition, in spite of its unusual chord combinations and surprising originality, is firmly based on tonality, although this

should not be strictly interpreted in terms of the major and minor system. The time will come when it will be realized that despite the atonal inclinations of modern music, the possibilities of building new structures on key systems have not been exhausted. The means used by this composer—the choice of instruments and the superb richness of the instrumental effects achieved despite the economy of the work—merit great attention in themselves. The content is suited to the form. It reveals a personality with something entirely new to say and one who is capable of communicating this content in a masterly and concentrated fashion. The work is extraordinarily rich in melodies.

The first and third movements are compelling in their rhythmic propulsion, metric incisiveness, and tonal brilliance; the third particularly evokes the spirit of a folk dance, with strummed pizzicatos accompanying solo "voices" in the central section. The delicate, haunting, and quite theatrical middle movement is extraordinary in different ways. Bartók found it particularly seductive: "[Its effects include] a double thread of seconds and ninths, [and] tremolo passages in the second violin played *pianissimo* and *con sordino* [with mute] provide a harmonic frame. There is also a kind of dialogue between the first violin and the viola. The strangely floating, passionate melodies of the viola alternate with spectral flashing motifs on the first violin. We find ourselves in a fairy world never dreamed of before."

György Ligeti [signature]

György Ligeti

Born: May 28, 1923, in Dicsöszentmárton, Transylvania, Hungary (now Tîrnăveni, Romania)

Died: June 12, 2006, in Vienna, Austria

Six Bagatelles for Wind Quintet

I *Allegro con spirito*
II *Rubato. Lamentoso*
III *Allegro grazioso* [attacca subito]
IV *Presto ruvido*
V *Adagio, Mesto* [attacca]
VI *Molto vivace. Capriccioso*

Work composed: 1953

Work dedicated: To Mrs. Maedi Wood; the Fifth movement is inscribed "Béla Bartók in memoriam."

Work premiered: October 6, 1969, in Södertälje, Sweden, by the Stockholm Philharmonic Wind Quintet

Instrumentation: Flute (doubling piccolo), oboe, clarinet, horn, and bassoon

G rowing up Jewish in a Hungary that was by turns dominated by Hitler and Stalin, György Ligeti did not experience life as a bed of roses. Unlike his father and his brother, he managed to survive internment in a labor camp. "The end of the war, and with it of the Nazi dictatorship, released an unprecedented pent-up energy and vigor, which found expression in a suddenly flourishing artistic and intellectual life," Ligeti recalled in an article in 1989. Budapest's musical community basked in important works by such composers as Stravinsky and Britten—and of course Bartók.

The Communist Party gradually assumed control, operating at the bidding of the Soviet Union and therefore Joseph Stalin, and in 1949 Hungary became officially a communist nation. Any potentially threatening literary, artistic, or musical works became invisible in the cultural isolation that ensued. The music of such composers as Debussy, Ravel, Britten, Stravinsky, and Schoenberg was silenced, as was much of Bartók, including all of his string quartets. Ligeti produced the stream of folk-based choral music that was de rigueur, but he remained curious about musical exploration. He had access to few models from the outer world, although at some point he was intrigued to find a score of Berg's Lyric Suite unaccountably lurking in the Budapest Music Academy's library. He worked quietly on experimental pieces, and he prudently kept them to himself.

The lack of outside influence was perhaps a blessing in disguise, as it forced Ligeti to generate his musical thinking entirely on his own, to construct an original musical language from the ground up. He reported:

> In 1951 I began to experiment with very simple structures of sonorities and rhythms as if to build up a new kind of music starting from nothing. My approach was frankly Cartesian, in that I regarded all the music I knew and loved as being, for my purpose, irrelevant and even invalid. I set myself such problems as: what can I do with a single note? with its octave? with an interval? with two intervals? What can I do with specific rhythmic interrelationships which could serve as the basic elements in a formation of rhythms and intervals? Several small pieces resulted, mostly for piano.

One of these was the piano suite Musica ricercata (1951–53), the eleven movements of which undertake precisely such investigations. As soon as he finished Musica ricercata, Ligeti selected six of its movements to arrange for wind quintet (with very slight alterations), the fulfillment of a request from the Jeney Quintet. The resulting Six Bagatelles were completed in 1953, but they were considered too bold to present before the public just then. Stalin's death that year may have led to a slight loosening of social strictures, but little would be gained—and much potentially lost—by testing the limits of the state's authority over matters artistic. Not until 1956 did the Jeney Quintet feel comfortable presenting Ligeti's set before the public, presenting the first five movements at a Festival of New Hungarian Music at the Franz Liszt Academy in Budapest. Even in such surroundings they omitted the final number as too audacious. (The premiere of Musica ricercata would follow six weeks later.) That year Ligeti emigrated to Germany, and the set would wait another thirteen years to be premiered in its entirety, given belatedly by the Stockholm Philharmonic Wind Quintet.

The Six Bagatelles are settings of movements 3, 5, 7, 8, 9, and 10 of Musica ricercata. (Movement 2, which Ligeti did not recast, would be heard widely years later, in 1999, as part of the soundtrack of Stanley Kubrick's disconcerting film *Eyes Wide Shut*.) From the distance of nearly six decades, it's hard to imagine these works offending; in the interstice, the set has become one of the most frequently programmed works of the entire wind-quintet repertoire. Arranged though they are from musical thoughts originally conceived for solo piano, they seem native to their new medium, capitalizing on the technical strengths of the individual instruments and even expanding the ensemble's range by having the flute double on piccolo in the first and last movements. Indeed, the wind settings strike me as in every case preferable to the piano originals, the pungent and acerbic possibilities of timbre investing them with greater depth of character than is possible from a piano. Ligeti allows himself increasing freedom in his employment of pitches as the set progresses: the first movement employs only four separate pitches (or their octave equivalents), the second movement six, the third movement eight, the fourth movement nine, the fifth movement ten, and the sixth movement eleven.

Ligeti has described four of the numbers as "pseudo-folkloric." "No actual folk songs are quoted," he said, "but Nos. 2 and 5 have an 'Hungarian diction' about them (No. 5 depicts mourning bells in memory of Bartók); No. 4, with its 'limping' dance music, is Balkan; and No. 3 depicts an artificial hybrid of Banat-Romanian and Serbian melodic idioms." That third movement is particularly seductive, its long-spun melody, harmonized in simple thirds and sixths, unrolling above a skittering accompaniment of staccato septuplets, the texture being lightened even further by the installation of a "bassoon mute" (a dignified term for sticking a cloth in the instrument's bell). Ligeti spoke of it as the most original movement of the set, at least in terms of the distinctive tone colors achieved through unusual positioning of the instruments in sonic relation to one another, as when the oboe displaces the flute from its accustomed spot at the top of the assemblage. The fourth movement—the Balkan dance, mostly in 7/8 meter—does indeed convey a folk spirit; most notes here carry accent marks, and the excited tone is underscored by the unusual heading *Presto ruvido* ("ruvido" meaning coarse or scratchy). So far as concerns the other movements, the first is bright and even jazzy. Stravinsky makes an appearance in the sixth; the bassoon's opening melody seems plucked from the pages of *The Firebird*, and when it's taken up by the rest of the ensemble they enrich it with piquant, Stravinskian semitones.

Ten Pieces for Wind Quintet

1. *Molto sostenuto e calmo [attacca]*
2. *Prestissimo minaccioso e burlesco [attacca]*
3. *Lento*

4. *Prestissimo leggiero e virtuoso*
5. *Presto staccatissimo e leggiero*
6. *Presto staccatissimo e leggiero*
7. *Vivo, energico*
8. *Allegro con delicatezza*
9. *Sostenuto, stridente*
10. *Presto bizzarro e rubato, so schnell wie möglich*

Work composed: August through December1968

Work dedicated: Commissioned by and dedicated to the Stockholm Philharmonic Wind Quintet. Individual movements are dedicated to the five members of the Stockholm Philharmonic Wind Quintet: the second movement to Thore Janson (clarinet), the fourth to Bengt Överström (flute), the sixth to Per Olof Gillblad (oboe), the eighth to Rolf Bengtsson (horn), and the tenth to Bruno Lavér (bassoon).

Work premiered: January 20, 1969, in Malmö, Sweden, by the Stockholm Philharmonic Wind Quintet

Instrumentation: Flute (doubling piccolo and alto flute), oboe (doubling oboe d'amore and English horn), clarinet, horn (double horn in F–B-flat), and bassoon

Ligeti became part of the great Hungarian exodus of 1956 and landed in Germany, where he avidly soaked up the thriving culture of contemporary music. Within a couple of years he became associated with the avant-garde center of Darmstadt and started producing captivating works of daring complexity, often within very free rhythmic frameworks. Before long he settled in Vienna, and he assumed Austrian citizenship in 1967. He was boosted to a prominent position among experimental composers thanks to his dramatic *Apparitions* for Orchestra (1960) and *Atmosphères* (1961), and the new-music community was watching him closely by the time he was thrust to popular fame in 1968. That's when, without the composer's knowledge or permission and to his utter horror, Stanley Kubrick incorporated three of his compositions—*Atmosphères*, *Lux Aeterna*, and Requiem—into the soundtrack of the MGM film *2001: A Space Odyssey*. (Ligeti was said to be particularly offended by having his music placed in proximity to works by Johann Strauss II and Richard Strauss, as they were in *2001*; these composers were apparently not to his taste.) Kubrick would make further use of Ligeti, in 1980 using his orchestral composition *Lontano* (among other pieces) to help create the creepy background in *The Shining* (along with excerpts of works by Bartók,

Penderecki, and Berlioz) and (as mentioned above) in 1999 employing a movement from *Musica ricercata* in the film *Eyes Wide Shut*.

Ligeti's scores usually project a sensual appeal to which audiences overwhelmingly respond, even though its vocabulary is not that of most other music. Indeed, his catalogue covers a broad variety of styles, reflecting his questing curiosity, and by the time he died in 2006 (in Vienna, where he spent the final years of his life) he was mourned as one of the central figures of late twentieth-century composition.

After the Stockholm Philharmonic Wind Quintet premiered the complete Six Bagatelles, in 1969, they tendered Ligeti a commission for a further work. By this time the composer was captivated by (as he put it) "interwoven polyphonic textures of lesser complexity" than those of his texturally spread-out orchestral works of the early 1960s. The discipline of writing again for a mere five instruments jibed with this more straitened approach, and Ligeti moved forward in close consultation with the members of the Swedish ensemble to make sure that what he wrote was really playable. "Courting danger," he said, "I wrote pieces that pushed the boundaries of possibility. This is not virtuosity for its own sake, but rather in the service of formal plans of tension and extreme expression. My goal is to create something new...from *within* the very sound of the music." The score is dense with textural instructions that clarify questions of timbre, attack, balance, rhythm, and breathing, in helpful detail. In the Six Bagatelles, Ligeti had expanded the basic wind-quintet possibilities by having the flutist double on piccolo; here alto flute is also added, and the oboist's responsibilities extend to both oboe d'amore and English horn. Sometimes one or two of the instruments sit out a piece.

Five of these short movements—Nos. 2, 4, 6, 8, and 10—particularly spotlight the individual instruments (they were respectively dedicated to each of the group's players), and they alternate with numbers of a more "ensemble" character. Ligeti's signature gauziness inhabits the first movement, though at the end the instruments join in a loud, penetrating unison. Many of these tiny movements, beginning with the second, project a burlesque character that the composer likened to a Tom and Jerry cartoon. Ligeti called special attention to an effect attained in the ninth movement, which features piccolo, oboe, and clarinet playing in unison or in close proximity in a high, strident register. Said the composer: "I deliberately exploited the effect of combination tones (specifically, difference tones): pitches not actually fingered by the instrumentalists, but which result from them playing together. I heard this acoustic phenomenon as a young child, when several girls with high voices would sing Hungarian folk songs in less than perfect unison: it was an amazing sound, much lower than the one being sung or played, and one does not know from which direction it is coming."

Trio for Violin, Horn, and Piano

> Andantino con tenerezza
> Vivacissimo molto ritmico
> Alla Marcia
> Lamento: Adagio

Work composed: 1982 (perhaps late 1981)

Work dedicated: "Hommage à Brahms"

Work premiered: August 7, 1982, at Bergedorf Castle, Hamburg, Germany, by violinist Saschko Gawriloff, hornist Hermann Baumann, and pianist Eckart Besch

Instrumentation: Violin, horn, and piano

Ligeti composed his Horn Trio on the suggestion of the pianist Eckart Besch (a colleague of his at the Hamburg Conservatory who performed in the work's premiere), to serve as a sort of companion piece to the Horn Trio of Johannes Brahms. Ligeti recalled of the conversation in which the subject was broached, "As soon as he pronounced the word 'horn' somewhere inside my head I heard the sound of a horn as if coming from a distant forest in a fairy tale, just as in a poem by Eichendorff." The musical world was gearing up to celebrate the 1983 sesquicentennial of the birth of Brahms, and Ligeti, who had been mulling over Besch's suggestion for quite some time and had written practically nothing in the four preceding years, finally plunged into the project by 1982.

Unlike many avant-garde composers of his day, Ligeti in no way disdained the music of his nineteenth-century predecessors. At the same time, he was firm in emphasizing that though his new trio was a salute to Brahms it was nonetheless entirely up-to-date in its language. Indeed, the Horn Trio reveals several fascinating conflations of historical and contemporary music, including the adaptation of a phrase from Beethoven to serve as a principal theme in the deeply felt fourth movement, though altered to sound modern rather than "Beethovenesque" (Ligeti termed this melody a "false quotation" from Beethoven's *Les adieux* Piano Sonata).

The piece draws on the language of expressionism and minimalism, but the composer protested that "the Trio cannot be pigeonholed into any neat stylistic category; it has odd angles and trick floors that do not fit in anywhere." He certainly did not like hearing it referred to as Postmodern. "Then there is a layer of cultural connotations—melted together, in the second movement, to produce an imaginary, synthetic folklore of Latin American and Balkan ele-ments," he observed. "Samba and rumba are based on asymmetrical meters, as is the *aksak* (Turkish: 'limping') dance rhythms of the Balkans." But these are allusions, as no actual folk quotations appear in this work.

Ligeti's approach to tuning is also imaginative and complex. The piano is tuned as accustomed, using a normal temperament, but the violin's strings are tuned in pure, untempered fifths; those pitches therefore do not quite correspond to the nominally identical ones of the piano. The horn called for is a modern valve horn, rather than the natural horn used in Brahms' Trio. Nonetheless, Ligeti said that he envisioned the instrument not as a single item but rather as "a collection of natural horns." He continued: "The sound would be much more beautiful on a true natural horn, but the horn player would then require a short pause to change crooks; as there is not sufficient time for this, I wrote the piece for valve horn. Nevertheless, I was thinking in terms of natural horns, pitched in various keys, and I indicate these in the score. In this way, mostly untempered overtones occur, which tend to throw the violinist's fingers off their mark. This is intentional, part of the riddle of this non-manifest musical language."

Bohuslav Martinů

Born: December 8, 1890, in Polička, Bohemia

Died: August 28, 1959, in Liestal, near Basel, Switzerland

H numbers: The "H numbers" attached to Martinů's works refer to the catalogue of the composer's music published in 1968 and revised in 2007 by the Belgian musicologist Harry Halbreich.

La Revue de cuisine Suite, H.161

Prologue
Tango
Charleston
Finale

Work composed: 1927 in Paris and Ostern, as part of the score for a ballet to a libretto by Jarmila Kröschlová

Work premiered: As a ballet production, on November 17, 1927, presented under the auspices of the Umělecká Beseda cultural society in Prague, with Jarmila Kröschlová's dance troupe and with Stanislav Novák conducting; the ballet suite for chamber ensemble, dedicated to Mrs. Božena Nebeská (the composer's landlady), was first played on January 5, 1930 (some sources give January 31, I think erroneously), at the Concerts Cortot at the Ecole Normale de Musique in Paris, with Dinan Alexanian conducting.

Instrumentation: Clarinet, bassoon, trumpet, violin, cello, and piano

Bohuslav Martinů entered the Prague Conservatory as a violinist at the age of sixteen, but he ended up being expelled for—as the official record put it—"incorrigible negligence." His horizons broadened in

1923, thanks to a modest fellowship that enabled him to study in Paris with the ever-patient Albert Roussel. In an article he published in 1937 in *La Revue musicale*, Martinů wrote: "With friendly and almost tender understanding, he divined, discovered, and strengthened all in me that was unconscious, concealed, and unknown. I went to him in search of order, clarity, balance, refinement of taste, accuracy, and sensibility of expression, the qualities in French art that I have always admired and with which I wished to become thoroughly intimate."

Martinů stayed in Paris for seventeen years, and he composed at full tilt practically from the moment he arrived. In 1927 he composed three one-act ballets. Two were not destined to reach the stage during his lifetime, but the third, *La Revue de cuisine*, was his first breakthrough to popular success. It began life under the title *Pokušení svatouška hrnce* ("Temptation of the Saintly Pot"), its sweetly absurdist scenario devised by Jarmila Kröschlová, who also provided the choreography. A noted figure of modern dance, she would go on to author *Movement Theory and Practice*, an influential treatise that applied the discipline of physical culture to dance, gymnastics, and mime with an emphasis on avoiding injury. Her libretto was divided into ten sections, and she attached a precise directive of timing for each part. She envisioned some segments as minuscule, such that Martinů's ballet score ran altogether to only about eighteen minutes. The slender plot suggests a *Peyton Place* in the kitchen cabinets. The Pot ("Le Chaudron") and its Lid ("Le Couvercle") are a couple obviously destined for each other, but the suave Twirling Stick ("Le Moulinet," a sort of whisk or stirring device for emulsifying) nonetheless sets out to seduce Pot. Dishcloth ("Le Torchon à vaisselle") similarly makes the moves on Lid, upon which Broom ("Le Balai") challenges Dishcloth to a duel. Twirling Stick makes considerable headway before Pot tires of him and realizes that Lid was her perfect match all along. To her alarm, Lid is nowhere to be found; but suddenly a gigantic foot materializes and kicks Lid back onstage, where he is amorously reunited with Pot. Twirling Stick returns to his Don Giovanni antics, this time focusing his attention on Dishcloth, and the two go off together—and that is the end.

Martinů devised a score that calls for only six instruments—violin, cello, clarinet, bassoon, trumpet, and piano—a modest group suited to the pared-down sensibilities of modern dance in the 1920s. The pianist Alfred Cortot asked Martinů to prepare a concert suite from the ballet for him to present on a series he oversaw at the Ecole Normale de Musique, and the resulting four-movement suite, which included most of the ballet score, was unveiled under the new title *La Revue de cuisine* (in Czech, *Kuchyňská revue*, and in English, *The Kitchen Revue*, though the French name is usually employed internationally). The Suite scored a huge hit at its Paris premiere, and the prestigious firm of Alphonse Leduc promptly committed to publish it along with a handful of Martinů's other compositions. In the early 1990s, the excised sections turned up at the Paul Sacher Foundation in Basel, so now enterprising chamber ensembles have the choice of playing either the composer-prepared Suite or the complete ballet score, which is only about four minutes longer.

Martinů had been grappling with how jazz might fit into his stylistic vocabulary, and particularly how he might balance it with the influences of traditional music that came to him more naturally. In 1925 he wrote in the Czech magazine *Dalibor*: "I often think about the extraordinarily pregnant rhythms of our Slavic folk songs, about our Slovak songs and their characteristic instrumental accompaniment, and it seems to me that it is unnecessary for us to resort to the jazz band. At the same time, I cannot deny the part [the jazz band] has been playing in mainstream life, which in turn dictates everything it needs for its artistic manifestations." Stravinsky was much on his mind, too, and Czech publications began publishing his admiring dispatches about that composer's oeuvre. *La Revue de cuisine* certainly traces part of its ancestry to *L'Histoire du soldat* (1918), Stravinsky's theatre-piece for narrator plus a roughly similar ensemble, a work that also happens to include short movements cast as popular dances.

The *Revue de cuisine* Suite opens with a Prologue (*Allegretto, Marche*) that comprises the three opening sections of the ballet: Prologue (*Allegretto*), a bagatelle that veers from the trumpet's G-major fanfare directly into the piano's momentarily C-major oom-pahs whose constant metric and harmonic shifts leave the listener quite untethered; Introduction (*Tempo di marche*), an off-kilter processional that nods in a neo-Classical direction; and "Dance of the Twirling Stick around the Pot," a perky clarinet solo. The motoric swirls of melodic figures, especially prominent toward the movement's end, are a Martinů hallmark.

A "Dance of the Pot and the Lid" being eliminated in the Suite, we continue to the Tango (*Danse d'amour, Lento*), a suggestive and sinuous item whose principal melody and repetitive rhythms at the beginning may remind us at least a bit of Ravel's famous *Boléro*. A Charleston follows: an introduction that begins rather slowly and gradually speeds up to *vivo* ("Lively") and a raucous "Tempo di Charleston," with clarinet and muted trumpet taking the lead.

Martinů now excises two further numbers from the complete ballet (a "Lament of the Pot" interlude and the Funeral March) and launches into his *Finale*. This comprises the ballet's two concluding numbers, "Expansive Dance (*Tempo di Marche*)," which revisits material from the Suite's very opening, though with the bassoon inserting a slight change in the trumpet's opening fanfare, apparently just for the heck of it—and we can not help marveling at the choice of the title "Expansive Dance" for a segment that lasts all of twenty seconds. It leads to what in the ballet is called "End of Story"

(*Allegretto*), its quodlibet style being custom-tailored to wrap up the plot lines, inconsequential though they are. Martinů offers a little *Petrushka*-style fantasy of imitative counterpoint on the fanfare theme, some neo-Classical banter, recollections of the Charleston, and allusions to folk song with an off-beat rhythmic accompaniment that the musicologist Michael Beckerman identifies as being specific to the Slovácko region, on the border between Moravia (today incorporated into the Czech Republic) and Slovakia.

The *Revue de cuisine* Suite claimed a special place in Martinů's heart. His friend and biographer Miloš Šafránek wrote that its score "was held by Martinů to be perfect (although he was not conscious of it when he was composing)....He expressed this opinion to me personally in the course of our conversations in Paris, in the years 1955 and 1956, and re-confirmed it in a letter to me dated April 4th, 1958.... 'That is just how it is'—he concluded this important communication—'that when a work is clearly in the composer's brain or expresses his character, the technique comes of itself.'"

String Quartet No. 5, H. 268

Allegro ma non troppo
Adagio
Allegro vivo
Lento—Allegro

Work composed: Late April and May 1938 in Paris

Work dedicated: The composer's autograph sketch carries no dedication, although some Martinů biographies erroneously state that it bears a dedication to Vitulka [Vitězslava] Kaprálová or to the Pro Arte Quartet. Martinů did prepare a fair copy particella score on which he inscribed a dedication to Kaprálová along with the notation "Paris, May, 1938."

Work premiered: According to Harry Halbreich's catalogue of Martinů's works, the composer reported in a letter to the Melantrich Verlag publishing company that this work was first played in July 1938 in Los Angeles by the Pro Arte Quartet. Martinů's friend and biographer Miloš Šafránek maintained that it was not played until May 25, 1958, in Prague, by the Novák Quartet.

Instrumentation: Two violins, viola, and cello

Martinů composed seven "official" string quartets from 1918 through 1947. In a 1946 letter to Miloš Šafránek, Martinů stated: "In pure chamber music I am always more myself. I cannot tell you with what happiness I begin to compose chamber music.... In a quartet one feels at home, intimately happy. Outside it is raining and growing dark, but the four parts are oblivious to it; they are independent, free, do what they like and yet form a harmonious ensemble, create some kind of new entity, a harmonious whole."

Of the seven, the Fifth String Quartet seems the most deeply personal in its expression. Although no written program is attached, it surely expresses something specific concerning the composer's relationship with Vítězslava Kaprálová (or, to use the diminutive, as he typically did, Vitulka Kaprálová). Martinů had been a married man since 1931; that year he had finally received his mother's grudging permission to marry Charlotte Quennehen, a French seamstress he had met more than four years earlier and with whom he had been living in Paris. She would remain his devoted wife until he died, twenty-eight years later, often wielding needle and thread to support them through periods of near destitution. Nonetheless, Martinů had several affairs born of serious emotional attachment, and one of them gave rise to the Fifth Quartet.

Vítězslava Kaprálová was an exceptionally gifted musician, twenty-five years younger than Martinů, the daughter of a composer (Václav Kaprál) and his singer-wife (Viktorie Kaprálová) from Brno, Moravia. Her teachers at the Prague Conservatory supported her application for a French government grant that took her to Paris in 1936. There she studied conducting with Charles Munch and composition, from October 1937 through February 1939, with Martinů. Soon they were traveling together to London, to Prague, to Martinů's hometown of Polička. The Martinů biographies are cagey, but the autobiography published in 1988 by her husband, Jiří Mucha (a noted writer and the son of the famous Art Nouveau artist Alfons—or Alphonse—Mucha), leaves no doubt that she and Martinů were romantically involved. Kaprálová married Mucha in April 1940, and less than two months later she died, at the age of only twenty-five, possibly of miliary tuberculosis.

She and Martinů were going through a trying time together in the spring of 1938, and from April 26 through May 20—precisely the weeks during which Martinů wrote his Fifth Quartet—Kaprálová was away from Paris, touring southern France, Monaco, and Italy with a young man for whom she also felt romantic inclinations. Martinů's twelve-page autograph sketch includes cartoon-like drawings and annotations alluding to their relationship, and in the sketch he names her as dedicatee. Not so the score as published, though in deference to the autograph sketch the firm of Editio Bärenreiter Praha does print her name as dedicatee in brackets.

In each of its four movements Martinů quotes a sinuous, chromatic motif from his opera *Julietta*, which had been unveiled to great success in Paris two years earlier. In the first three movements it's found in inner parts (viola in the first and third movements, second violin in the second), but in the finale we hear it as the movement's principal theme, articulated at the very outset by the first violin. This phrase became a fingerprint of Martinů's later works, and it seems that he came to identify it with Kaprálová herself, to whom he ended up presenting his piano sketch of the opera in January 1939. According to Kaprálová's husband, her last words were "It is Julietta"; he guessed that she was hearing Martinů's music in her head as she died.

The *Allegro ma non troppo* begins dramatically with accented chords, leaping intervals, and driving rhythms. Notwithstanding the dissonance of their "added notes," these opening measures establish the key of G minor, which will govern almost the entire quartet, even though Martinů attaches no key signature to any of the movements. The relentless momentum breaks for a gorgeous, lyric second theme that features the first violin soaring in the stratosphere. The chromatic motif turns in on itself contrapuntally, conveying a sense of inescapable density. Finally the movement exhausts itself, its final ten measures tracking an expansive *ritardando* while maintaining full volume and powerfully emotional tension.

An oppressive atmosphere inhabits the *Adagio*, where the first violin's tightly coiled melody is overlain by viola pizzicatos (and later, the peculiar timbre of sharp viola attacks *col legno*). In a central section the violins weave in claustrophobic counterpoint that builds to nearly unbearable emotional intensity. Martinů's sketch for this movement includes his notation of a passage from a song Kaprálová had composed the year before to a poem by the surrealist Vitězslav Nezval, "Sbohem a šáteček" ("Goodbye and Handkerchief"). If the slow movement seems beholden to Bartók in its eeriness, the final page—a short patch of sweet, C-major harmony returning immediately to a dreamy but somber mood—may evoke something of Shostakovich. But it is the future Shostakovich who is suggested, a Shostakovich more broken than when he composed his String Quartet No. 1 exactly when Martinů's Fifth was weeping its way into existence.

The *Allegro vivo* is an unbridled scherzo, its turbulent emotional state intensified by the quieter contrast of its shivering middle section. The finale begins with a *Lento* lamentation entrusted to the first violin, its sadness growing in hopelessness as the tempo shifts to a slightly less lugubrious *Adagio* and descending sequences sink ever downward. The four instruments now announce a forceful, syncopated theme in unison (and octaves), which Martinů dissects and uses to generate some short episodes of imitative counterpoint. As in the first movement, the energy dissipates and the tempo slows when the end approaches. The music again sinks down, down, down, but this time the volume increases, leaving an image of Martinů maintaining his composure only by clenching his fists and gritting his teeth.

Sources differ about when this work was premiered. Martinů's friend Miloš Šafránek believed it was not performed until 1958, when it was given by the Novák Quartet in Prague, but Harry Halbreich, author of the *catalogue raisonné* of the composer's music, cites a letter dated July 1938 in which Martinů told the publishing firm of Melantrich Verlag that it was played that year in Los Angeles, by the Pro Arte Quartet. What is certain is that Martinů declined to publish his Fifth Quartet throughout his lifetime, finally yielding only months before he died. He told Šafránek, "I have a bad opinion of it, as you know." Certainly his "bad opinion" had much to do with the personal pain of the incident that spawned it, but Aleš Březina, who co-edited the score of this quartet for Editio Bärenreiter Praha, astutely observes that the composer's uneasiness also had a strictly esthetic component, that he may have been uncomfortable with "the publication of a work which stood in such powerful contradiction to the lifelong artistic creed...[that stressed] objectivity of musical expression and moderation in the techniques used." On January 11, 1959, Martinů voiced such an idea in another letter to Šafránek: "I continue to differ with almost everyone in my opinions on emotional inspiration, even though this is the evidence; it is, in fact, also the reason I didn't want to put the quartet on the market." In other words, this masterly quartet proclaimed what Martinů himself was loath to admit.

Jacob Ludwig Felix Mendelssohn

Born: February 3, 1809, in Hamburg, Germany

Died: November 4, 1847, in Leipzig, Saxony (Germany)

About his surname: Following the Mendelssohn family's conversion from Judaism to Lutheranism—the children in 1816, the father in 1822—the members of the family appended the "Protestant-sounding" second name of Bartholdy to their surname. That name had already been adopted by Felix's Uncle Jakob Salomon (his mother's brother), who had preceded them in converting to Lutheranism; it was the surname of the family from whom he had purchased a dairy farm. The composer often signed his name as Felix Mendelssohn Bartholdy (without a hyphen), and that form of his name is frequently encountered in nineteenth- and early twentieth-century writings, though it is rarely used today.

Octet in E-flat major for Strings, Op. 20

Allegro moderato ma con fuoco
Andante
Scherzo: Allegro leggierissimo
Presto

Work composed: Summer and fall of 1825, completed on October 15; it was slightly revised—tightened in a few spans—prior to its publication in 1832.

Work dedicated: To his friend Eduard Rietz

Work premiered: October 1825, at a private gathering at the Mendelssohns' home on Leipziger-Strasse in Berlin; the first public performance took place on January 30, 1836, at the Leipzig Gewandhaus.

Instrumentation: Four violins, two violas, and two cellos

T he numbers don't lie: Felix Mendelssohn was born in February 1809, so when he composed his irreplaceable Octet for Strings, in the summer and fall of 1825, he was just midway between his sixteenth and seventeenth birthdays. He achieved absolute musical fluency at a young age, fluency as both a composer and a pianist. His talent was supported by privilege. He was born into a family that was both cultured and wealthy; his grandfather was the noted philosopher Moses Mendelssohn, and his father, Abraham, was a supremely successful banker, one remembered at least for his remark that he was destined to go down in history "as his father's son and his son's father." As a result, young Felix, his also gifted sister Fanny Cäcilie, plus their younger siblings Rebecka and Paul, enjoyed certain advantages as they moved through their childhood. Even as youngsters, the Mendelssohn children hobnobbed with the rich and famous; Felix, for example, struck up a bizarrely intimate friendship with the aged author Johann Wolfgang von Goethe, who seemed never to tire of his young interlocutor's boundless curiosity. Each of the Mendelssohn youngsters received a well-rounded education, with Felix mastering Classical and modern languages, writing poetry, and polishing his considerable skills as a watercolor painter and an artist in pen-and-ink. Felix and Fanny profited from the finest music instruction that money could buy, with Felix studying both piano and violin in addition to taking composition lessons from Goethe's music adviser Carl Friedrich Zelter, whose other students included Otto Nicolai, Carl Loewe, and Giacomo Meyerbeer. Most astonishingly, Felix had a private orchestra at his disposal to try out his new compositions at every-other-Sunday musicales in the family home in Berlin, an unthinkable boon for a developing composer.

He wrote the Octet as a birthday gift for his friend and violin teacher Eduard Rietz, and the florid first-violin part stands a compliment to that musician's abilities. Rietz was a native Berliner, born there in 1802, but the age disparity of seven years put him more or less on an intellectual par with young Felix. He was a frequent presence in the Mendelssohn home and is known to have been playing string quartets with Mendelssohn as early as 1820. In 1829 he would serve as concertmaster for the historic performance in which Mendelssohn conducted Bach's *St. Matthew Passion* in the first revival of that work since its composer's death. In fact, it was Rietz who copied out the entire score of that work so that it could be presented to Mendelssohn as a Christmas gift in 1823, and he also helped transcribe the instrumental parts for the premiere six years later. Eduard was on his way to becoming an accomplished conductor, too, when he was swept away by tuberculosis in 1832, a few months after his twenty-ninth birthday. (It was Franz Liszt who broke the news to Mendelssohn.) Mendelssohn was despondent, and he worked through his grief by writing a new slow movement for his String Quintet in A major (Op. 18) in memory of his departed friend—"lanky old Rietz," as Mendelssohn sometimes called him.

The string octet was in no way a classic chamber-music genre. Louis Spohr had produced the first of his four "double quartets" in 1823, but despite their identical combination of instruments they hew to a fundamentally different concept from Mendelssohn's: where Spohr's two string quartets operate as independent units, Mendelssohn uses his eight instruments as a single ensemble capable of any interactive permutations. In this regard, Mendelssohn's Octet seems to have more in common with the dozen string symphonies he had been composing during the preceding years, a connection underscored by the composer's instruction on the published score: "This Octet must be played by all the instruments in symphonic orchestral style. Pianos and fortes must be strictly observed and more strongly emphasized than is usual in pieces of this character." In 1829 he would arrange the Octet's *Scherzo* as an orchestral piece with wind and timpani parts so that it might be used as an alternative movement in his C-minor Symphony. This orchestrated version, which would make a delightful encore in a symphonic concert, goes almost unheard today, although it is not uncommon for orchestras to "scale up" the lines of the Octet to employ full orchestral string sections—an alteration that seems perfectly logical and idiomatic even if lacks the composer's specific benediction.

In the first two movements Mendelssohn pens a first-violin part filled with the sort of virtuosity that Rietz would soon face in the D-minor Violin Concerto Mendelssohn wrote for him. The *Allegro moderato ma con fuoco* (as the published score called it, a forceful change from the manuscript's *Allegro moderato*) tumbles forth with blistering energy, and the second movement injects deeply felt emotional undercurrents beneath the imaginatively scored ambling.

The *Scherzo*, which became celebrated as a stand-alone piece in Mendelssohn's lifetime, is a cousin to the analogous section of the *Midsummer Night's Dream* music. This movement also had a literary inspiration—the Walpurgisnacht scene from Goethe's *Faust*. We have little documentation about Mendelssohn's composing his Octet for Strings apart from a tantalizing comment from his sister Fanny, which was included in the Mendelssohn family history published by her son, Sebastian Hensel, in 1879 (appearing in English three years later). Wrote Sebastian:

> The ethereal, fanciful, and spirit-like scherzo in this [Octet] is something quite new. He tried to set to music the stanza from the Walpurgis-night Dream in 'Faust':—

> > The flight of the clouds and the veil of mist
> > Are lighted from above.
> > A breeze in the leaves, a wind in the reeds,
> > And all has vanished.

> 'And he has been really successful,' says Fanny of this Ottetto, in her biography of Felix. 'To me alone he told his idea: the whole piece is to be played staccato and pianissimo, the tremulandos coming in now and then, the trills passing away with the quickness of lightning; everything new and strange, and at the same time most insinuating and pleasing, one feels so near the world of spirits, carried away in the air, half inclined to snatch up a broomstick and follow the aërial procession. At the end the first violin takes a flight with feather-like lightness, and—all has vanished.'

The music of the *Scherzo* makes a further appearance as a passing allusion in the finale. Though cast as a sonata-rondo, this closing movement involves a great deal of working-out of the material through fugal procedures, beginning with a sputtering subject that works its way up through the texture from the second cello to the first violin. Later we encounter (again with imitative treatment) a broad theme that echoes the phrase "And He shall reign for ever and ever" from the *Hallelujah* Chorus in Handel's *Messiah*, a work with which Mendelssohn was almost surely familiar by that time. That a sixteen-year-old composer should have mastered such complicated techniques is in itself astonishing; that he should wield his skill with such debonair brilliance and good humor would seem incredible—but it's all there in the score.

String Quartet in A minor, Op. 13

> *Adagio—Allegro vivace*
> *Adagio non lento*
> *Intermezzo*
> *Presto*

Work composed: July through October 27, 1827

Work premiered: February 14, 1832, in Paris by violinists Pierre Baillot and Eugène Sauzay, violist Chrétien Urhan, and cellist Louis Norblin

Instrumentation: Two violins, two violas, and cello

In 1827, in the course of a family trip to the south of Germany, the eighteen-year-old Mendelssohn became romantically smitten, though it remains unclear precisely who was the object of his affection. It may have been Betty Pistor, a young lady who sang in a Friday-night chorus Mendelssohn accompanied in Berlin. The infatuation passed, but not before Mendelssohn, with adolescent hormones a-pumping, wrote a song setting of a poem by his friend Johann Gustav Droyson, "Frage" ("Questions"). Mendelssohn's nephew Sebastian Hensel said the composer himself wrote the poem, while Droyson's son said it was authentically his father's, though it was printed under his father's occasional *nom de plume* J. N. Voss. In any case, the text has to do with young love—"Is it true that you'll always be waiting for me beneath the arbor?"—hopeful, but requiring insistent reassurance as the singer repeats the three-syllable, three-note opening phrase "Ist es wahr?" ("Is it true?"). That motto would also serve as the central musical theme and emotional engine of Mendelssohn's Op. 13 String Quartet, which he composed shortly thereafter. The phrase is first heard following the slow introduction, and returns often, with great rhetorical effect. "You will hear its notes resound in the first and last movements, and sense its feeling in all four," Mendelssohn informed a friend.

Because it was the second of his quartets to be published, this work is often known as Mendelssohn's Quartet No. 2—deceptively so, since it preceded his Quartet "No. 1" (in E-flat major, Op. 12) by two years. A comment about the key of this piece is in order. The work as a whole is quite clearly in A minor, but because the first movement is in A major one sometimes sees the quartet identified as being in that key. A good solution might be to split the difference and to say that it's in A major/minor, which is accurate if a touch unorthodox. This underscores an important aspect of Mendelssohn's style: sometimes when he casts works in minor keys his heart seems nonetheless anchored in expressing ideas more commonly associated with the major mode. One is often struck in his minor-key pieces by how quickly he tends to modulate to the major, and how much time he likes to spend in those sunnier regions once he arrives there. Even when a piece of Mendelssohn's adheres mostly to the minor mode, its character may elude the ominous quality many composers find there. The sparkling A-minor finale of his otherwise A-major Symphony, the *Italian*, is a famous example, and one of the very few instances of a large scale, multimovement work that begins in the major and ends in the minor. We find this phenomenon in the minor-mode third movement of this quartet, which seems to have a twinkle in its eye as it presents its opening tune and then starts giggling in a mostly major central section.

Apart from that, though, the Op. 13 Quartet tends toward the passionate, as befits the idea that generated it, and nowhere more than in the second movement, an intense *Adagio non lento* that even incorporates a serious fugato section, recalling a musical procedure that Beethoven was exploring in his late quartets. The Mendelssohn family kept current on the cutting edge of the arts, and in music in the 1820s that meant especially the works of Beethoven. Mendelssohn avidly devoured Beethoven's late works and was astonished (of course) by the master's late string quartets, with their visionary expansion of form and other compositional procedures. The spirit of late Beethoven also infuses the larger conception of Mendelssohn's piece, in which thematic material from earlier in the quartet is recalled repeatedly. This is certainly true of the "Ist es wahr?" motif in general, but it is played out with considerable imagination as the whole raison d'être of the *Presto* finale. The movement opens with a powerful recitative proclamation, replete with dramatic tremolos; upon hearing it, it's hard not to think of Beethoven's Ninth Symphony and his Op. 132 Quartet—the latter being also in A minor, as is the context of this passage in Mendelssohn (although the recitative section itself seems intent on obscuring precisely what key it is in). The resemblance seemed a bit too clear to at least one early listener, a certain clueless Abbé Bernardin, who, seated next to Mendelssohn during a performance of this quartet in Paris, in 1832, leaned over at this point of the piece to share an insight: "He has that in one of his symphonies." "Who?" asked the puzzled Mendelssohn. "Why, Beethoven, the composer of this quartet," the Abbé responded. So reports Mendelssohn in a letter to his sister, noting that "this was a very dubious compliment." Following the recitative, Mendelssohn introduces a wealth of themes, many of which are at least closely related to melodies we have heard before. Hints of the second-movement fugato return, and at the movement's end we find ourselves plunged again into the music of the quartet's first-movement introduction. This brings Mendelssohn's musical narrative full circle—a trick he may have learned from Beethoven's song cycle *An die ferne Geliebte* or (even more à propos) the Op. 131 String Quartet.

String Quartet in D major, Op. 44, No. 1

Molto allegro vivace
Menuetto: Un poco allegretto
Andante espressivo ma con moto
Presto con brio

Work composed: Begun in April 1838 in Leipzig, completed on July 24 in Berlin

Work dedicated: To His Highness the Crown Prince of Sweden

Work premiered: February 16, 1839, at the Leipzig Gewandhaus by the violinists Ferdinand David and C. W. Ulrich, violist Carl Traugott Queisser, and cellist Andreas Grabau

Instrumentation: Two violins, viola, and cello

The three quartets presented in a group as Mendelssohn's Op. 44 fall midway along his twenty-four-year involvement with the string quartet, at about the same time he produced his D-minor Piano Concerto. In fact, that piece and the Op. 44 Quartets are the only major works he composed during the years 1837–38, for the very good reason that his life was brimful with other things, all of them positive. In 1835 he had been named music director of the Gewandhaus Orchestra in Leipzig, and for the dozen years he held that post he spent a great deal of his time fulfilling his obligations as a conductor, both at home and on tour, as well as appearing as a pianist, organist, and chamber musician in many nonorchestral performances. He didn't take the easy road: during the 1837–38 season, Mendelssohn put together a novel series of so-called historical concerts in Leipzig, in the course of which he and his musicians explored long-ignored repertoire from the Baroque period through the time of Beethoven. In addition, he got married on March 28, 1837, and following their honeymoon and some summer travels, he and his bride, Cécile, busied themselves setting up a new home in Leipzig before the arrival of their first son, in the winter of 1838.

In the midst of all this, he somehow found time to create three string quartets. When they were eventually published as a set (in parts in June 1839, as a complete score in November 1840, bearing a dedication to the Crown Prince of Sweden), they appeared in an order different from the order of their composition. The E-minor Quartet (Op. 44, No. 2) was written first, in 1837; the E-flat major (Op. 44, No. 3) was completed on February 6, 1838; and the D major (Op. 41, No. 1) was finished last, on July 24, 1838, in Berlin. The numbering of each is therefore misleading. As a set the Op. 44 Quartets have been sometimes criticized for their "classicized" tendencies. Indeed Mendelssohn's music of this period does hew closely to Classical forms, and for music-lovers who evaluate pieces principally for their groundbreaking properties this is cause for complaint. On the other hand, there are those of us who feel that the Classical composers did achieve a kind of perfection, but that even in the fullness of their output they left room for others to express worthy and interesting things within the forms they had developed. There is no profit in pretending that the Op. 44 Quartets had much to do with what qualified as avant-garde in the late 1830s, but they do exhibit a sense of Mendelssohn's conveying his instantly recognizable voice through compositional formulas that are comfortable and reassuring.

"I have just finished my third Quartet, in D major, and it pleases me greatly," wrote Mendelssohn to his friend the violinist Ferdinand David, on July 30, 1838. "I hope it may please you, too. I think it will, since it is more spirited and seems to me likely to be more grateful to the players than the others." The opening of the first movement, with its "spirited" tempo marking of *Molto allegro vivace*, fairly bristles with energy, with the first violin launching the principal theme against the crackling *tremolando* background of the other players. In fact, chamber musicians have been known to lament the symphonic flavor of this opening sonority, which does indeed stand far from the four-as-equals ideal of the quartet medium. *Cobbett's Cyclopedic Survey of Chamber Music*, that doughty repertoire guide from 1929, proclaims bluntly, "The first [quartet of Op. 44] is inclined to be too orchestral in the two outer movements." Yet *Cobbett's* allows that "this and the following quartets are of real distinction, the master-touch of the mature artist being evident throughout." In any case, the criticisms about the texture seem severe: it's not as if Mendelssohn writes nothing *but* that sort of music in this quartet. Considered in its entirety, the D-major Quartet is generally very clear—and reasonably democratic—in its textures, including several expanses of positively luminous four-part counterpoint.

In all three of the Op. 44 Quartets, Mendelssohn opts for the fast-slow ordering of the two middle movements. Mendelssohn may have been the all-time master of the scherzo, but in the D-major Quartet, he chooses to fill the second-movement slot not with a scherzo but rather with what he calls a minuet, harking back to the dance movement that reigned in the time of Haydn and Mozart. It's a gentle, restrained interlude, hardly a "fast movement" at all, notwithstanding the flowing first-violin decorations that waft through the contrasting trio at the movement's middle.

A gorgeous B-minor slow movement follows, a wistful (even haunting, in some interpretations) "song without words" of an *Andante*. Its opening also displays a vaguely antique character, a neo-Baroque effusion of harmonic suspensions over what might be heard as a standard basso-continuo foundation, which the cello often articulates *pizzicato*. At the movement's beginning the cello is joined by the viola in its pizzicatos; but when the opening music returns later, the viola is given a prominent voice of counterpoint (bowed) against the first violin's melody—a subtle masterstroke. Of the finale, there's no gainsaying *Cobbett's*; this rush of dance-like energy would probably sound right at home if it were played by a full orchestra. And yet, it makes wonderful chamber music, too, and those who hold special affection for "the intimate art" can only appreciate how Mendelssohn's lines, including touches of "brainy" canonic imitation, burst forth with winning clarity when this work is played by a top-drawer string quartet.

Piano Trio No. 1 in D minor, Op. 49

> *Molto allegro e agitato*
> *Andante con moto tranquillo*
> *Scherzo: Leggiero e vivace*
> *Finale: Allegro assai appassionato*

Work composed: February to July 18, 1839, mostly in Frankfurt; he immediately revised it and signed off on the definitive score in September 1839.

Work premiered: February 1, 1840, at the Leipzig Gewandhaus by violinist Ferdinand David, cellist Franz Karl Witmann, and the composer as pianist

Instrumentation: Violin, cello, and piano

"This is the master-trio of our time, even as Beethoven's in B-flat and D and Schubert's in E-flat were the masterpieces of their day; it is an exceedingly fine composition that, years hence, will still delight our grandchildren and great-grandchildren." So wrote Robert Schumann, one of the most perspicacious music critics of the Romantic era, when he first encountered Mendelssohn's D-minor Piano Trio a few months after it was finished. He continued:

> What more shall I say of about this Trio that everyone who has heard it has not already said? Most fortunate, certainly, are those who have heard it played by its creator in person, for even if there are more dashing virtuosos, hardly any other knows how to play Mendelssohn's works with such magical freshness as he himself. This should not make anyone afraid to play the Trio; in comparison to others, such as, for example, those of Schubert, it has fewer difficulties.... Moreover, it need hardly be said that the Trio is not a piece just for the pianist; the other players also have to play their roles in lively fashion and can count on gaining satisfaction and appreciation. So may the new work be effective from all perspectives, as it should, and may it serve us as evidence of its creator's artistic power, which now appears to be near its full bloom.

Schumann was right, of course: it remains a popular mainstay of chamber-music concerts to this day, rivaled among its contemporaries in the genre only by Mendelssohn's C-minor Piano Trio. On August 17, 1838, Mendelssohn wrote to his close friend the pianist and composer Ferdinand Hiller: "A very important branch of piano music, of which I am particularly fond—trios, quartets, and other things with accompaniment—is quite forgotten now, and I feel greatly the want of something new in that line. I should like to do a little towards this. It was with this in mind that I lately wrote the Sonata for Violin, and one for the cello, and I am thinking of writing a couple of trios."

In fact, Mendelssohn had already essayed the genre of the piano trio back in 1820, when he was all of eleven, though that piece is regrettably among his lost juvenilia; and he was rather overstating his point about the disappearance of chamber music with piano. It is true that Mendelssohn's and Robert Schumann's (and, in recent years, Clara Schumann's single contribution to the genre) are the only piano trios of their time that we are likely to find represented on concert programs today, but it is not to their detriment that a music-lover might plea for occasional airings of coeval piano trios by such figures as Heinrich Marschner (several of whose seven trios Schumann also admired), William Sterndale Bennet (who composed his A-major "Chamber Trio" in 1839), Ambroise Thomas (whose Op. 3 Trio, from about 1835, Schumann dismissed as a mere salon effusion), or Louis Spohr (whose remarkable piano trios all appeared in the decade of the 1840s).

The D-minor Trio offers abundant, arching melodies of Italianate bel canto inspiration, proclaimed with luxuriant sonorities and often introduced in the tenorial tones of the cello. The minor mode provides a sense of seriousness that can helpfully rein in Mendelssohn's native exuberance; but here, as is often his wont, the composer hardly feels constrained to abjure long stretches in the major (though, in the first movement, he surprisingly avoids the expected relative major key of F). The piano part is brilliant, as one might expect from a composer-pianist writing during an era of keyboard hypervirtuosity, though it does not dominate the strings as much as the keyboard part had in Mendelssohn's early chamber pieces (most notably in his Sextet for Piano and Strings of 1824). Mendelssohn revised the piano part somewhat after its provisional completion to incorporate certain new keyboard tricks associated with Chopin and Liszt—this apparently at Hiller's urging.

If the first movement stands as an amalgam of Romantic piano style and Classical structure, the second is purely of its time: a leisurely Romantic "song without words" (a Mendelssohn specialty), a heartfelt, intimate, uncomplicated piece that achieves a heightened emotional pitch in its middle. In the ensuing movement, a slightly syncopated *Scherzo*, we glimpse what was said to be Mendelssohn's forte as a pianist: brilliant finger staccato and lightning-fast wrist action. With the Schubert-inspired *Finale* we again return to the ostensible deep thoughts of the minor mode, though even here the strings sing out a warm-hearted cantabile melody in B-flat major halfway through.

That tune returns in a coda at the end, with the unusual marking *f e dolce* ("Loudly and sweetly"), transposed to D major, thus bringing the trio to a brilliant major-mode conclusion.

In 1898 the *Musical Times* ran an interview with the violinist Joseph Joachim. He had studied under Ferdinand David, who had played in the premieres of both of Mendelssohn's trios, and Joachim himself had considerable experience as a Mendelssohn interpreter. Joachim recalled a performance of the D-minor Trio given in London in 1844, in which he played violin, a Mr. Hancock played cello, and Mendelssohn served as pianist. "It so happened," recalled Joachim, "that only the violin and violoncello parts had been brought to the concert-room, and Mendelssohn was rather displeased at this; but he said, 'Never mind, put any book on the piano, and someone can turn from time to time, so that I need not look as though I played by heart.'" "Now-a-days," the *Musical Times* added, "when people put such importance on playing or conducting without a book...this might be considered a good moral lesson of a great musician's modesty. He evidently did not like to be in too great a prominence before his partners in the Trio. He was always truly generous!"

Piano Trio No. 2 in C minor, Op. 66

> *Allegro energico*
> *Andante espressivo*
> *Scherzo: Molto allegro quasi presto*
> *Allegro appassionato*

Work composed: February to April 30, 1845

Work dedicated: To the violinist and composer Ludwig (also known as Louis) Spohr, with whom Mendelssohn would go on to perform this work

Work premiered: December 20, 1845, at the Leipzig Gewandhaus by violinist Ferdinand David, cellist Franz Karl Witmann, and the composer as pianist

Instrumentation: Violin, cello, and piano

Doubtless Robert Schumann was correct in 1839 in proclaiming Mendelssohn's Piano Trio No. 1 to be "the master-trio of our time," but of course the Piano Trio No. 2 had not yet been written. The D-minor Piano Trio is as great a masterpiece as Schumann proclaimed it to be, and my impression is that it is the more frequently programmed of the two; but many connoisseurs feel that its composer would surpass it in his C-minor Trio, which followed six years later.

The first movement seems in certain ways uncharacteristic of Mendelssohn, whose music rarely sustains an analogous level of nervous tension. The anxiety is announced from the very opening, when the piano, soon seconded by the violin, proclaims the powerful theme above a pedal point in the cello. The second theme is a particularly glorious conception, a melody that holds the potential of joyous triumph in the relative major key of E-flat. Although Mendelssohn frequently cast compositions in the minor mode, he tended not to stay planted in the minor for long, veering preternaturally into the major mode for long expanses. Here he remains resolutely in the minor, and the E-flat-major theme is not allowed to dominate the proceedings. In its serious mien, the movement seems to look forward to Brahms; but, like Brahms, Mendelssohn was an ardent believer in certain Classical ideals. So it is that he develops his material within the framework of a perfectly proportioned sonata-form movement, drawing on motifs inherent in his themes to bind everything together tightly with a sense of inevitable unity. Mendelssohn was natively fluent in the language of counterpoint, and in the movement's coda he scores a technical bull's-eye of considerable intricacy by having the strings play an augmented (stretched-out) version of the main theme at the same time that the piano plays the theme in its normal proportions—no mean trick, and here one that mirrors related contrapuntal manipulation (in the form of thematic diminution and inversion) the composer had worked into the piano part earlier on.

While the piano is indeed fiery and impressive, listeners may not be aware of the precision Mendelssohn brings to its notation, distinguishing the character of his thematic development by specifying details of phrasing and articulation. In the second movement the piano is allowed to introduce the introspective, slightly nostalgic melody but then takes more of a back seat as the strings develop the material into an expressive, cantabile, triple-time outpouring in A-flat major; in practice, this unrolls as a sort of double structure, since the first half of the tune is presented, and then developed, before the melody's conclusion is articulated and developed.

Counterpoint is again prominent in the fleet *Scherzo*, a chattering toccata enlivened by fugato texture. If the opening recalls the bustling vigor of Mendelssohn's *Midsummer Night's Dream* scherzo, its middle section makes us think again of Brahms thanks to the constant shifting between major and minor modes, the powerfully accented downbeats (strengthened by trills), and what at moments evokes a "Hungarian Gypsy" flavor.

The finale begins less like Brahms than like Schumann, its leap of a ninth particularly recalling that composer's piano composition "Aufschwung" (Op. 12, No. 2). A moment of unalloyed Mendelssohn arrives soon

enough, however, with the introduction, in the piano, of a chorale—a favorite Mendelssohnian device for elevating the tone to one of spiritual devo-
tion. Examples of this rhetorical device surface strikingly in his oeuvre, with
famous examples including the *Reformation* Symphony, (Op. 107, of 1832),
the Prelude and Fugue in E minor for piano (Op. 35, No. 1, from 1832–36),
the slow movement of the D-major Cello Sonata (Op. 58, from 1843), and
several of the organ sonatas. Here the melody evokes the German Lutheran
chorale "Gelobet seist Du, Jesu Christ"—but it's really no more than an allusion. (Some scholars have instead heard the germ of the traditional chorales
"Vor deinen Thron tret' ich hiermit" and "Herr Gott, dich loben alle wir,"
but to my ears "Gelobet seist Du" seems a more obvious jumping-off point.)
Much as Brahms, in his ostensible folk-song settings, would often cite only
the beginning of a tune before spinning off into an essentially original melody,
Mendelssohn here writes his own chorale. After a good deal of deconstruc-
tion and reassembly, the melody returns at the movement's climax, hammered out loudly in rich piano chords against contrapuntal overlapping in
the strings—a moment in which the intimate medium of the piano trio seems
about ready to explode.

String Quintet No. 2 in B-flat major, Op. 87

Allegro vivace
Andante scherzando
Adagio e lento
Allegro molto vivace

Work composed: Summer 1845, in Soden (near Frankfurt), completed on July
8; it was published posthumously as his Op. 87.

Work premiered: November 1852

Instrumentation: Two violins, two violas, and cello

Mendelssohn's two string quintets, both for the identical combination of
two violins, two violas, and cello, are separated in his oeuvre by nearly two
decades. Together they practically frame his maturity as a composer, and listening to them back-to-back provides quite an education about the distance
the composer traveled in that span. In the Op. 87 Quintet, we find Mendelssohn revealing an older and wiser personality, often doubting the efficacy
of his achievements, searching for something beyond what came to him easily. He grew increasingly zealous about effecting revisions in his compositions,

and this quintet was among the works of his later years that he failed to bring to what he considered a completed state. As a result, it was not published until three years after his death, with the firm of Breitkopf & Härtel assigning it the opus number 87.

In 1845, Mendelssohn's career as a composer and conductor was continuing to flourish; he was considering competing job offers from two crowned heads (the Kings of Prussia and of Saxony), he was deriving satisfaction from his pet project of elevating the Leipzig Conservatory (which he had founded) into a world-class institution, and he enjoyed great happiness on the home front, the more so when he and his wife greeted the arrival of their fifth child, Lili. There is no way that the composer, who was only thirty-six years old, could have known when he wrote the B-flat-major Quintet that it would be among his last works, but the sad fact is that he had only two more years to live.

In this work, the exuberance of his early style remains in the outer movements, which seem practically born of the same breath as his Op. 18 Quintet, his Octet for Strings, and his String Quartet in D major (Op. 44, No. 1); in contrast, the inner two reveal the technical and emotive growth he had experienced in the intervening years. The first movement is dashing and athletic, with fleet triplets often propelling the accompanying parts. The first violin assumes what might be called a *concertante* role, somewhat dominating the proceedings. The classic wisdom is that, in chamber music, a composer should strive to equalize the individual parts as much as possible, involving each player in the presentation and working-out of themes. Mendelssohn was sometimes even-handed in this regard, but his personal style was not strictly that of the mainstream. As a result, certain of his works—and certainly the first and last movements of this quintet—can sometimes sound less like classic chamber music than like little string symphonies, reflecting a hierarchy in which the first violin spends far more time in the spotlight than the lower-lying "accompanying" instruments.

With the second movement, we enter a very different landscape. Mendelssohn is acknowledged as one of the all-time masters of the scherzo, but here he offers a curious one, an *Andante scherzando*. Scherzo means "joke," and it is natural that any piece cast in that form should be fast—even riotously fast. Here, however, we have a far more languorous scherzo—*Andante* implying a relaxed, "walking" tempo—and it falls to the performers to decide whether the movement will come across as charming (stressing the "scherzando" side of the equation) or eerily melancholy (underscoring the "andante").

The third movement stands as a monument to the shadow cast by Beethoven on the generation that followed him. The tense, rhapsodic expression of this *Adagio e lento* has a good deal in common with passages in Beethoven's quartets; and if one looks ahead rather than backward, one could just as easily see this as foreshadowing Brahms. Here Mendelssohn achieves an expressiveness of nearly operatic proportions, with the passages in which the first violin plays over shuddering tremolos in the lower strings reaching toward the melodrama of a "dark and stormy night" scenario. This leads *attaca*—that is, without a break—into the brief finale, which, like the opening movement, is mostly an exercise in bustling vibrancy, though with a beautiful theme for two violas thrown in for contrast.

The fortunes of the B-flat-major Quintet have fluctuated widely over the years. It proved hugely popular early on, especially in London, where, on February 14, 1859, it was the opening piece in the first of the renowned "Pops" concerts, a series that brought it back more than forty times, with unvarying success, before the "Pops" were discontinued forty-three years later. Mendelssohn was less pleased with it—an entirely characteristic stance from a composer typically given to self-criticism and endless revision as the years passed. In 1846 his friend Ignaz Moscheles (the pianist and composer) inscribed an entry in his journal describing an evening he spent with the Mendelssohns. "We also looked at the Viola Quintet in B-flat major," he wrote, "and Mendelssohn claimed that the last movement was not good." This is doubtless an accurate reflection of Mendelssohn's sentiments, and it is supported by the fact that he withheld it from publication during his lifetime. That does not automatically confirm that the work is deficient: even such an obviously splendid piece as the *Italian* Symphony remained unpublished at Mendelssohn's death due to his qualms about its quality. On the other hand, we can be reasonably sure that if Mendelssohn had lived longer he probably would have effected at least some, and perhaps many, revisions in his late string quintet. In the event, performers and audiences may approach this as a piece that reached only a provisionally finished state, though one that nonetheless bespeaks mastery, insightfulness, and a very personal allure.

String Quartet No. 6 in F minor, Op. 80

Allegro assai—Presto
Allegro assai
Adagio
Allegro molto

Work composed: Summer 1847

Work premiered: November 4, 1848, at the Leipzig Conservatory, in a concert marking the first anniversary of the composer's passing, by an ensemble headed by the violinist Joseph Joachim

Instrumentation: Two violins, viola, and cello

When Mendelssohn embarked on his F-minor Quartet, nine years had passed since he had worked seriously in the genre, and this final quartet is unlike any of the quartets that had come before. This work is marked by volatile contrasts and unanticipated turns of phrase, by a highly charged emotionality, and by a sense of agitation that borders on the combustible. It is hard not to feel that biography helps explain the new path that Mendelssohn suddenly travels in his F-minor Quartet.

By the end of 1846 the much fêted Mendelssohn had grown somewhat withdrawn from society, and the letters he wrote to his most intimate friends increasingly dealt with the deepest concerns of the artist, the shallowness of public acclaim, nostalgia for "the good old days," and mortality itself. There is no question that he suffered from some measure of exhaustion. Much in demand as a conductor and a pianist, he gave up public appearances in the spring of 1847, and at about the same time he wriggled out of as many teaching obligations at the Leipzig Conservatory as he could. At the end of a visit to England that spring, he was so depleted that he told his dear friend Karl Klingemann, "Another exhausting week like this and I'm a dead man!"

And then, returning to Germany, he was struck with horrific news: his beloved sister Fanny died with no warning, the victim of a stroke. Mendelssohn was bereft; they had been closest friends since his infancy. In the aftermath of this loss, he headed to Switzerland, where he had found solace and relaxation on earlier occasions. Traveling through Lucerne and Thun, he arrived at the breathtaking alpine village of Interlaken, where he remained until mid-September.

His English friend Henry Fothergill Chorley visited him there and reported that even in these holiday surroundings the composer seemed weary and aged. Though he was only thirty-eight, he was walking with a stoop. Mendelssohn returned to his home in Leipzig in mid-September, intending to conduct the first German performance of his oratorio *Elijah*, recently premiered in England. The concert was scheduled for November 3, in Berlin, but after Mendelssohn visited Fanny's former home in late September he was too despondent to follow through, and he canceled the concert. On October 7 he composed a mournful song about separation titled "Altdeutsches Frühlingslied" ("Old German Spring Song") and took it to his friend Livia Frege for its first private reading. As she sang it, he turned cold and pale and needed to lie down. Seemingly recovered, he returned home, where he suffered a stroke, just as Fanny had five months before, and their father and grandfather before them. A second stroke—this one more serious—arrived on November 1, partially paralyzing him; and another, on November 3, left him only one more day to live.

Mendelssohn composed his F-minor String Quartet rapidly during his summer in Switzerland. It is certainly sui generis among the composer's quartets. Whether it charts a new direction that ensuing work would have followed, as some commentators have suggested, we cannot know. It is worth remarking that although some of Mendelssohn's late music was assuming an increasingly somber quality, not everything from his pen veered toward melancholy. He told his friend Ignaz Moscheles that he hoped to write yet another string quartet, in D minor, whose first movement (a set of variations) he said would compare to the F-minor Quartet as "less gloomy, more comforting, and harmonically particularly distinguished." That piece never materialized, though he did leave two unattached movements, including a set of variations in E major, which were doubtless meant to be part of a complete quartet. In fact, those two movements do bear out the composer's description as being "less gloomy."

The first movement of Mendelssohn's last quartet (*Allegro assai*) opens with bristling tremolos, above which the first violin utters a terse theme first on the tonic, then on the subdominant, and yet again a third time, on the leading tone. This is a curious way to begin, all the more so if we are expecting the ingratiating, melodious method for which Mendelssohn's earlier quartets have typically prepared us. A fractured dialogue ensues: the tremolos suddenly give way to a high-pitched, almost shrieking gesture in the first violin, which is then assumed by the lower strings. The second theme is reached via unstable chord inversions that yield a sense of uncertainty about the direction in which the proceedings are heading. This section of the movement culminates on a powerful dominant seventh chord; but instead of resolving to the temporary tonic of A-flat, which any listener expects to hear at this moment, Mendelssohn instead cadences on a diminished seventh chord, an emotionally heightened sonority but one that is utterly noncommittal in terms of harmonic direction, and he enhances its drama by returning to his opening tremolos. Furious as this movement is, its sense of desperate rage increases by a degree when, at the very end, Mendelssohn injects an explosive crescendo and a coda, marked *Presto*, replete with brash octave writing, sharp dotted rhythms, and biting staccato attacks.

The second movement looks on the page rather like a minuet, though it is not so identified in the score. Neither does Mendelssohn call it a scherzo, even though at high speed—like the opening of the first movement, it is marked *Allegro assai*—it might be viewed as one. Scherzos certainly qualified as familiar territory for Mendelssohn, but this hardly resembles the fleet-footed movements that were his hallmark in earlier years. The harmonic curiosity continues in this movement, which begins on its dominant key rather than with the stability of its tonic, and the bass line's chromatic trajectory provides no certainty about the tonal center. Harmonic displacement is joined by rhythmic displacement as the composer proposes a syncopated theme, highly uncharacteristic of his earlier style. A measure of humor may be discovered in Mendelssohn's adroit working-out of material here, but on the whole it is a humor informed by sarcasm, a sort of bitter laughter. Against this, the trio section, with its obsessive repetitions of an ostinato bass line, inserts a feeling of intense claustrophobia.

With the *Adagio* we reach a moment of respite from the vehemence of the opening movements. Here instead is a deeply expressive elegy, at once peaceful and mournful, its depth of passion far surpassing the "song without words" character of many Mendelssohn slow movements. Its opening bars bear some kinship with the melody from the *Adagio molto e mesto* movement from Beethoven's String Quartet in F major (Op. 59, No. 1), a theme Beethoven had characterized in a sketchbook as "a weeping willow or acacia-tree on my brother's grave." Possibly Mendelssohn had this in mind, possibly not.

Restlessness returns with the finale, agitated in the outburst of its opening theme—again, with syncopation that sounds atypical compared to the composer's earlier quartets. After two statements of the principal theme, the first violin tries to inject calmer spirits into the action, without much success. The development section, set in the subdominant, involves breathless bantering with a rapid four-note motif, after which Mendelssohn has the cello, viola, and second violin play canonic entries against a pedal point played *tremolando* by the first violin—again, a curious but intriguing passage. Another "calm" violin theme is proposed but is quickly subsumed in the relentless drive of the syncopated principal theme. The conductor Julius Benedict, an English friend of Mendelssohn, captured the essential quality of this disturbing quartet: "It would be difficult to cite any piece of music which so completely impresses the listener with a sensation of gloomy foreboding, of anguish of mind, and of the most poetic melancholy, as does this masterly and eloquent composition."

Olivier Messiaen

Olivier-Eugène-Prosper-Charles Messiaen

Born: December 10, 1908, in Avignon, France

Died: April 28, 1992, in Paris, France

Quatuor pour la fin de temps ("Quartet for the End of Time")

Liturgie de cristal
Vocalise, pour l'Ange qui annonce la fin du Temps
Abîme des oiseaux
Intermède
Louange à l'Éternité de Jésus
Danse de la fureur, pour les sept trompettes
Fouillis d'arcs-en-ciel, pour l'Ange qui annonce la fin du Temps
Louange à l'Immortalité de Jésus

Work composed: 1940–41, in the prisoner-of-war camp at Görlitz, Silesia (then under German occupation, today in Poland); Messiaen had probably begun at least what would become the "Abîme des Oiseaux" movement shortly before being incarcerated.

Work dedicated: "In homage to the Angel of the Apocalypse, who raises his hand toward heaven, saying: 'There will be no more Time'"

Work premiered: In the Görlitz camp, on January 15, 1941, by four prisoners (violinist Jean Le Boulaire, cellist Etienne Pasquier, clarinetist Henri Akoka, and Messiaen himself as pianist)

Instrumentation: Violin, clarinet, cello, and piano

B orn into an intellectual family, Olivier Messiaen was engulfed in a heady cultural environment from his earliest years. His father was a professor and English-French translator whose output included a complete annotated French translation of Shakespeare, and the composer's mother was a poet. One might say that he was swept into the world of arts and letters even before he was born, as his mother dedicated a volume of her mystical poetry to him while he was still in utero. He showed an early aptitude for music, composing his first song at the age of eight, and by the time he was eleven he enrolled at the Paris Conservatoire, where he would earn *premiers prix* in four domains: organ, piano accompaniment, improvisation, and composition. His musical education there was of the highest order: his composition professors included Paul Dukas and Maurice Emmanuel (whose interest in Greek metrics would leave a strong mark on the student), and his principal organ teacher was Marcel Dupré.

Upon leaving the Conservatoire, he was named (in 1931) organist at the Eglise de la Trinité in the ninth arrondissement of Paris, where he would rule over the Cavaillé-Coll instrument in the loft for the rest of his life. As the 1930s progressed he accepted posts on the faculties of the Ecole Normale de Musique and the Schola Cantorum. In 1935 he helped found the short-lived contemporary music society La Spirale, and the following year he joined with his colleagues Yves Baudrier, Daniel-Lesur, and André Jolivet to establish the musical movement La Jeune France, hoping to re-inject a spirit of humanism and spirituality into French composition, which was stressing lighter, more cynical, even frivolous, attitudes during the interwar years.

In ensuing decades, Messiaen would gain renown as a composer of an individualistic bent, achieving works that combined an almost "tactile" sonic sensibility with a fascination for technical details, most astonishingly in the often-neglected area of rhythm. Young composers at the cutting edge—Boulez, Stockhausen, Xenakis, and Grisey among them—flocked to his classes at the Paris Conservatoire, at the Berkshire Music Center (Tanglewood), and at Darmstadt's renowned Ferienkurse für Neue Musik, ensuring that his very personal esthetic would leave a mark in musical history apart from his own output, which it unquestionably has.

The composer cited the Biblical glimpse of the apocalypse—Revelation of John, X: 1–7—as the direct inspiration for his *Quartet for the End of Time*: "And I saw another mighty angel come down from heaven, clothed with a cloud: and a rainbow was upon his head, and his face was as it were the sun, and his feet as pillars of fire." The Quartet's section titles relate the music of its seven movements (or at least several of them) to specific images from John's vision. Almost half the entries in his modest catalogue (which totals only about eighty works) are explicitly tied to biblical themes and celestial visions. Most of the remaining pieces are split among bird-related pieces, works of Asian inspiration, and technical studies.

Messiaen was drafted for military service soon after World War II began, and in May 1940 he unfortunately became a resident of Stalag VIII A of the German prisoner-of-war camp at Görlitz, Silesia. He spent nearly a year there, taking solace in the scores of musical classics he had managed to pack with his belongings, and a sympathetic guard sneaked in manuscript paper and pencils so that he could continue his composing. The result of this charity was the *Quartet for the End of Time*, its unorthodox combination of four instruments—violin, clarinet, cello, and piano—reflecting the available performing talent. The composer makes the most of the variety afforded by that ensemble: only half of the movements use all four instruments, with each of the other movements using a different combination (or, in the case of the "Abîme des oiseaux," only a solo clarinet). Messiaen, playing a broken-down piano, joined three of his fellow prisoners at the premiere, which took place in a frigid January before an audience of 5,000 literally captive listeners. "Never have I been heard with as much attention and understanding," the composer would recall.

The circumstances of the work's genesis have inspired some commentators to consider it an expression of the desperate straits in which Messiaen found himself. The composer always discouraged such an interpretation, insisting that it was "simply" a response to the biblical passage cited above. Nonetheless, matters involving mystics—for such Messiaen assuredly was—are rarely simple. In this case, the idea of the "end of time" may be understood not just as relating to the angel who proclaimed that "there will be no more Time," but also as underscoring Messiaen's stance toward rhythm—that is, musical time—which often explores paths generally left untouched by Western composers.

As was his custom, the composer affixed lengthy comments to his published score. Allow me to mix in quotations from those colorful paragraphs while paraphrasing his descriptions of the eight movements:

Liturgie de cristal ("Crystal liturgy")—The awakening of birds between 3 and 4 o'clock of the morning. "Transpose this to the religious plane, you will have the harmonious silence of heaven." Messiaen was passionate about birdsong. He began notating birdsong outdoors in 1923 and through the years he traveled widely on bird-watching expeditions to observe birds in their native habitats. He often captured their calls in the field using a tape recorder he might haul halfway around the word; he would then transcribe the tapes to provide musical material he could incorporate into his original works. Rather than use birdsong for its pastoral or sentimental implications, Messiaen incorporated it strictly for its esthetic content—birdsongs as musical themes. In this opening movement we hear the blackbird and the nightingale.

Vocalise pour l'Ange qui annonce la fin du Temps ("Vocalise for the Angel who Announces the End of Time")—The short opening and closing sections depict the power of the angel, crowned with a rainbow and garbed in storm clouds. In the middle are the irreproducible harmonies of heaven, including the piano's "waterfall of blue-orange harmonies." ("When I was a prisoner, the absence of nourishment led me to dream in color," Messiaen recalled.)

Abîme des oiseaux ("Abyss of the Birds")—The abyss is Time; we are trapped in its tedium. Birds stand as the opposite of Time in their joyful freedom. This entire movement is entrusted to the unaccompanied clarinet.

Intermède ("Interlude")—A light, exuberant break from the main topic, for clarinet, violin, and cello, though connected to the other movements through some melodic references.

Louange à l'Éternité de Jésus ("Praise of the Eternal Nature of Jesus")—Jesus is here viewed as the Word, existing apart from Time. "Majestically the melody unfolds itself at a distance both intimate and awesome." The movement (which does not use the clarinet) is marked "infinitely long, ecstatic," and though it occupies a mere three pages of the published score it may last some eight minutes in performance, its cello melody unfolding with immeasurable tenderness above the slowly reiterated chords on the piano.

Danse de la fureur, pour les sept trompettes ("Dance of Fury, for the Seven Trumpets")—"Rhythmically the most idiosyncratic of the set.... Music of stone, formidable sonority, movements as irresistible as steel, as huge blocks of livid fury or ice-like frenzy." The four instruments play always in unison (the pianist playing in octaves) in this "granitic" movement, suggesting "gongs and trumpets (the first six trumpets of the Apocalypse followed by various catastrophes, the trumpet of the seventh angel announcing the consummation of the mystery of God."

Fouillis d'arcs-en-ciel, pour l'Ange qui annonce la fin du Temps ("Cluster of Rainbows for the Angel Who Announces the End of Time")—The mighty angel appears enveloped in rainbows ("symbol of peace, of wisdom, of every quiver of luminosity and sound"). "In my dreaming I hear and see ordered melodies and chords, familiar hues and forms; then, following this transitory stage I pass into the unreal and submit ecstatically to a vortex, a dizzying interpenetration of superhuman sounds and colors. These fiery swords, these rivers of blue-orange lava, these sudden stars: Behold the cluster, behold the rainbows!" Cello and piano begin this movement alone, in dreamy tones, but the music springs into more energetic action when they are joined by violin and clarinet.

Louange à l'Immortalité de Jésus ("Praise of the Immortality of Jesus")—This second glorification, for just violin and piano, "addresses itself more specifically to...Jesus the man, to the Word made flesh.... Its slow rising to a supreme point is the ascension of man toward his God, of the son toward his Father, of the mortal newly made divine toward paradise.—And I repeat anew: 'All this is mere striving and childish stammering if one compares it to the overwhelming grandeur of the subject!'"

"Why are there eight movements?" asks Messiaen in his preface. "Seven is the perfect number, the six days of the creation sanctified by the divine Sabbath: the 7th day of rest extends into eternity and becomes the 8 of the indestructible light, the unalterable peace."

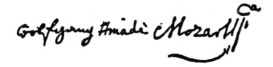

Johann Chrysostom Wolfgang Gottlieb Mozart

Born: January 27, 1756, in Salzburg, Austria

Died: December 5, 1791, in Vienna, Austria

About his name: He was baptized as Johann Chrysostom Wolfgang Gottlieb Mozart. He often used the Romanized forms Amadè or Amadé of the German Gottlieb, but rarely Amadeus, and when he did it usually seems to have been in jest.

K numbers: The "K numbers" attached to Mozart's compositions refer to the *Chronologisch-thematisches Verzeichniss sämmtlicher Tonwerke Wolfgang Amadè Mozart's (Chronological and Thematic Catalogue of the Complete Compositions of Wolfgang Amadè Mozart)*, published in 1862 by Ludwig von Köchel. The catalogue has gone through six editions since then, each of which has updated the chronology of Mozart's compositions and, in some cases, rendered decisions pro or con concerning their authenticity. Certain works are referred to with more than one Köchel number, the first referring to its traditional placement in the composer's output, the second to its updated chronological positioning as reflected in the catalogue's most recent (in this case the sixth) edition.

Flute Quartet in D major, K. 285

Allegro
Adagio
Rondeau

Work composed: December 1777 in Mannheim

Work premiered: Not known

Instrumentation: Flute, violin, viola, and cello

B y the time Mozart turned twenty-one, in January 1777, he had already experienced more of the world than most young adults of that era would approach in a lifetime. As a child prodigy, he had impressed musical connoisseurs and entertained crowned heads in many European capitals. Fortunately, he could still muster up some demand as a touring artist, and his travels provided important artistic cross-pollination with a musical avant-garde he rarely encountered at home.

Late that year, he and his mother embarked on a journey north and west from their home in Salzburg, stopping for three months in Mannheim. For more than thirty years Mannheim's court, overseen by the Elector Palatine, had stood as one of the most musical in all of Europe, and its orchestra was considered the greatest of its era. Johann Baptist Wendling, the orchestra's principal flutist since 1751, was an important player in the court's musical life, as were his brother (a violinist in the orchestra) and his wife and daughter (both of whom were famous sopranos). Wendling proposed that the Mozarts (son and mother) should accompany him and his oboist colleague Friedrich Ramm to Paris, where all were sure to find the welcome mat rolled out. Mozart was unenthusiastic about the idea. In the end, Wendling and Ramm left for Paris on February 15, and the Mozarts followed a month later, finding that Wendling had indeed paved the way for their generous reception in the French capital.

During Mozart's stay in Mannheim, Wendling's entourage included a wealthy Dutch/German gentleman named Dejean, who was attached to the East India Company and was also an accomplished amateur flutist. (Musicological digging has suggested that Mozart's spelling was a phonetic confusion and that the gentleman in question was actually Willem Britten de Jong.) Dejean—to continue with Mozart's spelling—commissioned the twenty-one-year-old composer to write several works for him: three "little, easy, short concertos" and several quartets for flute, violin, viola, and cello. For these, Dejean would pay the handsome sum of 200 florins. But there were distractions, most notably the Mannheim singer Aloisia Weber. Mozart developed a crush on her; eventually she would become his sister-in-law, rather than his wife. Back home in Salzburg, Mozart's father got edgy when he learned that his son was tardy in fulfilling Dejean's commission, and some spirited correspondence ensued. Grasping for an excuse, the composer wrote to him: "One is not disposed to work at all times. I could certainly scribble the whole day, but a piece of music goes out into the world, and, after all, I don't want

to feel ashamed for my name to be on it. And, as you know, I am quite inhib-
ited when I have to compose for an instrument which I cannot endure." This
comment, clearly made by a post-adolescent in a snit, is often cited as proof
that Mozart loathed the flute. It's weak evidence, especially since the composer never repeated anything to that effect in his remaining years, and since
he would spotlight the instrument sensitively in many of his symphonies and
operas. Would a composer who detested the flute have permitted it to serve
as the "title character" of *Die Zauberflöte*, where it is exalted as a repository of
magical powers of salvation?

It would seem that Mozart was blaming the flute for his own failure to fulfill Dejean's commission. By the time Dejean left Mannheim for Paris, Mozart
had completed only two of the three concertos (one of them being a reworking of an earlier composition for oboe—and neither of them particularly little, easy, or short) and one quartet, in D major (K. 285). Dejean pro-rated the
commission and paid Mozart only 96 of the 200 florins initially contracted.
It seems that a second quartet did materialize through this commission—the
two-movement G-major Flute Quartet (K. 285a), which Dejean may have
received a few months later when Mozart, continuing his tour, arrived in Paris
himself. The composer appears to have produced two further flute quartets in
the 1780s: one in C major (K.285b), probably early in the decade, though it
wasn't published until about 1788, and the authenticity of its authorship is
not ironclad; the other, in A major (K. 298), not earlier than 1786.

Dejean should have felt honored to own the D-major Flute Quartet.
There's nothing groundbreaking in the piece, but it displays Mozart's comfortable integration of themes and structures. The opening *Allegro* is an exercise
in ebullient graciousness, courtly chamber music in which each of the instruments has its say in support of the flute's perfectly balanced phrases. The middle movement is a B-minor *Adagio* in which the flute sings a haunting melody
over a pizzicato accompaniment (an accompaniment that, for all its simplicity, promises to expose the slightest variation of rhythmic pulse among the
string players). Prolonged harmonic resolutions reminiscent of Gluck intensify its sense of nostalgia. In fact, the movement lacks a "proper" resolution;
Mozart instead leaves it suspended in a mid-phrase sigh, breaking its tension
by launching into the concluding rondo—or *Rondeau*, as the composer put it,
his mind no doubt racing ahead to the Paris he would soon visit.

Oboe Quartet in F major, K. 370

> *Allegro*
> *Adagio*
> *Rondeau: Allegro*

Work composed: Apparently in early 1781 in Munich

Work premiered: Not known

Instrumentation: Oboe, violin, viola, and cello

When Mozart visited Mannheim in 1777, he was astonished by the playing of the oboist Friedrich Ramm, not least by, as he put it, "his pleasingly pure tone." Ramm must have been an exceptional musician: his employer, the Elector Palatine, allowed him the unusual privilege of touring as a soloist, letting his colleagues cover for him at home while he scored international successes as far away as Vienna, Berlin, Paris, and London. Mozart presented Ramm with a copy of a concerto (K. 271k) he had written earlier for another oboist, and he also wrote for Ramm (plus three colleagues) a Sinfonia Concertante for Four Wind Instruments and Orchestra (now lost), some arias with oboe obbligato, and the F-major Oboe Quartet, which apparently dates from early 1781.

This is a work of enormous charm and with a personality quite distinct from that of Mozart's string quartets. With the oboe occupying the prominent spot that otherwise would be inhabited by the first violin, Mozart confronts the compositional challenge of writing for a leading instrument that is more constricted in range than is the violin, and of balancing timbres from the heterogenous woodwind and string families. Range hardly proves a problem: Mozart leads the oboist through a full spectrum of nearly two-and-a-half octaves, all the way up to perilous high F (perilous on an eighteenth-century oboe, anyway). Balance doesn't prove problematic, either, since Mozart accepts that the oboe is bound to stand out as something of a soloist in this chamber constituency and simply treats the instrument as primus inter pares.

The three movements unroll in the classic fast-slow-fast pattern. The first (*Allegro*) is cast in familiar sonata form, and in its development section a brief fugal adventure inserts an academic aside into what is otherwise infused with a rococo esthetic. The *Adagio* is a poignant lament in D minor, so short that it doesn't allow for any real thematic development. The finale (*Rondeau: Allegro*) is especially memorable for a virtuosic passage in which the oboe meanders for a spell from the overriding 6/8 meter into a passage in 4/4 time (and notated as such!), while the strings continue below, in unchanging 6/8, as if nothing were amiss. This is a wry musical in-joke, and one should not be too hard on the players if they fail to exit that perplexing passage at precisely the same time. This musical experiment continued to intrigue Mozart. Three-and-a-half years later he tried something very similar in the finale of his Piano Concerto in B-flat-major (K. 456), where—again in a movement cast in 6/8—the woodwinds slip into 2/4 meter and eight measures later persuade the piano to follow them for a further phrase, while the strings stay true to the overriding 6/8 rhythm. We can appreciate in retrospect that these experiments were leading Mozart toward his crowning achievement in mixed meters, the ballroom scene in *Don Giovanni* (1787), where three orchestras play simultaneously in different meters, dramatically enriching the proceedings by underscoring the social stratification of the characters whose fates are at play at that moment of the drama.

Serenade in E-flat major for Wind Octet, K. 375b

Allegro maestoso
Menuetto-Trio-Menuetto da capo
Adagio
Menuetto-Trio-Menuetto da capo
Finale: Allegro

Work composed: October 1781 in Vienna; instrumentation expanded in 1782

Work premiered: In its original version, apparently on October 15, 1781, at the home of the Viennese court painter Joseph Hickel

Instrumentation: Originally a sextet comprising pairs of clarinets, horns, and bassoons, now identified as K. 375a; the following year Mozart added a pair of oboes to create the richer wind-octet version known as K. 375b, to which this essay refers.

> At 11 o'clock at night I was serenaded by two clarinets, two horns, and two bassoons playing my own music: I had written it for St. Theresa's Day for Frau von Hickel's sister, or rather the sister-in-law of Herr von Hickel, the court painter, at whose house it was performed for the first time. The six gentlemen who executed it are poor beggars who play together quite nicely all the same, especially the first clarinetist and the two horn players. But my chief reason for writing it was to let Herr von Strack, who goes there every day, hear something of my composition. And so I composed it rather carefully. It was well received, too, and played at three different places on St. Theresa's Night, because when they had finished it in one place they were taken somewhere else and paid to play it again. And so these musicians had the front gate opened for them, and when they had formed up in the yard, they gave me, just as I was about to undress for bed, the most delightful surprise in the world with the opening E-flat chord.

That Mozart documented his life through a barrage of letters to his father and other family members, and that so many of the letters have been preserved, is nothing less than a miracle of history. More than two centuries after they were written, these missives bring alive details of the composer's professional career and his daily life, year after year, piece after piece. Mozart had moved to Vienna from his native Salzburg not quite nine months before he penned that note to his father back home, on November 3, 1781. The whole background to this wind serenade is pretty much there in Mozart's own words; we'll only interrupt to clarify a few details.

Joseph Hickel, the court painter to whom Mozart refers, must have kept busy with his brush; in the course of his work at the Viennese court he painted some three thousand portraits, including one of Joseph Lange, an esteemed actor who in 1780 married Aloisia Weber, whom Mozart had once hoped to wed. (In the meantime, Mozart had married Aloisia's sister Constanze, which made him and Lange brothers-in-law.) Hickel's sister-in-law was named Therese. In Catholic Austria, saint's days were celebrated with roughly the vigor that we are likely to expend on birthdays; accordingly, St. Theresa's Day—October 15—would have been a big day in the Hickel household. The date on which Mozart got serenaded was, in fact, October 31, his own saint's day, the day designated to celebrate St. Wolfgang of Regensburg.

Being a newcomer to Vienna and intent on developing contacts that might help his career, Mozart (as he reports) seized the occasion not because of special affection for Hickel or his sister-in-law, but rather because he surmised that the festivities could double as an audition for Johann Kilian Strack. Strack (1724–93) had entered the service of the Austrian court in 1758. Initially he served as valet to Archduke Ferdinand, who was then three years old, but in 1765 he graduated to the adult world of Emperor Joseph II, for whom he arranged chamber-music performances, participating himself as a cellist. Strack's ears could obviously serve as entry to imperial musical life, and Mozart spotted an opportunity to ensnare them. Although he reported in a later missive that he visited Strack from time to time, it's not clear that Mozart ever scored great success with him. Haydn's early biographer C. F. Pohl maintained that Strack steadfastly prevented the music of both Haydn and Mozart from being including in the Emperor's chamber concerts.

It's hard to imagine how Strack could have failed to be seduced by this piece. Mozart cast it in a five-moment form, not an unusual blueprint for entertainment music (though many such pieces also include a march). The serenade is set up symmetrically: opening and closing *Allegros* frame a pair of minuets and, in the center, a gorgeous *Adagio*. The piece as a whole is light on harmonic contrast, since each of its movements is in the same key— E-flat major. Stentorian tonic chords launch the serenade, after which an E-flat persists for several measures more as a pedal point against which the clarinets and first bassoon engage in a bit of counterpoint; the clarinet's tune foreshadows the famous opening theme of Mozart's Symphony No. 40. Only at measure 25 does the music break into the body of the *Allegro* proper. Although the shift is clear to the listener, it's not so obvious from the score; Mozart achieves what sounds like a quicker meter only by writing in shorter notes—bassoons oom-pahing in eighth-notes on the bottom, oboes and horns offering little staccato fanfares, and clarinets swirling in sixteenth-notes. Nothing is earth-shattering in this movement, nor indeed in the serenade as a whole, but the prevailing sense of Classical balance is spiced up by occasional "sighing" motifs from the oboe, often with minor-mode overtones. The principal interest in the first minuet falls in its trio section, where the harmony is enriched with harmonic suspensions and touches of chromaticism.

Mozart, of course, could write an *Adagio* as well as (actually, better than) the next man, and the one he proposes here is supernal. The instruments take their turns introducing the languid melodies against gently pulsating accompaniments, yielding the instrumental equivalent of an action-stopping operatic ensemble of great introspection. The movement closes *pianissimo*, and the following *Menuetto* starts scarcely louder, at *piano*. Its four-bar phrases are bound together in groups of three, which succeed each other soft, loud, soft. The trio in this minuet comes across as a folk dance, its lighthearted melody being grounded by a drone. At some point a second trio became attached to the sextet version of this piece, but it doesn't appear in the composer's original autograph and may be considered specious; it has never been considered a part of the octet setting.

The *Finale* is as delightful a rondo as a listener could ask for. The rondo theme itself, based on boisterous homophony and sounding quite Haydnesque, alternates with episodes of distinct characters in which Mozart displays different possibilities of instrumental combinations and harmonic discovery. When the main theme is heard for the fourth and last time (counting the opening statement as only one, despite its repeat markings), it takes a turn-off into a tiny coda to bring everything to a rollicking close.

String Quartet in G major, K. 387

Allegro vivace assai
Menuetto: Allegretto—Trio
Andante cantabile
Molto allegro

Work composed: Completed December 31, 1782, in Vienna

Work dedicated: To Franz Joseph Haydn

Work premiered: Not known

Instrumentation: Two violins, viola, and cello

In the winter of 1782, the Viennese publishing firm of Artaria issued a set of
six new quartets by Franz Joseph Haydn, to which it attached the opus number 33. They proved so popular that they effectively jump-started what in the
preceding decade had become a ho-hum genre. Among those whose ears suddenly popped open to the possibilities of the string quartet was the twenty-
five-year-old Mozart, who had written sixteen string quartets between 1770
and 1773 and then, like Haydn, had paid the genre no further attention.

We don't know when Mozart made Haydn's acquaintance. It could have
occurred in the 1770s when they overlapped in visits to Vienna—Mozart
from Salzburg, Haydn from Esterháza or Eisenstadt. It's hard to imagine that
Mozart would not have managed to seek out Haydn during his first couple
of years living in Vienna, where he moved in 1781. Whenever the meeting
took place, we can be sure that they would have had plenty to talk about,
including the fact that Mozart was a good friend of Haydn's brother Michael,
a neighbor of the Mozarts in Salzburg, and also—without a doubt—the "new
and special way" in which Haydn was dealing just then with the medium of
the string quartet. Mozart and Haydn quickly became fast friends, and we
know that occasionally they participated together in private string-quartet
parties, the best documented of which was an evening in 1784 when the
participants were Haydn and Carl Ditters von Dittersdorf (playing violins),
Mozart (viola), and Johann Baptist Vanhal (cello)—four of Vienna's preeminent composers at that time.

Mozart must have studied Haydn's new quartets in the course of 1782,
and his imagination was spurred such that he decided to revisit the genre
himself. The first fruit of Mozart's renewed attention to the string quartet was
the G-major Quartet (K. 375), which he completed on the very last day of
1782. This work launched the ten great string quartets of Mozart's maturity,
one of the richest lodes in all of chamber music. In 1785 Mozart would assem-
ble the first six of those pieces into a collection that was published by Artaria,
the same firm that had issued Haydn's Op. 33, and when the first edition
appeared it began with one of the most moving dedications ever inscribed, in
this case in elegant Italian (as rendered in Robert Spaethling's fine translation of Mozart's writings):

Vienna, September 1, 1785

To my dear friend Haydn
    A father, having decided to send his children out into the wide world, felt
that he should entrust them to the protection and guidance of a famous Man

who by good fortune also was his best friend.—Here they are, distinguished Man and dearest Friend, my six children.—They are, to be truthful, the fruits of long and laborious efforts; however, the hope given to me by various Friends that my efforts will be at least somewhat rewarded encourages and flatters me to think that this offspring will be of comfort to me someday. You yourself, dearest friend, told me of your approbation of them during your last Visit here in our Capital. This acceptance gives me the courage to commend them to you and makes me hope that they would not be completely unworthy of your favor. May it please you to welcome them kindly and to be for them a Father, Guide, and Friend! From this moment on I hand over to you all my rights in them, begging you, however, to consider with indulgence their flaws, which a Father's uncritical eye may have overlooked, and in spite of them continue your generous Friendship toward one who so greatly appreciates it, while I remain, Dearest Friend, with all my heart, your most Sincere Friend,

W. A. Mozart

The autograph manuscript of Mozart's G-major Quartet looks like a composition exercise, not at all like a masterpiece already formed in the composer's mind and merely jotted down as an afterthought (as we are too accustomed to imagining Mozart's process). Here, instead, we find notes constantly changed, phrases rewritten, entire passages crossed out and replaced and sometimes replaced yet again. He was not exaggerating when he called these quartets "the fruits of long and laborious efforts."

The tempo marking for the first movement is *Allegro vivace assai*, an exhortation to very considerable haste that is often not followed literally in performance; in fact, this music seems to beg for a tempo on the relaxed side, and we leave it to the interpreters to do with it what they will. Some of the witty touches of Haydn's Op. 33 are to be found here, especially in the giggling figuration of the second subject, which at the end of the exposition (and again at the end of the recapitulation) is expanded into rising and falling gales of laughter. We may also spy a clever touch in the phrase that closes the exposition. This hushed, staccato comment is so simplistic as to claim no import whatsoever, yet it returns to punctuate each of the movement's principal sections. Still, this is not quite an example of Haydnesque wit. In Haydn, there is rarely question about whether a joke is a joke. Here, what I would point to as witty—that Mozart makes a mountain out of a musical molehill—some others hear quite differently, with at least one commentator highlighting this particular phrase as an example of the movement's "serious intensity."

About the second movement (*Menuetto*) there can be less doubt: where a minuet is most often the least involved movement in a Classical work, this one displays both heft and gravitas. Loud notes or phrases alternate with soft ones in quick succession, and the trio section, typically a bastion of bucolic repose, here is the opposite, beginning with a rising figure of *Sturm und Drang* bluster that harks back to Haydn's earlier quartets. The first two movements are overlain with a blur of dynamic markings, most of which underscore the idea of sudden contrast. In its opening page the third movement (*Andante cantabile*) seems as if it will follow course, as again *forte* and *piano* rub elbows. As this movement evolves, large spans do finally settle into gentle *piano*, but dynamic contrast remains essential, even in what is at heart a rhapsodic, overwhelmingly serene chapter of this quartet.

For his finale Mozart draws inspiration from the cerebral side of Haydn and plunges instead into counterpoint of an academic sort—not really a worked-out fugue so much as an exhibit of carefully crafted contrapuntal exercises that are separated by, and sometimes intertwined with, passages of entertaining amiability. The second violin introduces the first contrapuntal episode, which is based on a four-note motif of classic straightforwardness, and then the motif and counter-tunes are played out among the four instruments. After a homophonic interlude, the second contrapuntal episode, built on a dotted, syncopated rhythm, starts in the cello and works its way sequentially up through the quartet texture. A sweet melody in the first violin (marked *semplice*—"simple"—on its repeat) follows as the next interlude, which morphs into triumphant phrases that presage *Die Zauberflöte* by nearly a decade. As it turns out, this is a sonata form of sorts after all, although all the contrapuntal business may have blinded us to the fact. At this point Mozart repeats what we have heard until now—the exposition—and when he has done so he launches a sort of development section, again beginning with a counterpoint exercise. Second violin, viola, first violin, and cello in turn announce the new theme for this episode, which is nothing more than a rising chromatic scale extending over six notes. As it happens, we have already heard its mirror image—a falling six-note chromatic figure—as counterpoint in the first interlude of the exposition. In his telescoped "recapitulation" Mozart revisits his motifs with impressive skill that foreshadows (without rivaling) the contrapuntal tour de force he would create in 1788 in the finale of his *Jupiter* Symphony. The opening four-note figure pops out of the texture in surprising places, and, apparently mirroring the "inconsequential" phrase that punctuated the principal sections of the opening movement, the four-note motif reigns over the quiet and unassuming closing measures of this masterly quartet.

String Quartet in D minor, K. 421/417b

Allegro moderato
Andante

Menuetto: Allegretto

Allegretto ma non troppo—Più allegro

Work composed: Completed June 17, 1783, in Vienna

Work dedicated: To Franz Joseph Haydn

Work premiered: Not known

Instrumentation: Two violins, viola, and cello

The remarkable D-minor String Quartet was the second of the six Mozart dedicated to Franz Joseph Haydn, and there is no question that Haydn appreciated Mozart's tribute. We know that he heard three of the quartets (K. 387, K. 421, and K. 428) played at Mozart's home on January 15, 1785, and the remaining three (K. 458, K. 464, and K. 465) were on the menu when he paid a repeat visit on February 12. On that latter occasion the pieces were quite likely played by Mozart and his father, Leopold, who was visiting Vienna just then, joined by the Barons Anton and Bartholomäus Tinti, friends of Mozart from Masonic circles. On February 16 Leopold Mozart reported on the evening in a letter to his daughter, Nannerl, back in Salzburg, and it's easy to imagine him all but bursting his buttons with pride over the compliment paid by Haydn, who was then the most esteemed composer in all of Europe:

> On Saturday evening Herr Joseph Haydn and the two Barons Tinti came to see us and the new quartets were performed, or rather, the three new ones which Wolfgang has added to the other three which we have already. The new ones are somewhat easier, but at the same time excellent compositions. Haydn said to me: "Before God and as an honest man I tell you that your son is the greatest composer known to me either in person or by name. He has taste and, what is more, the most profound knowledge of composition."

The D-minor Quartet was born at the same time as Mozart's first child, Raimund Leopold—quite literally, according to the testimony of his wife, Constanze. She went into labor at 1:30 in the morning on June 17 and five hours later the baby emerged into the world. The early Mozart biographer Georg Nikolaus Nissen, whom Constanze married in 1809 (18 years after being widowed), quoted his wife as saying that Wolfgang was working on the D-minor Quartet through it all, interrupting his task at intervals to comfort her in moments of exceptional pain. The baby, Nissen recounted, arrived during the composition of the *Menuetto*. Constanze confirmed the accuracy of this story to Vincent and Mary Novello, the Mozart fans from England who traveled to meet her in Salzburg in 1829 and kept a careful account of their conversations. In fact, Vincent Novello noted in their travel journal that "several passages [were] indicative of her sufferings especially the Minuet (a part of which she sang to us)." You may decide for yourself whether Mozart was actually memorializing agonizing shrieks of childbirth in these pages or whether this presumed depiction was a familial legend the couple imposed on the piece after the fact. In this connection it may be relevant to observe that the manuscript of the D-minor Quartet bears fewer changes and corrections than the other quartets in the "Haydn" set, which might not be what you would expect of a piece being written while the composer's beloved wife endured labor pains across the room. In the event, it would not be a very happy reminiscence since, after a robust beginning, baby Raimund lived only two months, expiring on August 19.

The D-minor Quartet is a taut, compactly designed piece that conveys at least a sense of general pathos and more likely an atmosphere of fatalism. This quartet starts with a descending octave of the tonic note, D, played by the first violin, with the low-D destination reiterated so forcefully after the plunge as to seem powerful and unyielding—notwithstanding the fact that its first enunciation is marked *sotto voce*. A flavor of the late Baroque seems to inhabit this theme, a proud stoicism of the sort that appealed to Stravinsky in some of the Pergolesi (and assumed Pergolesi) tunes he appropriated for *Pulcinella*. The exposition works its way from the tonic D minor to the relative major (F major), a typical strategy for minor-key sonata forms, but a quite shocking modulation arrives as the movement twists into its development section by dropping a tone to E-flat minor, an arcane key that draws a still more covered timbre from the string instruments. Further mysterious modulations and touches of dense counterpoint ensue until we are ushered into the recapitulation, which maintains the movement's nervous edge to the bitter end.

We're ready for a break from such intensity, and the *Andante* provides that to a certain extent. It is serene compared with the opening movement, but it can't be said to convey happiness. Its middle section is frankly anguished, complete with strongly etched plummeting intervals of an octave or more, and even the music that surrounds that center—the end is basically a *da capo* revisiting of the beginning—is too hesitant to provide deep comfort.

The *Menuetto* is about as far from a court dance as one can imagine. It is densely polyphonic, conveying a minor-key forcefulness that prefigures what Mozart would achieve in the minuet of his G-minor Symphony (K. 550) five years later. Finally in the trio section the fever breaks, if only long enough for the first violin to intone a genial, yodeling ländler above a gentle pizzicato accompaniment from the other three instruments (with the viola doubling the melody at the end). After this the *Menuetto* returns for another go-round, and the leavening spirit of the trio instantly evaporates. In truth, the trio is the only expanse of the whole quartet that is entirely carefree; it accounts for perhaps a minute and a quarter of a work that runs nearly a half hour.

To conclude, Mozart provides a theme and variations on a siciliano melody that bears some kinship to an operatic item by Gluck. This movement corresponds strikingly in plan to the finale of Haydn's G-major Quartet (Op. 33, No. 5), although they cover entirely disparate expressive terrain. Mozart's first three variations grow increasingly complex, with the third achieving particular richness by directing the spotlight toward the deep-voiced viola, the instrument Mozart preferred to play in chamber music. The music shifts to the major mode for the fourth variation, but it proves to be a mere feint when the theme returns in the tonic key of D minor, now (in a coda marked *più mosso*) with an overlay of rhythmic outbursts (what were sixteenth-notes originally are now transformed into still more urgent triplets) that prefigure the tragic poignancy of Schubert's late quartets.

String Quartet in E-flat major, K. 428/421b

> *Allegro non troppo*
> *Andante con moto*
> *Menuetto: Allegro*
> *Allegro vivace*

Work composed: June or July 1783, in Vienna

Work dedicated: To Franz Joseph Haydn

Work premiered: Not known

Instrumentation: Two violins, viola, and cello

The third of Mozart's "Haydn" set, the String Quartet in E-flat major, K. 428/421b, was composed in Vienna in June or July 1783. That, at least, was the best guess of the Mozart scholar Alfred Einstein, although more recent musicologists have allowed that it might date from as late as January 1784. Since this is one of the two "Haydn" Quartets that lack a date on their autograph manuscripts (the other being K. 421/417b), we are not likely to attain more precision than that. The key of E-flat usually drew forth a mellow mood from Mozart, who used it often, and this quartet plays into that tendency. Even allowing for the breadth of possible interpretive approaches, this is probably the most consistently warmhearted quartet of the set, but we would be mistaken to imagine that warmheartedness is incompatible with originality and profundity. Rich lyricism pervades the first movement, which is launched by a statement of the sinuous principal melody by all four instruments in unison (or, more precisely, playing in unisons and octaves). This theme evokes a contour that Haydn employed on various occasions wherein the listener teeters uncertainly before finding a firm tonal footing; the *Allegretto* of Haydn's Symphony No. 82 (the *Bear*, of 1786) provides a nice example, as does the finale of his G-major String Quartet (Op. 77, No. 1). The puzzlement is quickly sorted out. The opening octave jump on an E-flat was not a red herring after all, and we are indeed in E-flat major. The potential of this theme becomes clear when it is reinterpreted in a harmonized context, with the four instruments conveying a strikingly lush texture, a sound so forward-looking that it anticipates Mendelssohn. And yet, as the movement progresses it shines forth as purely Mozartian. Where Haydn would have been inclined to fragment his principal themes and explore them through a development section made up of unanticipated turns, Mozart follows rather different inclinations and keeps his development section brief, valuing measured balance over constant analysis of his material. Haydn and Mozart may have been the most estimable mutual appreciation dyad in the history of music, but that didn't prevent each from being very much his own man.

If the first movement had its moment of foreshadowing Mendelssohn, the second would seem to look even further into the future, toward the realm of Brahms, thanks to its combination of a wistful dreaminess with a rich overlay of harmonic suspensions. This movement's key of A-flat major invites a somewhat veiled, nocturnal character from the strings; Mozart used it rarely, but when he did it underscored music of emotional intensity. The chromaticism that inhabited the principal theme of the first movement plays an important role here, too, and some listeners have fixated on a turn of phrase in the second movement's development section that even anticipates the advanced harmonic terrain of Wagner's *Tristan und Isolde*, which then lay three-quarters of a century in the future. (I wouldn't insist on the Wagner business too much. It strikes me as making a mountain of a molehill.)

The lullaby mood of the *Andante con moto* is swept away with the first notes of the *Menuetto*. Where the first movement had opened with a leap of an octave, here we have the same interval descending with a forceful accent, resembling nothing so much as a braying donkey. Musette-like notes held over several measures in the trio give that section a rustic cast, but the music that unrolls above those sustained tones is more doleful than cheerful: a fascinating, original, and unsettling conception.

In the finale Mozart does seem to be playing at being Haydn. The principal theme has a fragmented character of the sort we expect to hear in Haydn more than in Mozart, and sudden rhythmic displacements—even unanticipated silences—lend a sense of Haydnesque wit to the proceedings. The chromaticism that has marked so many phrases of this quartet is also to be found here in the form of numerous semitone sidesteps, especially remarkable just before the final visitation of the rondo tune.

Quintet in E-flat major for Piano and Winds, K. 452

Largo—Allegro moderato
Larghetto
Rondo: Allegro

Work composed: Completed March 30, 1784, in Vienna

Work premiered: April 1, 1784, at Vienna's Imperial and Royal National Court Theatre ("Burgtheater"), with the composer at the keyboard

Instrumentation: Piano, oboe, clarinet, horn, and bassoon

On April 10, 1784, Mozart wrote from his home in Vienna to his father in Salzburg to relay news about his recent professional triumphs. "The concert I gave in the theatre," he reported, "was most successful. I composed two grand concertos and then a quintet, which called forth the very greatest applause; I myself consider it the best thing I have ever written in my life. It is written for one oboe, one clarinet, one horn, one bassoon, and the pianoforte. How I wish you could have heard it! And how beautifully it was performed! Well, to tell the truth, I was really worn out by the end after playing so much—and it is greatly to my credit that the audience did not in any degree share the fatigue."

That's strong praise indeed, considering the source—even making allowances for the generosity associated with self-congratulation. The performance had taken place on April 1, at Vienna's Imperial and Royal National Court Theatre (commonly known as the "Burgtheater"), and it was liberally packed with music, in line with the custom of the day. Symphonies opened and closed the event (most likely a single symphony split in two), surrounding a succession of arias, a keyboard improvisation, two piano concertos (in B-flat major, K. 450, and in D major, K. 451), and the Quintet in E-flat major (K. 452).

At that time, Mozart had just begun to keep a catalogue of his compositions, inscribing a brief entry on each piece as he finished it. From this catalogue we learn that, as the winter of 1784 turned into spring, Mozart's creative schedule had settled into the predictable regularity of one masterpiece per week. The two piano concertos he premiered on his April 1 concert had been completed precisely a week apart—the B-flat-major on March 15, the D-major on March 22. Mozart signed off on the Quintet on March 30, which doubtless caused anxiety among the wind players who were scheduled to unveil it only two days later—the more so since the work's instrumentation was apparently unprecedented. Nonetheless, all parties must have acquitted themselves with distinction to earn the ovation Mozart described.

Two months later Mozart reported that the quintet got another airing, but beyond that its early performance history remains a mystery. Nonetheless, it must have been played enough to make an enduring impression in Vienna's musical community. In fact, Mozart's Quintet became a model of its genre—most prominently for Beethoven, whose own Quintet (Op. 16), in the same key and for the same instrumentation, followed in the same city a decade later.

Mozart's Piano-and-Winds Quintet is an intriguing hybrid that seems as much descended from the piano concerto as from classic chamber music. Piano concertos were much on the composer's mind when he wrote it; the two concertos that shared its premiere had been directly preceded by another piano concerto (in E-flat major, K. 449), and the series would immediately continue with a fourth (in G major, K. 453). In all of these concertos (as in many to follow), Mozart sometimes has the orchestra's woodwinds emerge from the symphonic texture to interact with the solo piano almost as equal partners in a sinfonia concertante (with its characteristic body of "group soloists"). The quintet's piano part is brilliant, much like what one would expect to find in a concerto, and the piano gets the honor of introducing most of the themes as they appear. In the context of the piece, the instrument's prominence seems logical, given its broad range and harmonic capabilities compared with the woodwinds; and it's worth recalling that Mozart was writing for his own use— and he was never inclined to hide his light under a bushel. On the other hand, the Quintet *is* chamber music at heart, and the four woodwinds are kept plenty busy throughout, even if their parts require less virtuosity than the piano's.

The Quintet's opening, however, would have been most unusual in a Mozart concerto: a broad introduction (*Largo*) in which the piano's initial musings yield to overlapping statements of the spacious theme by the horn, the bassoon, and finally the clarinet and oboe. Only twenty measures long, it serves as a masterful preamble that introduces all the players before the main body of the movement (*Allegro moderato*) springs nimbly to life. The second movement (*Larghetto*) is endowed with the sort of slow-movement poetry for which Mozart is renowned. It unrolls in a three-part structure that is particularly rich in thematic variety, and in which Mozart varies the return of the opening section in both orchestration and counterpoint. The horn shines in the movement's central section, introducing a lyrical melody that is enhanced by an especially prominent oboe obbligato, a hushed moment supported only by the piano's gentle accompaniment of repeated chords.

The third movement is a genial *Rondo*, though the composer also takes some inventive liberties with the classic rondo structure in which refrain-like ritornellos alternate predictably with contrasting episodes. The movement builds up to a point of harmonic instability that, in a concerto, would signal the time for a soloist to improvise a cadenza. Instead, Mozart involves all five players in an "ensemble cadenza" that, though written out in full, preserves an ex-tempore flavor, after which he brings matters to a brisk close with a coda that would find a welcome place in any opera buffa.

String Quartet in B-flat major, *Hunt*, K. 458

Allegro vivace assai
Menuetto moderato
Adagio
Allegro assai

Work composed: Completed September 9, 1784, in Vienna

Work dedicated: To Franz Joseph Haydn

Work premiered: Not known

Instrumentation: Two violins, viola, and cello

Mozart appears to have worked on at least some of his "Haydn" Quartets over an extended period, perhaps busying himself with more than one of them at a time. Not for nothing did he describe the project, in his dedication letter, as "the fruits of long and laborious efforts." But after he completed the first three of the set, from December 1782 through perhaps July 1783, he took a year's break from the genre, again focusing his attention on quartets from the summer of 1784 through January 1785. He was busy during the intervening year; apart from a lengthy visit to Salzburg during which he composed his Duos for Violin and Viola (K. 423 and 424), he and his wife moved to a new apartment and, during the Lenten season of 1784, he performed no fewer than seventeen concerts. A plethora of minor compositions crowd his catalogue—collections of dances, vocal ensembles, and so on—but also some enduring masterworks, including (apart from the Piano-and-Winds Quintet) his *Linz* Symphony (K. 425) and four piano concertos (K. 449–451 and K. 453).

The Quartet in B-flat major (K. 458) signaled his return to the "Haydn quartets" project. At some point the nickname *Hunt* became attached to this work—the name certainly did not emanate from Mozart—because of the genial opening theme in rollicking 6/8 time, which does indeed sound like something that might be sounded by a pair of horns. Mozart's tempo marking of *Allegro vivace assai* ("Very quick and rapid") may strike us as excessively hasty, just as it does in the corresponding movement of K. 387; in both cases, performers typically settle on a slightly more relaxed pulse. The "horn call" theme, which extends through an answering passage marked by flowing violin scales and a bit of yodeling from the first violin, has the advantage of being unforgettable. This makes it all the easier to appreciate the extent to which nearly all the music in the opening movement derives from what is heard at the very beginning.

The all-but-obligatory *Menuetto* stands as the second movement, as with the G-major Quartet (K. 387), and, as in that earlier piece, it is a serious-sounding movement rather than the mere toss-off that minuets could easily be. The trio section gives the strange impression that it is going to be a variation on the minuet itself, though it soon veers off in its own direction. Mozart's textural choice in this central section, with second violin and viola nonchalantly puttering away with staccato eighth-notes, provides a winning contrast to the long slurs that bind all four lines in the minuet itself.

Mozart usually reserves the marking *Adagio* for slow movements of emotional depth, which makes it entirely appropriate in this instance—the only time it appears in his "Haydn" Quartets. Again the second violin and viola tend to the accompanying—how these two instruments coordinate and interact is always a guide to assessing the technical finesse of a string quartet—leaving the first violin and cello to handle the more melodic material, which usually involves a descending motif that suggests a melancholy sigh. Mozart's codas are almost always magical, managing to summarize the entire emotional import of a movement, condense it into a few measures, and inject further intensification through a deft touch of harmonic or rhythmic variation. Here the coda occupies a mere two measures, and you should not even exhale while they're happening. They signal, in retrospect, that which was absolutely essential in this movement: a memory plucked from the end of principal theme, then a moment's rest, and finally the most ordinary of cadences rendered transcendent though the addition of delicate grace notes in the upper three parts and a final, ineffable sigh from the first violin. After this, the unassuming charm of the finale comes as a restorative balm.

String Quartet in C major, *Dissonance*, K. 465

Adagio—Allegro
Andante cantabile

Menuetto: Allegro
Allegro molto

Work composed: Completed January 14, 1785, in Vienna

Work dedicated: To Franz Joseph Haydn

Work premiered: Not known

Instrumentation: Two violins, viola, and cello

It is practically axiomatic that musical works with nicknames become more famous than ones without, usually for the simple reason that monikers makes it easier to put a face on them. The C-major Quartet (K. 465) fully deserves its renown, but I suspect it owes some of its popularity to the fact that it has a nickname; and that being the case, we might as well at least get the nickname right. In German it is known as the *Dissonanz* Quartet, and in English that translates to the *Dissonance* Quartet, *not* the *Dissonant* Quartet, as you are likely to see it referred to two times out of five. The name derives from the *Adagio* introduction to the first movement, a span of twenty-two measures in which the supple lines weave in such a way that their counterpoint gives rise to extraordinary harmonic piquancy. This is a no-man's-land of tonal ambiguity; even if your ear holds on to the recollection that the opening notes were a string of Cs—twelve eighth-notes of them—murmured gently by the cello, the music offers you no compelling reason to believe that those Cs in fact defined the tonic tone. The first harmonic triad built on those Cs is, in fact, a chord of A-flat major in its first inversion—hardly a stable declaration of tonicity, and in the event a false one. The A-flat of that chord (sounded by the viola) is itself dethroned after only two beats, when the first violin enters, two octaves above, playing the same melody in canon but altered so that its opening note is now A-natural instead of A-flat, the first of the introduction's cross-relations. And so this *Adagio* proceeds, winding its way through an obscure harmonic labyrinth, pulling the rug out from under our expectations practically note by note.

This is one of the most radical passages in all of Mozart, and it gave rise to a fair amount of consternation in its time. The Italian composer Giuseppe Sarti—previously a friend of Mozart, it seemed—proclaimed in his *Esame acustico fatto sopra due frammenti di Mozart* (which also gave K. 421 a drubbing) that it was the sort of music "that makes one put one's fingers in one's ears." This launched a *querelle* of the sort that esthetes of the time found irresistible. In 1829 the Belgian theorist and encyclopedist François-Joseph Fétis came up with a creative volley in this brouhaha by proposing a correction to the score. "The harshnesses arise from the lack of regularity in the imitations," he explained, "and I showed that by placing the entry of the first violin a beat later, Mozart *would have produced sound harmony* without injuring his conception" (italics his). A reasonable person might suppose that "injuring his conception" is precisely what such a drastic alteration would achieve; but Fétis resolutely insisted that his correction to "this passage, painful to the ears," was applauded by such luminaries of the Parisian musical firmament as Cherubini, Reicha, and Boieldieu, and the early Mozart biographer Alexandre Oulibichev wrote, "I shall always play the Introduction as thus corrected: it is henceforth sublime throughout, thanks to M. Fétis's happy emendation." Doing so today might incite a riot in the concert hall.

When this opening passage concludes, reaching (with considerable reluctance) a chord that can only be a dominant seventh poised to resolve to the tonic, we can hardly imagine what character the ensuing music will have. The classic solution for trumping a prelude of such intensity would be a fugue, which would maintain the intellectual heights while providing a structure stabilized by a sort of musical geometry. But Mozart takes a different tack here. Instead of trying to rival the profundity of his introduction, he responds, in the *Allegro* proper, with an opening theme of surpassing simplicity played over puttering eighth-notes in the most unencumbered C-major imaginable. What's more, the texture at the outset of this *Allegro* section extends to only three lines, with the cello sitting demurely on the sidelines until the theme has been presented. The effect is startling: it is as if you had groped your way out of a murky tunnel and emerged not just into the sunlight but into a sun-lit playground filled with happy children on a summer morning. This being the last of Mozart's "Haydn" Quartets, it is probably not a coincidence that this *Allegro* should echo a favorite technique of Haydn by employing essentially a single theme, with any secondary melodies serving as castaway footnotes.

In the *Andante* we have one of Mozart's most endearing slow movements. Gently throbbing figures and forward-pushing melodic decoration lend intensity to its gorgeous cantilena melody, but Mozart employs them with such subtlety that we are rarely aware of anything but the enveloping spirit of gracious, slightly nostalgic serenity. Only once, near the end, does a sob seem to make its way to the surface, but it is quickly suppressed by a coda of corrective poise. Nine months later Mozart would embark on writing *Le nozze di Figaro*, in which he would provide music of this sort in his most intimate glimpses of the Countess Almaviva, whose nobility sees her through a good deal of inner heartbreak.

The *Menuetto* is brusque and good-humored—proto-Beethoven, you might say—with displaced accents molding the end of its principal tune with jovial wit. The trio seems worried about something, and Mozart employs a strong dose of chromaticism to convey what ultimately proves to be a tempest in a teapot. This harmonic enrichment, along with the contrast between the major-mode *Menuetto* and the minor-mode trio—invites us to recall the effects Mozart used to make the opening of this quartet so powerful. Cheerfulness is certainly restored in the finale, richly endowed with melodies to an extent that is rare even in Mozart, but ultimately cast in a classic sonata form.

Haydn may have loved the quartets Mozart dedicated to him from the outset, but other listeners were a bit slower to catch on. The first major review of these pieces appeared in Cramer's *Magazin der Musik*, a Hamburg-based publication, in April 1787. Mozart, the critic found, "aims too high in his artful and truly beautiful compositions, in order to become a new creator, whereby it must be said that feeling and heart profit little; his new quartets for 2 violins, viola, and bass, which he has dedicated to Haydn, may well be called too highly seasoned—and whose palate can endure this for long? Forgive the simile from the cookery book." Surely the recipe for the *Dissonance* Quartet played a central role in earning that slap on the wrist.

Piano Quartet in G minor, K. 478

> *Allegro*
> *Andante*
> *Rondo: Allegro moderato*

Work composed: Completed October 16, 1785, in Vienna

Work premiered: Not known

Instrumentation: Violin, viola, cello, and piano

In Mozart's day, chamber music with piano did not usually present great technical hurdles to keyboard players. Intended principally for at-home music-making, such works typically would have been performed by amateur musicians, very often the daughters of upper- or middle-class families. Wise composers who kept at least one eye on the cash register knew that to write beyond the capabilities of such players was to court disaster in the marketplace. Fortunately, these amateur musicians were often quite accomplished; since music was one of rather few available diversions, they spent a good deal of time practicing it, and many reached a level of real accomplishment. On the other hand, one does not often find in eighteenth-century chamber music the sort of keyboard writing that can take our breath away in, for example, numerous piano concertos of the same period.

There were exceptions, however, and it comes as no surprise that Mozart stood out from the crowd. That there was peril in pushing the envelope is made evident in an anonymous account published in June of 1788 in the *Journal des Luxus und der Moden*:

> Some time ago, a single quartet by [Mozart] (for fortepiano, one violin, one viola, and violoncello) was engraved and published, which is very artistically composed and in performance needs the utmost precision in all the four parts, but even when well played, or so it seems, is able and intended to delight only connoisseurs of music, in a *musica di camera*. The cry soon made itself heard: "Mozart has written a very special new quartet, and such-and-such a princess or countess possesses and plays it!," and this excited curiosity and led to the rash resolve to produce this original composition at grand and noisy concerts and to make a parade with it *invita Minerva*. Many another piece keeps some countenance, even when indifferently performed; but in truth one can hardly bear listening to this product of Mozart's when it falls into mediocre amateurish hands and is negligently played.
>
> Now this is what happened innumerable times last winter; at nearly every place to which my travels led me and where I was taken to a concert, some young lady or pretentious middle-class demoiselle, or some other pert dilettante in a noisy gathering, came up with this engraved quartet and fancied that it would be enjoyed. But it *could* not please: everybody yawned with boredom over the incomprehensible *tintamarre* of four instruments which did not keep together for four bars on end, and whose senseless *concentus* never allowed any unity of feeling; but it *had* to please, it *had* to be praised!...
>
> What a difference when this much-advertised work of art is performed by four skilled musicians who have studied it carefully, in a quiet room where the sound of every note cannot escape the listening ear, and in the presence of only two or three attentive persons! But, of course, in this case no *éclat*, no brilliant, modish success is to be thought of, nor is conventional praise to be obtained! Here political ambition can have no part to play, nothing to gain, nothing to bestow, nothing to give and nothing to take—in contrast to *public* concerts of the modern kind, where such factors exert an almost constant influence.

It will be clear from this fascinating account that Mozart's piano quartets charted a new path. Although earlier works for this combination of instruments did exist, there was nothing to rival the level of compositional complexity or technical subtlety that Mozart put forth here. From the Mozart biography published in 1828 by Georg Nicolaus von Nissen (who married the composer's widow, Constanze), we learn that the publisher and sometime composer Franz Anton Hoffmeister had commissioned Mozart to write three piano quartets in 1785. Mozart set to work quickly on the first of them,

his G-minor Piano Quartet (K. 478). By the beginning of December, Hoffmeister had the parts engraved, and the composer proudly sent copies of the
violin and viola parts to his father, Leopold, back in Salzburg. Leopold probably looked at them askance: he was precisely the sort of commercially aware
musician who would have opted for something more marketable.

The key of G-minor often placed Mozart in a mood of *Sturm und Drang*—
most famously in his two symphonies in that key, but also in his String Quintet (K. 516). The first movement of this G-minor work may therefore be
considered typical in both its brooding opening, the frequent use of a two-
note "weeping" motif, and the overall impassioned flavor of its writing. The
composer trips up the listener (and sometimes the performers) with a curious
rhythmic displacement in his second theme, accenting certain notes in such
a way as to impersonate a 5/4 meter. The work's general richness of sound
owes much to the prominent role of the viola. The *Andante* is altogether
more placid, but its setting in the relative major key of B-flat belies that it,
too, is a far from happy movement. Its spirit is more one of nobility than true
tranquility, and a sense of private loneliness—perhaps even exhaustion—is
conveyed by a figure in which the strings pile up three repetitions of the
weeping figure. Even the last movement is tempered in its high jinks. Despite
its overflow of irresistible melodic material and a certain amount of ebullient, concerto-like piano figuration, this movement is not as sunny as one
might anticipate of a rondo-finale. The opening theme sounds tentative in
its tonality; as in many themes by Haydn (whose music Mozart, of course,
adored), the tune seems to be finding its way as we listen. Like the rest of the
piece, the finale is rich in appoggiaturas suggestive of sighing. Even a comical
little triadic tune, somewhat anticipating the famous slow-movement theme
of Haydn's *Surprise* Symphony, fails to override the emotional seriousness and
dramatic import that inform this entire quartet.

Piano Quartet in E-flat major, K. 493

Allegro
Larghetto
Allegretto

Work composed: Completed June 3, 1786, in Vienna

Work premiered: Not known, but this may be the piece to which the composer
referred in a letter written from Prague on January 15, 1787, in which he
discusses an excellent piano that his host there, Count Canal von Malabaila,

had put at his disposal and, in the next sentence, says that he and some friends played a little quartet for their own delight.

Instrumentation: Violin, viola, cello, and piano

Franz Anton Hoffmeister had high hopes when he commissioned Mozart to write three piano quartets in 1785, but he came to rue the day he had opened the door to this project. According to Mozart's biographer Georg Nicolaus von Nissen, "Mozart's first piano quartet, in G minor, was thought so little of at first that the publisher Hoffmeister gave the master the advance portion of the honorarium on the condition that he not compose the other two agreed-upon quartets and that Hoffmeister should be released from his contract." Yes, you read that right: Nissen said that Hoffmeister paid Mozart *not* to write any more piano quartets other than the one he had already finished. Although this recollection may be accurate in spirit, it seems to be slightly off in factual accuracy. It seems that by the time this arrangement was proposed, Mozart—thank heavens!—must have already gone on to complete the second of the three proposed works, his Piano Quartet in E-flat major (K. 493). He entered it on June 3, 1786, in the catalogue he kept of his musical compositions, immediately following his opera *Le nozze di Figaro.* When the E-flat-major Piano Quartet was published the next year, by the rival firm of Artaria, that company seems to have printed the piano, viola, and cello parts from plates it had purchased from Hoffmeister. That's a strong indictment, since it suggests that Hoffmeister decided to withdraw from the project even if it meant sacrificing nuts-and-bolts work that had already been expended on an edition. Artaria also made no money from the venture, and the third piano quartet was never written.

One may sense a dreamy quality in the opening movement, nowhere more than in the surprising modulation that heralds the development section. The melody at that point is a motif that simply pervades this movement, a figure that begins with a falling sixth, first heard as the second theme of the exposition. In the course of the movement it is transposed to many keys and is heard in a variety of instrumental combinations; at the very end, it even overlaps with itself in a bit of contrapuntal imitation. Where the G-minor Piano Quartet is taut and tense, the one in E-flat major tends toward luxuriance, which reaches its peak in the *Larghetto.* This is one of Mozart's most eloquent slow movements, so rich in reiterations that it truly seems a dialogue among the four participants.

Mozart had second thoughts about how to conclude this piece. He sketched out some delightful material that, for whatever reason, he decided not to follow through with; like the finale he *did* end up composing, it begins with a half-measure's upbeat. The finale as it stands is essentially a rondo, but Mozart grafts onto it aspects of a sonata structure as well. A second principal theme, replete with a touch of characterful syncopation, follows the initial rondo melody, and later a blustery minor-mode passage, sounding ever so much like a development section, provides an occasion for the pianist to sweep up and down the keyboard with impressively virtuosic figuration while pursuing harmonic modulations. Throughout this movement, we find Mozart practically on the verge of a piano concerto, with the piano "soloist" and the strings operating with the back-and-forth contrast normally found in a concerto more than the integrated style typical of chamber music.

Trio in E-flat major for Clarinet, Viola, and Piano, K. 498

Andante
Menuetto
Rondeaux: Allegretto

Work composed: Completed August 5, 1786, in Vienna

Work premiered: Shortly after its completion, by Anton Stadler (clarinet), Mozart (viola), and Franziska von Jacquin (piano)

Instrumentation: Clarinet, viola, and piano

Mozart was strongly drawn to mid-range instruments or to the lower ranges of treble-clef instruments, reveling in rich sonorities for their own sake. This accounts to no small extent for his love affair with the clarinet and basset horn, which he came to appreciate late in his brief career through the artistry of Anton Stadler.

Anton Stadler (1753–1812) and his brother Johann, also a clarinetist, performed as soloists in Vienna as early as 1773, and about that time entered the service of the Russian ambassador in that city. They started playing as freelancers at the Viennese Court in 1779, were granted salaried positions in the Imperial Wind Band three years later, and in 1787 were appointed as the regular clarinetists in the Court Orchestra. Anton Stadler became an especially close friend of Mozart—so close, in fact, that the composer was known to lend Stadler money when he himself lacked the resources to support his own family adequately. Mozart composed for Stadler a handful of supernal works: the Clarinet Quintet, the Clarinet Concerto, and obbligato parts to arias in *La clemenza di Tito*, in addition to this Trio for Clarinet, Viola, and Piano.

Mozart completed the Trio on August 5, 1786, and, according to the memoirs of the author Caroline Pichler, the piece was first performed by

Stadler, Mozart (playing viola), and Franziska von Jacquin (Mozart's favorite piano pupil). When it was published, in September 1788, it was advertised as a "Sonata for Harpsichord or Pianoforte with Violin and Viola Accompaniments." A note on the printed score reads, "The violin part can also be performed by a clarinet." This proposed alternative was a commercial decision of the publisher, who was well aware that there were many more violinists than clarinetists among the music-buyers at that time. Today, such a substitution would seem an unnecessary second choice. There is no question that Mozart intended this trio for the three instruments with which he enjoyed the closest personal affinity.

The piece displays a richness of sound nearly unprecedented in chamber music up to that time. Though the clarinet is capable of a wide range, it rarely ascends very high here, concentrating on its middle and lower registers, the latter being a particular Stadler specialty. The opening movement is an *Andante*, an unusual choice for launching a Classical piece but one that here seems perfectly suited to the warmth of sound and the intimacy of expression. The middle movement (*Menuetto*) is also unusual to the extent that it ends up bearing rather little resemblance to the spirit of courtliness evoked by that dance, a characteristic it shares with some of Mozart's Quartets dedicated to Haydn. This minuet is dark and serious, its musical material is sometimes deconstructed into short motifs, and the viola's scurrying interpolations contrast strangely with the clarinet's repeated four-note utterances in the central trio section. The finale arrives as a breath of spring air after such dense, even spooky "forest music." Its theme is not a folk song, but it could easily be mistaken for one. A few passing clouds darken even this landscape from time to time, but leisurely good spirits generally reign over the conclusion of this profoundly imaginative work.

This piece is nearly always purveyed with the nickname *Kegelstatt* attached to it. In Viennese German, the word refers to a skittles alley, skittles being a form of nine-pin bowling in which the player tries to knock down the pins by throwing, rather than rolling, a wooden ball or disk. Mozart was devoted to the game (and to the invigorating beverages that accompanied the execution of the sport), and legend has it that he composed this trio while engaged in a session of skittles. In fact, when Mozart entered this piece into the thematic catalogue he kept from 1784 until his death, he called it simply "Ein Terzett für Clavier, Clarinett und Viola." It appears that the skittles connection actually was to another composition of about the same time, the set of Duets for Two Horns (K. 487/496a), the autograph of which is inscribed "July 27, 1786 untern Kegelscheiben" ("while playing skittles"), and that at some point the *Kegelstatt* nickname gravitated to the Trio through a misunderstanding. I can't think of a good reason to perpetuate the mix-up.

String Quartet in D major, *Hoffmeister*, K. 499

Allegretto
Menuetto and Trio: Allegretto
Adagio
[Molto] Allegro

Work composed: Completed August 19, 1786, in Vienna

Work premiered: Not known

Instrumentation: Two violins, viola, and cello

The String Quartet in D major (K. 499) followed by nineteen months the last of Mozart's six Quartets dedicated to Haydn, and it would be followed by three further string quartets, the so-called *Prussian* Quartets of 1789–90. We don't know why Mozart wrote this piece, but it seems that his colleague Franz Anton Hoffmeister had something to do with it. (Apparently they remained friends even after the debacle with Mozart's piano quartets, discussed a couple of essays ago.) Hoffmeister was a composer who had arrived in Vienna in 1768 and, at the beginning of 1784, set himself up as a music publisher. By the next year he was running advertisements for his editions of music by a notable roster of Viennese composers, including Haydn, Mozart, Vanhal, Albrechtsberger, and Pleyel. In 1786 or 1787 Mozart borrowed the melody of Hoffmeister's song "An die Natur" to serve as the theme for the first-movement variations of his A-major Flute Quartet (K. 298; formerly mistaken chronology accounts for its low Köchel number, which I imagine will be reassigned in the next edition of the Köchel catalogue). It seems that Hoffmeister may have lent Mozart some money around the time the D-major String Quartet was written; it's not clear whether Mozart's piece was composed on commission from Hoffmeister or as repayment for that debt (if, indeed, either of those possibilities was the case).

The D-major Quartet stands somewhat on the intellectual side of Mozart's output. This is not to say that it lacks sensuous beauty and sheer delight; but while listening to it one is aware that the cortex is crackling and that Mozart is not pulling a single punch in working out his material with maximum inspiration and ingenuity. In terms of craftsmanship the lengthy first movement can stand up to any movement Mozart ever wrote. Its themes are differentiated through sharply etched contrasts in contour, rhythm, and dynamics, and the composer achieves perfectly balanced, democratic textures throughout. The opening melody is unquestionably the most influential one. It is initially presented (in unison) as an elaborated descending arpeggio of the tonic D-major triad, but Mozart spaces its notes in a way that invites a touch of ambiguity about just where the music is "planted." In the course of the movement, which ranges through a striking and sometimes disquieting array of almost Schubertian harmonic modulations, that theme is transmogrified, sometimes through inversion, sometimes by being torn apart and re-assembled. In the last measures of the exposition, a *staccato* "ticking" motif is introduced with deadpan innocence as a cadential figure. It's a treble transposition of what is heard in some Classical pieces as an accompanimental "Alberti bass," a repeating harmonic device that spells out a triad through the alternation of notes 1–5–3–5 of the scale—or inversions of the same—over and over. Negligible as this clockwork gesture seems, it takes over forcefully in the ensuing development section, where its eighth-notes are constantly intoned by varying pairs of instruments while the other two instruments explore mutations of other themes. It is astonishing that a thematic element introduced so late in the game should wield such importance in the unrolling of a piece. And yet this motif does precisely that; and, following the recapitulation, it even holds sway over a coda, to the extent of getting the very last word, high in the violins' tessitura.

In most four-movement Classical structures the second movement is a slow movement and the third a minuet-and-trio. Mozart reverses that plan here, following instead the layout he had used in three of the six "Haydn" Quartets. So it is that we are ushered into the brief *Menuetto*, with its lilting ländler flavor and sporting more independence of parts than we might expect of a minuet movement. The trio section provides scurrying contrast by way of triplets in the dark-hued tonic minor key (D minor), infusing some tightly constructed canonic counterpoint.

Interpreters often find an element of emotional restraint in the slow movement, a G-major *Adagio* in 3/4 meter. The musicologist Alec Hyatt King wrote tellingly of this movement, "It is rather reticent and suggests a mood of half-remembered grief." As in the first movement, Mozart closes *pianissimo*, in the ensemble's high register.

The finale is cast in 2/4 time, but before long the duple rhythm bubbles over in triplets, a Mozartian fingerprint that we have already encountered in the Trio of the minuet. Sudden stops and interruptions here recall the quartets of Haydn, and yet the atmosphere is not that of a Haydnesque joke. "The mood, again, is elusive," writes Hyatt King. "Is it one of wry humour, or one of veiled sadness, despite the major key?" About the tempo, we should note that the manuscript originally carried the marking *Allegro*. The word *molto* ("very") was later added—whether by Mozart or someone else has not been established—and when Hoffmeister published the first edition the movement was headed *Molto allegro*.

The D-major Quartet represents a crucial step in Mozart's modernity, and its special qualities were recognized already during his lifetime. On November

30, 1791, not quite a week before the composer's death, the *Musikalische Korre-spondenz der Teutschen Filarmonischen Gesellschaft*, a publication in Speyer, ran a review of this work and Mozart's Piano Quartet in E-flat major. "Both these quartets," said the critic, "are written with that fire of the imagination and that correctness which long since won for Herr M. the reputation of one of the best composers in Germany.... Even the Minuet in the former is composed with an ingenuity (being interwoven with canonic imitation) that one not infre-quently finds wanting in other such compositions, even by famous masters."

Piano Trio in B-flat major, K. 502

Allegro
Larghetto
Allegretto

Work composed: Completed November 18, 1786

Work premiered: Not known

Instrumentation: Violin, cello, and piano

The piano trio—the classic ensemble of violin, cello, and piano—was prefig-ured in numerous works of the Baroque period, particularly in France, where in sonatas for violin and basso continuo the continuo part gradually evolved into separately written-out, sometimes divergent parts for the harpsichord and the cello or viola da gamba. After the middle of the eighteenth century, piano trios started to emerge as pieces for amateurs to play, but the cello was slow to achieve full citizenship in the assemblage. In the early piano trios of Haydn (appearing in the 1760s and 1770s) and Mozart (his Divertimento in B-flat major for Piano Trio, K. 254, of 1776), there is little in the writing to distinguish the pieces from coeval sonatas for violin and piano (at that time usually still called "sonatas for the pianoforte with the accompaniment of a violin"), since the cello spends much of its time simply doubling the bass line assigned to the pianist's left hand.

By the mid-1780s, Haydn first, and then Mozart, began endowing the medium with greater equality. In 1784 Haydn embarked on the extraordinary series of twenty-nine piano trios that would occupy him through 1797; and in 1786 Mozart, who had not grappled with the medium since his Divertimento of 1776, returned to produce two piano trios, completed respectively on July 8 (in G major, K. 496) and November 18 (in B-flat major, K. 502). (In between he wrote a "cousin trio" for the quite different combination of clarinet, viola, and piano.) He would focus on piano trios yet again in 1788, when he produced another group: the Trios in E major (K. 542), C major (K. 548), and G major (K. 564, a slight work that appears to have been hastily assembled and that seems out of place next to its predecessors).

These pieces all relate to especially golden moments in Mozart's career. The 1786 piano trios arrived in the wake of his opera *Le nozze di Figaro* and immediately preceded his *Prague* Symphony, while the 1788 group were interlaced with the creation of his last three symphonies. As Mozart was under considerable financial duress, particularly in 1788, it seems likely that he wrote these works with an eye toward their commercial possibilities. Indeed, all but the last were published in short order, the two from 1786 by Franz Anton Hoffmeister and the first two from 1788 by Artaria. Even the titles attached to these pieces suggest the moment of flux in which we encounter the medium. On the title page of his manuscript for K. 496, Mozart labels the work "Sonata," implying the primacy of the violin and piano parts and the secondary nature of the cello. Yet when he finished composing the piece and entered it into the catalogue of his works, he called it instead a Terzett ("Trio"), which is also the name he attached to K. 502 on both its manuscript title page and in his catalogue. Hoffmeister issued both as "Terzette."

It is far from coincidental that the spirit breathed into keyboard trios in the 1780s corresponded with the unquestioned supplanting of the harpsichord by the pianoforte and by important technical advances in piano-building in Vienna. In 1788, Haydn asked his publishers to buy him an up-to-date Schantz piano so that he could craft a new set of piano trios specifically to highlight the capabilities of the latest instruments. His publishers acquiesced. As a noted keyboard virtuoso, Mozart was, if anything, even more attuned to the newly developed subtleties of Viennese pianos, and in the decade he resided in Vienna, from 1781 to 1791, he composed seventeen superlative piano concertos, of which three of the most irreplaceable—those in A major (K. 488), C minor (K. 491), and C major (K. 503)—date from the same year as the B-flat-major Piano Trio. This was also the period of his two great piano quartets, the second of which (in E-flat major, K. 493) preceded our trio by only five months.

The piano occupies a position of first among equals in K. 502, and for considerable expanses one could imagine this work being rendered as a solo concerto, or even a solo sonata. In the tightly constructed opening movement (*Allegro*), everything is based on a single theme—a very Haydnesque procedure but not so often a Mozartian one. It's a lighthearted, rather nonchalant melody. (A little motif uttered by the violin does take on a role as a subordinate theme, but the structural weight really is borne by the principal melody.) As the movement unrolls we are surprised to find that the theme offers as much opportunity as it does for harmonic and contrapuntal elaboration.

The *Larghetto* is structured as a relaxed rondo, with the recurring theme seeming prescient of reflective songs in Schubert's *Die schöne Müllerin*. The commentator Arthur Cohn accurately seized on its subdued nature when he wrote, "The slow movement is in major, but is itching to go into minor, not tonally, but with the melos itself." In the finale we find Mozart working out his material through a sonata-rondo form in which the principal theme not only recurs (*à la* rondo) but is also subjected to exploration through a finely wrought development section (*à la* sonata)—again with the unassuming melody harboring more possibilities for elaboration than we might have expected at first hearing. The second and third movements of this trio seem not far removed from the piano concertos Mozart was writing at about that time, not only in their formal plans and the flavor of their themes but also in the way the principal themes are adorned at their repetitions, not merely in the spirit of decoration but as a means of expanding the emotional terrain.

String Quintet in C major, K. 515

Allegro
Menuetto (Allegretto)—Trio
Andante
Allegro

Work composed: Completed April 19, 1787, in Vienna

Work premiered: Not known

Instrumentation: Two violins, two violas, and cello

Mozart's C-major String Quintet (K. 515) is the first of two the composer wrote in quick succession just prior to embarking on the composition of his opera *Don Giovanni*. The second, finished not quite a month later, on May 16, is the highly dramatic Quintet in G minor (K. 516), and the composer promptly offered them for sale on subscription, advertising in two newspapers that they were "beautifully and correctly written." Apparently there were few takers—perhaps none at all—because Mozart announced in a follow-up advertisement that he was delaying the works' appearance, and then the following year he sold the pieces as a pair to the Viennese publishing firm of Artaria. These two works stand somewhat as yin and yang to each other. If the G-minor Quintet, displaying both anguish and affection, comes across as one of the chamber works in which Mozart most readily reveals the fluctuating depths of his soul, the C-major is an altogether more amiable and optimistic work, a summa of the sort of civilized musical discourse that we value as a central attribute of the music of the Classical era.

If the C-major Quintet does not display the proto-Romantic tendencies of the G-minor, it nonetheless affords no small measure of delight and originality, not only in the masterful melodic, harmonic, and contrapuntal manipulation of materials (which we take for granted in Mozart) but also in the insightful deployment of forces in the presentation and bantering-about of melodies. From the very first measures, with the cello propelling the first phrase of the opening theme—nothing more than a rising arpeggiated triad—up through a distance of two octaves plus a major third, Mozart puts the listener on notice about the dimensions he is envisioning in this piece.

Countless Classical pieces have a slow second movement and a minuet-and-trio for a third, but in both this and its sister quintet the order is reversed. At least that's how Artaria published them in 1788. A complication arises from the fact that in Mozart's manuscript the pages are numbered such that the slow movement comes first and the minuet after; but since scholars doubt that the pagination is in Mozart's hand, many performers choose to rely on the published order, atypical though it is. The placement of this minuet is not its only unusual characteristic; one would also point to a distinctive dynamic technique in which the volume builds through a crescendo only to pull back to *piano* at the moment when the phrase reaches its climactic cadence. The movement's trio section also has an individual flavor. Whereas one might anticipate a charmed, bucolic interlude here, Mozart offers instead some ominous, chromatic writing and then surprises us by breaking out into a folksy ländler after all.

The gracious third movement is the slow one—not *very* slow, at *Andante*, though its original marking seems to have been *Larghetto*—and it's a great chamber-music moment for the first viola, which in the course of the movement is in the spotlight fully as much as the first violin. Imagine that it's Mozart playing, since the viola's was always the part he preferred handling in chamber-music gatherings. In the finale Mozart is paying homage to his dear friend Haydn, not only by adopting a sonata-rondo form (a favorite procedure for Haydn's finales) but also by allowing the first violin some moments of surpassing virtuosity and by fragmenting themes and tossing them about in absolutely fluent counterpoint.

String Quintet in G minor, K. 516

> *Allegro*
> *Menuetto (Allegretto)—Trio*

Adagio ma non troppo
Adagio—Allegro

Work composed: Completed May 16, 1787

Work premiered: Not known

Instrumentation: Two violins, two violas, and cello

Proto-Romantic tendencies come to the fore in Mozart's G-minor Quintet right from the first measures, which rustle with nervous tension. The movement unrolls with taut seriousness, its minor-key lugubriousness intensified when Mozart stays in G minor for his second subject (where he might more likely have moved to the major key for tonal contrast). The dynamics are usually hushed; although a few loud passages emerge in the course of this *Allegro*, the music always wants to return to *piano*. This renders all the more powerful the finale measures, which begin with tightly wound contrapuntal gestures and maintain a forceful *forte* to the end.

The second movement is a minuet, but in reality it is only ostensibly a dance, its angular music seeming angry, its offbeat accents tortured. The hushed slow movement (played with mutes) does nothing to dispel the troubled sensation, and midway through the atmosphere grows terribly uneasy due to offbeat flutterings in the inner voices. The *Adagio ma non troppo* ends, only to be followed by, improbably, another *Adagio*. The first violin declaims passionate phrases over a repeated-note accompaniment from the three inner voices; and the cello shows remarkable independence of purpose, sometimes echoing the violins' ideas but more often providing a bass line that stands apart from the rest of the texture through pizzicato articulation. This proves a long, despondent introduction that finally yields to a G-major rondo that seems unconvincing in its cheerfulness.

The musicologist Alexander Hyatt King, in his 1968 study *Mozart: Chamber Music*, considered the emotional response the composer's G-minor Quintet may evoke in listeners: "Reaction to such a personal work as this Quintet is inevitably subjective. To one hearer it may suggest despair; to another, poignant sadness; to another, passionate defiance, and so on. But whatever the event or experience reflected, the emotions expressed are violent and intense and its purport seems clear." Surely all the emotional reactions Hyatt King enumerates are entirely legitimate ones, and a listener's susceptibility to one or another of them is bound to be determined in large part by the nature of the interpretation. It may be that a demonic aspect is made to dominate, but on the whole I prefer a performance that underscores the work's tragic possibilities, pure and simple. Perhaps here we may glimpse the state of mind of a composer who had struggled hard to sustain the career he knew he deserved, yet could no longer avoid admitting that he was failing.

Piano Trio in C major, K. 548

Allegro
Andante cantabile
Allegro

Work composed: Completed July 14, 1788

Work premiered: Not known

Instrumentation: Violin, cello, and piano

The summer of 1788, when the C-major Piano Trio (K. 548) was born, was Mozart's "summer of the symphony." It gave rise to the tremendous final trilogy of his Symphonies No. 39 in E-flat major, No. 40 in G minor, and No. 41 in C major (the *Jupiter*), which continue to stand at the summit of the symphonic repertoire. Mozart seems to have scarcely broken a sweat in writing them. Incredibly, all three of these symphonies were produced in the space of about nine weeks that summer. We don't know precisely when he began writing the Symphony No. 39, but it was probably around the beginning of June, not quite a month after *Don Giovanni* was granted a lukewarm reception at its Vienna premiere. There is no question that he finished it on June 26 and that he went on to complete the succeeding symphonies on July 25 and August 10. Each is a very full-scale work that comprises the standard four movements of the late-Classical symphony. Twelve movements in nine weeks would mean that, on the average, Mozart expended five days and a few hours on the composition of each movement. Of course, that doesn't factor in that he was also writing other pieces at the same time, or that he was also giving piano lessons, tending a sick wife, entertaining friends, moving to a new apartment, and begging his fellow freemason Michael Puchberg for assistance that might see him and his family through what was turning into an extended financial crisis.

The C-major Piano Trio fell in the interstice between Mozart's Symphonies No. 39 and No. 40, as did the C-major "Sonata facile," K. 545, beloved of incipient pianists, and the great Prelude and Fugue in C minor for string quartet, K. 546. Commentators have sometimes linked this trio to the *Jupiter* Symphony, with which it shares a key; the two pieces were completed only three weeks apart. They may perhaps share a certain flavor of formality, and both have slow movements in 3/4 meter marked *Andante cantabile;* but apart from that not much is served by trying to argue the point very far.

The piano occupies a position of special prominence in K. 548, with its part not far removed from what we would expect of a Mozart piano concerto, but the string parts are also remarkably independent, even if they are ultimately less challenging. It's a large-scale work, opening with a unison fanfare of the sort we are not surprised to hear in a Mozart symphony, where it would presumably demand order in a crowded hall, but that is less usual in the intimate expanses of chamber music. This turns out not to be simply an attention-getting motif but rather the principal theme of the tightly constructed opening movement. We hear it in the major, we hear it in the minor, we hear it put through all sorts of paces in the ingenious development section, where it often alternates with a new motif, a gently sighing one that Mozart had not introduced in the exposition. In the end, this movement conveys a somewhat "intellectual" spirit, at least partly because of the tautness of the themes. In his influential Mozart biography of 1945, the musicologist Alfred Einstein dismissed this work for lacking "the vitality of invention" and the "thematic richness and conciseness" of what he considered Mozart's greatest piano trios. This judgment has dogged the piece ever since—unfairly, I think. Thematic richness is clearly not the point of this trio—Mozart sets the opposite as his challenge in the first movement—and on the whole this piece strikes me as one of Mozart's *most* concise achievements in the medium. *Chacun à son goût.*

The *Adagio cantabile,* in the subdominant key of F major, is also structured in a sonata form. As the movement's main thematic material is presented we hear an unusual sound for Classical piano trios: the cello playing solo in its high register, another step toward the chamber-musical democracy that will inform the medium in ensuing generations. Even Einstein had to admit that "the *Andante cantabile* is endlessly moving in its soft and delicate religious quality." So far as "vitality of invention" is concerned, I can't imagine quite what that would require that we don't find in this trio's finale, a jovial rondo on a spirited "hunting" theme in vivacious 6/8 time.

Divertimento in E-flat major for Violin, Viola, and Cello, K. 563

> *Allegro*
> *Adagio*
> *Menuetto (Allegretto)*
> *Andante*
> *Menuetto (Allegretto)*
> *Allegro*

Work composed: Completed September 27, 1788, in Vienna

Work premiered: Perhaps in Vienna shortly after its completion, but we know that Mozart (as violist) played this piece at the Hotel de Pologne in Dresden on April 13, 1789, assisted by violinist Anton Teyber and cellist Nikolaus Kraft.

Instrumentation: Violin, viola, and cello

The classic string trio of violin, viola, and cello reaches one of the summits of its genre in Mozart's E-flat-major Divertimento (K. 563). The work's title may lead the listener to expect a charmed bit of fluff, the word "divertimento" being derived from the Italian *divertire*, meaning "to amuse." Some have suggested that irony informed the choice of title, but it seems more likely that it simply reflects the layout of movements, since divertimentos often comprised more than the four movements that would have been standard in, say, a string quartet. Very typically they alternated slow movements and minuets just as Mozart does here. In fact, this is Mozart's longest chamber work, and on the whole it is no "lighter" than any of his other major chamber compositions.

Apart from a group of preludes he composed to accompany transcriptions of Bach preludes and fugues in 1782, this represents Mozart's only work to use the instrumentation of violin, viola, and cello. In September 1788 he did sketch the first movement of a String Trio in G major (K. 562e), just after the busy summer in which he completed his final triptych of symphonies and his C-major Piano Trio, but he abandoned that work quickly and started out fresh on what would become the E-flat-major Divertimento. The composer is utterly evenhanded in his distribution of the music, giving each player generous turns as both melodist and accompanist. In many string trios, the listener senses the sparseness of the texture. Here, one has to keep reminding oneself that it is not a string quartet playing, so brilliantly does Mozart solve the textural problem he poses to himself—and resorting only on very few occasions, such as the spectral opening of the *Adagio*'s development section, to double-stopping. As a performer, Mozart was most famous as a pianist, but he was also a professional-level string player who particularly enjoyed playing the viola. It therefore is not surprising that viola players have been known to point to this divertimento as containing one of the composer's most agreeable parts for their instrument.

It is widely held that Mozart composed this work for Michael Puchberg, his friend and fellow-Mason who at the time was prospering in the textiles business. Mozart was going through difficult financial straits, and beginning in 1787 or 1788 he began asking Puchberg for loans, a pathetic chapter that can be documented through the course of no fewer than nineteen letters. In one letter, the composer makes reference to a trio he had written for Puchberg; it is possible that the work in question was the Piano Trio in E major (K. 542), but more likely it was this divertimento, which Mozart referred to as the "Puchberg" Trio when he played it in Dresden on April 13, 1789.

From the first movement (*Allegro*), we are alerted to the fact that Mozart is taking this divertimento every bit as seriously as he did any of his string quartets or quintets. Here we have an elegantly crafted sonata-allegro movement built from memorable themes and, in its development, courageous in its harmonic modulations and captivating in its imitative counterpoint. The ensuing *Adagio* puts to rest any suspicions about this being "merely" a lighthearted piece. This is one of Mozart's great slow movements, a passionate expanse in warm-hearted A-flat major, with ornamental figures serving immense expressive purpose rather than simply embellishing the melodies. The cello's opening music, an arpeggiated triad moving upward (mirroring, in a way, the descending-triad principal theme of the opening *Allegro*), dominates much of the movement, and the eloquent, elongated coda that brings the *Adagio* to a close is almost entirely derived from this simple figure.

The first of two minuets follows, a sturdy affair with surprising syncopation built into its opening theme and with a gentle trio section to provide contrast. One could imagine this music scaled up to serve as the third movement of a Mozart symphony, so rich a texture does Mozart draw from his three instruments. Then comes another slow movement (but, at *Andante*, just moderately slow), a wondrous set of variations on a foursquare, thirty-two-bar tune that may have been a popular song of the day. Here Mozart's imagination is on full display; he never crafted variations finer than these, though he may have equaled them on a few occasions. Emotional breadth and technical facility are inseparable as he works his way through the second variation, where canons bustle beneath the soaring melody; the third, where the minor mode invites an atmosphere of mystery while the composer struts his stuff to sophisticates by writing the whole thing in three-part invertible counterpoint; and the fourth, where the viola sings a version of the theme as if it were the cantus firmus in a spectacular chorale prelude.

An adumbration of Schubert arrives with the second *Menuetto*, particularly in its two ländler-like trios. Rather than simply repeat the minuet section at the end, which would have been the standard practice, Mozart offers a run-through of the minuet and then adds a charming coda as a lagniappe.

The fourth movement (*Andante*) may have been based on a popular song, and so may the finale (*Allegro*). Whether there was a direct ancestor or not, it is certainly a species of folk-like tune Mozart employed often for finales at the end of his career, as in the last movements of his G-minor String Quintet (K. 516), his Piano Concerto in B-flat major (K. 595), and his Clarinet

Concerto (K. 622). In none of these, however, is the open-eyed simplicity of the theme allowed to wallow in banality. Here the listener is treated to all manner of contrapuntal cleverness, and the work concludes as a balm for not only the soul but also the intellect.

String Quartet in D major, K. 575

Allegretto
Andante
Menuetto (Allegretto)—Trio
Allegretto

Work composed: Completed June 1789, in Vienna

Work premiered: Probably May 22, 1790, at Mozart's apartment in Vienna

Instrumentation: Two violins, viola, and cello

Things were not going well for Mozart when, in April 1789, at the instigation of his friend and fellow-Mason Prince Karl Lichnowsky, he traveled from Vienna to Berlin to meet Friedrich Wilhelm II, the cello-playing monarch who in 1786 had succeeded his flute-playing uncle, Frederick the Great, as King of Prussia. Mozart and Lichnowsky set off on April 8, traveling toward Berlin through Prague, Dresden, and Leipzig. It's unclear precisely what happened, but it seems as if the two quarreled over something in the course of the journey, though apparently not before Lichnowsky presented Mozart at the Prussian Court at Potsdam on May 26. "I am lucky enough to find favor with the King," Mozart wrote home to Constanze. Georg Nikolaus Nissen (who wed Constanze after her husband's untimely death) wrote in his 1828 biography of the composer:

> As the news that Mozart was there spread through Berlin, he was made extremely welcome everywhere, but especially by Friedrich Wilhelm II. Not only was the King well known to hold music in high esteem, and to pay good money for it, but he was also an amateur with genuinely good taste, if he could not quite be called a connoisseur. For as long as his stay in Berlin lasted, Mozart had to improvise for him almost every day, and often also play quartets with members of the royal orchestra in the King's room.

When Mozart got back to Vienna on June 4, 1789, he had in hand a commission from the king for a set of six string quartets plus (for the king's daughter,

Princess Friederike) six easy piano sonatas. He would be paid for these, it seems, when the pieces were delivered.

This might have done much to help salvage Mozart's situation and he immediately set to work. He may have begun the first piece of the set, the D-major String Quartet (K. 575), while en route back home; in any case, it was completed before June was over and he entered it, with the notation "for His Majesty the King of Prussia," in his *Verzeichnüss aller meiner Werke* ("Catalogue of All my Works"), which he had begun to keep five years before. He may have started on the next quartet, but then the difficulties of his life interceded. His wife and son fell ill, and on July 12, requiring money for their treatment, Mozart sent a letter to his friend Michael Puchberg, who had already lent the composer significant sums. "Instead of paying off my debts, I come asking for more!" wrote Mozart, adding (implying a sort of collateral), "I am composing six easy keyboard sonatas for Princess Friederike and six quartets for the King, which I am going to have engraved at my own expense at Kozeluch's; the two dedications will bring in something as well."

Months passed and Mozart, growing increasingly depressed, got side-tracked with his new opera, *Così fan tutte*, which was his chief occupation from autumn 1789 through its premiere on January 26, 1790. But even after the premiere of *Così fan tutte* the King's commission remained stalled as Mozart's financial pressures mounted. In early May 1790, on the verge of moving to new lodgings and hoping to schedule some revenue-raising performances, he reported to Puchberg: "When I move from here I will have to pay 275 gulden toward my new apartment—besides, I need something to live on until my concerts are set to go and the quartets I'm working on are ready for the engraver." And then the following week, begging Puchberg for an extension regarding the debt repayment: "If only you knew what grief and worry all this causes me. It has kept me all this time from finishing my quartets....Next Saturday I intend to perform my quartets at home, and request the pleasure of your company and that of your wife." Presumably that private run-through—at Mozart's apartment on May 22, 1790—marked the premiere of this composition, and since we know that Mozart particularly enjoyed playing the viola part in quartets, the chances are good that he sat in the viola chair that day.

This work displays a distinct character among Mozart's quartets. The instrumental balance is unusual. Fresh in the enthusiasm of his royal commission, Mozart seemed intent on providing an especially felicitous cello part for his patron. But simply making the cello the group's chief melodist would have been too simplistic a solution. Instead, he paid particular attention to *all* the lower voices of the ensemble, with the result that the parts are written with great democracy and with instruments sometimes playing unexpected roles within the ensemble's texture.

Even apart from that, this work seems uncharacteristically subdued among Mozart's quartets, at least in its first two movements. "The beauty of the D-major quartet is of a delicate and chastened order," wrote Hermann Abert in the classic *Cobbett's Cyclopedic Survey of Chamber Music* (1929). The first movement displays the indication *sotto voce* at its outset and again later, and we also encounter the marking *dolce* ("sweet") as the movement proceeds; and both those directives, which are atypical for Mozart to attach explicitly to his music, reappear in the second movement.

Even the tempo markings steer clear of extremes. The quartet's overriding tempo is a moderately paced *Allegretto*, which is assigned to three of the four movements, though we should note that the composer actually labeled the first movement *Allegro* when he entered it in his *Verzeichnüss*. The slow movement is an *Andante*, similarly more moderate in speed than the *adagio* that Mozart assigned to many of his deepest musings. Though not lacking in melodic or rhythmic elegance, these movements display a construction that stresses symmetry rather than surprise, and the harmonic writing is considerably less chromatic than we might expect of "typical" Mozart.

The suavity of the opening movements is brushed away in the *Menuetto*—or, more precisely, in the second section of the minuet proper. Here we finally encounter a few brusque harmonic conflicts and rhythmic displacements that in this context seem disconcerting, perhaps even spooky. The trio section returns us to unencumbered melodic effusion, with the cello tapped to proclaim the tune first. The cello gets that privilege in the finale, too, playing high in its register. At last the emotional baggage of the early movements is set somewhat aside, allowing Mozart to serve up a thoroughly felicitous, highly contrapuntal rondo whose character may recall the subtle, worldly wit of *Così fan tutte*.

Clarinet Quintet in A major, K. 581

Allegro
Larghetto
Menuetto
Allegretto con variazioni

Work composed: Late September 1789, in Vienna

Work premiered: December 22, 1789, in a concert of the Composer's Society at Vienna's Royal Court Theatre, with Anton Stadler as clarinetist

Instrumentation: Clarinet, two violins, viola, and cello

Perhaps no piece of chamber music sets so autumnal a mood as Mozart's Clarinet Quintet—at least none before Brahms. Nostalgic longing came naturally to Mozart's musical expression, but he rarely vented it so freely, and at such uninterrupted length, as he did in this quintet, a major-key work with a minor-key aftertaste. In fact, Mozart wrote the piece in autumn, at the end of September 1789. The times were tumultuous. England was reeling from the war in America; France was in turmoil, the Bastille having fallen little more than two months earlier; and the rest of Europe was on sharper political pins and needles than usual.

Mozart was also distressed on a personal level. The novelty of his childhood successes were distant memories, and his Viennese public was applauding his piano-playing less loudly than they had only a few years earlier. In July, his wife, Constanze, fell dangerously ill. Her leg became ulcerated, requiring extensive—and expensive—medical attention away from home. While she was away, Mozart doubtless spent a good deal of time with his friends. One of his closest was the Austrian clarinetist Anton Stadler (1753–1812), whom we have already met in connection with Mozart's Trio for Clarinet, Viola, and Piano (K. 498). Though Stadler's character has been questioned—some have suggested that he took advantage of the Mozarts' hospitality, and even that he stole the composer's pawn tickets—Mozart steadfastly admired him, and apart from the K. 498 Trio he bestowed on him two of his very greatest instrumental masterpieces: his Clarinet Quintet (K. 581) and his Clarinet Concerto (K. 622).

Mozart wrote both the Quintet and the Concerto for a basset clarinet, which is essentially a standard instrument with an extended bass register. It is on such an instrument that Stadler probably played when the work was unveiled in a Christmas concert of Vienna's Tonkünstler-Societät. On that occasion, it separated the two halves of *Il natale d'Apollo*, a cantata (now long-forgotten) by Vincenzo Righini (also long-forgotten—or remembered, if at all, for writing an opera on the Don Giovanni theme precisely a decade before Mozart did).

In the Clarinet Quintet we hear Mozart at his most personal, allowing music to stream from his soul without answering to the terms of a commission or the exigencies of a public. It was written from an overflowing heart and offered as a gift. Mozart indulges himself with spacious pacing and luscious timbre. The themes of the luxurious first movement tend toward the wistful—or even the mournful—and the slow harmonic rhythm holds the vigor of the tempo marking (*Allegro*) in check. The clarinet's warm sonority goes hand in hand with the autumnal spirit, the more so since Mozart spends a great deal of time emphasizing the instrument's rich lower range. Having set the mood with an *Allegro* that is hardly an *Allegro*, Mozart turns to the profound soulfulness of the *Larghetto* in which the clarinet offers a hushed song supported, with great harmonic subtlety, by the muted quartet of strings. Other Mozart slow movements are introspective, but few make their appearance after an opening movement as relaxed as that of the Clarinet Quintet. Together, the two movements achieve an expanse of rarest poignancy from the composer who would survive only another two years.

Concerto-like dimensions rule over the third movement, too, a *Menuet to* with two trios. Despite making efforts to be good-humored, the *Menuet to* itself remains bittersweet. The strings dominate the first trio, anxiously, in the minor key; the clarinet joins the ensemble to restate the opening minuet (without repeats), and in the second trio its upturned phrases seem only to laugh with a pathetic, forced smile. The musical esthetics of Mozart's time exerted pressure for a happy ending, and Mozart complies with a finale in which six variations are derived from a forthright, folk-inflected theme. The movement explores the clarinet's technical capacities and the sonic possibilities of combining it in different ways with the string quartet. All the same, happiness seems to be an interloper, and Mozart allows the viola to inject ominous appoggiaturas in the minor-key third variation, and the clarinet and violin to exchange final nostalgic memories in the fifth, before closing with polite assurance that the clouds are sure to pass.

String Quartet in F major, K. 590

Allegretto moderato
Allegretto
Menuetto: Allegretto
Allegro

Work composed: June 1790

Work premiered: Not known

Instrumentation: Two violins, viola, and cello

Mozart's visit to Berlin in May 1789 netted him a handful of royal commissions from Friedrich Wilhelm II, King of Prussia: a set of six string quartets for the king and a group of easy piano sonatas for his daughter the princess. He was prompt in finishing the first quartet of the group, the one in D major (K. 575), and he played what may have been its first performance at his own apartment in Vienna on May 22, 1790. In the last weeks before that read-through Mozart had managed to finish the second quartet of the set, in B-flat major (K. 589), and the third of the Prussian or Berlin Quartets, in F major (K. 590) would follow the next month. Those would be his final string quartets. Although he made some sketches for quartets in G minor and E minor (neither of which were typical quartet keys at that time), he never did finish the set of six the King had commissioned, nor did he manage to write more than one of the sonatas the Princess had requested (assuming that Mozart's Sonata in D major, K. 576, was even intended for that project, since it hardly qualifies as easy). Rather than complete the quartet project and collect his payment, Mozart, driven by the need for ready money, tried instead to cash in on the work he had accomplished to date. "Dearest friend," he wrote to his patient friend and fellow-Mason Michael Puchberg, "if you could help me with my most urgent expenses, please do it;...I am forced to sell my quartets, all that hard work, for just a trifle, just to get some cash into my hands and meet my immediate obligations." The publishing rights were purchased by the publishing form of Artaria, but even that failed to benefit the composer. Artaria took its good time preparing the three quartets for publication, and they were not released for sale until December 28, 1791, three weeks after Mozart's death. No dedication to the King appeared on the published music; Friedrich Wilhelm and his daughter had apparently been content to let the whole business of the commission conveniently disappear. It seems likely that Mozart was depressed (as a diagnosis today might put it), or at the very least exhausted. Neither situation would be difficult for an impartial observer to understand.

It appears that Mozart never supplied the King with even the three quartets he managed to complete, but the evidence of that commission is nonetheless clear through the very prominent role that Mozart gives to the cello, the part the King would have played himself at one of his musical gatherings. Indeed, the three Prussian Quartets provide soloistic opportunities to all four instruments. Where the "quartet ideal" had by then evolved to a point where the four instruments normally worked toward homogenized integration, Mozart here explores how one might achieve a democratic texture while putting each instrument on prominent display at least some of the time. (When these pieces were published, Artaria advertised them as "concertante quartets," underscoring the soloistic aspect of the individual parts.) Of the three completed Prussian Quartets, the F-major is the most brilliant in this regard, with each of the parts sometimes approaching concerto-like sparkle. In the first movement we hear it in how all four instruments play the opening theme in unison (or in octaves), how the first violin plays that theme as a solo before it is bantered about by all the forces (including, prominently, by the cello in a high register), how the cello offers the second theme (moving upward from its low C to cover nearly three octaves), how in the movement's recapitulation the viola assumes the thematic passages the cello had intoned in the exposition.

Mozart initially called his slow movement an *Andante* but apparently replaced that marking with *Allegretto* to prevent players from lingering too much over its phrases, pensive though they are. A notable degree of impetus is built in thanks to the almost constant presence of an insistent, two-measure rhythmic motif, which represents the kernel of the melodic theme that generates the entire movement. At the end the first violin ascends to a high C located well into the stratosphere, a very unusual demand from Mozart. The *Menuetto* seems to start very much where the *Allegretto* leaves off, with the first violin emitting a high-pitched (if not quite so stratospheric) melody in a light-textured context. Here we discover Mozart playing rhythmic tricks, trying out an asymmetrical balance by casting his theme in seven-bar phrases. In the finale we find him at his most Haydnesque, beginning with a jocular theme that resembles any number of melodies from Haydn finales (particularly prefiguring that of Haydn's G-major *Gypsy Rondo* Piano Trio, to be written five years later), continuing with a blustery, minor-key tempest-in-a-teapot, and extending to the sort of sonata-rondo architecture Haydn so enjoyed. This movement is chock full of surprises; as in many of Haydn's finest pieces, surprise seems to play a role in its own right, and you can never assume that what would logically lie around the bend is what you're likely to find when you get there.

String Quintet in D major, K. 593

> *Larghetto—Allegro*
> *Adagio*
> *Menuetto (Allegretto)*
> *Allegro*

Work composed: Completed in December 1790, perhaps begun a few months earlier

Work premiered: Not known

Instrumentation: Two violins, two violas, and cello

Although we lack watertight information about the first performance of the D-major String Quintet, we do know something about its early performance history. During the summer of 1829 the English music publisher Vincent Novello and his wife, Mary, traveled around Europe visiting the late Mozart's surviving family and friends. They kept a detailed diary of their encounters, and fortunately their manuscript remained tucked away and unnoticed among the family's papers for several generations. It was rediscovered only in 1944, at the home of a great-granddaughter of the Novellos, and when it was finally published, in 1955—by Novello & Co., which is still in business to this day—it furnished a trove of information about Mozart and his circle.

One of the notable figures the Novellos had sought out was the Abbé Maximilian Stadler, a cleric and composer who made Mozart's acquaintance no later than 1781. (He apparently was not related to the clarinetist Anton Stadler, for whom Mozart wrote several works.) When the Novellos interviewed Stadler he spoke of Mozart's deep friendship with Haydn. Reads their diary: "Mozart and Haydn frequently played together with Stadler in Mozart's Quintettos; particularly mentioned the 5th in D major, singing the Bass part"—at which point Vincent Novello jots down the opening motif of K. 593. He concludes by noting that they also played "the one in C major and still more that in G minor." This ensemble must have convened very shortly after the completion of the D-major Quintet, since the catalogue Mozart kept of his compositions lists the work as being completed in December, and Haydn left for his first residency in London on December 15. It seems entirely possible—even likely—that the chamber-music gathering to which Stadler alluded was the first time Mozart's Quintet was heard. Stadler was mostly a keyboard player, and we're not sure which part he played in the quintets. Perhaps it was violin, since he studied that instrument as a young man. In that case, he and Haydn would have shared the violin parts while Mozart supplied one of the viola lines, since he preferred to play that instrument in chamber gatherings. Oh, to have been a fly on the wall!

The work opens in a Haydnesque mood. The cello announces a simple D-major arpeggio, as nonchalantly as if it were a hiccup. The four upper strings respond quietly with a richly harmonized phrase that evaporates before the sentence is concluded. The tempo is slow. For Mozart the marking of *Larghetto* often signals relaxed introspection, but we shouldn't read too much into that heading since in his catalogue the composer identifies that particular passage as *Adagio*. As in the slow introductions to Haydn's London symphonies, we are left groping for stability in this hazy landscape of melodic fragmentation and harmonic instability. The two musical ideas alternate for a minute and a half before coming to rest on the dominant seventh chord. Mozart resolves into the tonic (D major) and into an *Allegro*, though one that doesn't seem to want to go terribly fast and that allows for a threatening detour into the minor mode before the exposition is over. He also changes his meter signature with the onset of the *Allegro* such that the opening triple pulses now become duple. The expected sonata form plays out, with further minor-mode references and some finely wrought counterpoint in the development section. Everything seems on a more or less predictable path when— what's this? Just as the movement seems preparing to end, the introduction returns, now transformed in its harmonic contours. Following this surprising turn of events, the principal tune of the *Allegro* section revives for one more go-through. As in Haydn's *Joke* Quartet this delivers an irresolute conclusion. Only after a certain amount of silence do we feel comfortable trusting that it is indeed the movement's end.

Next comes a movement dense with incidents, a triple-meter *Adagio* that, again, seems Haydnesque in the constricted contours of its opening. Near the end of the first "paragraph" the first violin, answered by first viola, intones a chromatically enriched ascending line, immediately echoed by first viola; and then the two violins move back down again with a descending chromatic figure. In retrospect we will understand that this is a harbinger of still more serious chromaticism in the movement's development section. Before we get to that Mozart shocks us with an anguished passage in the minor mode, with the first violin giving voice to its lamenting melody against shivering chords in the middle strings and an upward-rising figure in the cello that is surely meant to remind us of the cello's opening arpeggio eructation in the first movement. A few measures of circle-of-fifths modulation follow as the first violin prolongs its melody; but as common as that device is, Mozart here elaborates the texture to dramatic and eerie effect. The movement's most shocking passage is still held in check. Mozart will release it gradually, entering by way of an insouciant descending motif articulated first by the three upper lines, then by the three lower, then upper, then lower, and finally cascading down through the entire quintet texture, from top to bottom. This idea leads to another circle-of-fifths pattern, comforting in its harmonic familiarity but again elaborated with astonishing imagination. Not the least of this moment's effects is the cello's pizzicatos at precisely this poignant juncture. Chromaticism continues to hold its grip on this movement until, on the final page, the language simplifies and we feel finally grounded.

After such a far-reaching adventure the *Menuetto* seems unthreatening. Nonetheless, it's far from a piece of fluff, energized as it is by syncopated accents and, in its final measures, a close canon that pits the violins against the violas and cello. The hushed trio section is simpler still, with arpeggiated violin figuration often set above a plucked accompaniment of chords in the lower instruments.

Mozart still had chromaticism on his mind when he started his finale. It opens with a descending chromatic scale from the first violin, which then recurs periodically in the course of the movement. When the piece was published, by the Viennese firm of Artaria, this figure was massaged into a differently tooled passage, still descending, still with chromatic inflections, yet rendered perhaps more playful by turning the unvarnished chromatic scale into a skipping pattern of intervals. Most musicologists now seem to believe that the unadorned chromatic line is the only authentic one, and that the skipping pattern was an emendation from another party, perhaps someone in Artaria's employ. Toward the end, Mozart inserts some learned passages of imitative counterpoint without making much ado about them, leaving this *finale* to stress unalloyed good humor and to provide the sense of certainty that had been withheld in the first two movements.

String Quintet in E-flat major, K. 614

Allegro di molto
Andante
Menuetto (Allegretto)
Allegro

Work composed: Completed April 12, 1791

Work premiered: Not known

Instrumentation: Two violins, two violas, and cello

We know nothing for sure about why Mozart composed this final string quintet, and no details have come down about its early performance history. Manuscript sketches exist for two attempts at a first movement of another String Quintet in E-flat major, one sketch running seventy-one measures, the other only nineteen—but nothing really links them to the work at hand. In 1793 the Artaria firm published this quintet posthumously (along with its predecessor, the D-major Quintet, K. 593) in an edition bearing the inscription "Composto per un Amatore Ongarese" ("Composed for a Hungarian Aficionado"). Some Mozart scholars, apparently beginning with E. F. Schmidt, have wondered if the two quintets might have been commissioned by the violinist-turned-fabric salesman Johann Tost, remembered chiefly through his commissions of works by Haydn and Spohr. But Tost was born in Moravia, not Hungary, and there were so many authentic Hungarian music patrons in Mozart's Vienna that it hardly seems necessary to cast the net wider. Among the scholars who picked up on the Tost idea have been such estimable figures as Otto Erich Deutsch and H. C. Robbins Landon. The latter notes in his book *Mozart's Last Year: 1791* that in 1800 Mozart's widow did mention, in a letter to the publisher Johann Anton André, Jr.: "There is a Herr v[on] Tost here—he lives in the Singerstrasse—who says he has autograph scores by Mozart. It is true that M. worked for him. He has promised me the themes." We don't know of any other Mozart-Tost connection, so if you want to suppose this was the piece that linked them you are welcome to do so.

The first movement opens with an imaginative texture: the two violas unsupported by the other instruments, announcing the "horn-call" theme (in appropriately jaunty 6/8 meter) that dominates the movement. In fact, the only other theme that merits that appellation appears late in the movement, in the recapitulation; again, it is introduced by the first viola.

The B-flat-major *Andante* unrolls as freely treated variations on a theme, the melody being somewhat reminiscent of Belmonte's aria "Wen der Freude Thränen fliessen" from Act Two of *Die Entführung aus dem Serail*, which Mozart had composed eleven years earlier. The third movement is a more-or-less standard *Menuetto* with trio, though a bit unusual in that the Trio displays the character of a pastoral ländler. In that central section the cello plays a nearly unbroken drone on the note E-flat, above which the violins and violas weave with subtle agility, the first violin and first viola finally ending up joining forces to play their final phrases in tandem, an octave apart. For the finale Mozart gives us one of his irresistible sonata-rondo movements, strikingly Haydnesque in its unpredictable wit, working its way up to an unanticipated but wonderful fugato passage in the development episode. Here, and elsewhere in the movement, we find Mozart spinning out the most inventive and inspired counterpoint as if it was second nature, which in his case it was.

Carl Nielsen

Carl August Nielsen

Born: June 9, 1865, in Sortelung, near Nørre Lyndelse, Funen, Denmark

Died: October 3, 1931, in Copenhagen, Denmark

Wind Quintet, Op. 43

Allegro ben moderato
Menuet
Praeludium: Adagio—Tema con variazioni

Work composed: 1921–early 1922

Work dedicated: To the Wind Quintet of the Royal Orchestra, Copenhagen, "most amicably"

Work premiered: April 30, 1922, at a private concert in Göteborg; the first public performance was given on October 9 of that year in Copenhagen, by the Wind Quintet of the Royal Orchestra, Copenhagen.

Instrumentation: Flute, oboe (doubling English horn), clarinet, horn, and bassoon

Born into a large family of slender means, Carl Nielsen rose to become the most honored of Denmark's composers. He hailed from outside a small town smack in the middle of Funen, an island that sits latitudinally in the center of the country, a few miles south of the city of Odense. As a composer, Nielsen grew to be "world famous in Denmark" during his lifetime, but his works failed to generate much interest elsewhere until the 1950s. Listeners in Great Britain were the first beyond Scandinavia to get on the Nielsen bandwagon, and some English commentators began to rank him on a level with Mahler and Sibelius as a symphonist. Though his language was diverse, his works often exhibit a sense of health and wholesomeness, of optimism and affirmation—a cliché in Nielsen commentary, perhaps, but nonetheless a characteristic that proved seductive at a time when much contemporary music left listeners baffled.

One evening in the fall of 1921 he placed a phone call to Christian Christiansen, a pianist friend who just then happened to be rehearsing (as accompanist) with four-fifths of the Wind Quintet of the Royal Orchestra, Copenhagen, for a performance of Mozart's Sinfonia Concertante for Four Winds (K. 297b, and since consigned to the category of spurious Mozartiana). As Nielsen and his friend chatted, the four wind players continued to play in the background, and Nielsen was so taken by the sounds that he asked Christiansen if he could pop over to listen in person, which he did.

Nielsen, who had just completed his Fifth Symphony, instantly decided that his next work would be for the Wind Quintet of the Royal Orchestra, Copenhagen. While working on the piece he consulted closely with the five members—flutist Paul Hagemann, oboist Svend Christian Felumb, clarinetist Aage Oxenvad, hornist Og Hans Sørensen, and bassoonist Knud Lassen—with the goal of seizing not only the characters of their instruments but also the specific musical personalities of the players. As befitted such a project, the result was a work of terrific variety—ranging from languorous to stately to humorous—and of more than usually pointed individuality in its voices. Nielsen was so taken by the ensemble that he determined to continue by writing a solo concerto for each of its members. That led to the composition of his Flute Concerto in 1926 for Gilbert Jespersen (who had by then replaced Hagemann as the ensemble's flutist) and his Clarinet Concerto in 1928 for Oxenvad; oboists, hornists, and bassoonists have special reason to mourn that Nielsen did not live to see his incentive through to the end.

Haydnesque good spirits (even lightly Stravinskyian neo-Classicism) and neo-Baroquism pervade this piece. The first movement unrolls in a rather traditional sonata form, altogether in a relaxed mood, its vigor being decidedly pastoral; following the bassoon's opening solo, the first sally of the upper winds even resembles a birdcall. The charmingly contrapuntal Menuet recalls the Baroque with a studied quaintness that is also to be found in Nielsen's marvelous but (except in Denmark) scandalously neglected opera Maskarade (1906).

The finale is the longest of the movements. Nielsen opens it with a serious, two-minute Praeludium in which the oboist darkens the texture by switching to English horn, the alto member of the oboe family. There follows a theme and, with the oboist playing oboe again, a set of eleven wide-ranging variations. The melody is a chorale hymn-tune Nielsen had written several years earlier, "Min Jesus, lad mit hjerte faa" ("My Jesus, let my heart be thine"). It is indeed a beautiful chorale, and it had become an instant success among Danish churchgoers, but Nielsen makes a point not to treat it as an item invested with sanctity. In a program note he prepared for the premiere, he wrote (using the third person): "The theme for these variations is the tune of one of Carl Nielsen's spiritual songs, which is here made the basis of a number of variations, now gay and grotesque, now elegiac and solemn, ending with the theme itself, simply and gently expressed." It is in these variations that Nielsen's characterization of his individual musicians reached its apex, but at the end the ensemble returns to strictly democratic balance to again enunciate the unembellished chorale, this time re-orchestrated to employ oboe rather than English horn.

Musically, Nielsen often seems a latter-day relative of Brahms, though a chess player might view him as displaced from that figure by a knight's move: a step to the side and a stride into the future. Though anchored in classical values, he allowed his compositions to develop organically in their own directions, never sacrificing an allegiance to tonality but loosening its grip on the large-scale aspects of compositions. So does he arrive at a tonal organization that doesn't center on any single tonic: the first movement of the Wind Quintet is in E major, the second in A major (with the trio section hovering between D minor and F major), and the third (following its introduction in C minor) in A major.

The Wind Quintet is one of the most frequently performed pieces in the entire Nielsen catalogue. It was the first of his compositions to be released on a sound recording outside Denmark, via 78-r.p.m. platters made by the ensemble that had introduced it. When the composer died he was accorded a state funeral at the Free Church in Copenhagen and among the pieces performed at the service was the hymn "Min Jesus, lad mit hjerte faa." At the ensuing burial, the Wind Quintet of the Royal Orchestra, Copenhagen played the chorale and variations on that melody that make up the finale of the Wind Quintet. In the score, the final, straightforward rendition of the melody is marked *Andante festivo*. Possibly on that occasion it was simply *Andante*.

Francis Poulenc

Born: January 7, 1899, in Paris, France

Died: January 30, 1963, in Paris

Trio for Oboe, Bassoon, and Piano

Lent—Presto
Andante con moto
Rondo (Très vif)

Work composed: **Principally from February through April 1926**

Work dedicated: **To Manuel de Falla**

Work premiered: **May 2, 1926, at the Salle des Agriculteurs in Paris, by Roland Lamorlette (oboe), Gustave Dhérin (bassoon), and the composer (playing piano)**

Instrumentation: **Oboe, bassoon, and piano**

Francis Poulenc stands as a delightful paradox among twentieth-century composers. Many highbrows have been eager to dismiss his music: it generally has a lightweight harmonic flavor to it, and even when he was sowing his wild oats, as a young composer in the Jazz Age, he was always running a lap behind Stravinsky. On the other hand, musicians and audiences tend to love his music: its technical panache is undeniable, its neo-Classicism is comforting, its wit makes them laugh out loud. And in his sacred music, as well as his more serious songs and certainly his masterful opera *Dialogues des Carmélites*, Poulenc achieves a rare level of direct, sincere, profoundly spiritual expression.

He enjoyed the benefit of finding himself at the right place at the right time. Born into fortunate circumstances only a year before the onset of the twentieth century—his father and uncles founded the pharmaceutical firm that would evolve into the mega-corporation Rhône-Poulenc—he came of age in a Paris whose cultural geography was re-mapped monthly under the assault of Stravinsky's colorful music, Diaghilev's exotic ballets, Apollinaire's unpredictable poems, Picasso's angular paintings, and Satie's slyly subversive scores.

Poulenc may have begun his Trio as early as 1924, but it was mostly composed between February and April 1926 in Cannes, on the Riviera, and carries a dedication to the Spanish composer Manuel de Falla. Upon receiving a copy of the score, Falla wrote to Poulenc: "I was overjoyed to receive the Trio—MY TRIO!—so eagerly awaited. I like it so much that, at the very first opportunity, we will perform it in Seville (keeping the piano part for myself, of course)." He did indeed see to it that the piece was played in Spain in 1929. By that time the trio had been issued in a recording on the French Columbia label, with Poulenc playing the piano part along with oboist Roland Lamorlette and bassoonist Gustave Dhérin, the same ensemble that had performed the premiere, at an Auric-Poulenc concert in the Salle des Agriculteurs in Paris on May 2, 1926.

The Trio displays everything we love most about Poulenc: lyrical generosity, trenchant irony, formal concision, delight in Classical models, elegant balance of voices, naturalness of expression, and, above all, a terrific sense of humor. "For those who believe that I don't care about matters of form," remarked Poulenc, "I don't hesitate to unmask my secrets here: the first movement follows the plan of an allegro by Haydn, and the Rondo finale is carved out of the scherzo of the Second Concerto for Piano and Orchestra by Saint-Saëns."

Following a mock-ponderous introduction (*Lent*) of recitative-like motifs, the first movement breaks forth in a rollicking *Presto*: at its outset it invites comparison with Groucho Marx's "Hooray for Captain Spaulding," after which irresistible themes unroll in profusion. (The film *Animal Crackers*, in which that song is sung, appeared in 1930, four years after Poulenc's Trio, and the song was written by composer Harry Ruby and lyricist Bert Kalmar, though they were not mentioned in the film credits.) An undated letter, perhaps written in April 1926, makes it clear that Poulenc shared his new score with no less a colleague than Igor Stravinsky, who offered some constructive criticism. Poulenc responded to Stravinsky's comments: "How kind of you to have given me all of that good advice. I have modified the first tempo in the trio. It is completely different." What the tempo started out as we don't know.

The second movement is gracious and songlike, and would seem to evoke a Mozart andante but for an entirely modern structural twist: it begins in B-flat major and ends in F minor (the dominant minor), a progression that would not be logical to an analyst but that, in context, sounds just right. The finale sparkles with giggling delight—or perhaps we should say "jigging delight," since its triple-duple meter happily evokes that ancient dance.

Serge Prokofieff [signature]

Sergei Sergeievich Prokofiev

Born: April 11 (old style)/23 (new style), 1891—so he always said, though his birth certificate said April 15/27)—in Sontsovka, in the Ekaterinoslav district of Ukraine

Died: March 5, 1953, in Moscow, Russia, USSR

Overture on Hebrew Themes, Op. 34

Work composed: 1919

Work premiered: **January 26, 1920, in New York, by Zimro (a chamber ensemble)**

Instrumentation: Clarinet, two violins, viola, cello, and piano

When Russian composers began developing a distinctly national style in the nineteenth century, they drew much inspiration from the diverse fabric of their ethnic cultures. Jews represented a significant subculture through much of Russian history, often coexisting uneasily, viewed suspiciously as outsiders. Sympathy for "the outsider" seems to have fueled many composers who borrowed Jewish melodies or composed new melodies that sounded like Jewish traditional music. Prokofiev provided one of the most enduring of these "Russian-Jewish" pieces in 1919 in his Overture on Hebrew Themes.

When the Bolshevik Revolution hit, Prokofiev decided to ride out the storm elsewhere, so in May 1918 he left for what he thought would be a visit of several months to New York. As it happened, the Revolution did not blow over quite as he imagined, with the result that Prokofiev spent the first half of his career abroad—first in New York but mostly in Paris, until 1936. He would then return to Russia definitively, precisely when Soviet musical life was becoming consolidated under the iron-fisted auspices of the Union of Soviet Composers. Prokofiev weathered the challenge reasonably well until 1948, when he was censured by the Central Committee of the Communist Party (along with quite a few other prominent composers) for writing music "marked with formalist perversions...alien to the Soviet people." Had he survived until the cultural thaw of the post-Stalin era, it is conceivable that his physical condition might have improved along with his professional fortune. As it was, he did not: Prokofiev and Stalin died on the same day.

The Overture on Hebrew Themes dates from Prokofiev's time in New York, where, in the autumn of 1919, he encountered a group of his classmates from the St. Petersburg Conservatory. They had formed an ensemble called Zimro, consisting of string quartet, clarinet, and piano, and they had come to New York hoping to raise money to fund a new conservatory in Jerusalem by playing chamber music on Jewish themes. They hoped Prokofiev would compose a piece for them. Prokofiev at first declined, protesting that he was not Jewish, that he didn't know any Jewish themes, and that in any case he was not drawn to composing pieces on pre-existing melodies; but his friends provided a collection of melodies for him and before long he found this irresistible piece forming in his mind. It scored a success when Zimro premiered it in New York in January 1920, thanks to the imagination the composer uses in melding the serpentine, modal klezmer flavor of its clarinet theme to the burgeoning Modernism of the moment.

Prokofiev considered his Overture to be a mere trifle, essentially composing it in two days and polishing it in another ten. Nonetheless, it proved very successful with audiences—so much so, in fact, that in 1934 he prepared an orchestral transcription of the piece, which is occasionally presented today as his Op. 34a. That version in no way displaced the original chamber setting, which benefits from a certain earthiness and an uncanny balance of distinct timbres.

String Quartet No. 2 in F major (on Kabardinian Themes), Op. 92

Allegro sostenuto
Adagio
Allegro—Andante molto

Work composed: 1941

Work premiered: September 5, 1942, in Moscow, by the Beethoven Quartet

Instrumentation: Two violins, viola, and cello

After Prokofiev returned to live in Moscow, in 1936, his artistic experiments continued in the shadow of politically acceptable style. There is no question that important masterpieces resulted from this second half of his career; nonetheless, it is in his pre-Soviet oeuvre that Prokofiev-the-experimenter makes his most dependable appearances. His two string quartets reflect these two periods accurately. His First, written during an American concert tour in 1930, forthrightly reflects his pioneering, distinctive Modernism. The Second, composed in a remote region of the Soviet Union in 1941–42, maintains a good measure of Prokofiev's genuine voice, but it melds his originality with the considerable demands of state-approved Social Realism.

He was living at a country home outside Moscow when, on June 22, 1941, the Nazis broke their nonaggression pact and invaded Russia. German troops swept eastward, blockading Leningrad and stopping only twenty miles short of Moscow when winter storms impeded their advance. Expecting that Moscow would fall, the Soviet Committee on Artistic Affairs evacuated the city's artistic luminaries to safer surroundings. On August 8, 1941, Prokofiev therefore joined a group of musicians (including his friend Nikolai Myaskovsky), theatre people (including Chekhov's widow, by then an elderly actress), and other artistic types on a three-day train trip to Nalchik, the capital of the Kabarda-Balkar Autonomous Republic in the northern Caucasus, about nine hundred miles south of Moscow. In late November the Nalchik artists' colony moved on to Tbilisi, keeping a step ahead of the advancing Nazi forces.

By that time Prokofiev was engrossed in his String Quartet No. 2, which would occupy him from November 2 through mid-December 1941. The work was directly inspired by the Kabardinian folk music he encountered in Nalchik. "The material proved to be very fresh and original," he wrote. "I felt that the combination of new, untouched Oriental folklore with the most classical of classic forms, the string quartet, could yield interesting and unexpected results." Indeed it is a fusion of "folk" and "classical." The quartet retains a strong semblance of the original folk rhythms and textures. On the other hand, the piece is cast in recognizable Western structures with their attendant large-scale harmonic relationships. Several Kabardinian tunes are encountered along the way. Myaskovsky, who found the piece "simply monstrously, even 'nightmarishly' interesting," would use two of them in his coeval Symphony No. 23.

When Prokofiev's Second String Quartet was premiered, by the Beethoven Quartet in Moscow on September 5, 1942, the performance started late, delayed by a Nazi air-raid. A few critics complained that the composer had taken too much liberty with the folk tunes, that he had actually written an original piece rather than settle for a folk-song recital, but on the whole the quartet was a triumph, enjoying what Prokofiev termed "an extremely turbulent success."

Joseph Maurice Ravel

Born: March 7, 1875, in Ciboure, Basses-Pyrenées, France

Died: December 28, 1937, in Paris, France

String Quartet in F major

Allegro moderato
Assez vif—Très rhythmé
Très lent
Vif et agité

Work composed: 1902–03

Work dedicated: À mon cher maître Gabriel Fauré

Work premiered: March 5, 1904, in the concert hall of the Schola Cantorum in Paris, by the Heymann Quartet

Instrumentation: Two violins, viola, and cello

When Maurice Ravel's String Quartet was introduced, at a concert of the Société Nationale de Musique on March 5, 1904, the composer was on the verge of his twenty-ninth birthday and was just finishing his study with Gabriel Fauré at the Paris Conservatoire. In truth, he was no longer an official student of that great master, whom Ravel adored. In July 1900 he had been expelled from Fauré's composition classes according to the decree of the Conservatoire's ruling board, a judgment based on the fact that he had failed to demonstrate competence in writing an academic fugue. But kindly Fauré suspected that Ravel had a distinctive talent, even if it didn't involve writing fugues, and he allowed him to remain in his composition class as an auditor, which Ravel did through 1903. Ravel expressed his gratefulness to Fauré through the dedications of two works of that period: *Jeux d'eau* (for piano, 1900) and the String Quartet.

Debussy had written his only string quartet in 1893, Ravel wrote his only quartet a decade later, and the two have been linked in the public's mind ever since. Reviewing the premiere of Ravel's Quartet in *Le Temps* (April 19, 1904), Pierre Lalo wrote, "In its harmonies and successions of chords, in its sonority and form...and in all the sensations which it evokes, it offers an incredible resemblance with the music of M. Debussy." If you purchase a recording of one of these quartets, chances are that it will be coupled with the other. There is no question that they display similarities, most strikingly their use of an evolved form of cyclic structuring that owed much to César Franck. This is perhaps more apparent in Debussy's Quartet, where a single theme (or a descendant thereof) generates each of the work's four movements. Ravel employs greater freedom in his approach, but even here melodic motifs in the third and fourth movements are derived from material in the opening movement. Then, too, the general sound of the two quartets is strikingly similar: by employing a complete panoply of string effects, both composers move into a new chamber esthetic that would delight in instrumental color as an essential arrow in the composer's quiver.

This is not to say that Ravel was not concerned with structural issues when he embarked on this piece. In a 1931 interview with the Amsterdam newspaper *De Telegraaf*, he went so far as to characterize his Quartet as an early display of neo-Classicism—one, moreover, that was inherently distinct from Debussy's. "After our extreme modernism," he said, "a return to classicism was to be expected. After a flood comes the ebb tide, and after a revolution we see the reaction. Stravinsky is often considered the leader of neoclassicism, but don't forget that my String Quartet was already conceived in terms of four-part counterpoint, whereas Debussy's Quartet is purely harmonic in conception."

Fauré was befuddled by the formal liberty of the finale, and perhaps by its unorthodox 5/8 meter. Any "outside references" this quartet makes are strictly musical, as when, in the second movement, pizzicatos and cross-rhythms (the outer two instruments play in 3/4 meter while the inner two proceed in 6/8) evoke the sounds of bells, or perhaps a Javanese gamelan. Ravel's musical dialogue is complex but tightly organized, and he creates stunning coloristic effects at every turn by harnessing the four instruments in unanticipated ways.

Critical reception was generally supportive, although some early listeners predictably failed to grasp what was going on. Such was the critic for the *New York Tribune*, who was appalled when he heard the work in 1906: "In his String Quartet, M. Ravel is content with one theme which has the emotional potency of one of those tunes which the curious may hear in a Chinese theater, shrieked out by an ear-splitting clarinet. This theme serves him for four movements during which there is about as much emotional nuance as warms a problem in algebra. It is a drastic dose of wormwood and assafoetida." (The former herb is best known as an ingredient in absinthe; the latter is a foul-smelling fennel derivative known in some popular circles as "devils' dung.") Following the premiere, Jean Marnold, in *Le Mercure de France*, observed: "A healthy and sensitive temperament of a pure musician is developing here…a spontaneous art or the unfailing nature of instinct ensures the communication of his thinking. One should remember the name of Maurice Ravel. He is one of the masters of tomorrow." This, in 1904, was right on target.

Some reference books state that Ravel effected substantial changes to his Quartet before it was published, in 1910, by the eminent firm of Durand. Not so. Ravel's Quartet was published promptly after its premiere, in 1904, by Gabriel Astruc, a far from inconsequential music publisher, impresario, and (later) music publicist. Six years later the rights were transferred to the still more prestigious house of Durand, which brought out what it advertised as a "new edition reviewed and corrected by the author." The correction amounted to precisely two notes.

Piano Trio

> *Modéré*
> *Pantoum: Assez vif*
> *Passacaille: Très large*
> *Finale: Animé*

Work composed: Between April 3 and August 7, 1914, in Saint-Jean-de-Luz, France

Work dedicated: To André Gédalge, Ravel's former counterpoint teacher at the Paris Conservatoire

Work premiered: January 25, 1915, at a concert of the Société Musicale Indépendente in the Salle Gaveau, Paris, by pianist Alfredo Casella, violinist Gabriel Willaume (some evidence suggests that George Enescu may have taken his place), and cellist Louis Feuillard

Instrumentation: Violin, cello, and piano

Quintessentially refined Parisian though he became, Maurice Ravel never relinquished his attachment to the Basque country of southwestern France in which he was born, about five miles from the Spanish border. He typically spent his summer vacations in those familiar climes, specifically in the village of Saint-Jean-de-Luz, which sits directly across the River Nivelle from the even smaller Cibours, where Ravel was born. That's where he was during the spring and summer of 1914, principally occupied with his piano suite *Le Tombeau de Couperin*, his "Basque-flavored" piano concerto *Zaspiak-bat*, and his Piano Trio. He would abandon *Zaspiak-bat*, although he presumably resurrected some of its material in his later Piano Concerto in G (1929–31), and some say that this vanished score also furnished the opening theme of the Piano Trio.

These were, in any case, his principal musical concerns during his vacation that year. Much of his mind was centered on the gathering clouds of war as the German armies mobilized and World War I prepared to explode onto the scene. On June 28 the assassination in Sarajevo of Archduke Franz Ferdinand provided the spark for the European tinderbox, and by August nations were declaring war on one another. Ravel reported to his friends that he was pushing as hard as he could to finish his Piano Trio before he himself got involved in the action. This he managed to do, and the following January he volunteered for military service.

Writing a piano trio had been on his mind for some years. He first made reference to working on a trio in a letter to his friend Cipa Godebski in March 1908; whether this project evolved in any direct way into the eventual Piano Trio is unclear. Ravel didn't focus his energies on such a composition until his work on this piece, which, according to his notation on the manuscript, occupied him from April 3 through August 7, 1914. Already on March 21 of that year Ravel had written to Mrs. Alfredo Casella (whose composer-husband would play the piano part in the work's premiere the following January), "I am working on the trio despite the cold, the storms, the thunder, the rain, and the hail." Apparently he was already sketching musical thoughts for the piece by that time.

Ravel's disciple Roland-Manuel, in his study of the composer, pointed out the problems of balance always presented to those who throw their hat in the ring of the piano trio, with its potentially conflicting mix of string and piano sonorities. Roland-Manuel felt that only Saint-Saëns had actually succeeded in the medium. "So," he wrote, "Ravel placed himself under Saint-Saëns' discipline, delighted to deal in material thus contrasted and to build upon recalcitrant foundations.... In the most successful movements, especially the first and the Passacaglia, the incompatibility of opposing sonorities is solved with consummate lightness and distinction." He was perhaps echoing his teacher's sentiments, since Ravel himself was known to dismiss this achievement modestly as "C'est du Saint-Saëns."

In 1928 the Aeolian Company convinced Ravel to prepare a brief autobiography to accompany their release of piano rolls of his music that he and some colleagues were recording. He dictated his remarks to Roland-Manuel, whose unedited manuscript of the autobiography yields no more than this about the work played here: "The Trio, whose first theme has a Basque flavor, was composed entirely in 1914, at Saint-Jean-de-Luz." The musicologist Mark DeVoto has identified the opening movement's rhythm as being derived from the *zortzico*, a Basque dance with a characteristic alternation of meters with the complicating addition of extra beats.

The second movement, which serves as a scherzo, carries the unusual designation *Pantoum*. That's a French variant of the literary term pantun, which refers to a Malayan poetic structure wherein diverse strains of thought are expressed in parallel. French artistic types drawn to exoticism—Hugo, Baudelaire, and Verlaine among them—had dabbled in this form, and Ravel was intrigued enough to adapt some of its principles in structuring not only this movement but also a section of the coeval *Tombeau de Couperin*. Strict pantun form involves the interlacing of material: the second and fourth lines of one stanza are repeated as the first and third lines of the next stanza, with the flow of plot or whatever ideas are being expressed continuing through it all. Ravel does not try to duplicate a pantun slavishly, but a close analysis of this movement does turn up subtle interlacing of material; at the very least the general idea is conveyed through the mixing of binary and ternary rhythms.

The sober third movement (*Passacaille*) provides respite from the bustling *Pantoum*, flowing peacefully in the classic French form of the passacaille, in which a melody repeats over and over as the composer weaves elaborations around it. The slowly paced eight-measure melody is transformed in the course of the movement, but it is nearly always present in one voice or another. Here we find a suggestion of palindrome: at the beginning the melody is articulated first by the piano, then by the cello, and finally by the violin, whereas at the end the melody is intoned in precisely the reverse order.

The rhythm of the sumptuous *Final*, flitting constantly between 5/4 and 7/4 time, may also have some connection to Basque folklore. Its opening theme can be viewed to some extent as an inversion of the principal theme of the first movement. The instrumental writing here is virtuosic. Ravel was an accomplished pianist himself, but he did not even pretend that the piano writing in his Trio was within his grasp. Responding to a request from an English presenter, Ravel declared himself "absolutely incapable of playing the piano part."

Sonata for Violin and Cello

Allegro
Très vif
Lent
Vif, avec entrain

Work composed: Between 1920 and 1922

Work dedicated: To the memory of Claude Debussy. Ravel was very clear about this in a letter to his publisher, although his incomplete manuscript is inscribed "to Maurice Maréchal, in remembrance of the beautiful premiere on April 6, 1922, from his devoted Maurice Ravel."

Work premiered: The first movement, on January 24, 1921, in Paris at a concert organized by the Société Musicale Indépendente in tribute to the late Claude Debussy; the complete sonata, on April 6, 1922, at the Salle Pleyel in Paris, by violinist Hélène Jourdan-Morhange and cellist Maurice Maréchal

Instrumentation: Violin and cello

"I believe this Sonata marks a turning point in the evolution of my career. Economy of means is here carried to its extreme limits; there are no harmonies to charm the ear, but a pronounced reaction in favor of melody." So said Maurice Ravel of his Sonata for Violin and Cello in the biographical sketch he dictated to his disciple Roland-Manuel in 1928, a brief but fascinating document that was first published a decade later in *La Revue musicale*. The Sonata was composed in the early 1920s, coevally with Ravel's opera *L'Enfant et les sortilèges*, and if the opera still refers to the lush textures that infused his earlier works, including such beloved classics as *Daphnis et Chloé* and *Valses nobles et sentimentales*, the Sonata epitomizes the austerity that would lie ahead in his Sonata for Violin and Piano (1923–27), his Chansons madécasses (1925–26), his two piano concertos (1929–31), and, in certain respects, his *Boléro* (1928). The Sonata for Violin and Cello shows the composer at his most uncompromising. Wrote Roland-Manuel, "This remarkable sonata, bristling with virtuosity and a lyricism which spits like an angry cat, is one of the most significant—and least flattering—works in Ravel's new manner."

The Sonata's genesis can be traced to an invitation from Henri Prunières, the founder and editor of *La Revue musicale*, for Ravel to contribute a short composition to a special issue of the magazine commemorating Claude Debussy, who had died in 1918. Ravel immediately consented to join a roster of nine other contributors: Bela Bartók, Paul Dukas, Manuel de Falla, Eugène

Goossens, Gian Francesco Malipiero, Albert Roussel, Erik Satie, Florent Schmitt, and Igor Stravinsky. (The artist Raoul Dufy contributed the frontispiece.) Their compositions were published by the magazine on December 1, 1920, and were all performed at a Debussy memorial concert sponsored by the Société Musicale Indépendente on January 24, 1921.

The Ravel piece played on that occasion was the first movement—*Allegro*—of the Sonata for Violin and Cello. Ravel continued to develop his Sonata for nearly another year and a half, a long gestation period for a piece that lasts only twenty minutes. On September 22, 1921, he wrote to Roland-Manuel, "This confounded Duo is giving me a lot of trouble." A week later things were looking up: "I am beginning to see my way through the Duo." On February 3, 1922: "The Duo was finished, but I then saw that the scherzo was much too long, so I am beginning it again with some new material."

The medium of the string duo poses unique challenges to any composer. Lushness is really not an option; duos are stark practically by definition. Multiple stopping (playing simultaneous notes on more than one string) can stretch the texture of the string instruments, but one might argue that to compose a duo that duplicates the texture of a trio or a quartet is to miss the very point of writing a duo. Only in the climax of the second movement does Ravel make great use of multiple stopping; elsewhere he pursues the method he described in his biographical sketch, stressing melodic lines over full harmonic textures.

Although Ravel composed the first movement as a tribute to Debussy, he did not try to mimic that composer. In fact, the unusual tautness of its tone might be taken to reflect Ravel's occasional complaint that Debussy was too frequently lax in formal matters. From the opening measures Ravel explores the conflict between the intervals of the major and minor third, suggesting some arcane modality; this, along with a melodic emphasis on the wide interval of the major seventh, becomes a distinctive sound of the entire piece. Ravel also unifies his composition through the technique of cyclic thematic unrolling, another quintessentially French preoccupation. In this work, two themes from the opening *Allegro* resurface in each of the following movements, though markedly transformed and developed through new tempos, meters, instrumental timbres, or other means.

The scherzo (*Très vif*) comes next, launched by a vigorous interchange of pizzicato notes between the two parts. Ravel soon begins contrasting pizzicato notes with bowed ones (including, as we have already mentioned, some imposing chords achieved through multiple stopping) and injects further energy through the use of spiccato, with the players bouncing their bows on the strings to yield nimble attacks. This is a quicksilver but complicated little movement. The rhythm grows complex as duple-time measures are interpolated into the overriding triple meter, and the harmonic language is proudly bitonal; for several sections, Ravel even attaches different key signatures to the violin and cello parts.

The third movement (*Lent*) is as close as this piece gets to the spirit of elegy, though in the middle the music builds to an anguished *fortissimo* underpinning the players' widely disjunct melodies. The finale (*Vif, avec entrain*—that is, "Fast, with hearty spirit") is a brilliant romp with more than a bit of Stravinskian bite, although the composer said at one point that here he was imitating a rondo by Mozart. (Specifically the Rondo finale of Mozart's F-major Sonata for Piano Four-Hands, K. 497, Roland-Manuel would add.) Duple and triple meters again alternate to keep the ear ever alert; a dissonant fugato passage cleverly caps off the contrapuntal writing that pervades the piece; and the melodic writing is so audacious that Ravel even works in a nine-tone row, which is probably as close as he ever got to writing a twelve-tone row. After all this overt modernism, who could anticipate the work's final sonority, a completely consonant C-major chord?

When the piece was premiered in its four-movement entirety, in 1922, it was presented under the title Duo for Violin and Cello; only when it was published later the same year was it rechristened Sonata, perhaps a nod to the sense of large scale that it conveys in performance. It was received uneasily at its first performance. Most listeners were shocked by a harshness they had not previously associated with the composer. Ravel could handle the criticism. To his dear friend Cipa Godebski he wrote: "I hear that you did not care for my Sonata for violin and cello and that you had the courage to say so. I am very glad to hear it, because that proves, as indeed I already suspected, that it's not only for reasons of friendship or snobbery that you like my works. And I much prefer this spontaneous impression to that of the good lady who, after congratulating me on my 'modesty,' found my work 'original' and 'witty'—which is exactly what she said about my Trio."

Steve (Stephen Michael) Reich

Born: October 3, 1936, in New York City

Different Trains (interviews), for String Quartet and Tape

I *America—Before the War*
II *Europe—During the War*
III *After the War*
(*The movements are played without break*)

Work composed: 1988, commissioned by Betty Freeman

Work premiered: November 2, 1988, at the Queen Elizabeth Hall at the South Bank Centre in London, by the Kronos Quartet

Instrumentation: Two violins, viola, and cello, all amplified, plus a pre-recorded two-track stereo CD

C oncert music reached something of an impasse in the 1950s and 1960s. The dominant current of music's mainstream adhered to some take or another on serialism—a manipulation of tones according to a rigorous, sometimes mathematical, balance—and the traditional harmonic processes of tonality were very much on the outs among composers who claimed sophistication. General audiences often felt baffled and alienated, and the divide between the intellectual aspirations of composers and the interests of a large body of listeners was growing wider.

In the late 1960s a new way of making and hearing music burst onto the scene, a style that was dubbed Minimalism. Four Americans, born within eighteen months of each other in 1937–38, emerged as the leading voices of classic Minimalism: La Monte Young, Terry Riley, Steve Reich, and Philip Glass. The materials of Minimalist music were reduced to bare essentials, and its composers reveled in doing much with little—as opposed to the champions of complexity, some of whom fell into the trap of doing little with much. Early Minimalism typically involved pulsating rhythmic and/or melodic repetition that transformed very gradually over a long time frame through small incremental changes; or, alternatively, their individual sounds might themselves be sustained far longer than the ear was accustomed to. In either case, the effect could be at once static and energized, its sounds vivid and eminently apprehensible.

Of the four pioneer Minimalists, Steve Reich has traveled the furthest. His training included work with the composers William Bergsma and Vincent Persichetti at the Juilliard School and with Luciano Berio and Darius Milhaud at Mills College, and he went on to study African drumming in Ghana, Balinese gamelan in Indonesia, and Hebrew cantillation in Israel. Since he was a trained percussionist, it seemed natural that his early Minimalist works should emphasize minute gradations of rhythmic dissonance, which he achieved particularly by having identical musical lines move gradually in and out of phase.

His parents divorced when he was an infant, and, as a youngster, he found himself shuttling on transcontinental trains back and forth between the two of them, the father in New York, the mother in Los Angeles. His governess accompanied him on these trips, which took place from 1939 to 1942. Years later, he was struck by how dissimilar his excursions were from train trips taking place at the same time in Europe by unwilling passengers being transported in boxcars to concentration camps. As he wrote in 1988, "I now look back and think that, if I had been in Europe during this period, as a Jew I would have had to ride very different trains." The conflict of these circumstances became the engine for the work that he accordingly titled *Different Trains*.

The production and coordination of this piece is complex. The performers are a standard string quartet, each instrument being amplified. They play against a pre-recorded soundtrack—which the work's publisher makes available for performances—in which one track is given over to the sounds of three further string quartets and the other to snippets of spoken conversation. Reich emphasizes in the published score: "*There should be no ambiguity as to what is pre-recorded and what is live. The live players have the main parts throughout the piece and should be clearly heard.*" Great responsibility lies on the shoulders of the sound technician, who controls the balances.

When first published, the three movements of this work were identified only by Roman numerals, but the composer later attached more descriptive headings. The three movements are of roughly similar length, ranging from about seven and a half minutes (the second movement) to ten minutes (the third movement); the tempos and performance time obviously cannot vary from performance to performance, given the defined nature of the pre-recorded material. (Surely no tempo marking has ever been more precise than in the first movement: "♩ = 94.2.") In the opening movement ("America—Before the War"), the words are taken from interviews Reich conducted with his governess and with a Pullman porter who used to work on the route he rode. In the second movement ("Europe—During the War"), the voices are those of three Holocaust survivors who had ridden trains to Nazi concentration camps, their words drawn from historical archives. All of the voices appear in the final movement ("After the War").

The music of the string quartet, and of the pre-recorded quartets, is developed out of the spoken texts, which are fragmented and reassembled through electronic sampling. The rhythms and inflections of the statements are doubled, then mimicked, then developed by the instruments, with the viola corresponding at first to the voices of women, cello to the voices of men. Although, on a strictly musical level, the words serve as cells of rhythm and pitch, we must nonetheless remain alert to the import of what these people are saying. On top of everything Reich superimposes the pre-recorded sounds of train whistles and sirens; these are specific to the topics of the movements, with the American trains emitting a luxurious moan in comparison to the spiky blasts of the ones in wartime Europe.

The first movement grows hypnotic, sometimes pleasantly monotonous, as the listener is lulled by the rumbling and swaying of the locomotive, its rhythm persisting unchanged for long stretches. The voices reminisce in a tone of admiring nostalgia: "one of the fastest trains," "from New York to Los Angeles," "1939," "1940," "1941, I guess it must've been." In contrast, the second movement is frenetic; its underlying tempo is not very much faster—trains are trains—but the European-accented voices are filled with anxiety: "and he pointed right at me," "into those cattle wagons," "They tattooed a number on our arm."

The pace actually increases slightly in the last movement, where the voices of the first movement return to mingle with those of the Holocaust survivors: "and the war was over," "going to America," "from New York to Los Angeles." One of the Europeans asks, "Are you sure?"; and another voice responds "the war is over." The inflection of the second suggests finality, if perhaps not enough to erase the ascending question of the first. "But today, they're all gone," says the Pullman porter. Although we know he's speaking of the passenger trains that once flashed across the American landscape, we have been transformed in the course of this piece, and we cannot help thinking of the millions of hapless victims of war who are also "all gone."

The Holocaust, that endless source of the unimaginable, is brought very near to us in this piece, but so are aspects of the era that preceded it and the one that came after. *Different Trains* courses on, its rhythms mechanical. It follows the flow of time, which will not be interrupted by even the most momentous of events.

Silvestre Revueltas (signature)

Silvestre Revueltas Sánchez

Born: December 31, 1899, in Santiago Papasquiaro, Durango, Mexico

Died: October 5, 1940, in Mexico City, Mexico

Música de Feria ("Music of the Fair")

Allegro—Vivo—Lento—Allegro—Presto

Work composed: Completed March 25, 1932

Work dedicated: To Dr. Manuel Guevara Oropeza

Work premiered: November 7, 1933, at the Teatro Hidalgo in Mexico City, by the Cuarteto Clásico Nacional (violinists Ezequiel Sierra and David Saloma, violist David Elizarrarás, and cellist Teófilo Ariza)

Instrumentation: Two violins, viola, and cello

Silvestre Revueltas entered the world at the dawn of the twentieth century—literally, since he was born on the very last day of 1899—and in his short, messy life of only four decades he staked an essential place in the currents of Modernism that were then emerging in his country. Mexico was enduring growing pains. A popular uprising in 1910 marked the beginning of the Mexican Revolution. After dragging on for a chaotic and blood-drenched decade, it officially ended in 1920, when the four-year presidency of Álvaro Obregón initiated an era friendly to educational and artistic advances. The most visible flowering of a stabilized Mexico was the movement known as the Mexican School of Painting, with its star participants Diego Rivera, José Clemente Orozco, and David Alfaro Siqueiros.

This was the rapidly evolving nation in which Revueltas grew up, the oldest of twelve siblings who included several artistic achievers. By 1917,

Mexican schools were in such disarray that his father sent him to study in the United States, along with his brother Fermín (who became a noted painter, though he lived only to the age of thirty-five). For much of his life Silvestre Revueltas would shuffle back and forth between the United States and Mexico; in that sense he personally encapsulated the spirit of Pan-Americanism that was much championed by his friend Aaron Copland. In Chicago his violin studies included stints with two notable musicians from Central Europe, Paweł Kochański and Otakar Ševčík. Under their guidance he grew into a very accomplished performer, and when he was in Mexico he would often play solo recitals in halls newly decorated by the popular Mexican muralists. In 1924 he met Carlos Chávez, and Revueltas became a leading interpreter at the concerts of new music Chávez began producing in Mexico City, concerts that introduced the nation to important scores by Debussy, Schoenberg, Varèse, Milhaud, and Hindemith, among others. Wrote Revueltas of this sudden infusion of radical music in the concert scene, "Under the circumstances the reaction was violent, and we met with taunts, hisses, protests, insults, and the angry indignation of a public long-ensconced and of the same old critics." In the mid-1930s, he and Chávez had a falling out, the reason for which remains a subject of speculation. To this day both have their partisans to argue in favor of each one's standing as Mexico's greatest composer.

Not much time remained for Revueltas. He filled it intensely with work, composing compulsively while continuing his teaching and conducting, and he grew increasingly involved in political concerns. His end arrived in poignant circumstance. On October 4, 1940, his ballet *El renacuajo paseador* ("The Strolling Tadpole"), which he had composed in 1933, received its belated premiere at the Palacio de Bellas Artes in Mexico City. Rather than attend the premiere Revueltas, who had been going through one of his inebriated phases, spent the evening downing beers in his apartment and eventually headed out dressed less warmly than the weather merited. By the time he staggered back home he was already suffering from an acute attack of bronchial pneumonia, and he was transported to a hospital barely in time to die. The poet Octavio Paz, writing in the magazine *Taller* in 1941, was among the cultural luminaries who paid tribute to him: "He had found the mysterious point where art and life touch and enrich each other, the taut nerve of creation.... All his music seems preceded by something that is not happiness, as some believe, nor satire nor irony, as others think. This element... is his joyful empathy for people, animals, and things. It is this empathy that makes the significance of the works of this man—so naked, so defenseless, so wounded by heaven and mankind—surpass in significance a great part of contemporary music."

His modestly sized catalogue includes about a dozen works of chamber music. His overall output is quite impressive given that it represents only about ten years of work—work that coincided with full schedules of teaching, travel, and political activism, not to mention periods seriously impacted by his alcoholism and even, beginning in 1936, sporadic confinement to a psychiatric hospital.

He wrote his First String Quartet in 1930 and dedicated it to Chávez. His Second and Third followed the ensuing year, as did *Música de Feria*. All of them bristle with the rhythmic point of the Modernist scores he championed as a performer. The Second, subtitled *Magueyes*, sounds especially rich in regional flavor; the composer allowed that it could be considered "a Mexican sketch, but without overstepping into the area of the folkloric." "More like a fantasy," he continued. "At its base is a fragment of a folksong. It displays nothing of the folkloric, neither in a serious nor a transcendental way." That's not entirely clear, is it? Perhaps that has something to do with the title: *magueyes* are the agave plants from which is derived tequila.

Whereas the first three quartets are multimovement works, Revueltas' final work for this medium is cast much more tightly in a single movement running only eight or nine minutes. Nowhere on the score is the piece actually called a string quartet, and it is probably just as well not to refer to it as his String Quartet No. 4, although it is effectively that. Its title is *Música de Feria*, which the publisher translates as "Music of the Fair." In this vibrant music it is hard not to imagine the cheerful chaos that regularly surrounds Mexican markets; ramp it up to a "fair," suggesting a commercial gathering of more special occasion, and the effect reaches an even higher pitch of excitement and exhilaration. Further words from Octavio Paz' tribute seem especially pertinent to this piece: "The name of Silvestre Revueltas resounds within me like a great flash of light, like a sharp arrow that scatters into feathers and sounds, into lights, colors, birds, wisps of smoke, to crash against the naked heart of heaven. It was like the flavor of the village, of the people themselves, when 'people' refers to community and not to mere multitude. It was like a village festival: the church bombarded by fireworks, rendered silver by the cascade of shining water, fortress both blunt and innocent...the magical garden, with its fountain and its kiosk filled with heroic music sour and out of tune...and the peanuts, in pyramids, next to the oranges...."

Though the primacy of melody is never doubted in this work, the four instruments are equally deployed throughout, their constantly shifting rhythms suggesting the buzzing activity of Mexican public celebration. The score covers 296 measures, during which the meter signature changes more than a hundred times, at several points in every successive measure. Phrases of folkish songs or dances drift in and out as the listener is escorted through the colorful opening scene. The tempo breaks: the first violin whistles in harmonics and then leads the ensemble in a wistful, swaying melody. (Is this a love scene, or only a siesta?) The *Allegro* returns, again busy with scurrying sixteenth-notes and ever-shifting cross-rhythms; the effect is Bartókian. The pages of the fast sections are dense with notes and practically devoid of rests: the fair is constantly abuzz. After it bustles on for a while, Revueltas suddenly draws the curtain on this evocative scene with a pair of highly seasoned bitonal chords.

Charles Camille Saint-Saëns

Born: October 9, 1835, in Paris, France

Died: December 16, 1921, in Algiers, Algeria

Septet in E-flat major for Two Violins, Viola, Cello, Double Bass, Trumpet, and Piano, Op. 65

Préambule: Allegro moderato
Menuet: Tempo di minuetto moderato
Intermède: Andante
Gavotte et Finale: Allegro non troppo

Work composed: The *Préambule* in December 1879, the remainder in December 1880

Work dedicated: To Émile Lemoine

Work premiered: The *Préambule* was performed independently on January 6, 1880, by the La Trompette concert society in Paris (the composer serving as pianist), and the complete work on December 28, 1880, under the auspices of the same.

Instrumentation: Two violins, viola, cello, double bass, trumpet, and piano

Monsieur Saint-Saëns possesses one of the most astonishing musical organizations I know of. He is a musician armed with every weapon. He is a master of his craft as no one else is.... He plays, and plays with the orchestra as he does the piano. One can say no more." So remarked the composer Charles Gounod of his fellow French composer, and in marveling over his talents, Gounod might have noted that Saint-Saëns was also a highly accomplished organist (who for two decades ruled over the loft at the Madeleine), a champion of forgotten earlier music and of contemporary composers, an inspiring teacher, a gifted writer, a world traveler, and an avid and informed aficionado of such disciplines as Classical languages, astronomy, archaeology, philosophy, and even the occult sciences.

He was one of the most precocious geniuses in the history of music. When he was ten, he played his formal debut recital at Paris's Salle Pleyel, a program that included piano concertos by Mozart and Beethoven. The applause was resounding, so he topped off the event by offering to play any of Beethoven's piano sonatas from memory, as an encore. "He knows everything, but lacks inexperience," lamented his friend Hector Berlioz. He lived to the advanced age of eighty-six, and although some viewed him as a curious relic of antiquity, listeners with open ears could hardly overlook that his style continued to develop practically until the day he died, while on vacation in Algiers. He left no musical genre untouched. Opera, oratorio, theatre music, ballet, choral works, songs, symphonies, concertos, symphonic poems, band compositions, piano music, organ works, chamber music—they all boast notable entries in his catalogue, and he even became the very first composer to write a film score, to accompany a silent movie made in 1908.

In 1860 the violist Émile Lemoine founded a Parisian music society called La Trompette ("The Trumpet"). Its mission was to present a varied scope of chamber music. Saint-Saëns began appearing as pianist with the group in 1875, and at some point Lemoine started pestering him to write a chamber work that included a trumpet part along with the more usual instruments, out of deference to the group's name. The composer insisted that he would sooner write "a piece for guitar and 13 trombones." Nonetheless, he eventually did come around to the idea of the trumpet-centered chamber piece, which today stands as a curiosity of instrumentation that balances its forces with far greater success than one might anticipate. Portions of this appealing and entertaining work rank high on the scale of musical humor.

The *Préambule* is sprung from the ancient French tradition of prelude improvisation: a bit of this, a bit of that, all strung together into a fanciful curtain-raiser. It opens with a great flourish of unison scales, leading to the trumpet's entrance on a sustained note. Ideas follow rapidly, and none are developed at length: a touch of imitative counterpoint, cadenza-like piano figuration, a harmonic progression of book-learned Classicism, a hysterical fugato, a spacious "development-style" passage, and so on.

The *Menuet* refers to some of the *Préambule's* material but mostly proceeds according to its own ideas. The central trio is a gem of light lyricism in which the piano embroiders the strings' melody with a filigree of decoration. The cello intones the main theme of the relatively serious *Intermède*, an idea immediately taken up in succession by the viola, the violins, and the trumpet, all against a recurrent rhythmic figure in the piano. The movement's overall effect is rather Schumannesque, devolving into a curious coda that sounds like a transition to something but instead ends with a full stop. The *Finale* is a rollicking dance movement, perhaps something the late nineteenth century would have thought of as Handelian. Again, Saint-Saëns keeps the listener alert: one moment, the pianist plays bravura material that might be drawn from one of the composer's fleet-fingered piano concertos, and before you know it, he's trying out another fugue. The trumpet joins in for a final go-round with its colleagues, bringing everything to a broadly smiling conclusion.

Hugo Wolf, reviewing a performance of this work in Vienna on January 1, 1887, found the composition entirely enjoyable: "What was most engaging about this piece, distinguished by its skillful exploitation of the trumpet, was its brevity. A bit longer, and it would be a bore. This shrewd moderation and pithiness is admirable, and absolutely not to be underestimated. How many a German composer might envy Saint-Saëns this virtue!" Near the end of Saint-Saëns' life, the members of the Académie des Beaux Arts in Paris threw a huge celebration to honor their fellow Academician. That glittering event marked the last time he would appear in public as a pianist. The piece performed on that final occasion was none other than this Septet.

Arnold (Franz Walter) Schoenberg

Born: September 13, 1874, in Vienna, Austria

Died: July 13, 1951, in Los Angeles, California

Name: He was given the name Arnold Franz Walter Schönberg at birth and used that German spelling into the 1930s; once he moved to America, however, he converted to the spelling "Schoenberg," which is normally used today in English-speaking lands.

Verklärte Nacht ("Transfigured Night"), Op. 4

Work composed: September through December 1, 1899

Work premiered: March 18, 1902, in Vienna's Kleine Musikvereinssaal, by the Rosé String Quartet, with two colleagues from the Court Opera Orchestra, Franz Jelinek (second viola) and Franz Schmidt (second cello). The concert program's face-page identified the work as *Sextet nach Richard Dehmels Gedicht "Die verklärte Nacht"* ("Sextet after Richard Dehmal's poem 'The Transfigured Night'")

Instrumentation: Two violins, two violas, and two cellos

With *Verklärte Nacht* the twenty-five-year-old Arnold Schoenberg essayed a somewhat novel idea. Although tone poems were already widely represented in the symphonic repertoire, this was one of the first times that a composer tried to depict a detailed literary program through chamber music. Schoenberg's inspiration was the poem "Verklärte Nacht" by the German writer Richard Dehmel (1863–1920), published in the poet's 1896 collection, *Weib und Welt* ("Woman and World").

The poem, which was printed as a sort of preface in the original edition of Schoenberg's score (but was not supplied to the audience at the premiere), is an emotionally simmering, poignant text, of which this is the general plot: In a moonlit forest walk a man and a woman who are in love. She tells the man that before she met him, consumed with hopelessness and desiring a baby, she had an affair with another man; she is now ashamed to find herself carrying their child. But her new lover invokes the moonlight that bathes the universe, mirrors his love, binds them together, and will transform the baby into their own child.

Echoing the method of a classic tone poem, Schoenberg casts *Verklärte Nacht* in a single large span, with discrete sections corresponding to the events in the poem. His student Egon Wellesz was the first to propose that the piece be considered as a five-section structure, although later commentators have added personalized spins when interpreting the construction. As Wellesz saw it: "the first, third, and fifth [sections] are of more epic nature and so portray the deep feelings of the people wandering about in the cold moonlit night. The second contains the passionate plaint of the woman, the fourth the sustained answer of the man, which shows much depth and warmth of understanding."

At the opening we hear the sadness of the couple as they walk—*sehr langsam* ("very slowly")—through the moonlit forest, their steps depicted by the trudging repeated notes of the second viola and second cello: unison low Ds, then soon an ascending scale figure. Their gentle melancholy is evident in the D-minor theme—*immer leise* ("always gently") and *pianissimo*—of mournful, descending scale fragments intoned through four measures by the first viola and first cello and then taken up also by the violins.

The tempo becomes more animated—*etwas bewegter* ("with somewhat more motion")—with a new theme offered initially in the first viola, and then taken up successively by second violin, first violin, and first cello. The couple continues to walk, perhaps up a hill, since the repeated notes now turn into ascending scale patterns, played in tremolos. The characters stop—the bass line disappears for several measures—and the woman grows agitated as she reveals her secret; second cello drops out for several measures as she begins, while first violin and first viola sing high in their tessituras, mostly *pianissimo* but at one point swelling in an impassioned wail to touch *forte* for the briefest moment. As the couple strolls on, the man apparently digesting the information, the "walking" pattern of the opening returns, sometimes quivering with agitated tremolos. The music builds toward a climactic outpouring of emotion, after which Schoenberg releases a passionate, tender melody in suddenly luminous E major, played by the upper strings over a bass line so slow to change that it might be considered a series of pedal points. But the sense of comfort proves short-lived, and nervous anguish takes over again.

A stately, noble D-major section, *Sehr breit und langsam* ("very broadly and slow"), beginning *forte*, is surely meant to evoke the man's generous, loving response. The pain that had characterized the piece earlier is now banished, and rapturous passion infuses what remains. The transfiguration finds its musical reflection when, near the end, Schoenberg reassigns the descending motif from the opening to the high strings, most prominently to the first violin. They bring the work to a peaceful conclusion by intoning the music in their top register, against gentle rustlings in the other instruments. That this takes place over an extended pedal point on low D clarifies that when Schoenberg wrote *Verklärte Nacht* he was still attached to the idea that a piece should be anchored by a tonic note; that his excursions from that center have been so audacious alerts us that his thoughts could soon head to other possibilities of tonal organization.

String Quartet No. 2 in F-sharp minor, Op. 10

> I.
> II.
> III. *Litanei* (*Stefan George*)
> IV. *Entrückung* (*Stefan George*)

Work composed: Spring and summer of 1908, with sketches begun the year before

Work dedicated: To "Meiner Frau," that is, to the composer's first wife, Mathilde

Work premiered: December 21, 1908, at the Bösendorfer Hall in Vienna, by the Rosé String Quartet with the soprano Marie Gutheil-Schoder

Instrumentation: Two violins, viola, and cello, plus soprano singer

Though it does not yet reflect the dodecaphony that has proved impervious to broad popularity, Schoenberg's String Quartet No. 2 nonetheless makes many listeners uncomfortable. It might be viewed as a summation of the spirit of its time and place: Vienna, the proud capital of the European musical mainstream at the turn of the twentieth century, when harmonic development stood on the brink of breakdown, when centuries of accepted musical order seemed poised to crash into some other world that could not quite yet be imagined.

In his String Quartet No. 2, Schoenberg took the plunge. Its first three movements represent the last time the composer would adhere to a key as it is traditionally understood. The first is clearly grounded (and notated with three sharps) in the key of F-sharp minor, which is the key that is assigned to identify the quartet as a whole. The second movement has something to do with D minor, and the third gravitates toward E-flat minor. With the fourth movement, Schoenberg steps into the breach, banishing key signatures forever and writing in a highly chromatic, pan-tonal style in which no single note is granted a priori precedence over any other. But even here, pitches are not completely separated from structural concerns. "In the third and fourth movements," the composer later wrote, "the key is presented distinctly at all main dividing points of the formal organization. Yet the overwhelming multitude of dissonances cannot be balanced any longer by occasional returns to such tonal triads as represent a key. It seemed inadequate to force a movement into the Procrustean bed of tonality without supporting it by harmonic progressions that pertain to it. This was my concern, and it should have occupied the mind of all my contemporaries also."

The critic Ludwig Karpath was on hand for the quartet's premiere, which took place in Vienna on December 21, 1908. Two weeks later, in the magazine *Signale für die Musikalische Welt*, he published a review so breathtaking in its indictment that it bears quoting as an indicator of the confusion that greeted Schoenberg's revolution:

> I shall restrict myself to the statement that it developed into such an unholy scandal as had never happened before in a Vienna concert hall. All through the individual movements there was sustained and riotous laughter and, in the middle of the final movement, people shouted with all their might, "Stop!" "We've had enough!" "Don't try to make fools of us!" I must regretfully confess that I also found myself compelled to utter such cries for the first time in my twenty years of professional experience. Most certainly, a critic is beholden not to express his displeasure in a concert hall. If I nevertheless found it impossible to restrain myself, I merely state as evidence that I was suffering physical pain, and despite all my best intentions to overcome even the very worst, was in such severe torment that I simply could not help crying out.

Looking back on the event nearly three decades later, Schoenberg allowed: "Although there were … some personal enemies of mine, who used the occasion to annoy me … [,] I have to admit, that these riots were justified without the hatred of my enemies, because they were a natural reaction of a conservatively educated audience to a new kind of music."

The quartet's opening movement, structured along the lines of traditional sonata forms, is filled with questing neuroticism. A clue about Schoenberg's mind-set at the time is embedded in the prominent rhythmic motif of the opening theme; presumably it transcribes the pattern that Schoenberg's wife, Mathilde, always used when she whistled to attract the composer's attention from a distance. Mathilde, however, had just then embarked on an affair with the painter Richard Gerstl, which led to her separation from her astonished husband. The memory of her whistled signal would have inspired anguish rather than joy. They later reconciled, and Schoenberg dedicated the quartet to her. (Before the year was out Gerstl committed suicide in a fashion most grisly: having created a series of self-portraits that manifested escalating anguish, he destroyed all the artworks in his studio, stabbed himself in the chest, and then hanged himself before a mirror he had used when painting his self-portraits.)

The second movement, a scherzo-and-trio, develops the Expressionistic mood into a near panic. Suddenly, just before the juncture where the trio returns to the main scherzo section, the ensemble (beginning with the second violin) begins to banter about the old German song "Ach, du lieber Augustin, alles ist hin" ("Oh, my dear Augustine, it's all over now"), in juxtaposition with other thematic material. It could refer to Schoenberg's marriage, of course, or perhaps to tonality. It could be an intrusion of impudence. Or it could be a fleeting memory recaptured, much as Mahler—a composer adored by Schoenberg—had lit on "Frère Jacques" to fuel the third movement of his Symphony No. 1. In fact, "Ach, du lieber Augustin" had contributed to a potent memory of Mahler's. During his consultation with Dr. Sigmund Freud in 1910, he related how, as a boy, he had fled his house when a particularly violent scene occurred between his mother and his abusive father. "It became unbearable for the little one, and he ran away from home," recorded Freud. "But just at that moment the well-known Viennese song 'Ach du lieber Augustin' rang out from a hurdy-gurdy. Mahler thought that from this moment on, deep tragedy and superficial entertainment were tied together indissolubly in his soul and that one mood was inevitably tied to the other."

It seems oxymoronic for a string quartet to include more than four participants, but since Schoenberg was stretching the boundaries so far anyway, he had little compunction about including a soprano singer in the quartet's last two movements. In both, she sings poems from the collection *Die Siebente Ring* ("The Seventh Ring"), by Stefan George, a poet much admired by Schoenberg and his contemporaries in Vienna. The poem for the third movement, "Litanei" ("Litany"), expresses a yearning to be freed from the constraints that passion imposes; it's set as five variations with a coda, its theme being fundamentally derived from material already heard in the preceding movements. "Entrückung" ("Remoteness"), sung in the fourth movement, seems to describe an out-of-body experience as the soul soars off through "air of another planet," as the poem puts it. Schoenberg later wrote: "The visionary poet here foretold sensations which perhaps soon will be affirmed. Becoming relieved from gravitation—passing through clouds into thinner and thinner air, forgetting all the troubles of life on earth—that is attempted to be illustrated in [the movement's] introduction." This movement's up-in-the-air character is perfectly matched by the uprootedness of its highly extracted tonality, and it is all but impossible not to read these pages as marking Schoenberg's own musical leap to "another planet."

Franz Peter Schubert

Born: January 31, 1797, in Liechtenthal, then a suburb of Vienna, Austria, now incorporated into the city

Died: November 19, 1828, in Vienna

D numbers: The "D numbers" attached to Schubert's compositions relate to their entries in *Schubert: Thematic Catalogue of All His Works in Chronological Order*, published in 1951 by Otto Erich Deutsch

Quintet in A major, *Die Forelle* ("The Trout"), D. 667

Allegro vivace
Andante
Scherzo. Presto—Trio
Thema. Andantino—Variazioni I-V—Allegretto
Allegro giusto

Work composed: Begun during the summer of 1819 in Steyr, Upper Austria, and completed that fall in Vienna

Work premiered: Apparently late 1819 in Steyr

Instrumentation: Violin, viola, cello, double bass, and piano

In the summer of 1819, the twenty-two-year-old Franz Schubert went on a vacation with his close friend Johann Michael Vogl to Steyr in Upper Austria, a bit southeast of Linz, at the confluence of the rivers Steyr and Enns, a tributary of the Danube. Vogl, who was twenty-nine years Schubert's elder, had been born in that area and since 1794 had been a baritone at the

Court Opera in Vienna, where his distinctions included singing the role of Don Pizarro in the 1814 premiere of Beethoven's *Fidelio*. In the summers of 1819, 1823, and 1825 Schubert accompanied Vogl on vacations to Upper Austria, where the singer still enjoyed a circle of friends.

The composer would recall that summer as a serenely happy time, the days filled with hikes and picnics, the evenings with chamber music at the home of Sylvester Paumgartner, who was the assistant manager of iron mines in the region. Paumgartner was a great music lover, and he possessed a notable collection of musical scores and instruments. He also was an amateur cellist, though it was said that he didn't play very well. He held musical soirées at his home on the main square in Steyr, and Vogl sometimes stayed with him during his visits. Actually, Vogl and Schubert did not lodge with him during their 1819 trip, although they would on both of their later trips to town. In any case, during this first trip they spent many evenings making music at Paumgartner's home on the town square, a building that today is adorned with a historical marker identifying it as the site that gave rise to Schubert's *Trout* Quintet.

Paumgartner seems to have been particularly enamored of a quintet by Johann Nepomuk Hummel (actually a quintet arrangement of his D-minor Septet, Op. 74), the unusual instrumentation of which—violin, viola, cello, double bass, and piano—apparently coincided with the forces provided by his fellow musical aficionados in Steyr. Schubert leaped at Paumgartner's invitation to compose a companion piece and was delighted to accede to the only stipulation apart from the instrumentation: that the new work incorporate the melody of Paumgartner's favorite Schubert song, "Die Forelle" ("The Trout"), which had been written two years earlier and which tells the tale of a fisherman ensnaring a wriggling trout to an alarmed onlooker's distress. While still on vacation the composer set down some sketches for the resulting composition, forever known as the *Trout* Quintet, and he completed the piece immediately on his return to Vienna in September. In fact, the dating of this work is not a watertight matter since the documentary evidence concerning its genesis, which principally consists of a recollection penned by one of Schubert's friends forty years after the fact, could be taken to refer to any of the composer's three visits to Steyr. Even the manuscript of the *Trout* Quintet has gone missing. And yet there are compelling musical arguments that support connecting this work to the first of Schubert's Steyr vacations. Over the course of several years Schubert wrote out five versions of his song "Die Forelle," each differing in subtle details from the others, and the theme he uses in the *Trout* Quintet aligns most perfectly to a version of the song that he inscribed in 1818—which is to say, the most up-to-date version that existed in 1819, but not in 1823 or 1825. Then, too, the *Trout* Quintet displays certain distinctive features of structure and harmonic behavior, and even aspects of keyboard writing (such as the prevalence of using the piano as a melody instrument, the two hands doubling the same line an octave apart) that coincide with other pieces he composed in 1818 but that he was no longer employing in the 1820s.

Schubert's variations on "Die Forelle" are confined to the fourth of the quintet's five movements, but references to the song also appear in the bubbling arpeggios (usually ascending) that pervade the piano part in the song and that are to be found in every movement of the Quintet except the third. The Quintet is plotted rather after the fashion of a by-then-old-fashioned serenade, alternating fast movements with slower ones. The opening *Allegro vivace* takes off with a flourish—a grand chord from the ensemble and a rising "Trout" arpeggio from the piano. The action takes its time moving into full gear, but before long the viola and cello set up a pulse that provides a vigorous underpinning to Schubert's spacious melodies. Three leisurely tunes provide the stuff for the next movement, a liberally ornamented *Andante* that achieves a deeply Schubertian sense of melancholy; and, at the center of the work, the *Scherzo* positively bristles with energy derived from the upturned eyebrow of its initial four-note motif.

Next comes the set of six variations on the song's opening strain (or five variations plus a coda). The opening statement is reserved for the warm-voiced strings alone, and in the first three variations the piano, the viola and cello (as a pair), and the double bass stand out respectively. With the fourth variation, Schubert embarks on a more profound transformation of the melody; its blustery minor-key opening yields easily to major-key taming. In the fifth variation, the cello further adapts the theme into an emotional high point that encompasses concern and nostalgia. But these shadows are swept away by the final variation, where the piano finally sings forth with the leaping accompaniment that was original to the song. Again mirroring the simple good humor of a Haydnesque serenade, Schubert ends his quintet with an invigorating *Allegro giusto* finale, replete with references to the high-kicking "Hungarian Gypsy" style.

Paumgartner and his friends apparently played the work in Steyr at the end of 1819, and most likely they continued to bring it out from time to time for their own edification; but the piece was unknown to the outer world until after the composer's untimely death. In 1829, the publisher Joseph Czerny brought out the first edition of this much-loved chamber work. In an advertisement, he proclaimed confidently, "The quintet having already been performed in several circles at the publisher's instigation, and declared to be a masterpiece by the connoisseurs present, we deem it our duty to draw the musical public's attention to this latest work by the unforgettable composer."

Octet in F major, D. 803

Adagio—Allegro
Adagio
Allegro vivace—Trio
Andante und Variationen
Menuetto: Allegretto—Trio
Andante molto—Allegro

Work composed: February through March 1, 1824

Work premiered: Shortly after completion at a private concert at the home of Count Troyer, in Vienna; the first public performance was on April 16, 1827, at a Vienna Musikverein concert, probably played by Ignaz Schuppanzigh and Carl Holz (violins), Franz Weiss (viola), Joseph Linke (cello), Josef Melzer (double bass), Georg Klein (clarinet), August Mittag (bassoon), and Friedrich Hradezky (horn).

Instrumentation: Two violins, viola, cello, double bass, clarinet, bassoon, and horn

Franz Schubert idolized Beethoven, twenty-seven years his senior; but, though they both lived in Vienna and though Beethoven unquestionably knew of Schubert, there is no firm evidence that they ever met. Contemporary accounts differ, variously suggesting that Schubert paid a brief visit to Beethoven in 1822 (accompanied by the publisher Anton Diabelli), that he came with a group to salute the composer on his deathbed, or that after Beethoven's death Schubert expressed regret that he had never spoken to his great predecessor. At least there is no question that Schubert did serve as a torchbearer at Beethoven's burial at the Währing cemetery and that in 1888 the remains of both were moved to Vienna's Central Cemetery, where they have reposed next to each other ever since. Even if they escaped personal acquaintance while alive, the history of Schubert's Octet demonstrates how closely his work became intertwined with Beethoven's.

Beethoven's 1799 Septet for Strings and Winds (Op. 20) was enormously popular. Among its admirers was Count Ferdinand Troyer, an avocational clarinetist who served as a chamberlain to Beethoven's pupil and patron Archduke Rudolph. Troyer commissioned Schubert to compose a piece "exactly like Beethoven's Septet," which, in formal terms, Schubert did, completing his work on March 1, 1824. Both pieces have six movements in the same order, except that Beethoven's minuet-and-trio and scherzo-and-trio reverse their positions in Schubert. Schubert's instrumentation is essentially

Beethoven's—violin, viola, cello, double bass, clarinet, horn, bassoon—but with a second violin added. In deference to Troyer, Schubert sees to it that the clarinet enjoys a degree of prominence, as it had in Beethoven's Septet, though Schubert demands technical feats from the first violinist and horn player, too.

Schubert's Octet belongs to a period characterized by intense works, including his A-minor and D-minor String Quartets. But in contrast to their brooding darkness, the Octet seems good-natured—a reminder that musical compositions are not necessarily works of autobiography. A harmonically adventurous *Adagio* introduction of eighteen bars (exactly the same length as the introduction to Beethoven's Septet), gives way to an energetic *Allegro*. The clarinet comes to the fore in the second movement, a sublime *Adagio*; and the third movement, a scherzo (*Allegro vivace*) and trio, exudes a bluff bumptiousness.

The next two movements—a relaxed theme-and-variations and a minuet-and-trio—did not figure in the work's initial publication, but we would sorely miss them if they were excluded today. The genial theme of the five variations had begun life as a love duet in Schubert's 1815 singspiel *Die Freunde von Salamanka* ("The Friends from Salamanca"). Only in the introduction (*Andante molto*) of the sixth movement does Schubert inject a somber note; but the cello's nervous rumblings are completely erased by the grand sweep of the *Allegro* finale, even when the pace slows down midway to rest up for its ultra-energetic conclusion.

The Octet was performed at a private residence shortly after its completion, with Troyer playing the clarinet part. The string contingent included the quartet headed by Ignaz Schuppanzigh, the violinist who had championed Beethoven's quartets and who, as it happens, had played in the premiere of Beethoven's Septet. Schuppanzigh reassembled most of the players for a performance of the Octet for the Vienna Musikverein at the Red Hedgehog Inn's recital rooms at 4:30 in the afternoon of April 16, 1827—just two and a half weeks after Beethoven's death. At that public premiere it shared the bill with Beethoven's song cycle *An die ferne Geliebte* and an arrangement (for two pianos and string quartet) of Beethoven's *Emperor* Concerto. After that airing, the Vienna *Theaterzeitung* described the Octet as "commensurate with the author's talent, luminous, agreeable, and interesting; only it is possible that too great a claim may be made on the hearers' attention by its long duration." "If the themes do not fail to recall familiar ideas by some distant resemblances," the reviewer continued, probably alluding to Beethoven, "they are nevertheless worked out with individual originality, and Herr Schubert has proved himself...as a gallant and felicitous composer." Notwithstanding this praise the piece remained unpublished until 1853, twenty-five years after Schubert's death.

String Quartet in A minor, *Rosamunde*, D. 804

Allegro ma non troppo
Andante
Menuetto: Allegretto—Trio
Allegro moderato

Work composed: February and early March 1824

Work dedicated: To Ignaz Schuppanzigh

Work premiered: March 14, 1824, at Vienna's Musikverein, by the Schuppanzigh Quartet

Instrumentation: Two violins, viola, and cello

Schubert's experience of chamber music dated to his earliest years, when he played intimate works at home with his father and brothers. His principal instruments were the violin and the piano, but, like Mozart and Beethoven before him, he gravitated toward the viola part when playing string quartets. In the course of his short career he would compose fifteen string quartets (not counting lost or incomplete works), the first seven or eight of which he produced between 1812 and 1814, while he was a student at the Kaiserlich-königlich Stadtkonvikt (Imperial and Royal City College); some of these bear corrections in the hand of his composition teacher, Antonio Salieri.

While still in his mid-twenties, Schubert enjoyed a modicum of respect as a composer, though he was appreciated principally for his small-scale works, such as lieder and piano pieces, rather than the operas and symphonies he kept hoping would make a mark in musical Vienna. In truth, his career was propped up to a large extent by his adoring circle of artistically inclined friends, with the result that his works were performed frequently, but in modest surroundings, for a relatively small, repeat audience. In any case, his career certainly wasn't bringing in much money, and poor health only contributed to the unsteadiness of his situation. Late in 1822 he contracted syphilis, and within months he grew so ill that he required a lengthy hospitalization. His symptoms subsided somewhat, but he could have had no delusions about where the disease was likely to lead; the time between diagnosis and death rarely exceeded ten years. On March 31, 1824, he wrote to a friend: "In a word, I feel myself to be the most unhappy and wretched creature in the world. Imagine a man whose health will never be right again and who, in sheer despair over this, ever makes things worse and worse, instead of better; imagine a man, I say, whose most brilliant hopes have been perished, to whom the felicity of love and friendship have nothing to offer but pain."

Schubert's A-minor String Quartet (D. 804) received its public premiere on March 14, 1824—just two and a half weeks before the composer penned those desperate words—by a quartet led by the violinist Ignaz Schuppanzigh, Beethoven's portly, much-abused musical champion; it was his ensemble that had introduced many of that master's quartets, the most recent of which were appearing at about the same time. Schubert's friend Moritz von Schwind found that the quartet was "on the whole very gentle, but in the manner that one remembers the melody, as in songs, full of emotion and quite emphatic." To the extent that the press took note of the performance, its response was at least not out-and-out negative. Vienna's *Allgemeine musikalische Zeitung* suspended a verdict by declaring, "One will have to hear this composition on more than one occasion in order to be able to offer a thorough judgment of it," and the critic for Leipzig's similarly named, and famously conservative, *Allgemeine Musikalische Zeitung* allowed of the piece that "for a firstborn [it was] not to be despised." It was far from a firstborn of course, but it *was* the first of Schubert's string quartets to be played in public. In any case, the work had been born quickly: Schubert had begun working on it only in February or March of that year.

Immediately on this work's heels Schubert embarked on his D-minor Quartet (D. 810), but it was not premiered until almost two years later, on February 1, 1826. Schubert intended to write a third quartet as well, and to publish the three under a single opus number. Death interceded. In the event, the A-minor was the only one of all his string quartets published in his lifetime, and it appeared as his Op. 29, No. 1—curiously so, in retrospect, since there is no Op. 29, No. 2. Schubert would go on to write one further string quartet—in G major—after the D-minor, but that was separate from the triptych project he had fleetingly envisioned.

The A-minor Quartet derives its nickname (not bestowed by Schubert) from the fact that its second movement employs a theme from the incidental music he wrote for the much-reviled four-act play *Rosamunde, Fürstin von Zypern* ("Rosamunde, Princess of Cyprus"), by the very bad author Wilhelmine von Chézy. The play opened at the Theater an der Wien on December 20, 1823, and endured for only one further performance. But *Rosamunde* had one thing going for it: the ten selections (entr'actes, solos, choruses, even two ballet sequences, adding up to nearly an hour of music) that Schubert provided to help it along.

Schubert often allowed himself astonishing structural spaciousness, especially in his later works. In this regard, the A-minor Quartet is greatly reined in; the shortest of Schubert's three late quartets, it achieves a perfect balance of form and content. The first movement (*Allegro ma non troppo*) opens with an "accompanying" figure that evokes, but does not exactly quote, Schubert's famous lied "Gretchen am Spinnrade." Above this the first violin introduces the main theme, a lyric outpouring of surpassing sadness constructed out of a simple, descending minor triad, enhanced by a trill in the middle. A second theme provides real contrast only in its major tonality; again of a lyrical bent, it cannot be said to be an overly happy tune. In his development section, Schubert explores the pessimistic landscape of numerous minor keys, and the recapitulation includes a wealth of surprising modulations, its minor-key conclusion confirming the overall dolefulness of the movement.

Next comes the *Rosamunde* movement, which employs a tune from the third entr'acte, an *Andantino* in B-flat major that had marked the entrance of a shepherdess with her flock. Its wistful melody resurfaces not only in this quartet (in slightly altered form, and transposed to C major) but also in the composer's Impromptu in B-flat major for piano (D. 935). Here, the gentle melody alternates with tragic sections in a sort of large-scale rondo, and even a "yodeling" interlude shows not much peasant merriment. One listens in vain for the ensuing minuet to inject a lighter spirit. Again, the key of A minor reigns, and here it introduces music with a dispiriting extramusical reference. When Schubert composed the movement's principal theme, for his song "Die Götter Griechenland" ("The Gods of Greece"), it corresponded to Schiller's words "Schöne Welt, wo bist du?" ("Lovely world, where art thou?"). The cello seems at odds with the other instruments through most of this minuet, lending a further sensation of psychological dissonance to a movement of overriding eeriness. From von Schwind's account of the premiere, we learn that this work "received much applause, especially the minuet, which is extraordinarily delicate and natural." The finale hints at its outset that greater happiness may lie in store—or perhaps resignation or "acceptance of tragedy" would be a more accurate description. Its gracious ländler rhythms notwithstanding, this is music of tremendous poignancy, as positive a character as is perhaps appropriate for the conclusion of so serious a work.

String Quartet in D minor, *Der Tod und das Mädchen* ("Death and the Maiden"), D. 810

Allegro
Andante con moto
Scherzo: Allegro molto—Trio
Presto

Work composed: Completed in March 1824, probably revised in January 1826

Work premiered: February 1, 1826, at the Vienna home of Josef Barth; the first public performance took place posthumously on March 12, 1833, in Berlin at one of the so-called Musical Gatherings of Karl Möser.

Instrumentation: Two violins, viola, and cello

Schubert's A-minor Quartet had employed quotations from his *Rosamunde* music and his song "Die Götter Griechenland," as well as an allusion to his song "Gretchen am Spinnrade." In the D-minor he also quotes himself: its second movement is a set of variations on his song "Der Tod und das Mädchen" ("Death and the Maiden," to a text by Matthias Claudius), from 1817. The "Death and the Maiden" quotation all but forces interpreters and listeners to approach the D-minor Quartet as a morbid work, which may not have been Schubert's idea at all; he certainly never suggested it as a title for the composition as a whole. Nonetheless, the spacious first movement—nearly five hundred measures long—is an intense piece, and it gets off to a rousing start with the *fortissimo* proclamation of a motif that will dominate the opening movement: a shaking-of-the-fist that is the spiritual cousin of the opening of Beethoven's Fifth Symphony. Schubert's triplets pervade the entire first movement, even providing a nervous underpinning to the lyrical second theme.

In Claudius' poem for "Der Tod und das Mädchen," Death gently but firmly conveys to a young girl that her protestations will be of no avail and that he cannot be dissuaded from taking her with him. The theme Schubert uses in this quartet—a simple melody of few notes, never ranging far from the home base of the tonic G—is slightly modified from what the piano articulates in the introduction to the song. Here it provides the material for five strict variations of increasing intensity. Following a homophonic statement of the theme by all four instruments, the first variation moves the melody to the second violin, which plays it in throbbing triplets beneath a chirping descant from the first violin. The descant continues in the second variation, with the first violin now tracing octaves above the melody in the cello. A more homophonic texture again reigns over the ensuing, blustery variation. With the fourth variation everything grows suddenly quiet, even potently sentimental, as the first violin weaves major-mode "heartstring" music high above the rest of the ensemble. The fifth and final variation becomes ominous as the cello persists in playing an unvarying drone throughout the first half of the theme. A major-key run-through of the melody in the coda does little to dispel the overall sadness of this movement.

The *Scherzo* returns to the angry intensity of the opening movement, with some alleviation provided by the carefree leisure of the trio. (The Schubert biographer Brian Newbould cites the movement's opening measures as another example of self-quotation, the source in this case being one of the composer's German Dances, D. 790.) The finale is cast as a tarantella or saltarello, leading (by way of a Brahmsian "big statement" sort of chorale-theme, marked *con sforza*, "forcefully") to an exhausting, *prestissimo* close. Some commentators, building on the "Death and the Maiden" idea, view it as a *danse macabre*, a dance of the Grim Reaper. In the course of the movement the second violin articulates a seductive counter-melody from Schubert's "Erlkönig," another song about a young person ceding to Death-as-Friend. In this context, it may well be an intentional reference.

String Quartet in G major, D. 887

Allegro molto moderato
Andante un poco moto
Scherzo: Allegro vivace
Allegro assai

Work composed: June 20–30, 1826, in the Vienna suburb of Währing; those dates, which appear on the autograph, may not take into consideration earlier sketching.

Work premiered: March 7, 1827, at a private gathering, probably at the home of Schubert's composer-friend Franz Lachner, on which occasion three friends joined the composer, who played the viola part. The first movement is thought to have figured in a public all-Schubert concert at the hall of the Austrian Philharmonic Society in Vienna on March 26, 1828 (played by violinists Joseph Michael Böhm and Carl Holz, violist Franz Weiss, and cellist Joseph Linke), but the complete work was not played publicly until December 8, 1850, when the Hellmesberger Quartet performed it at a concert of the Philharmonic Society in Vienna.

Instrumentation: Two violins, viola, and cello

Schubert's D-minor String Quartet followed fast on the heels of the one in A minor, but after that more than two years passed before he would again approach this medium, in June 1826. The months preceding had not been happy ones for Schubert. Desperately in need of income, he had applied in April for the position of Second Court Kapellmeister; but the position would be abolished. To make matters worse, at about the time of this quartet, symptoms of Schubert's syphilis returned after a remission of a year and a half. He was having little success getting his major works into print. A letter from the publisher Heinrich Probst of Leipzig summed up the situation as gracefully as it could: "The public does not yet sufficiently and generally understand the peculiar, often ingenious, but perhaps now and then somewhat curious procedures of your mind's creations." Professionally and personally, Schubert was in a tough situation but he apparently tried not to let the situation get the better of him. An invitation to join a friend for a vacation in Gmunden met with this response from Schubert: "I cannot possibly get to Gmunden or anywhere else, for I have no money at all, and altogether things go very badly with me. I do not fret about it, and am cheerful!"

The G-major Quartet, the result of a ten-day flurry of work, is quite unlike any quartet Schubert had written before. Since it is his last quartet, we can only wonder to what extent its "somewhat curious procedures" signal the path that future Schubert quartets might have traced. Schubert's late quartets are coeval to Beethoven's late quartets; the G-major is an almost exact contemporary to Beethoven's final quartet (in F major, Op. 135). The differences are striking. Where Beethoven's late quartets fracture the time-honored layouts of movements, Schubert retains the standard four-movement form of the traditional quartet. Beethoven obsessed over counterpoint of the most abstract type and pushed variation techniques to previously unimagined complexity. Schubert, in contrast, was never so drawn to counterpoint as Beethoven was, and he is not overly concerned with it here; and his own interest in variation forms, which had contributed so importantly to his D-minor Quartet, seems to have evaporated by the time he embarked on this piece.

What Schubert does choose to explore in his G-major Quartet is the relationship between major and minor modes, an interest that informs both surface and structural behavior in this work. We hear this in the opening measures, where G-major chords erupt into G-minor chords; here the duality of the major-minor conflict, always an engine of Schubertian thoughts, is moved front and center. The musicologist Jack Westrup spoke of "Schubert's equation of major and minor" and described these measures as "a neutral opening, but one charged with great possibilities." Indeed, when Schubert reaches the recapitulation of this big-boned, discursive movement, he confirms that sense of "equating" major with minor by reversing the order in which those sonorities are heard. Schubert's treatment of sonority is also captivating in this opening movement. He seems to be thinking beyond the "normal" capacity of a string quartet, and near the end he actually has the four instruments employ multiple-stopping to the extent that they are sounding fifteen of their sixteen strings at the same moment.

In the elegiac *Andante* our composer explores other major-minor implications, now in the key of E minor. A friend reported that the melancholy principal melody of this second movement was derived from a Swedish song

Schubert had heard sung by a touring concert artist, but later scholars have pretty much agreed that the friend was wrong, and that she really meant to refer to Schubert's E-flat-major Piano Trio. Nonetheless, it would be easy to imagine the theme as a song—but, of course, one could say that of so many melodies Schubert devised for his instrumental works. Schubert characteristically does not allow his listeners to glide uninterrupted as the movement unrolls, instead interrupting its flow with passionate, even terrifying outbursts. The third-movement *Scherzo* lightens the emotional climate somewhat, particularly in the ländler-like expanses of its trio section, though even this can sound either bucolic or ghostly, depending on the performance.

In the bustling fourth movement, a sort of tarantella, Schubert plays with the implications in a different way. In the rondo theme of that finale we hear the descending minor triad first, expanded rhythmically into an arpeggio rather than as a single chord, and after that we are instantly confronted with the major mode, usually expanded into a scale. Schubert has therefore underscored his harmonic juxtaposition of G major and G minor by applying a new rhythmic framework, enlarging the telescoped single sonority of a chord to the more extended, but no less defined, tonality expressed by arpeggios and scales.

This dense and powerful work did nothing to help reverse Schubert's fortunes, although the Leipzig *Allgemeine musikalische Zeitung*, reporting the all-Schubert concert on March 26, 1828, at which the first movement of this quartet was probably premiered, mentioned that the new quartet movement was "full of spirit and originality." This was among the group of pieces that Schubert offered to the publisher Schott in February 1828, along with the *Death and the Maiden* Quartet, the F-minor Fantasia for Piano Four-Hands, one of his piano trios, the C-major Fantasia for Violin and Piano, the second set of piano impromptus, and a number of shorter works. Schott regretted that they couldn't find a place for these works in their catalogue. What were they thinking?

Piano Trio in B-flat major, D. 898

Allegro moderato
Andante un poco mosso
Scherzo: Allegro
Rondo: Allegro vivace

Notturno in E-flat major, D. 897

Works composed: Perhaps in October 1827

Works premiered: The Trio on January 28, 1828, in Vienna, in a private performance; it was published in 1836 by the Viennese firm of Diabelli, as Schubert's Op. 99. We lack early performance history about the Notturno.

Instrumentation: Violin, cello, and piano

Schubert wrote two piano trios, both of them intimate yet towering masterpieces, both summations of his music at its best, both created by a young composer who was only thirty years old, both the products of a genius who had little more than a year left to live. We know that Schubert's Piano Trio in E-flat major was completed in November 1827, since he inscribed that date on his manuscript. Dating its B-flat-major companion is trickier, but evidence suggests that it was composed immediately beforehand.

Schubert seems to have esteemed the E-flat-major work more highly, since he chose it to be the centerpiece of the only public all-Schubert concert to be held during his lifetime, in March 1828. It is a splendid piece, but it has come into a fair share of criticism for being overly luxurious in its length, and modern performances usually involve some judicious trimming. The B-flat-major Trio, on the other hand, comes across as more perfect in its proportions, although it, too, is leisurely, evolving over the course of some forty minutes. But what forty minutes they are! Nowhere does Schubert's melodic inspiration wear thin, and the work's structural felicities keep the alert listener perpetually engaged. Robert Schumann described it as "passive, lyrical, and feminine," as compared with the "more spirited, masculine, and dramatic tone" of the one in E-flat major. "One glance at Schubert's Trio," he continued of this piece, "and the troubles of our human existence disappear and all the world is fresh and bright again."

"Charming" is not always a compliment, but the B-flat-major Trio manages to be profoundly charming without ever descending to cheap nostalgia or kitsch. It is for such a piece that the Viennese press into service the word *gemütlich*, with its overtones of hearth and home, of unpretentious honesty, of unthreatening benevolence. The first movement opens with a positive, noble theme, played by the strings in octaves and propelled by upward bursts of notes. The cello, playing in its high register, introduces the spacious second melody to provide lyric contrast. As in the much earlier *Trout* Quintet, the piano often doubles its lines in the two hands when entrusted with melodic material. Formalists will take delight in Schubert's inventive manipulation of sonata form, especially when the recapitulation makes not one, not two, but three false starts in different "wrong keys" before finally plowing forward in the tonic B-flat.

The cello again takes responsibility for the songful, gently rocking utterance that opens the second movement, which (like the first) involves some "wrong-key" explorations toward its conclusion. This follows a brooding central section that simmers with unease, but not enough to derail the movement in that direction. This exquisite *Andante un poco mosso* came as an afterthought. Initially Schubert had written a dreamlike *Adagio* in which time seems to stop. The replacement movement holds up more strongly in the context, but the original *Adagio* continued in an independent life of its own as Schubert's Notturno in E-flat major (D. 897), that being the title assigned to it in 1845 by its posthumous publisher. Musicological research has confirmed that the paper on which it is written displays the same watermarks as other works from the period of the two piano trios, which helps cement its connection. That *Adagio*/Notturno has encountered some bad press through the years, dismissed as "justly neglected," "unfortunately long-winded," or "flaccid." I don't understand the objections. Of course Schubert is among the most rhapsodic of composers, and tight structures are rarely the point of his compositions. But a slow movement that lasts eight minutes (as the Notturno does) can hardly be taken to task for inordinate rambling, especially when it encapsulates such sublime material as this one does. Once heard, Schubert's Notturno is not soon forgotten. Strummed chords on the piano introduce a statement of the soft, elegiac theme played by the two string instruments; then the forces immediately trade places for the piano to repeat the theme against a pizzicato accompaniment by the strings. Time seems to have stopped for the first two minutes of the piece, and then the spell is interrupted by a vigorous variation, replete with rather haughty arpeggios in the piano. This winds down into a searching chromatic passage, which in turn leads to a second variation; now the principal theme is embellished only lightly by a much less effusive piano. Schubert further investigates these aspects of the movement's personality—the elegiac, the stentorian, the "well integrated," and the questing—until the piece fades away beneath the piano's embellishment of gentle trills.

Back to the B-flat-major Trio. Where the opening movement was built on rising phrases, the *Scherzo* plays with a falling motif, often injecting rhythmic displacements to humorous effect. The trio section is a spacious waltz, but its airy quality is blown away with the return of the *Scherzo's* whirlwind. Schubert calls his finale a *Rondo*, but it isn't a terribly strict one since the main theme undergoes considerable alteration when it returns periodically to punctuate the proceedings. The musicologist Alfred Einstein seems to have been the first to note that the rondo theme bears considerable resemblance to Schubert's song "Skolie," composed in 1815, a gather-ye-rosebuds sort of song that admonishes the listener to "take delight in the brief life of the flower before its fragrance disappears." Few works of Schubert's final fruition provide more poignant illustration of that sentiment.

Piano Trio in E-flat major, D. 929

Allegro moderato
Andante un poco mosso
Scherzo: Allegro
Rondo: Allegro vivace

Work composed: Autumn 1827, completed that November; it was published posthumously, in October 1828, by the Leipzig firm of Probst, as Schubert's Op. 100.

Work premiered: December 26, 1827, at the Musikverein in Vienna, by violinist Ignaz Schuppanzigh, cellist Joseph Linke, and pianist Carl Maria von Bocklet

Instrumentation: Violin, cello, and piano

Schubert's B-flat-major Piano Trio met with no immediate success, although its gracious, convivial spirit eventually won it the upper hand in popular affection. The more intellectual E-flat-major Piano Trio fared better when it was new, and the composer had the opportunity to hear it on at least two occasions, both times in the hall of Vienna's Musikverein played by the same group of musicians: violinist Ignaz Schuppanzigh (whose string quartet had done yeoman's service in ushering Beethoven's quartets onto the stage), cellist Joseph Linke (the cellist of Schuppanzigh's quartet), and pianist Carl Maria von Bocklet (to whom Schubert had dedicated his D-major Piano Sonata, D. 850, in 1825). Following the Trio's premiere, on December 26, 1827, the players revived it on March 26, 1828, as the centerpiece of the only public all-Schubert concert ever held during the composer's lifetime. Two weeks later, in a letter to the Leipzig publisher H. A. Probst, Schubert reported of the concert that the "trio for pianoforte, violin, and violoncello in particular found general approval, so much so, indeed, that I have been invited to give a second concert (rather as a repeat performance)." That encore performance seems not to have materialized, but at least Schubert had the opportunity to enjoy the fruits of his effort twice. What's more, it apparently became the only one of his pieces to be published outside Austria in his lifetime, since Probst released an edition in Leipzig in October 1828. Whether Schubert received a copy of the printing before his death is not known, but at the least he knew such a publication was imminent. He must have viewed it is an important advance in his career.

Schubert rarely gives the impression of being in a hurry, and, true to form, this trio unrolls over a very generous span of time, usually lasting more than forty minutes. The composer himself sensed that it could use some editing, and he effected a lengthy cut in the finale, the longest of the four movements, though this material was restored by the editors of the complete edition of Schubert's works. Elsewhere, passages are sometimes repeated wholesale or with rather little alteration. Despite its length, the E-flat-major Trio is clear in matters of form, and the recurrence of the second movement's theme at several points in the finale does much to convey a sense of overriding cohesiveness.

Within the individual movements, Schubert develops his material in a characteristically sectional manner, with the contrasting moods of different expanses clearly demarcated. The first movement is largely derived from the contours of the opening motif (proclaimed at the outset by all three instruments in unison), from a counter-statement (first by the cello), and from a gentler second theme (introduced by the two string instruments). The movement is cast in a more-or-less classic sonata form, though its working-out is spread over a vast landscape of competing tonalities and is characterized by an unrelenting sense of forward propulsion.

The slow movement is magical, sounding from the outset quite like a Schubert song in which the cello sings the melody against the grim staccato of the piano's accompaniment. In fact, the melody *is* that of a song, though not one by Schubert. His friend Leopold Sonnleithner said that the tune was taken from a Swedish song named "Se solen sjunker" ("The Sun Has Set"), which Schubert heard sung by the tenor Isaak Albert Berg in Vienna in 1827. Sonnleithner's report long remained the only record of the existence of "The Sun Has Set," which sank into total oblivion in the ensuing years. But in 1978 the musicologist Manfred Willfort rediscovered the old song and was therefore able to demonstrate that although Schubert did not quote the tune verbatim, he did draw substantial inspiration from it, in terms of both its melody and its slowly treading accompaniment. Schubert develops a second melody from a figure (highlighted by widely leaping pitches) embedded within the tune, and this not only gives rise to a contrasting section but also plays a role in the movement's emotionally distraught development.

After these two somewhat rhapsodic outpourings, Schubert is ready to tighten the score through the imposition of canon, one of music's most precise and unforgiving procedures. Some of the *Scherzo* is worked out in strict canon at the distance of a measure; in other places, Schubert allows himself the luxury of merely writing in close imitation that gives the impression of canon without actually being one (which is easier than "the real thing"). Compared to the gossamer lightness of this opening, the movement's trio section is startlingly gruff—a rude peasant dance interrupting a ballet of Biedermeier nymphs.

We have already mentioned that the finale is so vast—it covers nearly 750 measures in moderate tempo, lasting a good thirteen minutes in most performances—that Schubert himself thought it might well be shortened and suggested how it could be abbreviated. It begins so unpretentiously that the listener would never expect that something so substantial lies ahead. But, as the musicologist Jack Westrup observed, "Schubert's apparently innocent beginnings often turn out to be the signpost for a good deal of less innocent activity." The music ranges widely through the harmonic spectrum, spending almost no time in the home key of E-flat after the opening bit. We reach the development section, and suddenly, against a background of falling piano chords, the Swedish melody from the slow movement makes a return appearance in the cello. Further harmonic exploration ensues, and after several more minutes the cello's Swedish song resurfaces yet again, this time against the almost-tonic key of E-flat minor. Schubert effects a switch back to the major mode, placing us in the key that allows the movement to zero in on its conclusion. It does so with repetitive, swaggering, triumphant figures that put one in mind of a Rossini opera.

It remains only to cast a glance at a letter Schubert penned to the publisher Probst in Leipzig, on August 1, 1828, when he was getting worried about delays in the publication schedule. "I beg you to make sure that the edition is free from errors," he wrote. "This work will not be dedicated to any one person, but rather to all who find pleasure in it. That is the most profitable form of dedication."

String Quintet in C major, D. 956

> *Allegro ma non troppo*
> *Adagio*
> *Scherzo: Presto—Trio: Andante sostenuto*
> *Allegretto*

Work composed: September and perhaps early October 1828, while living at his brother's apartment in the Town of Ronsperg, in the suburbs of Vienna; when it was published, in 1853, it was assigned the opus number 163.

Work premiered: The first documented performance was on November 17, 1850, in Vienna, played by Joseph Hellmesberger's string quartet, assisted by the cellist Josef Stransky.

Instrumentation: Two violins, viola, and two cellos

"It is arguable," wrote Benjamin Britten in 1964, "that the richest and most productive eighteen months in our musical history is the time when

Beethoven had just died, when the other nineteenth-century giants, Wagner, Verdi, and Brahms had not begun; I mean the period in which Franz Schubert wrote his *Winterreise*, the C-major Symphony, his last three piano sonatas, the C-major Quintet, as well as a dozen other glorious pieces. The very creation of these works in that space of time seems hardly credible; but the standard of inspiration, of magic, is miraculous and past all explanation."

And yet one might argue that nowhere in this lineup do the special qualities of late Schubert—by which we mean, tragically, a Schubert just entering his fourth decade—come together more magically than in the String Quintet. This was his only effort in the genre (his *Trout* Quintet being for the very different ensemble of violin, viola, cello, double bass, and piano), and it is worth remarking that for his instrumentation Schubert turned here to the eighteenth-century precedent of Luigi Boccherini, who wrote more than a hundred quintets for string quartet with an extra cello, as opposed to the geographically closer models of Mozart and Beethoven, whose quintets (admired by Schubert) called for string quartet with an extra viola. We can't know exactly what informed Schubert's decision, but it lent an added air of profundity to the resulting work. Nonetheless, what is profound is not necessarily turgid; once Schubert settled on his instrumental combination he found imaginative ways to exploit its possibilities through intriguing pairings or other transparent subgroups within the ensemble as a whole.

A fine example comes at the very outset. Apparent simplicity: a C-major chord swelling from *piano* to *forte*, at which point it is transformed into an ambiguous and ominous diminished-seventh chord and then recedes back to *piano* before proceeding on and coming to rest on a G-major chord, the dominant, eerily high-pitched. But what is most striking, perhaps, is that in these opening measures Schubert employs only one of his two cellos; his quintet begins as a standard string quartet. Then, in the eleventh measure, he responds with a second phrase that essentially mirrors the first, though transposed to D minor; and only here does he finally move into the depths of the available ensemble, with the first violin sitting it out while the second violin (playing on its lowest string), viola, and the two cellos make a sound that contrasts starkly with the opening. A *pianissimo* figure is then batted back and forth for a couple of measures between two instrumental units: viola and two cellos on one hand, viola and two violins on the other—with the viola's double duty tricking the listener into imagining that a string sextet is at work. And so it goes in the kaleidoscopic texture of this subtle masterpiece of chamber music.

One must not be in a hurry when encountering late Schubert. Most of these supernal works take no pains to travel the direct route from here to there, but rather luxuriate in agreeable scenery where surprises lie around many bends of the road. Performances of the Quintet typically last between fifty minutes and an hour, and of the four movements only the last often clocks in at less than ten minutes. All the same, the Quintet sounds compact, never bloated or overlong, thanks to the constantly shifting trajectories of harmony, the surfeit of irresistible melodies, and the changing textures occasioned by the composer's ingenious scoring.

The opening movement is delicious, but most chamber music aficionados agree that the second movement, the *Adagio*, is the soul of this piece. Set in E major, it stands harmonically in a "thirds relationship" to the Quintet's overall tonic of C major. The same interval also informs the principal theme itself, which the second violin and the viola introduce harmonized in thirds, sometimes abetted by the first cello, while the second cello lays a foundation in soft pizzicatos and the first violin utters an overlay of gentle *pianissimo* chirps. But such a description doesn't begin to suggest the hovering beauty of this *Adagio*, a sublimity interrupted by a tortured middle section in F minor (a mere semitone above the movement's overall tonic) before transcendence reaffirms itself—with further elaborate decoration—at the end. The pianist Arthur Rubinstein, the cellist Alfredo Piatti, and the novelist Thomas Mann were among those who have expressed the desire that they might die while listening to this movement. I appreciate the sentiment, though I myself would prefer to stick around, if only to hear this piece one more time.

As ethereal as is the *Adagio*, so is the ensuing *Scherzo* vivacious and bumptious—manic, one might even say. Its opening is muscular, rather like proto-Brahms. The trio section (*Andante sostenuto*) bears the same harmonic relationship to what surrounds it as the F-minor section had to the E-major parts of the *Adagio*. Here the rise of a semitone moves us from C major to D-flat, this time retaining the major mode; the psychological lift is dramatic. The tempo relaxes drastically, and the chorale-like writing takes on somber, hymn-like overtones, after which the raucous *Scherzo* returns for another go-round.

This is not the last we will have heard of the push-and-pull of harmonic regions separated by a semitone. The forthright Hungarian and Austrian dance-tunes of the finale might lead us to believe that all will be clear sailing to the end; and indeed, much of the concluding movement basks in the sort of generous melody and spacious development we have come to expect of the composer. But in the last couple of pages Schubert escalates the intensity by accelerating the tempo (*Più allegro*), landing for a while in the minor mode, and peppering the score with accents. From there to the end an ambiguous spirit reigns, and in the final measures we hear a struggle between the notes C and D-flat—the semitone disparity that has been played out through the large structures of the preceding movements and that leaves us with the feeling that danger may lurk behind the trees even in the most pleasant of landscapes.

On October 2, 1828, Schubert wrote to a publisher (who declined to put out an edition of the piece) that "the quintet rehearsal will only begin in the next few days." We don't know if that rehearsal took place. If it did, it would likely have been the only time Schubert heard this piece. Little more than six weeks later he was dead at the age of thirty-one.

Clara Josephine Wieck Schumann

Born: September 13, 1819, in Leipzig, Saxony (Germany)

Died: May 20, 1896, in Frankfurt am Main, Germany

Surname: Schumann, following her marriage in 1840

Piano Trio in G minor, Op. 17

Allegro moderato
Scherzo: Tempo di Menuetto
Andante
Allegretto

Work composed: From May to September 12, 1846

Work dedicated: The published Trio carries no dedication, although the composer is reported to have planned to dedicate it to Fanny Mendelssohn Hensel, who died before it appeared.

Work premiered: January 15, 1847, in Vienna

Instrumentation: Violin, cello, and piano

The venerable Walter Willson Cobbett, writing in his classic *Cobbett's Cyclopedic Survey of Chamber Music* in 1929, provided the following commentary on Clara Schumann's Piano Trio, here quoted in its entirety:

This composition, in which Haydn's influence is felt, is of modest calibre, and its interest for us Londoners lies in the fact that it proceeds from the pen of a chamber music player who delighted audiences at the "Pops" during many weeks of each season for a series of years by her poetic interpretations of classical works by the great masters, especially those written by her husband. Such an example of allied greatness in husband and wife is perhaps unique in the annals of chamber music. Madame Schumann's reputation as a teacher of the piano was so great that to be known as a pupil of hers was alone a high distinction.

How nice—and how likely that he never looked at a score of her G-minor Piano Trio, let alone bothered to play through it. There is no Haydn here, though there is plenty that is redolent of Robert Schumann, or (a bit more removed) Mendelssohn. This is a capital piece of chamber music, and a few recent commentators have suggested that in many respects it surpasses her husband's essays in the genre of the piano trio. Perhaps we need not be too severe on Cobbett for the whiff of chauvinism that inhabits his assessment. He was, after all, merely carrying on a tradition that could scarcely imagine a woman as a significant composer. She would have been accustomed to it. In 1860, for example, her friend the violinist Joseph Joachim once told her that he had just heard a piece by Moritz Hauptmann, but that "I would rather have heard your Trio. I recollect a fugato in the last movement and remember that Mendelssohn once had a big laugh because I would not believe that a woman could have composed something so sound and serious."

Clara Wieck was one of the superlative pianists of her generation, admired for an approach that stressed seriousness of purpose over flashy barnstorming—"the Holy Grail in the quest of the critic," as George Bernard Shaw described her. But she also composed practically from the outset of her career. She made her debut as a pianist at the Leipzig Gewandhaus in 1828, at the age of nine, and published her first works—a set of polonaises—three years later. By the time she ceased composing, in 1855 (which, one notes with interest, coincided with her husband's death), her opus numbers reached to twenty-three. The Piano Trio is unquestionably one of her finest achievements, rich in inspiration, classically disciplined in structure, imaginative in its details, and a model of how to successfully balance the participating instruments.

This fresh-sounding work was produced during an extremely trying period in the composer's life. She began work on it in May 1846, in Dresden, where she had just recently introduced her husband's new Piano Concerto in A minor, and finished it that September 12, on her sixth wedding anniversary (and therefore, the eve of her twenty-seventh birthday). She had given birth to her fourth child only a few months earlier, and in her confinement had lost some important concert opportunities. She was making up for lost time by learning new works and preparing for numerous public appearances. Despite all this activity, both Robert and Clara were feeling depressed throughout the summer. Clara suffered a miscarriage, and the couple cut short a vacation that they failed to find stimulating. Still, Clara's achieving her Trio served as an inspiration for Robert, who shortly embarked on his own D-minor Piano Trio. Those two trios—Clara's in G-minor and Robert's in D-minor—would often be paired on programs during the later nineteenth century.

Following the first rehearsal of Clara's Trio, which took place on October 2, 1846, the composer wrote in her diary: "There is nothing greater than the joy of composing something oneself, and then listening to it. There are some pretty passages in the Trio, and I think it is fairly successful as far as the form goes." But she would prove to be as critical of her own music as she was of that by others (excepting her husband's, of which she was an unswerving advocate). She was gratified when the publishing house of Breitkopf & Härtel wrote to ask her if they might publish the piece, but when it finally appeared in print, a year after she finished writing it, Clara's diary entry took a deflated tone: "I received the printed copies of my Trio today, but I did not care for it particularly; after Robert's in D minor, it sounded effeminate and sentimental." This was neither the first nor the last time she would dismiss her own achievements almost reflexively when they might have threatened to rival her husband's work.

The texture is rather light, especially when compared with the density that typified her husband's works, but it would be hard to condemn this characteristic as a deficiency. Since the three instruments nearly always play together, much of this transparency must occur thanks to the deft piano writing. The *Allegro moderato* is a relaxed sonata-form movement. A sighing quality inhabits its opening material, and the working-out of its second, syncopated theme displays piano figuration that can only be described as "Schumannesque" (meaning that these traits correspond to the sorts of ideas we also find in her husband's music). Scotch snaps (rhythmic figures in which a beat is divided into a quick attack and a longer follow-up note) enliven the *Scherzo*, though that term seems to overstate the liveliness of mood that is really inherent in such dreamy music as this. Perhaps it was its *Tempo di Menuetto* marking that made Cobbett think the music should resemble Haydn.

The *Andante* is perhaps the Trio's most enchanting portion; all players have a go at its spacious theme, which is introduced by the piano, handed off to the violin, and then given to the cello when it is reprised near the movement's end. Extremes of velocity have had no place in this work so far, and this moderation of tempo carries even through the finale, an *Allegretto*. But there is musical drama here all the same, nowhere more than in this closing movement's imitative passages, the ones that mightily impressed Mendelssohn.

Robert Schumann

Born: June 8, 1810, in Zwickau, Saxony (Germany)

Died: July 29, 1856, in Endenich, near Bonn, Germany

String Quartet in A minor, Op. 41, No. 1

Introduzione: Andante espressivo—Allegro
Scherzo: Presto—Intermezzo
Adagio
Presto

Work composed: June 4–24, 1842

Work dedicated: To his friend Felix Mendelssohn Bartholdy

Work premiered: September 13, 1842, in a private performance in Leipzig

Instrumentation: Two violins, viola, and cello

Robert Schumann was eighteen when he traveled to Leipzig from his home in Zwickau to make arrangements to enter law school. During that preliminary visit he made the acquaintance of Friedrich Wieck (a well-known piano teacher) and his talented eight-year-old piano-playing daughter, Clara, who seems to have made little, if any, impression on him. Law school didn't work out, but lessons with Wieck did, and Schumann soon became a fixture in his household. In the spring of 1835 love began to complicate the balance of Robert and Clara's friendship. Clara, now fifteen, had been away on a concert tour for the preceding half-year, and a spark ignited between the two of them on her return. Robert, who kept a detailed diary, reported that they exchanged their first kiss on November 25 and that quite a few followed in quick succession thereafter.

Wieck did what he could to put an end to the affair. After dragging on for several years, the matter ended up in court, and the proceedings were simplified by centering the case on a single issue: if Wieck could prove that Robert was a habitual drunkard, he could prevent the marriage. This Wieck failed to do, and on September 12, 1840, Clara (one day short of her twenty-first birthday) became Mrs. Robert Schumann in a low-key ceremony at a village church outside Leipzig.

Rather than inhibit his work, this crisis seemed to inspire Schumann's creativity, particularly in the area of the lied. In 1840 he composed 138 songs, slightly more than half of all the songs he would write in his entire career. Before that year, piano music had been his chief concern. By 1841, he would become obsessed with symphonic music, and the following year would find him engrossed in writing chamber music. This was Schumann's style—to obsessively explore a genre until he felt he had reached the current limit of his abilities and curiosity, and then to move on to other musical fields.

The composer began the year 1842 engrossed in the study of counterpoint and fugue. In February he recorded in the "household book," which he and Clara maintained for several years, that he found himself having "quartettish thoughts," and ensuing entries confirm that his interest continued apace. On April 1 he reported, "Constantly quartets. Studied Mozart"; on April 28, "Quartets by Beethoven"; on May 6, "Studied quartets by Haydn." In June and July those quartettish thoughts coalesced into his own Three String Quartets (Op. 41); his June 4 entry in the household book states tersely, "Quartet in A minor begun."

Schumann worked at a frenzied pace, developing two quartets concurrently—those in A minor (Op. 41, No. 1) and F major (Op. 41, No. 2)—and immediately continuing with the Quartet in A major (Op. 41, No. 3). All three were finished within the space of about seven weeks, meaning that he composed these magnificent pieces at the rate of about four days per movement. "The whole of July was a pleasant month," he wrote, "aside from a few days and also nights of reveries. But I have also been active on a new species and have almost completed, and also written down, two quartets for strings, in A minor and F major." Shortly after their return from an August vacation, Clara was greeted with a memorable present to mark her twenty-third birthday, on September 13, 1842: the at-home premiere of all three of her husband's new string quartets. Already in the summer of 1842, following read-throughs, Schumann had advised his publishing firm Breitkopf & Härtel, "We have played the quartets frequently at [Ferdinand] David's house, and they seem to give pleasure to players and hearers, and especially also to Mendelssohn. You may rest assured that I have spared no pains to produce something really good—sometimes I think it is even my best."

Haydn, Mozart, and Beethoven may have been on Schumann's mind in the months before he penned his quartets, but the *Introduzione* of the A-minor Quartet makes clear that Bach also hovered in his consciousness— or perhaps it was Bach as filtered through Beethoven. Indeed, Schumann had plunged into counterpoint exercises earlier that year, and we hear the fruits in a movement such as this, where the four instruments weave in dense imitation. The overall quiet of the *Andante espressivo* introduction is disturbed by numerous markings of *sforzando*. Schumann initially instructed the players to use mutes during this section but later removed that marking. Four *stringendo* measures follow, an emphatic curtain-raiser of a fanfare signaling that the main body of the movement is about to begin. These four measures have a curious history. Originally, Schumann wrote them as the opening bars of his Second Quartet, which he was composing at the same time. For some reason, he made the extraordinary decision to excise them from the Second Quartet and drop them verbatim into the First; in his final manuscript, they appear in squashed handwriting at the juncture of the opening introduction and the sonata-form exposition. In both contexts these measures lead to music in F major, so they work equally well in a harmonic sense. The effect they wield is, however, strikingly different.

An exposition based on F major would hardly be anticipated in a quartet identified as being in A minor, but this unorthodox move served as further argument that he was viewing this work as linked to the ensuing quartet, which really is in F major. The leisurely *Allegro* theme, swaying gently in compound meter, gives way to some further studious counterpoint—here a brief canon announced by the viola—and a second principal theme, a spikier melody given out initially by the second violin. That second theme becomes the shuttlecock in further contrapuntal volleys during the development, and the movement concludes in a conventional recapitulation.

That Mendelssohn should have liked this quartet, as Schumann reported, should come as no surprise, given the Mendelssohnian flavor of the *Scherzo*. Schumann, however, puts his special twist on the proceedings, vesting his sprightly theme in sometimes lyrical, sometimes forceful garb, and achieving his signature wistfulness in the trio section (here marked *Intermezzo*). Contrasting moods also characterize the ensuing *Adagio*, a vintage display of his dreamy "Eusebius" mood. Where the principal section of the first movement had been introduced by four emphatic measures, this *Adagio* begins with a corresponding prelude of very different character: three wistful measures whose ambiguous, chromatic tonality is only resolved with the enunciation of the main theme in measure four, itself a nostalgic effusion. After exploring the theme's possibilities, Schumann concludes his slow movement much as he had begun it, drifting off into a coda that recalls his opening bars of dream music.

For his finale, Schumann offers a technical surprise: the entire movement grows out of a single unbridled theme. Normally a contrasting theme would provide additional core material. In this case the second theme does provide some contrast, but in fact it's essentially an inversion of the main tune. Much of the requisite contrast of this movement comes from a sophisticated manipulation of rhythm, most astonishingly when Schumann suddenly modulates from A minor to A major and down-shifts to *Moderato* for a brief interlude comprising a sort of musette-style "bagpipe drone" and a page of chorale-like homophony before the quartet gallops forcefully to its conclusion.

String Quartet in A major, Op. 41, No. 3

> *Andante espressivo—Allegro molto moderato*
> *Assai agitato*
> *Adagio molto*
> *Finale: Allegro molto vivace*

Work composed: July 8–22, 1842

Work dedicated: To his friend Felix Mendelssohn Bartholdy

Work premiered: September 13, 1842, in a private performance in Leipzig

Instrumentation: Two violins, viola, and cello

As a group Schumann's Three String Quartets (Op. 41) display remarkable unity, the three components flowing forth rather as a cycle. The works are related through their key structure; their overall trajectory of A minor—F major—A major would have made compelling logic according to the thirds-relationships that were captivating German composers at that time. The works share a propensity for volatility of character, and sudden shifts (even within individual movements) may be interpreted as the musical expression of Schumann's much-discussed dual musical personality as embodied by the fictionalized alter-egos of the Dionysian, extroverted Florestan and the Apollonian, introverted Eusebius to whom he gave voice in his published writings.

While the first two quartets adhere to recognizably Classical norms, Schumann concludes his cycle with effusive Romanticism in this quartet, which has historically been the most frequently programmed of the set. Perhaps the composer, having grown comfortable with the quartet medium through writing the first two pieces, now felt more at home giving free rein to his expressive urges; or perhaps wafting toward effusiveness was his overall conception for the cycle all along.

Despite its generally rhapsodic character and the variety of tempo markings within individual movements, the Third Quartet does not (or at least does not need to) come across as chaotic. Schumann employs the interval of the descending fifth as a unifying element—you can hear it in the piece's opening tones, and it will reappear often at prominent junctures—and he develops his melodic material with a Beethovenian density that early audiences must have found remarkable. A work such as this serves as a waypost between the styles of Beethoven and of Schumann's protégé Brahms, nowhere more clearly than in the second movement (*Assai agitato*), which serves as the quartet's scherzo. The confounding of a clear meter at the movement's outset would become a Brahmsian fingerprint, as would the imaginative deployment of variation form. Schumann's scherzo unrolls as a set of five variations (all in the key of F-sharp minor) plus a dreamy coda that wavers between the unlikely neighbors E-flat major and F-sharp major. The material is not presented in the order one would expect, however, which would be with the unadorned theme followed by increasingly ornate elaborations. Instead, Schumann seems to start in the midst of his variations, and only in the fourth section does he present the basic theme in what would seem its straightforward form. Lest we miss the point, Schumann allots the melody at that point to the first violin, the quartet's most prominent line, and reinforces it in canon in the viola.

The slow movement (*Adagio molto*) begins in an aura of hymnic sanctity and then moves on to a still more haunted section based on dotted rhythms (with ominous contrapuntal motifs winding about). When these theme-groups return Schumann tellingly alters their details. Rhythmic surprise has informed this entire quartet, beginning with the pulsating syncopation of the *Allegro molto moderato* section of the first movement. Now, in the *Finale* (*Allegro molto vivace*), we are treated to a smorgasbord of free rhythmic play to offset the solidity of the main theme, which stomps loudly on an off-beat. We hear a lot of this memorable tune. It returns seven times following its initial presentation, and each of its statements is separated by a contrasting section to yield a large-scale rondo structure.

Piano Quintet in E-flat major, Op. 44

> *Allegro brillante*
> *In modo d'una Marcia. Un poco largamente—Agitato*
> *Scherzo molto vivace—Trio I—Trio II*
> *Allegro, ma non troppo*

Work composed: Sketched September 23-28, 1842; completed by the beginning of December

Work dedicated: To Clara Schumann, the composer's wife

Work premiered: December 6, 1842, in Leipzig, at the home of Carl and Henriette Vogt; Clara Schumann was to have been the pianist, but as she fell ill on the day of the concert, Felix Mendelssohn filled in to sight-read the piano part. The public premiere took place on the morning of January 8, 1843, at the Leipzig Gewandhaus, with Clara as pianist.

Instrumentation: Two violins, viola, cello, and piano

Schumann began the year 1842 engrossed in the study of counterpoint and fugue. June and July he gave over to composing his Three String Quartets, and then, following a vacation with his wife, on September 23 he embarked on his Piano Quintet, crafted to spotlight her pianistic strengths. Practically without a break, he went on to begin his Piano Quartet on October 24. He completed it a month later, after what he complained of as "dreadful sleepless nights." Two further chamber works ensued in short order—a piano trio (it would eventually become his Phantasiestücke, Op. 88) and his haunting Andante and Variations for Two Pianos, Two Cellos, and Horn (WoO 10)—and then Schumann's interest veered toward choral music.

Schumann's is the earliest of the standard works in the repertoire for piano plus string quartet, and its popularity would give rise to a tradition that includes notable piano quintets by Spohr, Brahms, Franck, Dvořák, Borodin, Fauré, Sibelius, Dohnányi, Elgar, Granados, Reger, d'Indy, Ornstein, Bartók, Webern, Martinů, Shostakovich, Ginastera, Schnittke, Rochberg, Feldman, and Carter, to cite a very partial list—though only a handful of these are encountered often. Whereas later composers would seek greater democracy in the participation of the five instruments, Schumann seems to have viewed the piano and the string quartet as more or less balancing one another. The pianist works hard in this piece, scarcely relaxing for a single measure.

Some commentators have found the contour of the seventh prelude from Book Two of Bach's *Well-Tempered Clavier* reflected in the opening theme of the first movement, taken to be a reference (conscious or not) to Robert and Clara Schumann's studies of that composer. This theme will dominate the whole sonata-form movement (indeed, the entire Quintet), its upward jumps popping out all over the place, though not in the irresistibly tender second theme, which is first presented by cello and viola.

The ebullience of the first movement throws into higher relief the very different flavor of the second movement, a C-minor march that seems to be a somber funeral procession, an extreme contrast we may choose to view as emblematic of the composer's manic-depressive mood swings. The major-key episode that follows can come across as otherworldly, with first violin playing a tentative melody against sustained cello counterpoint and a flickering accompaniment. The movement unrolls as a rondo, with the funeral march returning, then giving way to a more blustery section (*Agitato*) based on themes already heard, and veering again (with consummate inspiration) into the march, now invested with high anxiety. The music quiets down to revisit the otherworldly theme and then, one last time, the solemn march.

In Schumann's original sketch, a G-minor *Adagio* was to follow at this point, but this strategy was dropped as he refined the piece, which reduced the quintet from five to four movements. Instead we proceed directly to the whirling scales of the *Scherzo*, with two trios providing respite of different kinds. In the first Schumann shows off his skill in counterpoint as the first violin and viola spin out a lyrical canon. The second trio contains bustling, proto-Brahmsian music that contrasts with its surroundings in both mood and meter. It is widely related that this second trio replaced what Schumann originally presented in that spot, his response to a suggestion by Felix Mendelssohn that a certain part of the quintet lacked liveliness. (Mendelssohn had substituted for Clara at the premiere, at the eleventh hour.) It's a dubious tale, and even if it contains an essence of truth, the source from which it's drawn fails to identify which trio was replaced, or, for that matter, in which of the middle movements the replacement span fell. Both movements as we know them adhere closely to the way Schumann planned them in his initial sketches, although the *Scherzo*'s first trio did pick up some extra piano figuration at some point, perhaps the "liveliness" in question.

The finale is a brilliant piece of composition, a strong-boned, imaginative sonata-rondo into which the composer works two fugal passages. The second, arriving after a pregnant pause near the end, is a breathtaking double fugue in three parts that spectacularly incorporates themes from the opening and closing movements, thereby helping to unify the whole quintet. Writing in her diary just as the piece was completed, Clara described this quintet as "magnificent—a work filled with energy and freshness," which it certainly is.

Piano Quartet in E-flat major, Op. 47

Sostenuto assai—Allegro ma non troppo
Scherzo: Molto vivace
Andante cantabile
Finale: Vivace

Work composed: 1842

Work dedicated: To Count Mathieu Wielhorsky

Work premiered: December 8, 1844, in Leipzig, by violinist Ferdinand David (who would premiere Mendelssohn's E-minor Violin Concerto the following year), violist Niels Gade (the soon-to-be-famous Danish composer), Wielhorsky as cellist, and Clara Schumann as pianist.

Instrumentation: Violin, viola, cello, and piano

Robert Schumann and his music are so full of surprises that it seems unfair to codify his life and achievements in terms of rehashed truisms. And yet Schumann did characterize his musical opinions as the duality of his sub-egos, the fiery Florestan and the dreamy Eusebius (though also the more temperate middleman of Magister Raro), and it's hard to resist reducing his musical expression to those extremes. His Piano Quintet (Op. 44) and Piano Quartet (Op. 47), written back-to-back in 1842, seem to take sides with those two main characters: generally speaking, the Piano Quartet is a "Eusebius piece," the introverted sibling of the flashier, "Florestan-style" Piano Quintet.

Like the Piano Quintet, the Piano Quartet was written with the composer's wife, Clara, specifically in mind. But another musician was also important in Schumann's conception of the work: Count Mathieu (also called Matvei) Wielhorsky, a cellist and concert impresario in St. Petersburg who urged the composer toward this piece. Though Wielhorsky was an amateur when it came to performing, the role his instrument plays here suggests that he must have achieved a level of serious accomplishment. In this work Schumann treats the cello as a prominent participant in the activity, though, when all is said and done, the piano still reigns supreme in the texture. The medium of the piano quartet was an unusual one; probably Mozart's two sublime essays in the genre and perhaps Beethoven's piano-quartet version of his Op. 16 Quintet for Piano and Winds were the only ones Schumann would have known.

Writing in her diary, Clara described the Piano Quartet as "a beautiful work, so youthful and fresh, as if it were his first." Her "as if it were his first" remark is curious, since, for all intents and purposes, it was his first; but possibly she was remembering a C-minor Piano Quartet Schumann had sketched when he was a teenager. Whereas many composers were working in the medium of the piano trio (violin, cello, and piano), the addition of a viola lent certain challenges to the task. Its extra voice increased the opportunity for complicated contrapuntal interweaving, but it also added to the density of the ensemble's middle range—an especially significant problem for Schumann, who on the best of days rarely erred on the side of transparency in his textures. Considerable skill is required to keep such forces melded into a like-minded ensemble, rather than drifting toward a "piano versus strings" texture that suggests a concerto on a shoestring.

The quartet begins with a hushed exhalation of rich chords, which shortly give way to a well-measured *Allegro ma non troppo* and the first broad melody, which is introduced by the cello. Schumann reverses the usual order of the internal movements, saving his slow movement until after a rapid *Scherzo*. Though marked *Molto vivace*, the *Scherzo* is hardly buoyant in a Mendelssohnian way; a slightly sinister undercurrent emerges intermittently throughout the *Scherzo* proper and its two contrasting trio sections.

In the third movement (*Andante cantabile*), the cello again emerges (after the briefest of introductions) to sing one of Schumann's most sublime melodies, perfect in its balance, soulfulness, and apparent simplicity. The melody is handed off in turn to the violin and then the piano, which applies elegant embellishment. A central section seems almost prayerful and chorale-like, profoundly comforting. The original song-melody returns, this time with violin filigree; and at the very end the cellist surreptitiously tunes the instrument's lowest string down a step to the otherwise inaccessible low B-flat, providing a thirteen-bar pedal-point support for the suspended animation of the movement's coda. "Alas!" wrote the Schumann biographer Robert Haven Schauffler in 1945, "the long solo which opens the movement, too saccharine in feeling and too mechanical in construction, is the weakest part of the work." Surely most music-lovers would disagree, and in the strongest terms. This is one of the magical Schumann moments in which the entire universe seems to hold its breath. The Eusebius of the *Andante cantabile* is replaced by Florestan for the *Finale*, an outpouring of thematic exuberance that grows from a fugue-like opening and incorporates an episode recalling the *Andante*'s magical coda.

Citing bad reviews of supernal masterpieces is easy sport, but it's hard to resist wondering what was going on the mind of the redoubtable Henry Fothergill Chorley when he reported on a London performance of Schumann's Piano Quartet featuring the pianist Edward Dannreuther. His judgment appeared in the June 20, 1863, edition of the *Athenaeum*, in the column titled "Musical and Dramatic Gossip": "This is no music for us; nor shall we ever become reconciled to the hardihood of ugliness which is therein paraded by way of originality.... [Dannreuther played well] in spite of the uncouthness of the work on which his labour was wasted. He will do well, however, save when presenting himself before a young German audience, to eschew Schumann's music, for that has as small chance of establishing itself in England as it had in 1848, when this very quartett was introduced [here] by Herr Eduard Röckel."

He was quite mistaken, of course, and Schumann's Piano Quartet went on to occupy hallowed ground in the concerts halls of England and everywhere else.

Piano Trio No. 2 in F major, Op. 80

Sehr lebhaft (*"Very lively"*)
Mit innigem Ausdruck (*"With earnestly affectionate expression"*)
In mässiger Bewegung (*"With moderate motion"*)
Nicht zu rasch (*"Not too quick"*)

Work composed: August 2 through early November 1847

Work premiered: February 22, 1850, at the Leipzig Gewandhaus, by violinist Ferdinand David, cellist Julius Rietz, and pianist Clara Schumann

Instrumentation: Violin, cello, and piano

Near the end of his "chamber music year" of 1842, immediately after completing his Three String Quartets, his Piano Quintet, and his Piano Quartet, Schumann moved on to yet another of the central chamber ensembles, the piano trio. At that point he drafted four movements that he planned as a Piano Trio in A minor, but he failed to see it through to finished form. Some years later he revisited this score and adapted it into a set of Fantasiestücke ("Fantasy Pieces"), unassuming character pieces that he published, in 1850, as his Op. 88.

By that time he had already composed two of his three full-scale piano trios, the ones in D minor (Op. 63) and F major (Op. 80), which, despite their distant opus numbers, were created in close succession. The immediate impetus for their composition seems to have been the creation of Clara Schumann's Piano Trio in G minor during the summer of 1846—possibly an element of competition was at play—and less than a year later Robert was busy producing his responses, the First Trio in June 1847, the Second from August until the beginning of November. The D-minor Trio, Schumann wrote to his composer-friend Carl Reinecke, was born of "a time of gloomy moods," while the F-major was "of a completely different character than [the one] in D—it makes a breezier and more ingratiating impression."

His Third Piano Trio, in G minor (Op. 110), would follow in the autumn of 1851, and along with nearly all of Schumann's late works, posterity long dismissed it as the product of a mind in decline. Indeed Schumann's mind would decline, but he remained productive as a composer practically until the point when he committed himself to an insane asylum, in March 1854. It is true that the final entries in the last three years of his catalogue can be hit-or-miss, but many of them prove abundantly interesting and hardly one of them lacks at least some segments that merit a detour. Nobody doubts that Schumann was in command of his faculties when he revised his D-minor Symphony into the version in which it is nearly always heard today. He did that in December 1851, just weeks after completing the G-minor Trio. In recent years, biased assumptions about Schumann's post-1850 work have been increasingly questioned, and the G-minor Trio accordingly has begun to enjoy revived attention from chamber musicians.

Nonetheless, the earlier two do seem more consistent in their inspiration, and they remain far the more popular, with the F-major proving a particular audience favorite thanks to its friendly demeanor. The first movement bustles forth with healthy vigor, its themes laid out with a well-grounded firmness that Brahms must have appreciated. A heart-in-throat high point comes when, over suddenly quiet piano arpeggios, the violin intones a near-quotation from Schumann's "Intermezzo," the second song in his *Liederkreis* (Op. 39), composed in May 1840, just at the time when he was struggling to gain Clara as his bride. There the music is set to Joseph von Eichendorff's words "Dein Bildniss wunderselig / Hab ich im Herzensgrund" ("I bear your beautiful likeness in the depths of my heart"). It's not hard to imagine that Robert intended this allusion as a "message of love" to Clara—a "Liebesbotschaft," as the composers of lieder would often have it—and it may be no mere coincidence that in 1849 Clara wrote of this trio with words reminiscent of Eichendorff's: "It is one of the pieces of Robert's that delights and warms the depths of my soul from beginning to end. I love it passionately, and would like to go on playing it again and again."

"I always look forward to the beginning of the Adagio," Schumann wrote to his composer-friend Carl Reinecke, "and, when it comes, to the Allegretto (instead of a Scherzo)." In the score, Schumann labels those two sections not with those Italian terms but rather with the German markings *Mit innigem Ausdruck* and *In mässiger Bewegung*, and both are marked by particularly adept touches of counterpoint, reflections of a skill Schumann had acquired through much perseverance. We might translate "Mit innigem Ausdruck" as "With earnestly affectionate expression." The adjective *innig* encapsulates a quintessentially Schumannesque quality, and he uses it often in his music. Langenscheidt's dictionary offers a string of English equivalents for it—tender, affectionate; ardent, fervent; heartfelt, sincere—and taken all together these suggest the richness this word conveys. It is the perfect directive for the violin's utterance at the movement's opening, a faraway melody that is technically nothing more than a mere descending scale and yet is suffused with wistfulness. Its duple rhythms are slightly at odds with the gently repeated triplets in the pianist's right hand, and against it the cello plays a counterpoint of rising figures. The cello's counter-melody sounds almost offhanded, as if tossed off as an improvised obbligato; but it turns out to be more finely crafted than at first we suspect, when the left hand of the piano part quietly intones it in a canon that lasts for about six measures. A great deal of art is embedded in this innocent opening. Short sections of contrast follow—a see-sawing melody that sounds folkish in its modality, a perky outburst from the piano, as if suddenly wakened from the dream—but it is the music attached to the opening that ultimately carries the spirit of this slow movement.

Canons inform the following movement, too, right from the opening phrases of the piano, then cello, then violin. As Schumann emphasized to Reinecke, this is decidedly not a scherzo; instead it's a relaxed intermezzo (Schumann's tempo marking means "With moderate motion"), and although it's less gauzy than the preceding movement, thanks in no small part to the staccato character of the piano's bass line (many attacks are actually marked *sforzando*), it does prolong the general aura of poetic dreaming. The first movement included an allusion to Schumann's *Liederkreis*. The low-lying string chords of the third movement's coda evoke a different Schumann cycle, *Frauenliebe und -leben*, also from 1840 and also credibly heard as articulating his love for Clara. The charge of sentimentality has sometimes been lobbed in Schumann's direction, and such moments as these may invite performers to err in a syrupy direction. But there is nothing inherently maudlin about the sincere expression of love. The pianist Fanny Davies, who in the 1880s spent two years as a pupil of Clara Schumann's in Frankfurt, related her teacher's admonition: "Schumann is nothing if he is not rhythmic. He is a poet, full of sentiment and fantasy, but he is never sentimental; you must never make his music sound sentimental." Less risk of this is run in the finale ("Not too quick"), where again Schumann takes pains to work in a dose of contrapuntal imitation. Despite the energy of its moments, this temperate conclusion achieves real jubilation only in its final measures.

Dmitri Dmitrievich Shostakovich

Born: September 12 (old style)/25 (new style), 1906, in St. Petersburg, Russia

Died: August 9, 1975, in Moscow, Russia, USSR

Piano Quintet in G minor, Op. 57

Prelude: Lento—Poco più mosso—Lento [attacca]
Fugue: Adagio
Scherzo: Allegretto
Intermezzo: Lento
Finale: Allegretto

Work composed: Summer 1940, completed on September 14, in Moscow, on request from the Beethoven String Quartet

Work premiered: November 23, 1940, in the Small Hall of the Moscow Conservatory, by the composer (as pianist) and the Beethoven String Quartet (violinists Dmitri Tsyganov and Vasili Shirinsky, violist Vadim Borisovsky, and cellist Sergei Shirinsky)

Instrumentation: **Two violins, viola, cello, and piano**

Dmitri Shostakovich spent practically his whole career falling in and out of favor with the Soviet authorities in a game of totalitarian badminton that left the shuttlecock in shambles. Only the most perverse novelist could have dreamed up the life that lay ahead following the success of his pert Symphony No. 1 (1924–25): how in 1930 Shostakovich's satirical opera *The Nose* would run afoul of Soviet politicos, being denounced by the Russian Association of Proletarian Musicians for its "bourgeois decadence"; how he would redeem himself through his charming Piano Concerto No. 1 in

1933; how his fortunes would crash again in early 1936, when Stalin saw and loathed his opera *Lady Macbeth of Mtsensk* and reduced him to nothingness until the composer contritely offered his Fifth Symphony (1937) as "the creative reply of a Soviet artist to justified criticism" (not really Shostakovich's words, though often attributed to him). The adventures continued through the rest of his life. In the wake of his rehabilitation he was awarded the Stalin Prize twice in succession, in 1940 and 1941; in 1945, his star fell again when his Ninth Symphony struck the bureaucrats as an insufficient reflection of the glory of Russia's victory over the Nazis; he rebounded with yet another Stalin Prize in 1949, but nonetheless squirreled away private masterpieces in his desk drawer until Soviet cultural policies began to thaw after the dictator's death in 1953. Only in 1960 would he feel confident enough to hazard the series of searing, poignant works rich in musical autobiography that would characterize the final years of his earthly tragedy.

Shostakovich held the music of Bach close to his heart. Nonetheless, the evidence of that love comes more from his music than through his words. If he spoke of Bach to his students and colleagues (and he doubtless did), few of his comments have been preserved. His pupil Boris Tishchenko quoted Shostakovich, a great connoisseur of the music of Mahler, as saying, "I used to consider *Das Lied von der Erde* the best work ever written, but now it seems to me that Bach's music is even more forceful." Another student, Yuri Abramovich Levitin, recalled that in 1938, after Shostakovich was hospitalized due to a near-breakdown (the result of political bullying), the composer proclaimed: "I have decided to start working again, so as not to lose my qualifications as a composer. I am going to write a prelude and a fugue every day. I shall take into consideration the experience of Johann Sebastian Bach." Two Bach violin sonatas were played at his funeral—badly, by all accounts. As a pianist, he apparently had a good deal of Bach under his fingers. In 1950, he headed the Soviet delegation that traveled to the German Democratic Republic (East Germany) for the Bach bicentennial celebrations; on that occasion he performed as one of the pianists in Bach's Concerto for Three Keyboard Instruments and also served as a judge at the International Bach Competition. Following the competition, where he was bowled over by the playing of Tatyana Nikolaeva, he would compose his Forty-eight Preludes and Fugues for Piano, a modern equivalent to Bach's *Well-Tempered Clavier*.

Bach sometimes lurks about the fringes of others of his pieces, but Shostakovich's Piano Quintet offers the most direct and eloquent testimony of the inspiration he drew from the Leipzig master. The opening two movements (you may consider them a single, bipartite movement, if you prefer) stand as a prelude-and-fugue pair. (Prokofiev objected to this opening as being too "Bachian" for his taste.) The *Intermezzo* also evokes Bach in its spare texture, in which long melodic lines weave above an incessant, crisply punctuated "walking bass" line. One wonders if Shostakovich was turning to the technical model of Bach as a means of grounding his tendency toward the emotional self-expression that had already gotten him into plenty of trouble.

In 1939 Shostakovich was temporarily in political favor, and it was safe for the Beethoven String Quartet to approach him to request a new chamber work. To the group's first violinist he responded immediately, "I shall definitely write you a quintet and play it with you." It would be an enduring relationship: from then on, all his string quartets except the last would be premiered by the Beethoven Quartet.

The Piano Quintet came into being during the summer of 1940, and Shostakovich premiered it with the ensemble in Moscow, on November 23 of that year. (He would record it with the Beethoven Quartet twenty years later.) The audience received it ecstatically, demanding an encore of the *Scherzo* and the *Finale*. It is a beautifully balanced, finely wrought work. Compared with Shostakovich's other chamber works, the Quintet's impact derives relatively little from intense soul-searching, although the slow-paced *Fugue* is certainly moving, emerging without a break from the pent-up drama of the *Prelude*. Instead, we encounter more "positive" aspects of the composer's emotional arsenal: the naive sassiness of the *Scherzo*, the ecstatic melodies of the *Intermezzo*; the optimism of the dance-march *Finale*, complete with a quotation from a tune associated with the entrance of clowns in Russian circuses. But even in this concluding movement, Shostakovich is given to undercutting the overriding emotion, and the piece ends by fading into an unpretentious wisp of a coda.

Piano Trio No. 2 in E minor, Op. 67

Andante—Moderato
Allegro con brio
Largo [attacca]
Allegretto

Work composed: February 15 through August 13, 1944, at the Composers' House at Ivanovo, Russia

Work dedicated: To the memory of Ivan Ivanovich Sollertinsky, Shostakovich's musicologist-friend, who had died four days before the composer embarked on this work

Work premiered: November 14, 1944, at the Great Hall of the Leningrad Philharmonic, by violinist Dmitri Tsyganov, cellist Sergei Shirinsky, and the composer (as pianist)

Instrumentation: Violin, cello, and piano

Following the 1936 brouhaha over *Lady Macbeth of Mtsensk*, Shostakovich increasingly split his composing into parallel universes: one for public consumption, the other for personal expression. His chamber music probably constitutes the most complete body of "the real Shostakovich," the music he wanted to write, rather than the music he was allowed to write.

The transcendent E-minor Piano Trio was his Piano Trio No. 2 (his first, a one-movement piece in C minor, was a student work, composed in 1923 and published as his Op. 8). This trio was composed in memory of Ivan Ivanovich Sollertinsky, who died on February 11, 1944, at the age of only forty-one, of a heart attack while in evacuation in Siberia with the Leningrad Philharmonic, which he was then serving as artistic director. A brilliant musicologist, music critic, linguist, professor (at Leningrad University), and administrator, Sollertinsky had become a close friend of the composer in 1927, had opened Shostakovich's eyes to the glory of Mahler, and had stood by him through the darkest days. "I cannot express in words all of the grief I felt when I received the news of the death of Ivan Ivanovich...who was my closest friend," Shostakovich wrote to Sollertinsky's widow. "I owe all my education to him."

Shostakovich had already begun thinking about writing a piano trio, but he started over when news of Sollertinsky's death arrived. The work's elegiac portions are a fitting tribute to such a brave friend. But the piece is much more than just an elegy: it is rich in variety, and its diversity itself stands as an appropriate tribute to the man who championed all aspects of Shostakovich's art. This is, moreover, a wartime work—the death camps of Majdanek and Treblinka had recently been discovered in the wake of the Nazis' retreat from the eastern front—and its macabre aspects surely evoke the emotional extremes that might be juxtaposed even in daily life during such a time.

The cello launches this work in an unlikely fashion, playing an *Andante* lamentation in harmonics, at pitches so high that when the violin enters, in canon, it serves briefly as a bass to the cello's melody. The piano, deep in its register, soon takes over that role, and the violin assumes the aspect of reality, as opposed to the shadowy *Doppelgänger* of the cello's wincing harmonics. To the piano goes the honor of articulating the movement's main theme (*Moderato*), against a repeated-note accompaniment in the strings. It's a nervous movement, flitting between transparent neo-Baroque happiness, folk-like depictions of Russian life, muted reflection, and even angry defiance.

From E minor we shift brashly to F-sharp major for the often riotous, sometimes menacing scherzo, built from a theme whose nonchalantly cast-off triads sound sarcastic. Though the movement is headed *Allegro con brio* ("Fast with spirit"), the string parts carry such indications as *marcatissimo, pesante* ("strongly accented, heavy"), suggesting the stylistic schizophrenia particularly associated with this composer. Shostakovich's sardonic inclinations are largely set aside in the contrasting trio section, a giddy waltz in G major. The speed of this movement can prove problematic. Yakov Milkis, a violist in the Leningrad Philharmonic, reported having asked the composer about the tempos in this piece. "As a general rule," Milkis said,

> the metronome markings in the score were always faster than the tempos taken during performance.... For instance, take the Second Piano Trio. There the metronome marking of the scherzo is so fast as to render it virtually unperformable. Once, while I was studying this trio, I happened to be in Komarovo when Dmitri Dmitriyevich was also staying there. I plucked up the courage to ask him about the markings, not only the fast speed of the scherzo, but the very slow speed indicated for the third movement. He answered, "You know, take no notice. I use this rickety old metronome, and I know I should have thrown it out years ago, as it's completely unreliable, but I have got so attached to it that I keep it. But you, as a musician, should just play as you feel the music and take no notice of those markings, take no notice."

The *Largo*, in the dark key of B-flat minor, is one of Shostakovich's great threnodies. As he had in his Piano Quintet of 1940, the composer here draws inspiration from Bach, setting the movement's opening as a vast, emotionally desolate passacaglia: the piano repeats its deep-voiced, eight-measure chordal progression six times as the strings weave in counterpoint above.

A quiet drumming figure in the piano leads us from this reverie directly into the finale, which, like the scherzo, juxtaposes joy and sorrow in such a way as to intensify emotions in both directions. Ian MacDonald, writing in *The New Shostakovich*, says that "horrified by stories that SS guards had made their victims dance beside their own graves, Shostakovich created a directly programmatic image of it." Although Shostakovich was not Jewish, he felt a strong affinity with what he considered the most persecuted people of Europe (and, of course, virulent anti-Semitism was sanctioned by the Soviet government). The "Jewish" tune that pervades this finale, introduced pizzicato by the violin, would make a return appearance in Shostakovich's autobiographical String Quartet No. 8.

This shell-shocked, or otherwise stunned, *danse macabre* unrolls propulsively through contrasting passages of broad lyricism, roughly suggesting the structure of a rondo. A curious dollop of densely contrapuntal atonality casts it into relief along the way. At the end, the dance gives way to a return of material we have heard before: memories of the first movement's theme, the muted anguish of stratospheric strings, a fleeting glimpse of the piano's passacaglia from the slow movement.

Written as a memorial in part for Sollertinsky, in part for all the subjugated of the world, this trio would eventually be pressed into service for the composer's own obsequies. When he died and his body was laid out to be honored by the public in the Grand Hall of the Moscow Conservatory, the slow movement of the E-minor Piano Trio was one of the works played to accompany the sad proceedings.

String Quartet No. 3 in F major, Op. 73

Allegretto
Moderato con moto
Allegro non troppo
Adagio [attacca]
Moderato—Adagio

Work composed: January 26 through August 2, 1946, mostly in Moscow, but completed in Kellomäki (shortly renamed Komarovo), near St. Petersburg

Work dedicated: To the members of the Beethoven String Quartet

Work premiered: December 16, 1946, at the Small Hall of the Moscow Conservatory, by the Beethoven String Quartet (violinists Dmitri Tsyganov and Vasili Shirinsky, violist Vadim Borisovsky, and cellist Sergei Shirinsky)

Instrumentation: Two violins, viola, and cello

Shostakovich's fifteen string quartets constitute the most continuous distillation of what we take to be his most personal expression, relatively removed from the official scrutiny that attached to his more "public" symphonies. He composed his First String Quartet in 1938 and waited until 1944 to write his Second; between then and 1974, when he completed his Fifteenth, we find a nearly unbroken outpouring of these pieces, composed for (as he put it) "one of the hardest musical mediums."

World War II had finally come to a close. Shostakovich had produced three symphonies relating to that excruciating period: in 1941, his Seventh, the *Leningrad*, much of it composed during the Nazi siege of that city; in 1943, his Eighth, a gloomy work in which we sense the composer's despondency over the depths to which humanity had descended; and in 1945, his Ninth, in which elation over the conclusion of the war reaches a level of giddiness.

The Ninth threatened to bring down the hand of officialdom yet again. The commissars who passed judgment on such things would have preferred something more grandiose to mark the great victory of the Soviet people. In the event, Shostakovich was spared formal censure, but the threat of condemnation caused him deep anxiety.

He plunged forward into his Third String Quartet, making good progress on it in January 1946 and then setting it aside for several months before returning to complete it that summer. He was composing it expressly for the Beethoven String Quartet, with whose members Shostakovich had been friendly for two decades by that time. They had premiered his Second String Quartet in 1944, on the same concert at which two of its members joined the composer to unveil his E-minor Piano Trio. Upon completing the new quartet, Shostakovich wrote to Sergei Shirinsky, the group's cellist: "It seems to me that I have never been so pleased with one of my works as with this quartet. Probably I am mistaken, but for the time being this is exactly how I feel." His opinion was seconded by the musicologist and critic Daniel Zhitomirsky, who the following year wrote: "In the wealth and versatility of its ideas, the Third Quartet surpasses everything the composer has composed in the sphere of chamber music." That seems possibly unfair to the E-minor Trio, but at least it was an unassailable assessment in comparing the Third with the quartets that had preceded it.

Both of those earlier quartets had followed a standard four-movement layout; perhaps Shostakovich was thinking of late Beethoven when he cast the Third in five movements. It remains nonetheless firmly rooted in its Classicism by adhering to such long-established structures as sonata form, fugue (an extended double fugue, even, beginning in the middle of the first movement), rondo, and passacaglia (in the third movement). The composer initially placed descriptive headings at the beginning of each movement: "Calm unawareness of the future cataclysm," for the first; "Rumblings of unrest and anticipation" for the second; "The forces of war are unleashed" for the third; "Homage to the Dead" for the *Adagio*; and, at the end, "Why, and for what?" No explanation is recorded for his decision to delete them, but they don't appear in the published score. Perhaps he felt they were too specific in suggesting an interpretation to the listener. Perhaps he felt they weren't specific enough. Perhaps he felt that the less he said the better: he was painfully aware of what trouble could ensue when people started arguing about his intentions. It was just as well. In between his completing this quartet and its premiere four and a half months later, rumblings resurfaced about his Seventh Symphony, and Shostakovich was probably relieved that his by-then-deleted-subtitles no longer risked rubbing anyone the wrong way.

If the Third Quartet is meant to suggest a narrative, the plot is in no way clear. Much of the piece comes across as parodistic: Is the opening really as insouciant as it seems? Is a waltz just a waltz and is a march just a march?

What are we to make of the trio section of the second movement, where the four instruments play in such quiet staccato that sometimes the music seems scarcely to be there at all? Violent argument enters the discourse (as in the third movement) and at points it reaches the realm of personal anguish and (in the great *Adagio*) funereal tragedy.

The violist Fyodor Druzhinin, who joined the Beethoven Quartet in 1964, left a moving reminiscence involving this piece:

> Only once did we see Shostakovich visibly moved by his own music. We were rehearsing the Third Quartet. He'd promised to stop us when he had any remarks to make. Dmitri Dmitriyevich sat in an armchair with the score opened out. But after each movement ended he just waved us on, saying, "Keep playing!" So we performed the whole Quartet. When we finished playing he sat quite still in silence like a wounded bird, tears streaming down his face. This was the only time that I saw Shostakovich so open and defenseless.

String Quartet No. 8 in C minor, Op. 110

Largo
Allegro molto
Allegretto
Largo
Largo
(*The movements are played without pause*)

Work composed: July 12–14, 1960, at Gohrisch, near Dresden, German Democratic Republic

Work dedicated: "In memory of the victims of fascism and war"

Work premiered: October 2, 1960, in Glinka Hall in Leningrad, by the Beethoven String Quartet (violinists Dmitri Tsyganov and Vasili Shirinsky, violist Vadim Borisovsky, and cellist Sergei Shirinsky)

Instrumentation: Two violins, viola, and cello

Shostakovich's Seventh and Eighth String Quartets—both composed in 1960 and standing at the midpoint of his fifteen contributions to the genre—make a profoundly moving pair. The composer dedicated the Seventh to the memory of his first wife, and its music is bathed in nostalgia. The Eighth is an anguished outcry, and its effect is so extraordinary that many connoisseurs consider it the apex of his chamber music.

The circumstances of the work's composition help explain its musical character. Shostakovich wrote it rapidly, in only three summer days, while visiting the German city of Dresden to compose music for a film about the city's destruction in World War II. Devastation was still abundantly evident a decade and a half after the fact. "[It made] a terrific impact on me," Shostakovich recalled, "the frightful and senseless destruction"; and he inscribed his score "In memory of the victims of fascism and war."

On another occasion, however, the composer said of the Eighth Quartet, "I dedicated it to myself," alerting listeners to meaningful subtleties that might elude the Soviet censors. In fact, the Eighth Quartet is unusually rich in allusions to the composer's other works. References—some extended, some fleeting—recall Shostakovich's First and Fifth Symphonies, his E-minor Piano Trio, his First Cello Concerto, and a love aria from *Lady Macbeth of Mtsensk* (the opera that had earned him disgrace from Soviet officialdom), as well as a traditional prisoner's song ("Tortured by Heavy Bondage") that Russian audiences would have recognized. The Quartet's first four notes constitute a musical signature. This device, which Shostakovich also employed in several other works, is easily decoded when one realizes that some notes of the musical scale are named differently in German and in English: D and C represent the same notes in both languages, but what we call E-flat and B-natural are respectively known in German as Es (the phonic equivalent of "S") and H. Imagining oneself in Germany for a moment—where the composer was when he wrote the piece, and where his name is transliterated as Schostakowitsch—one sees that the first four letters of "D. Schostakowitsch" could be rendered as a musical motto by the notes D–S–C–H, which English-speakers know as D–E-flat–C–B-natural. One is tempted to view the Eighth Quartet as a cryptic autobiography, though interpreting its references would involve considerable speculation. It seems likely, however, that Shostakovich included himself as one of "the victims of fascism and war," and perhaps this can be read to suggest that the Soviet leaders were victimizers just as the German ones were.

The D–S–C–H motif proves central to the work's musical strategy. The five movements are played *attacca* (without pause). At the very opening, the theme is introduced respectively by cello, viola, second violin, and first violin, transposed so that within eleven measures its notes have been intoned on all twelve semitones of the octave. Suspicions that Shostakovich may be preparing to flirt with twelve-tone processes are dispelled as the movement settles into the key of C minor. He intensifies this somber tonality by sometimes allowing the E-flat (or "S") of his motif to drift upward to E-natural, offering a passing glimpse of major-key optimism; but that hope inevitably returns to the gloomier minor. This major-minor conflict pervades the entire quartet, though the D–S–C–H motif appears prominently only in the first, third, and fifth movements.

The opening *Largo* explores the contrapuntal possibilities of Shostakovich's signature theme. The ensuing *Allegro molto* breaks forth with a brilliant opening and proceeds to employ a lengthy quotation from the composer's E-minor Piano Trio—specifically, a leering *danse macabre* that grows ever more terrifying as one of its fragmented phrases repeats incessantly, unable to move forward. The third movement, a drunken waltz (*Allegretto*), is more pathetic than amusing, especially when its scratchy timbres are interrupted by desperate shrieks from the second violin. In the solemn expanse of the ensuing *Largo*, the viola intones the "Dies irae," the ancient chant from the Mass for the Dead. The prisoner's song also appears, and the love music from *Lady Macbeth of Mtsensk*, but everything is interrupted by a succession of three-note outbursts: The rat-a-tat of gunfire? The Gestapo or KGB pounding at the door? (A woman who lived through the most oppressive years of the Soviet regime once told me that people in a restaurant or tavern would make three loud knocks surreptitiously on the underside of a tabletop to signal that a known KGB agent was in their midst. Others I have asked about this say it's hogwash. I don't know one way or the other.) The concluding movement (another *Largo*) recapitulates the D–S–C–H motif and other material that had sounded in the opening movement, twenty exhausting minutes earlier, as well as hints of the "Dies irae." The tones of the instruments, now suffocated by mutes, die away into silence.

When it was new, this work became widely associated with the Borodin String Quartet, whose members were the first to champion Shostakovich's quartets through recordings. While learning the Eighth Quartet, the ensemble played it for the composer at his home, hoping he might offer suggestions for its interpretation. They received none: on hearing his creation, Shostakovich simply buried his head into his hands and wept. Apparently the tears Shostakovich's shed when the Beethoven String Quartet rehearsed his Third Quartet (recounted above) were not the only ones his string quartets occasioned.

String Quartet No. 14 in F-sharp major, Op. 142

> *Allegretto*
> *Adagio [attacca]*
> *Allegretto—Adagio*

Work composed: March 23 through April 23, 1973, begun at Repino (near St. Petersburg) and completed in Copenhagen

Work dedicated: To Sergei Pyotrovich Shirinsky, cellist of the Beethoven String Quartet

Work premiered: October 30, 1973, at the USSR Composer's Union in Moscow, by the Beethoven String Quartet (violinists Dmitri Tsyganov and Nikolai Zabavnikov, violist Fyodor Druzhinin, and cellist Sergei Shirinsky)

Instrumentation: Two violins, viola, and cello

Shostakovich dedicated his Quartets Nos. 11 to 14 to the individual members of the Beethoven String Quartet, the ensemble that premiered all but the first and last of his quartets (though with personnel changes near the end): which is to say that those works are dedicated sequentially to the second violinist Vasili Shirinski (in memoriam; he had died in 1965 and was replaced by Nikolai Zabavnikov), to the first violinist Dmitri Tsyganov, to the violist Vadim Borissovsky (who had retired in 1964 and was replaced by Fyodor Druzhinin), and—for the Fourteenth—to the cellist Sergei Shirinsky. Shirinsky would die the following year, in October 1974, following a rehearsal of Shostakovich's Quartet No. 15. In each of these four late quartets Shostakovich accords a special prominence to the part of the dedicatee—or, in the case of the Eleventh, he poignantly "spotlights" a sometimes missing second violin. The Quartet No. 14 is accordingly a "Cello Quartet," though not to an exaggerated extent. Shostakovich reinforced this dedication by translating the name "Sergei" into German musical notation for use as a theme in the finale; and he also quotes in that movement a phrase from his opera *Katerina Izmailova* (the revised version of his ill-fated *Lady Macbeth of Mtsensk*), in which it was set to the words "Seryozha, my dear one"—Seryozha being a diminutive form of Sergei.

Shostakovich's health deteriorated perilously in his last years. Shortly after completing his Symphony No. 15 in July 1971 he suffered his second heart attack, which left him utterly exhausted ("dried up," as he explained to his friend Isaak Glikman). He passed eighteen months in convalescence, and only in the spring of 1973 was he able to resume composing, at which point he dedicated himself to his Quartet No. 14. He completed it in Copenhagen, en route to the United States, where he would receive an honorary doctorate from Northwestern University, be honored with a medal from Lincoln Center for the Performing Arts, attend *Aida* at the Metropolitan Opera, appear in a televised press conference speaking on behalf of Soviet composers and in favor of cultural exchange, and be diagnosed with an incurable progressive neurological disorder (this on top of his heart problems).

Elizabeth Wilson's fascinating collection of interviews, *Shostakovich: A Life Remembered*, includes a reminiscence by the Beethoven Quartet's then violist, Fyodor Druzhinin, that provides a firsthand look at the birth of this work, following a read-through at which the composer played the second violin part at the piano, since Zabavnikov was out sick:

> When the rehearsal was over, Dmitri Dmitrievich was visibly excited. He got up and addressed us with these words: "My dear friends, this has been for me one of the happiest moments of my life: first of all, because I think that the Quartet has turned out well, Sergei…and secondly I have had the good fortune to play in the Beethoven Quartet, even if I only played with one finger! And how did you like my Italian bit?" We immediately knew what he meant by this last remark, as in the second movement and in the Finale's coda there is a short but wonderfully beautiful and sensual melody. It evokes a nagging but unquenchable ache of the heart, perhaps because this vocal phrase verges on banality.

An impressive emotional expanse is traveled in the course of this quartet. Following the opening repeated F-sharps from the viola, we hear the principal theme enunciated by the cello, as one might expect from a cello-centric work. This melody has been termed "Haydnesque," but just how this theme is conveyed is, of course, a matter of interpretation. It can certainly be dispatched with offhand ease, but as the piece progresses it will be displayed in various guises. I like to think of it as a tune that might be whistled (though of course a cello is not much of a "whistling" instrument at heart); and although the whistling is carefree at the opening, this tune will later take on a more ominous mien—"whistling in the dark," perhaps—especially when it is played in violin harmonics just after the cellist's unaccompanied passage two-thirds the way through. Shostakovich often masked his anxiety in cheerfulness, sometimes in mordant, obviously forced merriment; here the theme, crafted to appear lighthearted by itself, fools nobody when heard in context.

The second and third movements are linked into a single span—not an uncommon trait of Shostakovich's late works—and they ask to be heard more as a single movement than as separate entities. The *Adagio* is a deeply expressive expanse, hushed and dreamlike, very intimate, yet also profoundly noble in its melancholy dignity; the finale, itself bipartite, involves a return of thematic material from the *Adagio* as well as from the opening *Allegretto*. The movements also balance each other in their references to Shostakovich's predecessors in music history: the opening notes of the *Adagio* mirror Wagner's *Tristan und Isolde*, while the conclusion of the finale anchors the piece (which largely tends toward a minor-mode feeling) in the luminous and unusual key of F-sharp major, probably not coincidentally the tonality of the unfinished Symphony No. 10 by Mahler, with whose music Shostakovich felt the deepest affinity.

String Quartet No. 15 in E-flat minor, Op. 144

Elegy (*Adagio*)
Serenade (*Adagio*)
Intermezzo (*Adagio*)
Nocturne (*Adagio*)
Marche funèbre (*Adagio molto*)
Epilogue (*Adagio—Adagio molto*)
(*The movements are performed without pause*)

Work composed: 1974, completed on May 17 in a hospital in Moscow

Work premiered: October 25, 1974, at the Leningrad Composers' Club, by
the Taneyev String Quartet (violinists Vladimir Ovcharek and Grigori Lutsky,
violins Vissarion Soloviev, and cellist Iosif Levinzon)

Instrumentation: Two violins, viola, and cello

Shostakovich expressed the wish that he might compose twenty-four string
quartets, one in each of the major and minor keys; but it was not to be. With
his Fifteenth String Quartet, written in 1974 (his penultimate year), he
arrived at his final work in the genre. The Fourteenth had been dedicated to
Sergei Shirinsky, cellist of the Beethoven String Quartet, who would die in
October 1974 just after a rehearsal of the composer's Quartet No. 15. Shostakovich was eager to have the work premiered, fearing that if it were delayed
he might not be still alive to hear it. That's why the first performance of
that final quartet was entrusted to a different ensemble, the Taneyev Quartet,
which played it in Leningrad, although the Beethoven Quartet was able to
regroup with a new cellist in time to perform the work's Moscow premiere.

Death had become very much part of Shostakovich's sphere, and his own
health was ranging from poor to precarious. In 1966 he had a heart attack;
another followed in 1971. In the end it was cancer that got him, first appearing in the lungs, then spreading to his kidneys, liver, and circulatory system.
Despite necessary hospital stays, he pushed himself as much as his weakened
state allowed, traveling to Western Europe in 1972 and to the United States
in 1973, while continuing to compose as much as he could.

A spirit of doom hovers over the Quartet No. 15. In the book *On Death
and Dying* (written in 1969, just five years before this Shostakovich quartet),
Elizabeth Kübler-Ross enunciated what would become well known as the five
stages of grief a terminally ill patient is likely to go through on the path
toward death: denial, anger, bargaining, depression, and acceptance. Shostakovich has not quite reached acceptance in this quartet; he would achieve

that shortly, in his leisurely, transcendent Viola Sonata. Certainly depression informs the Fifteenth Quartet, and in places, anger. His friends Dmitri and Ludmila Sollertinsky said of this quartet: "Shostakovich was writing about a subject that wholly preoccupied him at the time and of thoughts which obsessed him: the meaning of life and its end; death and immortality; the role of the artist and his work; himself. This theme was so close to him and so engrossed him that he continued to reflect on it after completing the quartet. It still needed concrete form."

The Fifteenth is quite unlike any of Shostakovich's other quartets, or indeed any quartet by any other composer. Each of its six movements maintains the same dark key of E-flat minor. All share the tempo marking of *Adagio*, with the fifth movement allowing for an alteration to the still-slower *Adagio molto* (which also returns at the end of the *Epilogue*). The six movements are all connected without breaks into a single thirty-five-minute span; a listener may not feel certain about precisely where one movement yields to the next. Its drama is intensely personal.

The first movement, *Elegy*, opens with a fugato passage, deliberate almost to the point of sluggishness, in which the subject sounds chant-like, covering as it does a terribly restricted melodic and harmonic range. But rather than being monotonous, the hushed music of this movement proves mesmerizing as it sets a tone of deep introspection. As we adapt to the very slow pace we become attuned to small changes in the shifting combinations of instruments, with often one, two, or three playing at any point, rather than all four. The desolate, static landscape is interrupted by a succession of extraordinary shrieks, perhaps suggesting piercing pain, perhaps the calls of disagreeable birds or animals. These startling outbursts, which mark the beginning of the second movement (*Serenade*), are achieved through a progression of overlapping notes played by the various instruments, in every case a tone that is attacked very softly (*ppp*) and then grows into a loud and shattering release (marked *sffff*). Just at the moment when one instrument reaches the end of its note the next instrument enters, with the "hand-off" being all but imperceptible. (It may strike Shostakovich aficionados that this music picks up where the composer's Thirteenth Quartet left off.) Other themes follow: an offbeat, stumbling melody (hardly more than an accented rhythmic pattern) first played by the cello, and an actual tune that is lyrical but uncomfortably foreboding.

The third movement (*Intermezzo*) begins with what sounds like a cadenza for first violin over the cello's drone bass on the tonic note of E-flat. Perhaps Shostakovich is in his "bargaining phase" here, with the cello refusing to adapt to the arguments being offered above it. In the title *Intermezzo* we may detect a touch of Shostakovich's signature irony, since that heading would normally announce a light bagatelle between weightier sections. Nothing in this quartet is light, although this is at least the shortest of the movements. It gives way to the fourth (*Nocturne*), which is launched by a languid, muted melody in the viola, ineffably sad, with the other players weaving misty webs of sound above and below it. Just where this movement is headed seems uncertain; it suggests wandering through a dreamscape that is clear in the moment but vague in the long term.

Near the end of the *Nocturne* we hear the ominous rhythm of a slow march tapped out pizzicato. This heralds the suddenly slower *Marche funèbre*, which arrives unmistakably in fully voiced minor chords. Nonetheless, much of this movement is given over to unaccompanied passages for the quartet's individual members—short funeral orations, perhaps, punctuated by the signature rhythm of the dead-march. The march passes by, and a chord played by the whole quartet, swelling in a *crescendo* in the style of the second-movement shrieks, ushers us into the *Epilogue*. Memories of earlier movements abound here, not only in the quotations of themes and motifs but also in the emotional allusions. An extraordinary passage (extraordinary even in this context in which everything is extraordinary) provides some twenty seconds of scurrying sounds that have been compared to wind whistling through a graveyard; the idea of a soul flickering on the verge of the unknown posthumous ether may cross a listener's mind during these measures. Certainly the moments that remain trace a route to nothingness, or perhaps to a transformation we are unable to glimpse.

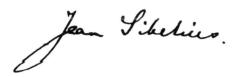

Jean Sibelius

Born: December 8, 1865, in Tavastehus, otherwise known as Hämeenlinna, Finland

Died: September 20, 1957, in Järvenpää, Finland

String Quartet in D minor, Op. 56, *Voces intimae* ("Intimate Voices")

Andante—Allegro molto moderato
Vivace
Adagio di molto
Allegro (ma pesante)
Allegro

Work composed: From November 1908 (in Järvenpää) to April 15, 1909 (in London)

Work premiered: April 25, 1910, at Helsinki Conservatory, by violinists Viktor Nováček and Sulo Hurstinen, violist Carl Lindelöf, and cellist Bror Persfelt

Instrumentation: Two violins, viola, and cello

Jean Sibelius was passionate about chamber music from his earliest years, and his catalogue lists among his juvenilia four works for string quartet (some of them fragmentary), as well as four piano trios and pieces for various other small ensembles. Three string quartets date from what we might consider his maturity, though the first two are admittedly on the cusp: the First, in A minor, in 1889; the Second, in B-flat major (Op. 4), in 1890; and the Third, in D minor (the only one heard with any regularity), in 1908–09.

Chamber music, scaled as it is for a small group of performers and ideally presented before an audience of limited size, is a natural vessel for intimate musical expressions. Certain composers are especially drawn to a confessional spirit in their music. Tchaikovsky was certainly one such—"Oh, how difficult it is to make anyone see and feel in music what we see and feel ourselves!" he once wrote to his patron Nadezhda von Meck—and in this D-minor String Quartet we see that Sibelius was another.

Subtitled *Voces intimae* ("Intimate Voices"), this quartet was Sibelius' last substantial piece of chamber music, though he would live for nearly another half-century. He was in Berlin when he finished it, and he wrote to his wife back in Finland: "It turned out to be quite wonderful. It is the sort of thing that will make one smile even on one's deathbed." Well, perhaps: but one wonders if Sibelius was exercising the famously restrained Far-North sense of humor when he made that comment. As it happens, his own deathbed was much on his mind when he composed *Voces intimae*. He was suffering from a throat ailment that persistently eluded medical diagnosis. Being preternaturally drawn to pessimism, Sibelius had no doubt whatsoever that it was cancer and apparently spent a good deal of time pondering the misery that lay ahead for him. In the end his problem turned out to be a benign tumor and the composer faced no greater inconvenience than having his physicians pester him about lightening up on cigars and alcohol. The latter he was particularly loath to contemplate, which is one of the reasons he composed practically nothing during the last thirty years of his life, which were subdued by alcoholism and depression.

The quartet's title invites us to suppose that Sibelius is here pouring his apprehensions into tones, giving musical form to the "intimate voices" of his imagination. It certainly appears that something more-or-less specific is going on in this piece, although exactly what that might be remains a mystery. It stands as a unique achievement in Sibelius' oeuvre, composed between his Third and Fourth Symphonies, connecting more in structural matters to his Sixth and Seventh Symphonies, yet seeming in the end quite unlike anything else he wrote. It is cast in five movements, with the "extra" one (since string quartets usually have four movements) being a second scherzo movement.

We pass through a broad psychological landscape as this disturbing piece unrolls, yet the tone is overwhelmingly severe. The first movement is nervous, bitter, angry, even desolate, but those sentiments give way to a dreamlike quality in the second movement, which flows out of the first without pause. Melodic and textural fragmentation prevents this first scherzo from seeming truly dancelike. The emotional heart of the quartet is the third movement, a vast *Adagio di molto* which the Sibelius scholar Erik Tawaststjerna said "symbolizes the tension between the physical world and the world beyond." "With the *adagio* of this quartet," he continued, "Sibelius puts much of his Nordic reticence on one side and, in revealing more of his inner feeling, the music assumes a special warmth." A heavy-footed theme fuels the fourth movement (*pesante* means "weighty"), and the finale pushes forward as a sort of perpetual-motion machine that, for all its vigor, never seems less than deadly serious. Upon completing this work, Sibelius wrote in his diary: "The Quartet [is] finished. I—my heart bleeds—why this sort of tragedy in life. Oh! Oh! Oh! That I should exist."

Bedřich Smetana

Born: March 2, 1824, in Litomyšl, Bohemia

Died: May 12, 1884, in Prague, Bohemia

Piano Trio in G minor, Op. 15

Moderato assai
Allegro, ma non agitato
Finale: Presto

Work composed: September through November 22, 1855, labeled his Opus 9 on completion; revised in 1857 and again prior to the work's publication, in 1880, when it was assigned the new opus number 15.

Work dedicated: To the memory of the composer's daughter Bedřiška

Work premiered: December 3, 1855, at the Konvikt Hall in Prague, with the composer as pianist, joined by violinist Antonín Bennewitz and cellist Julius Goltermann; on that occasion it shared the bill with Schubert's C-major String Quintet and Schumann's Piano Quintet. In its first revised version it was introduced on February 11, 1858, in Göteborg, Sweden, again with the composer at the keyboard.

Instrumentation: Violin, cello, and piano

The G-minor Piano Trio takes us to the beginning of Bedřich Smetana's career, to a moment when he was struggling to achieve recognition and acceptance as a composer. Times were difficult in Bohemia just then. Civil war had broken out in many areas of the Habsburg Empire, including Bohemia, and in 1846 Smetana found himself stirred into political activism; he fought with other forward-looking, mostly young Bohemians at the barricades and also wrote several musical compositions to inspire his comrades in arms. He was devastated by the movement's failure. The installation of a repressive, dictatorial regime surely played a part in his decision to leave Bohemia in 1856, shortly after the composition of his G-minor Piano Trio, to seek opportunities in Sweden.

In 1849 Smetana married Kateřina Kolářová, and they became the parents of four daughters in quick succession. The eldest of these, Bedřiška (her father's namesake), showed early signs of musical precocity, just as her father had. He nicknamed her Fritzi and encouraged her inclinations to sing and play the piano, both of which she was doing with a marked degree of musical sensitivity by the time she was four.

The G-minor Piano Trio was Smetana's first great achievement as a composer. The only large-scale works he had completed previously were a Piano Sonata (also in G minor), his *Jubel-Ouvertüre*, and his *Triumph-Symphonie* (of 1853–54); he had composed the last to honor Emperor Franz Joseph, whom the Bohemian revolutionaries had hoped would buoy their cause. Nothing in those works approaches the consistent quality of the G-minor Trio, although the Piano Sonata did furnish musical material for the Trio's finale. Perhaps Smetana would have achieved his first masterpiece in any case, but it seems clear that his surge of inspiration was born of a specific event. On June 9, 1854, the Smetanas' second daughter, Gabriela, died; on September 6, 1855, Bedřiška followed her to the tomb, a victim of scarlet fever. Thanks to Bedřiška's musical aptitude, her father had particularly adored her, and he was devastated by the loss. The Smetanas' fourth daughter, Kateřina, had been born less than two weeks before Bedřiška died; she, too, would perish the following year. Only the third daughter, Žofie, would live a full life. What's more, Smetana's wife was diagnosed with tuberculosis in 1855; she would live only until 1859. Shocking though such a scenario sounds to us today, infant mortality was tragically common in the nineteenth century: many of the composer's own siblings and half-siblings failed to reach adulthood. But the prevalence of infant mortality did not lessen the grief of a parent's loss. "Nothing can replace Fritzi," Smetana wrote in his diary, "the angel whom death has stolen from us." He immediately embarked on the composition of his G-minor Piano Trio, which he dedicated "in memory of our eldest child Bedřiška, whose rare musical talent gave us such delight; too early snatched from us by death at the age of 4½ years."

There is no mistaking the serious mien of this trio. All three of its movements are in the key of G minor, and those sections that unroll in the major mode do so out of the necessities of musical contrast without really doing much to change the somber mood. Falling intervals, especially the interval of the descending fifth, predominate in the themes, suggesting the sounds of weeping or at least sighs. Such a sinking theme is cried out, *espressivo*, right at the opening by the violin, playing on its husky-toned G string; against this the cello soon intones a yearning theme in beautifully crafted counterpoint. Although the composer never revealed an explicit program through which this piece could be construed as a portrait of his departed daughter, he did once maintain that the second theme of the first movement alludes to a tune that Bedřiška particularly loved. This *Moderato assai* is overwhelmingly intense in its emotion, even including a rather angry fugato passage. But an elegiac spirit also peeks through, especially in the more lyric sections spotlighting the violin almost as a soloist: in these passages one glimpses the sounds that would ultimately define Smetana's musical language—a rhythmically vibrant melding of vaguely modal harmony with triumphant melody. A brief solo passage for piano in the middle of the movement sounds strikingly Chopinesque, reminding the listener of Smetana-the-pianist's early infatuation with that composer's music as well as with the compositions of Liszt and Schumann. Chopin's nobility is also echoed in an elegant theme introduced by the cello and quickly taken up by all three instruments before being transformed into the punchy coda.

Staying in the tonic key of G minor for the second movement is an unusual choice; a listener might have expected a move to a contrasting tonal center. The movement is laid out as a scherzo with two trios ("alternativos," Smetana calls them, using a term that was by then old-fashioned). If Chopin had seemed a kindred soul in the first movement, Schumann would appear to have inspired the second, or perhaps Mendelssohn in the scurrying of the opening section. The writing achieves a luscious texture, and its dreamy quality spells Romantic music pure and simple.

The *Finale* opens in bustling compound rhythm, with the strings energizing the texture further through occasional plucks of pizzicato. A gorgeous, reflective theme is introduced by the cello and then answered immediately by the other instruments (the piano embellishing it with Chopinesque figuration). Near the end, Smetana inserts a funereal section, a slow march (actually marked *grave, quasi marcia*) that the piano punctuates with what we may hear as the tolling of bells.

Despite the obvious emotion behind the piece and the skill Smetana displayed in working out his material, the work was received coolly by critics at its premiere, in December 1855. Only when Liszt extolled the work, after hearing it at the Smetanas' home during a visit to Prague the following year, did its fortunes change. Encouraged by this, Smetana returned to his score and effected a number of revisions once he was installed in his new job as a music teacher in Göteborg, Sweden. He retouched it further prior to publication in 1880, and it is in this ultimate version that work went on to become the repertoire staple it is today.

String Quartet No. 1 in E minor, *Z mého života* ("From My Life")

Allegro vivo appassionato
Allegro moderato à la Polka
Largo sostenuto
Vivace

Work composed: October through December 1876

Work premiered: In a private performance in Prague in 1878, with Antonín Dvořák playing the viola part; the public premiere took place on March 29, 1879, at a concert of the Umělecká Beseda cultural group at Konvikt Hall in Prague, played by violinists Ferdinand Lachner and Jan Pelikán, violist Josef Krehan, and cellist Alois Neruda.

Instrumentation: Two violins, viola, and cello

From the mid-nineteenth century through the early twentieth, one of the big debates in the musical world was whether music should attempt to communicate a specific program—whether it was proper for composers to depict extra-musical scenes or ideas in their compositions, yielding "program music," or if they should instead write "absolute music" in which sonic discourse operates strictly on its own terms without reference to anything apart from music itself. The genre of the symphonic poem would become the hottest flashpoint in this altercation after Franz Liszt started writing such works in the 1840s.

As a young composer Smetana felt strongly attracted to Liszt and his ideals. In 1848, long before his own musical career took off, Smetana wrote to Liszt, whom he did not yet know personally, asking for a donation to help him found a music school, and he sweetened his pitch by asking Liszt to accept the dedication of a piano cycle he had composed. Liszt sent no money but he did respond with warm encouragement about Smetana's music. By 1851, thanks to Liszt's door-opening skills, Smetana managed to get his piano cycle accepted by a publisher in Leipzig—it appeared as his Op. 1—signaling the beginning of his career as a truly professional composer. Liszt continued as a mentor to Smetana, and twice in the course of his travels Smetana visited Liszt in Weimar. He also began composing symphonic poems in a generally Lisztian mold; in fact, Smetana remains most reliably represented in the repertoire today through *Má vlast* ("My Fatherland"), his cycle of six symphonic poems from the 1870s that includes the much-played *Vltava* ("The Moldau"), the ever-popular musical depiction of the river that flows through Prague.

Most symphonic poems were based on a literary source though occasionally they leaned on pictorial imagery instead. A few examples were even pressed into service as vehicles for autobiography, as Richard Strauss did in *Ein Heldenleben* (1897–98) and, to embarrassing effect, *Symphonia domestica* (1902–03). Explicit autobiography never gained as prominent a foothold in the realm of chamber music, but it actually does seem to have arrived there first, in Smetana's String Quartet No. 1, composed in 1876 and unambiguously titled *From My Life*. Perhaps because of Strauss' forcefulness in the orchestral realm, the idea of an autobiographical symphonic poem may strike us as somehow less curious than a corresponding essay in chamber music. On the other hand, music-lovers have no compunction about suggesting that a composition—a chamber work as easily as a symphonic one—may reveal its composer's depth of feeling or state of mind, and that is not very far removed from the idea of music as explicit autobiography. What's more, we are accustomed to granting that chamber music provides a particularly intimate forum for musical expression, and for that reason, too, we should not be astonished to find a composer trying to convey a piece of his life story through a chamber work.

Smetana was fifty-two years old when he wrote his String Quartet No. 1 and he had reason to think about writing his musical autobiography because by then he had experienced an interesting life with an unusual twist: two years before, in 1874, he had gone deaf. An immediate upshot was that he had to curtail his activities as conductor of the Provisional Theatre in Prague, a post he had held since 1866, and in a letter that September he informed the theatre's management of what was happening: "It was in July . . . that I noticed that in one of my ears the notes in the higher octaves were pitched differently than in the other and that at times I had a tingling feeling in my ears and heard a noise as though I was standing by a mighty waterfall. My condition changed continuously up to the end of July when it became a permanent state of affairs and it was accompanied by spells of giddiness so that I staggered to and fro and could walk straight only with the greatest concentration." In August he began to experience aural hallucinations and then, he reported to his devoted friend Josef Srb-Debrnov, "on the 20th of October I lost my hearing completely."

This was the immediate instigation for his First String Quartet, the technical demands of which met with some objections when the piece was first played through privately at Srb-Debrnov's apartment. Smetana kept few secrets from Srb-Debrnov, and on April 12, 1878, he detailed the program of this work to his friend. Here are some extracts:

> With me the form of every composition is dictated by the subject itself and thus the Quartet, too, shaped its own form. My intention was to paint a tone picture

of my life. The first movement depicts my youthful leanings towards art, the Romantic atmosphere, the inexpressible yearning for something I could neither express nor define, and also a kind of warning of my future fortune.... The long insistent note in my finale owes its origin to this. It is the fateful ringing in my ears of the high-pitched tones which, in 1874, announced the beginning of my deafness. I permitted myself this little joke because it was so disastrous to me.

The second movement, a quasi-polka, brings to my mind the joyful days of youth when I composed dance tunes and was known everywhere as a passionate lover of dancing.... The third movement—*Largo sostenuto*—reminds me of the happiness of my first love, the girl who later became my first wife.

The fourth movement describes the discovery that I could treat national elements in music, and my joy in following this path until it was checked by the catastrophe of the onset of my deafness, the outlook into the sad future, the tiny rays of hope of recovery; but remembering all the promise of my early career, nonetheless a feeling of painful regret.

That is roughly the aim of this composition, which is almost a private one and therefore deliberately written for four instruments conversing among themselves about the things that have so momentously affected me. Nothing more than that.

Smetana would go on to write a further string quartet, in 1882–83, which he completed about a year before he descended into complete insanity (the result of syphilis) and had to be moved to an asylum, where he died within weeks. Although it is not headed by a programmatic title, some commentators imagine that Smetana's Second String Quartet, which conveys considerable unease, is essentially a prolongation of his musical memoir. Whether that's correct or not, there's no question that *From My Life* did inspire a small handful of autobiographical chamber works from later Czech composers, most famously the Second String Quartet (revealingly titled *Intimate Letters*) by Leoš Janáček, and the Fifth String Quartet by Bohuslav Martinů.

Igor Stravinsky [signature]

Igor Fyodorovich Stravinsky

Born: June 5 (old style)/June 18 (new style), 1882, in Oranienbaum (now called Lomonosov) in the North-west Saint Petersburg Region of Russia

Died: April 6, 1971, in New York City

Three Pieces for String Quartet

I. ♩ = 126
II. ♩ = 76
III. ♩ = 40

Work composed: 1914 in Salvan, Switzerland, the first piece on April 26, 1914; the second on July 2; the third on July 25–26; the set was revised in December 1918.

Work dedicated: At the time of the premiere this set was dedicated to the Swiss artist Alexandre Cingria; when published, in 1922, the score bore a dedication to the conductor Ernest Ansermet.

Work premiered: May 13 (some sources say May 19), 1915, in Paris, apparently by the Flonzaley Quartet

Instrumentation: Two violins, viola, and cello

In January 1914, Stravinsky moved his growing family to Switzerland, hoping the altitude in the Alps east of Geneva would provide relief for his wife, who was suffering from tuberculosis. From there he watched war clouds gather over Europe. World War I broke out that August, and the Stravinskys settled in for the long haul in the Land of Neutrality.

During that spring and summer in Switzerland the composer produced his first essay in chamber music, the Three Pieces for String Quartet. Plans began immediately for publication in Berlin, the first step being the preparation of individual parts for the Flonzaley Quartet to use when they premiered the piece in their upcoming international tour, presenting them under the rubric *Grotesques*. Apparently the war intervened before even the parts, let alone a full score, could be prepared, so the Flonzaley Quartet played from manuscript at the premiere and the piece remained unpublished until 1922. In 1914 Stravinsky also produced an arrangement of the Three Pieces for piano four-hands, and in December 1918 he revised the string-quartet version. In 1928 he would revisit these pieces again, orchestrating them to serve as the first three of his Four Etudes for Orchestra, the additional piece being a transcription of an Etude for Pianola he had written in 1917. That's when he supplied descriptive titles to the movements, with the Three Pieces turning into "Dance," "Eccentric," and "Canticle."

The Three Pieces were brief and, on the surface, unassuming. The first lasted a minute at most, the second perhaps two minutes, the third perhaps four; and they carried the entirely objective titles "I. $\quarternote$ = 126," "II. $\quarternote$ = 76," and "III. $\quarternote$ = 40." The critic and author Paul Griffiths, in his book *The String Quartet: A History*, precisely grasps the historical significance of these several minutes. He writes: "Stravinsky's work, for the first time in the history of the genre, is determinedly not a 'string quartet' but a series of pieces to be played by four strings. There is no acknowledgment of a tradition or a form, and the lack of any such acknowledgment seems iconoclastic because of our own experience of the genre's traditions.... The notion of quartet dialogue has no place here, nor have subtleties of blend: the texture is completely fragmented, with each instrument sounding for itself."

The intrepid Flonzaley Quartet played their premiere in Paris on May 13, 1915 (some sources say May 19); introduced them to America in Chicago on November 8, 1915; and brought them to New York's Aeolian Hall three weeks later. Conservative critics were aghast. "If this type of passage has any proper place in the art of the string quartet, then the end is near," wrote one, citing a spot in the second movement. On the other hand, forward-looking listeners found them stimulating. Following the New York concert the poet Amy Lowell even penned a poetic triptych that tried to "reproduce the sound and movement of the music as far as is possible in another medium."

The first movement, the minute-long $\quarternote$ = 126 (later "Dance"), is a sort of repetitive bitonal march consisting of a four-note melody repeated incessantly above a drone bass. One imagines a medieval pipe-and-tabor musician intoning a tune on a flute with so few holes that it could be fingered with just one hand while simultaneously beating a drum accompaniment with his other hand. But things are not so simplistic as they may seem at first glance. A complicated bit of a rhythmic play is going on here: a twenty-three-beat melody repeating over an unvarying metric plan of one 3/4 measure plus two 2/4 measures. Three of these three-measure units obviously add up to twenty-one beats, so a rhythmic displacement inevitably occurs when the length of the tune (twenty-three beats) and the length of the metric underpinning (twenty-one beats) fail to coincide. This keeps the piece ever intriguing, despite its paucity of thematic material. The Stravinsky scholar Stephen Walsh has offered a splendid metaphor: "a permanently revolving target (the main tune) at which the second violin hurls missiles, always hitting it at a different point until it eventually stops hitting it on the head." Amy Lowell's poem conjures up something essential to this movement's spirit:

> ...Bang! Bump! Tong!
> Petticoats,
> Stockings,
> Sabots,
> Delirium flapping its thigh-bones;
> Red, blue, yellow,
> Drunkenness steaming in colors;...

The second movement, ♩ = 76 (later "Eccentric"), recalls the Russian passion for the circus and may suggest the puppet-show music from *Petrushka*. Stravinsky related this mercurial music to a clown named Little Tich he had seen perform in London in the summer of 1914. "The jerky, spastic movement, the ups and downs, the rhythm—even the mood or joke of the music—was suggested by the art of this great clown," he wrote. In the sketchbook documenting Stravinsky's 1918 revision of the Three Pieces we find the words "a female dancer on horseback" inscribed next to a recurrence of the little trumpet-like motif that sounds a few moments into the piece. But the circus connection seems to have been strictly Stravinsky's creation, since elsewhere in the sketch he notes of that very motif that it derived from "a Breton song given to me by Shura [Alexandre] Benois. A clarinetist, sitting on a stone, during a strong rain, played full force and the music was danced."

The set concludes with ♩ = 40 (later "Canticle"), a solemn chant, again with a tightly constrained melody. The composer described it as "choral and religious in character." ("The nave is blue with incense, / Writhing, twisting, / Snaking over the heads of the chanting priests," was Ms. Lowell's interpretation.) As in the first movement, this is an exercise in economy of means.

The principal theme, a five-measure chant phrase, embraces only three different pitches within the tight compass of a minor third. The chant's progress alternates with slightly more urgent phrases, suggesting the responsorial style of much liturgical music. This movement claimed a special place in its composer's heart, and he would later point to its last twenty measures as "some of my best music of that time."

L'*Histoire du Soldat* ("The Soldier's Tale")

PART ONE
The Soldier's March
Scene One: Airs by a Stream
Interlude: The Soldier's March (repeated)
Scene Two: Pastorale
Interlude: Airs by a Stream (repeated)
Scene Three: Airs by a Stream (repeated again)

PART TWO
The Soldier's March (altered version)
The Royal March
Scene Four: The Little Concert
Scene Five
   Three Dances: Tango; Waltz; Ragtime
   The Devil's Dance
   Little Chorale
   The Devil's Song
   The Great Chorale
Scene Six
   Triumphal March of the Devil

Suite from L'*Histoire du Soldat* ("The Soldier's Tale"), arranged by the composer for Clarinet, Violin, and Piano

The Soldier's March
The Soldier's Violin (Scene of the Soldier at the Stream)
A Little Concert
Tango—Waltz—Ragtime
The Devil's Dance

Work composed: 1918; the trio arrangement dates from autumn 1919

Work dedicated: To Werner Reinhart

Work premiered: September 28, 1918, at the Théâtre Municipal de Lausanne, Switzerland, with Ernest Ansermet conducting; the trio version was first heard on November 8, 1919, in Lausanne.

Orchestration: The complete ballet requires clarinet, bassoon, cornet, trombone, violin, double-bass, two snare drums (in different sizes) with snare releases, triangle, tambourine, field drum with snare release, bass drum, cymbal, tambourine, triangle (with one musician playing all the percussion instruments), the seven musicians being joined by actor/dancers and a narrator; the trio setting uses clarinet, violin, and piano.

At the close of World War I, it must often have seemed in Europe that the only thing not in short supply was necessity. Nations were displaced, fortunes were decimated, and—for many—life's luxuries remained on hold. Notwithstanding his early successes for Serge Diaghilev's Ballets Russes (which already included the ballets *The Firebird, Petrushka, The Rite of Spring,* and *Les noces*), Igor Stravinsky was in as dire straits as everyone else, somehow scraping by in Switzerland. The political conflict had cut off Stravinsky's access to his family's estate in Russia and his publisher, Serge Koussevitzky's Édition Russe de Musique (which, despite its French name and Russian focus, was headquartered in war-torn Berlin), had stopped sending royalties. Even if there had been a way to get money through, not much would have been forthcoming, since concert and ballet performances had all but dried up.

Desperate times call for desperate solutions; Necessity proved herself, yet again, to be the Mother of Invention. Several years earlier, the conductor Ernest Ansermet had introduced Stravinsky to Charles F. Ramuz, a Swiss novelist, and Stravinsky and Ramuz found themselves to be compatible as friends and collaborators. Since Ramuz's royalties weren't arriving either, the pair devised a scheme to write a stage work that could be produced on the cheap, requiring only a handful of performers and portable enough to be mounted on tour with minimal effort. The result was *L'Histoire du Soldat* ("The Soldier's Tale"), a quirky musical-theatre work for seven instrumentalists plus actor/dancers and narrator, which Stravinsky and Ramuz worked out while hunkered down in the town of Morges in 1918.

It received its first performance on September 28 of that year, in spiffier surroundings than the creators might have dared hoped for—the Théâtre Municipal de Lausanne. Sets and costumes were devised by René Auberjonois, and Ernest Ansermet conducted a group of distinguished instrumentalists while university-student actor/dancers did their best in the featured stage parts. A contemporary account by Jean Villard-Gilles (who recited the part of the Devil in the premiere) suggests the colorful spirit of the preparations for the first production of *The Soldier's Tale*:

> Stravinsky and Ramuz were in charge of daily rehearsals—the former always in a frenzy of enthusiasm, inventiveness, joy, indignation, headache; leaping on the piano as if it were a dangerous foe that had to be subdued by a bout of fisticuffs, then bounding on to the stage, swallowing glasses of kirsch whose after-effects had to be combated with the aid of aspirin: the latter, calm, attentive, friendly, rather bashful when giving advice, seeing things from our point of view, trying (like us) to find the right answers, showing an indomitable patience, and following with malicious enjoyment the genial capers of his collaborator.

The production came together on a shoestring, but, against all odds, it was a success. Nonetheless, the tour that was to have ensued (which had been the rationale of the piece in the first place) never took place, derailed by an influenza epidemic. In 1920, the impresario Serge Diaghilev entertained the idea of mounting it as a "proper" ballet, with designs by Picasso, including sandwich-man outfits for the dancers. This came to naught, but slowly the work's reputation began to spread and it became established as a curious little masterpiece. Whether offered as a miniature ballet or as a simple concert work with narration, *The Soldier's Tale* is strictly sui generis.

Eleven numbers make up the piece; some are repeated in the course of the show, and several consist of multiple, discrete sections. Together they tell a story amalgamated by Ramuz from an anthology of Russian folk tales that had been assembled by Alexander Afanasiev. Ramuz's libretto/scenario is structured in two parts, each comprising three scenes. In the first scene, a soldier on leave trades his magic fiddle to the devil, launching a bizarre sequence of magical encounters in which he gains wealth and then learns to despise it, wishing only that he had his fiddle back. In the second part, the soldier does manage to regain his violin, as well as the hand of a princess; but, in the end, he unwisely crosses over into the devil's territory once more, and loses his fiddle again. The music is minutely intertwined with the stage action, carefully matching the dramatic trajectory of the play. Though only two of the eleven musical numbers bear key signatures, Stravinsky's tonality remains clearly rooted. References to popular musical genres are clear—the tango, the waltz, the ragtime, even the Spanish pasodoble of "The Royal March." As befits the slender forces, Stravinsky's score is taut, pithy, ultra-condensed, and more than a little cynical.

A year after creating *The Soldier's Tale*, Stravinsky drew from the score a five-movement suite that he orchestrated for the reduced grouping of clarinet, violin, and piano. The violin was indispensable, since the plot hinges on that instrument. The clarinet was essential in a different way; the original production of *The Soldier's Tale* had been underwritten by Werner Reinhart, an "altruistic gentleman" (as Stravinsky put it) who happened to be an amateur clarinetist as well as a philanthropist. Whether Stravinsky made this adaptation as a gracious gesture to his sponsor or in the hope that Reinhart would pay him extra for it remains unclear. That the third instrument is a piano is ironic in light of Stravinsky's remarks, in his *Chronicle of My Life* (1936), about his instrumentation for the original *L'Histoire du Soldat*: "I had to avoid it [the piano] for two reasons: either my score would have seemed like a piano arrangement—and that would have given evidence of a certain lack of financial means, not at all in keeping with our intentions—or I should have had to use it as a solo instrument, exploiting every possibility of its technique." In the event, he did end up making what is basically a piano arrangement after all.

Octet

Sinfonia
Tema con variazioni
Finale: Tempo giusto

Work composed: Begun near the end of 1922 in Biarritz and completed May 20, 1923, in Paris; revised slightly in 1952

Work premiered: October 18, 1923, with Stravinsky conducting, on a concert series overseen by Serge Koussevitzky at the Paris Opera House

Instrumentation: Flute, clarinet, two bassoons, two trumpets, and two trombones

"I began to write this music without knowing what its sound medium would be," stated Stravinsky in *Chronicle of My Life* (1936), "that is to say, what instrumental form it would take. I only decided that point after finishing the first part, when I saw clearly what ensemble was demanded by the contrapuntal material, the character, and the structure of what I had composed." But Stravinsky was greatly given to revision, and just as his Octet (or Octuor, to use its original French name) underwent some alterations thirty years after it was composed, so did his story of the work's genesis get a makeover. The changes to the score were minimal: corrections of a few misprints that had crept into the original parts, the slowing down of one metronome marking, refinements of dynamics—the sorts of changes Stravinsky sometimes made in order to qualify for copyright extension. The transformation of the background story was more fundamental. In Stravinsky's *Dialogues and a Diary* (1963), he reported that the vision of his unorthodox ensemble came to him in a dream. "I awoke from this little concert in a state of great delight and anticipation and the next morning began to compose the Octuor, which I had had no thought of the day before."

Stravinsky went to lengths to stress the objective quality of his Octet. In an article he published in a Brooklyn monthly magazine called *The Arts* (January 1924), he explained: "My Octuor is not an 'emotive' work but a musical composition based on objective elements which are sufficient in themselves. The reasons why I composed this kind of music for an octuor of flute, clarinet, bassoons, trumpets, and trombones are the following: First, because this ensemble forms a complete sonorous scale and consequently furnishes me with a sufficiently rich register; second, because the difference of the volume of these instruments renders more evident the musical architecture. And this is the most important question in all my recent musical compositions. I have excluded from this work all sorts of nuances, which I have replaced by the play of these volumes." It is, in short, a piece to be played but not interpreted. Its dry, astringent wit stands on its own.

This is surely a work of chamber music, but its rhythms and its mercurial changes of meters can prove maddening. It is therefore one of the few pieces in the chamber repertoire that is regularly led by a conductor. Stravinsky himself conducted the work's premiere.

The *Sinfonia* opens with a slow exordium (*Lento*) that the composer likened to the measured introductions of Haydn's late symphonies. All the instruments pause on a sustained chord of relative consonance and then march briskly into the body of the movement (*Allegro moderato*), a sort of sonatina with a recognizable exposition and recapitulation, the latter including some playful fuguing in the brass, but without much of a development. One is reminded of Stravinsky's remark that, on the whole, he'd prefer Classical symphonies if their development sections were simply cut out.

Stravinsky had scarcely employed the theme-and-variations form before he embarked on the second movement of the Octet—the Gavotte with two variations in his ballet *Pulcinella* (1919–20) is simply an arrangement from an eighteenth-century harpsichord sonata by Carlo Ignazio Monza— but you would never guess it from the mastery he displays in working out the possibilities of his material. Here he comes up with a hybrid take on the standard procedure by recalling Variation A as a recurrent visitor; you might call this a theme-and-variations rondo. The composer stated that his favorite part of the whole piece was Variation E, a slow, mysterious fugato based on an inversion of the original tune. In this dense, organ-like writing one recalls Prokofiev's quip that Stravinsky sounds like "Bach on the wrong notes," an impression that also carries over to the *Finale*, which follows without pause. Indeed, Stravinsky said of the *Finale*, "Bach's Two-part Inventions were somewhere in the remote back of my mind while composing this movement."

[signature]

Karol Maciej Szymanowski

Born: October 6, 1882, in Tymoszówka, Poland (now Ukraine, near Kiev)

Died: March 29, 1937, in Lausanne, Switzerland

String Quartet No. 1 in C major, Op. 37

Lento assai
Andantino semplice (In modo d'una canzone) [attacca]
Vivace—Scherzando alla Burlesca (Vivace ma non troppo)

Work composed: Autumn 1917

Work dedicated: To the French musicologist and critic Henry Prunières

Work premiered: April 1924, in the Concert Hall of the Warsaw Conservatory, by the String Quartet of the Warsaw Philharmonic

Instrumentation: Two violins, viola, and cello

Szymanowski's First String Quartet dates from precisely the period when the Russian Revolution broke out. It appears that he composed most of it just prior to his family's war-enforced displacement from their ancestral home in the town of Tymoszówka, Poland. He had recently completed his Third Symphony (*The Song of the Night*, 1914–16), First Violin Concerto (1916), and Third Piano Sonata (1917), middle-period works that are infused with his distinctive blend of musical influences from Germany and Austria (Wagner, Mahler, Schoenberg), Russia (Scriabin), and France (Debussy, Ravel). His biographer Christopher Palmer has described this as "a transitional piece which in its new linear and formal clarity and contrapuntal consistency flows back in the classical mainstream (or is it forward to neo-classicism?) and clears the decks for Szymanowski's forthcoming discovery and assimilation of folksong."

The String Quartet No. 1 reflects the provisional state of a piece that was never really completed, though it stands as a satisfactory entity as it is. He intended for the *Scherzando alla Burlesca* to serve as the second movement, after the opening *Lento assai*. The *Andantino semplice* would follow, and the piece would conclude with a fugal fourth movement. This seems like an odd choice, since the *Scherzando alla Burlesca* is already largely fugal; but of course the two fugal movements would have been separated in the re-ordered context. In any case, in the turmoil surrounding the Revolution and his displacement, Szymanowski retreated more and more into the extensive novel he was writing—*Ephebos*, which might be described as a paean to homosexual love (bordering on pedophilia) inspired by his travels in southern Italy, Sicily, and North Africa. Thus occupied, he never managed to produce the fugue he envisioned. He held on to his plan for years but the finale continued to elude him. In 1924 he finally allowed the piece to be premiered in its three-movement form, and immediately after that he released it to be published, though he maintained that he still hoped to write the desired finale and that the publisher would attach it to the printed score when the time came. The time never came.

Although the opening tempo markings are useful in identifying the movements of this quartet, they don't really convey the overall pace or character of each movement since the music tends to roam through disparate terrains of tempo and mood. The first movement, for example, does begin *Lento assai* ("Very slow"), but by its eighth measure Szymanowski instructs the players to speed up, then to relax to the opening tempo, then to proceed to an *Allegro moderato*, then (via a *sostenuto* measure) to a *tempo risoluto*, to a *tranquillo* passage, and so on—all this on the first three pages of the score. Szymanowski's early attraction to the ultra-chromaticism of turn-of-the-century Vienna (think of Schoenberg's *Verklärte Nacht*) is much on display in the opening movement; near its conclusion he even offers a near-quotation from Wagner's *Tristan und Isolde*. All the same, he then goes and ends the movement on a C-major chord, the most tonal gesture imaginable, and he has the four musicians play it pizzicato and as loudly as possible, with each player plucking all four of the instrument's strings to yield a sixteen-part texture.

The second movement, *Andantino semplice (In modo d'una canzone)*, is a hauntingly beautiful expanse of a mysterious cast that, again, owes much to the general tenor of last-gasp-Romanticism. The murmuring inner lines of the middle section evoke Debussy, as do prominent whole-tone steps in the first violin's melody that lies far above.

The concluding movement is a fugue with a striking twist: each of the four parts is written in a different key. The first violin plays in A major, the second violin in F-sharp major, the viola in E-flat major, and the cello in C major, with each line bearing its own key signature to support the respective key. Together, the scales of these four keys include all twelve tones of the chromatic scale. For the central section, introduced by widely spaced, broken chords in the cello (shades of Rimsky-Korsakov's *Scheherazade*), the parts all move up a step to B major, A-flat major, F major, and D major; but for the recapitulation they return, via further harmonic complications, to their original pitch levels. This piece was written just as bitonality was growing popular among edgy composers, but it's far more common for bitonality to be notated through the insertion of accidentals within an overriding key signature, or on a canvas of no sharps or flats at all, than with the different signatures for each part. (One composer who did follow Szymanowski's lead, perhaps without knowing it, was Gustav Holst, in his Terzetto for Flute, Oboe, and Viola, Op. 44, of 1925; each of its two movements uses a different combination of three keys for its three instruments.) This third movement follows the second one *attacca*, which is to say without a break. Szymanowski does separate them, however, by seven measures of transition (*Vivace*), of which four consist entirely of silences and the rest comprise three-note unison articulations of three eighth-notes each time, the first group set *piano*, the second in a blustery, Beethovenian *fortissimo*. The four-keyed fugal finale ensues, cast in a sort of sonata form. The music seems to sputter out near the end as a whistling, sardonic joke (adumbrations of Shostakovich), and the final two sonorities echo the conclusion of the first movement by being utterly tonal, again yielding an ending on a C-major chord and again pizzicato, but this time played *pianississimo*, with only three notes per instrument.

String Quartet No. 2, Op. 56

> *Moderato dolce e tranquillo*
> *Vivace, scherzando*
> *Lento*

Work composed: 1927

Work dedicated: To Dr. Olgierd and Juli Sokołowski

Work premiered: May 14, 1929, in the concert hall of the Warsaw Conservatory, by the Warsaw String Quartet

Instrumentation: Two violins, viola, and cello

Szymanowski spent the decade of the 1920s in Poland, though traveling frequently to the musical centers of Western Europe (especially Paris) as the

leading emissary of Polish music. In 1927 he was offered the directorships
of two conservatories, those of Cairo—which he turned down with some
regret, since the warm climate might have helped his persistent respiratory
problems—and of Warsaw, which he accepted, seeing in it the opportunity
to reinvigorate Polish musical education. This he would achieve, but with
difficulty; and, exhausted by the political pressures of his mission, he resigned
in 1929.

By the mid-1920s he had grown enraptured with folk music, especially
that of the Tatra Gorals, in the mountainous region of Poland. In 1926, these
sounds inspired his ballet *Harnasie* (Op. 55), which is filled with quotations
from folk songs and dances. The work that occupied him the following year,
the String Quartet No. 2 (Op. 56), makes more subtle use of the same sources.
Instead of direct citations, Szymanowski here employs their musical materials as building blocks for a new compositional vocabulary. The scales of their
music therefore become the scales of the Second Quartet: curious modalities
with the second and fourth degrees of the scale sharpened (sometimes leading
to out-and-out bitonality), often underscored by discordant drones reminiscent of rustic bagpipes. Said the composer, "It is important to know how to
take the eternally beating 'heart of the people' into one's hand—outside the
sphere of apodictic estheticism—and to recreate in the shape of a perfect and
easily comprehensible work of art what emerges among the people themselves
as an independent creative power, unrestricted by any kind of dogma." This
would become a central concern of his later work, worked out through such
large-scale compositions as his Symphony No. 4 and Violin Concerto No. 2.

Szymanowski achieves a highly personal expression in this quartet. This
may result from the work's situation at a sort of crossroads (and synthesis)
of many of the influences that wafted through his music: classical formal-
ism, nationalistic folk inspiration, structure-by-sonority (à la Debussy or
Scriabin), percussive rhythmic propulsion. The first movement is broadly a
sonata-allegro, though the composer seeks creative modernist adaptations of
the classic formal layout. The opening theme (in the first violin and cello) is
haunting, disembodied in a way that recalls Ravel, and the inner voices add
ominous fluttering. Alarm intensifies in the second section, and an uneasy
spirit reigns throughout the masterful working-out of material.

Folk influence surfaces prominently in the second movement, an
energetic *Vivace* whose secondary marking of *scherzando* seems more lightweight than the piece really wants to be. The movement unrolls loosely as
a rondo with variations, and it includes expanses of canonic writing. Strict
counterpoint stands at the heart of the third movement, which is built as a
double fugue in four parts: the first subject resembles a theme Szymanowski
had used in the *Harnasie* ballet, which had itself been derived from a folk
melody. Though it opens *Lento*, this final movement is actually a succession

of segments in many tempos, some of them quick; in essence, it follows the model of Bartók's String Quartet No. 2 in positioning what is at heart a slow movement as a finale—one of practically lunar bleakness. Indeed, Bartók is the composer who comes most to mind to a listener searching for stylistic comparisons. The two composers, born a year apart, were pursuing strikingly parallel paths of artistic development.

Szymanowski composed his Second Quartet for a competition held by the Musical Fund Society in Philadelphia, which sought to reward an exceptional new chamber work for any combination of instruments. In the event, the Society declared two composers as equal winners, neither of whom was Szymanowski. The prizes went instead to Alfredo Casella, for his Serenade for Five Instruments, and to Bartók, for his String Quartet No. 3.

Pyotr Ilyich Tchaikovsky

Born: April 25 (old style)/May 7 (new style), 1840, at Votkinsk, in the district of Viatka, Russia, some 700 miles east-northeast of Moscow

Died: October 25 (old style)/November 6 (new style), 1893, in St. Petersburg, Russia

String Quartet No. 1 in D major, Op. 11

Moderato e simplice
Andante cantabile
Scherzo: Allegro non tanto e con fuoco
Finale: Allegro giusto

Work composed: February 1871 in Moscow

Work dedicated: To the composer's friend Serge Ratschinsky, a botanist with literary pretensions

Work premiered: March 16 (old style)/28 (new style), 1871, at the Nobles' Club in Moscow, played by a quartet of members of the Russian Musical Society: the violinists Ferdinand Laub and Ippolit Prianishnikov, the violist Ludwig Minkus (the noted ballet composer), and the cellist Wilhelm Fitzenhagen

Instrumentation: Two violins, viola, and cello

Pyotr Ilyich Tchaikovsky enrolled at the St. Petersburg Conservatory immediately when it opened in 1862 as an ambitious institution directed by the pianist Anton Rubinstein. By the time he graduated, in 1865, he had developed into a composer who boasted a polished technique and seemed to have something distinctive to express. Anton's younger brother, Nikolai

Rubinstein, also a pianist, set about founding a conservatory in Moscow to complement Anton's establishment in St. Petersburg. In 1865 Nikolai traveled to St. Petersburg to recruit faculty, bringing back to his incipient Moscow Conservatory Anton's protégé Tchaikovsky to be a music theory professor.

When he penned his Quartet No. 1, Tchaikovsky was barely squeaking by on his salary from the Moscow Conservatory and the extra income he derived from private teaching. An all-Tchaikovsky concert seemed like just the thing to raise his profile and his professional prospects, but the idea of hiring an orchestra for such an occasion was unrealistic. Instead, he set his sights on a more modest program of solo and chamber works, and accordingly wrote this quartet quickly in February 1871. The concert, which took place in Moscow on March 16/28, 1871, was a success both artistically and financially; Tchaikovsky took special pleasure from the fact that the senior literary lion Ivan Turgenev attended, thanks to enthusiastic comments about Tchaikovsky he had heard while abroad. When the quartet was presented in St. Petersburg that October the composer reported that it "created a *furore*." It was also one of his earliest works to gain performances abroad, reaching both Boston and London in 1876, with the distinguished violinist Leopold Auer introducing it in the latter city.

When Tchaikovsky composed his String Quartet No. 1 he was going through a relatively nationalistic phase, here evident in the second of the work's four movements. It employs a Russian folk tune, "Sidel Vanya," that the composer had heard and written down two years earlier while visiting his sister in Kamenka, Ukraine. He had already gotten use out of the tune, having set it in 1869 as the forty-seventh of his Fifty Russian Folksongs for piano four-hands, a collection that would go on to serve as a source for works as diverse as his opera *The Snow Maiden*, his Serenade for String Orchestra, and his overture *1812*.

The words of the folk song start off "Vanya sat on a sofa and smoked a pipe of tobacco," but the melody is far more gorgeous than you might expect from lyrics like that. It manages to combine elegance with a sense of the primitive or folkish—the former thanks to its beautifully crafted melodic contour and its hushed dynamics (the four instruments play with mutes through the whole movement), the latter through a striking amalgam of duple and triple meters plus a few modal harmonies. The tune alternates with another beautiful theme, and much of the fascination of this deceptively simple piece involves the subtle alterations Tchaikovsky introduces in the accompanying parts when the themes recur.

In December 1876 the novelist Leo Tolstoy, seated next to the composer at a private performance, foundered in tears upon hearing this movement played. "Never have I been so flattered in my life," wrote Tchaikovsky, "nor felt so proud of my work." Indeed, the quartet was the first of his compositions to achieve widespread acclaim—and particularly the *Andante cantabile* movement, which became an independent chestnut appearing in all sorts of arrangements by other musicians. People tended to follow Tolstoy's lachrymose lead in whatever guise the piece was presented. Writing of a concert presented just following Tchaikovsky's death, the Grand Duke Konstantin Konstantinovich, president of the Russian Musical Society, wrote: "[Leopold] Auer played the Violin Concerto, and then, for an encore, played the *Andante* from the String Quartet in a transcription for violin and orchestra. It was marvelous, and it seems that many in the audience wept." The arrangement Auer played was one of the first to be made of this movement—he had been programming it since 1873—but other transcriptions quickly followed from the violinist Ferdinand Laub and the cellist Wilhelm Fitzenhagen (the future dedicatee of the composer's Variations on a Rococo Theme), both of whom had participated in the quartet's premiere. A catalogue of Tchaikovsky's works issued in 1897 by the composer's principal Moscow publisher, Pyotr Ivanovich Jürgenson, offered no fewer than eight versions of this movement available through that imprint alone, and that was just a fraction of all the published editions that were floating around by that time.

What surrounds the *Andante cantabile* is also of a high caliber. The opening movement, *Moderato e simplice* (to use the composer's odd misspelling of what is often, understandably, corrected to *semplice*) opens with uncomplicated chords in a syncopated, pulsating figure, recalling on one hand Schubert's *Death and the Maiden* Quartet, on the other an accordion. Then follows the muted *Andante cantabile*, and after that a forceful *Scherzo* filled with boisterous rhythms. Its contrasting trio section begins dancelike, with the cello rumbling in the cellar, but evolves into eeriness. The spirit of folk dance inhabits the grandly scaled *Finale*, too, replete as it is with repeated rhythms and bumptious accents. The final two movements may not quite fulfill the promise of the opening two, but there is nothing to object to in them, and that in itself is a considerable compliment to a first endeavor in a challenging medium.

In an 1873 article in *The Voice*, the music critic Herman Laroche, who followed Tchaikovsky's musical development assiduously, singled out the First String Quartet for marking an advance in its composer's management of form. "This is particularly true of the first Allegro," he wrote, "whose themes are at a decent, average level but which is written so coherently and fluently that it makes a graceful impression such as could not have been made with more significant themes but less rounded form.... In general the string quartet, with its radiant mood, represents a rather rare exception among the works of Mr. Tchaikovsky, in whose soul melancholy and disillusionment predominate, sometimes reaching a tone of somber hopelessness."

String Quartet No. 3 in E-flat minor, Op. 30

Andante sostenuto—Allegro moderato—Sostenuto
Allegretto vivo e scherzando
Andante funebre e doloroso ma con moto
Finale: Allegro non troppo e risoluto

Work composed: From January through February 18 (old style)/March 2 (new style), 1876; begun in Paris and completed in Moscow.

Work dedicated: To the memory of the violinist Ferdinand Laub, a fellow-professor of Tchaikovsky at the Moscow Conservatory

Work premiered: In a private performance on March 14/26, 1876, in Moscow, at the home of Nikolai Rubinstein; the first public performance took place March 30/April 11, 1876, at the Moscow Conservatory, played by violinists Josef (or Jan) Hřímalý and Adolf Brodsky, violist Yuri Gerber, and cellist Wilhelm Fitzenhagen.

Instrumentation: Two violins, viola, and cello

Notwithstanding the charm of the First String Quartet, the Third is considered by many connoisseurs to be Tchaikovsky's greatest contribution to the genre. It is certainly imposing, both in length (lasting about thirty-five minutes) and in emotional gravity, particularly in its first and third movements—which, as it happens, account for almost three-quarters of its running time. Tchaikovsky dedicated this quartet to the memory of the recently deceased Ferdinand Laub, the Czech violinist who was Tchaikovsky's colleague on the faculty of the Moscow Conservatory and who, as leader of the Russian Musical Society's quartet, had participated in the premieres of the composer's first two string quartets. As it turned out, this piece would institute a tradition whereby Russian composers would write chamber music compositions as memorials, although as the practice took root it would center on piano trios rather than string quartets.

Tchaikovsky was almost always given to grave self-doubts about his compositions, and the premiere of this Third Quartet, at a soirée at the home of his colleague Nikolai Rubinstein, gave him a predictable opportunity to let loose with misgivings, which he did to his brother the following day: "I think I'm all written out. I've begun to repeat myself and can't come up with anything new. Can I really have sung my swansong? Have I really nowhere else to go?" He was mistaken, as he generally was during these crises of uncertainty. Before the year was up he would compose his symphonic fantasy *Francesca da Rimini* and his Variations on a Rococo Theme for Cello and Orchestra (although those, in turn, would provide further opportunities for Tchaikovsky to question his instincts); and he would complete his ballet score *Swan Lake* in April 1876, only two months after finishing this quartet. The ballet had occupied him since the preceding August, and he took a break from it in order to compose the Third Quartet, which shares something of its tragic spirit. Audiences didn't show any reservations about the Quartet, but Tchaikovsky nonetheless revised it immediately.

The opening movement is expansive by chamber-music standards, encompassing some 600 measures. Two sustained slow sections (*Andante sostenuto*) of deeply confessional character frame this movement, in both cases focusing on an impassioned melody of almost desperate sadness. These surround a central section (*Allegro moderato*) of contrasting urgency. The Baltimore journalist H. L. Mencken was doubtless thinking of music like this when he referred slightingly to "the sonorous but maudlin stuff of such fellows as Tschaikovsky." Mencken could be both amusing and dead wrong—sometimes the former and very often the latter when it came to music; but a loaded word like "maudlin" is a relative one, greatly dependent on the both the perceived and the perceiver, and standards may have changed since his time. Even hard-to-please Stravinsky, who cited Tchaikovsky as one of the few Russian composers whose music he actually liked, observed that Tchaikovsky "is reproached for 'vulgarity.'" He continued: "But it seems to me that to be 'vulgar' is not to be in one's proper place, and surely Tchaikovsky's art, devoid as it is of all pretentiousness, cannot be accused of this fault....The 'pathos' in his music is a part of his nature, not the pretension of an artistic ideal." In any case, comments like Mencken's may have as much to do with an interpretation as they do with a composition in any objective sense. For example, the musicologist Jean-Alexandre Ménétrier found that the central section of this movement exhibited "an icy, Nordic sensibility"—a possibility, but a more heated interpretation is also plausible.

The second movement (*Allegretto vivo e scherzando*) is a fleeting, balletic, potentially acerbic scherzo, little more than a palate-cleanser between the Quartet's two "major" movements. The third movement (*Andante funebre e doloroso, ma con moto*) is the most obvious memorial portion of this piece: a ten-minute lament in which the muted strings produce a haunted tone from the rasping bite of the opening measures. Muting of strings most usually accompanies quiet music, but here Tchaikovsky marks the opening nine measures *forte* and then repeats them *fortissimo*. The string tone sounds accordingly raw, even downright hoarse. Into this unaccustomed sonic landscape the composer infuses not just the sorts of tragic outpourings one finds in *Swan Lake* and the soon-to-follow opera *Evgeny Onegin*, but even funereal allusions to liturgical chanting. The overriding key of E-flat minor veers into the relative major—G-flat major—for a poignant melody introduced by the first violin, *piangendo e molto espressivo* ("weeping, and very expressively"). At the movement's end the chant music returns, a solemn send-off followed only by ultra-high-pitched chords that die away into nothingness.

The *Finale* follows the lead of the scherzo in not trying to compete with the big movements: consider it simply an energetic postlude, though with a brief recollection of the quartet's opening tragic theme—a movement infused with the spirit of dance and recalling more than a little the impetuous finale of the composer's celebrated First Piano Concerto. The wife of Adolf Brodsky, the violinist who played in this work's premiere, reported that Tchaikovsky joined the Brodskys for a simple dinner *à trois* one night at their home in Leipzig. After dinner the other members of the Brodsky Quartet materialized and surprised the master with a performance of his Third Quartet. "I saw the tears run down his cheek as he listened," she related in her memoirs, "and then, passing from one performer to the other, he expressed again and again his gratitude for the happy hour they had given him. Then turning to Brodsky he said in his naïve way: 'I did not know I had composed such a fine quartet. I never liked the finale, but now I see it is really good.'"

The Quartet No. 3 was enthusiastically cheered at its premiere, as it was in two further performances that took place within the following week. "It pleased everyone *very* much," Tchaikovsky wrote to his brother. "During the Andante (andante funebre e doloroso) many, so I'm old, were in tears. If this is true, then it's a great triumph." The work remained popular throughout Tchaikovsky's lifetime, and when he died it was featured in several concerts presented in his memory.

Piano Trio in A minor, Op. 50

Pezzo elegiaco: Moderato assai—Allegro giusto
Tema con variazioni: Andante con moto
Variazione finale e Coda: Allegro risoluto e con fuoco—Andante con moto

Work composed: December 1881 to January 28 (old style)/February 9 (new style), 1882, then revised in April 1882

Work dedicated: "To the memory of a great artist," by which Tchaikovsky meant the pianist Nikolai Grigorevich Rubinstein, who founded the Moscow Conservatory

Work premiered: March 11/23, 1882, in a private concert at the Moscow Conservatory, played by pianist Sergei Taneyev, violinist Josef (Jan) Hřímalý, and cellist Wilhelm Fitzenhagen; the first public performance (with the work now in its revised form) took place October 18/30, 1882, by the same musicians, at a concert of the Russian Musical Society in Moscow.

Instrumentation: Violin, cello, and piano

Though the piano trio had been a popular genre in Western Europe since the time of Haydn and Mozart, it had failed to take root in Russia during the nineteenth century. In 1880 Nadezhda von Meck (Tchaikovsky's evasive patron, who supported him from 1877 to 1890) urged him to write a piece for her resident trio, but Tchaikovsky declined. "There is no tonal blend," he protested in a letter to her, "indeed the piano cannot blend with the rest, having an elasticity of tone that separates from any other body of sound.... To my mind, the piano can be effective in only three situations: (1) alone, (2) in a contest with the orchestra, (3) as accompaniment, i.e. the background of a picture." His protest rings a bit hollow, given the rich succession of well-balanced trios by such composers as Beethoven, Schubert, Mendelssohn, Schumann, and Brahms, all of which works Tchaikovsky must have known. His avoidance probably had more to do with his being occupied at the moment plotting ideas for two operas (*Vanka the Bartender*, which he aborted, and *Mazeppa*, which he completed three years later); or perhaps it resulted from his jealousy concerning Mme. von Meck's house pianist, whom he viewed as a rival protégé—a brilliant Parisian teenager named Claude Debussy, who had just then produced a youthful piano trio.

All the same, Mme. von Meck had planted the seed of an idea, and it soon germinated. Several months later, Tchaikovsky was deeply saddened by the death of Nikolai Rubinstein, who had often spurred Tchaikovsky's development by assessing his music with brutal honesty. Sometimes that bluntness caused pain, most famously in the case of the First Piano Concerto, which Rubinstein had dismissed with astonishing rudeness. But Tchaikovsky revered Rubinstein as a friend and mentor, and he resolved to commemorate him by writing a composition with a piano part so virtuosic that it would have been worthy of Rubinstein as a performer. Perhaps the fact that Rubinstein had composed five piano trios (most exceptionally for a Russian) helped focus Tchaikovsky's thoughts on the medium he would apply to this enterprise.

At the end of 1881 Mme. von Meck received news that her ensemble might get a piece of Tchaikovsky's after all. "Do you remember that you once counseled me to write a trio for piano, violin, and cello," Tchaikovsky inquired in a letter (the only way he was permitted to communicate with his patron), "and do you remember my reply in which I openly declared to you my antipathy for this combination of instruments? Now suddenly, despite this antipathy, I have conceived the idea of testing myself in this sort of music, which so far I have not touched. I have already written the beginning of a trio. Whether I will finish it, whether it will come out successfully, I do not know, but I would very much wish to bring what I have begun to a successful conclusion." This he did, and quickly. On March 11/23, 1882—the precise anniversary of Rubinstein's death—Tchaikovsky's Piano Trio was unveiled in a private concert at the Moscow Conservatory.

It proved to be an ambitious piece; though cast in only two movements, the Trio takes nearly fifty minutes to perform. Tchaikovsky's musician-colleagues were unstinting in their praise, though few failed to remark on the work's considerable duration. Reviewers were more mixed in their reaction, with the strongest objections coming from the German critic Eduard Hanslick, an avowed Tchaikovsky-hater, who maintained that "it belongs to the category of suicidal compositions, which kill themselves by their merciless length." Though always sensitive to criticism, Tchaikovsky took these comments in stride; he knew that structural tightness was not one of his strengths. Eventually he marked several passages as optional, including a fugue in the second movement. Most modern performances, however, follow the uncut score.

The first movement (*Pezzo elegiaco*) is an elegy in which three highly expressive melodies unroll within a free adaptation of a classic sonata form. Its unusually prominent and very difficult piano part confirms that Tchaikovsky was more interested in setting the instrument apart in a concerto-like, "Rubinsteinian" style than in achieving the subtle blend of the most admired German or French trio composers. Rubinstein's memory is also recalled in the second movement, an enormous theme-and-variations structure growing out of a melody whose folk-like character would have pleased the late composer. Critics tried to discern a narrative in which each of the movement's eleven variations depicted a specific episode in Rubinstein's life, but Tchaikovsky rebuffed such attempts. "How amusing!" he wrote, "to compose music without the slightest desire to represent something, and suddenly to discover that it represents this or that; it is what Molière's Bourgeois Gentilhomme must have felt when he learned that he had been speaking in prose all of his life." The opening variations proceed predictably, with the second turning the duple-time theme into a triple-time waltz and the fourth transposing it into the minor mode. The fifth offers a charming music-box effect high on the piano keyboard before giving way to a spacious waltz (a Tchaikovsky specialty) and, in the seventh variation, an expanded texture that seems almost symphonic. The optional fugue follows, full of octave work for the pianist. The ninth variation reflects muted introspection, the tenth is a buoyant mazurka (again stressing the piano), and the eleventh serves to recapitulate the theme in its original form, though with an altered accompaniment.

A final exploration of the possibilities of variation form comes in the concluding section (*Variazione finale e Coda*), so extensive that some commentators consider it an independent movement. The composer appears to have held on to the conception of this as a two-movement trio, although his revisions of April 1882 make clear that he considered the second movement to be subdivided into two demarcated sections. In this final segment of the work Tchaikovsky employs his variations theme as the second subject of a sonata-form finale. The section is worked out according to classic procedures before finally fading away in a funereal recall of the opening movement.

Tchaikovsky's Trio wasted no time entering the chamber-music repertoire and seems to have linked the genre of the piano trio to the spirit of commemorating musical luminaries, at least in the minds of Russian composers. In 1893, Rachmaninoff would dedicate his D-minor *Trio élégiaque* to the memory of Tchaikovsky, and Anton Arensky would compose his Trio No. 1 as a tribute to the departed cellist Karl Davïdov. A half-century later, Dmitri Shostakovich would memorialize his mentor, the musicologist Ivan Sollertinsky, through his E-minor Piano Trio. Tchaikovsky's Trio had obviously fulfilled its intent supremely, both as a memorial to a specific "great artist" and as the wellspring for the ensuing convention of like-minded chamber-music legacies.

String Sextet in D minor, *Souvenir de Florence*, Op. 70

Allegro con spirito
Adagio cantabile e con moto
Allegro moderato
Allegro vivace

Work composed: Begun in June 1887 in Borzhom, Tiflis Province (now Georgia), but mostly composed from June 12 (old style)/24 (new style)–July 25/August 6, 1890; revised in December 1891 and (mostly) January 1892 and completed in its final form by January 29/February 10, 1892.

Work dedicated: To the St. Petersburg Chamber Music Society

Work premiered: In a private performance on November 25/December 7, 1890, in St. Petersburg, with violinists Evgeni Albrekht and Franz Hildenbrandt, violists Oskar Gille and Bruno Heine, and cellists Aleksandr Verzhbilovich and Aleksandr Kuznetsov; the public premiere followed three days later at an all-Tchaikovsky concert of the St. Petersburg Chamber Music Society, with the same performers; the revised version was first presented on November 24/December 6, 1892, by the Russian Musical Society in St. Petersburg with violinists Leopold Auer and

Hildenbrandt, violists Emmanuel Kruger and Sergei Korguev, and cellists Verzh-bilovich and Dmitri Bzul.

Instrumentation: Two violins, two violas, and two cellos

In October 1886 the St. Petersburg Chamber Music Society elected Tchaikovsky as an honorary member and formally asked him to compose a piece for its musicians to unveil. As was typically the case, the composer delayed in fulfilling the request; but once a seed was sown in Tchaikovsky's mind it tended to grow, however slowly. The following June he set down some preliminary sketches for a string sextet, but it failed to hold his interest for more than a few days. The project lay dormant until the winter of 1890, when the composer was in Florence, working assiduously on his opera *The Queen of Spades*. Tchaikovsky found himself jotting down a melody that would eventually evolve into the sextet's slow movement, where the melody is spun out over a pizzicato accompaniment. This theme is, in fact, the "souvenir of Florence" to which the title refers; nothing else in the piece particularly evokes Italy.

As soon as Tchaikovsky finished his opera he plunged full-time into composing the sextet. Back in Russia, he wrote to his brother, in June 1890: "I started working on [the sextet] three days ago and am writing with difficulty, handicapped by lack of ideas and the new form. One needs six independent but, at the same time, homogenous voices. This is frightfully difficult. Haydn never managed to conquer this problem and never wrote anything but quartets for chamber music." In fact, there existed few precedents for the ensemble of two violins, two violas, and two cellos, apart from the prominent examples of Brahms' two Sextets, which had been premiered in 1860 and 1866, and Dvořák's Sextet, unveiled in 1879. He confessed to his friend Aleksandr Ziloti that he feared he was imagining the piece in orchestral terms and then forcing his ideas into the procrustean limits of the six intended instruments.

By July 25/August 6 he had completed the composition and the scoring. He concealed his struggle working in the sextet medium when he wrote about the piece to his patron, Nadezhda von Meck: "Knowing that you love chamber music I rejoice in the thought of you hearing my sextet....I truly hope that this music will please you; I have written it with extreme enthusiasm and pleasure, without the slightest effort." Sadly, his relationship with Mme. von Meck ended only a few days after he penned those words. They had been connected for thirteen years, since early 1877, though with the very curious proviso that he never attempt to meet her in person. During that time they had exchanged a flood of effusive correspondence and she had deposited 500 rubles in Tchaikovsky's bank account every month, an act of benefaction that freed him up significantly to pursue his artistic goals without having to undertake "work for hire" to pay the bills. Suddenly, with no warning, she wrote in September 1890 to inform him that her apparently limitless fortune was no longer what it had been and that their relationship would cease immediately, a break that hurt the composer profoundly—by that time for reasons more emotional than financial.

The medium of the sextet continued to worry Tchaikovsky, and he insisted that the St. Petersburg Chamber Music Society give the piece only a provisional reading that might serve as a springboard for necessary revisions. "I will not publish it at this time," Tchaikovsky wrote to the Society's chairman, "not until you and your companions learn it, and correct everything in it that is unidiomatic, not good, ill-sounding.... Only then, after hearing your performance and taking into consideration all your corrections and advice, will I revise the sextet and submit it to the engraver." A very private reading took place on November 25/December 7, 1890, and those present (including the composers Alexander Glazunov and Anatoly Lyadov) agreed that the work's third and fourth movements were far from successful. Nonetheless, the concert at the Chamber Music Society went on as planned three days later. Tchaikovsky pondered his options for another year, eventually rewriting the third and fourth movements and effecting smaller changes elsewhere. The revised *Souvenir de Florence* finally received its public premiere at the end of 1892, when it was enthusiastically received. At the work's ensuing performance, the St. Petersburg Chamber Music Society presented the composer its medal of merit, to thunderous applause. The critic Herman Laroche reported that "when he had finished his string sextet, he declared that 'I should like to compose forthwith another sextet,' probably because he felt that the sextet had turned out successfully, and because he was attracted to the unaccustomed complement of instruments." It was not to be; this would be the last entry in the catalogue of Tchaikovsky's chamber music.

Despite its minor key, *Souvenir de Florence* is an ebullient and untroubled composition, a last sunny spell before Tchaikovsky's anguished emotional decline toward the Sixth Symphony (the *Pathétique*). Here we glimpse Tchaikovsky's neo-Classical proclivities, making *Souvenir de Florence* an obvious cousin to such of the composer's efforts as the Serenade for Strings and the Orchestral Suites. Its passionate first movement follows a traditional sonata form, more clearly plotted than many of Tchaikovsky's well-known works, strikingly "classic" for a work so late in his chronology. The *Adagio cantabile e con moto* shows off the composer's melodic gift in both the *Souvenir de Florence* tune (which immediately follows a short, harmonically fragrant introduction) and the beautifully intertwined counter-themes. A thirty-measure-long central section (*Moderato*) serves as an imaginative exercise in orchestration, in which subtly shifting instrumental balances provide the musical interest as variations of timbre temporarily challenge the primacy of melody, harmony, and rhythm. The third movement scherzo/intermezzo (*Allegro moderato*, with its lighter-than-air, balletic trio section) and espe‑ cially the high-spirited finale (*Allegro vivace*) show the influence of Slavic traditional music. The last movement is, however, far removed from a mere folk dance. Tchaikovsky finds ample opportunity to show off his contrapuntal prowess and develops one of the movement's later episodes into a fugue, an appropriately erudite gesture given that the piece owed its very existence to an honorary award from a music society.

Joan Peabody Tower

Born: September 6, 1938, in New Rochelle, New York

PETROUSHS
        K
        A
        T
        E
        S

Work composed: 1980

Work dedicated: Written for the tenth anniversary of the Da Capo Chamber Players

Work premiered: March 23, 1980, in Alice Tully Hall, Lincoln Center, New York City, by the Da Capo Chamber Players (flutist Patricia Spencer, clarinetist Laura Flax, violinist Joel Lester, cellist André Emelianoff, and the composer as pianist)

Instrumentation: Flute, clarinet, violin, cello, and piano

Name: On the score the title is given as above, but the piece is usually referred to in more standard, one-line form, as just *Petroushskates.*

Born in a suburb of New York City to a family of ancient New England lineage, Joan Tower entered a very different world at the age of nine. Her father was a consultant for mining companies, and in 1947 the family moved to La Paz, Bolivia, high in the Andes, where he assumed the management of a collection of tin mines. "My whole world turned inside out," said Tower in an interview. "We had servants of Incan descent who lived with us, and they would celebrate the Saint's Days—and there were a lot of Saint's Days!—with fantastic festivals, lots of music and dancing. My nurse would take me…and whatever percussion instruments we'd find there, I'd play them. That's where my love for percussion, dance, and rhythm developed."

For many years Tower was enmeshed in the inner workings of New York City's modern-music scene. In 1969 she founded the Da Capo Chamber Players, which more than four decades later remains one of the nation's most respected contemporary-music ensembles; for fifteen years she played a literally hands-on role, serving as the group's pianist. In 1984, she was offered a three-year term as composer-in-residence at the St. Louis Symphony. She balked. Up until that point her work had focused almost exclusively on chamber music, and although she had written a well-received orchestral movement titled *Sequoia*, she hardly pictured her interests or aspirations changing radically in the symphonic direction. Nonetheless, she relinquished her keyboard duties in the Da Capo Chamber Players and took the position in St. Louis. It proved to be a critical stepping-stone in a career that would flower in breadth, though chamber music would remain central to her activities and she would remain overwhelmingly a composer of instrumental music, for whatever size ensemble.

The makeup of the Da Capo Chamber Players—flute, clarinet, violin, cello, and piano—paralleled the instrumental forces specified in one of the seminal works of the twentieth century, Arnold Schoenberg's *Pierrot Lunaire*, a cycle written in 1912 in which that quintet of instruments is joined by a reciter using *Sprechstimme*, a style of delivery that falls in the crack between speech and song. Indeed, this formulation, without the vocal part, would become known in general musical parlance as the "Pierrot ensemble." It is ironic that Schoenberg's model should have so deeply influenced the course of Tower's career, since she does not find herself much attracted to his music. On the other hand, she explains that she is more likely to be influenced by an individual work than by a composer in some general sense. For example, she observes: "In spite of my unsympathetic regard for the work of Arnold Schoenberg, whose music is so unlike my own, I remember one beautiful moment in his Chamber Symphony, Op. 9. This slow, stately motive in rising fourths has stuck in my ears throughout the years and has appeared and reappeared in different guises in several of my works." Connections to other composers are clearly stated through such of her titles as *Piano Concerto (Homage to Beethoven)*, from 1985, or *Très Lent (Hommage à Messiaen)*, a 1994 work for cello and piano. "Even though my own music does not sound like Beethoven's in any obvious way," she has said, "in it there is a basic idea at work which came from him, something I call the 'balancing of musical energies.'" And elsewhere: "I think most composers would have to admit that they live, to various degrees, in the sound-worlds of other composers both old and new, and that what they consciously or unconsciously take from them enables them to discover what they themselves are interested in."

The composer who most frequently leaps to mind in her music is Stravinsky. She points to the pulsing rhythms of the strings not far into *The Rite of Spring* as "something that has been distributed throughout some of my pieces." The very title of her *Petroushskates* signals the inspiration of Stravinsky's 1911 ballet score *Petroushka* (to use the French form of its title). But what of the "skates"? Tower explains:

> In an attempt to understand why figure skating, especially pair skating, was so beautiful and moving to me, I discovered a musical corollary I had been working on for a while—the idea of a seamless action—something I had started to explore in *Amazon* [an orchestral piece from 1979]. I also always loved *Petroushka* and wanted to create an homage to Stravinsky and that piece in particular. As it turned out, the figure skating pairs became a whole company of skaters, thereby creating a sort of musical carnival on ice.

The music leaps brightly into action with shimmering, Minimalist repetitions of sixteenth-notes. The clarinet sews the seam to a mysterious slow episode and instrumental outbursts that briefly suggest the alarm expressed by the hapless puppet Petroushka. But most of the time, Tower's writing is relentlessly energetic: shades of Stravinsky, to be sure, but perhaps also of the percussion-rich festivities of her Andean youth. And then, after a *decrescendo* of piano trills, the music simply disappears. Tower has described herself as a "choreographer of sound," often manipulating her material—whether individual melodic lines, chords, or complexes of carefully wrought sonorities—in a way that the listener can instantly perceive as spatial, much as a choreographer manipulates dancers (or figure skaters). "I think in terms of 'center' and 'up' and 'down' and 'fast' and 'slow,'" she has said, "except in my case you're hearing these things instead of seeing them."

As a devoted aficionado of competitive figure skating, I must voice a single disappointment with *Petroushskates*. The score says that it runs approximately five minutes, and in performance it sometimes reaches a half-minute or so beyond that. U.S. Figure Skating, which writes the rule-book for the sport in the United States (in line with the International Olympic Committee), limits the free skate (or "long program") in pairs competitions to an absolute maximum of four minutes and forty seconds. But for that extra minute (or even just twenty seconds), this sparkling chamber work could serve as a pairs-skating soundtrack par excellence.

C. M. von Weber.

Carl Maria Friedrich Ernst von Weber

Born: Probably on November 19, 1786, in Eutin, Holstein, Germany (in what is now the northernmost state of Schleswig-Holstein). He grew up celebrating December 18 as his birthday but in later life became aware that the official registry for his hometown revealed November 20 to be the date of his baptism.

Died: June 5, 1826, in London, England. He was buried in London, but his remains were transferred to Dresden in 1844.

Trio for Flute, Cello, and Piano, Op. 63 (J. 259)

Allegro moderato
Scherzo: Allegro vivace
Schäfers Klage ("Shepherd's Lament"): Andante espressivo
Finale: Allegro

Work composed: The third movement possibly as early as 1813, the remainder in 1818–19, completed on July 25, 1819, at his summer home at Hosterwitz on the Elbe

Work dedicated: To Philipp Junghe, Weber's friend and physician in Prague

Work premiered: At a read-through at the home of Louis Spohr in Frankfurt, on November 21, 1819

Instrumentation: Flute, cello, and piano; published editions often allow violin to be used instead of flute as a practical substitution, but there is no question that the flute is what Weber envisioned for the topmost line.

J numbers: The "J numbers" attached to Weber's works were assigned by the musicologist Friedrich Wilhelm Jähns in his volume *Carl Maria von Weber*

in seinem Werk: Chronologisch-thematisches Verzeichniss seiner sämmtlicher Compositionen (Berlin, 1871).

Carl Maria von Weber spent much of his career in the orbit of opera. He served as music director at a succession of civic and court theatres and opera houses—Breslau, Carlsruhe, Prague, and Dresden—but it was as a composer of opera that he made his most enduring mark. Weber worked on ten of them in his too-brief life. Not all were completed, and not everything he did complete of them appears to have survived, but at least *Der Freischütz* is honored as a true classic. It was Weber's work in opera that earned him the historical position he enjoys as a pillar of German Romanticism, as a defining figure in a fantasy-rich movement that managed to link such ethereal illusions as fairies, haunted forests, and magic bullets with such real ones as German nationalism.

The first part of the Flute Trio to be written seems to have been its eventual third movement, the *Schäfers Klage* ("Shepherd's Lament"), which is widely believed to be a revision of a lost Adagio and Variations for Flute, Viola (perhaps Cello), and Piano that he composed in 1815 while living in Prague. But the piece had already begun its history before then. On October 16, 1814 (according to John Warrack's Weber biography of 1968; in his preface to the 1977 Eulenberg edition of the score Warrrack changes the year to 1813), Weber entered in his diary a mention of the "Andante and Variations for Jungh," referring to his friend and physician Dr. Jungh of Prague, who was an accomplished amateur cellist. It therefore would appear that a version for cello and piano fit somewhere into this movement's genealogy, quite likely as the original version of 1813. Warrack suggests that the flute-viola (or cello)-and-piano version of this movement was written for the father-and-son flutists Caspar and Anton Fürstenau, though he doesn't explain why it's not for two flutes, which one would expect if that were the case. Elsewhere in the same book he seems to posit that this slow movement was originally composed in 1814 for Dr. Jungh and was revised in March 1815 as an interim step on its path to becoming the third movement of the Flute Trio.

If there is room for confusion about that movement, the chronology of the other three is crystal clear. Weber's diary for 1819 reveals that he did preparatory work on the other movements in April and May and then completed the piece in a flurry of inspiration in July. By this time Weber had left Prague for Dresden. His last act in Prague was to get married, and following a six-week honeymoon the Webers (Carl Maria and Caroline) moved into their new home in Dresden in the last weeks of 1817. After a busy winter season they spent the summer of 1818 at a bucolic summer retreat at Hosterwitz near

Pillnitz, just to the east of Dresden. Weber was frustrated that his work on *Der Freischütz* kept being interrupted by demands for celebratory works for court events, and by the end of the summer he returned to Dresden exhausted.

The next year was a disaster. A daughter was born on December 22, 1818, and Caroline, having endured a difficult pregnancy, was slow to recover. Six days after the baby's birth the Webers received word that Caroline's father had died. In mid-March, Carl Maria was also brought low by illness—he was showing signs of the tuberculosis that would eventually kill him—and he remained in bed for six weeks, until he and his wife could return to their summer place in Hosterwitz. While Carl Maria was sick the daughter died and Caroline collapsed with grief. In Hosterwitz, he started work on a new opera, *Alcindor*, commissioned to celebrate the wedding of Prince Friedrich August to the Archduchess Caroline of Austria. Suddenly word arrived that the King of Prussia had canceled his commission for the opera. Much though he had been excited about the *Alcindor* project, Weber actually seemed relieved. Rather than return immediately to work on *Der Freischütz*, he let loose with a freshet of smaller scaled pieces completed in quick succession, including the Flute Trio (achieved on July 25) and the piano solo *Aufforderung zum Tanze* ("Invitation to the Dance," on July 28).

Much of the Flute Trio has a melancholy flavor, which might reflect Weber's depletion after a string of horrendous months but in any case was in tune with prevailing early Romantic sentiments. The first movement opens with haunted music in the minor mode but before long segues into a bubbling second theme that seems to have popped out of the Hunting Chorus of *Der Freischütz*. Warrack's Weber biography describes the *Allegro moderato* as "perhaps the most successful of his sonata movements in setting a Romantic character in classical form." Yet as sonata forms go, this one is unusual; in the recapitulation the two principal themes are presented in reverse order from how we have encountered them in the exposition. The following *Scherzo* is also founded on great emotional contrast: a powerful, jagged, minor-key opening yields to a major-key section that is all sweetness and light. One expects a discrete trio section in a scherzo, but that is not Weber's plan; he amalgamates the contrasting characters that would have attached to the scherzo and trio into a single through-composed span. This alternation of gruff Beethovenian scherzo and what reminds one of a bel canto *cabaletta* (*à la* Rossini, perhaps) leaves emotional ambiguity in its wake.

The *Schäfers Klage* follows, based on a guileless melody that has been variously identified as the folk songs "In einem kühlen Grunde" and "Dort droben auf jenem Berge." (Actually, they would be fake folk songs, as the first is founded on a folk-like poem authored by Joseph Freiherr von Eichendorff and the second is from the famous collection *Des Knaben Wunderhorn*, in which Clemens Brentano and Achim von Arnim passed off largely original poems as folk texts.) Here, too, deep currents run beneath the surface simplicity. Charming as the tune is, it generates a movement underpinned by anxiety thanks largely to unanticipated throbbing in the piano left hand and chromatically intense elaborations in all three parts. The *Finale* jams no fewer than four distinct melodic motifs into its opening few measures (with further themes yet to come), again with intimations of *Der Freischütz*, especially of Caspar's Drinking Song. The movement unrolls episodically, even passing through a fugato section; you may have the impression of listening to an operatic potpourri.

Weber's Flute Trio inhabits a tonal world that, though based overall on the tonic of G, largely falls between the cracks of major and minor. It leaves a listener uncertain about its emotional intent, much as many of Schubert's best chamber works do, although in Weber the contrasts between manic and depressive are delineated without much middle ground in between. Overwhelmingly dejected expanses make way for passages of almost defiant gaiety. In the end it's hard to know quite what to make of this Trio, a fascinating if troubling achievement that is not quite like anything else in the chamber repertoire.

Anton Webern

Anton Friedrich Wilhelm Webern

Born: December 3, 1883, in Vienna

Died: September 15, 1945, in Mittersill, near Salzburg, Austria

Name: He was born Anton Friedrich Wilhelm von Webern, but he dropped the aristocratic "von" in 1918, when Austria declared such distinctions illegal.

Fünf Sätze für Streichquartett ("Five Movements for String Quartet"), Op. 5

Heftig bewegt
Sehr langsam
Sehr bewegt
Sehr langsam
In zarter Bewegung

Work composed: Completed on June 16, 1909

Work premiered: February 8, 1910, in Vienna by an ad hoc ensemble put together for that purpose

Instrumentation: Two violins, viola, and cello

Today we admire Webern as the most exquisite of composers, but of the musical creators who emerged at the dawn of the twentieth century he must have seemed the most completely enigmatic. The compositions of Schoenberg, Berg, Stravinsky, and Bartók were groundbreaking, but Webern's coeval works were at least as audacious in their departure from received traditions. (Perhaps only Ives was as radical, but his music went mostly unheard at the time.) Nonetheless, even the styles of revolutionary composers tend to evolve gradually. Webern's earliest pieces, such as his *Lang-samer Satz* ("Slow Piece") for String Quartet (1905, but not published until 1965), reveal a mastery of late-Romantic musical processes and the fin-de-siè-cle sentiment of decadence and neurosis that is also to be found in works writ-ten then by Mahler, Schoenberg, Zemlinsky, and others. Before the century's opening decade had passed, Webern reached a more advanced modernism that combined harmonic freedom, melodic severity, and an apparent sparse-ness of material that earned his scores the description "aphoristic."

Webern received a thorough training in harmony, counterpoint, and musicology at the University of Vienna, which in 1906 awarded him a Ph.D. (for which he wrote a dissertation on the Renaissance composer Heinrich Isaac). But the most decisive step in his musical upbringing came in the autumn of 1904, when, along with Alban Berg, he began studying composi-tion with Arnold Schoenberg, who was just nine years older than Webern. Schoenberg stopped offering formal classes after a year, frustrated that most of his pupils showed no aptitude for composition. But the talented students, including both Webern and Berg, stuck with him. Schoenberg's teaching regime frequently involved his students' actually performing the music under discussion. Webern typically played cello in these explorations, and in 1910 (in a letter to his brother-in-law) he recalled these experiences by declar-ing that "quartet playing is the most glorious music-making there is." Years later, Webern would write thoughtfully of Schoenberg's tutelage: "Schoen-berg demands, above all, that what the pupil writes for his lessons should not consist of any old notes written down to fill out an academic form, but should be something achieved as the result of his need for self-expression. So he has, in fact, to create—even in the musical examples written during the most primitive initial stages.... With the utmost energy, he tracks down the pupil's personality, seeking to deepen it, to help it break through—in short, 'to give the pupil the courage and the strength to find an attitude to things which will make everything he looks at into an exceptional case, because of the *way* he looks at it.' It is an education in utter truthfulness with oneself."

Still, it was natural that Webern's development should in some way reflect his teacher's progress in adapting traditional tonic-anchored harmony into a method whereby music might be constructed from a cell containing each of the twelve notes of the chromatic scale. By the time Webern composed his Five Movements for String Quartet (Op. 5), he was himself grappling with the challenge of writing music that was governed by neither tonality nor thematic development, both of which were topics of pressing interest to Schoenberg. Only in the first of the Five Movements does a theme undergo the sort of transformation we can think of as "development"; elsewhere, the listener senses that highly regulated, sometimes sudden, changes of tim-bre, balance, and dynamics are more central to the conception of the piece than any melody. Here we also encounter what would reign as a hallmark of Webern's music: extreme brevity. The entire span of the Five Movements is a mere eleven minutes. The second movement comprises only thirteen measures (though at exceedingly slow tempo) and a leisurely interpretation of the third lasts perhaps forty-five seconds.

The Five Movements were composed in 1909, just as Webern's studies with Schoenberg were winding down, and they were premiered on February 8, 1910, in Vienna. Webern had already written one piece he titled String Quartet, and he would produce another (his Op. 28) between 1936 and 1938. But this composition he did not call a string quartet: he apparently chose the title Five Movements (after considerable worrying) to emphasize that it was not in any way a classic string quartet but that the independent sections were nonetheless to be viewed as attached entities. In 1929 he created an adaptation of the Five Movements for string orchestra, in which form the piece is not uncommonly heard today.

In either version the listener is faced with a spirit of the ephemeral as Webern's sounds slip away almost quicker than they can be grasped. Many have found his music perplexing, yet it is undeniably beautiful if it is well performed. Webern himself didn't see what was so mystifying about his music. "In fifty years," he said, "one will find it obvious; children will understand it and sing it." He was a bit wide of the mark in that prediction, but at the very least he grew to be revered by all self-respecting Serialists, many jazz visionaries, and even hard-to-please Stravinsky, to whom goes the last appreciation of Webern: "We must hail not only this great composer but a real hero. Doomed to a total failure in a deaf world of ignorance and indifference, he inexorably kept on cutting out his diamonds, his dazzling diamonds, the mines of which he knew to perfection."

Hugo Filipp Jakob Wolf

Born: March 13, 1860, in Windischgraz, Styria, Austria, which is today Slovenj Gradec, Slovenia

Died: February 22, 1903, in Vienna

String Quartet in D minor

> Grave—Allegro (Leidenschaftlich bewegt)
> Scherzo (Resolut)
> Adagio (Langsam)
> Finale (Sehr lebhaft)

Work composed: December 31, 1878, through September 1884

Work premiered: February 3, 1903, in Vienna, by the Prill Quartet

Instrumentation: Two violins, viola, and cello

The early String Quartet in D minor represented a typical chapter in Hugo Wolf's tragic life. His attempts to get it performed publicly added up to an exercise in frustration. The score was even lost for a while but, rediscovered by music-lovers attached to the short-lived Hugo Wolf Society, it was finally given its premiere (by the Prill Quartet) on February 3, 1903, less than three weeks before the composer's death. By then Wolf was in no condition to enjoy it. His mental stability had been disintegrating for several years, exacerbated by tertiary syphilis. Following a failed suicide attempt in 1899, he asked to be committed to a mental institution, where he sank into ever deepening insanity and finally died at the age of only forty-two.

He began his D-minor String Quartet on the last day of 1878. He was in emotional turmoil from a failed love affair, and he was already experiencing the mood swings that would become increasingly unmanageable with passing years. He was completely uprooted in his living situation, moving constantly from one address to another; that fall he had touched down at seven different addresses in a single six-week period. His String Quartet took almost six years to reach its finished form, factoring in much starting and stopping, but by 1881 it was ready to be played in a private gathering at the home of Natalie Bauer-Lechner (remembered by music-lovers as Mahler's confidante). Since she was a professional violinist she presumably took part in the reading, which Wolf found appalling. Writing in the third person, he reported that he "had to watch with secret shuddering how the four assassins, who at a sign from himself swung their murderous instruments, horribly mutilated his child." Possibly his quartet was a three-movement piece at that point; or possibly it included a fourth-movement finale that Wolf later destroyed. In any case, he did not compose the movement that today stands as the *Finale* until September 1884.

At the head of the score stands the exhortation "Entbehren sollst du, sollst entbehren!" ("You must renounce, must renounce!"—or, as a loose but appealing translation has it, "Thou shalt abstain, renounce, refrain!"). It's a quotation from Goethe's *Faust*, Part One, and it falls where Faust is giving in to Mephistopheles' temptation and, decrying what he views as the deception of life and love, decides to cast his lot with the devil. Placing this motto on such an ambitious score—forty-five minutes is a lot for a string quartet—may be taken as the brash act of a young man, the more so when the young man in question was surely aware that his idol Richard Wagner had suggested that those very words should be attached to the beginning of Beethoven's Ninth Symphony.

The first movement opens with a powerful, passionate introduction (*Grave*) in which the first violin proclaims an almost frantic recitative that, like the Goethe quotation, is built on an exclamation mark. The wide melodic intervals, the surprising placement of entrances, the dotted rhythms, and the fiercely determined character are so over-the-top as to evoke Beethoven's *Grosse Fuge*. Memories of that astonishing piece, and also of Schubert's *Death and the Maiden* Quartet, continue to haunt this monumental movement as it breaks into its main section, a very extended sonata-form expanse marked *Leidenschaftlich bewegt* ("Passionately lively"), full of unanticipated juxtapositions of material, including reappearances of fragments from the opening "recitative."

Discrepancies between source materials and the first published edition have led to dissent concerning the ordering of the two middle movements. Majority practice seems to favor placing the *Scherzo* as the second movement. Marked *Resolut* ("Resolutely"), this pitiless *Scherzo* bears striking affinities to the corresponding movement of Beethoven's *Serioso* Quartet in F minor (Op. 95). The character grows rather less forbidding in the central trio section.

If Beethoven references have been most prominent until now, the *Adagio* begins with sounds straight out of Wagner—specifically, the white purity of glistening, high-pitched triads unrolling in slow motion, as remembered from the Prelude to *Lohengrin*. These stratospheric violin tones return periodically to punctuate the proceedings. The opening music gives way to a spacious cantilena—inspired, perhaps, by the more tender aspect of Beethoven, with post-Wagnerian chromaticism—though the flow is repeatedly interrupted by rhythmically nervous interjections.

After the soul-searching and turbulence of the first three movements, Wolf's *Finale* (*Sehr lebhaft*; "Very lively") seems considerably less troubled—though with its dense fugal passages it is certainly not less Beethovenian. If we take Wolf's "Faust motto" seriously we may choose to view the *Finale* as reflecting Faust's relief at having come to terms with his options, at having arrived at some decision—although we know it's the wrong one.

In 1884 Wolf approached both the recently founded Rosé Quartet and the Vienna Wagner Society about presenting his quartet, without success. (One wonders about the subliminal message that is sent to any ensemble which, about to evaluate a new score, is greeted with an exhortation to "abstain, renounce, refrain!") A year later a friend urged him to send it again to the Rosés, notwithstanding the earlier rejection. When no acknowledgment arrived, Wolf started to speak ill of that ensemble for ignoring him, and he made overtures toward the rival Kretschmann Quartet, which also came to naught. Then in October 1885 he finally received a letter from the Rosé Quartet:

> Dear Mr. Wolf,
> We have played through your D-minor Quartet with attention and have reached the unanimous decision to deposit this work for you with—the porter at the Imperial and Royal Opera House (Operngasse). Would you please be so kind as to pick it up as soon as possible. He could easily misplace it. With heartiest greetings,
>
> The Quartet,
> [signed] Rosé, Loh, Bachrich, Hummer

Ouch. The letter was actually signed by Siegmund Bachrich, the group's violist, who took the liberty of inscribing the "signatures" of his three colleagues along with his own. It seems that this stinging exercise of wit was meant as retribution against things Wolf had written in his capacity as music critic for the *Wiener Salonblatt*, to which he contributed from 1884 to 1887. Bachrich had composed two operettas that Wolf reviewed savagely. If that weren't enough, Bachrich then became a recurrent character in Wolf's columns, mentioned in entirely gratuitous contexts as an object of derision. Bachrich's moment for revenge had arrived.

Wolf responded by discussing the incident very publicly in his October 23 column, which he titled "Unanimously: No!" "When I offered a piece of my chamber music to the Rosé Quartet, I was reckless enough, unfortunately, to entertain the wish that they might play it," he reported. "A two-voiced rejection, to be sure, in gentle thirds, a third voice associating itself with the others in decorous contrapuntal turns... with the fourth, a neutral power, counting rests, would have affected me far more sympathetically than this barbarically rough, inquisitorially stern and utterly inhuman, unmusically unanimous condemnation from the mouth of an awesome assemblage of four acute and experienced judges of high art." Following this exchange, Wolf-the-critic tended to find the performances of the Rosé Quartet at least in part "not to our taste."

All this ill will did nothing to help get the piece performed by anybody, and Wolf's String Quartet accordingly went unheard until the last weeks of the composer's life. Reviews reflected differences of opinion, but the most interesting account was the balanced assessment of Max Reger, a sympathetic champion of Wolf, if one who held him to a high standard. "First," wrote Reger, "a lack of knowledge of the technical design of the string quartet can be observed on occasion; and, when it occurs, it cannot be denied and is very noticeable. Then the melody is still somewhat unfree in some passages. One senses what the composer wanted but did not accomplish because he lacked the pure technical ability. Here and there something is amiss in the purity of the writing style. The austere, deeply felt passion of the tonal idiom, a captivating temperament bursting forth on its stormy path especially in the outer movements, makes up for this. And everywhere one turns one also encounters the genuine Wolf in passages that he alone could create."

Serenade in G major for String Quartet ("Italian Serenade")

Work composed: May 2–4, 1887; this piece is often heard in the transcription for small orchestra that the composer prepared in 1892.

Work premiered: The original string quartet version was premiered in Vienna in 1904

Instrumentation: Two violins, viola, and cello

The heart-rending terminus of Wolf's stormy life seems all the sadder when contrasted with such a sunny bagatelle as his G-major Serenade for String Quartet, composed in a mere three days in May of 1887, a decade before he crumbled into insanity. This piece is often referred to under the title "Italian Serenade," but that usage is questionable. In the *Hugo Wolf Gesamtausgabe*, the scholarly edition of his complete works, editor Hans Jancik calls it only "Serenade," which is how it is identified on all of Wolf's sketches and manuscripts. The "Italian" business comes from a letter Wolf wrote to his friend Oskar Grohe on April 2, 1892, in which he referred to the piece as "an Italian Serenade"; and he gave that title—*Italian Serenade*—to the orchestral version he arranged that year. But when speaking of the quartet setting it is probably more accurate to refer to it simply as Serenade in G major.

In the spring of 1887 Wolf was engrossed in writing songs on poems by the German Romantic poet Joseph Freiherr von Eichendorff. The musicologist Eric Sams has proposed that the Serenade may have some deep-seated connection to Eichendorff's novella *Aus dem Leben eines Taugenichts* ("The Life of a Good-for-Nothing"). It tells the tale of a young musician who shuffles off the coil of workaday demands to seek adventures, some of which take place in a castle in Italy, where an orchestra plays a serenade that proves pivotal in the plot. One of Wolf's Eichendorff settings of that period, *Der Soldat I* (composed in March of that year), also bears some relationship to the plot of the novella, and it prefigures some of the music in the Serenade.

This lighthearted piece is cast as a sort of quick rondo, marked *Äussert lebhaft* (Very lively), replete with Wolf's signature brand of post-Wagnerian harmony. Its thematic gestures tellingly illustrate a lover's serenade, not without a generous measure of irony and caricature. We hear the serenader strumming a G-major chord on his guitar for several measures at the opening, doubtless checking his tuning, but then Wolf swerves amusingly and without warning into E-flat. The main body of the piece can be taken as the serenade itself, poured out with considerable passion; we may imagine that the dialogue among the four instruments represents a conversation between the lovers. The cello breaks into a rather pompous declaration in recitative, and after further exchange of "sweet nothings," the serenade concludes with an allusion to the strumming that had launched it six minutes earlier.

In April and May of 1892 Wolf set about transcribing the piece for a small orchestra of two flutes, two oboes, two clarinets, two bassoons, two horns, and strings, including a solo viola, which Wolf initially intended to share the spotlight with the English horn, though he ended up dispensing with the latter entirely. His plan was to have this serve as the first part of a (probably) three-movement orchestral suite, but although he sketched some material for the other two movements, neither was brought to a state approaching completion. Max Reger prepared the manuscript of the orchestral version to submit to the publishers—and in the process corrected a few obvious errors in the score. This led some commentators to describe Reger's involvement as that of a full-fledged arranger, a vast overstatement not borne out by a study of the manuscript and the first edition; but occasionally one still finds references to the Wolf-Reger *Italian Serenade*. Opinions are split about the relative merits of the two versions of the Serenade; some listeners prefer the rich and imaginative scoring of the orchestral version to the more homogenized string-quartet setting, while others feels that the denser textures of the orchestral version work at cross-purposes to Wolf's fleet writing. It's hardly worth debating. Both settings are charming, amusing, and lighter than air.